20/12 .

Land, Poverty and Livelihoods in an Era of Globalization

A host of internationally eminent scholars are brought together to explore the structural causes of rural poverty and income inequality as well as the processes of social exclusion and political subordination encountered by the peasantry and rural workers. Utilizing new empirical evidence from ten countries and in-depth analysis of key country studies, a comparative analysis of agrarian reforms and their impact on rural poverty in Africa, Asia, Latin America and transition countries is undertaken. This volume provides a critical analysis and framework for the study of neoliberal land policies in the current phase of globalization.

Land, Poverty and Livelihoods in an Era of Globalization determines that the currently dominant neoliberal economic and social policies do not tackle the main causes of rural poverty and are thus unable to significantly reduce, let alone eliminate, this major development problem. The book undertakes a critical analysis of past agrarian reform policies as well as of current neoliberal land policies. It seeks to propose an agrarian reform policy embedded in an appropriate development strategy which is able to significantly reduce, and hopefully eliminate, rural poverty.

A. Haroon Akram-Lodhi is Professor of International Development Studies at Trent University, Peterborough, Canada. **Saturnino M. Borras Jr** is Canada Research Chair in International Development Studies, St Mary's University, Halifax, Nova Scotia, Canada. **Cristóbal Kay** is Associate Professor of Rural Development and Development Studies at the Institute of Social Studies, The Hague, the Netherlands.

Routledge ISS studies in rural livelihoods

Editorial Board: A. Haroon Akram-Lodhi (Trent University), Saturnino M. Borras Jr (St Mary's University), Cristóbal Kay (Chair) (Institute of Social Studies) and Max Spoor (Institute of Social Studies).

Routledge and the Institute of Social Studies (ISS) in The Hague, the Netherlands have come together to publish a new book series in rural livelihoods. The series will include themes such as land policies and land rights, water issues, food policy and politics, rural poverty, agrarian transformation, migration, rural-oriented social movements, rural conflict and violence, among others. All books in the series will offer rigorous, empirically grounded, cross-national comparative and inter-regional analysis. The books will be theoretically stimulating, but will also be accessible to policy practitioners and civil society activists.

1 **Land, Poverty and Livelihoods in an Era of Globalization**
Perspectives from developing and transition countries
Edited by A. Haroon Akram-Lodhi, Saturnino M. Borras Jr and Cristóbal Kay

Land, Poverty and Livelihoods in an Era of Globalization

Perspectives from developing and transition countries

Edited by A. Haroon Akram-Lodhi, Saturnino M. Borras Jr and Cristóbal Kay

LONDON AND NEW YORK

First published 2007
by Routledge
2 Park Square, Milton Park, Abingdon, Oxon OX14 4RN

Simultaneously published in the USA and Canada
by Routledge
270 Madison Ave, New York, NY 10016

Reprinted 2007

Routledge is an imprint of the Taylor & Francis Group, an informa business

© 2007 Selection and editorial matter, A. Haroon Akram-Lodhi,
Saturnino M. Borras Jr and Cristóbal Kay; individual chapters, the
contributors

Typeset in Baskerville by Wearset Ltd, Boldon, Tyne and Wear
Printed and bound in Great Britain by MPG Books Ltd, Bodmin,
Cornwall

British Library Cataloguing in Publication Data
A catalogue record for this book is available from the British Library

Library of Congress Cataloging in Publication Data
A catalog record for this book has been requested

ISBN10: 0-415-41449-0 (hbk)
ISBN10: 0-203-96225-7 (ebk)

ISBN13: 978-0-415-41449-4 (hbk)
ISBN13: 978-0-203-96225-1 (ebk)

Contents

Illustrations

Figures

Tables

Contributors

A. Haroon Akram-Lodhi is Professor of International Development Studies at Trent University, Peterborough, Canada. His research focuses upon the gendered political economy of agrarian change in Asia, with special reference to Pakistan, Vietnam and Fiji, and his work in this area has been published in numerous peer-reviewed journals and books. His most recent book, which he co-edited, is *Globalization, Neoconservative Failures and Democratic Alternatives: Essays in Honour of John Loxley*.

Saturnino M. Borras, Jr. is Canada Research Chair in International Development Studies at St. Mary's University, Halifax, Canada. He is the author of numerous articles and books, the most recent of which is *On Just Grounds: Struggling for Agrarian Justice and Citizenship Rights in the Rural Philippines*, co-edited with Jennifer Franco. His current research interests include transnational agrarian movements and redistributive reform in 'non-private lands'.

Ray Bush is Chair of African Studies and Development Politics at the University of Leeds. He has published extensively on development-related issues, with a focus on Northern African and Middle Eastern countries. Among his books are *Counter-Revolution in Egypt's Countryside: Land and Farmers in the Era of Economic Reform* and *Economic Crisis and the Politics of Reform in Egypt*.

Danilo Carranza is Coordinator of the Research and Policy Analysis Program at the Philippine Ecumenical Action for Community Empowerment Foundation, one of the oldest and largest networks of non-governmental and peasant organizations struggling for rural development and democratization, as well as being the author of several articles on land reform and peasant movements in the Philippines.

Carmen Diana Deere is Professor of Food and Resource Economics and Latin American Studies and Director of the Center for Latin American Studies at the University of Florida, Gainesville. The former President of the Latin American Studies Association, she has published extensively on gender and rural development in Latin America, and is the author of several books, including *Household and Class Relations: Peasants and Land-lords in Northern Peru* and the award-winning *Empowering Women: Land and Property Rights in Latin America*, written with Magdalena León.

Jan Kees van Donge is Senior Lecturer in Public Policy and Development Management at the Institute of Social Studies in The Hague, the Netherlands, having previously worked for 20 years at African universities in Zambia, Tanzania and Malawi. His present research interests are in the field civil service reform in Africa, the long term effects of democratization, and ultra poverty in rural Africa.

George Eiseb works at the University of Namibia. He has participated extensively in research on land issues in Namibia, and was a member of the Permanent Technical Team on Land Reform that designed a new land reform policy for the government of Namibia.

Mwangi wa Githinji is Assistant Professor of Economics at the University of Massachusetts-Amherst. He has acted as a consultant for the United Nations on poverty, gender and human development issues. In addition to publishing several articles, he authored the book *Ten Millionaires and Ten Million Beggars: A Study of Income and Development in Kenya.*

Cristóbal Kay is Associate Professor of Rural Development and Development Studies at the Institute of Social Studies in The Hague, the Netherlands. As well as contributing to a wide variety of peer-reviewed journals he recently co-edited the books *Disappearing Peasantries? Rural Labour in Africa, Asia and Latin America* and *Latin America Transformed: Globalization and Modernity*. He is currently doing research on rural poverty as well as continuing his work on Latin American theories of development.

Azizur Rahman Khan is Adjunct Professor of International and Public Affairs in the School of International and Public Affairs at Columbia University in New York. He has published numerous journal articles, chapters, and books, among the most recent of which is *Inequality and Poverty in China in the Age* of *Globalization*, written with Carl Riskin. Ongoing research interests include income distribution, employment and poverty in developing countries, globalization and its effects on the developing countries, and problems of transition and systemic reform in developing countries.

Terry McKinley is Acting Director of the International Poverty Centre in Brasilia and is a Policy Adviser on Poverty Reduction and Economic Policies in the Bureau for Development Policy, both with the United Nations Development Programme. His work emphasizes the need to develop economic policies that promote growth, employment and redistribution. His books include *Implementing a Human Development Strategy* written with Keith Griffin, *The Distribution of Wealth in Rural China* and *Macroeconomic Policy, Growth and Poverty Reduction.*

Alfons Mosimane lectures in the Faculty of Agriculture and is Head of the Life Science Division of the Multi Disciplinary Research Center of the University of Namibia. His research is principally on exclusion and inclusion with respect to natural resource use, and he has recently published work in this area.

Leonilde Servolo de Medeiros is Professor at the Graduate Center for Development, Agriculture and Society of the Rural Federal University of Rio de Janeiro, Brazil. She has written many books and articles about Brazilian rural social movements and the agrarian reform settlements, and is currently conducting research on the Landless Worker's Movement and the trade union movement of family farmers.

Gebru Mersha is Assistant Professor and past Chairperson of the Department of Political Science and International Relations at Addis Ababa University. He has published several articles on agrarian relations, state farms and the state in Ethiopia, and is currently working on the theme of alternative agrarian structures and their implications for capital formation in Ethiopia.

Sam Moyo is Executive Director of African Institute of Agrarian Studies. In addition to publishing articles on land reform in Zimbabwe he has written *The Land Question in Zimbabwe, Land Reform Under Structural Adjustment in Zimbabwe: Land Use Change in the Mashonaland Provinces* and has most recently co-edited *Reclaiming the Land: The Resurgence of Rural Movements in Africa, Asia and Latin America.*

Ricardo Reyes is Coordinator of the Partnership for Agrarian Reform and Rural Development Services, a Philippine coalition of non-governmental and peasant organizations that advocate land and rural reform. He is the author of numerous articles on agrarian change, social movements, political parties, democratization, and elections in the Philippines.

Max Spoor is Associate Professor at the Institute of Social Studies, The Hague, the Netherlands, Co-ordinator of the Centre for the Study of Transition and Development (CESTRAD), and affiliated Professor at CIDOB and IBEI, Barcelona. He edited *Globalisation, Poverty and Conflict: A Critical 'Development' Reader*, and, most recently, *Dragons with Clay Feet? Transition, Sustainable Land Use and Rural Environment in China and Vietnam*, together with Nico Heerink and Futian Qu, titles which reflect his current research interests.

Miguel Urioste is Director, Fundación TIERRA in La Paz, Bolivia. A former member of the *Cámara de Diputados*, or Parliament, he has undertaken extensive consultancy work on rural poverty and development and has published numerous books and articles, including *Desarrollo Rural con Participación Popular*.

Foreword

The United Nations Development Programme (UNDP) has joined efforts with the Institute of Social Studies (ISS) in The Hague to support the publication of this landmark volume of country studies and analytical papers on 'Land Policies, Poverty and Public Action'. Both UNDP's Poverty Group in New York and the UNDP-supported International Poverty Centre in Brasilia have been active supporters of these studies through a joint UNDP–ISS global project initiated in 2004.

The rationale for UNDP's support of the studies was its recognition that sharp inequalities in access to land have remained a major cause of extreme poverty in many developing countries. It also recognized that neither the state-led nor the market-led land reform model has been successful in resolving these inequalities. Thus arose the principal question for the studies: is there a feasible model of land reform that can both satisfy legitimate and urgent demands for social justice and promote an agrarian system that is economically viable?

Land reform emerged recently as a critical issue in many UNDP-supported national studies on 'Economic Policies and Poverty Reduction'. One of the primary objectives of these studies was the formulation of policies that could generate growth with equity, or 'pro-poor growth', as it has been most recently called. Once the logic of 'pro-poor growth' was accepted, it led to the recognition that in many developing countries, this objective could not be achieved without accelerated rural development. Moreover, in many contexts, rural development could not be achieved, it was recognized, without meaningful land reform.

One clear result of the studies in this volume is that severe inequality in land distribution is a basic issue of social injustice. Hence, an economic calculus of the benefits and costs of land reform is not sufficient. More tellingly, land reform is inevitably controversial. The reason: it invariably alters the distribution of economic power in a country and, by implication, the distribution of political power.

Within this context, the state-led model of land reform – despite having been widely criticized in recent years – has much to commend it. Redistributing economic power in rural areas will require the strong support of the central state, particularly with regard to advancing the interests of the landless and land-deprived. Their demand for land often remains latent until they recognize a genuine opportunity for success. For this purpose, they need to be well organized and the central state needs to be supportive of their efforts.

The state-led model has been criticized for being 'market-distorting' and inefficient. It is true that if successful, such reform will disrupt normal – and unequal – market relations. But once the transfer of land is completed, vibrant market relations can re-establish themselves – but, now, on the basis of a more equitable distribution of wealth. Whether the state-led model leads to an inefficient agrarian system depends, in good measure, on the magnitude of material support that the state provides in the wake of the overhaul of land ownership. If adequate resources do not back up land reform, it is, indeed, more likely to be inefficient. A change in ownership might well unleash a surge of hitherto repressed productivity, but these gains are unlikely to be sustained unless they are buttressed by augmented public investment, credit and technical assistance.

In recent years, the state-led model of land reform has been supplanted as the dominant paradigm by a market-led model. This has been due primarily to forceful lobbying by international financial institutions. But has the market-led model proved superior? In the first place, it has not led, in fact, to a genuine redistribution of wealth. Large landholders must be willing to sell land, and when they do, they must receive 100 per cent of its market value. So, they are fully compensated. By contrast, the landless must be willing to assume a liability, namely, a state loan, in order to buy the land. In order to pay off the loan, not only must the beneficiaries work hard but also general agricultural conditions must remain prosperous.

In general, despite good intentions, the market-led model has underestimated the power of large local landholders (who wield considerable political as well as economic power), and overestimated the power of the landless and land-deprived. The result, in most cases, has been that economic power has trumped the equity objectives of these programmes.

As a consequence, land reform initiatives have turned into localized, underfunded programmes that perhaps have been poverty-alleviating, but certainly not poverty-eliminating. Large landholders sell little land or low-quality land. And when they do sell good land, they command high prices. The decentralization of market-led programmes down to local government (ostensibly to avoid problems of a centralized bureaucracy) has usually catered to the power of local landed elites. In addition, the artificial organizations that the landless form as a prerequisite of these programmes end up wielding little real influence.

Because the market-led model has had only limited success, and has generated, understandably, little enthusiasm among the landless, international financial institutions have recently shifted to a more pragmatic approach. In the name of 'national ownership' of land policies, these institutions have asserted that national governments now have the freedom to choose the most appropriate model. In several countries, both market-led and state-led programmes now coexist. But most multilateral financing still backs, of course, the market-led programmes. So, despite rhetoric to the contrary, the state-led programmes start out with a handicap.

Since both land reform models have had only mixed success, is it possible to envision an alternative? In other words, is there a 'productivity-enhancing Redistributive Alternative'? Although the specifics would have to be articulated within each country, the general outline of such an alternative is not difficult to identify. The general policy lessons that can be derived from the country studies in the UNDP–ISS global project can be formulated as 'Four Pillars'.

The First Pillar is that the rural poor have to form their own *independent* organizations. Such organizations cannot be formed by outside forces, no matter how well meaning. A common theme among land reform programmes that have been relatively successful is their reliance on 'relentless pressure from blow' exerted by the mass mobilization of the landless.

The Second Pillar is that a broad pro-reform national political coalition must have consolidated a firm hold on state power. The coalition has to be strong enough to reject compromise with political factions representing large landholders (who are often very influential at the national level). The coalition also has to be able to uphold the interests of the landless in the face of the growing political influence of large export-oriented agribusiness.

The Third Pillar is that the redistribution of land must be accompanied by substantial public investment, state loans and technical assistance. This should be the main contribution of multilateral and bilateral donors. Definitely, they should not be meddling in the internal politics of a country, such as supporting particular mass organizations or particular political coalitions. But they could play an important role in helping ensure that redistributive land reform will be economically sustainable.

The Fourth Pillar is that land reform has to be part of a more ambitious, growth-oriented development strategy. Economic policies, in particular, have to be geared to promoting 'pro-poor growth'. Restrictive neoliberal economic policies have been an impediment to success in land reform because of their inability to deliver the general conditions of agricultural prosperity that would sustain redistributive reform. Securing more equitable access to landed assets is not likely to be sustainable if growth of the rural economy is impeded. The economic returns to land would remain inadequate.

A 'scaled-up' national development strategy geared to the Millennium Development Goals could help provide a macro environment able to underpin and sustain the significant shift in economic and political power that a broad-based land reform programme would entail. Deprived of such a conducive environment and disconnected from a growth-oriented development strategy, land reform initiatives are likely to degenerate into slow-paced, anemic and, ultimately, ineffectual poverty alleviating programmes.

Terry McKinley
Director a.i.
International Poverty Centre
Brasilia

Preface

In the first six months of 2006 the governments of Bolivia and Venezuela announced plans to introduce wide-ranging reforms governing access to and control over land, in order to enhance the capacity of the poor and the marginalized to construct a livelihood. During the same period, the Food and Agriculture Organization (FAO) of the United Nations (UN) convened the International Conference on Agrarian Reform and Rural Development in Porto Alegre, Brazil, which was the first such major intervention hosted within the UN system in 25 years, and which reaffirmed the need to wider, more secure and sustainable access to land in order to secure poverty eradication and sustainable development. While the conference was underway, *La Via Campesina*, the international peasants' movement, was involved in a major confrontation with the Brazilian government over the grabbing of land by international biotechnology companies engaged in research designed to promote monocropping. Finally, six weeks later the national general secretary of the Philippines peasant movement, UNORKA, was assassinated, in an escalation of violence that had, at its heart, the issue of deepening conflicts over land between peasants, governments and international corporations. In short, 2006 saw a sharp reassertion of the primacy of land reform for all major actors involved in the global politics of development.

In this light, the decision of Terry McKinley, the Macro, Growth and Structural Policies Advisor of the United Nations Development Programme in New York, to organize an international workshop on Land Reform and Poverty Reduction was a prescient one. The workshop took place in February of 2005 at the Institute of Social Studies (ISS) in The Hague, and this book is the direct outcome of it. The ISS was, in many respects, a logical place to hold the workshop, in that, since its foundation, it has been concerned with issues of land, rural poverty and social justice, a concern reflected in the work of Ernst Feder, David Baytelman, Raymond Apthorpe, Henk van Roosmalen, Martin Doornbos, Wicky Meynen, Kurt Martin and Ken Post, as well as that of many current researchers. We are grateful to Terry McKinley for all his efforts in ensuring that both the workshop and this book saw the light of day.

This book is the first of a multi-volume series, Routledge ISS Studies in Rural Livelihoods. Each book in this series will focus on a key theme in rural livelihoods studies, and will seek to explore that theme, in a fresh yet critical manner, from a historical, comparative and policy perspective. We wish to express our thanks to Rob Langham and Terry Clague at Routledge for their commitment both to this book and the series.

A. Haroon Akram-Lodhi
Saturnino M. Borras, Jr
Cristóbal Kay
The Hague

Abbreviations and acronyms

AALS	Affirmative Action Loans Scheme
A&D land	alienable and disposable land
ABRA	*Associação Brasileira de Reforma Agrária* or Brazilian Association of Agrarian Reform
ADB	Asian Development Bank
ARC	Agrarian Reform Community
CA	Compulsory Acquisition
CARP	Comprehensive Agrarian Reform Programme
CBFM	Community-based Forest Management
CBO	community-based organization
CFCP	*Crédito Fundiário de Combate à Pobreza* or Land Credit and Poverty Reduction Programme
CIDOB	*Confederación de Pueblos Indígenas de Bolivia* or Confederation of Indigenous Peoples of Bolivia
CLOA	Certificate of Land Ownership Award
CMARPRP	Community-Managed Agrarian Reform and Poverty Reduction Programme
CNBB	*Conferência Nacional dos Bispos do Brasil* or National Conference of Bishops
CNRA	*Consejo Nacional de Reforma Agraria* or National Council of Agrarian Reform
CONTAG	*Confederação Nacional dos Trabalhadores na Agricultura* or National Confederation of Agricultural Workers
CPT	*Comissão Pastoral da Terra* or Pastoral Land Commission
CSO	civil society organization
CSUTCB	*Confederación Sindical Única de Trabajadores Campesinos de Bolivia* or Confederation of Peasant Trade Unions of Bolivia
CUT	*Central Única dos Trabalhadores*
DAR	Department of Agrarian Reform
DENR	Department of Environment and Natural Resources
DTA	Democratic Turnhalle Alliance
EBRP	*Estrategia Boliviana de Reducción de Pobreza* or Bolivian Strategy of Poverty Reduction

ELF	Eritrean Liberation Front
ENDAR	*Estrategia Nacional de Desarrollo Agropecuario y Rural* or National Strategy of Agricultural and Rural Development
EPLF	Eritrean People's Liberation Forces
EPRDF	Ethiopian People's Revolutionary Democratic Front
ESAP	Economic Structural Adjustment Programme
FAO	Food and Agriculture Organization
FES	*Función Económica y Social* or Social and Economic Function
FSU	Former Soviet Union
FTLRP	Fast-Track Land Reform Programme
GAO	Gross Agricultural Output
GDP	Gross Domestic Product
GoE	Government of Egypt
GoZ	Government of Zimbabwe
HEPR	Hunger Eradication and Poverty Reduction
HIES	Household Income and Expenditure Survey
HIPC	Highly Indebted Poor Countries
ICFU	Indigenous Commercial Farmers Union
Ich'at	Ethiopian Oppressed Peoples' Revolutionary Struggle
IFI	International Financial Institution
IMF	International Monetary Fund
INC	*Instituto Nacional de Colonización* or National Institute of Colonization
INCRA	*Instituto Nacional de Colonização e Reforma Agrária* or National Institute of Colonization and Agrarian Reform
INRA	*Instituto Nacional de Reforma Agraria* or National Institute of Agrarian Reform
LCHR	Land Centre for Human Rights
LSCF	Large-Scale Commercial Farms
LSMS	Living Standards Measurement Surveys
MAIPO	*Ministerio de Asuntos Indígenas y Pueblos Originarios* or Ministry of Indigenous Affairs and Indigenous Peoples
MALR	Ministry of Agriculture and Land Reclamation
MAS	*Movimiento al Socialismo* or Movement toward Socialism
MIRAD	*Ministério da Reforma Agrária e Desenvolvimento* or Ministry for Agrarian Reform and Development
MLAR	market-led agrarian reform
MNC	multinational company
MNR	*Movimiento Nacionalista Revolucionario* or National Revolutionary Movement
MST	*Movimiento dos Trabalhadores Rurais sem Terra* or Landless Rural Workers' Movement
NCA	National Constituent Assembly
NGO	non-government organization
NAPC	National Anti-Poverty Commission

NUDO	National Union of Democrats
ODA	Overseas Development Assistance
OLF	Oromo Liberation Front
OLT	Operation Land Transfer
PNRA	*Plano Nacional da Reforma Agrária* or National Agrarian Reform Plan
PT	*Partido dos Trabalhadores* or Workers' Party
RNF(E)	rural non-farm (employment)
SAP	Structural Adjustment Programme
SCC	State Cadastre Committee
SDO	Stock Distribution Option
SIA	Agricultural Superintendency
SWAPO	South West African People's Organization
TCO	*Tierras Comunitarias de Origen* or Original Community Territory or Community Lands of Origin
TDA	*Títulos da Dívida Agrária* or Agrarian Reform Bonds
TPLF	Tigrian Peoples Liberation Front
UDP	*Unidad Democrática Popular* or Popular Democratic Unity
UDR	*União Democrática Ruralista* or Rural Democratic Union
UNDP	United Nations Development Programme
UNORKA	*Pambansang Ugnayan ng Nagsasariling Lokal na mga Samahang Mamamayan sa Kanayunan* or National Coordination of Autonomous Local Rural People's Organizations
USAID	United States Assistance for International Development
USSR	Union of Soviet Socialist Republics
VLT	Voluntary Land Transfer
VOS	Voluntary Offer-to-Sell
VHLSS	Vietnam Household Living Standards Survey
VLSS	Vietnam Living Standards Surveys
WB	World Bank
WTO	World Trade Organization
ZCFU	Zimbabwe Commercial Farmers Union
ZCTU	Zimbabwean Congress of Trade Unions
ZFU	Zimbabwe Farmers' Union
ZIMPREST	Zimbabwe Programme for Economic and Social Transformation
ZNLWVA	Zimbabwe National Liberation War Veterans Association

1 Agrarian reform and rural development

Historical overview and current issues

Saturnino M. Borras Jr, Cristóbal Kay and A. Haroon Akram-Lodhi

Introduction

Land reform is back on the policy agenda of international development institutions as well as of many nation states.[1] Globally, poverty still has primarily a rural face, with two-thirds of the world's poor constituted by the rural poor. Its persistence has defied policy makers for decades despite sustained efforts by national governments, international institutions and civil society. Effective control over productive resources, especially land, by the rural poor is crucial to their capacity to construct a rural livelihood and overcome poverty. This is because in many agrarian settings a significant portion of the income of the rural poor still comes from farming, despite far-reaching livelihood diversification processes that occurred in different places over time.[2] Hence, lack of access to land is strongly related to poverty and inequality.[3] It is therefore not altogether surprising that the World Bank's 2006 *World Development Report*, focusing on the question of equity, has underscored the importance of land access (World Bank, 2005: chapter 8). However, policy discussions around the Millennium Development Goals are yet to systematically and significantly include the issue of wealth and power redistribution in the rural areas, i.e. agrarian reform, especially in a situation where the majority of the world's poor are rural poor (CPRC, 2005). The need for land reform in the context of the global campaign against poverty has also been one of the key conclusions of the International Conference on Agrarian Reform and Rural Development (ICARRD) held on 6–10 March 2006 in Porto Alegre, Brazil, sponsored by the Food and Agriculture Organisation (FAO) of the United Nations and the Brazilian government (see, e.g. Cotula *et al.*, 2006; Leite with Avila, 2006; Merlet *et al.*, 2006).

But unlike in past theorising and practice of land reform, where the central state took a commanding role, in contemporary thinking about land policies a decisive role is assigned to 'free' market forces in land re-allocation and use.[4] More than a decade into its experimentation and implementation, the new type of land reform should be examined more systematically, both in theory and practice, as to whether it has delivered what it has promised, and if not, why not. Yet, it is important that a parallel critical evaluation of ongoing conventional state-directed land reforms, wherever these have been implemented, must be carried out as well. The end goal is to produce empirically grounded conceptual reflection on land policies and their relevance to rural poverty eradication within the changed and changing global, national and local context.

This book gathers evidence on the impact of the different land policies, and the varying strategies and approaches to implement them, on reducing poverty and social exclusion in the rural areas, with an end view of identifying possible sets of workable alternative policy options in contemporary developing countries and transition economies. This volume maps out and critically analyses the different types of land policies that have been carried out in a number of national settings. It has been guided by a broad conceptualisation of redistributive land reform that includes land titling, restitution of indigenous lands, indigenous land claims, land settlement, tenancy and rental arrangements, farm consolidation and parcelisation, along with the complementary measures necessary to facilitate the success of redistributive reform. Finally, this introductory chapter puts the discussion in this volume within the broader historical perspective and identifies common themes that have been the subject of the country case studies.

The ten countries examined in this study are Armenia, Bolivia, Brazil, Egypt, Ethiopia, Namibia, the Philippines, Uzbekistan, Vietnam and Zimbabwe. These ten countries, cutting across regions, represent broad types of historical contexts within which different land policies have been carried out more recently. The historical context is important to take into consideration partly because it provides us with a good idea about the character of the pre-existing agrarian structure and its relationship with existing poverty – the main objects of the redistributive agenda in any land reform.

The first type involves those countries that have not seen significant land reform in the past but where, since the 1990s, land reform has emerged as an important component of the national development policy and political agendas and has seen greater degrees of implementation. In this research project, this is represented by Brazil and the Philippines. Both countries have seen state-driven attempts to redistribute some lands in the 1950s–1970s, but with less than significant outcomes in terms of the quantity of lands redistributed. Both countries have witnessed strong militant peasant movements in the 1950s–1960s, experienced military dictatorship and regime national transition almost at the same time, in the mid-1980s, coinciding with the resurgence of militant rural social movements demanding land reform (Fox, 1990; Lara and Morales, 1990; Franco, 2001). Carmen Diana Deere and Leonilde Servolo de Medeiros as well as Saturnino Borras Jr., Danilo Carranza and Ricardo Reyes analyse land policies in Brazil and the Philippines, respectively, and explain why and how land reform has been resurrected in these countries from the mid-1980s onward, and with what outcomes. As shown in these studies, both countries have also witnessed the introduction of broadly pro-market approaches to land reform beginning in the later part of the 1990s – side by side with a state-driven land reform programme – and Deere and Medeiros as well as Borras *et al.* examine such approaches and their initial outcomes, particularly looking into their impact on poverty and inequality. Finally, both countries have active contemporary agrarian reform movements, and these are analysed within an 'interactive framework' in the study of state–society relations (Fox, 1993, 2004).

The second type pertains to those national settings that have had significant land reforms in the past within broadly capitalist-oriented development frameworks, but which are now experiencing important ongoing changes in land policies with profound implications for the peasantry. In this book, this type is represented by Bolivia and Egypt, as both countries underwent important land reforms in the 1950s–1960s, although these major land reforms did not result in significant degrees of poverty reduction in either country, and both nations are currently confronted by important changes in land policy regimes. Cristóbal Kay and Miguel Urioste, as well as Ray Bush, examine past land policies and their impact on poverty in Bolivia and Egypt, respectively. They also critically analyse the key features of contemporary adjustments being made in land policies in these countries, and their impact on poverty and social exclusion.

The third type involves those countries that have undergone socialist construction in the past, but are now currently promoting varying forms and degrees of market-oriented land policies. In this research undertaking, this type is represented by Armenia, Ethiopia, Uzbekistan and Vietnam. These countries, with different historical backgrounds, had carried out socialist-oriented land reforms in the past, biased in favour of a combination of farm collectives and state farms. Since the early 1990s, all of these nations started to carry out, in varying extent and pace, broadly pro-market land policies, giving importance to individualised property rights over land, with varying outcomes and implications. Max Spoor (Armenia), Gebru Mersha and Mwangi wa Gĩthĩnji (Ethiopia), Azizur Rahman Khan (Uzbekistan), and A. Haroon Akram-Lodhi (Vietnam) examine the historical evolution of the land policies in these four countries, the recent market-oriented changes in land policies, and their subsequent impact on poverty and inequality.

The fourth type pertains to those countries lacking a long history of land policies, whose ongoing land policies are very much framed within the post-colonial context. This type is represented, in this volume, by Zimbabwe and Namibia. In both countries, land policies have been shaped by the way colonialism ended, as well as the character of the nationalist governments that took over state power. Both have somehow adopted, or were forced to adopt, generally market-oriented land policies, although Zimbabwe started to break away from this framework when the Mugabe government launched its 'fast-track' state-instigated land redistribution campaign in 1996. Sam Moyo (Zimbabwe) as well as Jan Kees van Donge, George Eiseb and Alfons Mosimane (Namibia) examine the evolution of the pro-market land policies and their impact on poverty and social exclusion. They critically analyse the continuing legacy of colonialism far beyond its formal end, as manifested partly in the persistent control over vast tracts of land by white settlers of European origin.

Historical contextualisation of the emergence of varying types of agrarian structures within countries, as done in each of the country case studies in this volume, is important for a better understanding of land-based social relations and state–society interactions around land policies. However, examining land policies on a global level is equally relevant and important for a fuller understanding of the broader and longer historical context within which land reforms appeared, disappeared and reappeared in the development policy agendas. This will be discussed in the succeeding section.

Revisiting past land reforms

The terms 'land reform' and 'agrarian reform' are commonly interchanged to mean the same thing, i.e. to reform existing agrarian structure. However, some scholars find it useful to distinguish these terms, i.e. land reform pertains to the reform of the distribution of landed property rights, while agrarian reform refers to land reform and complementary socio-economic and political reforms (see, e.g. Thiesenhusen, 1989: 7–9). By making this distinction, analysts hoped that highlighting this fact would draw the attention of policy makers to the importance of these complementary measures for improving the chances of success of the reform. In this chapter, we are aware of this distinction, although we will use the two terms interchangeably.

Cycles of land reforms took place in many parts of the world during the distant past. In its varying form and scale, land reform was carried out during ancient times, beginning with the Greeks and Romans. Much later, the French Revolution ushered in the era of modern types of land reform after the ancient regime and feudalism were overthrown in that country. Major land reforms were also carried out in many parts of Europe, including Russia where, prior to the 1917 Bolshevik assumption of state power, at least two significant land reform initiatives took place. But it was the past century that witnessed the most numerous land reforms in human history, starting with the 1910 Mexican revolution. Prior to the Second World War, land reform was also implemented in the communist Union of Soviet Socialist Republics (USSR) where the role of land reform and peasants in the broader industrial development was hotly debated in the

1920s and early 1930s. Land reform became a favoured policy of most countries immediately after the Second World War, a condition that lasted for a few decades, ending decisively in the early 1980s.[5] The reasons for initiating land reform varied between and within nations during the period of the 1940s–1980s, although two dominant categories could be noted, namely, economic and socio-political reasons.

Economic reasons

The economic basis for land reform was quite a powerful imperative for many of these initiatives. This is founded on the interlinked assumptions that large farms under-utilise land, while small farms are wasteful of labour, resulting in low levels of land and labour productivity and consequently leading to poverty.[6] Many agrarian settings are marked by significant degrees of unemployment and under-employment of labour and relative scarcity of land. Hence, from an economic perspective, it is sensible to raise land productivity rather than try to increase labour productivity.[7] There were no major disagreements among scholars on the issue that many of the pre-existing large farms were generally inefficient and needed restructuring, although the main preoccupation that underpinned debates on land reform then was the question of national economic development. It is on the question of strategic perspective, i.e. what type of development paradigm land reform is to serve or be taken to, or to what developmental end should the rural surplus be made to serve, that positions diverge. This has a direct relationship to the closely linked debate on what type of organisation of production should be adopted, i.e. individual or collective farms.

Through time, and amid rich theoretical exchanges and practical experiences, diverse conceptual positions and empirical insights were put forward, revolving around the contentious issues of the role of agriculture in national development, ideological frameworks, and types of organisation of production, among others.[8] There are however two persistently dominant positions. On the one side, there is the position that land reform should eventually take the course of the industrial–urban path to national development, generally favouring a more collectivist type of land reform,[9] and on the other side, the agriculture–rural path to development, generally favouring a land reform that promotes individual small family farms.[10] Moreover and not altogether de-linked from the above-mentioned dichotomy, land reforms during the past century were also divided by their ideological perspectives, namely, capitalist- or socialist-oriented, although each camp is quite diverse. Broadly, in the former, land reform was used to develop private property rights further as a key institution in capitalist development, while in the latter land reform was used to liquidate private property rights to strengthen a socialist development largely driven by the state.[11]

In most non-socialist settings, the types of organisation of production created during and after land reform were very much determined by the character of the pre-existing agrarian structure. It was mainly the collectivist types of land reform communities that emerged in much of Latin America, partly due to the character of pre-existing landholdings, where large farmholdings were directly operated by landlords and where the contribution by peasants was mainly labour. In general, individual family farms emerged in East Asian land reforms partly because the pre-reform farms were smaller and usually under sharecropping arrangements with tenant-farmers.

Meanwhile, in most socialist settings, two types of organisation of the reform sector came into being: state farms and collective/cooperative farms – and these were determined largely by both the conditions prior to the revolutionary takeover of farms and the strategic developmental goals and approaches of the socialist central state. In some cases, the socialist state just took over plantations from corporate owners, foreign and domestic, recruited workers and continued the operation of these new state farms. In other cases, the state expropriated lands and redistributed them to peasants who were in turn organised into cooperatives. In Cuba after the revolution of 1959, both forms of land expropriation and organisation of farms occurred, although state farms predominated (Ghai *et al.*, 1988). However, in the 1990s, the pre-existing organisations of production have started to be transformed, affecting state farms in particular, which have been broken up into smaller landholdings that are operated through cooperatives with aspirations for greater production and marketing efficiency (Deere, 2000).

While it may seem that the forms of organisations that emerged out of land reforms in both capitalist and socialist settings were clustered neatly either as state- or privately owned, individual or collectivist, in reality, the situations were diverse. Peasants subverted or revised, or acquiesced to, state-imposed membership of cooperatives or collectives; individual farmers joined together for purposes of achieving economies of scale in input and output markets; land rights were rented out and sold despite the legal ban on the practice; workers' efficiency levels fluctuated in state-controlled industrial farming complexes, mechanisation was developed in some places and not in others, and so on – with the overall effects resulting in almost always unintended and unexpected outcomes of official policies.[12]

Socio-political reasons

But while the economic basis of land reform was a crucial reason for carrying out land reform, a variety of socio-political imperatives had in fact and on most occasions provided the critical push for such policies to be adopted and implemented by national governments. There were at least six interlinked broad types of socio-political reasons. First, on the eve of and immediately after the Second World War, the decolonisation process spread like a prairie fire in much of what used to be called the Third World. Land reform became an integral component of these processes in many national settings, such as in Algeria and Egypt, where emerging nationalist governments took over colonial lands and distributed these, or some of these, to their landless rural citizens. The decolonisation process continued into the late 1950s and until the 1970s in some former colonies where, to varying extents, land reform also found its way onto the main agenda of the emerging nationalist governments, such as in Indonesia with the Basic Agrarian Law of 1960 and Zimbabwe with its land reform of 1980.[13]

Second, geo-political and ideological imperatives in the context of the build-up towards and during the Cold War provided crucial context and reason for the rise of land reform in the international and national policy agendas. The post-war 'division' of the world into the capitalist and socialist blocs had made the United States rush to consolidate its ideological and political hold in East Asia, which was fronting the vast territories of the communist USSR and China. Land reform was a key component in the American consolidation of this region, where it imposed and financed sweeping land reforms in Japan, South Korea and Taiwan partly in reaction to the revolutionary land reform being carried out in China.[14] The subsequent Cold War became an arena where the capitalist and socialist ideological perspectives battled against each other on different contentious themes, among which was the question of how to address the issue of rural poverty, through what type of land reform, and within what broader development framework. As communist- and socialist-inspired national liberation movements gained ground, some of which were able to seize state power, the capitalist bloc took on the agenda of land reform with greater ideological vigour and an increased sense of political urgency. American agents led by Wolf Ladejinsky crisscrossed the world to pressure national governments to carry out (a capitalist version of) 'pre-emptive' land reform (see Walinsky, 1977; Ross, 1998: chapter 5; Putzel, 1992). Towards this end, the US instigated the formation of the Alliance for Progress in Latin America and the Caribbean in the 1960s where land reform took centre-stage in the alliance's agenda. In short, land reform was used by the two contending camps as key policy ammunition (and as a shield) during the Cold War.

Third, land reform also became a crucial component of the national projects of victorious peasant-based revolutions. The prominence of land reform in this context is due partly to the fact that the demand for land by peasants was quite strongly internalised within the revolutionary government. But its prominence was also partly due to the revolutionary government's desire to consolidate its political legitimacy and to quell possible reactionary counter-revolution on the one hand, and the central state's need to proceed with its developmental project, to be financed to a significant extent by 'squeezing' agriculture of surplus factors of production. It was in this context that land reforms emerged and were implemented in Mexico, Bolivia, Nicaragua and Vietnam (Tannenbaum, 1929; Grindle, 1986; Collins *et al.*, 1982; Paige, 1975; Wolf, 1969). The Guatemalan land reform emerged in a relatively similar context, but it was a case that saw immediate reversal through a counter-revolution (see Handy, 1994).

Fourth, in reaction to external and internal political pressure, land reform was used by central states to 'manage' rural unrest. While some of this unrest was communist-inspired, many should be seen as parts of ongoing cycles of peasant revolt against unjust and exploitative conditions, and their struggles for social justice, as in the cases of the Huk and Mau-Mau rebellions in the Philippines and Kenya. The conflagration of forcible land occupations, often met with violence from state and non-state actors, that marked the countryside of many countries after the Second World War, such as those in Peru, the Philippines, northern Mexico, Indonesia (see Wolf, 1969; Stavenhagen, 1971; Hobsbawm, 1974; Landsberger, 1974; Kerkvliet, 1993; Huizer, 2001; Kay, 2001; Redclift, 1978), and even in Italy, Portugal and southern Spain, unsettled national governments. The subsequent patches of successful regional land redistribution outcomes within these countries were testimonies to the efforts of central states to respond, albeit selectively and partially, to these pockets of rural unrest.

Fifth, in other cases, land reform was used to legitimise and/or consolidate the claim to state power by one faction of the elite against another. This happened immediately after a military takeover of state power, as in Peru in the late 1960s, where the new government tried to debase possible elite challengers by expropriating their landholdings and to court popular support by redistributing lands to peasants (Kay, 1983), or in the Philippines during the Marcos authoritarian regime (Putzel, 1992; Riedinger, 1995). This also happened when Left political parties gained electoral victories, such as those in Chile in the early 1970s (Castillo and Lehmann, 1983), as well as in the states of Kerala and West Bengal in India.[15]

Finally, land reform was used by the central state in its continuing state-building process. Land reform, and the usually accompanying land titling and colonisation programmes, required systematic and standardised cadastral maps, land titles, and peasant household registration, and so on. These in turn fed into the need of the central state to extend its administrative, political and military-police presence and authority into the more remote parts of its claimed territory, as well as into its need to develop its tax base. Taken altogether, these processes form part of the central state's effort, in the words of James Scott (1998), to 'simplify' and render 'legible' the otherwise numerous complex social relationships in 'non-state spaces'.

Different land reforms were passed into law, implemented, and resulted in varied and uneven outcomes between and within countries over time. Some land reforms redistributed more lands, either collectively or individually, to more peasant households than others, such as those in Cuba, China, Japan, South Korea, Kerala, Bolivia, Taiwan, Peru and Mexico on the one side, and Venezuela, Brazil, Bangladesh and Pakistan on the other. Some of the land reforms able to redistribute significant quantities of land to a significant number of agricultural households actually led to a substantial reduction in rural poverty, such as those in South Korea and Kerala, although other countries in the same category did not witness any significant rural poverty reduction, such as Bolivia. Moreover, the countries that carried out significant land reform and where the state provided massive direct and indirect support in the input and output markets of the rural economy, as well as in pro-poor social policies (e.g. health, education), were able to reduce rural poverty quite dramatically, as in the cases of Taiwan, China and Cuba. Meanwhile, the countries that undertook important land reforms but whose national governments failed to carry out massive and sustained support in the input and output markets for the reformed rural sectors were unable to radically reduce the level of poverty in their countryside, as in the case of Bolivia and Mexico.[16]

Furthermore, four issues relevant to the discussion above should be noted. First, none of the various competing brands of and approaches to land reform had the monopoly of cases that resulted in widespread land redistribution and poverty eradication. Second, in general land reforms were carried out in many developing countries amid the dominant 'protectionist', 'inward-looking' development strategies developed and promoted by countries in the socialist bloc as well as those in the capitalist world. Land reform had become an integral component of these inward-looking, protectionist policies for a variety of reasons, including the central state's aspiration to create a domestic market for its industrial sector (see, e.g. Kay, 2002; Wuyts, 1994). It is not surprising therefore that the peak period of import-substituting industrialisation (ISI) was also the era of land reformism in many countries. The timing of land reform in the context of a country's industrialisation drive can be very crucial and may have direct bearing on the probability of success in land redistribution as well as in post-land redistribution national development, as, for example, in the contrasting cases of Latin America and East Asia (Kay, 2002). Third, some of these land reforms were later subjected to counter-reform where, to varying extents, redistributed lands, or portions of these, were returned to the previous owners and other sectors close to the new status quo. In varying circumstances and extents of reform reversal, Guatemala, Chile and Nicaragua share this similar experience. Fourth, most of the land reforms, but especially the capitalist-oriented ones, while they involved significant degrees of state initiative and intervention, had also witnessed the important roles played by non-state actors – i.e. peasant movements and their allies. These issues bring us to the question of policy and political strategies of carrying out land reform, a topic that occupies an important portion of the current discourse on land policies.

Different land reforms were implemented by state and non-state actors through different political strategies between and within countries over time. Some were implemented through varying strands of centralised authoritarian methods, such as in many East Asian land reforms (Tai, 1974), China and Peru, while others were implemented through more democratic approaches, as in the cases of Kerala and West Bengal in India (Herring, 1983). While some analysts would present a dichotomy marked by 'state-led' on the one side, and 'peasant-led' on the other (see, e.g. de Janvry, Sadoulet and Wolford, 2001), it may be more useful to look at these political processes within an 'interactive state/society' perspective because resolving claims and counter-claims for property rights involves not only a peasant–state relationship, but also relations within the state and between different groups in society (Borras, 2001; Herring, 1983; Fox, 1993, 2004). The interactive state/society framework seems to offer a better analytical lens to explain political processes in land reform, whether in single party-ruled socialist countries such as in China during the first wave of communist land reform in the early 1950s (Shillinglaw, 1974), or politically open countries with ruling communist/socialist parties that implemented land reform, as in Chile under Allende, or in West Bengal and Kerala in India (Kay and Silva, 1992; Ghose, 1983b). In these cases, land reform implementation relied on the ruling parties and the central state, but these, in turn, relied heavily on the mobilisation of the rural masses to actually implement land reform and make it work. Meanwhile, land reforms undertaken in capitalist-oriented, open political settings, relied to a large extent on the autonomy and capacity of the central state to carry out its promise of and mandate for land reform. But the central state in turn relied largely on the support and mobilisation of the affected rural population (Barraclough, 2001). In many settings, of course, the state simply took the lead from the peasants who unilaterally occupied lands, forcing the central state to legitimise such actions, as in the case of the Bolivian land reform of 1953 (Urioste, 2001).

The 1980s interregnum

Meanwhile, in the 1980s, land reform had had an abrupt and heavy fall from grace. It was eliminated from official development policy agendas of international institutions and nation states. While in most cases nation states did not actually pass new laws to stop or halt land reforms, many of them decided to place existing land reform laws and policies in dormant status: land reform laws continue to exist, at least officially, but no significant funds were allotted to nor administrative machineries set up or maintained for their implementation. In short, there was no 'political will' to implement the land reform law. The cases of land reform laws in Indonesia (see, e.g. Wiradi, 2005; Bachriadi and Sardjono, 2005; Bachriadi and Fauzi, 2006) and Bolivia are examples of this (Kay and Urioste, this volume). It was at this historical juncture that the broadly pro-market land policy reforms would find their seeds. The subsequent paradigm shift in terms of land reform occurred due to various factors, or the convergence of such factors, as will be discussed below.

Among such factors is the debt crisis that started in the early 1980s that crippled the fiscal capabilities of the national governments of most developing countries and slowed down their economic growth and development. The subsequent rise of neoliberalism and its advocacy to cut back public spending and at the same time to raise taxes largely in order to pay off debts or just to scale down if not stop borrowing altogether pushed land reform out of the official agenda of many national governments because it is a policy that required substantial state financing, including regular appropriation to maintain a huge bureaucracy, while at the same time it is believed to erode some sections of pre-existing tax base.[17]

Second, the economic crisis of agriculture in general,[18] and the land reform sector in particular, that included widespread social discontent about the 'actually existing' land reforms, both in socialist and capitalist settings, forced governments and external development agencies to introduce varying forms and degrees of adjustments. In some socialist countries as well as in capitalist settings that resorted to collectivist land reform, experiments on (state and) collective farms did not usually result in the intended gains in production and productivity levels, both for the households and for the purposes of national development campaigns. These farm collectives were also hounded by the persistent problem of rent-seeking activities by state officials and farm collective leaders. These conditions provided constant pressure for de-collectivisation, which was eventually matched by the central state's eagerness to rescind on their responsibility for the (economic) performance of the reformed sector.[19]

Third, beginning in the 1970s, technological advances directly and indirectly related to agriculture gained more ground: more fertiliser and pesticide use, proliferation of improved seeds and high-yield varieties, farm mechanisation, relative improvement in physical infrastructure in the rural areas such as road, irrigation and electrification – the Green Revolution package of technology (see, e.g. Griffin, 1974). There were optimistic celebrations about the prospects of eradicating rural poverty and hunger via technological innovation. While in some instances, both in policy discourse and in actual practice, technological advances and land reform were not seen to contradict each other, the rise in significance of technological advances in the input and output markets of agriculture gave additional incentive for modernising, entrepreneurially minded landlords to resist land reform, and provided governments with less politically contentious policy alternatives toward rural poverty reduction.[20]

Fourth, in the 1980s, especially toward the later part of that decade, most communist- and socialist-inspired national liberation movements had been waning, with others completely dissipated, for various internal and external reasons. The conflagration of unrest manifested in peasant land occupations that marked much of the rural world in the 1950s through the 1970s was not immediately visible during this decade. From a distance, there was relative silence and calm. Of course one reason for this was the demobilisation of the previously militant mass of peasants after they received lands from the state land reform programmes during the preceding decade or two. The relative absence of visible forms of significant peasant unrest and militancy in the rural areas during this decade helped encourage national governments to relegate land reforms to a dormant status if not remove them from the official agenda altogether.

Finally, the end of the Cold War towards the later part of the 1980s signalled some form of closure of the ideological rivalry between socialist versus capitalist paths to development. There was a general perception that there was no more immediate communist and socialist threat to the capitalist world, and so, there was no more urgent need for 'Ladejinskys' to crisscross the world to promote pre-emptive land reforms. In the 1980s, restructuring of property rights and farm work incentive structures in state and collective farms were slowly introduced in countries that would later be labelled collectively as 'transition economies'. These reforms have been broadly market-oriented, giving individuals and households more flexibility in some bundles of landed property rights and providing them greater control over their farm surplus and on how to dispose of it. But as will be shown by Akram-Lodhi (Vietnam, this volume), Khan (Uzbekistan, this volume) and Spoor (Armenia, this volume), it would only be in the 1990s, after the decisive collapse of the actually existing socialism in Eastern Europe, that such market-oriented reforms would gain enormous ground (see, e.g. Akram-Lodhi, 2005; Spoor, 2003; Deere, 2000).

These five factors, separately and jointly, adversely impacted on land reform, resulting in the latter's decisive exclusion from the official development agendas. This policy elimination was carried out with relative ease partly because of the 'chequered' record of land reform, especially in terms of its declared goal of poverty eradication – and, arguably, because those that wanted land reform off the official development policy agenda were successful in waging hegemonic policy discourse, projecting land reform as a 'failure', especially in terms of eradicating poverty in the countryside (see Borras, 2003b).

The resurrection and 'metamorphosis' of land reform in the 1990s

In the 1990s, however, land reform was resurrected in the development policy agendas of international development institutions as well as those of many nation states. It was a confluence of events and convergence of factors that put land back on the agenda.

First, around the mid-1990s, pockets of dramatic land-based political conflicts caught the attention of the world. Three of these were most important, namely, the Chiapas uprising in southern Mexico, the state-instigated land invasions by black landless poor of white commercial farms in Zimbabwe, and the resurgence of militant peasant land occupations in Brazil reminiscent of the actions by the peasant leagues of the 1950s but much greater in scale and political sophistication (Brass, 2003; Harvey, 1998; Moyo, 2000; Moyo and Yeros, 2005; Ghimire, 2005; Petras, 1998, 1997; Veltmeyer, 2005, 1997; Wright and Wolford, 2003; Meszaros, 2000; Branford and Rocha, 2002). National governments were compelled to address these boiling social pressures 'from below', while the international development community grappled with the meanings and implications of such complex conflicts, resulting in the convergence of international and national efforts to address these land-based grievances. But as Borras *et al.* (this volume) and Kay and Urioste (this volume) will explain, these resurgent peasant mobilisations also occurred in many other places, such as in the Philippines and Bolivia, as well as in Honduras, South Africa and Indonesia, although these did not receive the same scale and extent of (inter)national media attention as the three cases cited above.[21] Altogether, these phenomena validate what Ronald Herring (2003) observed, that land reform was taken off the 'policy agendas' of national governments and international agencies, but it never left the 'political agendas' of peasants and their organisations. Herring explained that even 'dead land reforms are not dead; they become nodes around which future peasant mobilisations emerge because promises unkept keep movements alive'. It is also important to note that these peasant actions have been broadened in many parts of the world by mobilisations for land and democratic rights by indigenous peoples, such as those in Bolivia and Ecuador (see, e.g. Yashar, 1999, 2005; Korovkin, 2000) and by peasant women (see, e.g. Razavi, 2003), as well as by the urban poor in countries like Brazil and South Africa. These changed contexts and sets of actors have also transformed the perceptions about land reform and rural livelihoods (Gwynne and Kay, 2004), facilitating the emergence of (new) sets of policy agendas, such as renewed efforts in land titling and cadastral records that would subsequently attract greater development policy and academic interest (Zoomers and van der Haar, 2000; Kay, 1998).

Second, in some countries ravaged by political conflict, negotiated settlements or regime transitions occurred, where the question of solving poverty and social exclusion was made part of the peace-building processes or democratic (re)constructions, especially those in the countryside.[22] Hence, for example, land reform was resurrected in the official agendas of the El Salvadorean and Guatemalan governments as part of their post-conflict peace-building process (de Bremond, 2006; Foley, 1997; Pearce, 1998; Diskin, 1989; Gauster, 2006). The same was attempted a few years back in Colombia, although without much success in terms of sustaining it in the official agenda (Ross, 2003). Moreover, it was within a post-authoritarian regime transition context that land reforms were resurrected in the official policy agendas in the mid-1980s in Brazil and the

Philippines (see Deere and Medeiros, as well as Borras *et al.*, this volume; see also Fox, 1990; Houtzager, 2000; Franco, 2001; Riedinger, 1995). It was also in the same context that the land reform agenda took prominence in post-apartheid South Africa, where, alongside the adopted policies of land distribution and leasehold reform, the policy of land restitution was officially inaugurated (Ntsebeza, 2006).[23] It is also in this similar context that the heated land policy debate erupted in post-dictatorship Indonesia (Lucas and Warren, 2003; Aspinal, 2004).

Third, beginning in the early 1990s, when several countries abandoned socialism, they were confronted by the difficult question of what to do with the huge state and collective farms. The challenge of sensible transition for these farms has put the question of landed property rights among the top policy agendas of concerned national governments and international development institutions (see Spoor, this volume; Deininger, 1995, 2002; Spoor, 2003; Spoor and Visser, 2004; Mersha and Gĩthĩnji, this volume). Also, other socialist countries, as mentioned earlier, started to adjust the incentive structure in their agricultural sector, ushering in a new era of varying forms and bundles of land-based property rights and market exchange in several socialist countries (see, e.g. Akram-Lodhi, 2004, 2005; Kerkvliet, 2005, 1994, for Vietnam).

Finally, the rise of neoliberalism and its aspiration to achieve complete ideological hegemony in all aspects of development questions and initiatives has brought the issue of land under a new – but different – spotlight. The problems with earlier neoliberal policy prescriptions became more apparent in the late 1980s, particularly the inherent limits and flaws of income-centred and growth-oriented approaches to poverty eradication and development. The persistent poverty and growing inequality have put into question the neoliberal paradigm. The emergence of this problem forced mainstream economists to introduce adjustments to their development policy model. It is in this context that the issue of poor people's access to productive assets, including land, was (re)introduced. The assumption is that poor people are poor because they do not have access to productive resources. Closely linked to this is the popularisation of the notion of 'insecurity' in the context of rural livelihoods and economic investments in the countryside. The consensus among mainstream economists was that many rural poor people have insecure access to land resources, leading to their unstable livelihoods and low level of investments. The imperative of developing formal private and individualised landed property rights through land titling programmes in public lands, as well as land sales and rental arrangements in private lands, have thus become more urgent and necessary. It has been popularly assumed that these property rights-related campaigns will not only make poor people's access to land secure, but that they will also make financial investments in the rural economy more attractive (see Deininger and Binswanger, 1999; World Bank, 2003, 2005). Furthermore, the interest in land and in the institutional regulations about its ownership, control and use is also linked to the efforts of the transnational corporate sector, especially those engaged in the agro-food and timber sectors, to expand their production (and trade) hegemony in developing countries and transition economies (see Friedmann, 2005; Goodman and Watts, 1997; McMichael, 1995; Magdoff *et al.*, 1998; Lappé *et al.*, 1998; van den Hombergh, 2004; Borras, forthcoming). And so land was rushed back onto the development policy agendas of mainstream international development institutions, and then re-channelled widely to national government agencies, and even to NGOs.

Altogether, the four factors and events have put land back onto official development policy discourses and agendas. However, the content and context of the policy revival are significantly different from those of the past land reform policy initiatives. The terms of the current policy discourse on land are dominated by the broadly pro-market mainstream economists. The previous, ideologically grounded debates around 'capitalist-versus socialist-oriented', 'individualist versus collectivist' land reforms were now supplanted by the new discourses propagated by those who rejected the conventional notion of expropriationary land reform. And so we are currently confronted by debate formulations such as: 'state- versus market-led', 'coercive versus voluntary', 'centralised versus decentralised', or 'top-down/supply-driven versus bottom-up/demand-driven' land reforms (see Borras, 2003a, 2003b, 2005).[24] Instead of uncritically accepting these presented dichotomies, we take such constructions as problematic.

Moreover, among the ongoing land reforms diversity in approach is apparent: from 'state-instigated' as in Zimbabwe (see, e.g. Moyo, this volume; Palmer, 2000b; Moyo, 2000; Worby 2001), to 'peasant-led' as in Brazil (Wright and Wolford, 2003; Wolford, 2003; Rosset, 2001; Petras, 1998; Veltmeyer, 2005),[25] to 'state-society-driven' as in the Philippines (Borras, 2001; Franco, forthcoming; Franco and Borras, 2005), to 'market-led', as in some pilot programmes in Colombia, Brazil, South Africa and the Philippines (Deininger, 1999). It is thus important to examine from a comparative perspective the ongoing land reforms in different parts of the world, highlighting both their similarities and differences; this research undertaking aspires to contribute toward this effort by drawing lessons from the discussion of the ten country cases.

In short, past land reforms, despite their diversity in ideological provenance and orientation, had been united on several common economic and socio-political themes. Nevertheless, past land reform discourse and practice also missed, to a significant degree, a number of issues now considered as crucial to the success or failure of land reform itself, and of any broad-based sustainable development more generally. The way different development issues, broadly categorised as economic and socio-political, have become important contexts for and objects of land reforms, has been altered over time, as partly shown in Table 1.1. If we take a simplified

Table 1.1 Changes in the economic and socio-political bases of, and imperatives for, land reforms

Pre-1980s period	1990s onward
Economic	
Existing large landed estates are economically inefficient; must be restructured via land reform	Continuing relevance/currency
Creation of privatised and individualised landed property rights to boost investments in rural economy	Continuing – and has seen greater expansion in coverage
	Issues related to inefficiency (and accountability) in (former) socialist state farms and e.g. Eastern Europe, central Asia, Vietnam, China
	Issues related to efficiency in farm collectives brought about by past land reforms, cooperatives, e.g. Mexico and Peru
Socio-Political	
Decolonisation	While to a large extent it is not a burning issue with the same intensity as decades ago, decolonisation process-related issues have persisted in many countries, such as Zimbabwe
Cold War	Not any more
Central state's 'management' of the rural unrest usually instigated by liberation movements for revolutionary societal/state transformation	Diminished substantially as liberation movements waned. But rural unrest persisted usually not in the context of armed groups wanting to seize state power but to push for radical reforms, e.g. Chiapas, Brazil
As a strategy to legitimise and/or consolidate one elite faction's hold on state power against another, e.g. Left electoral victories, military coup d'état.	Continuing, e.g. Zimbabwe, tenancy reform by the Left Front in West Bengal

As an integral component of the central state's 'modernisation', i.e. standardised cadastral maps, etc. for taxation purposes, etc.

Continuing, and has seen unprecedented degree of technological sophistication (e.g. satellite/digital mapping, computerised databanking)

New issues

i   Post-conflict democratic construction and consolidation, e.g. post-apartheid South Africa, post-civil war El Salvador (de Bremond, 2006; Pearce, 1998; Foley, 1997), Colombia (Ross, 2003) and Rwanda (Liversage, 2003).

ii   Advancement of knowledge about the distinct rights of indigenous peoples (e.g. Yashar, 1999, 2005; Korovkin, 2000; Corpuz and Cariño, 2004; Assies *et al*., 1998)

iii   Advancement of knowledge about *gender* and *land* rights issues, see, e.g. Razavi (2003); Agarwal (1994), Kabeer (1995), Deere (1985) and Deere and León (2001)

iv   Greater knowledge about the relationship between land and the environment (see, e.g. Leach *et al*, 1999; Li, 2002; Peluso, 1992; Roth, 2004; Bachriadi and Sardjono, 2005; Herring, 2002)

v   Persistence and resurgence of violence (see, e.g. Pons-Vignon and Lecomte, 2004; Peluso, 2002; Via Campesina, 2005, 2006)

vi   Emerging '[human] rights-based approaches' to development (see, e.g. Franco, 2006; Johnson and Forsyth, 2002).

vii   The phenomenal rise of NGOs as important actors in development questions at the local, national and international levels (see, e.g. Borras, 2006c; IPC for Food Sovereignty, 2006) periodisation of pre-1980s' and post-1990s' land reforms (with the 1980s as an 'interregnum'), then we would see that many old issues have remained relevant and important up to this time, while others have in varying degrees waned in importance or even disappeared. Still, many development issues that were not critical in the past have emerged to be important issues at present, and certainly, in the future, as in the cases of gender, indigenous peoples, violence and the environment. While land reforms were admittedly treated as integral components of broad development strategies whose strategic aims eventually included eradicating poverty, in general the relationship between land reform and poverty reduction were more theoretically assumed than empirically demonstrated.

When land reform was resurrected in development policy discourse from the 1990s, it had undergone a metamorphosis, at least as far as the dominant groups in the academic and policy practitioner's circles are concerned. The neoliberal paradigm on land policies is the dominant current in today's development policy discourse and practice. These land policies have been conceptualised and promoted within a changed global, national and local context. Development strategies changed from having a 'protectionist and inward-looking perspective', to a 'free trade and outward-looking orientation', or from state-directed to market-oriented. The land policies that emerged in the 1990s, and the various meanings and purposes accorded to these by different competing groups, should be seen as integral components of these processes of global neoliberal reforms – as explained for example by Bush (this volume) in the context of Egypt.[26]

These land policies have been theorised for and carried out in four broad types of settings. First, 'public and/or communal' lands are the chief targets for privatisation. Mainstream economic policies are arguing and advocating for the systematic privatisation and individualisation of property rights in public/communal lands in order to transform these land resources into active capital. Thus, renewed interest and initiatives at land titling, registration and (decentralised land) administration have seen an unprecedented level and extent.[27] The current efforts are different from past initiatives on at least two counts: i) the scale in terms of spaces being covered, or aspired to be covered, is enormous and unprecedented; and ii) the degree of technical sophistication in terms of (satellite/digital) mapping and (computerised) data-banking has been unparallelled in human history. Moreover, while the mainstream policies at times recognise the relevance of pre-existing communal forms of property ownership, they nevertheless advocate for individualised property rights within these blocks of common landed properties, e.g. individual plots where the right to use can be freely traded (World Bank, 2003; but see Cousins and Claassens, 2006; Juul and Lund, 2002). This policy, aimed at homogenising property rights regimes across diverse national and subnational settings, is currently being implemented through various policies and projects, with varied outcomes.[28]

Second, state and collective farms, both in capitalist settings and in 'transition economies,' are also important targets for farm privatisation and parcelisation. Mainstream economists believe that collective farms established in settings where significant capitalist-oriented land reforms were implemented in the past had produced institutions that have hampered, not promoted, incentives for individuals to become economically efficient and competitive farmers, and have impeded the emergence of a more fluid land market. Thus, they have advocated for the privatisation and individualisation of property rights in these farms, as a key incentive for farms to produce more and to produce efficiently. This is the case, for example, in Mexico and Peru. Moreover, and for broadly similar reasons, the policy of privatisation and individualisation of state collective farms in transition economies was also advocated and (unevenly) carried out in different countries (Deininger, 1995; Spoor, 2003; Wegren, 2004). The initial outcomes varied between countries: it did not seem to have the intended outcome of vibrant land markets in the reformed (privatised-parcelised) *ejidos* in Mexico (Nuijten, 2003) for example, although it seems to have resulted in increased production and productivity levels, albeit amid increasing inequality, in Vietnam (Akram-Lodhi, 2005).[29]

The first two policies discussed so far are directed towards non-private lands – in order to create private, individualised landed property rights. The discussion that follows will be on the two policies directed towards private lands.

Third, private productive farms are to be reformed only under certain conditions and within a specific economic orientation. For mainstream economists and development policy experts one of the reasons for the low production and productivity level in rural economies is because of the persistence of 'distortions' in the land market where inefficient producers continue to own and control lands while the more efficient ones (and those that have potential to become efficient producers) could not access land (World Bank, 2003). These distortions, according to the mainstream view, are caused by various factors including many land reform-related laws that limit land rental and sales transactions in the market. For the mainstream view, the principal policy for this type of setting is the promotion of non-coercive sharecropping tenancy reform, through leasehold arrangements. This policy is believed to be more sensible and practical towards achieving the most economically efficient land resource use and allocation, and it does not entail any major state fiscal requirement. It will also contribute to the development of a vibrant land market. Sadoulet *et al.* (2001: 196–197) explain that land markets 'have welfare effects, even though rental is not a transfer of wealth'. They contend that this is because 'in the long-run, access to land via tenancy may help the landless capitalise the returns to otherwise idle assets [e.g. family labour], accumulate wealth, and move up an "agricultural ladder" toward land ownership'. Klaus Deininger of the World Bank's land policy unit supports this assumption and argues that only in settings where a rental arrangement is not feasible should land reform through land sales be considered (1999: 666). For the mainstream view, this policy should be carried out simultaneously with other related policies including those that lift the 'ceiling' on land ownership and ban on land rental and sales, as well as the legal prohibitions on share tenancy practices (World Bank, 2003; see also Baranyi *et al.*, 2004: 33).

The fourth pertains to private farms, but with different policy treatment. The mainstream view still believes that large inefficient farms should be redistributed to tenant-farmers and farmworkers, so that small family farms, believed to be more economically efficient, can be created. But the approach to carrying out this reform is quite different from the conventional framework. This policy aims to substitute the conventional coercive land reform with a voluntary policy. As mentioned above, the favoured policy toward private farms is the promotion of a share tenancy arrangement; only in circumstances where there are 'willing sellers' and 'willing buyers' of land should land sales be allowed. The features of this pro-market 'land reform' are, according to its advocates, the opposite of the features of conventional land reforms: voluntary not coercive, demand-driven not supply-driven, private not state land transactions, decentralised not centralised, top-down/centralised versus bottom-up/decentralised, and so on. This policy, popularly known as Market-Led Agrarian Reform (MLAR), is a scheme whereby landlords are paid 100 per cent spot-cash for 100 per cent of the market value of the land, where the cost of the land transfer is shouldered fully by the buyer, and where landlords unwilling to part with their estates will not be coerced to sell their lands (Deininger and Binswanger, 1999; World Bank, 2003, 2005: 156–175; but see Borras, 2003a, 2003b, 2005; Navarro, 1998).

In varying policy adaptations and scales, this policy model has been implemented in several countries, such as Brazil, Colombia, South Africa and the Philippines. Its initial outcomes, or the meanings of these outcomes especially in terms of reducing poverty and social exclusion in the countryside, are interpreted differently by different scholars and policy practitioners. For the optimistic claims, see Buainain *et al.* (1999), Deininger (1999), Deininger and Binswanger (1999); and for critical insights, see Rosset, Patel and Courville (2006), Barros *et al.* (2003), Sauer (2003), Levin and Weiner (1997), Lahiff (2003), Bhandari (2006), Lebert (2001), El-Ghonemy (2001), Riedinger *et al.* (2000), Reyes (1999) and Borras (2003a, 2003b, 2005, 2006b).[30] This policy has been actively opposed by several rural-oriented civil society groups, coordinated internationally by *La Via Campesina*, the Foodfirst Information and Action Network or FIAN, and the Land Research and Action Network or LRAN (see Baranyi *et al.*, 2004; Borras, 2004; IPC, 2006).

In short, policies in the four broad types of settings are based upon the use of markets as a principal means of reallocating land resources under formal property rights that are 'secure' so as to entice capital inflows into the rural economy. The World Bank calls these policies collectively 'pro-poor land policies'. The initial outcomes of these land policies in various countries were comprehensively reviewed by the World Bank in its August 2003 Policy Research Report *Land Policies for Growth and Poverty Reduction*. This report is now an important document in the formulation of land policies in many developing and transition economies, as well as having a major influence on debates around such policies. In fact, in November 2004 the European Union Council of Ministers approved its own similar, but not the same, version of a blueprint of land policy guidelines for its overseas development assistance,[31] and so have all other major multilateral and bilateral development agencies. The framework of this World Bank report has been reiterated in the *World Development Report 2006* (see chapter 8).

Common themes and competing perspectives

The economic and socio-political imperatives for, bases and impact of, land reforms are the common themes to all country case studies in this multidisciplinary research. These themes are examined not separately from each other, but in a relational way. In this research undertaking, land and landed property rights are treated not merely as factors of economic production, but as resources that have social, cultural and political dimensions. Understanding the relationships between these different dimensions of land and the policies around them necessarily requires a closer examination of the roles of the 'free' market, state and civil society – and how they shape one another towards a 'pro-poor' (re)allocation of land resources. Each country case study in this book is analysed from within this framework.

Viewed from this perspective, the contemporary debate about agrarian reform is marked by four broadly distinct and competing views about land reform – as summarised in Table 1.2.[32] The faultlines between these four are the differences on which types of land reform and which strategies to employ in order to achieve their objectives, especially on reducing poverty and social exclusion in the countryside. It must be noted that these are ideal types. They are useful as an analytical typology, but the reality does not always neatly fit with each type. This typology, in turn, serves as general analytic signposts for the country studies in this book.

The first common theme is the role of 'free' markets in the (re)allocation of land resources between different social classes and groups in society as well as in sectors in the national economy. All the chapters in this volume examine whether and how and to what extent the forces of the 'free' market have (re)distributed access to and control over land resources that favour the rural poor. All the chapters critically examine the empirical materials from the various countries that have been studied

Table 1.2 Key features of various contending perspectives in agrarian reform

Perspective	Features
Market-led	Main consideration is economic efficiency/productivity gains; gives secondary/marginal role to central states; peasants/beneficiaries who are supposed to be in the 'driver's seat' of the reform are actually subordinated to dominant market actors; in reality, 'market-led' means 'landlord/merchant/TNC-led' in many agrarian settings today
State-led	Main consideration is usually related to securing/maintaining political legitimacy, though developmental agendas are also important; 'strong political will' necessary to carry out land reform agenda; usually treats peasants/beneficiaries as necessary administrative adjuncts; subordinates market actors, or selectively deals with market actors depending on which actors are more influential within the state
Peasant-led	Main assumption is that 'state is too captive to societal elite interests', while market forces are basically dominated by elite interests; thus, the only way to achieve pro-poor agrarian reform is for peasants and their organisations to themselves take the initiative to implement agrarian reform
State/society-driven	Main assumptions: it does not romanticise the 'omnipotence' of peasants/beneficiaries and their organisations; it does not assign a commanding role to the central state; it does not provide sole importance to economic productivity-enhancement issues, although it recognises the relevance of each of these perspectives; analyses state, peasant movements, and market forces not as separate groups, but as actors inherently linked to each other by their association to the politics and economics of land resources. It has three key features: '*peasants/beneficiaries-led*', '*state-supported*', and '*economic productivity-enhancing*'

against the backdrop of an existing mainstream assumption about the superiority of the forces of the 'free' market in land resource (re)distribution. As partly explained in the country case studies in this research such as the Uzbekistan, Vietnamese and Armenian cases (by Khan, Spoor and Akram-Lodhi, respectively, this volume), this perspective is the one that views land reform as a policy that can and should facilitate the provision of privatised and individualised property rights to as many people in as much land space as possible – through *market-led* and *market-oriented* mechanisms of transferring property rights and of governing land markets. This is represented by mainstream economists and, to a large extent, by development policy experts. This perspective does not altogether rule out the role of the state, but that role is being modified, from being 'key' to a 'facilitative' one, and assigned with the tasks of: providing the necessary legal institutional frameworks for these market mechanisms to emerge and operate, providing information accessible to 'stakeholders' to create a 'level playing field', and promoting transparency and accountability. The state, especially its local government units, is also required to promote and enter into 'partnerships' with the civil society and private sectors. Deininger (1999) and World Bank (2003) represent this view.

The second common theme is the role of the state in the 'pro-poor' (re)allocation of land resources. All chapters in this book examine how and to what extent central states played a role in the (re)distribution of land resources between different social classes and groups in society and between different sectors of the economy. All the chapters critically examine the state and its role in pro-poor land policies partly in dialogue with an existing school of thought in the agrarian reform literature that identifies the central state as the leading actor in any pro-poor redistributive reform policies such as land reform. This perspective follows the conventional framework, which views land reform as a policy that should provide secure access to and control over land resources to the landless and near-landless rural poor – through a *state-led* mechanism to expropriate land from big landlords and to redistribute them to peasants. As partly explained in the country cases in this study, such as the Ethiopian, Zimbabwean and the Philippine cases (Mersha and Gĩthĩnji, Moyo, and Borras *et al.*, respectively, this volume), a state-led strategy is quite diverse, (historically) ranging from authoritarian to 'democratic' approaches (see, e.g. Tai, 1974; Riedinger, 1995). While this perspective follows, in many cases, the economic basis of the market-led view, it also places the question of land reform firmly in the context of social justice, explicitly calling for the reform of inefficient, unjust and exploitative pre-existing agrarian structures. Founded on the belief that the market by itself will not redistribute, but rather may even further the concentration of wealth and power in society, this view calls for the central state to muster strong 'political will' and mobilise significant funds to finance large-scale land reform. Tai (1974) represents this view, while the recent re-assertion made by Barraclough (2001) can also be identified with this perspective.

The third common theme examined in this book is the role of peasant movements and mobilisations for land. All the case studies in this volume analyse the role played by peasants' actions, albeit the degree and extent of analytic treatment varies from one country study to another, depending on the prevailing conditions in each. For example, this theme receives greater attention in Brazil and the Philippines (see Deere and Medeiros, and Borras *et al.*, respectively, this volume), as compared to Armenia and Uzbekistan (see Spoor and Khan, respectively, this volume). However, all the essays acknowledge the importance of peasants' actions in land policy-making and implementation, and have to address an existing distinct view in the agrarian reform literature that assigns a key role to peasants' actions in any pro-poor land policy making and implementation. The perspective sees land reform in ways very much similar to that of the state-led perspective, i.e. to provide secure access to and control over land resources to landless and near-landless poor in the context of social justice and with the explicit goal of reforming the inefficient, unjust and exploitative agrarian structure – but through a *peasant-led* approach. Following the state-led view that the market by itself will not redistribute wealth and power, this approach, however, is founded on the belief that the state by itself cannot be relied upon to carry out reform either because it is usually captive to the dominant classes and groups in society that are also opposed to redistributive reforms like land reform. The peasant-led approach is exemplified by the ideological and political discourse of the *Movimiento dos Trabalhadores Rurais Sem Terra* (MST, or Landless Rural Workers' Movement) in Brazil in particular, and *La Via Campesina* more generally,[33] and scholars closely sympathetic to this view, such as James Petras (1997, 1998) and Henry Veltmeyer (1997, 2005).[34]

The fourth common theme addressed by all chapters is the *interaction* between state and society. As mentioned earlier, while it is important to analyse the separate, distinct roles of the 'free' market, state and peasant movements, it is equally crucial to examine them as inherently interlinked actors – focusing on the interaction between them. All the case studies examine this theme within the perspective of *state/society-driven* land policy-making and implementation processes that views an 'interactive' state–society relationship that largely determines the character, content, pace and direction of land reform policy. The class character of the state is taken into serious consideration in this view, as demonstrated by Petras and Veltmeyer (2003). This view also advocates for secure access to and control over land resources by the landless and near-landless rural poor within a social justice framework. It has three key features: '*peasants/beneficiaries-led*', '*state-supported*', and '*economic productivity-enhancing*'. While it highlights the importance of political mobilisations 'from below', it also puts equal weight to the reformist initiatives by state actors 'from above'. It is founded on the belief that, left alone, markets will not only not lead to pro-poor redistributive reforms, they are even likely to further inequality and poverty. Nevertheless, it does not altogether dismiss the positive role of the market, although the latter needs to be governed by the state (see Wade, 2004, 1990). Herring (1983) represents this view.

The treatment of these different themes and the subsequent competing perspectives as to their role in agrarian reform and rural development has evolved amid changing contexts for, and contested meanings of, land reform[35] (as summarised in Table 1.1). Assessing the outcomes of the diverse types of land policies initiated from the 1990s onwards in terms of redistributing land to landless and near-landless peasants and in reducing rural poverty via different approaches is as difficult a task as assessing past land reforms. Again, the record of contemporary land reforms is varied and uneven between and within countries, as will be shown and explained in the various chapters in this book. A crossnational comparative analysis of these processes and outcomes, and their implications for agrarian reform policy making in particular and to the study of agrarian change more generally will be explored in the concluding chapter of this book.

Notes

1 We are grateful to the participants at the workshop in February 2005 held at the Institute of Social Studies (ISS), especially Terry McKinley and Carmen Diana Deere, as well as to the two anonymous Routledge reviewers for their critical comments and suggestions that have greatly improved the quality of this chapter.

2 A recent comprehensive crossnational comparative study is Bryceson *et al.* (2000). The explanation by Ellis (2000) about livelihood diversification due to necessity or by choice offers relevant analytic insights, as do Lahiff and Scoones (2000) and Bebbington (1999).

3 Important studies on the relationship between lack of access to land and poverty include Griffin (1976, 1974) and El-Ghonemy (1990); more recent re-arguments within a broadly similar framework but amid a changing context include Herring (2003); see also Kay (2005). De Janvry, Gordillo, Platteau, and Sadoulet (2001) is a recent collection of (generally economic) studies that include both mainstream scholars and others who do not necessarily or fully subscribe to the current mainstream economic doctrines.

4 Deininger and Binswanger (1999) and World Bank (2003) are the landmark publications key to understanding the main features of the contemporary mainstream land policies. The World Development Report 2006 (on equity and development) has addressed the issue of land access, but has not put forward any new insights and has simply repeated the arguments and claims in other World Bank documents and by other mainstream economists, dismissing the growing body of literature that is critical of these arguments and claims (World Bank, 2005: chapter 8).

5 Some works that provide relevant crossnational and historical overviews include Tuma (1965), Jones (1991), King (1977), Tai (1974), Christodoulou (1990), Jacoby (1971), Prosterman *et al.* (1990), Warriner (1969), Paige (1975), Moore (1967), and Sobhan (1993). For recent conceptual and methodological discussion of comparative studies in land reform, see Borras (2006b).

6 Refer, for example, to the influential study edited by Barraclough (1973) in the case of Latin America. But see Johnston (forthcoming) and Rigg (2006) for fresh arguments on labour-related issues in the land reform debate.

7 Refer to the discussions by Berry and Cline (1979), Barraclough and Domike (1966), Dorner and Kanel (1971). For more recent discussion on the economic basis see Binswanger and Deininger (1997, 1996) and Deininger and Binswanger (1999).

8 Refer, for example, to the relevant insights offered by Lehmann (1974), Harriss (1982), Ghose (1983a), Ghimire (2001), Kay (2002), Karshenas (2004) and Wuyts (1994).

9 Refer, for example, to Byres (1974); and more recently, Byres (2004a, 2004b) and Bernstein (2004, 2003, 2002).

10 Refer, for example, to Lipton (1974), and more recently, to Griffin *et al.* (2002).

11 For analytic insights in the context of socialist settings in Latin America, Asia and Africa, refer to FitzGerald (1985) for the Sandinista Nicaraguan case, Saith

(1985) for the Chinese case, O'Laughlin (1996, 1995) for the case of Mozambique, Abate and Kiros (1983) for the Ethiopian case, and Fagan *et al.* (1986) for a transnational, comparative perspective.

12 See James Scott (1998) for an insightful overview account of farm mechanisation in the USSR in the 1920s–1930s, as well as in the efforts to construct modern socialist farms and villages in Tanzania and Ethiopia in the 1970s–1980s. Benedict Kerkvliet's (2005) study of the Vietnamese peasants under farm collective and post-collective eras is equally revealing and insightful.

13 See Tsing (2002) for an historical analysis of the promulgation and subsequent implications of the Agrarian Law of 1960 in Indonesia. Refer to Bratton (1990) for the historical background and initial implementation of the Zimbabwean land reform.

14 Of course there are other important reasons, both internal and external to these countries, for carrying out land reform other than in reaction to the communist threat from China and the USSR. For varying analysis, see Kay (2002), Griffin *et al.* (2002), Tai (1974) and King (1977).

15 See various analyses by Raj and Tharakan (1983), Ghose (1983b), Herring (1983), Banerjee *et al.* (2002), Harriss (1993), Baruah (1990) and Lieten (1996).

16 Important crossnational comparative studies, albeit from varying perspectives and disciplines, include de Janvry (1981), de Janvry and Sadoulet (1989), Thiesenhusen (1989, 1995), Dorner (1992), Kay (1998, 2004) for Latin America, Herring (1983) and Tai (1974) for Asia, and more generally, Ghose (1983a), Tuma (1965), Sobhan (1993), Christodoulou (1990), and King (1977).

17 The general analytic insights found in Gwynne and Kay (2004) offer relevant views that put this issue in a better historical and broader context. Refer also to Spoor (1997).

18 For a critical reflection on the performance of agriculture during the much-maligned period prior to neoliberalism, refer to Spoor (2002) for a specific study of the Latin American experience.

19 For relevant insights, see Kerkvliet (2005) for Vietnam and O'Brien (1996) for China; see also Mersha and Gîthînji for Ethiopia (this volume).

20 For insightful analysis of the changing political economy of global food regimes, the invention and proliferation of the Green Revolution ideology and how, in different ways and to varying extents, these impacted on the land question in most developing countries during this period, refer to Lappé *et al.*, (1998), Friedmann (2005), Boyce (1993) and Ross (1998).

21 Refer to Franco and Borras (2005), Urioste (2001), Greenberg (2004) and Lucas and Warren (2003), respectively.

22 See also Pons-Vignon and Lecomte (2004). It is also within this broad context that we should understand the renewed calls for land reform during the many regime transitions when, for various reasons, centralized authoritarian regimes in many developing countries collapsed and political processes for greater (rural) democratization gained some ground (see, e.g. the edited volume on rural democratization by Fox, 1990).

23 For critical analyses, see Levin and Weiner (1997), Bernstein (1998), Lahiff (2003), and Cousins (1997).

24 It is broadly within this context that decentralised approaches to natural resources management have become very important in development policy discourse – for critical studies, refer to Ribot and Larson (2005).

25 Refer also to the insightful discussion in Grindle (1986: chapter 1).

26 See, for example, the argument advanced by Fortin (2005) in the specific context of sub-Saharan Africa, and Bush (2002) in the context of Egypt.

27 The mainstream arguments for such renewed efforts on land titling, registration and related policies are captured quite clearly by Bryant (1996); see also de Soto (2000).

28 For preliminary critical studies in the context of Africa, see Toulmin and Quan (2000), Platteau (1996), Quan (2000), Palmer (2000a), Berry (2002), McAuslan (2000), and Matondi and Moyo (2003); for Latin America, see Jansen and Roquas (1998), Hernaiz *et al.* (2000), and Zoomers and van der Haar (2000); for a view from Asia, see Borras (2006a).

29 Among contemporary scholars who have carried out empirical studies and theorising on land markets within an economic perspective, perhaps Michael Carter is among the few who have offered sophisticated analysis based on his examination of Latin American cases (see, e.g. 2000; Carter and Salgado, 2001; Carter and Mesbah, 1993). Refer also to the various studies in Zoomers and van der Haar (2000).

30 For a relevant critical insight based on the experience of southern Mexico, refer to Bobrow-Strain (2004). Refer also to the critical insights offered by Paasch (2003) and the joint critique put forward by *La Via Campesina* and the Foodfirst Information and Action Network or FIAN (FIAN-Via Campesina, 2003).

31 For critical reflections on the European Union (draft) land policy, see Monsalve (2004).

32 For a Latin American view, see Veltmeyer (2005) for a similar, but not the same, typology involving the first three types discussed in this section.

33 For an analysis of the issue of agrarian reform focusing on *La Via Campesina*, see Borras (2004).

34 For excellent background on *Via Campesina*'s history, politics and ideology, see Desmarais (2001, forthcoming), Edelman (2003) and Borras (2004). Refer also to de Janvry, Sadoulet and Wolford (2001) for their analysis of the Brazilian landless movement.

35 See, for example, the discussion by Borras and Franco (2005) about the contested meanings of 'land reform' in the context of highly productive, capital-intensive, agribusiness plantations.

References

Abate, A. and F. Kiros (1983). 'Agrarian Reform, Structural Changes and Rural Development', in A. K. Ghose, ed., *Agrarian Reform in Contemporary Developing Countries*, pp. 141–184. Geneva: International Labour Organization; New York: St Martin's Press.

Agarwal, B. (1994). *A Field of One's Own: Gender and Land Rights in South Asia.* Cambridge: Cambridge University Press.

Aguilar, F. Jr (2005). 'Rural Land Struggles in Asia: Overview of Selected Contexts', in S. Moyo and P. Yeros, eds, *Reclaiming the Land: The Resurgence of Rural Movements in Africa, Asia and Latin America*, pp. 208–234. London: Zed.

Akram-Lodhi, H. (2005). 'Vietnam's Agriculture: Processes of Rich Peasant Accumulation and Mechanisms of Social Differentiation', *Journal of Agrarian Change*, vol. 5, no. 1, pp. 73–116.

Akram-Lodhi, H. (2004). 'Are Landlords Taking Back the Land: An Essay on the Agrarian Transition of Vietnam', *European Journal of Development Research*, vol. 16, no. 2, pp. 757–789.

Aspinal, E. (2004). 'Indonesia: Transformation of Civil Society and Democratic

Breakthrough', in M. Alagappa, ed., *Civil Society and Political Change in Asia*, pp. 61–96. Stanford: Stanford University Press.

Assies, W., G. van der Haar and A. J. Hoekma (1998). *The Challenge of Diversity: Indigenous Peoples and Reform of the State in Latin America*. Amsterdam: CEDLA.

Bachriadi, D. and N. Fauzi (2006). 'The Resurgence of Agrarian Movements in Indonesia'. Paper presented at the International Conference on Land, Poverty, Social Justice and Development, Institute of Social Studies (ISS), The Hague, the Netherlands, 9–14 January 2006 (www.iss.nl – see 'publications' – downloaded 18 May 2006).

Bachriadi, D. and M. A. Sardjono (2005). 'Conversion or Occupation: The Possibility of Returning Local Communities' Control over Forest Lands in Indonesia'. Paper prepared for and presented at the International Exchange in Environmental Governance, Community Resource Management and Conflict Resolution, Institute of International Studies, University of California Berkeley.

Banerjee, A., P. Gertler and M. Ghatak (2002). 'Empowerment and Efficiency: Tenancy Reform in West Bengal', *Journal of Political Economy*, vol. 110, no. 2, pp. 239–280.

Baranyi, S., C. D. Deere and M. Morales (2004). *Scoping Study on Land Policy Research in Latin America*. Ottawa: North-South Institute and the International Development Research Centre (IDRC).

Barraclough, S. (2001). 'The Role of the State and Other Actors in Land Reform', in K. Ghimire, ed., *Land Reform and Peasant Livelihoods: The Social Dynamics of Rural Poverty and Agrarian Reform in Developing Countries*, pp. 26–64. Geneva: URISD; London: ITDG.

Barraclough, S. (ed.) (1973). *Agrarian Structure in Latin America: A Resume of the CIDA Land Tenure Studies of Argentina, Brazil, Chile, Colombia, Ecuador, Guatemala, Peru*. Lexington: Lexington Books.

Barraclough, S. and A. Domike (1966). 'Agrarian Structure in Seven Latin American Countries', *Land Economics*, vol. 42, no. 4, pp. 391–424.

Barros, F., S. Sauer and S. Schwartzman (eds) (2003). *The Negative Impacts of World Bank Market-based Land Reform*. Brazil: Comissao Pastoral da Terra, Movimento dos Trabalhadores Rurais Sem Terra (MST), Foodfirst Information and Action Network (FIAN).

Baruah, S. (1990). 'The End of the Road in Land Reform? Limits to Redistribution in West Bengal', *Development and Change*, vol. 21, no. 1, pp. 119–146.

Bebbington, Anthony (1999). 'Capitals and Capabilities: A Framework for Analyzing Peasant Viability, Rural Livelihoods and Poverty', *World Development*, vol. 27, no. 12, pp. 2021–2044.

Bernstein, H. (2004). 'Changing before Our Very Eyes: Agrarian Questions and the Politics of Land in Capitalism Today', *Journal of Agrarian Change*, vol. 4, nos 1 and 2, pp. 190–225.

Bernstein, H. (2003). 'Land Reform in Southern Africa in World-Historical Perspective', *Review of African Political Economy*, vol. 96, pp. 21–46.

Bernstein, H. (2002). 'Land Reform: Taking a Long(er) View', *Journal of Agrarian Change*, vol. 2, no. 4, pp. 433–463.

Bernstein, H. (1998). 'Social Change in the South African Countryside? Land and Production, Poverty and Power', *Journal of Peasant Studies*, vol. 25, no. 4, pp. 1–32.

Berry, A. and W. Cline (1979). *Agrarian Structure and Productivity in Developing Countries*. Baltimore: Johns Hopkins University Press.

Berry, S. (2002). 'Debating the Land Question in Africa', *Comparative Study in Society and History*, vol. 44, no. 4, pp. 638–668.

Bhandari, R. (2006). 'Searching for a Weapon of Mass Production in Nepal: Can Market-Assisted Land Reforms Live Up to their Promise?' *Journal of Deveoping Societies*, vol. 22, no. 2, pp. 111–143.

Binswanger, H. and K. Deininger (1997). 'Explaining Agricultural and Agrarian Policies in Developing Countries'. Paper presented at the FAO Technical Consultation of Decentralization and Rural Development, Rome, 16–18 December 1997.

Binswanger, H. and K. Deininger (1996). 'South African Land Policy: The Legacy of History and Current Options', in J. v. Zyl, J. Kirsten and H. P. Binswanger, eds, *Agricultural Land Reform in South Africa: Policies, Markets and Mechanisms*, pp. 64–104. Oxford: Oxford University Press.

Bobrow-Strain, A. (2004). '(Dis)Accords: The Politics of Market-assisted Land Reforms in Chiapas, Mexico', *World Development*, vol. 32, no. 6, pp. 887–903.

Borras, S. Jr (forthcoming). ' "Free Market", Export-led Development Strategy and Its Impact on Rural Livelihoods, Poverty and Inequality: The Philippine Experience Seen from a Southeast Asian Perspective', *Review of International Political Economy*.

Borras, S. Jr (2006a). 'Redistributive Land Reform in Public (Forest) Lands? Rethinking Theory and Practice with Evidence from the Philippines', *Progress in Development Studies*, vol. 6, no. 2, pp. 123–145

Borras, S. Jr (2006b). 'The Philippine Land Reform in Comparative Perspective: Conceptual and Methodological Implications', *Journal of Agrarian Change*, vol. 6, no. 1, pp. 69–101.

Borras, S. Jr (2006c). 'Land, Empowerment and the Rural Poor: Challenges to Civil Society and Development Agencies'. Rome: IFAD. Also downloadable at: www.icarrd.org.

Borras, S. Jr (2005). 'Can Redistributive Reform be Achieved via Market-based Land Transfer Schemes? Lessons and Evidence from the Philippines', *Journal of Development Studies*, vol. 41, no. 1, pp. 90–134.

Borras, S. Jr (2004). 'La Via Campesina: An Evolving Transnational Social Movement', *TNI Briefing Series* No. 2004/6. Amsterdam: Transnational Institute (for PDF version, see www.tni.org).

Borras, S. Jr (2003a). 'Questioning Market-led Agrarian Reform: Experiences from Brazil, Colombia and South Africa', *Journal of Agrarian Change*, vol. 3, no. 3, pp. 367–394.

Borras, S. Jr (2003b). 'Questioning the Pro-market Critique of State-led Agrarian Reform', *European Journal of Development Research*, vol. 15, no. 2, pp. 105–128.

Borras, S. Jr (2003c). 'Inclusion-Exclusion in Public Policies and Policy Analyses: The Case of Philippine Land Reform, 1972–2002', *Journal of International Development*, vol. 15, no. 8, pp. 1049–1065.

Borras, S. Jr (2001). 'State–Society Relations in Land Reform Implementation in the Philippines', *Development and Change*, vol. 32, no. 3, pp. 545–575.

Borras, S. Jr. and J. Franco (2005). 'Struggles for Land and Livelihood in Agribusiness Plantations in the Philippines', *Critical Asian Studies*, vol. 37, no. 3, pp. 331–361.

Boyce, J. (1993). *The Political Economy of Growth and Impoverishment in the Marcos Era*. Quezon City: Ateneo de Manila University Press.

Branford, S. and J. Rocha (2002). *Cutting the Wire: The Story of Landless Movement in Brazil.* London: Latin American Bureau.

Brass, T. (ed.) (2003). *Latin American Peasants.* London: Frank Cass.

Bratton, M. (1990). 'Ten Years after Land Redistribution in Zimbabwe, 1980–1990', in R. Prosterman, M. Temple and T. Hanstad, eds, *Agrarian Reform and Grassroots Development: Ten Case Studies,* pp. 265–291. Boulder: Lynne Rienner.

Bryant, C. (1996). 'Strategic Change through Sensible Projects', *World Development,* vol. 24, no. 9, pp. 1539–1550.

Bryceson, D., C. Kay and J. Mooij (eds) (2000). *Disappearing Peasantries? Rural Labour in Africa, Asia and Latin America.* London: Intermediate Technology Publications.

Buainain, M. A., J. M. da Silveira, H. M. Souza and M. Magalhães (1999). 'Community-based Land Reform Implementation in Brazil: A New Way of Reaching out to the Marginalized?'. Paper presented at the GDN Conference in Bonn, Germany, December 1999. www.gdnet.org/bonn99/confpapers.f1ml (downloaded 1 March 2001).

Bush, R. (ed.) (2002). *Counter-revolution in Egypt's Countryside: Land and Farmers in the Era of Economic Reform.* London: Zed.

Byres, T. (2004a). 'Introduction: Contextualizing and Interrogating the GKI Case for Redistributive Land Reform', *Journal of Agrarian Change,* vol. 4, nos 1 and 2, pp. 1–16.

Byres, T. (2004b). 'Neo-classical Neo-populism 25 Years on: Déjà Vu and Déjà Passé: Towards a Critique', *Journal of Agrarian Change,* vol. 4, nos 1 and 2, pp. 17–44

Byres, T. (1974). 'Land Reform, Industrialization and the Marketed Surplus in India: An Essay on the Power of Rural Bias', in D. Lehmann, ed., *Peasants, Landlords and Governments: Agrarian Reform in the Third World,* pp. 221–261. New York: Holmes and Meier Publishers.

Carter, M. (2000). 'Old Questions and New Realities: Land in Post-Liberal Economies', in A. Zoomers and G. v.d. Haar, eds, *Current Land Policy in Latin America: Regulating Land Tenure under Neo-liberalism,* pp. 29–44. Amsterdam: Royal Tropical Institute (KIT).

Carter, M. and R. Salgado (2001). 'Land Market Liberalization and the Agrarian Question in Latin America', in A. de Janvry, G. Gordillo, J. P. Platteau and E. Sadoulet, eds, *Access to Land, Rural Poverty, and Public Action,* pp. 246–278. Oxford: Oxford University Press.

Carter, M. and D. Mesbah (1993). 'Can Land Market Reform Mitigate the Exclusionary Aspects of Rapid Agro-export Growth?', *World Development,* vol. 21, no. 7, pp. 1085–1100.

Castillo, L. and D. Lehmann (1983). 'Agrarian Reform and Structural Change in Chile, 1965–79', in A. K. Ghose, ed., *Agrarian Reform in Contemporary Developing Countries,* pp. 240–272. Geneva: International Labour Organization; New York: St Martin's Press.

Christodoulou, D. (1990). *The Unpromised Land: Agrarian Reform and Conflict Worldwide.* London: Zed.

Collins, J. with F. Moore Lappé and N. Allen (1982). *What Difference Could a Revolution Make? Food and Farming in the New Nicaragua.* San Francisco: Institute for Food and Development Policy.

Corpuz-Tauli, V. and J. Cariño (2004). *Reclaiming Balance: Indigenous Peoples, Conflict Resolution and Sustainable Development.* Baguio City: Tebtebba Foundation.

Cotula, L., C. Toulmin and J. Quan (2006). 'Policies and Practices for Securing and Improving Access'. Paper presented at the International Conference on Agrarian Reform and Rural Development (ICARRD), 6–10 March 2006, Porto Alegre, Brazil (www.icarrd.org – downloaded 18 May 2006).

Cousins, B. (1997). 'How Do Rights Become Real? Formal and Informal Institutions in South Africa's Land Reform', *IDS Bulletin*, vol. 28, no. 4, pp. 59–67.

Cousins, B. and A. Claassens (2006). 'More than simply 'socially embedded': recognizing the distinctiveness of African land rights.' Keynote address at the international symposium on 'At the frontier of land issues: social embeddedness of rights and public policy'. Montpellier, May 17–19, 2006.

CPRC (2005). *The Chronic Poverty Report 2005–05.* Manchester: Chronic Poverty Research Centre, University of Manchester.

de Bremond, Ariane (2006). 'The *Programa de Transferencia de Tierras* (PTT) and Livelihoods in the Making of a Future: State–Market Hybrids and the Post-war Resettlement of Agrarian Landscapes in El Salvador'. Paper presented at the International Conference on Land, Poverty, Social Justice and Development, 9–14 January 2006, Institute of Social Studies (ISS), The Hague, Netherlands.

de Janvry, A. (1981). *The Agrarian Question and Reformism in Latin America.* Baltimore: Johns Hopkins University Press.

de Janvry, A. and E. Sadoulet (1989). 'A Study in Resistance to Institutional Change: The Lost Game of Latin American Land Reform', *World Development*, vol. 17, no. 9, pp. 1397–1407.

de Janvry, A., G. Gordillo, J.-P. Platteau and E. Sadoulet (eds) (2001). *Access to Land, Rural Poverty, and Public Action.* Oxford: Oxford University Press.

de Janvry, A., E. Sadoulet and W. Wolford (2001). 'The Changing Role of the State in Latin American Land Reform', in de Janvry, G. Gordillo, J. P. Platteau and E. Sadoulet, eds, *Access to Land, Rural Poverty, and Public Action*, pp. 279–303. Oxford: Oxford University Press.

de Soto, H. (2000). *The Mystery of Capital: Why Capitalism Triumphs in the West and Fails Everywhere Else.* New York: Basic Books.

Deere, C. D. (2000). 'Towards a Reconstruction of Cuba's Agrarian Transformation: Peasantization, De-peasantization and Re-peasantization', in D. Bryceson, C. Kay and J. Mooij, eds, *Disappearing Peasantries? – Rural Labour in Africa, Asia and Latin America*, pp. 139–158. London: ITDG.

Deere, C. D. (1985). 'Rural Women and State Policy: The Latin American Agrarian Reform Experience', *World Development*, vol. 13, no. 9, pp. 1037–1053.

Deere, C. D. and M. León (2001). 'Who Owns the Land: Gender and Land-Titling Programmes in Latin America', *Journal of Agrarian Change*, vol. 1, no. 3, pp. 440–467.

Deininger, K. (2002). 'Agrarian Reforms in Eastern European Countries: Lessons from International Experience', *Journal of International Development*, vol. 14, no. 7, pp. 987–1003.

Deininger, K. (1999). 'Making Negotiated Land Reform Work: Initial Experience from Colombia, Brazil and South Africa', *World Development*, vol. 27, no. 4, pp. 651–672.

Deininger, K. (1995). 'Collective Agricultural Production: A Solution for Transition Economies?', *World Development*, vol. 23, no. 8, pp. 1317–1334.

Deininger, K. and H. Binswanger (1999). 'The Evolution of the World Bank's Land Policy: Principles, Experience and Future Challenges', *The World Bank Research Observer*, vol. 14, no. 2, pp. 247–276.

Desmarais, A. (forthcoming). 'The Power of Peasants: Reflections on the Meanings of the Via Campesina', *Journal of Rural Studies*.

Desmarais, A. (2001). 'The *Via Campesina*: Consolidating an International Peasant and Farm Movement', *Journal of Peasant Studies*, vol. 29, no. 2, pp. 91–124.

Diskin, M. (1989). 'El Salvador: Reform Prevents Change', in W. Thiesenhusen, ed., *Searching for Agrarian Reform in Latin America*, pp. 429–450. Boston: Unwin Hyman.

Dorner, P. (1992). *Latin American Land Reforms in Theory and Practice*. Madison: University of Wisconsin Press.

Dorner, P. and D. Kanel (1971). 'The Economic Case for Land Reform', in *Land Reform, Land Settlements and Cooperatives*, 1971, no. 1, pp. 1–16

Edelman, M. (2003). 'Transnational Peasant and Farmer Movements and Networks', in M. Kaldor, H. Anheier and M. Glasius, eds, *Global Civil Society*, pp. 185–220. Oxford: Oxford University Press.

El-Ghonemy, R. (2001). 'The Political Economy of Market-based Land Reform', in K. Ghimire, ed., *Land Reform and Peasant Livelihoods: The Social Dynamics of Rural Poverty and Agrarian Reform in Developing Countries*, pp. 105–133. Geneva: UNRISD; London: ITDG.

El-Ghonemy, R. (1990). *The Political Economy of Rural Poverty: The Case for Land Reform*. New York/London: Routledge.

Ellis, F. (2000). *Rural Livelihoods and Diversity in Developing Countries*. Oxford: Oxford University Press.

Fagan, R., C. D. Deere and J. L. Corragio (eds) (1986). *Transition and Development: Problems of Third World Socialism*. New York: Monthly Review Press.

FIAN-Via Campesina (2003). 'Commentary on Land and Rural Development Policies of the World Bank'. Heidelberg/Honduras: FIAN.

FitzGerald, E. V. K. (1985). 'Agrarian Reform as a Model of Accumulation: The Case of Nicaragua since 1979', *Journal of Development Studies*, vol. 22, no. 1, pp. 208–220.

Foley, M. (1997). 'Land and Peace in Postwar El Salvador: Structural Adjustment, Land Reform and Social Peace in the Salvadoran Countryside'. Research for the Washington Office on Latin America (WOLA) on the World Bank and agrarian policy in post-war El Salvador.

Fortin, E. (2005). 'Reforming Land Rights: The World Bank and the Globalisation of Agriculture', *Social and Legal Studies*, vol. 14, no. 2, pp. 147–177.

Fox, J. (2004). 'Empowerment and Institutional Change: Mapping "Virtuous Circles" of State–Society Interaction', in R. Alsop, ed., *Power, Rights and Poverty: Concepts and Connections*, pp. 68–92. Washington, DC: World Bank.

Fox, J. (1993). *The Politics of Food in Mexico: State Power and Social Mobilization*. Ithaca: Cornell University Press.

Fox, J. (ed.) (1990). *The Challenges of Rural Democratisation: Perspectives from Latin America and the Philippines*. London: Frank Cass.

Franco, J. (2006). 'Making Land Rights Accessible: Potentials and Challenges of a Human Rights Approach to Land Issues'. Paper presented at the Conference on Land Rights sponsored by the Norwegian Foreign Ministry, 22–23 March, Oslo. Also downloadable at: www.peace.tni.org.

Franco, J. (Forthcoming). 'Making Land Rights Accessible: Social Movement Innovation and Political-Legal Strategies in the Philippines.' *Journal of Development Studies.*

Franco, J. (2001). *Elections and Democratization in the Philippines.* New York: Routledge.

Franco, J. and S. Borras Jr. (eds) (2005). *On Just Grounds: Struggling for Agrarian Justice and Citizenship Rights in the Rural Philippines.* Quezon City: Institute for Popular Democracy; Amsterdam: Transnational Institute.

Friedmann, H. (2005). 'Feeding the Empire: The Pathologies of Globalized Agriculture', in L. Panitch and C. Leys, eds, *The Empire Reloaded.* New York: New York University Press.

Gauster, S. (2006). 'Impacts of the World Bank's Land (Reform) Policies in Guatemala'. Paper presented at the International Conference on Land, Poverty, Social Justice and Development, 9–14 January 2006, Institute of Social Studies (ISS), The Hague, Netherlands.

Ghai, D., C. Kay and P. Peek (1988). *Labour and Development in Rural Cuba.* London: Macmillan.

Ghimire, K. (ed.) (2005). *Civil Society and the Market Question: Dynamics of Rural Development and Popular Mobilization.* London: Palgrave; Geneva: UNRISD.

Ghimire, K. (ed.) (2001). *Land Reform and Peasant Livelihoods: The Social Dynamics of Rural Poverty and Agrarian Reform in Developing Countries.* Geneva: UNRISD; London: ITDG.

Ghose, A. K. (ed.) (1983a). *Agrarian Reform in Contemporary Countries.* Geneva: International Labour Organization; New York: St Martin's Press.

Ghose, A. K. (1983b). 'Agrarian Reform in West Bengal: Objectives, Achievements and Limitations', in A. K. Ghose, ed., *Agrarian Reform in Contemporary Developing Countries,* pp. 91–140. Geneva: International Labour Organization; New York: St Martin's Press.

Goodman, D. and M. Watts (1997). *Globalising Food: Agrarian Questions and Global Restructuring.* London: Routledge.

Greenberg, S. (2004). *The Landless People's Movement and the Failure of Post-Apartheid Land Reform.* Durban: KwaZulu-Natal, School of Development Studies.

Griffin, K. (1976). *Land Concentration and Rural Poverty.* London: Macmillan Press.

Griffin, K. (1974). *The Political Economy of Agrarian Change: An Essay on the Green Revolution.* London: Macmillan Press.

Griffin, K., A. R. Khan and A. Ickowitz (2002). 'Poverty and Distribution of Land', *Journal of Agrarian Change,* vol. 2, no. 3, pp. 279–330.

Grindle, M. (1986). *State and Countryside: Development Policy and Agrarian Politics in Latin America.* Baltimore: Johns Hopkins University Press.

Gwynne, R. and C. Kay (2004). *Latin America Transformed: Globalization and Modernity.* London: Arnold (second edition).

Handy, J. (1994). *Revolution in the Countryside: Rural Conflict and Agrarian Reform in Guatemala, 1944–1954.* Chapel Hill: University of North Carolina Press.

Harriss, J. (1993). 'What IS Happening in Rural West Bengal? Agrarian Reform, Growth and Distribution', *Economic and Political Weekly,* XXVIII, pp. 1237–1247.

Harriss, J. (ed.) (1982). *Rural Development: Theories of Peasant Economy and Agrarian Change.* London: Routledge.

Harvey, N. (1998). *The Chiapas Rebellion: The Struggle for Land and Democracy.* Durham: Duke University Press.

Herring, R. (2003). 'Beyond the Political Impossibility Theorem of Agrarian Reform', in P. Houtzager and M. Moore, eds, *Changing Paths: International Development and the New Politics of Inclusion*, pp. 58–87. Ann Arbor: University of Michigan Press.

Herring, R. (2002). 'State Property Rights in Nature (With Special Reference to India)', in F. Richards, ed., *Land, Property, and the Environment*, pp. 263–297. Oakland: Institute for Contemporary Studies.

Herring, R. (1983). *Land to the Tiller: The Political Economy of Agrarian Reform in South Asia*. New Haven: Yale University Press.

Hernáiz, I., D. Pacheco, R. Guerrero and H. Miranda (2000). *Análisis Crítico del Proceso de Catastro Rural Legal y Saneamiento Integrado al Catastro Legal en el Departamento de Chuquisaca (KADASTER e INRA)*, La Paz and Sucre: Fundación TIERRA.

Hobsbawm, E. (1974). 'Peasant Land Occupations', *Past and Present*, no. 62, pp. 120–152.

Houtzager, P. (2000). 'Social Movements amidst Democratic Transitions: Lessons from the Brazilian Countryside', *Journal of Development Studies*, vol. 36, no. 5, pp. 59–88.

Huizer, G. (2001). 'Peasant Mobilization for Land Reform: Historical Case Studies and Theoretical Considerations', in K. Ghimire, ed., *Land Reform and Peasant Livelihoods: The Social Dynamics of Rural Poverty and Agrarian Reform in Developing Countries*, pp. 164–198. London: ITDG.

IPC for Food Sovereignty (2006). 'Agrarian Reform in the Context of Food Sovereignty, the Right to Food and Cultural Diversity: Land, Territory and Dignity'. Paper presented by the International Planning Committee (IPC) for Food Sovereignty, a broad coalition of civil society organisations that includes *La Via Campesina*, at the International Conference on Agrarian Reform and Rural Development (ICARRD), 6–10 March 2006, Porto Alegre, Brazil. www.icarrd.org (downloaded 18 May 2006).

Jacoby, E. with C. Jacoby (1971). *Man and Land: The Fundamental Issue in Development*. London: André Deutsch.

Jansen, K. and E. Roquas (1998). 'Modernizing Insecurity: The Land Titling Project in Honduras', *Development and Change*, vol. 29, no. 1, pp. 81–106.

Johnson, C. and T. Forsyth (2002). 'In the Eyes of the State: Negotiating a "Rights-based Approach" to Forest Conservation in Thailand', *World Development*, vol. 30, no. 9, pp. 1591–1605.

Johnston, D. and H. Le Roux (forthcoming). 'On Shaky Foundations? The Implications for Land Reform of Unreconstructed Thinking about Households', *European Journal of Development Research*.

Jones, P. M. (1991). 'The "Agrarian Law": Schemes for Land Redistribution during the French Revolution', *Past and Present*, no. 133, pp. 96–133.

Juul, K. and C. Lund (2002). 'Negotiating Property in Africa: Introduction', in K. Kristine and C. Lund, eds. *Negotiating Property in Africa*, pp. 1–10. Portsmouth, NH: Heinemann.

Kabeer, N. (1995). *Reversed Realities: Gender Hierarchies in Development Thought*. London: Verso.

Karshenas, M. (2004). 'Urban Bias, Intersectoral Resource Flows and the Macroeconomic Implications of Agrarian Relations: The Historical Experience of Japan and Taiwan', *Journal of Agrarian Change*, vol. 4, nos 1 and 2, pp. 170–189.

Kay, C. (2005). 'Reflections on Rural Poverty in Latin America', *European Journal of Development Research*, vol. 17, no. 2, pp. 317–346.

Kay, C. (2004). 'Rural Livelihoods and Peasant Futures', in R. Gwynne and C. Kay, eds, *Latin America Transformed: Globalization and Modernity*, pp. 232–250. London: Arnold (second edition).

Kay, C. (2002). 'Why East Asia Overtook Latin America: Agrarian Reform, Industrialization and Development', *Third World Quarterly*, vol. 23, no. 6, pp. 1073–1102.

Kay, C. (2001). 'Reflections on Rural Violence in Latin America', *Third World Quarterly*, vol. 22, no. 5, pp. 741–775.

Kay, C. (1998). 'Latin America's Agrarian Reform: Lights and Shadows', *Land Reform, Land Settlements and Cooperatives*, 1998, no. 2, pp. 9–31.

Kay, C. (1983). 'The Agrarian Reform in Peru: An Assessment', in A. K. Ghose (ed.). *Agrarian Reform in Contemporary Developing Countries*, pp. 185–239. London/New York: Croom Helm/St Martin's Press.

Kay, C. and P. Silva (eds). (1992). *Development and Social Change in the Chilean Countryside: From the Pre-Land Reform Period to the Democratic Consolidation*. Amsterdam: CEDLA.

Kerkvliet, B. (2005). *The Power of Everyday Politics: How Vietnamese Peasants Transformed National Policy*. Ithaca: Cornell University Press.

Kerkvliet, B. (1993). 'Claiming the Land: Take-overs by Villagers in the Philippines with Comparisons to Indonesia, Peru, Portugal, and Russia', *Journal of Peasant Studies*, vol. 20, no. 3, pp. 459–493.

Kerkvliet, B. (ed.) (1994). 'Dilemmas of Development: Vietnam Update 1994', *Political and Social Change Monograph*, no. 22, Canberra: Australian National University.

King, R. (1977). *Land Reform: A World Survey*. London: B. Bell and Sons Ltd.

Korovkin, T. (2000). 'Weak Weapons, Strong Weapons: Hidden Resistance and Political Protest in Rural Ecuador', *Journal of Peasant Studies*, vol. 27, no. 3, pp. 1–29.

Lahiff, E. (2003). 'Land Reform and Sustainable Livelihood in South Africa's Eastern Cape Province'. *IDS Research Paper*, no. 9, Brighton: Institute of Development Studies, March 2003.

Lahiff, E. and I. Scoones (2000). 'Sustainable Livelihoods in Southern Africa: Institutions, Governance and Policy Processes', *Sustainable Livelihood Southern Africa (SLSA) Research Paper 2*, Brighton: Institute of Development Studies.

Landsberger, H. (ed.) (1974). *Rural Protest: Peasant Movements and Social Change*. London: Macmillan.

Lappé, F. M., J. Collins and P. Rosset (1998). *World Hunger: Twelve Myths*. Berkeley: Food First Books (second edition).

Lara, F. Jr. and H. Morales Jr. (1990). 'The Peasant Movement and the Challenge of Democratisation in the Philippines', in J. Fox, ed, *The Challenge of Rural Democratisation: Perspectives from Latin America and the Philippines, Journal of Development Studies*, (special issue) vol. 26, no. 4, pp. 143–162.

Leach, M., R. Mearns and I. Scoones (1999). 'Environmental Entitlement: Dynamics and Institutions in Community-based Natural Resource Management', *World Development*, vol. 27, no. 2, pp. 225–247.

Lebert, T. (2001). 'Tinkering at the Edges: Land Reform in South Africa – 1994 to 2001'. Paper prepared for the International Conference on Access to Land: Innovative Agrarian Reforms for Sustainability and Poverty Reduction, 19–23 March 2001, Bonn, Germany.

Lehmann, D. (ed.) (1974). *Peasants, Landlords and Governments: Agrarian Reform in the Third World*. New York: Holmes and Meier Publishers.

Leite, S. with R. Avila (2006). 'Agrarian Reform, Social Justice and Sustainable Development'. Paper presented at the International Conference on Agrarian Reform and Rural Development (ICARRD), 6–10 March 2006, Porto Alegre, Brazil (www.icarrd.org – downloaded 18 May 2006).

Levin, R. and D. Weiner (eds) (1997). *Struggles for Land in Mpumalanga, South Africa.* NJ/Eritrea: Africa World Press.

Lieten, G. K. (1996). 'Land Reforms at Centre Stage: The Evidence on West Bengal', *Development and Change*, vol. 26, no. 1, pp. 111–130.

Li, T. (2002). 'Engaging Simplifications: Community-based Resource Management, Market Processes and State Agendas in Upland Southeast Asia', *World Development*, vol. 30, no. 2, pp. 265–283.

Lipton, M. (1974). 'Towards a Theory on Land Reform', in D. Lehmann, ed., *Peasants, Landlords and Governments: Agrarian Reform in the Third World*, pp. 269–315. New York: Holmes and Meier Publishers.

Liversage, H. (2003). 'Overview of Rwanda's Land Policy and Land Law and Key Challenges for Implementation'. Rwanda: MINITERE/DFID.

Lucas, A. and C. Warren (2003). 'The State, the People and their Mediators: The Struggle over Agrarian Law Reform in Post New Order Indonesia', *Indonesia*, no. 76 (October 2003).

Magdoff, F., F. Buttel and J. B. Foster (eds) (1998). 'Hungry for Profit: Agriculture, Food, and Ecology', *Monthly Review*, vol. 5, no. 3.

Matondi, P. and S. Moyo (2003). 'Experiences with Market Based Land Reform in Zimbabwe', in F. Barros *et al.*, eds, *The Negative Impacts of World Bank Market-based Land Reform*, pp. 323–402. Brazil: CPT and MST.

McAuslan, P. (2000). 'Only the Name of the Country Changes: The Diaspora of "European" Land Law in Commonwealth Africa', in C. Toulmin and J. Quan, eds, *Evolving Land Rights, Policy and Tenure in Africa.* London: DFID/IIED/NRI.

McMichael, P. (ed.) (1995). Food and Agrarian Order in the World Economy. Westport, CT: Praeger.

Merlet, M. S. Thirion and V. Garces (2006). 'States and Civil Society: Access to Land and Rural Development and Capacity Building for New Forms of Governance'. Paper presented at the International Conference on Agrarian Reform and Rural Development (ICARRD), 6–10 March 2006, Porto Alegre, Brazil (www.icarrd.org – downloaded 18 May 2006).

Meszaros, G. (2000). 'No Ordinary Revolution: Brazil's Landless Workers' Movement', *Race and Class*, vol. 42, no. 2, pp. 1–18.

Monsalve, S. (2004). 'EU Land Policy Guidelines and the Human Right Approach to Land'. Paper presented at a seminar on the European Union Land Policies for Developing Countries, Brussels, 17 April 2004, sponsored by Foodfirst Information and Action Network (FIAN).

Moore, B. Jr. (1967). *Social Origins of Dictatorship and Democracy: Lord and Peasant in the Modern World.* Harmondsworth: Penguin.

Moyo, S. (2000). 'The Political Economy of Land Acquisition and Redistribution in Zimbabwe, 1990–1999', *Journal of Southern African Studies*, vol. 26, no. 1, pp. 5–28.

Moyo, S. and P. Yeros (2005). 'The Resurgence of Rural Movements under Neoliberalism', in S. Moyo and P. Yeros, eds, *Reclaiming the Land: The Resurgence of Rural Movements in Africa, Asia and Latin America*, pp. 8–66. London: Zed.

Navarro, Z. (1998). 'The "Cédula da Terra" Guiding Project – Comments on the

Social and Political-Institutional Conditions of Its Recent Development'. www.dataterra.org.br.

Ntsebeza, L. (2006). *Democracy Compromised: Chiefs and the Politics of the Land in South Africa.* Leiden: Brill.

Nuijten, M. (2003). 'Family Property and the Limits of Intervention: The Article 27 Reforms and the PROCEDE Programme in Mexico', *Development and Change,* vol. 34, no. 3, pp. 475–497.

O'Brien, K. (1996). 'Rightful Resistance', *World Politics,* vol. 49, no. 1, pp. 31–55.

O'Laughlin, B. (1996). 'Through a Divided Glass: Dualism, Class and the Agrarian Questions in Mozambique', *Journal of Peasant Studies,* vol. 23, no. 4, pp. 1–39.

O'Laughlin, B. (1995). 'Past and Present Options: Land Reform in Mozambique', *Review of African Political Economy,* no. 63, pp. 99–106.

Paasch, A. (2003). 'The Failure of Market-assisted Land Reforms and Some Necessary Consequences: Comments on the World Bank's Policy Research Report'. www.worldbank.org/landpolicy/ (downloaded 05 May 2004).

Paige, J. (1975). *Agrarian Revolution: Social Movements and Export Agriculture in the Underdeveloped World.* New York: Free Press.

Palmer, R. (2000a). 'Land Policy in Africa: Lessons from Recent Policy and Implementation Processes', in C. Toulmin and J. Quan, eds, *Evolving Land Rights, Policy and Tenure in Africa,* pp. 267–288. London: DFID/IIED/NRI.

Palmer, R. (2000b). 'Mugabe's "Land Grab" in Regional Perspective', in T. A. S. Bowyer-Bower and C. Stoneman, eds, *Land Reform in Zimbabwe: Constraints and Prospects,* pp. 15–23. Aldershot: Ashgate.

Pearce, J. (1998). 'From Civil War to Civil Society: Has the End of the Cold War Brought Peace in Central America?', *International Affairs,*vol. 74, no. 3, pp. 587–615.

Peluso, N. (2002). 'Some Questions about Violence and Decentralization: A Preliminary Exploration of the Case of Indonesia'. Paper presented at the Conference on Decentralization and the Environment, Bellagio, Italy, 8–22 February. Washington, DC: World Resources Institute.

Peluso, N. (1992). *Rich Forests, Poor People: Resource Control and Resistance in Java.* Berkeley: University of California Press.

Petras, J. (1998). 'The Political and Social Basis of Regional Variation in Land Occupations in Brazil', *Journal of Peasant Studies,* vol. 25, no. 4, pp. 124–133.

Petras, J. (1997). 'Latin America: The Resurgence of the Left', *New Left Review,* no. 223, pp. 17–47.

Petras, J. and H. Veltmeyer (2003). 'The Peasantry and the State in Latin America: A Troubled Past, an Uncertain Future,' in T. Brass, ed. *Latin American Peasants,* pp. 41–82. London: Frank Cass.

Platteau, J.-P. (1996). 'The Evolutionary Theory of Land Rights as Applied to Sub-Saharan Africa: A Critical Assessment', *Development and Change,* vol. 27, no. 1, pp. 29–86.

Pons-Vignon, N. and H.-B. S. Lecomte (2004). 'Land, Violent Conflict and Development', OECD Development Centre *Working Paper,* no. 233.

Prosterman, R., M. Temple and T. Hanstad (eds) (1990). *Agrarian Reform and Grassroots Development: Ten Cases.* Boulder: Lynne Rienner Publishers.

Putzel, J. (2000). 'Land Reforms in Asia: Lessons from the Past for the 21st Century', *LSE Working Paper Series,* no. 00–04. London: London School of Economics.

Putzel, J. (1992). *A Captive Land: The Politics of Agrarian Reform in the Philippines.*

London: Catholic Institute for International Relations; New York: Monthly Review Press; Quezon City: Ateneo de Manila University Press.

Quan, J. (2000). 'Land Tenure, Economic Growth and Poverty in Sub-Saharan Africa', in C. Toulmin and J. Quan, eds, *Evolving Land Rights, Policy and Tenure in Africa*, pp. 31–49. London: DFID/IIED/NRI.

Raj, K. N. and M. Tharakan (1983). 'Agrarian Reform in Kerala and Its Impact on the Rural Economy', in A. K. Ghose, ed., *Agrarian Reform in Contemporary Developing Countries*, pp. 31–90. Geneva: International Labour Organisation; New York: St Martin's Press.

Razavi, S. (ed.) (2003). 'Agrarian Change, Gender and Land Rights', *Journal of Agrarian Change*, (special issue) vol. 3, nos 1 and 2, pp. 2–32.

Redclift, M. (1978). *Agrarian Reform and Peasant Organization on the Ecuadorian Coast*. London: University of London/Athlone Press.

Reyes, R. (1999). 'Market-assisted Land Reform: An Indecent Proposal'. www.philsol.nl (downloaded 25 April 2005).

Ribot, J. and A. Larson (2005). *Democratic Decentralisation through a Natural Resource Lens*. New York: Routledge.

Riedinger, J. (1995). *Agrarian Reform in the Philippines: Democratic Transitions and Redistributive Reform*. Stanford: Stanford University Press.

Riedinger, J., W.-Y. Yang and K. Brook (2000). 'Market-based Land Reform: An Imperfect Solution', in H. Morales Jr. and J. Putzel, eds, (2001). *Power in the Village: Agrarian Reform, Rural Politics, Institutional Change and Globalization*, pp. 363–378. Quezon City: University of the Philippines Press.

Rigg, J. (2006). 'Land, Farming, Livelihoods, and Poverty: Rethinking the Links in the Rural South', *World Development*, vol. 34, no. 1, pp. 180–202.

Ross, E. (2003). 'Modernisation, Clearance and the Continuum of Violence in Colombia'. *ISS Working Paper Series*, no. 383, The Hague: Institute of Social Studies.

Ross, E. (1998). *The Malthus Factor: Poverty, Politics and Population in Capitalist Development*. London: Zed.

Rosset, P. (2001). 'Tides Shift on Agrarian Reform: New Movements Show the Way', *Backgrounder*, vol. 7, no. 1, pp. 1–8. Berkeley: Foodfirst Institute.

Rosset, P., R. Patel and M. Courville (2006). *Promised Land: Competing Visions of Agrarian Reform*. Berkeley: Food First Books.

Roth, R. (2004). 'On the Colonial Margins and in the Global Hotspots: Park-People Conflicts in Highland Thailand', *Asia Pacific Viewpoint*, vol. 45, no. 1, pp. 13–32.

Sadoulet, E., R. Murgai and A. de Janvry (2001). 'Access to Land via Land Rental Markets', in A. de Janvry, G. Gordillo, J. P. Platteau and E. Sadoulet, eds, *Access to Land, Rural Poverty, and Public Action*, pp. 196–229. Oxford: Oxford University Press.

Saith, A. (1985). 'Primitive Accumulation, Agrarian Reform and Socialist Transitions: An Argument', *Journal of Development Studies*, vol. 22, no. 1, pp. 1–48.

Sauer, S. (2003). 'A Ticket to Land: The World Bank's Market-based Land Reform in Brazil', in F. Barros *et al.*, eds, *The Negative Impacts of World Bank Market-based Land Reform*, pp. 45–102. Brazil: Comissão Pastoral da Terra, Movimento dos Trabalhadores Rurais Sem Terra (MST), Foodfirst Information and Action Network (FIAN).

Scott, J. (1998). *Seeing Like a State: How Certain Schemes to Improve the Human Condition Have Failed*. New Haven: Yale University Press.

Shillinglaw, G. (1974). 'Land Reform and Peasant Mobilization in Southern China, 1947–1950', in D. Lehmann, ed., *Peasants, Landlords and Governments: Agrarian Reform in the Third World*, pp. 118–155. New York: Holmes and Meier Publishers.

Sobhan, R. (1993). *Agrarian Reform and Social Transformation*. London: Zed.

Spoor, M. (ed.) (2003). *Transition, Institutions, and the Rural Sector*. New York: Lexington.

Spoor, M. (2002). 'Policy Regimes and Performance of the Agricultural Sector in Latin America and the Caribbean during the Last Three Decades', *Journal of Agrarian Change*, vol. 2, no. 3, pp. 381–400.

Spoor, M. (ed.) (1997). *The 'Market Panacea': Agrarian Transformation in Developing Countries and Former Socialist Economies*. London: Intermediate Technology Publications.

Spoor, M. and O. Visser (2004). 'Restructuring Postponed: Large Russian Farm Enterprises "Coping with the Market"', *Journal of Peasant Studies*, vol. 31, nos 3 and 4, pp. 515–551.

Stavenhagen, R. (ed.) (1971). *Agrarian Problems and Peasant Movements in Latin America*. New York: Anchor Books.

Tai, H.-C. (1974). *Land Reform and Politics: A Comparative Analysis*. Berkeley: University of California Press.

Tannenbaum, F. (1929). *The Mexican Agrarian Revolution*. New York: Archon Books (published again in 1968).

Thiesenhusen, W. (1995). *Broken Promises: Agrarian Reform and the Latin American Campesino*. Boulder: Westview.

Thiesenhusen, W. (ed.) (1989). *Searching for Agrarian Reform in Latin America*. Boston: Unwin Hyman.

Toulmin, C. and J. Quan (eds) (2000). *Evolving Land Rights, Policy and Tenure in Africa*. London: DFID/IIED/NRI.

Tsing, A. (2002). 'Land as Law: Negotiating the Meaning of Property in Indonesia', in F. Richards, ed., *Land, Property, and the Environment*, pp. 94–137. Oakland: Institute for Contemporary Studies.

Tuma, E. (1965). *Twenty-six Centuries of Agrarian Reform: A Comparative Analysis*. Berkeley: University of California Press.

Urioste, M. (2001). 'Bolivia: Reform and Resistance in the Countryside (1982–2000)'. London: University of London, Institute of Latin American Studies Occasional Papers, no. 23.

van den Hombergh, H. (2004). *No Stone Unturned: Building Blocks of Environmentalist Campaigning versus Transnational Industrial Forestry in Costa Rica*. Amsterdam: Dutch University Press.

Veltmeyer, H. (2005). 'The Dynamics of Land Occupations in Latin America', in S. Moyo and P. Yeros, eds, *Reclaiming the Land: The Resurgence of Rural Movements in Africa, Asia and Latin America*, pp. 285–316. London: Zed.

Veltmeyer, H. (1997). 'New Social Movements in Latin America: The Dynamics of Class and Identity', *Journal of Peasant Studies*, vol. 25, no. 1, pp. 139–169.

Via Campesina (2006). *Violations of Peasants' Human Rights, 2006 Annual Report*. Jakarta: Via Campesina. www.viacampesina.org (downloaded 18 May 2006).

Via Campesina (2005). *Violations of Peasants' Human Rights, 2005 Annual Report*. Jakarta: Via Campesina. www.viacampesina.org (downloaded 18 May 2006).

Wade, R. (2004). 'Is Globalization Reducing Poverty and Inequality?', *World Development*, vol. 32, no. 4, pp. 567–589.

Wade, R. (1990). *Governing the Market: Economic Theory and the Role of Government in East Asian Industrialization.* Princeton: Princeton University Press.

Walinsky, L. (ed.) (1977). *Agrarian Reform as Unfinished Business: The Selected Papers of Wolf Ladejinsky.* Oxford: Oxford University Press.

Warriner, D. (1969). *Land Reform in Principle and Practice.* Oxford: Clarendon Press.

Wegren, S. (2004). 'From Communism to Capitalism? Russia's Agrarian Relations in the Twentieth Century and Beyond,' *Journal of Peasant Studies,* vol. 31, nos. 3 and 4, pp. 363–399.

Wiradi, G. (2005). 'Agrarian Reform Movement in Indonesia: Past and Present'. Paper presented at the workshop on 'Food Sovereignty and Agrarian Reform Movement in Indonesia, organised by the CCFD, Paris, 3 February 2005.

Wolf, E. (1969). *Peasant Wars of the Twentieth Century.* New York/London: Harper and Row.

Wolford, W. (2003). 'Producing Community: The MST and Land Reform Settlements in Brazil', *Journal of Agrarian Change,* vol. 3, no. 4, pp. 500–520.

Worby, E. (2001). 'A Redivided Land? New Agrarian Conflicts and Questions in Zimbabwe', *Journal of Agrarian Change,* vol. 1, no. 4, pp. 475–509.

World Bank (2005). *World Development Report 2006: Equity and Development.* Washington, DC: World Bank; New York: Oxford University Press.

World Bank (2003). *Land Policies for Growth and Poverty Reduction.* Washington, DC: World Bank; Oxford: Oxford University Press.

Wright, A. and W. Wolford (2003). *To Inherit the Earth: The Landless Movement and the Struggle for a New Brazil.* Oakland: Food First Books.

Wuyts, M. (1994). 'Accumulation, Industrialisation and the Peasantry: A Reinterpretation of the Tanzanian Experience', *Journal of Peasant Studies,* vol. 21, no. 2, pp. 159–193.

Yashar, D. (2005). *Contesting Citizenship in Latin America; The Rise of Indigenous Movements and the Postliberal Challenge,* Cambridge and New York: Cambridge University Press.

Yashar, D. (1999). 'Democracy, Indigenous Movements, and the Postliberal Challenge in Latin America', *World Politics,* vol. 52, no. 1, pp. 76–104.

Zoomers, A. and G. van der Haar (eds) (2000). *Current Land Policy in Latin America: Regulating Land Tenure Under Neo-Liberalism.* Amsterdam: Royal Tropical Institute (KIT).

2 Bolivia's unfinished agrarian reform

Rural poverty and development policies[1]

Cristóbal Kay and Miguel Urioste

Introduction

The Bolivian revolution of 1952 was a turning point in the country's history. The revolutionary upheaval in the countryside resulted in one of the most drastic agrarian reforms in Latin America. Together with the Cuban revolution of 1959, it signalled an era of land reforms throughout most of Latin America during the 1960s and 1970s. Almost half a century had elapsed since the Mexican revolution of 1910–1917, in which the peasantry were major protagonists, before they were able again to overturn the traditional landlord system but this time in Bolivia. However, Bolivia's agrarian reform of 1953 generated highly contradictory processes whose consequences have assumed dramatic proportions in recent years. Despite Bolivia's long history of agrarian reform, the land question is at the centre of the contemporary political debate like in no other Latin American country, especially since the early 1990s when the land issue became enmeshed with the ethnic and indigenous question. This chapter explores the various forces unleashed by the agrarian reform, some paradoxical and conflicting, which have subsequently led to the design of a so-called 'second agrarian reform' in the 1990s which, however, was never fully implemented. It also seeks to explain the reasons for the persistent rural poverty and the renewed relevance of the land question in Bolivia. The chapter closes with some reflections on the whole process started by the 1952 revolution as well as a few recommendations for a development strategy capable of dealing with the land and poverty problems.

Bolivia achieved independence from Spain and became a Republic in 1825 but with a marked exclusionary character. The emergent state explicitly denied citizenship rights to the indigenous population which, at that time, represented 80 per cent of the Bolivian population. When the Republic was founded, indigenous forms of social organisation, of land tenancy and labour use – shaped by colonial patterns of domination – were not flourishing. On the contrary, in many cases – and especially with respect to access to land – they were deteriorating (Klein, 2003).

The colonial regime subordinated and utilised the forms of organisation and labour relations of the *ayllus*,[2] with the aim of supplying the silver
mines of Potosí with an unpaid workforce by means of forced labour
(Klein, 1993). Rather than destroying indigenous forms of territorial
organisation, the Spanish Conquest subordinated them to its own interests
and many ancient *ayllus* came to be known as '*comunidades*' (communities)
according to the old medieval Spanish usage of the term. The *caciques* or
heads of the *ayllus* became known as '*taseros*' (assessors) and had the task
of collecting taxes from the indigenous subjects of the Crown (Klein,
2003). These pre-colonial forms still prevail today, 500 years later, in some
parts of the western Andes, where there are significant overlaps between
existing local political administrative and territorial structures (*provincias,
cantones, secciones, municipios*) and the earlier territorial forms of organisation (*señorios, ayllus, markas*).

In 1870, half a century after the founding of Bolivia, the *hacienda* (large
landed estate) regime began to develop by usurping lands belonging to
the indigenous communities, a process euphemistically known as '*ex-vincu-
lación*' (de-linking). Parliamentary records of the time reflect the intense
debate which took place and the final shape of the public policies on the
indigenous question and on access to the land-territory (*tierra-territorio*).
'Land in indigenous hands is dead land' was the saying of those who
wanted to end the regime of communities and who pressed for the compulsory transfer of community lands in the Andean highlands and the
valleys to the minority *criollo-mestizo* (people of Spanish descent and mixed
race) groups who controlled the state apparatus (Pearse, 1975; Langer,
1989).

This dispossession – by means of a supposedly public auction – changed
the property structure, access to and use of land, and the local political
administrative organisation. By the end of the nineteenth century the best
agricultural and grazing land of most indigenous communities had
become the property of the *hacienda*. As in many other Latin American
countries, the *hacienda* symbolised modernity. On the one hand, it meant
the incorporation of new technologies to improve yields and surpluses
and, on the other, it meant the appropriation of land-rent by means of the
labour services of '*pongos*', '*colonos*' and '*peones*', who were obliged to work
for the landlord or *patrón* in return for the provisional and precarious
usufruct of a family parcel on the *hacienda* (Larson, 1988).

The *hacienda* regime, which lasted for almost a century until the middle
of the twentieth century, met with particular resistance from the indigenous quechuas and aymaras who refused to give up their claims to the land
which had been expropriated from them. Attempts to recuperate their
land included judicial action, indigenous uprisings and reducing food
supplies for the market. The growing discontent of the 1940s and peasant
rebellions, following the deaths of thousands of indigenous people in the
Chaco War,[3] led to the Agrarian Reform Law of 1953 which brought an

end to the regime of servitude (Calderón and Dandler, 1986; Rivera, 1987). This law juridically recognises the '*Solar Campesino*' (peasant house-hold plot) as a vital space for the construction of the family dwelling, corrals for livestock, and stores for agricultural equipment. The '*solar*' forms the nucleus of the 'small property' which spread rapidly throughout the whole western Andean region in a complex process of fragmentation of landed property rights, of labour and the partial incorporation into the market economy, within the framework of the political and administration organisation of the community. Under the 1953 agrarian reform the state recognised *de facto* – if not *de jure* – the 'original communities' (those which were not expropriated during the Republic), the 'communities ex-*hacienda*' (constituted by *peones* or labourers from the ex-*latifundios* or large landed estates) and the 'new communities', created following the agrarian reform at the instigation of landless rural families. The juridical recognition of the peasant and indigenous communities had to wait until the Land Law of 1996 (also called 'Ley INRA').

The 1953 agrarian reform law was not part of a prophylactic policy against the spread of communism as occurred in other Latin American countries after the Cuban revolution. Nor was it a planned public policy. What distinguishes the Bolivian agrarian reform is its endogenous charac-ter, its strong roots in the indigenous identity, its outwardly redistributive orientation and the lack of clear public policies to support rural develop-ment. This lack led to the failure of the process in terms of achieving a sustainable improvement in rural family incomes and a strengthening of national food security.

However, the Bolivian agrarian reform was a notable success when seen as an economic and social process which historically restored indigenous territorial claims. In addition to freeing the labour force, it led to a dynamic economic expansion for the first generation of peasant land reform beneficiaries until the early 1960s, and in particular to the strengthening of their communal organisation. The indigenous popu-lation, on gaining free and direct access to the land, to their own forms of organisation under the rubric of 'agrarian trade unions' and to political hegemony over rural territorial space, were transformed into the central actors of the revolution, organising armed militias to consolidate and defend their recently recovered land. But the rapid abandonment of the agrarian reform of 1953 by public institutions and by the very party which had propelled it, the MNR (*Movimiento Nacionalista Revolucionario* or National Revolutionary Movement) condemned it to failure in terms of achieving a form of inclusionary and sustainable rural development.

In the following years, the state privileged the construction of roads from the western Andes (the highland and valley regions) to the eastern plains or lowlands (the *llanos* or *tierras bajas* region), investing there in an infrastructure for agricultural and livestock production, in sugar and oil refineries and in forestry, thereby opening up the eastern plains to national development. In the 1960s and 1970s important colonisation programmes were introduced, leading to the settlement of indigenous aymaras and quechuas from the western Andes to the eastern lowlands (Wennergren and Whitaker, 1975). However, the spontaneous colonisation (following the roads) was just as important as state-sponsored colonisation schemes. Remarkably, spontaneous settlers were economically more successfully than those settlements which had been established by the state (Zeballos, 1975). It is thus not surprising that spontaneous colonisation becomes dominant, especially after the state abandons the state-sponsored colonisation schemes in the early 1990s. But this expansion of the agricultural frontier towards the east was accompanied by an arbitrary process of reconcentration of land ownership in the hands of a minority of *mestizos*,[4] both civilian and military, who supported the government of the day (Gill, 1987).

The 'conquest of the east' consolidated two productive structures, corresponding to two forms of land ownership. In the western Andes, family production remained linked to the small landed property under the organisational aegis of the indigenous communities, while in the eastern plains capitalist agro-enterprises underwent a rapid expansion, concentrating most of the land suitable for crops and pasture. Since then, these two extreme models have turned their backs on each other, coexisting without interacting, while competing for the attention of the state. However, it is the indigenous population from the western Andes which provided most of the labour force for the eastern plains.

At the beginning of the 1990s, the colonisation programme of the agrarian reform collapsed as a public policy. The human settlement programmes were stalled by the profitable cultivation of coca leaves in the tropical regions and, with the support of international bodies and the environmental movements, large parks and forest reserves were created with the aim of reducing environmental degradation supposedly caused by human settlements. While these did stem the expansion of the spontaneous colonisation of peasants-indigenous people expelled from the Andean highlands and valleys in search of land in the eastern plains, it did not affect the interests of large entrepreneurs and owners of *latifundios* who continued to leave large tracts of land unexploited.

The failure of the 1953 reform is not only seen in terms of the unequal distribution of land in the plains, but also in the way the administration of the land became a victim to corruption and bureaucracy (Hernáiz, 1993). In one such instance, in 1992 even a Minister of State attempted to appropriate free of charge 100,000 hectares of some of the best land in the plains for the cultivation of soya. Nor is this an isolated case. Political favouritism and patronage gave rise to a black market in land in the east of Bolivia. These events prompted in 1992 the 'intervention' of the *Consejo Nacional de Reforma Agraria* – CNRA (National Council of Agrarian Reform) and the *Instituto Nacional de Colonización* – INC (National Institute of Colonisation) which brought to an end the first stage of the agrarian reform from 1953 to 1992 (Hernáiz, 2002). Aside from the initial radical changes in favour of peasants in the Andean region, the Bolivian agrarian reform failed to achieve its objective of reducing rural poverty. So, what is to guarantee that a second agrarian reform will do any better?

In the 1990s, with the rise of structural adjustment policies, international agencies have been advocating throughout Latin America the paradigm of a 'market in land' as a solution to the 'failure of redistributive agrarian reforms'. Since then many countries have encouraged the free purchase and sale of community lands and family peasant properties and have focused their attention on clarifying private property land rights. The premise is that once private ownership is assured, the market can allocate the factors of production (land, labour and capital) more efficiently than the state, and thereby achieve growth (Deininger and Binswanger, 2001; but see also Borras, Kay and Akram-Lodhi, this volume).

In 1996 a new land law – the INRA law (*Instituto Nacional de Reforma Agraria* or National Institute of Agrarian Reform) – was passed with the aim of clarifying and regularising land rights, a process which is called *saneamiento* or land titling process (Fundación TIERRA, 1997). However, unlike in other countries of the region where the land titling process has been restricted to registering property rights, the Bolivian law is more ambitious and complex. Faced with the administrative chaos and widespread illegal land rights, especially in the eastern plains, the new law insists on identifying the technical or legal reasons for annulling or confirming land ownership. This process has been advancing slowly and without much conviction since 1996. The process, which has now been going on for ten years, has experienced many technical, financial and political difficulties.

The mapping of poverty in Bolivia: regional, ethnic and gender dimensions

As in other Latin American countries, the main demographic characteristic of the past half century has been the rapid growth of cities due to a sustained process of out-migration from countryside to city. What are striking are the high levels of poverty and the extreme unequal distribution of income. As is common throughout Latin America the incidence of rural poverty is much higher than urban poverty but the difference is particularly acute in Bolivia. Bolivia has one of the worst income distributions of Latin America having a Gini coefficient of 0.614 in 2002. Income inequality was also more severe in the rural sector (0.632) than in the urban sector (0.554) (ECLAC, 2004: 301–305).

Regional distribution of poverty: highlands, valleys and plains

In Bolivia there are three main geographical zones: highland or highland plateau (*altiplano*), valleys (*valles*) and plains (*llanos*), also known as the Andean region, the sub-Andean region and the lowlands (*tierras bajas*), respectively – see Figure 2.1. The highland accounts for 28 per cent of total land area, the valleys 13 per cent and the plains 59 per cent. In demographic terms, 42 per cent of the population live in the highland, 29 per cent in the valleys and 29 per cent in the plains. The highland and valleys account for seven out of every ten people who live in the rural area of Bolivia. In sum, the highland and valleys account for less than half of the territory but are home to the majority of the rural population, living in very unfavourable ecological and environmental conditions.

Regional distribution of poverty has one constant feature, the poorest region is the highland, followed by the valleys and then by the plains. The incidence of poverty is much higher in the highland (69.8 per cent) and valleys (69.2 per cent) than in the plains (53.9 per cent) as can be seen in

Figure 2.1 Map of Bolivia and its three geographical zones.

Table 2.1. In terms of extreme poverty (or destitution), it can be observed that the gap is even greater between the highlands and valleys as compared to the plains. While 43.6 per cent and 42.5 per cent of the highland and valley population respectively experience extreme poverty, this figure drops to 23.0 per cent in the plains. These regional differences as well as the internal characteristics of each sector mean that the poor are not a homogeneous group. Rural poverty replicates the regional differences mentioned at the national level. While 59.4 per cent and 63.9 per cent of the highland and valley rural population live in extreme poverty, this figure drops to 32.2 per cent in the plains as can be seen in Table 2.1. There is also a marked asymmetry in the incidence of poverty between the rural and the urban population. While in the rural area more than 80 per cent of the people live in poverty, in the cities less than 40 per cent of the population do so.

One criterion which clearly helps to distinguish the factors which determine poverty in each region is access to land. In the highland and valleys, the peasants and indigenous population have access to poorer quality and less land. In the plains, by contrast, there is a greater abundance of fertile land, although it is not always in the hands of poor peasants and indigenous people but in those of medium-sized and large landowners (Roca, 2001). On the other hand, in the plains part of the peasant-indigenous population marginally share in the benefits of agro-industry, being

Table 2.1 National and rural poverty profile by region in Bolivia, 2002

Description	Number of persons (thousands)	Persons (%)	Income per capita of households (Bolivianos)	Incidence of poverty (%)	Incidence of extreme poverty (%)
Total national	8,488	100.0	378	64.6	36.8
Highlands	3,404	40.1	288	69.8	43.6
Valleys	2,398	28.3	334	69.2	42.5
Plains	2,686	31.6	532	53.9	23.0
Rural Area	3,212	100.0	142	82.2	55.0
Highlands	1,377	42.9	128	86.1	59.4
Valleys	1,128	35.1	115	84.8	63.9
Plains	708	22.0	215	70.3	32.2
Migration					
Non-migrant	1,759	66.4	120	85.4	60.7
Migrant	891	33.6	201	72.4	38.6

Source: Elaborated with information from the Instituto Nacional de Estadística, *Encuesta de Hogares y Medición de Condiciones de Vida*, La Paz: INE, November 2002.

Notes
Incidence of poverty refers to the population that is below the poverty line which is calculated according to the minimum income required to satisfy basic needs. *Incidence of extreme poverty* refers to the population whose income is so low that even if they allocate it exclusively to food it would not satisfy the minimum nutritional requirements.

employed as wage labourers (*peones*) and seasonal workers, while those settled in the colonised lands (the '*asentados*') draw some benefit from the land by participating in market activities. It is interesting to note that the migrant population in the place of reception has a higher per capita income and a lower incidence of poverty. For example, the migrants have a per capita income of 201 Bolivianos compared to the non-migrants' 120 Bolivianos as can be seen in Table 2.1. In other words the migrants have 70 per cent more income than the non-migrants. The migrants are peasants from the highland and valleys who have emigrated to the plains.

Another way of comparing differences between the poor across regions is by comparing their links with the economy, which determine the way in which they use their assets and participate in production. In the highland and valleys they usually produce non-marketed goods for their own subsistence with the exception of some milk and meat, while in the plains the peasants and colonisers produce agricultural inputs for the agro-industries, so that they are largely producing commodities for a fully commercialised economy (Roca, 2001). Rural inhabitants are not only vulnerable because of their precarious economic and productive situation but because the seasonal and fluctuating nature of their agricultural activities makes the end result risky and uncertain. In sectors which are more linked to the market, such as the plains, small producers are at the mercy of price fluctuations, while in the highland and valleys, risks are linked to changing climatic conditions which, according to the peasants, have recently become much more unstable.

Ethnic and gender composition of rural poverty

Poverty is not only mainly rural but also indigenous and feminine. This situation is even more marked in Bolivia as 62 per cent of the total population over 15 years of age self-identify as indigenous, a figure which increases to 78 per cent in the rural area. In Bolivia 80 per cent of the indigenous population fall below the poverty line in comparison to 40 per cent of the non-indigenous population (CEPAL, 2002). This situation is not a coincidence but has historical roots. Up until the agrarian reform of 1953 the indigenous people, especially those in the highland and valleys, were practically subordinated to the *haciendas* by relations of servitude, a fact which constrained their development as a social group and as individual citizens. Bolivia currently has 35 indigenous groups mainly concentrated in the lowlands, although lowland groups are much fewer in terms of actual numbers. The indigenous people of the Amazonian lowlands used to be, and still often are, hunter-gatherers. They are also different culturally as well as in their social organisation and settlement pattern to the aymara and quechua peasantry. The guaraní is another distinctive indigenous group whose members mainly live in the southern lowlands in the Chaco region which borders with Paraguay. Despite the widespread cultural diversity, the indigenous quechuas and aymaras make up 90 per cent of the total Bolivian indigenous population. Quechuas account for 30.7 per cent, followed by aymaras with 25.2 per cent of the country's total population (including the non-indigenous population). The other indigenous groups are much less numerous (6.1 per cent) (INE, 2001). The indigenous population largely inhabits the western region, precisely those Andean territories which are the poorest in the country. To generalise roughly, one can say that the highlands are inhabited by aymaras, the valleys by quechuas and the plains by other indigenous or native peoples from the east and Amazonia.

Statistics show that, while rural poverty affects the entire indigenous-peasant population, women confront greater impoverishment because of their role in the production of foodstuffs, reproduction and care of children, production of a monetary income and household tasks. Rural women have been most affected by the lack of recognition of their status as producers, a fact which excludes them from state and private actions and which has prevented them from gaining access to land ownership, credit, technology and other public services. Data from INRA show that a large part of the property titles assigned under the 1953 agrarian reform were in the name of the male head of household. Nevertheless one of the clauses of the 1953 agrarian reform was quite visionary by defining beneficiaries without distinguishing by sex, yet another clause limited beneficiaries on the *haciendas* to widows with small children (Deere and León, 2001: 74). The agrarian reform was thus contradictory and in practice it has failed to overcome gender discrimination as only 17.2 per cent of agrarian reform and colonisation beneficiaries were women up until 1994 (ibid.: 75). Although the 1996 INRA law include a statement of principle or intent for granting land titles to women, until now this has been marginal. What is missing in the Ley INRA is a pro-active mechanism to incorporate women such as titling to couples and priority to female household heads. The delay in processing land titles and land redistribution with respect to women also means deferring the application of a policy designed to overcome the gender discrimination as set out in the 1953 agrarian reform law (Salazar, 2003).

The Civil Code specifies that inheritance – in this case the land – should be distributed equally between sons and daughters but, in practice, men have accumulated more land than women. This has its origin in traditional social practices which have discriminated against women. Agricultural work has been considered to be men's work; the sexual division of labour assigned women to the domestic and reproductive space and men to the productive public space. This vision has prevented the extent of and the multiple ways in which peasant-indigenous women participate in economic activities from being seen and their contribution from being reflected in the official statistics.

Many studies concur in pointing out how property and security of land rights strengthens, protects and increases the bargaining power of women in both public and private spheres. It gives them economic security and opens up the possibility of empowering them socially and politically (Agarwal, 1994). Women tend to invest the income which they earn in the home, in the welfare of their children, more than men do. Granting land to women means improving family well-being. Moreover, women stand out as producers of basic foodstuffs for the family basket and as such, women's access to land is linked to food security (Deere and León, 2001). In the rural area, economic activity revolves around the family: the family is the unit of consumption and production so it is difficult to estimate the incidence of rural poverty by gender. What is certain is that peasant families as a unit suffer poverty, and that this falls most heavily on women when men migrate in search of non-rural income or simply reside permanently or temporarily in urban centres. Where indigenous women gain access to wage work, they tend to occupy low-status jobs both in terms of the type of activity undertaken and the level of income received (Valenzuela, 2004).

The above can be summarised by saying that there is a clear correlation between poverty, living in a rural area (especially the highland and valleys), belonging to an indigenous group and being a woman. Such a condition is both consequence and cause of the social exclusion of the indigenous population. This issue is the subject of debate among rural actors, policy planners, non-governmental organisations and international bodies. Political parties prefer to evade their responsibilities when it comes to defining public policies of rural development. Rural social conflicts, marches, road blockades, land seizures, which have intensified since 2000, expose the profound crisis of a nation which at its birth excluded the indigenous majority and which today attempts to construct a new social pact by means of the Constituent Assembly, originally envisaged for 2005 but postponed until 2006 due to the country's continuing political instability.

Critique of poverty approaches

One of the characteristics of Bolivia in the past 20 years is the fact that income, employment and productivity have stagnated, thereby leading different governments to propose reducing extreme poverty by means of 'pro-poor' strategies. Within this framework, and under the auspices of international agencies, in 2001 the Bolivian Strategy of Poverty Reduction (EBRP) as a policy for combating poverty was set up, with the financial support of resources arising from the cancellation of the foreign debt for Highly Indebted Poor Countries (HIPC), approximately US$1,400 million. The disappointing results of the poverty reduction strategy in Bolivia over the past five years (Komives et al., 2005) is giving greater credence to an almost forgotten vision, i.e. that one cannot devise strategies to combat poverty if the structural conditions which produce it are not addressed. Within such a perspective the distribution of resources and power within and between countries becomes paramount.

It became commonplace to think that only by working with the poor would one find a solution to their poverty. The adoption of this point of view meant the abandonment of the focus on a modern globalising society which generates so many poor and continues increasingly to produce them. The basic condition was neither to question nor to intervene in the organisation and functioning of society, understood as a set of relations in which social actors with divergent and contradictory interests are engaged. Some of the current prevalent poverty approaches think of the poor and not of the society. The 'question of poverty' has concealed and annulled the 'social question'. The political consequence of such an ideological distortion has been to substitute the 'struggle against poverty' for that of social struggles. This 'poortology' (*pobretología*) is nothing other than a perverse focus which assumes the abandonment of the social struggle. It assumes that the causes of poverty lie in the poor themselves, that poverty is external to or outside the society which produces it, that one can combat poverty without affecting the society and wider international relations.

In Latin America, the conviction has grown that poverty and its growth are due to the absence of social policies, forgetting that throughout history in any model of society the main criterion of equality and equity is the distribution of wealth. There will always be greater inequality where there is less social redistribution. In Bolivia the concentration of wealth is taking place in a context where democratic institutions are maintained which, with few exceptions, serve to legitimate anti-democratic procedures, functions, processes and relations. The kind of deformed democracy prevailing in Latin America and Bolivia has made it possible to legitimate greater impoverishment and a growing gap between rich and poor. Democracy is being emptied of real content because – in spite of popular participation – it masks the causes and consequences of the crisis of participation and political representation.

Although the Bolivian Strategy of Poverty Reduction (EBRP) is a tool for redistributing resources and transferring political power, within the framework of Popular Participation,[5] it does not draw attention to the structural causes of poverty but to the shortcomings, seemingly envisaged as immanent, of the traditional rural population. Rural poverty is chronic not because the peasant-indigenous population lacks the ability to generate a surplus but because their conditions of production do not permit the sustainable development of their family enterprises. Those rural territories which used to be poor continue to be so. Many factors influence this picture: environmental factors, land fragmentation, the loss of nutrients in the soil through over-exploitation and the almost complete abandonment of the system of rotating crops and leaving land fallow. In addition their crops are permanently vulnerable to frosts and drought and they lack institutional access to new technologies, adequate finance, secure markets and information systems. The persistence of extreme rural poverty is practically endemic. The limited results of the policies to combat poverty require that analysis refocus on the problem of access to resources, inequality and development strategies (Kay, 2005a).

Main characteristics of the rural sector

The mono-export dynamic, initially centred on silver and more recently on tin, dominated Bolivian international economic relations until the collapse of the price of tin in the 1980s. For a century and a half, Bolivia, since its creation in 1825, almost exclusively lived off the income generated by mineral exports and by indigenous tribute. The collapse of the state mines in 1985 and the dismissal of over 30,000 miners generated a new wave of demands for access to natural resources, especially land. But by then more than 30 years had passed since the start of the agrarian reform, so that all the land in Bolivia already had new owners. The hyper-inflation (1983 to 1985) and the high level of unemployment from the closure of the state mines was – together with the liberalisation of agricultural imports – the detonator which put the issue of land access back on the national agenda. But it did so in a chaotic and contradictory way. It was precisely in 1984 that the Confederation of Peasant Trade Unions of Bolivia (*Confederación Sindical Única de Trabajadores Campesinos de Bolivia* or CSUTCB), which at that time brought together most peasants-indigenous people in Bolivia, which pressed for a new law to replace the agrarian reform of 1953. This proposal, known as the Fundamental Agrarian Law, reflected the most elaborate statement at the time of the peasant-indigenous movement of Bolivia (Urioste, 1984). However, this proposal was not approved by Congress, although some points were included in the INRA law of 1996.

Throughout its history Bolivia has mainly exported natural resources. The latest trends are the increasing importance of hydrocarbons – especially natural gas – and the production of soya in the lowland department of Santa Cruz.[6] There has been an enormous change in the geographical distribution of agricultural production since the 1953 agrarian reform. Until the middle of the twentieth century, agriculture was the most important subsistence economy for the indigenous communities in the Andean region as at that time the settlement of the eastern lowlands had not yet occurred. According to Demeure (1999) in 1950 the cultivated area in Santa Cruz was only 60,000 hectares increasing to over a million after the structural reforms of the mid-1980s. New crops, such as soya, sunflower, wheat, cotton and sorghum, now account for 80 per cent of the cultivated land in Santa Cruz and 60 per cent is devoted to the production of soya. By contrast, according to the same source, the growth of the cultivated area in the highlands has been quite moderate, around 30 per cent. Productivity in the Andean region has stagnated, with the exception of some small innovations in potato production with the introduction of mineral fertilisers and agricultural machinery and the cultivation of quinua.

Change in the agrarian sector is not only characterised by transformations in production but also in consumption. As a consequence the contribution of the peasant sector to the national food supply has fallen dramatically from 70 per cent to 45 per cent over the last couple of decades (Delegación de la Comisión Europea, 2003). This means that the traditional supplies of food to the domestic market, largely by the peasant beneficiaries of the 1953 agrarian reform, have been displaced by imports, especially from neighbouring countries. Food imports have increased to meet the needs of the middle-class urban population for more sophisticated products (INE, 2003). Up until the policies of structural adjustment of 1985, the internal supply was able to meet the demand of the Bolivian population but, with the ability to freely import foodstuffs as from 1985, the peasant economy declined as it could not compete with better quality and cheaper imports (Banco Central de Bolivia, 2004). The expansionary phase of food production of the peasant-indigenous farm sector since the agrarian reform comes to an end in the mid-1980s with the shift to the new economic policy of neoliberalism (van Dijk, 1998).

The changes in agricultural activity in the country, namely the stagnation of production in the Andean region and the impressive development of agriculture in the eastern department of Santa Cruz, both in terms of quantity and diversification of crops, are shown in Table 2.2.

Causes, impacts and limitations of the first agrarian reform of 1953

At the time of independence in 1825 Bolivia had approximately 11,000 communities registered. Over a century later, only 3,783 communities remained as a result of the devastating effect of the *latifundista* feudal regime imposed by the *criollos*. Land ownership was highly concentrated: in 1950 0.72 per cent of properties or 615 estates with an average size of 26.400 hectares controlled almost half of the owned land while 60 per cent of properties smaller than five hectares only had 0.23 per cent of the owned land (Ministerio de Agricultura, 1985). The large landed estates (*haciendas* or *latifundios*) possessed on average 1,500 hectares of land of which only about 35 hectares were cultivated. By contrast, a peasant community possessed 1,900 hectares on average of which 45 hectares were cultivated. The main difference is that the estate was the property of a single family whereas the community belonged to several hundred families (Demeure, 1999).

The 1953 agrarian reform is the most important milestone in the history of the republic for transforming the rural sector. Its radical nature

Table 2.2 Regional evolution of principal crops in Bolivia (in hectares), 1950–1997

Crop/year	1950 (a)	1972 (b)	1991 (c)	1997 (c)
Andean region (d)				
Maize	94,291	157,500	180,625	166,144
Potato	111,680	107,200	135,881	121,914
Onions	61,194	101,000	95,297	86,508
Wheat	82,950	61,066	77,933	81,536
Quinua	18,998	15,000	38,791	38,680
Broadbeans	9,226	21,000	27,210	27,649
Alfalfa	6,325	15,200	17,705	20,880
Total	384,664	477,966	573,442	543,311
Growth index	100	122	140	130
Department of Santa Cruz				
Maize	19,177	57,940	43,500	99,300
Wheat	1,755	2,097	38,493	76,860
Rice	10,151	34,220	72,318	83,776
Sugar cane	10,548	37,500	67,458	75,120
Cotton	109	68,222	16,523	52,000
Soya	0	1,100	183,865	513,190
Sunflower	0	150	10,217	89,000
Sorghum	0	0	28,000	45,000
Total	41,740	201,229	460,374	1,034,246
Growth index	100	482	1,103	2,478

Sources: (a) Censo Agropecuario, La Paz (1950); (b) Ministerio de Agricultura, *Diagnóstico de Sector Agropecuario*, La Paz (1974); (c) Instituto Nacional de Estadística, La Paz, several years; (d) The Andean region includes the departments of La Paz, Oruro, Cochabamba, Chuquisaca, Potosí and Tarija.

lay in abolishing servitude or '*pongueaje*' – which had been the bedrock of the colonial *haciendas* – and transferring land to the families of peasant communities, largely to the *colonos* or labour-service tenants (McEwan, 1975). These changes reconfigured the social and spatial organisation of the valleys and highlands giving rise to new collective identities organised into 'agrarian trade unions' (Lagos, 1994).[7] The agrarian reform resulted from a protracted struggle on the part of the indigenous people to recover their communal lands which had been seized and transformed into *latifundios* with the indigenous people converted into serfs. The 1952 revolution was preceded by widespread mobilisation as *haciendas* were occupied, '*patrones*' (landlords) expelled and armed indigenous militias organised (Heath *et al.*, 1969; Dandler, 1984). It was the revolution of 1952 led by the MNR, a newly created poly-class party with a strong nationalist and popular tendency, which finally brought about the desired change in Bolivia (Dunkerley, 1984).

In essence, the agrarian reform was not seen by the party which introduced it as restoring the legitimate rights of the indigenous population and indigenous communities were still not legally recognised (Urioste,

1992). Rather the feudal regime of the *hacienda* was identified as a brake on the capitalist development of agriculture and the development of a free wage labour system. The prevailing ideology was one of jettisoning the traditional economy and moving to a modern one. In line with this conception, an attempt was made to accelerate capitalist development in the countryside and it also explains why the 1953 law legitimated disguised forms of neo-*latifundism,* under the generic heading of 'enterprises'. The land titles distributed to the beneficiaries of the agrarian reform did not constitute firm property rights. The majority of peasants and indigenous communities are simply in possession of the land as proceedings with respect to ownership are incomplete, and thereby insecure, as will be discussed further on (Valderrama, 2002; Oporto, 2003).[8]

The 1953 agrarian reform had opposite effects in the western and eastern regions of the country. While in the west the *latifundia* disappeared, in the east new *latifundia* emerged as a result of giveaways of huge tracts of 'public lands' (Healy, 2004). The consolidation of a new unequal land tenure structure over the last few decades can be seen in Table 2.3. It shows that the medium properties (average size 132 hectares) and the so-called 'enterprise' properties (average size 1,596 hectares) received half of the distributed land which is in the hands of a sixth of the beneficiaries. The medium and 'enterprise' properties or large farms generally belong to non-indigenous owners from different parts of Bolivia who obtained for free large tracts of land as *estancias* (livestock estates) or *haciendas* (mainly crop estates) in the east, thereby creating a new rural elite. Meanwhile the remaining five-sixths of beneficiaries, largely indigenous people, received the other half of the land with a significant presence of Original Community Territory or Community Lands of Origin (*Tierras Comunitarias*

Table 2.3 Land distributed by the agrarian reform according to type of beneficiary and property in Bolivia, 1953–2002

Type of property	Beneficiaries (numbers)	Percentage	Land surface (hectares)	Percentage	Average size (hectares)
Small	279,523	32.48	5,043,204	5.41	18
Medium	125,029	14.53	16,532,904	17.74	132
Enterprise (*Empresa*)	19,486	2.26	31,097,404	33.37	1,596
Peasant plot (*Solar*)	4,026	0.47	23,881	0.03	6
Communal property	342,491	39.80	12,829,088	13.77	37
TCO[1]	77,714	9.03	26,718,826	28.68	344
Without information	12,358	1.44	931,485	1.00	75
Total	860,627	100.00	93,176,792	100.00	108

Source: H. Oporto, '¿De la Reforma Agraria a la guerra por la tierra?', *Opiniones y Análisis*, No. 65, 2003, pp. 131–172. La Paz: FUNDEMOS.

Notes
TCO or *Tierras Comunitarias de Origen* (Community Lands of Origen), i.e. indigenous territories which are largely concentrated in the Amazonian region.

de Origen – TCO).[9] These data underline the unequal distribution of land arising from the 1953 agrarian reform, which is a major anomaly and which the INRA law of 1996 has failed to address, as will be discussed further on (Ballivián and Zeballos, 2003; Vargas, 2003; Arze and Kruse, 2004).

Large agro-industries have been established in the east of Bolivia, mainly because of the economic advantages of the lowlands with their better agro-ecological conditions. This more progressive agricultural sector is the one which is most connected to the national and external markets. The effects of such an agrarian structure not only relate to land ownership but also to the fact that large landowners have greater access to credit. The eastern lands have acquired more value added through their concentration of large public investment and state loans which were largely written off; forms of finance which were not directed to peasants, indigenous groups or small producers (Vargas, 2004). Large and medium property owners in the east have sought to consolidate their land rights, to secure tax reductions and low rates of interest. Their property rights are being questioned in part because of the lack of transparency at the time when they received free grants of public land some years ago. Their priority is now that of safeguarding their properties in the face of fears of expropriation on the part of the state, and the mass migration and settlement of poor peasants from the west to the east.

The neoliberal turn from 1985 onwards

The new economic model of 1985

From 1952 to 1985, Bolivia adopted a model of 'state capitalism' in which the state was the main motor of growth. Accordingly, the most important enterprises in the country were state-owned, especially the mines, foundries, hydrocarbon deposits, electricity, railways and air transport. In addition the state was also involved in less strategic sectors, such as services and commerce (Campero, 1999). An economy organised in this way generates dependency on the part of certain private sectors which provide goods and services. Other private sectors, such as agriculture and mining, secured large credits from state banks which they never repaid. Another feature was the high proportion of state employment, which in terms of salaries accounted for the equivalent of 10 per cent of GDP (Morales and Pacheco, 1999). The state became the main employer. Over time, this institutional arrangement led to a high level of economic inefficiency and to disputes between the political parties for privileged control of the state apparatus.

Nevertheless there was a high rate of economic growth between 1960 and 1970. This was largely due to the high price of raw materials on the international market (tin and oil) and to credits being more easily obtained from private international banks, a fact which led to the indebt-edness of Bolivia. However, at the beginning of the 1980s this same dependency would lead to the one of the worst crises. The combination of a strangling external debt, military-assisted coups d'état, and the staunch opposition to the leftist government of the UDP (Unidad Democrática Popular) (1982–1985) which blocked attempts to remedy the delicate eco-nomic situation, unleashed a rampant hyperinflation (Thorp, 1998). The situation became unsustainable and a new government led by the MNR (1985–1989) introduced shock measures. In August 1985, the new govern-ment issued the Supreme Decree 21060 which marked a point of radical change for the Bolivian economy. After the stabilisation measures came the liberalisation of commodity, financial and labour markets (Stallings and Peres, 2000). The return to liberalism was sealed with the transfer of state enterprises to the private sector and by reducing the role of the state to a minimum. In practice, the public agricultural sector was dismantled and has still not recovered.

Impact of the new model on the agrarian sector

Macro-economic data from 1985 onwards show that the contribution of the agricultural sector to GDP has remained at around 14 per cent, which is similar to the situation prior to the new economic policy. With the liber-alisation of markets, the economic situation of smallholders in the west worsened while new incentives were created for agro-industry in the east. Peasants had to compete with cheap imports and stagnating yields pre-vented them from participating in the export economy (Arze and Kruse, 2004). According to a World Bank report (2002: 30), 'the rural economy is increasingly polarised between the small peasant sector producing food-stuffs, on the one hand, and the agro-enterprise sector producing cash crops for export, on the other'. In the Andean region, especially in the highlands, 80 per cent of the peasant sector is trapped in a vicious circle: intensive agriculture, degradation of the land and increasingly meagre economic returns (ibid.). However, 20 per cent of peasants seem to have been able to break out of this negative cycle, improving productivity and income, even in the highlands, as their farms had either better quality land, access to irrigation, were located in areas with fewer climatic risks, and/or benefited from closer proximity to urban centres.

In the east or lowlands, large properties have continued to grow and expand. The large estate owners and others seeking land have continued to monopolise land by means of their influence over the state apparatus and fraudulent titles, at least until 1996 when a new land law was passed. Land was not therefore distributed according to need or to considerations of economic and social efficiency but according to the interests of small powerful groups with the inevitable exclusion of other agricultural actors. Neither the producers from the Andean region nor the indigenous groups of the lowlands participated in the endowment or adjudication of the main lands in the east, the latter possibly because their territories were not threatened at this time. The permanent swallowing up of indigenous land in the lowlands, especially by timber companies, led to their organisation into what is known today as the Confederation of Indigenous Peoples of Bolivia (*Confederación de Pueblos Indígenas de Bolivia* – CIDOB).[10] This means that in the east there are three clear actors engaged in a conflict over land: large property owners, indigenous people of the lowlands and the '*collas*' colonisers, i.e. those coming from the western part of the country.

From 1985 onwards, the deepening crisis in Andean agriculture and the accumulation of land in the east for speculative and commercial purposes increased social discontent over the level of inequality and state toleration of land trafficking. In short, regional tensions between west and east intensified along with demands to resolve the conflict over land. At the beginning of the 1990s, the 1953 agrarian reform was unable to provide a lasting solution to the problems of land distribution and titling. The early abandonment of the agrarian reform as a public policy, its focus on solving problems of access to land in the west, and the limited inclusion of Andean farmers to lands in the eastern plains, served to aggravate the Bolivian agrarian conflict to the extent that it was necessary to hurriedly draw up a second agrarian reform and to close down the CNRA and INC because of the arbitrary way in which they had distributed land (Urioste, 2003). However, the INRA law of 1996 never enjoyed the formal status of being a 'second agrarian reform' as will be analysed next.

The second agrarian reform of 1996

The Road to the INRA Law of 1996

After the 1953 agrarian reform devolved land to the communities in the Andean region, agriculture in the highlands and valleys experienced a slight recovery. However the subsequent population growth and subdivision of properties into very small pieces of land led to the emergence of *minifundios* which were economically and technically unsustainable. Furthermore, these subdivisions were rarely publicly registered so that property rights were unclear in the eyes of the state, although not to the peasants concerned. In the eastern region, Chaco and Amazonia, government employees condoned many illegal transfers of land by political supporters of the government (mainly that of the military government of Hugo Banzer 1971–1978); later, the CNRA ended up legalising many of these property transfers. In 1992 massive corruption in the distribution and titling of lands came to light and led the government of Jaime Paz (1989–1993) to close down the CNRA and to set up a commission to put an end to the chaos in land administration. Subsequently the government of Gonzalo Sánchez de Lozada (1993–1997) signed an agreement with the World Bank to draw up a new land law. This so-called INRA Law of 1996 was supposedly part of wider set of laws which were passed in Latin America at that time with the aim of encouraging a market in land, as a new paradigm of access to and distribution of land (Urioste, 2002; see, e.g. Deere and Medeiros, this volume).

Following the intervention of CNRA and the INC, a new land law was drawn up between 1992 and 1996. Initially the main actors involved in the process were peasants, colonisers, indigenous groups and agricultural producers, each one of whom brought their own perspective to the dialogue. In the final stages, the peasants and indigenous groups from the west broke off the dialogue with the government, questioning the passage of the law by Congress. However, the indigenous groups in the east maintained contact and showed a keen interest in its application, thereby succeeding in getting more of their demands included in the new law. While the 1953 agrarian reform law focused on the Andean west, the new law has tended to reflect more the situation of the plains in the east.

The INRA law retains the preferential rights of peasants and indigenous groups to ownership of the land and creates the concept of Community Lands of Origin (TCO) for handing over titles to vast indigenous territories in favour of the original inhabitants (Almaraz, 2002). As from the passage of this new law in 1996, a process was set in motion of revising the legality of each of the property titles handed out by the agrarian reform since 1953. This issue has been generating a great deal of conflict in the last few years with no end in sight. This process of regularisation of land titles ('*saneamiento*') aims to correct the technical and juridical distortions of land ownership in order to continue redistributing land to the peasant and indigenous population who possess either none or an insufficient amount. However, as will be seen in the tables below, this process has been advancing very slowly and is contested by some powerful groups in the east who own large tracts of land which are left unexploited. Many of these properties form part of the black market in land to secure cheap mortgages from banks or for speculative purposes.

The process of regularisation of land titles

The process of regularisation of agricultural property lies at the heart of the new agrarian process begun in 1996. The guiding principle for the regularisation of land titles ('*saneamiento*') is to establish the fulfilment of the Social and Economic Function (*Función Económica y Social* – FES) and the legality of the adjudication or acquisition of property titles within a time span of ten years from 1996 (Superintendencia Agraria, 2001a). If it can be established that the large farm 'enterprise' does not fulfil these requisites then the property would revert back to the state and the land would become available for redistribution to those in need of it. Nine years of applying the

INRA law and, despite important financial support from international bodies, progress has been poor and has been confined to the eastern lowlands and southern valley regions. There have been major demands for TCO titles. This is motivated not only by the desire to secure ownership rights but also to reconstitute the *ayllus*, the ancient indigenous form of organisation, as a platform for presenting claims of an ethnic character. In general a process of regularisation is not envisaged in the Andean region.

The total land surface of Bolivia is almost 110 million hectares as can be seen in Table 2.4. When areas of water, salt flats and urban conglomeration are discounted, this leaves an area of 107 million hectares which are subject to regularisation. In almost nine years, until December 2004, only 14.1 million hectares had been regularised or only 13 per cent of the total land available for regularisation (category D in Table 2.4). At this rate it will take almost 60 years for the process to be concluded. Those property owners who have completed the whole process of land titling have only 23 per cent of the land that has been regularised (category E in Table 2.4) while 28 per cent of the regularised land is state land, most of which concerns forestry (category L in Table 2.4). The remaining 49 per cent of reg-

Table 2.4 Land property regularisation process in Bolivia, 1996–2004

Categories		Land (hectares)	Percentage	
Total land surface	A	109,858,100	–	
Urban areas	B	713,398	–	
Water areas and salt flats	C	1,880,607	–	
Available for regularisation	A−B−C	107,264,095	100.00	
Regularised surface	D=E+F+L	14,078,866	13.12	100
With RFS*	E	3,262,140		23
State lands	L	3,894,892		28
With titles or certificates	F	6,921,844		49
Surface in process of regularisation	G=H+I+K	37,183,670	34.67	100
SAN-TCO**	H	16,218,452		44
CAT-SAN**	I	6,787,183		18
SAN-SIM**	K	14,178,035		38
Surface to be regularised	M=A−B−C−D−G	56,001,558	52.21	100
Protected areas	N	13,486,396		24
Reserves and forestry concessions	O	5,581,062		10
Farm surface	P=M−N−O	36,934,100		66

Source: Instituto Nacional de Reforma Agraria (INRA), *Estado del Proceso de Saneamiento*, La Paz: INRA, 2004.

Notes
* RFS stands for *Resoluciones Finales de Saneamiento* (Final Resolutions of Regularisations) which means that the final property right has been granted and thus the regularisation process has been completed.
** SAN-TCO, CAT-SAN and SAN-SIM are different modalities of land regularisation. SAN-TCO stands for *Saneamiento de Tierras Comunitarias de Origen* (Regularisation of Community Lands of Origen), CAT-SAN means *Saneamiento Integrado al Catastro Legal* (Regularisation Integrated to the Legal Registry), and SAN-SIM is *Saneamiento Simple* (Simple Regularisation).

ularised land has resulted in land titles or certificates to individuals or communities (TCO) which still have to obtain the final resolution of regularisation (category F in Table 2.4).

Another 37.2 million hectares are currently undergoing regularisation which represents 35 per cent of the land subject to regularisation (category G in Table 2.4). This leaves 56 million hectares or 52 per cent still to be regularised (category M in Table 2.4), of which 66 per cent is farmland (category P in Table 2.4). These data reveal the delays and the operational difficulties which INRA has experienced in applying the law and explains why land ownership and the lack of legal security has become a very conflictive issue.

As can be seen in Table 2.5, it is clear that the process of regularisation has prioritised small property owners as these beneficiaries received 89 per cent of all titles and certificates but covering a land area of only 5 per cent. However, it is the TCOs which are the real winners as they account for 70 per cent of the land area that has been regularised. Fifty-five titles or certificates were given under the Community Lands of Origin arrangement and the average size is close to 78,000 hectares but each TCO comprises several hundred families and much of the land is of poor quality. Nevertheless, this represents a very significant if still incomplete progress.

Another aim of the INRA law is to recover land which has been wrongfully acquired by *latifundistas*. However, up to now the process of regularisation has not really touched on this question. As such a limited amount of land has been recovered by the state, there is very little new land available to redistribute for agricultural purposes. According to the World Bank (Banco Mundial, 2004), tax reductions on the ownership of rural enterprises, which were introduced by President Banzer in 1998, have acted as a disincentive to the redistribution and rational use of the land.[11]

Table 2.5 Titled and certified land by type of property in Bolivia, 1996–2004

Type of property	Titles and certificates		Beneficiaries		Land surface		Average size (hectares)
	No.	%	No.	%	Thousands of hectares	%	
Enterprise property	95	0.82	145	0.64	196	3.05	1,352
Medium property	222	1.91	319	1.40	361	5.61	1,132
Small property	10,284	88.59	14,069	61.64	318	4.94	23
Communal property	523	4.51	7,507	32.89	1,031	16.01	137
Peasant plot	430	3.70	728	3.19	10	0.15	14
Community Lands of Origin (TCO)	55	0.47	58	0.25	4,523	70.25	77,983
Total	11,609	100.00	22,826	100.00	6,439	100.00	–

Source: Instituto Nacional de Reforma Agraria, *Estado del Proceso de Saneamiento 2004*, La Paz: INRA, 2005.

The lack of results is giving rise to numerous conflicts. From the start of the process in 1996, the political will to prioritise the issue has been lacking and the administrative capacity of the institutions responsible for carrying it out is questionable. However, the promptness with which titles were handed out to families and peasant communities during the Carlos Mesa presidency (October 2003 to June 2005) stands out as over half of the total land titles granted since 1996 have been issued by his government (*Gaceta Agraria*, La Paz: INRA, 2005).

Evaluation of the second agrarian reform of 1996

Despite the initially rather favourable conditions for putting the INRA law into practice, an evaluation carried out by the Agricultural Superintendency (SIA) after five years found the results to have been disappointing and poor (Superintendencia Agraria, 2001b). The situation has changed little since then. First, the land titling process or '*saneamiento*' has experienced significant delays in application so that those state lands which could be massively redistributed have not yet been identified. Second, land in private hands which does not meet the constitutional requirement of serving a Social and Economic Function has not been identified either. Again this means that this land is not available for redistribution, as the law specifies. Finally, the slowness of the whole process has not enabled existing land rights to be confirmed, an indispensable condition for ensuring the legal security of producers in the rural areas of Bolivia.

According to the evaluation the main reasons for this situation were: first, the government authorities lacked political will so that land issues were not prioritised; and second, the existence of severe management shortcomings in the responsible government bodies, particularly the INRA (Superintendencia Agraria, 2001b). Furthermore, the Agricultural Superintendency made the following three recommendations. First, to accelerate the process of regularisation by identifying those state lands available for distribution and by returning those lands which do not fulfil a Social and Economic Function to the state for redistribution. Second, to guarantee legal security of those owners and legal possessors of land who adhere to the law of the land, as an indispensable condition for guaranteeing the investments made in the sector and revitalising commercial and export production. Third, to guarantee respect for and application of the law, so as to prevent legal violations and the consolidation of rights by means of pressure and the illegal use of force, whatever its origin, irrespective of any political considerations (ibid.). As a way of expediting the regularisation of small properties, it recommends drawing on the positive experience of internal regularisation within indigenous communities (CSUTCOPYCC, 2002).[12]

As can be seen, the problems with the slow progress of the 'second agrarian reform' were already identified several years ago (Hernáiz and

Pacheco, 2001; Almaraz, 2003). We fully agree with these assessments as well as with the recommendations mentioned above. We wholeheartedly endorse the implementation of these sensible recommendations while being aware that political circumstances may cause further delays or even prevent their execution.

The INRA law of 1996: directed by the state or by the market?

Many Latin American countries reoriented their agrarian policies in the 1990s. The new policies and associated legislative reforms share a clear affinity with the neoliberal paradigm which has been gaining ground in the region since the 1980s. They aim to establish greater security of land tenure and to promote a market in land, with the aim of increasing productivity and creating a more viable agricultural sector. In line with this they favour individual property ownership and the reduction of the role of the state in land distribution in favour of the market (van der Haar and Zoomers, 2003; Assies 2006; see also Deere and Medeiros on Brazil, this volume).

These changes are seen by some observers as representing a necessary revision of agrarian policies which were counter-productive and obsolete, speaking of a 'reform of the reform'. At the same time, they are criticised by others as 'counter-reforms' which will undo the gains of the existing agrarian reforms (Kay, 2002). Certainly, the neoliberal orientation implies a clear break with previous agrarian reforms, based on an active role by the state and the redistribution of land tenure in favour of those in most need, protecting peasant or 'social' property. Such a break is particularly seen in three areas. First, the forced expropriation of land and its free redistribution according to social criteria to landless peasants is reduced or abandoned altogether. Second, the collectivist orientation of the previous agrarian reforms is abandoned. Finally, restrictions which were placed on 'social property' regarding their subdivision or privatisation have been lifted (Zoomers and van der Haar, 2000).

However, this characterisation does not apply to the Bolivian case. On the contrary, the refusal of powerful groups and those who accumulate land to adhere to the process of regularisation in Bolivia goes to show that the new land law of 1996 (INRA) does indeed privilege the interests of peasants and indigenous people. The difficulties experienced in applying the process arise from the strong political and economic power exercised by non-indigenous Bolivians and foreigners who have been accumulating land in the eastern plains for many years. Despite all the problems discussed above, the process of regularisation since 1996 has mainly favoured the indigenous people of the lowlands and to a lesser extent the peasant communities of the valleys.

Policies to combat rural poverty

At the start of the 1990s, after the worst hyperinflation in the country's history, the free market model gained ground as the main instrument in the allocation of economic resources. The country was undergoing a wave of structural transformations directed towards macro-economic stabilisation, privatisation and decentralisation. At the same time, poverty, inequality and exclusion became more visible so that civil society demanded more participation and that greater attention be given to social and economic problems. Faced with this situation, the state had not only to find the financial resources for its social programmes but to create institutions and mechanisms of participation.

Popular Participation

The Law of Popular Participation of 1994 and the Law of Decentralisation of 1995 mark the start of one of the most influential changes towards redefining the role of the state in rural areas. The Law of Popular Participation enabled the transfer of resources (20 per cent of income from the internal fiscal revenue) and powers to the 314 municipalities so that they themselves, using participatory channels, define policies and local development priorities through Municipal Development Plans (*Planes de Desarrollo Municipal* or PDMs) and Annual Operational Plans (*Planes Operativos Anuales* or POAs). This idea had been taking root for more than 13 years. On the one hand, strong civic departmental committees had been demanding decentralisation to allow regional power groups to control public financial resources, which until then were administered centrally; on the other hand, peasant movements and indigenous peoples pressed for local political-administrative autonomy. The municipalisation of the country was conceived from the start as the main plank in a process of departmental administrative decentralisation, assigning important duties to each department and its respective bodies. To put this into action, participatory planning mechanisms were introduced in each municipality, leading to thousands of projects with citizen participation (Urioste, 2002).

Popular Participation has partly corrected an enormous historical imbalance by setting the budget according to the number of inhabitants in the municipality. At the same time it has devolved significant political power to the peasant and indigenous communities, although with certain restrictions; the candidacy for mayor being until the municipal elections of 2004 limited to the political parties. The recent 2004 Law of Citizen Groups and Indigenous Peoples (*Ley de Agrupaciones Ciudadanas y Pueblos Indígenas*) extends political participation to other organisations which are closer to the citizenry and to the peasant communities and indigenous peoples. The idea is to create a more legitimate form of local government.

In balance, the merits of Popular Participation outweigh the weaknesses, especially the scarce attention paid to productive projects. The lack of articulation between municipal and national policies is another weak spot whose rectification goes beyond redesigning the local and involves harmonising national policies among themselves and adopting a long-term focus (Ameller, 2002; Ayo, 2004). Nevertheless, Popular Participation has undoubtedly been a factor in the empowerment of indigenous people as can be witnessed by their increasing representation and involvement in local, regional and national affairs (Albó, 2002a; Albó, 2002b; Urioste, 2004).[13]

National dialogue and the Bolivian Strategy of Poverty Reduction (EBRP)

After the first steps towards Popular Participation, civil society, the state and even some international aid agencies were convinced of the need to develop public policies to combat poverty with widespread public participation. In 1997 the First National Dialogue took place, an event which brought together the most important organised groups of civil society. There was the government, worker federations, the Catholic Church, peasant organisations and representatives from different political parties. Undoubtedly this experience was valued for its inclusionary character, but it did not lead to effective social agreements. There was no real national debate, nor did the documents produced reflect the diversity of viewpoints aired.

The Second National Dialogue in the year 2000 involved consultations at municipal, departmental and national level so that the different actors could each contribute their perspective in drawing up a strategy to combat poverty. This event was also seen as a way of gaining access to the World Bank's HIPC funds which were given as grants on condition that they were used to reduce poverty. At that time it was hoped to institutionalise this form of dialogue as a permanent way of bolstering participation in policy making, a goal which has not been fully realised nor received sufficient backing.

At the end of 2001 the process of consulting the citizens found expression in a new law, the Law of National Dialogue. The aim was to strengthen channels of popular participation and decentralisation and, most importantly, to allocate the resources provided by the HIPC in line with the criteria of efficiency, equity, participation and transparency. An important condition was that resources were to be assigned on a progressive basis to benefit the poorest municipalities, according to the principle of giving more to those who needed it most. Such measures had to be in line with the Bolivian Strategy of Poverty Reduction (UDAPE, 2003).

The Bolivian Strategy of Poverty Reduction (*Estrategia Boliviana de Reducción de Pobreza* or EBRP) starts from the premise that poverty, inequity and social exclusion are the most important problems affecting the country. The strategy attempts to synthesise contributions arising from the dialogue and to translate them into public policies to combat poverty (Komives *et al.*, 2004). However, social conflicts which have been exacerbated since 2000 have led to a questioning of this approach. It is perceived by radical leaders as forming part of state policy, but more particularly as being imposed by international organisations, such as the World Bank and the International Monetary Fund, and as being far removed from the everyday reality of poor rural dwellers (Molenaers and Renard, 2003).

An official evaluation of the strategy in 2003, carried out by Carlos Mesa's government, acknowledges that it has not succeeded in reducing poverty (UDAPE, 2003). Three substantial changes were proposed: first, to recognise the limitations of a pattern of development restricted to achieving economic growth and based on the trickle-down assumption as this does not guarantee a reduction of poverty; second, to regard social and productive actors as protagonists of their own development and not as passive subjects on the receiving end of social and economic policies; and third, to abandon the paternalism implicit in existing policies and to forge strategic and durable alliances between social and productive actors and the state (Komives *et al.*, 2005). In December 2004 the government changed the name of the Bolivian Strategy of Poverty Reduction to that of Bolivian Strategy of Development, with all that this implies (Ministerio de Desarrollo Económico, 2005). But by June 2005 the Mesa government resigned after a series of protest movements. The head of the Supreme Court became the interim president with the mandate to call for new elections in December 2005. The political instability has put on hold several development programmes and at the time of writing it is unclear when and whether the country's political crisis will be resolved.

National Strategy of Agricultural and Rural Development (ENDAR)

The National Strategy of Agricultural and Rural Development (*Estrategia Nacional de Desarrollo Agropecuario y Rural* – ENDAR) is an attempt by the last two governments to intervene in the rural environment with a different logic, one which not only provides policy guidelines but also attempts to find ways of resolving the high level of conflict existing in the country as a whole. In some way it responds to the demands of peasant and indigenous organisations to prioritise the productive development of agriculture. The Mesa government sees this strategy as complementing the EBRP by adding productive and agricultural concerns.

The strategy aims to increase the incomes of agricultural producers within a framework of social, economic, cultural and gender equity, giving them the means and knowledge required to compete in a sustainable way in the national and international markets for goods and services. The strategic objective is to insert the agricultural enterprise sector, and to a lesser extent the traditional sector, into the market, especially the external market. In addition the strategy also takes into account that rural development must be seen in relation to the urban sector, given that over half of peasant incomes stem from non-agricultural activities (Ministerio de Desarrollo Sostenible y Planificación, 2004). The government has constantly modified this plan over the past years without as yet being able to reach an agreement with agricultural producers. Criticisms have come from several directions, for its emphasis on external markets, and for its exclusion of small agricultural producers in the highlands and valleys, who are still involved in a subsistence economy.

Within the peasantry it is the small producers linked to agricultural exports who form the main reference point for the ENDAR plan. This is seen in such proposals as the development of productive networks, associations of producers, and the expansion of export markets. However, the strategy is mainly directed towards those profitable producers in areas where there is proven productive potential. There have been attempts to correct this weakness in later versions of the policy but without much success (Ministerio de Asuntos Campesinos y Agropecuarios, 2004). This is because the structural guidelines maintain the classical focus on agricultural commodity chains in which those who benefit are those who already have control of certain sectors of the system, largely the capitalist farmers, agro-industries and transnational corporations (Urioste, 2003). Furthermore, the topic of land and territory, the conflict over property rights and land regularisation and redistribution are all addressed very marginally by ENDAR, thereby exposing one of its major limitations as well as the lack of coordination between public policies (Kay, 2005b).

Policies of the Ministry of Indigenous Affairs and Indigenous Peoples (MAIPO)

Another relevant public institutional actor is the Ministry of Indigenous Affairs and Indigenous Peoples (*Ministerio de Asuntos Indígenas y Pueblos Originarios* – MAIPO), which indigenous leaders consider as theirs, a body which belongs to them by right. Such a ministry had formed a central demand of their social struggles. Its work is specifically directed towards drawing up intercultural productive policies, within a framework of decentralisation, and to strengthening the rights of indigenous peoples, especially in relation to natural resources as set out in the International ILO Convention 169 of 1989, which Bolivia ratified in 1991.

This ministry works closely with indigenous and peasant organisations across the country. It helps to identify the special needs of the indigenous peoples so as to enable them to secure collective property rights over indigenous territories. It adopts a more cultural, organisational and rights-based approach in terms of reconstructing indigenous territorial identities and is working towards achieving a better indigenous representation in the future Constituent Assembly originally planned for 2005 but postponed to

2006 due to the political crisis. The ministry is grossly underfunded and almost its entire budget comes from international development cooperation funds.

Migration policies and access to land

In the 1960s the Bolivian state promoted the mass migration of indigenous peasant colonisers from the highland and valleys to the eastern lowlands (Royden and Wennergren, 1977; Ormachea and Fernández, 1989). The 'march to the east' was a state policy explicitly designed to transfer the rural surplus population of the highlands and valleys to the plains in order to develop agro-industry and expand the agricultural frontier following the programme of the INC at first but later happening spontaneously (Soria, 1996; Ministerio de Desarrollo Sostenible y Planificación, 2002). These pioneers opened the way for a large number of human settlements. It is estimated today that more than 60,000 emigrant families have settled in the eastern lands of Bolivia (Roca, 2001). However, the migration of peasants from the Andean region is still continuing in a spontaneous, chaotic and disorderly way.

The main trends of the internal migratory flows show the population transfer from the highlands to the plains, although the most important work destination is no longer the rural area of the department but the city of Santa Cruz (Anonymous, 2005). This may be explained by the saturation of rural settlements and by the lack of land for new colonisers. International migration has also increased in the last couple of decades, mainly to Argentina and other neighbouring countries. But the economic crisis of Argentina at the beginning of this decade led to a falling off of remittances from Bolivian emigrants to their families in rural communities. In addition emigrants are returning to Bolivia increasing the pressure on employment and access to land (Hinojosa, Pérez and Cortez, 2002; Hinojosa, 2004). The country requires a policy of human settlements, which takes account of the economic, social and cultural characteristics of its population, as well as its physical conditions and eco-systems, so that the relationships established do not exacerbate the poverty of migrants (Instituto PRISMA, 2004).

Conclusions: the unfinished agrarian reform and rural poverty

It has been shown that poverty in Bolivia is mainly rural. Being indigenous, a peasant and a woman increase the risk of being trapped in extreme poverty. Extreme poverty is largely concentrated in the western Andean region, although there is also widespread rural poverty in the eastern plains. While the agrarian reform of 1953 was a turning point in the country's history, it has been unable to overcome rural poverty. Nevertheless, living conditions in the countryside have improved in terms of access to education, health and housing, especially since the 1994 legislation on municipal decentralisation and popular participation. However, family income from agriculture has decreased in both relative and absolute terms. This is more evident in the highlands than in the lowlands.

Half a century after the introduction of the agrarian reform, the rural indigenous peasant population has doubled, despite migration to the eastern lowlands. Demographic pressures have led to over-exploitation and soil erosion in Andean communities. The agrarian reform had a totally different character in the eastern lowlands than in the western Andean region. In the plains, land was freely granted in a disorderly, unplanned and corrupt way to those non-indigenous citizens who demanded it. Many never worked it while retaining ownership over it. The majority who worked the land succeeded in transforming lowland agriculture into the motor of regional growth.

With the 1953 agrarian reform underway, the Bolivian state had neither the capacity nor the will to invest in transforming productive conditions in rural areas. There has been little progress in building access roads to the communities or in providing irrigation systems; and electricity is only recently reaching rural communities. The neglect of the Bolivian rural area, especially in the Andean region, combined with the opening up of the market to food imports as required by structural adjustment programmes since 1985, led to a notable decrease in the ability of indigenous-peasants to supply foodstuffs to urban areas due to their lack of competitiveness. By contrast, in the plains the expansion of industrial crops, principally cotton in the 1970s and soya in the 1990s, and their insertion in international markets in accordance with regional integration agreements, enabled competitive pricing and led to the sustained and rapid expansion of the agricultural frontier over the past 30 years. The continued expansion of soya in a region without clear property rights is the main source of conflict over land, more so than the peasant migration from the west.

Bolivia is characterised by a dual model of land tenure with a corresponding dual system of production. These two models – *minifundio* and subsistence agriculture in the west and capitalist enterprises linked to the *latifundio* in the east – do not interact or complement each other. However, it is the migration of labour from the highlands and valleys to the eastern lowlands which provided the necessary labour to clear the land for productive purposes. Capitalist agriculture in the east is not only the result of private initiative but also of public development policies over three decades. For the majority of property owners who benefited from free grants of land at the start of the agricultural expansion in the east, land has had almost no cost.

This situation started to change in 1996 with the promulgation of the new Land Law (INRA). The rapid expansion of industrial crops in the eastern lowlands led to a speculation in land values and the awakening of indigenous peoples with a long 'march for land and dignity' (which was the main slogan) in 1990. This mobilisation raised the question of the indigenous territories and their legal recognition as TCOs six years later in the 1996 INRA law. The titling of the TCO is a central part of the land regularisation begun ten years ago. The process is complex, slow and full of obstacles but it is a step in the right direction.

The conflict over land in the eastern lowlands has a marked ethnic character. Indigenous landless peasants from the Andean region – quechuas and aymaras – continue to migrate and settle on unexploited land in the east whose non-indigenous owners claim rights over it even though they do not work the land. These non-indigenous owners resist the land seizures of the Bolivian Landless Movement (MST – *Movimiento sin Tierra de Bolivia*) and demand respect for private property. The land conflict has sharpened the regional confrontation between east and west (*cambas* against *collas*). The medium and large landowners complain that the INRA law is generating two classes of citizens: one, the indigenous people with preferential and privileged rights, who do not have to work the land to retain their property, nor do they pay tax on land; and two, the agricultural entrepreneurs (as they refer to themselves), with property titles, who pay taxes, generate employment and create wealth but suffer legal insecurity and violation of their property rights (Barragán, 2004). In turn, the indigenous peasants of the highlands complain that the INRA law has taken for granted the free distribution of land benefiting their sector, especially of *colla* colonisers in the lowlands, and that these lands end up being put on the market. The land then does not belong to those who work it but to those who have the money to buy it, violating one of the principles of the 1953 agrarian reform.

In recent years a climate of violence and confrontation around the issue of access to land has resulted in the death of several indigenous peasants. There are no mechanisms of conflict resolution. Land policies are not linked to rural development policies such as the ENDAR and more tangentially the EBRP. In general no link is made between sectoral public policies relating to energy, roads, health, education and those relating to agriculture, land titling, the environment, the creation of markets and food security. Despite the multisector discourse, public policies continue to be compartmentalised. ENDAR has prioritised the commodity chains approach to the detriment of a spatial approach to territorial development, which has been shown to be more effective and to meet more fully the demands of the local rural population.

In general small rural producers continue to be regarded as non-viable within the framework of an open international economy. Most plans and government proposals, as well as international development agencies, see them as passive recipients of aid and compensatory policies. Secure access to productive land which is capable of generating a surplus and the introduction of rural territorial development are goals which are yet to be achieved in Bolivia. This implies that the agrarian reform is not yet concluded but remains a priority for both society and the state.

In conclusion, the 1996 INRA law has not served as a second agrarian reform and does not form an integral part of the rural development programmes. Regularisation, in terms of the reversion of land back to the state in cases of irregularities or noncompliance with the economic and social function by large landowners, is seen as a problem and not a solution. The increasing problem of landlessness and the continuing high levels of rural poverty make it imperative to fully implement the provisions contained in the INRA law, thereby transforming it into a genuine second agrarian reform. We estimate that about 100,000 landless families would need to be settled in the eastern lowlands to relieve some of the most pressing demands for land. This would require roughly five million hectares, some of which might be found from still available public lands but most of which will have to come by recovering land from those landlords who do not comply with the INRA law. While such land redistribution would not eliminate rural poverty, it would certainly begin to tackle the escalating problem of landlessness, reduce extreme poverty and enhance food security. A drastic reduction of rural poverty would require a new development strategy, which is able to substantially raise rural investment particularly in the peasant sector, as well as a series of other productivity, employment and equity-enhancing measures. To bring about such a transformation requires major political changes and the achievement of a wide national consensus for the implementation of such a radical programme.

Postscript

The text above was written before Evo Morales became president in January 2006. It is of interest to observe that our recommendation for the implementation of a genuine 'second agrarian reform' has become government policy. However, it remains to be seen to what extent his government will be able to execute it but at least it will not be for lack of political will. Evo Morales won the presidential elections in December 2005 with an absolute majority of 53.7 per cent of the votes, which is the highest percentage ever achieved by a candidate since the revolution of 1952. His election to power is a momentous event in the country's history as for the first time an indigenous person has gained the presidency. He first gained notoriety as leader of the coca growers' union and later became the founder and leader of the Movement toward Socialism (*Movimiento al Socialismo* or MAS). With his victory the prospects for implementing some of the policy recommendations made in this text have become more hopeful.

During the election campaign the MAS proposed a '*Pacto por la Tierra*' ('Pact for Land') which has the following four key propositions. First, it guarantees the legal rights of those properties which fulfil productive activities in a proven and sustainable manner. Second, it guarantees social justice in the access to land. It will sentence land speculators, hoarders and traffickers by reverting the land to the state by applying the Constitution and agrarian legislation. Third, it seeks to strengthen the national agrarian institutions so that they can pursue more effectively the social demands of the people. Finally, it proposes to articulate the land redistribution policies with the promotion and diversification of production policies. The MAS also intends to use the available legislation, mainly the Ley INRA, to check the legality of the land transfers, to speed up the process of land titling regularisation, giving priority to areas of conflict and to give land titles to indigenous and peasant communities. It also envisages the creation of an agrarian ombudsman for the avoidance and peaceful resolution of land conflicts. Furthermore, the MAS intends to reform the land tax system as well as to regulate the transfer, mortgage and sale of land and also to implement a national programme of human settlement.

Previously the MAS had a critical, although ambiguous position, regarding the Ley INRA which it considered of neoliberal inspiration. However, it now recognises the potential of this legislation for land redistribution. As mentioned, it is in the eastern region of the country, particularly in the department of Santa Cruz, where today's *latifundio* is concentrated. However, any attempt at land reform will encounter militant opposition from the landlords. At the same time as the presidential elections, there have also been for the first time elections of the nine *prefectos*, the departmental governors, who were previously appointed by the president. The elected governor of Santa Cruz belongs to the opposition and represents the interests of the dominant class in the region. Furthermore, Santa Cruz is leading a group of provinces which are seeking greater autonomy from the central state. This is a matter which is going to be discussed later in 2006 with the election of a Constituent Assembly (*Asamblea Constituyente*) whose task it will be to rewrite the country's Constitution. But it is likely that the departments will achieve greater autonomy and this will make it more difficult for the government to redistribute land.

Since assuming the presidency in early 2006, the government of Evo Morales has declared that it will speed up the process of regularisation of property titles as well as extend its term for another five years when it expires in October 2006. More fundamentally, in May 2006 the government announced that it will present to Congress new legislation which will reform certain aspects of the Ley INRA so as to facilitate the implementation of the second agrarian reform. While the government has a majority in the Chamber of Deputies it lacks such a majority in the Senate and thus will have to enter into negotiations with other political parties for the approval of the reforms. It is to be hoped that the government succeeds in completing the agrarian reform process which started over half a century ago. This is a necessary step for tackling the even more difficult task of

eliminating rural poverty which will require a series of supportive measures for regenerating the peasant economy and improving the living conditions of peasants and rural workers.

Notes

1 Essay written for the United Nations Development Programme (UNDP) global
research project on 'Land Policies, Poverty Reduction and Public Action:
Experiences from Africa, Asia and Latin America' and presented in the
ISS–UNDP Workshop held at the Institute of Social Studies (ISS), 18 and 19
February 2005. We are grateful for the assistance provided by Floriana Soria
and Gonzalo Colque of the Fundación TIERRA as well as by Saturnino Borras
Jr. of the ISS. We much appreciate Carmen Diana Deere's and Haroon Akram-
Lodhi's most helpful comments on the draft version of this chapter.

2 *Ayllus*, or self-governing Indian communities, are pre-Colombian forms of
social, political and economic organisation, operating within a specific territory, and usually including several hamlets (*caseríos*) in continuous geographic
units.

3 The Chaco War (1932–1935) between Bolivia and Paraguay resulted in the loss
of a large part of Bolivia's vast Chaco territory to Paraguay and tens of thousands of people died.

4 *Mestizos* are people of mixed race, generally of mixed Spanish and Indian
descent.

5 The Law of Popular Participation came into force in 1994 and provides a
framework for consultation of civil society at local, regional and national level.

6 A *Departamento*, which we translated as department, is a political administrative
unit which in many countries is called a province.

7 The peasant communities within the expropriated estate adopted this termi-
nology of the 'agrarian trade union' (*sindicato agrarios*) for their organisation
following the experience of the militant trade unions of mine workers as well
as due to the influence of political parties.

8 Peasant communities assumed forms of territorial control which did not
necessarily coincide with the political division of the state. Living in a community is precisely what enables the group to survive in this rugged and fragile
environment. Up until the beginning of the 1990s, their form of organisation
was largely that of a trade union (*sindicato agrario*). After this time, some groups
decided to resurrect pre-agrarian reform forms of organisation. These differences are reflected in the division of the national peasant organisations: one of
a trade-union type (*Confederación Sindical Unica de Trabajadores Campesinos de
Bolivia* – CSUTCB) and the other of a more traditional type in terms of its
indigenous identity, the National Council of Markas and Ayllus of the Qulla-
suyo (*Consejo Nacional de Markas y Ayllus del Qullasuyu*).

9 The titling process of TCOs, which is one of the positive outcomes of the 1996
INRA law, seeks the restitution of land to the communities and their legal
recognition by the state. The regularisation process of those communities
which had shifted to individual household farming are creating communal
property rights regarding their external boundaries but family property rights
internally.

10 This organisation was originally called *Confederación de Indígenas del Oriente de
Bolivia*, hence CIDOB. When it changed to its current name it decided to keep
its acronym.

11 The 1996 INRA law introduced a tax on the market value of land (including
improvements made on the farm like irrigation, fencing and buildings) for

medium and large properties. But landlords managed to change and drastically reduce this tax to the extent that today few, if any, pay any significant land tax.

12 However, the land titling process in indigenous communities is not without problems. Many indigenous families in the rural communities are pressing for mixed property rights to both communal property and private family property within a communal territorial jurisdiction. This demand is not incorporated into the 1996 INRA law which requires a clear choice between collective ownership and individual ownership. However, those families who are more linked to the market and who have access to better-quality and irrigated land seek individual family property rights and the annulment of all forms of collective property or communal control.

13 It is the merit of the Popular Participation law that it gave juridical recognition to the peasant and indigenous communities under the form of Territorial Base Organizations (OTB – *Organizaciones Territoriales de Base*).

Bibliography

Agarwal, B. (1994). *A Field of One's Own: Gender and Land Rights in South Asia.* Cambridge and New York: Cambridge University Press.

Albó, X. (2002a). *Pueblos Indios en la Política.* La Paz: Plural editores.

Albó, X. (2002b). 'From indian and campesino leaders to councillors and parliamentary deputies', in R. Sieder, ed., *Multiculturalism in Latin America: Indigenous Rights, Diversity and Democracy*, pp. 74–102. Houndmills and New York: Palgrave Macmillan.

Almaraz, A. (ed.) (2002). *Tierras Comunitarias de Origen: Saneamiento y Titulación – Guía para el Patrocinio Jurídico.* Santa Cruz: Centro de Estudios Jurídicos e Investigación Social (CEJIS).

Almaraz, A. (2003). *Reglamento de la Ley INRA: Análisis, Evolución y Normas Vigentes.* Separata de la Revista Artículo Primero, Santa Cruz: Centro de Estudios Jurídicos e Investigación Social (CEJIS).

Ameller, V. (2002). *Diálogo para la descentralización: Provocaciones, Avances y Desengaños.* La Paz: Agencia Suiza para el Desarrollo y la Cooperación (COSUDE).

Anonymous (2005). 'El país de las migraciones', *Temas de Debate: Boletín del Programa de Investigaciones Estratégicas de Bolivia*, vol. 3, no. 3, pp. 1–4, La Paz: PIEB.

Arce, M. (1954). *Monografía Estadística Indígena de Bolivia.* La Paz: S.C.I.D.E.

Arze, C. and T. Kruse (2004). 'The consequences of neoliberal reforms', *NACLA Report on the Americas*, vol. 38, no. 3, pp. 23–28.

Assies, W. (2006). 'Bolivia: land tenure legalization in a pluricultural and multiethnic country'. Paper presented at the International Conference on Land, Poverty, Social Justice and Development, 9–14 January, The Hague: Institute of Social Studies (available at: www.iss.nl).

Ayo, D. (ed.) (2004). *Voces críticas de la Descentralización: Una Década de Participación Popular.* La Paz: Plural editores.

Ballivián, D. P. and H. Zeballos (2003). *Diagnóstico de la Reforma Agraria Boliviana 50 Años Después de la Promulgación de la Ley.* La Paz: Instituto Nacional de Reforma Agraria (INRA).

Banco Central de Bolivia (2004). *Memoria 2003.* La Paz: Banco Central de Bolivia (BCB).

Banco Mundial (2004). *Bolivia. Estrategia de Asistencia al País 2004/2005.* Spanish translation of document No. 26838-BO 'Report and Recommendation of the

President of the International Bank for Reconstruction and Development to the Executive Directors on a Country Assistance of the World Bank for the Republic of Bolivia', Washington, DC: World Bank.

Barragán, R. (2004). '"La media luna": autonomías regionales y comités cívicos', *Tinkazos*, vol. 7, no. 16, pp. 9–43.

Calderón, F. and J. Dandler (eds) (1986). *Bolivia: la Fuerza Histórica del Campesinado*, second edition. Geneva: United Nations Research Institute for Social Development (UNRISD) and La Paz: Centro de Estudios de la Realidad Económica y Social (CERES).

Calderón, F. and R. Laserna (1997). *La Fuerza de la Equidad: El Desarrollo Humano en Bolivia*. La Paz: Los Amigos del Libro.

Campero, F. (1999). *Bolivia en el Siglo XX: La Formación de la Bolivia Contemporánea.* La Paz: Harvard Club de Bolivia.

CEDLA (2003). 'Consideraciones sobre la Estrategia Nacional de Desarrollo Agropecuario y Rural', *Observatorio de Políticas Públicas Agropecuarias*, vol. 1, no. 3.

CEPAL (2002). *Panorama Social de América Latina 2002*, Santiago: Naciones Unidas, Comisión Económica para América Latina y el Caribe (CEPAL).

CSUTCOPYCC (2002). *Saneamiento Interno en Nuestras Comunidades.* Central Sindical Única de Trabajadores Campesinos Originarios de la Provincia Yamparaez Carrillo Caliza (CSUTCOPYCC).

Dandler, J. (1984). *El Sindicalismo Agrario en Bolivia; los Cambios Estructurales en Ucureña (1935–1952).* La Paz: Centro de Estudios de la Realidad Económica y Social (CERES).

Deere, C. D. and M. León (2001). *Empowering Women: Land and Property Rights in Latin America.* Pittsburgh: University of Pittsburgh Press.

Deininger, K. and H. Binswanger (2001). 'The evolution of the World Bank's land policy', in A. de Janvry, G. Gordillo, J.-P. Platteau and E. Sadoulet, eds, *Access to Land, Rural Poverty, and Public Action*, pp. 406–440. Oxford and New York: Oxford University Press.

Delegación de la Comisión Europea (2000). *Bolivia: Disponibilidad Nacional de Alimentos, Patrón de Consumo y Cambios Tendenciales del Sector Agropecuario.* La Paz: Delegación de la Comisión Europea.

Demeure, J. (1999). 'Agricultura, de la Subsistencia a la Competencia Internacional', in F. Campero, ed., *Bolivia en el Siglo XX: La Formación de la Bolivia Contemporánea*, pp. 269–290. La Paz: Harvard Club de Bolivia.

Diez, A. (2003). *Propiedad Colectiva y Propiedad Individual.* Lima: manuscript.

Dunkerley, J. (1984). *Rebellion in Their Veins: Political Struggle in Bolivia 1952–1982.* London: Verso Editions.

ECLAC (Economic Commission for Latin America and the Caribbean) (2004). *Social Panorama of Latin America, 2002–2003.* Santiago: United Nations, ECLAC.

Fundación TIERRA (1997). *Con los Pies en la Tierra: Reflexiones sobre la Ley INRA.* La Paz: Fundación TIERRA (Taller de Iniciativas en Estudios Rurales y Reforma Agraria).

Gill, L. (1987). *Peasants, Entrepreneurs, and Social Change: Frontier Development in Lowland Bolivia.* Boulder: Westview Press.

Healy, K. (2004). 'Towards an Andean rural development paradigm?', *NACLA Report on the Americas*, vol. 38, no. 3, pp. 28–33.

Heath, D, C. Erasmus and H. Buechler (1969). *Land Reform and Social Revolution in Bolivia.* New York: Praeger.

Hernáiz, I. (1993). *La Corrupción de la Reforma Agraria.* La Paz: Fundación TIERRA.

Hernáiz, I. (2002). *Concentración de la Tierra.* La Paz: Fundación TIERRA.

Hernáiz, I. and D. Pacheco (2001). *La Ley INRA en el Espejo de la Historia: Propuestas de Modificación.* La Paz: Fundación TIERRA.

Hernáiz, I., D. Pacheco, R. Guerrero and H. Miranda (2000). *Análisis Crítico del Proceso de Catastro Rural Legal y Saneamiento Integrado al Catastro Legal en el Departamento de Chuquisaca (KADASTER e INRA).* La Paz and Sucre: Fundación TIERRA.

Hernani, W. (2002). *Mercado Laboral, Pobreza y Desigualdad en Bolivia.* La Paz: Instituto Nacional de Estadística (INE).

Hinojosa, A. (ed.) (2004). *Migraciones Transnacionales: Visiones de Norte y Sudamérica.* La Paz: Plural editores.

Hinojosa, A., L. Pérez and G. Cortez (2002). *Idas y Venidas: Campesinos Tarijeños en el Norte Argentino.* La Paz: Programa de Investigación Estratégica en Bolivia (PIEB).

Instituto Nacional de Estadística – INE (2001). *Censo Nacional de Población y Vivienda.* La Paz: INE.

Instituto Nacional de Estadística (2002). *Encuesta de Hogares Medición de Condiciones de Vida.* La Paz: INE.

Instituto Nacional de Estadística (2003). *Bolivia: Características Sociodemográficas de la Población.* La Paz: INE.

Instituto Nacional de Estadística (2004). *Anuario Estadístico 2003.* La Paz: INE.

Instituto Nacional de Reforma Agraria – INRA (2005). *Estado del Proceso de Saneamiento 2004.* La Paz: INRA.

Instituto PRISMA (2002). *Población, Migración y Desarrollo en Bolivia.* La Paz: Instituto PRISMA.

Kay, C. (2002). 'Agrarian reform and the neoliberal counter-reform in Latin America', in J. Chase, ed., *The Spaces of Neoliberalism: Land, Place and Family in Latin America*, pp. 25–52, Bloomfield: Kumarian Press.

Kay, C. (2005a). 'Reflections on rural poverty in Latin America', *The European Journal of Development Research*, vol. 17, no. 2, pp. 317–346.

Kay, C. (2005b). 'Pobreza y Estrategias de Desarrollo Rural en Bolivia: ¿Está impulsando la ENDAR las capacidades campesinas?', *Debate Agrario: Análisis y Alternativas*, no. 38, pp. 109–139.

Klein, H. S. (1993). *Haciendas and Ayllus: Rural Society in the Bolivian Andes in the Eighteenth and Nineteenth Centuries.* Stanford: Stanford University Press.

Klein, H. S. (2003). *A Concise History of Bolivia.* Cambridge: Cambridge University Press.

Komives, K., J. C. Aguilar and others (2004). 'Estrategia Boliviana de Reducción de la Pobreza: ¿La Nueva Brillante Idea?', Stockholm: Agencia Sueca de Desarrollo Internacional (ASDI) y La Haya: Institute of Social Studies (ISS).

Komives, K., J. C. Aguilar, G. Dijkstra and C. Kay (2005). 'Bolivia: ¿Más de lo Mismo?- Evaluación de las Estrategias de Reducción de la Pobreza en América Latina: Informe País Bolivia, 2004', Stockholm: Agencia Sueca de Desarrollo Internacional (ASDI) y La Haya: Institute of Social Studies (ISS).

Lagos, M. L. (1994). *Autonomy and Power: The Dynamics of Class and Culture in Rural Bolivia.* Philadelphia: University of Pennsylvania Press.

Landa, F. (2002). *Pobreza y Distribución del Ingreso en Bolivia entre 1999–2002.* La Paz: Unidad de Análisis de Políticas Sociales y Económicas (UDAPE).

Langer, E. D. (1989). *Economic Change and Rural Resistance in Southern Bolivia 1880–1930.* Stanford: Stanford University Press.

Larson, B. (1988). *Colonialism and Agrarian Transformation in Bolivia: Cochabamba, 1550–1900*. Princeton: Princeton University Press.

McEwan, W. J. (1975). *Changing Rural Society: A Study of Communities in Bolivia*. New York: Oxford University Press.

Maletta, H. (1980). *La Fuerza de Trabajo en Bolivia 1900–1976: Análisis Crítico de la Información Censal*. La Paz: Oficina Internacional del Trabajo (OIT) and Ministerio del Trabajo, Proyecto 'Migraciones Laborales y Empleo'.

Matus, M. (2003). 'Obstáculos y Promesas del Desarrollo en Bolivia: Claves Históricas y Territoriales', in J. Prats, ed., *El Desarrollo Posible, las Instituciones Necesarias*. Colección Diagnósticos Institucionales. La Paz: IIG, Plural editores.

Ministerio de Agricultura (1985). *Censo Nacional Agropecuario, 1950*. La Paz: Ministerio de Agricultura.

Ministerio de Asuntos Campesinos y Agropecuarios (MACA) (2004). *Estrategia Nacional de Desarrollo Agropecuario y Rural (ENDAR)*. La Paz: MACA.

Ministerio de Desarrollo Económico (2005). *Bases para la Estrategia Boliviana de Desarrollo*. La Paz: Consejo Nacional de Política Económica (CONAPE).

Ministerio de Desarrollo Sostenible y Planificación (2002). *Migración Interna. Estudios de los Movimientos Poblacionales en Bolivia*. La Paz: CODEPO.

Ministerio de Desarrollo Sostenible y Planificación (2004). *Estrategia Nacional de Desarrollo Rural Agropecuario y Rural (ENDAR)*. La Paz: Ministerio de Desarrollo Sostenible.

Molenaers, N. and R. Renard (2003). 'Participation and PRSP: the Bolivian case revisited', *European Journal of Development Research*, vol. 15, no. 2, pp. 133–161.

Morales, J. and N. Pacheco (1999). 'Economía, el Retorno de los Liberales', in F. Campero, ed., *Bolivia en el Siglo XX: La Formación de la Bolivia Contemporánea*, pp. 155–192. La Paz: Harvard Club de Bolivia.

Muller y Asociados (2004). *Estadísticas Socio-económicas 2003*. La Paz: Muller y Asociados.

Oporto, H. (2003). '¿De la Reforma Agraria a la guerra por la tierra?,' *Opiniones y Análisis*, no. 65, pp. 131–172. La Paz: FUNDEMOS.

Ormachea, E. and Fernández, E. (eds) (1989). *Amazonía Boliviana y Campesinado*. La Paz: Cooperativa Agrícola Integral 'Campesino'.

Pearse, A. (1975). 'Peasants and revolution in Bolivia', in A. Pearse, *The Latin American Peasant*, pp. 119–116. London: Frank Cass.

Programa de las Naciones Unidas para el Desarrollo (PNUD) (1998). *Desarrollo Humano en Bolivia*. La Paz: PNUD.

Programa de las Naciones Unidas para el Desarrollo (2003). *Informe sobre el Desarrollo Humano*. Madrid: Grupo Mundi-Prensa.

Programa de las Naciones Unidas para el Desarrollo (2004). *Informe Nacional de Desarrollo Humano 2004: Interculturalismo y Globalización – La Bolivia Posible*. La Paz: PNUD.

Rivera, S. (1987). *'Oppressed but not Defeated': Peasant Struggles Among the Aymara and Quechua in Bolivia, 1900–1980*. Geneva: United Nations Research Institute for Social Development (UNRISD) and La Paz: Centro de Estudios de la Realidad Económica y Social (CERES).

Roca, J. L. (2001). *Economía y Sociedad en el Oriente Boliviano (Siglos XVI–XX)*. Santa Cruz: Cooperativa de telecomunicaciones SC – COTAS.

Royden, Y. and B. Wennergren (1977). 'Los problemas de la colonización en

Bolivia: características y resultados de la colonización dirigida y espontánea en el oriente', *Revista Económica*, vol. 3, no. 12, pp. 48–54.

Salazar, R. (2003). *Tierra en la Tierra, las Mujeres ¿Dónde Están?*. La Paz: Fundación TIERRA.

Soria, C. A. (1996). *Esperanza y Realidades: Colonización en Santa Cruz*, Cuadernos de Investigación 49. La Paz: Centro de Investigación y Promoción del Campesinado (CIPCA).

Stallings, B. and E. Peres (2000). *Growth, Employment, and Equity: The Impact of the Economic Reforms in Latin America and the Caribbean*. Washington, DC: Brookings Institution Press.

Superintendencia Agraria (1997). *Hacia el Uso Sostenible de la Tierra*. La Paz: Superintendencia Agraria (SIA).

Superintendencia Agraria (2001a). *Bases para el Relanzamiento del Proceso Agrario Nacional*. La Paz: SIA.

Superintendencia Agraria (2001b). *Evaluación de Cinco Años de Aplicación del Nuevo Proceso Agrario Nacional*. La Paz: SIA.

Thorp, R. (1998). *Progress, Poverty and Exclusion: An Economic History of Latin America in the 20th Century*. Washington, DC: Inter-American Development Bank (IDB).

Unidad de Análisis de Políticas Sociales y Económicas – UDAPE (2003). *Estrategia Boliviana de Reducción de la Pobreza: Informe de Avance y Perspectivas*. La Paz: UDAPE.

Unidad de Análisis de Políticas Sociales y Económicas (2004). *Dossier de Estadísticas Sociales y Económicas*, vol. 14. La Paz: UDAPE.

Urioste, M. (1984). *El Estado Anticampesino*. La Paz: Instituto Latinoamericano de Investigaciones Sociales (ILDIS).

Urioste, M. (1987). *Segunda Reforma Agraria. Campesinos, Tierra y Educación Popular*. La Paz: Centro de Estudios para el Desarrollo Laboral y Agrario (CEDLA).

Urioste, M. (1992). *Fortalecer las Comunidades: Una Utopía Democrática y Posible*. La Paz: Fundación TIERRA.

Urioste, M. (2002). *Desarrollo Rural con Participación Popular*. La Paz: Fundación TIERRA.

Urioste, M. (2003). *La Reforma Agraria Abandonada: Valles y Altiplano*. La Paz, Fundación TIERRA. An updated version has been published under the title 'Bolivia: la reforma agraria abandonada: los valles y el altiplano', in *Debate Agrario*, Lima: CEPES, no. 37, 2004, pp. 161–182.

Urioste, M. (2004). 'Ninguno de los indígenas que están en el Parlamento hoy en día hubiera llegado a ese nivel si no era a través del proceso de participación popular', in D. Ayo, ed., *Voces Críticas de la Descentralización: Una Década de Participación Popular*, pp. 333–361. La Paz: Plural Editores.

Urioste, M. and R. Barragán (2005). *Los Nietos de la Reforma Agraria*. La Paz: Fundación TIERRA.

Urquiola, M. (1999). 'La distribución de la población en el siglo XX', in F. Campero, ed., *Bolivia en el Siglo XX: La Formación de la Bolivia Contemforánea*, pp. 193–217. La Paz: Harvard Club de Bolivia.

Valderrama, C. (2002). *Estadísticas Agrarias: Tenencia de la Tierra en Bolivia*. La Paz: INRA-DANIDA (Danish International Development Agency).

Valenzuela, R. (2004). *Inequidad, Ciudadanía y Pueblos Indígenas en Bolivia*. Santiago: NNUU, Comisión Económica para América Latina y el Caribe (CEPAL).

van der Haar, G. and A. Zoomers (2003). 'Las políticas de tierra en América

Latina: tendencias y problemáticas actuales', *Artículo Primero*, no. 14, pp. 177–189. Special issue on 'Reforma Agraria, 50 años: TCO y tierras campesinas.' Santa Cruz: Centro de Estudios Jurídicos e Investigación Social (CEJIS).

van Dijk, P. (ed.) (1998). *The Bolivian Experiment: Structural Adjustment and Poverty Alleviation*. Amsterdam: Centre for Latin American Research and Documentation (CEDLA).

Vargas, J. D. (ed.) (2003). *Proceso Agrario en Bolivia y América Latina: 50 años de la Reforma Agraria en Bolivia*. La Paz: Plural editores.

Vargas, J. D. (ed.) (2004). *La Reforma Agraria desde las Regiones. Tierra y Territorio. 50 años de la Reforma Agraria en Bolivia*. La Paz: Plural editores.

Various Authors (1981). *Apuntes sobre Colonización*. La Paz: Centro de Estudios y Proyectos (Serie: Estudios Rurales).

Wennergren, E. B. and M. D. Whitaker (1975). *The Status of Bolivian Agriculture*. New York: Praeger Publishers.

World Bank (2002). *Report and Recommendations of the President of the IBRD to the Executive Directors on a Country Assitance of the World Bank for the Republic of Bolivia*. Washington, DC: World Bank.

Zeballos, H. (1975). *From the Uplands to the Lowlands: An Economic Analysis of Bolivian Rural–Rural Migration*, unpublished Ph.D. dissertation, Department of Agricultural Economics, University of Wisconsin, Madison.

Zoomers, A. and G. van der Haar (eds) (2000). *Current Land Policies in Latin America: Regulating Land Tenure under Neo-liberalism*. Amsterdam: KIT and Frankfurt: Vervuert.

3 Agrarian reform and poverty reduction

Lessons from Brazil

Carmen Diana Deere and
Leonilde Servolo de Medeiros

Introduction

Brazil is among the countries in Latin America with the most extreme concentration of land, in a region noted for having the worst distribution of land in the world. It also has one of the worst income distributions, with a large share of its rural population – almost two-thirds – living in poverty.

Following the general Latin American pattern, during the period of its state-driven industrialisation process, Brazil passed its first agrarian reform law. Efforts at land distribution until the mid-1980s, however, were minimal and largely focused on colonisation of the agrarian frontier. In the 1990s, nonetheless, Brazil was one of the few Latin American countries carrying out a redistributive agrarian reform, largely driven by pressures from the landless movement. At the same time, Brazil experimented with World Bank-inspired market-led land reform. Moreover, in 2003 Brazil elected its first leftist, working-class president, Luis Inácio Lula da Silva, who pledged to carry out a comprehensive agrarian reform.

This chapter presents an assessment of Brazilian efforts at land redistribution over the past 20 years. It seeks to explain why agrarian reform has been on the agenda in Brazil when in the rest of the region the process was considered to be over, as well as why in the late 1990s the government was expropriating land at a faster rate than ever before in its history, while also pursuing market-led land redistribution. The chapter also seeks to draw lessons from Brazil's experience with 3,000-plus land reform settlements, particularly with respect to poverty reduction. A main concern of the chapter is with what measures have worked and under what conditions.

The prelude to agrarian reform efforts

Beginning in the late 1940s, land struggles throughout Brazil, particularly those of dispossessed squatters and tenants on large estates, began to gain visibility. Incipient steps in recognition of rural workers' rights included their gaining the right to organise and the 1963 Rural Workers' Statute, whereby rural wage workers gained similar rights to those achieved by urban workers in the 1930s. Nonetheless, demands for agrarian reform met with fierce resistance. These disputes were part of the political crisis that led to the military coup of 1964.

One of the paradoxes of Brazilian agrarian policy is that the Land Statute – the agrarian reform law that has oriented the land policy of the different governments up through the current period – was adopted after the military coup of April 1964. The Land Statute opened up the possibility for the state to expropriate land, with compensation, when it was in the social interest, specifically, in the case of land conflicts.

The objective of this legislation was the gradual extinction of extremely small parcels (*minifundios*) and the large landed estate (*latifundios*), both of which were considered to be the source of rural social tensions.[1] The ideal model became the rural enterprise (which could include family-run enterprises) characterised by an adequate level of land use and productivity which complied with labor legislation and preserved the environment. The methods for transforming *latifundios* into enterprises included their expropriation due to the social interest in the case of land conflicts, progressive taxation, and support for production, including credit, technical assistance, cooperative development, etc.

By the end of the 1960s, the military regime's interest in colonisation far surpassed that in land redistribution. In subsequent years land conflicts were largely solved by violence and repression rather than by land expropriation. The military regime opted to confront the backwardness of agriculture via technological modernisation without changing property relations. The principle mechanism to spur modernisation became the availability of cheap and ample credit combined with tax incentives of various kinds.

Modernisation was accompanied by the massive displacement of workers who had formerly lived and worked on the large estates. The dispossessed former residents of these estates moved to the peripheries of the cities where they became part of the temporary, seasonal labour force for capitalist agricultural enterprises. In addition, tax incentives to stimulate the colonisation of the agricultural frontier led to significant deforestation and the expansion of cattle production as well as encroachment on the lands of indigenous peoples. The result was the intensification of land conflicts throughout Brazil, but particularly in the Amazon region, as huge areas of land were appropriated by large enterprises pertaining to the industrial and financial sectors.

The principal organisation for rural workers in this period was the National Confederation of Agricultural Workers, CONTAG (*Confederação Nacional dos Trabalhadores na Agricultura*). In a context of heavy repression, its involvement in these land conflicts was largely procedural. The Catholic Church was the main institution denouncing rural violence and supporting the organisation of rural workers both morally and materially.

The Pastoral Land Commission (*Comissão Pastoral da Terra*, CPT), created in 1975 by progressive Catholic bishops, came to play a major role in legitimising forms of resistance by the poor and their struggle for land, as well as in training a new generation of rural leaders. The critique of traditional unionism as embodied in CONTAG grew out of these efforts. A new, combative rural unionism emerged focused on the mobilisation of rural workers. These oppositionary forces played a major role in the land conflicts of the late 1970s and early 1980s (Medeiros, 2002).

The redefinition of the agrarian question in the 1980s

If the land struggles of the 1950s to 1970s were primarily struggles of resistance to dispossession, by the end of the 1970s new actors had emerged, making the agrarian question even more complex. The construction of large hydroelectric dams throughout the country displaced many small farmers and small towns. Initially demanding restitution of lands in the same region, the resistance movement was soon demanding an end to compulsory dislocations and eventually questioning the very logic behind the construction of large dams.

In the western frontier state of Acre, traditional rubber-tappers began protesting the destruction of native forests and their conversion to pasture lands in the wake of the expansion of the cattle industry. They were successful in merging their demand to maintain traditional access to forest land with the demands of environmentalists, gaining national and international recognition for their cause. In other regions of the country such as the south, other demands emerged, for example, for access to credit and better prices among small farmers who were attempting to modernise. In addition, there were growing confrontations between small farmers and agro-industry (particularly in chicken, hog, tobacco and grape production) over prices and the conditions of their integration. Rural wage workers, for their part, increasingly mobilised and drew attention to their precarious conditions, including low wages, long work days and their lack of access to basic workers' rights and benefits.

In this context of broadening rural conflict – just as the country was going through a process of political opening and redemocratisation – agrarian reform was once again placed on the agenda. At its Third National Congress in 1979, agrarian reform emerged as one of the principal demands of CONTAG. The National Conference of Bishops (CNBB, *Conferência Nacional dos Bispos do Brasil*) positioned the church against the concentration of land, land speculation and the exploitation of workers.

This is the period in which land occupations began as a form of struggle, eventually giving rise to the formation of the Movement of Landless Rural Workers (MST, *Movimiento dos Trabalhadores Rurais sem Terra*). The landless movement was initially formed by small farmers who had either lost their land or who were unable to increase their access to land

and were being excluded from the process of modernisation. Land occupations became the means to draw attention to their plight and to pressure the state to carry out an agrarian reform. These began in the state of Rio Grande do Sul in the late 1970s, spreading to neighboring states in the early 1980s, and were to become the principal means of struggle for agrarian reform. Moreover, these land occupations also became the means of constructing a political identity – the landless – and a specific organisation, the MST (Grzybowski, 1987; Medeiros, 1989; Wright and Wolford, 2003).

These rural conflicts were taking place at the same time that urban mobilisations were intensifying around demands that ranged from political amnesty for political prisoners and exiles, to demands for salary increases. Notable among the latter was the 1978 strike of the metallurgy workers in the industrial area of São Paulo that led to the rise of Luis Inácio da Silva (Lula) as a political figure and the formation of the Workers' Party (PT, *Partido dos Trabalhadores*). These struggles slowly but steadily merged into the demand for political opening and redemocratisation of the country, eroding the legitimacy of the military regime. The large-scale urban and rural popular mobilisations that marked the end of the military regime raised expectations regarding the possibility of agrarian reform.

The agrarian reform of the new republic

Even before the democratic government took office, a working group was formed to elaborate a proposal for a National Agrarian Reform Plan. Its composition was broad, including advisors of the rural unions and members of the Brazilian Association of Agrarian Reform (ABRA, *Associação Brasileira de Reforma Agrária*, an organisation of intellectuals committed to agrarian reform). The Sarney government soon created a Ministry for Agrarian Reform and Development (MIRAD, *Ministério da Reforma Agrária e Desenvolvimento*), and a political figure linked to the Catholic Church and sympathetic to agrarian reform, was named as minister. INCRA (*Instituto Nacional de Colonização e Reforma Agrária*), the land reform agency, was brought under MIRAD, and an historic defender of agrarian reform (one of the authors of the Land Statute and founder and president of ABRA) was named as its president.

The proposal for a National Agrarian Reform Plan (PNRA, *Plano Nacional da Reforma Agrária*) was symbolically presented to the Fourth Congress of CONTAG in May 1985. The same evening that the proposal was presented, the MST carried out a number of occupations in western Santa Catarina state, calling attention to its unhappiness with the agrarian reform proposal and its lack of confidence in the government implementing even a weak agrarian reform. These actions marked the beginning of a political dispute over the content of the agrarian reform that has characterised the subsequent 20 years.

In the proposal, the principal means of obtaining land for redistribution was its expropriation in the social interest. Landowners were to be compensated based on the declared value for tax purposes. Since such valuations tended to be notoriously below market value, the proposal implicitly assumed that expropriation would penalise landowners for not utilising their land in the social interest (Medeiros, 2002). Alternative means of obtaining land for the reform included colonisation, the recuperation of illegally titled national lands, and via a progressive tax on underutilised lands.

In terms of concrete goals, the proposal was to settle seven million of the estimated 10.5 million landless households in a period of 15 years. It was assumed that the remainder would be employed as wage workers in the capitalist agricultural sector where working conditions would improve once surplus rural workers were settled on agrarian reform lands.

The PNRA proposal took the Land Statute to its ultimate consequences – expropriation in the social interest – and was strongly supported by CONTAG. But the proposal was contested by other organisations, such as the MST, that considered it to be too timid. If these groups opposed the proposal because they wanted a deeper and more rapid agrarian reform, other organisations, representing agrarian capitalists and landowners, tried to block it altogether. Among them were the Brazilian Rural Society (SRB, *Sociedade Rural Brasileira*) and the National Confederation of Agriculture (CNA, *Confederação Nacional da Agricultura*). But the proposal also caused fissures within these organisations. A new organisation of rural entrepreneurs, the Rural Democratic Union (UDR, *União Democrática Ruralista*), was formed, which urged its members to use force to resist land occupations, gaining it attention in the national press as well as supporters in the National Congress.

The landowning sector essentially defended their right to negotiate the sale of land to the state as an alternative to expropriation (and its punitive implication). They also contested the definition of a 'productive' enterprise. They were successful in incorporating into the final version of the PNRA that any farm in production was exempt from expropriation, irrespective of its size or use.

INCRA did begin carrying out expropriations, principally in long-standing areas of agrarian conflict in the northeast and north. Land conflicts continued as did the incidence of violence in the countryside. The church-affiliated CPT continued to be the main voice denouncing such violence nationwide.

The convocation of the National Constituent Assembly in 1987 was the next act in the saga over agrarian reform. Notwithstanding strong popular pressure to strengthen the provisions in the new constitution in favour of an ample agrarian reform, landlord opposition managed to stop the bulk of such efforts. Nevertheless, there were a number of advances in the new constitution, particularly with respect to social rights, including the extension of social security provisions to rural workers (including those in family agriculture) and with respect to women's rights to land (they were now mentioned explicitly as potential beneficiaries), but also with regard to the legal basis for agrarian reform.

Previous Brazilian constitutions made only passing reference to the social function of land. The 1988 constitution states explicitly that land should serve a social function (Art. 5, xxiii), and also defines such, following the precedent set in the Land Statute: that land should be utilised rationally and in a manner protective of the environment; that labour regulations must be adhered to; and that the well-being of both owners and workers should be taken into account. In addition, the constitution provides for expropriations in the social interest to be compensated for in agrarian reform bonds (to be indexed so that their real value is preserved) payable over 20 years with the valorisation of land determined by what the owner declares for tax purposes. Exempt from expropriation are small and medium (those smaller than 15 rural modules) as well as productive properties and the definition of the latter would continue to be a point of contention.

It took almost five years before the necessary implementing legislation was adopted by the Congress, largely at the insistence of the Workers' Party. The Agrarian Law of February 1993 (No. 8629) opened up some possibilities to deepen the agrarian reform, while it closed others. For example, it established that preferentially, public lands were to be used for the agrarian reform. Some controversial points were maintained such as the tension between the social function criteria of land and the definition of productive properties that were exempt from expropriation. This had the effect of strengthening the role of the judiciary in settling contested expropriations.

Rural workers' organisations and the land settlements of the new republic

In total, between 1985 and 1994, 140,065 families were settled on *assentamentos*, more than during the whole 21-year period of military government, but this was a pittance compared to the numbers demanding land (which was estimated at between 3.3 and six million families). A large number of the agrarian reform settlements created were in the northeast and north, where many of the beneficiaries were peasant families who had been fighting their dispossession.

While the numbers may seem insignificant, the experiences generated on these land reform settlements were important for the future course of agrarian reform. The MST-organised *assentamentos* in the south are an important example. The MST was quite aware of the importance of successfully organising production on these new settlements so that they would serve as a model, demonstrating the potential of agrarian reform.

In the late 1980s they began experimenting with various forms of collective production and cooperatives of various types. Moreover, they emphasised not only political education, but also formal education and the eradication of adult illiteracy. They also began to demand state resources to develop infrastructure and agro-industrial projects on the settlements. In addition, they began to rotate talented local leaders to other regions of the country in order to organise new land occupations and thus to expand the movement nationally. As these experiences matured, the lessons learned were applied to the growing number of *assentamentos* of the 1990s.

With respect to the rural unions, they were initially weakened by their faith that the government would carry out an agrarian reform of its own volition. CONTAG slowly came to recognise that the agrarian reform was moving forward only because of the MST-led land occupations. CONTAG was also weakened politically by the organisation and growing strength of the rural department within the CUT (*Central Única dos Trabalhadores*) which captured the most progressive union forces. It was this latter group that, once it had gained control of numerous municipal-level unions and various state federations, also began to carry out land occupations.

The expansion of the struggle and of agrarian reform beneficiaries

The priority of the government of Fernando Henrique Cardoso upon taking office in 1996 was growth and employment generation. Agrarian reform was considered necessary not only to secure social peace but also because it was thought that employment could more readily be generated in agriculture and at a lower cost than in other sectors of the economy. The government's initial plan was to settle 280,000 families on *assentamentos* within four years (Cardoso, 1994). This was a rather timid goal, given the demand for land, but not insignificant when compared with previous governments. The goal was to create viable family farmers and the government thus pledged to provide each beneficiary family with a financing package that included a settlement grant and three credit lines under PROCERA (the agrarian reform credit programme instituted in 1986) for working capital and investments in social and productive infrastructure, as well as technical assistance.

But agrarian reform quickly lost political momentum within the government as Cardoso's top priority shifted to stabilising the economy and combating inflation. In this unfavorable context, the pressure of the social movements intensified, particularly that of the MST, which increased the pace of land occupations. Two, practically sequential massacres of rural workers (Corumbiara in August 1995 and Eldorado dos Carajás in April 1996) highlighted how traditional forms of violence continued to be used against rural workers and served to reactivate the public debate regarding agrarian reform. Moreover, international pressure came to bear on the Cardoso government, particularly from human rights groups. These events marked a turning point for the Cardoso government. A new Ministry Extraordinaire of Land Policy was then created and INCRA was once again removed from the province of the Ministry of Agriculture and brought under this new ministry.

In tandem, the MST intensified its mobilisations as well as efforts to win over public opinion to its cause. The high point of this period was the National March for Agrarian Reform, Employment and Justice (known as the March of the Landless) that from diverse points of this vast country, converged on the capital of Brasilia in 1997 on the first anniversary of the massacre of Eldorado das Carajás. A three-month-long march, it resulted in the demands of the landless – and their impressive degree of organisation – being reported on the front page of newspapers and prime-time television for its duration. It also served as a catalyst for the manifestation of diverse anti-government sentiments, many expressed for the first time, particularly with respect to the impact of Cardoso's economic policies.

Facing escalating anti-government social mobilisations, the Cardoso government responded by trying to isolate the MST in order to reduce its role as the main protagonist in agrarian reform. At the same time, it sought to take the initiative with respect to agrarian reform. As Medeiros (2002) argues, a new institutionality resulted from this effort. Often the result of temporary decrees or complementary legislation, it demonstrates the urgency and importance that the agrarian question had assumed for the state. This new institutionality was inscribed in a broader reform of the state around the pillars of decentralisation, shrinkage of government and privatisation.

Some of the new measures intended to accelerate the acquisition of land for new rural settlements and to lower the high cost of indemnisation for expropriated properties by confronting the multiple ways utilised by landowners to avoid expropriation. For example, one measure prohibited the subdivision of an estate once notification had been given of its forthcoming inspection, to prevent an estate from being divided up among family members into units smaller than those eligible for expropriation (ibid.). In order to encourage the sale of unproductive land and its more efficient use, in 1996 the government increased the land tax on unused land, with the precise rate depending both on farm size and the degree of land utilisation. This measure was complemented by efforts to modernise the rural land cadastre and institute a national land registry, measures that would also allow more precise identification of illegally titled national lands and increase the supply of public land available for redistribution (Reydon and Plata, 2002).

Another series of measures intended to curtail the actions of the rural social movements, particularly the MST, were carried out by the government. Among the most important of these was the decree that prohibited the inspection of properties that had been the target of a land occupation, thus ending once and for all the possibility that occupations would lead to expropriation. Another sought to end a common form of protest against the slowness of INCRA's procedures, the occupation of its local or state headquarters. If a public building was occupied, negotiations on whatever issue was in dispute were to be suspended immediately. Another measure prohibited the disbursement of public funds, at whatever level of government, to individuals who participated in any kind of occupation of land or public property. The new measures thus sought to end what had been the most successful means of carrying out an agrarian reform from below: the land occupations. These measures were accompanied by what the MST considered to be persecution of the movement, with a number of its leaders jailed on various charges and it being accused of the misappropriation of credit provided to the land reform settlements.

To retake the initiative on agrarian reform, the Cardoso government launched a new beneficiary selection process whereby those seeking land could apply directly to INCRA by filling out a form at the post office. The social movements responded by urging their members to apply for land, and over three-quarters of a million people signed up.

In tandem, the government began a process of decentralisation of the functions of INCRA, a highly centralised and hierarchal institution, in order to speed up and simplify the process of land acquisition (INCRA, 1998). Key to this was the decentralisation of many administrative functions from the headquarters in Brasilia to the regional superintendencies, intended to accelerate the process of decision-making. There was also a concerted effort to involve the state and municipal governments in the agrarian reform.

These initiatives were consolidated in the 1999 program known as 'The New Rural World' the main theme of which was 'to bring quality to the *assentamentos*' (MEPF, 1999). Agrarian reform beneficiaries were equated with family farmers and the aim became to treat both of these sectors in a parallel fashion in the policies executed by the newly created state and municipal-level Sustainable Development Councils. In partnership with the federal government, these were to define the lands to be acquired for the agrarian reform and how these would be obtained, taking into account cost–benefit analysis with respect to needed infrastructure, credit, technical assistance, etc.

It was also envisioned that some of the traditional activities of INCRA (such as topographical studies, the demarcation of individual plots, the construction of basic infrastructure, the production plan of the *assentamento*, etc.) would be privatised by giving grants to the *assentamento* associations themselves to contract these services. Another objective was to rapidly 'emancipate' the settlements from state tutelage (within two or three years after the demarcation of plots), transforming the agrarian reform beneficiaries into full family farmers. This also meant that beneficiaries would commence to pay their land debt shortly thereafter.[2] In the government's new view, agrarian reform beneficiaries were to be viewed as mini-entrepreneurs who must adjust to market competition.

The experiments in market-led land reform

As explained by Borras, Kay and Akram Lodhi in the introductory chapter of this book, in the 1990s the World Bank rediscovered agrarian reform as a mechanism to combat poverty worldwide. Drawing on the critique of traditional land reform efforts, the Bank proposed an alternative reform model based on direct negotiations between landowners and those demanding land. It was argued that such a market-led model would result in a more rapid and efficient redistribution of land with much less political conflict.

The first experiment with this policy began in the northeast of Brazil in the state of Ceará in 1996. The next year the government expanded the programme to four other states in this region in what came to be known as the *Cédula da Terra* programme. The programme was based on the constitution of associations of small farmers or landless workers who were to identify a farm for sale and then take their proposal for its purchase to either a bank or the state-level land agency. The price was to be negotiated directly between buyer and seller, but was subject to the approval of the relevant government agency based on the analysis of the average market price in the region for land of similar location, fertility and potential economic use. In addition, the government agency was to verify that there was a clear title to the property; that the land could be employed in a sustainable manner and that it could be exploited profitably with a minimum of additional investment, generating a sufficient income for the beneficiaries; that the infrastructure, water availability and market access were sufficient; and that the property was of adequate size to accommodate the number of proposed beneficiary families (Buainain *et al.*, 1999).

Once these conditions were met the association would receive a ten-year mortgage (with a three-year grace period) via an intermediary financial institution to purchase the land. The beneficiaries were then eligible for another loan for working capital and for grant funding to cover settlement costs, the purchase of technical assistance, and for social and productive infrastructure investments. The US$90 million World Bank loan to the government was for the financing of the grant component, with the land credit coming from US$60 million in counterpart funding by the Brazilian government. The aim was to benefit 15,000 families over three years (1998–2000) with 400,000 hectares of land (Teófilo *et al.*, 2002).

Even before this experiment in market-led reform was evaluated, negotiations with the World Bank began to extend the programme to other regions of the country, through the creation of a Land Bank (*Banco da Terra*). The Land Bank proposal differed from the *Cédula da Terra* programme in that fighting poverty was not one of its objectives. Thus potential beneficiaries with higher household incomes than allowed under the latter program could participate. Moreover, all the financing was in the form of loans.

From the government's perspective, the market-led programme was attractive primarily due to the continued pressure of the social movements to increase the pace of expropriations in addition to the high costs of these, the latter largely the result of the actions of the judiciary. There was also a favourable context for land market transactions at this point in time due to the fall in land prices as a result of the macro stability engendered by the Plan Real which decreased land prices in some regions to the order of 60 per cent (Reydon and Plata, 2002).

The main voice of opposition to the Land Bank was the National Forum for Agrarian Reform and Justice in the Countryside, a grouping of 32 social movements and non-governmental and religious organisations constituted in 1995. Its members opposed it for slightly different reasons. The opposition of CONTAG was framed in terms of the need to defend land expropriations in the social interest. It also favoured a maximum size limit on landholdings and an end to excessive compensations to expropriated landowners by the judiciary. The MST denounced the Land Bank as a subterfuge to demobilise the rural social movements as well as a travesty, since it would reward landlords for their unjust concentration of land. Moreover, given the power of the landlord class at the state and local level, such devolution of state responsibility for agrarian reform would put land reform precisely in the hands of those who have traditionally opposed it while strengthening traditional patron–client relations.

The forum engaged in a major campaign against the proposed Land Bank, drawing support from international allies opposed to the World Bank model, such as *La Via Campesina* and FIAN (the Foodfirst Information and Action Network), to give visibility and prestige to the campaign. Nationally, Congressional hearings were held and meetings demanded with the World Bank office in Brazil. Finally, the forum requested that the World Bank undertake a formal inspection of the *Cédula da Terra* programme, a mechanism provided for by the bank's charter. Among the main concerns raised by the forum was that the market-led programme would gradually replace traditional reform by expropriation. Another was with respect to the conditions of the land mortgages, for it seemed unlikely that the beneficiaries of these programmes would be able to repay their loans given the crisis facing Brazilian agriculture. In states such as Ceará, Maranhão and Bahia, many of the associations of beneficiaries had been formed at the behest of landowners simply hoping to profit from the state's financing of land transactions. Moreover, there was concern that the programme was having the result of raising land prices, reverting the previous tendency towards their reduction. Finally, another major criticism focused on the lack of participation of the rural workers' organisations in the programme (Wolff and Sauer, 2001; Fox, 2001).

The World Bank turned down the request for an inspection panel for reasons of legal technicality (Fox, 2001). But it did agree to amend the loan agreement so that lands that would otherwise be eligible for expropriation be excluded from the Land Bank programme. At the same time, in the face of the mounting criticism of the Land Bank programme, the bank again pursued the support of CONTAG. Since the mid-1990s CONTAG had supported the idea of a complementary land programme aimed at sharecroppers, renters and smallholders with insufficient land. Key to their demands was that such a programme only encompass lands not subject to expropriation and that, to ensure the viability of the programme, the mortgages be on highly subsidised terms.

The result was a new US$400 million programme entitled the Land Credit and Poverty Reduction Programme (CFCP, *Crédito Fundiário de Combate à Pobreza*), which would only encompass lands not potentially subject to expropriation such as farms less than 15 fiscal modules in size. The new programme targeted the rural poor in 14 states (including all those of the northeast, the three southern states and Minas Gerais and Espírito Santo). The terms of the loans also included subsidised interest rates and incentives for prompt repayment.[3] The programme was to be administered by the state and municipal-level Sustainable Rural Development Councils in which CONTAG participates and aimed to benefit 50,000 families between 2002 and 2004.

The support of CONTAG, an active participant in the forum, was crucial to the legitimisation of the World Bank project. It also resulted in growing tensions between CONTAG and the MST in terms of who had the right to speak on behalf of rural workers and in this context the forum became increasingly fractionalised.

Outcomes of the agrarian reform

As Table 3.1 shows, during the Cardoso regime the number of beneficiaries of redistributive agrarian reform more than doubled compared with

Table 3.1 Agrarian reform beneficiary families by period and region

Region	1964–1994	1995–September 2002
North	135,138 (61.8%)	219,087 (37.8%)
Northeast	41,444 (19.0%)	191,319 (33%)
Centre-west	26,196 (12.0%)	105,549 (18.2%)
Southeast	7,914 (3.6%)	29,083 (5%)
South	7,842 (3.6%)	34,695 (6%)
Total	218,534 (100%)	579,733 (100%)

Source: MDA/INCRA (2002).

Note
Excludes beneficiaries of the land bank and land credit and poverty reduction programmes.

the previous 30 years.[4] The area expropriated since 1964 amounts to approximately 20 million hectares, approximately 6 per cent of the farmland reported in the 1995–1996 agricultural census (MDA/INCRA, 2001). The bulk of this land is located in the north and constitutes land whose tenure was regularised rather than subject to expropriation.

The beneficiary numbers have been hotly disputed (Spavorek, 2003). Moreover, the creation of agrarian reform settlements over the course of the last 20 years has not produced a major change in land tenancy or in the concentration of land (Assuncão, 2006). In their study of six agrarian reform zones in nine states, Leite *et al.* (2004: 67) found that only in one, Pará, did the area in *assentamentos* constitute a significant share of total lands, 25 percent. In the other states, the land settlements represented 5 per cent or less of the total farm area. At best, there has been some change in the structure of landholdings at the local level.

Turning to the beneficiaries of the process, they come from a diverse set of origins: squatters whose right to land was challenged by owners or presumed owners; the children of destitute family farmers who, unable to obtain land through traditional means, opted for joining the occupations and land encampments to reproduce themselves as family farmers; and sharecroppers seeking their own piece of land. In addition, there were farmers displaced by the dams or whose livelihoods were being threatened by deforestation, rural and urban wage workers living in the urban peripheries, as well as retired workers seeking a place to live and access to land to complement their meagre incomes.

Those demanding land were also organised by a diverse group of actors who were often in competition for their loyalties. As already noted, depending on the region and time period, they could be mobilised by the MST or other organisations demanding land rights; by the rural unions; by the different groups organising those affected by the hydroelectric projects; by the CPT, etc. Others were mobilised by local political actors, such as mayors or councilmen who, when confronted with the possibility of the creation of *assentamentos* in their municipalities, jumped into the fray to create political alliances. There were even situations where mayors who, having observed successful *assentamentos* in neighbouring municipalities, organised land occupations in their own in order to encourage the formation of such land settlements for municipal development purposes. Case studies also reveal situations where, given the dynamism of the occupation process, groups of workers organised themselves, without any links to outside movements, and managed to remain autonomous from any organised group (Medeiros, 2002).

Studies of the *assentamentos* suggest that the great majority were constituted as a result of a land conflict. As Leite *et al.* (2004) show, the expropriations ended up being concentrated in certain areas where the occupations had been most densely concentrated. This partly reflects the manner in which the occupations fed on their own success – successful occupations in one area providing a powerful example to others in the region desiring land. Those areas where large numbers of *assentamentos* are concentrated represent what could be called agrarian reform zones.

The absence of planning with respect to the creation of these settlements led to a lack of provision of the necessary infrastructure, even in the areas of greatest *assentamento* concentration. A common characteristic of many of these is that access is a problem due to the precarious road network in the interior of the country, making it difficult for them to access markets. Numerous studies also reveal the precarious state of their access to health and education services (Neto and Bamat, 1998; Bruno and Medeiros, 2001; Spavorek, 2003; Medeiros and Leite, 2004; Leite *et al.*, 2004). Notwithstanding these unfavourable conditions there have been significant, positive changes.

Impact on growth, incomes and the standard of living

The presence of *assentamentos* has generated positive changes at the local, municipal level. Due to the concentration of land settlements in certain municipalities, in some of these an important share of the rural population consists of agrarian reform beneficiaries, which has political repercussions, since their demands for social and physical infrastructure cannot be easily ignored.

The *assentamentos* represent a change in the use of space, transforming areas that once consisted of extensive pastures or of decaying monoculture production. In general, in the areas were *assentamentos* have been created through expropriation, the former farms were unproductive, being either abandoned or at best characterised by a lack of productive dynamism. The constitution of *assentamentos* has usually brought about a diversification of agricultural production and the introduction of new activities. The expansion of the labour market and the increased demand for consumption items has dynamised local commerce, and even the banking sector, in turn contributing to the generation of greater fiscal revenue for the municipalities.

The agrarian reform beneficiaries, besides a plot upon which to grow part of their subsistence requirements, also gain access to a range of other benefits from which they had previously been excluded: funds to build a house, to purchase foodstuffs until the harvests come in, and for working capital.[5] While access to these benefits among the settlements has been uneven, when available, these resources stimulate a number of other local activities (the sale of inputs and agricultural implements, construction materials, small appliances, etc.) and hence economic activity. In addition, the agrarian reform beneficiaries establish a dialogue with the different agencies of the state and financial agents or other intermediaries, notably the Bank of Brazil, whose personnel begin to frequent long-neglected areas, in turn stimulating the demand for local services.

With respect to the organisation of production, the great majority of *assentamentos* are characterised by individual, family-based production. The 1996 agrarian reform census of 1,425 settlements found that 87 per cent of the beneficiaries engaged only in individual production, 5 per cent in collective production, and 8 per cent in a mixture of the two (INCRA/CRUB/UnB, 1998: Table 1.11). The majority of production cooperatives are in the south, as this had been the preferred form of the MST in its initial years. Even though some of these production cooperatives have been quite successful, the idea of collective production has not generally been well received in this or other regions of the country. While the MST leadership continues to favour production cooperatives, it has not insisted upon them, and instead, has promoted other forms of cooperatives, such as for marketing.

In terms of productivity on the *assentamentos*, the results vary significantly by region and crop. Notwithstanding, most studies suggest that the results have generally been satisfactory (Leite *et al.*, 2004: 160–161). In terms of income generation, the standard rural poverty line in Brazil consists of two minimum wages per family (R$/302 or US$100 in 2000).[6] The most rigorous study of income levels on the settlements was carried out by researchers at the National Rural University in Rio de Janeiro on 92 settlements constituted between 1985 and 1997 in six agrarian reform zones (Leite *et al.*, 2004). This survey of 1,568 households found that the mean gross monthly income was R$/312, just slightly above the poverty line. There was tremendous variation by state, with the range being an average R$/117 in Ceará in the northeast to R$/439 in Santa Catarina in the south.

Perhaps more telling is the data on the distribution of incomes. Only one-third of the beneficiaries were above the poverty line, although this is in many ways quite an accomplishment, given the slowness of the state in providing the settlements with the promised assistance. While at the time of the survey, 75 per cent of the beneficiaries had received the promised subsistence subsidy, 81 per cent the production subsidy, and 73 per cent the housing subsidy, on average such assistance was not received until four to five years after the beneficiaries were settled on the land (Leite *et al.*, 2004: Table A3.15).

That two-thirds of the agrarian reform beneficiaries are still poor by conventional measures could lead to the conclusion that not much has been accomplished through the distribution of land. Yet, given the precarious and low standard of living in rural Brazil, all studies have found that beneficiaries consider themselves to be much better off in the *assentamentos* than in their previous situations. Leite *et al.* (2004: Table A7.5) found that almost two-thirds of the beneficiaries considered that they had increased their household incomes on the *assentamentos* compared with what they had previously earned. This improvement in the situation of the beneficiaries is also evident in terms of other indicators of the standard of living, such as the quality of housing, access to electricity and potable water, ownership of small appliances, etc. These findings bolster the argument of the social movements that the best way to tackle hunger and poverty in Brazil is by redistributing land.

Another potential indicator of the relative success of the agrarian reform is in terms of desertion rates on the *assentamentos*. Although these are often reported in the press as being extremely high, there have been few in-depth studies of the process. Most studies report some evidence of families or family members leaving the *assentamentos*, mainly young people who leave in search of educational or employment opportunities or other lifestyles (Leite *et al.*, 2004). Bruno and Medeiros's (2001) study of this process found that among the most frequently cited reasons for abandoning the settlements was their lack of promised infrastructure, the difficulties of transport, lack of access to schooling or health services and the lack of support for agricultural production. Another problem was indebtedness related to the lack of appropriate infrastructure and production support, sometimes combined with the difficulty of adapting to a new logic based on the use of credit. Another factor has been landlord pressure and threats, particularly in areas where not all the land has been regularised. Finally, others have felt abandoned by the state or the social movements once the initial euphoria of gaining access to land had passed and the initially high expectations of life on the settlement not met. These factors are, of course, all interrelated.

Bruno and Medeiros (2001) note that abandonment of the settlements tended to be greater in their initial years, with the population then stabilising. They also caution that abandonment does not necessarily imply that an *assentamento* has failed. While the rate of abandonment is higher on the more precarious settlements, it also takes place on successful ones, as families move on in search of better opportunities once their situation on the *assentamento* has stabilised them economically.

Turning to the political dimension of the process, various studies have shown that the experience of organising around the struggle for land has produced new leaders who, once this objective was achieved, have moved on to struggle for social and political rights (Medeiros and Leite, 2004; Leite *et al.*, 2004). Moreover, just the act of expropriation begins to change relations of power, since landowners – who may or may not be members of the local elite – must negotiate with the state. The constitution of new *assentamentos* in many cases becomes a political event as negotiations take place between the state, the social movements and local governments over who is to become an agrarian reform beneficiary. All of this destabilises traditional clientele relationships which are challenged or renegotiated, although at times they are also reproduced.

Agrarian reform beneficiaries are increasingly standing for local elections as councilmen/women and even mayors. Their participation is evident in civil society, whether in the rural unions, local cooperatives, or councils of various types. To act in these spaces is to have a voice to speak for and as agrarian reform beneficiaries and to gain social legitimacy. In the process, the beneficiaries also contribute to the formation of public opinion. In elected roles they sometimes challenge local elites and change the terms of local politics – as being in favor or against the agrarian reform and the beneficiaries. This process is particularly evident in the regions where the MST is strong due to its recognised ability to train new leaders and prepare them for political and economic debate.

State-led versus market-led reform

As yet no rigorous studies have been carried out comparing redistributive and market-led agrarian reform in even one region of Brazil. Moreover, the latter has yet to be rigorously evaluated. A small household survey of 232 beneficiary families of the *Cédula da Terra* programme was commissioned by NEAD/MDA and the World Bank shortly after this programme was initiated, and this study was often cited by the Cardoso government to argue that the program was a success.[7] A second study, this one at the behest of the organisations comprising the National Forum for Agrarian Reform, was carried out in 2001 (Dias and Sauer, 2002, referred to below as the 'forum study'). Among the main results of the forum study was that the majority of the farms purchased under the project were medium-size farms; in all states, however, some farms had been purchased which were abandoned and above the minimum farm size to be exempt from expropriation. Moreover, the lands purchased under the programme had not been cheap; rather, beneficiaries were paying dearly for poor-quality land. This study highlighted how land prices were often determined politically, such as when landlords or their friends controlled the associations of beneficiaries and in fact determined the price of land, a situation that is also observed in the Philippines (see Borras, Carranza and Reyes, this volume). The study also showed that these associations often have very little autonomy in the process of either land selection or negotiating its price, nor in its final use. Rather, in many cases, traditional patterns of paternalism were being reproduced, a point also emphasised in the Buainain *et al.* (1999) evaluation. This latter study found that half of the associations created in the first stage of the project had been created solely for the purpose of purchasing land and that few of the beneficiaries were aware of the conditions under which they were purchasing land, such as interest rates or that the loan constituted a mortgage (cited in Pereira, 2004).

In his analysis of these studies, Pereira (2004: 172) emphasises the extreme poverty of the beneficiaries and how they were attracted to the programme by the possibility of acquiring land in a period when the social movements were being persecuted and traditional means of becoming an agrarian reform beneficiary seemed remote. Another damning conclusion was that a decentralised agrarian reform is no more efficient than one that is centralised. Government agencies at the local and state level were not delivering on their promises regarding the timely provision of infrastructure or credit. Moreover, access to technical assistance and extension was quite precarious.

The forum study found there to be a fairly high rate of desertion from these projects, in some as high as 50 per cent. The high dropout rate places an even greater burden on those who remain, since they must assume the land debt for the whole property (which is a collective responsibility). The main reason for the high dropout rate in most cases was the lack of minimum conditions for production, related to the poor quality of lands purchased and the dearth of productive infrastructure, combined with insufficient state support. The 2003 study by Buainain *et al.* (cited in Pereira, 2004) also pointed to the high rate of desertion on the projects, particularly of those where the associations had been artificially created.

The forum study concluded that few beneficiaries had improved their standard of living. Moreover, few were engaging in commercial production and thus had little chance of repaying their debt for land and housing. Ironically, in a few cases the local bureaucrats monitoring the process forced the associations to engage in collective production of commercial crops in order to generate income to repay these debts.

The 2003 study by Buainain *et al.* included a household income survey of 313 beneficiaries on projects created between 1997 and 1999. According to this report: 'The families that entered the program today generate an income from agricultural production higher than they did before the project, but that not always is sufficient for their subsistence . . .' (Buainain *et al.*, 2003: 172, cited in Pereira, 2004: 189). This study found that the infrastructure grants had often not been used well, with social infrastructure receiving priority over productive infrastructure, and moreover, that access to technical assistance and production credit continued to be deficient. Notwithstanding these troubling reports, the final 2003 World Bank on the *Cédula da Terra* project was quite upbeat about the possibilities of beneficiaries repaying their loans (cited in Pereira, 2004: 192).

Agrarian reform under the Lula government

In his four bids for the presidency as the candidate of the Workers' Party (PT), Lula's campaign platform always included the need for a large-scale and relatively quick agrarian reform. In his 2002 campaign Lula promised that among his priorities would be an 'ample' agrarian reform as the lynchpin of a new model of rural development (Coligação, 2002: 13). He also projected a vision of how the family farming and agro-export sectors might be complementary, foreseeing the alliances that would eventually constitute his government.

With his inauguration in January 2003, the rural social movements expected agrarian reform to be among his first initiatives. Instead, during his first six months in office Lula gave priority to launching a campaign to end hunger. The rural social movements initially welcomed this initiative, seeing the potential, if it was linked to the deepening of the agrarian reform, for creating a market for *assentamento* production. But they viewed with alarm the fact that INCRA's budget for land acquisition was reduced during 2003 as compared with the last year of the Cardoso administration, and that in the first semester of that year only 9,500 families were settled on *assentamentos* (Zibechi, 2003). Moreover, the technical commission charged with drafting a new National Agrarian Reform Plan (PNRA), promised in Lula's campaign platform, was not appointed until July. The technical commission concluded its work in October and the Lula government accepted most, but not all, of the commission's recommendations, adopting the PNRA-II in November 2003.

The main goal set forth in the PNRA-II is to carry out a sustainable agrarian reform of 'quality'. Thus, while the targeted number of new beneficiaries is relatively modest (400,000 families in four years) compared to the expectations of the rural social movements, the aim is to provide them – as well as previous land reform beneficiaries – with the conditions to assure their sustainable development. Hence the plan places great emphasis on the need for an integral agrarian reform, one that besides land provides the agrarian reform settlements with the needed social and physical infrastructure and access to credit, technical assistance, marketing channels, etc., to assure that the beneficiaries will be able to earn adequate levels of income. The principal means of acquiring land for new settlements was envisioned as expropriation with compensation (MDA, 2003).

Compared with the Cardoso period, the PNRA-II de-emphasises market-based mechanisms of land acquisition. The Land Bank programme had been previously abolished by the Lula government, but in the PNRA-II three different land financing programmes are continued or initiated: the World Bank-funded Land Credit and Poverty Reduction program (the CFCP); a new World Bank-financed programme aimed at enabling rural youth to purchase farms; and a credit line to enable smallholders to expand their holdings and consolidate family farms. The target is for 130,000 families to acquire land through these three modalities over four years. In the PNRA-II these programs are seen as complementary to land reform via expropriation since the state will only finance land purchases of farms under the size limit (15 family modules) potentially subject to expropriation.

The PNRA-II also includes a major land titling program, aiming to give secure titles to 500,000 squatters (*posseiros*) on public lands over four years. In support of this activity, the plan embraces one of the unmet goals of the Cardoso government, to finally develop a comprehensive national land cadastre and registry. A modernised cadastral system is seen as crucial to effectively target lands for expropriation, to prevent further, illegal usurpation of public lands, and to create an effective system of land taxation.

What is novel in the PNRA-II is its emphasis on diversity and social inclusion. Thus its aims include the promotion of gender equality in the agrarian reform process, primarily by making the joint adjudication and titling of lands to couples obligatory irrespective of marital status, and increasing rural women's access to credit. The PNRA-II also reflects the Lula government's commitment to inclusion of under-represented racial and ethnic minorities: it aims to renew efforts to identify and title the historic landholdings of Quilombo communities (formed of runaway slaves in the nineteenth and earlier centuries); promises to continue the process of demarcation of indigenous territories and to give priority to resettling non-indigenous squatters; and gives special attention to the populations that have been displaced by dams and other large infrastructure projects, to the precarious situation of the Amazonian river population, and to furthering the policy of Extractive Reserves for sustainable forestry development in the Amazon.

Another innovation of the PNRA-II is its emphasis on territorial development. Critical of the Cardoso policy of unplanned development, the Lula government intended to resurrect state planning with respect to settlement development. The idea was for the state to take the initiative in identifying areas that are conducive to agricultural development and where large numbers of settlements are already concentrated, channeling state resources to these zones for the dual purpose of developing new *assentamentos* while consolidating earlier ones.

Finally, another important aspect of the Lula government's intended approach to agrarian reform was its overarching concern with creating viable, sustainable agrarian reform settlements that would generate employment, reduce poverty and raise incomes. This theme is not new as evidenced in the policy documents of the Cardoso government. Where it differs, however, is in the Lula government's unprecedented attention to environmental matters as well as a concern with agricultural price and marketing policy as shown in the intended symbiosis between the programme to end hunger and the consolidation of the agrarian reform. The challenge for the Lula government, as with its predecessor, is with implementation.

The PNRA-II and the demands of the rural social movements

The main critique of the rural social movements and the National Forum for Agrarian Reform and Social Justice in the Countryside which encompasses them and other supporters of redistributive agrarian reform, is that the Lula government's agrarian reform will not transform the agrarian structure.[8] In their analysis, Lula could have chosen to change the model of development from one centered on agro-exports and favouring agribusiness, to one focused on the internal market and favouring family-based agriculture. Instead, given the important role played by agro-exports (particularly, soya) in generating a positive trade balance, and Lula's commitment to meeting Brazil's external debt obligations, his government has chosen to continue Cardoso's macro-economic policies and privileged treatment of the export sector while pursuing social policies of inclusion. Thus critics from the Left consider Lula's approach to agrarian reform not significantly different from that of his predecessor, labelling it 'compensatory social policy'.

The rural social movements and progressive critics are, of course, aware of the constraints under which the Lula government is operating. First, it is a coalition government. While Lula was elected with a substantial majority (61.3 per cent of the vote), his coalition does not control the Congress. In order to govern, Lula had to enter into a broad-based alliance which means that among his allies in government are precisely those who have historically been vehemently opposed to agrarian reform. This alliance was reflected in the appointments to Lula's cabinet, with many of the crucial economic positions filled by members of conservative parties, determined to maintain the status quo. Continuity with previous economic policy was maintained although the Minister of Finance, Antonio Palocci, who coordinates economic policy, was a long-time member of the Workers' Party.

Important to our analysis, the Lula government maintained the separation and division of labor between the Ministry of Agriculture and the Ministry of Agrarian Development instituted under the previous government, whereby the former focuses on commercial agriculture (particularly, agro-exports) and the latter on family farming and agrarian reform. A well-known defender of agri-business, Roberto Rodrigues (a former president of the Brazilian Rural Society and former vice-president of the CNA) was appointed Minister of Agriculture. Miguel Rossetto, a representative of a minority tendency within the PT, was appointed Minister of Agrarian Development, while the presidency of INCRA went to a long-standing advocate of redistributive agrarian reform, Marcelo Resende, who had close ties to the progressive wing of the Catholic Church.

Lula's election and just the prospect of a serious agrarian reform effort provoked the ire of large landowners who immediately began to organise to combat land occupations (CPT, 2003). In addition, the mainstream press became even more anti-agrarian reform than usual. A new factor in the political equation is that agro-exporters, who at various times in the past had distanced themselves from the traditional landed oligarchy, in the current conjuncture seem to have come to its defence. According to the MST's João Pedro Stedile, 'the agro-export sector has become main defender of traditional elites because the economic frontier for agro-export production is now the unproductive *latifundio*. With land prices rising in interior, agribusiness is now competing with the rural social movements for potential land.'[9] This competition extends beyond the traditional *latifundio* to include the Amazon forest.

A second major constraint recognised by the social movements is the limited capacity of the state to carry out a massive agrarian reform.[10] Under Cardoso, INCRA was reduced in size from a peak of 12,000 employees in the 1970s to 4,800 currently. Moreover, INCRA personnel were badly demoralised by low pay and the lack of a career track.[11] Other state programmes crucial to the reform effort where either eliminated (such as Lumiar, the state-funded technical assistance program whereby private contractors provided technical assistance to the settlements), or largely privatised (such as CONAB, the state marketing agency). Thus the capacity of the state to both consolidate the existing *assentamentos* and to considerably expand their numbers is questionable.

The scope of the agrarian reform was one of the major points of contention between the Lula government and the rural social movements. In the Plínio proposal it was estimated that the potential demand for land – in terms of the number of families living in extreme poverty – was to the order of 3.3 to 6.1 million (Equipe Técnica, 2003). The effective demand for land was estimated as comprising nearly one million families, taking into account the number in encampments,[12] and that 839,715 families applied for land when the Cardoso government provided them with the opportunity to register as potential beneficiaries through the post office.

The technical team drafting the PNRA-II proposed that in the budgetary planning period 2003–2007 the government aimed to settle one million families. In the PNRA-II, the government adopted a more modest target for 2003–2006, of 400,000 beneficiary families.[13] An additional 150,000 would be settled in 2007, bringing the total for the budgetary planning period running through that year to 550,000 (MDA, 2003: 14), a far cry from the one million demanded by the social movements. The PNRA-II does provide for the families living in the encampments to be among the first settled, thus meeting one of the demands of the rural social movements. Nonetheless, implementing this policy continues to be one of the main points of tension between the social movements and the government.

One of the arguments stressed by Lula's government is that it plans to carry out an integral agrarian reform, one of quality, and that assuring that beneficiaries earn an adequate standard of living is more important than generating a large number of beneficiaries. Critics argue that there is no contradiction between a massive agrarian reform and one of quality for to carry out an agrarian reform of quality, it must in fact be massive, since that is the only way to change the correlation of forces so that public services reach the poor.

There is also the question of whether there is sufficient land of good quality available for a more massive agrarian reform. In the PNRA-II proposal it was estimated that approximately 35 million hectares of land would have to be expropriated to settle one million families, assuming an average of 35 hectares per family (Equipe Técnica, 2003: Table 5.4.2). According to the estimates in that report, 120 million hectares of unproductive land are held by large estates and could be expropriated based on the economic criteria delineated in the federal constitution alone. Some 4.3 million hectares of public land could also be made available for redistribution in addition to 111 million hectares of unclaimed land (*terras devolutas*) – net of that portion presently occupied by squatters with holdings under 100 hectares. Thus the total stock of land potentially available for agrarian reform purposes is to the order of 235 million hectares, more than sufficient to meet the demand for land. The problem is that the location of the demand for and supply of land are not always the same, nor is this land always potentially good agricultural land or located in the targeted agrarian reform zones.

In the proposal, a series of measures were recommended to increase the potential stock of land for agrarian reform purposes, most of which were endorsed in the PNRA-II. The standard of what constitutes unproductive land is based both on the degree of capacity utilisation (80 per cent of a holding) and minimum average yields. The latter criteria were determined in the 1970s and the government proposed to revise these upwards by administrative action. The MDA finally presented its proposal in early 2005, but it requires endorsement by the Ministry of Agriculture and as of April 2006 had still not been approved. Moreover, there was no indication that President Lula was going to intervene in the matter. This means that the possibility for the state to expropriate lands in the more modernised agricultural areas, such as the south and southeast, remains very limited. Hence, the main way that the state can acquire land for agrarian reform purposes in these regions is via expensive land purchases. This is one of the reasons many of the families in encampments have not been settled on new *assentamentos*.

Two measures that would allow land to be expropriated without compensation have been controversial, one focusing on land worked by slave labour and another regarding land where drug crops are discovered. The latter bill was passed, but only after constitutional provisions were watered down so that farms found growing illegal drug crops would not be confiscated, but rather, only the specific land parcels on an estate planted with such crops. The bill authorising confiscation of land worked by slave labour has languished in the Congress and as of April 2006 has not been approved. Given the composition of the Congress, it is doubtful that this measure will ever become law.

The Plínio proposal also gave attention to how the cost of acquiring land through expropriation could be lowered by changing the financing structure of the agrarian reform bonds (the TDAs, *Títulos da Dívida Agrária*). Since 1991 the TDAs have been indexed to the prime rate of the financial market plus a 6 per cent margin, rather than prices in local land markets. This is very favorable to landowners and, of course, has made the agrarian reform more expensive. The proposal to reform the financing structure was incorporated into the PNRA-II, but has not been presented to the congress since it would be opposed by those not interested in discussing the terms of indemnification at all.

One of the major differences between the Plínio proposal and the PNRA-II regards the role of market-led land redistribution. Reflecting the position of the MST and CPT, which led the struggle against the World Bank model, market-led mechanisms of land redistribution are not mentioned in the Plínio proposal. But CONTAG, which negotiated its own market-led programme during the previous administration, was not represented in the technical commission that drafted the proposal. Largely reflecting its demands and other organised groups of small farmers, while the Land Bank programme was eliminated, the CFCP was retained in the PNRA-II.

Implementing the reform

During the Lula government's first year in office only 36,301 families were settled on *assentamentos* (see Table 3.2), many of them families who had begun the process of acquiring land during the previous administration. The slow progess was due to a number of factors, among them budgetary concerns. The Lula government was committed to generating a budget surplus to meet (and even surpass) IMF targets and thus funds for land

Table 3.2 Targeted number of beneficiary families and numbers settled

	Target	Actual
Via land settlements		
2003	30,000	36,301
2004	115,000	81,254
2005	115,000	127,506
2006	140,000	–
Total	400,000	245,061 (to date)
Via land credit		
2003	17,500	9,138
2004	37,500	6,466
2005	37,500	8,142
2006	37,500	–
Total	130,000	23,746 (to date)

Notes and sources
For targets, MDA (2003); for land settlements, Brasil (2006). The data on the land credit programme was provided to the authors by Caio Galvão de França, Coordinador General, NEAD, 11 January 2006. Brasil (2006) only reports a total, three-year figure of 24,500 for this programme.

acquisition were slashed in 2003 along with funding for a number of other social programs, with priority given to expenditures on the anti-hunger campaign. Equally important were disagreements within Lula's own team over the pace and content of the agrarian reform.

In response to pressure from the rural social movements, in July of that year, besides developing the National Agrarian Reform Plan, President Lula promised to step up land redistribution measures and that the budget for land acquisition in 2004 would be the largest in the history of the agrarian reform. Lula made good on his promises, with the initial 2004 MDA budget increasing substantially from the previous year, to R$1.4 billion. But to make sure that the pace of agrarian reform actions did, indeed, pick up, the MST increased its land occupations in April, with 109 taking place that month, bringing the total to a near record 165 occupations for the first trimester of 2004.[14] By then, the lack of financing was not the major constraint. Rather, the capacity of the state to execute the agrarian reform seemed a more formidable barrier. This is evident in that through the end of 2004, the Lula government had only settled 117,555 families, 81 per cent of the targeted number. In 2005 the pace finally did pick up, and an additional 127,506 families became agrarian reform beneficiaries. This favourable result was also due to the intense pressure of the rural social movements, which in April of that year had carried out another 'Red April' with simultaneous occupations nationwide.

All told, the Lula government claimed that by the end of 2005 it had met 94 per cent of the target set forth with respect to agrarian reform beneficiaries in the PNRA-II (see Table 3.2). With an average of 81,687 families settled per year in the 2003–2005 period, it has exceeded the pace of the reform under the Cardoso government, which had been 67,588 families annually. Moreover, it boasts that it has acquired more land for agrarian reform purposes, 22.5 million hectares, than in the eight years of the Cardoso government (19.6 million) (Brasil, 2006).

As in previous periods, the number of families actually benefiting through the agrarian reform has been a source of contention. The MST contends that the government's numbers include families whose land titles have been 'regularised' (particularly in the north, were squatters predominate) or have been resettled due to the construction of dams who are not real agrarian reform beneficiaries, as well as families settled on vacant lots in existing settlements rather than in new agrarian reform settlements. They draw attention to the fact that the new beneficiaries include few of those waiting for land in the encampments.[15]

In addition, while the Lula government may have acquired more land for agrarian reform purposes than the previous government, critics such as Teixeira (2006) and de Oliveira (2006) contend that the majority of this land is public land. Reportedly, only 8.7 per cent of the 22.5 million hectares acquired by INCRA has been acquired through expropriation. Moreover, they argue that less land has actually been acquired through expropriation under Lula (1.9 million hectares) than in the last three years of the Cardoso government (2.1 million hectares). Further, much of the land acquired by the Lula government for land settlements is in the Amazon region, specifically in Pará where land conflicts have intensified in recent years as a result of the expansion of soya production.

With respect to territorial planning, as of 2005, 107 such zones had been identified (MDA/SDT, 2006). Nonetheless, it has been as difficult for the Lula government as for its predecessor to take the initiative in planning new settlement development. As various studies have shown, it is only in specific areas with very particular conditions where something approximating planned reformed areas exist, primarily as a result of the intense pressure of the rural social movements.

Turning to the process of support for the beneficiaries, in 2003, 192,430 families received their installation grants, with many of these being families settled during the Cardoso period who never received any of the initial financing due them at all (MDA, 2004). In 2004, the value invested per family more than doubled, but the number of families receiving installation credits was smaller – 43,905 – leading the social movements to increase their pressure on the government (MDA/INCRA, 2005b). Data on the availability of installation credits during 2005 is not yet available.

The land credit programme got off to a slow start primarily because, in response to the criticisms of the previous programme, the Lula government decided to review the terms of financing and what could be financed under the various credit lines, in addition to extending the programme in several innovative directions. The legislation orienting the programme, approved in March 2004, lowered the cost of the credit for land purchases from between 30 to 50 per cent, depending on the region and the income level of the beneficiaries. The grant portion of the financing (for the CFCP as well as the youth program) may now include six months' worth of subsistence expenses for the beneficiary family, technical assistance, and investments in productive infrastructure including environmentally oriented investments. As an incentive to make sure these groups negotiate the lowest possible purchase price, the amount of grant funding is determined by the gap between state-oriented land prices for the region and the negotiated sales price.

Also, the land credit programme is a decentralised programme, overseen by the local and state-level Sustainable Rural Development Councils. While the Secretariat for Agrarian Reordering of the MDA monitors the programme, it can do little about the pace of implementation which ultimately depends on the ability of the rural social movements and local NGOs to organise groups of workers to initiate the search for suitable land to purchase.

Enthusiasm for the land credit programme and its various components varies by state. For example, interest in the youth programme and the consolidation of the family farming programme is greatest in the south, and it is in this region where these programmes were targeted to begin. Also, the land credit programme has considerable support from the farmers' union FETRAF-SUL (*Federação da Agricultura Familiar Sul*) in this region, a union formed in 2001.[16] As of December 2005, 24,500 families had benefited through the CFCP programme (Brasil, 2006) (see Table 3.2). The target in the PNRA-II had been to benefit 92,500 through this programme by the end of 2005, suggesting that it is the land credit programmes rather than redistributionary agrarian reform which the Lula government has been slow to implement.

Turning now to the programs that potentially benefit all groups of family farmers – settlers on the *assentamentos*, beneficiaries of the land credit programmes, and traditional family farmers – PRONAF financing for production and investment costs[17] has increased considerably under the Lula government.[18] The government also resumed state-financed technical assistance to the *assentamentos*, funding that concluded in 2000 when the Cardoso government ended the Lumiar programme of decentralised technical assistance. Discussions between the rural social movements and ministry officials on the form and content of technical assistance resulted in consensus that it had to move away from the top-down approach of the past to include the active participation of the beneficiaries as well as respect for traditional practices that are often more ecologically benevolent. By the end of 2004, 427,419 families had received technical assistance, with this figure increasing to 450,700 during 2005 (Brasil, 2006).

Finally, another initiative of the Lula government which should assist in the consolidation of the *assentamentos* and that is supportive to family farming is the national electrification programme. By the end of 2005 some 75,100 families on the *assentamentos* had benefited through this programme which includes free home connections and service, and it is expected that electrification will reach all existing agrarian reform land settlements by the end of 2006 (ibid., 2006).

In sum, while the agrarian reform of the Lula government has not been a failure, it has been a disappointment to the rural social movements. The insufficiency of resources, the frailty of INCRA, the formidable legal obstacles to expropriations, have produced a meager process of agrarian reform, particularly when compared with the expectations generated during the electoral campaign. While the rural social movements are not happy with the pace or scope of the agrarian reform, they also recognise that much has changed with a PT government – a government they helped to elect.[19]

Among the main changes is that the actions of the social movements are no longer 'criminalised' as under the Cardoso government. Rather, there is an implicit understanding that the social movements will keep up their pressure to ensure that the agrarian reform be implemented, but that their actions will take place within the confines of the law. The various repressive decrees of the Cardoso government have not been lifted, although the Lula government has not really enforced them. For example, land that is occupied will still not be subject to INCRA inspection (*vistoria*) until two years have passed and those that take part in a land or building occupation continue to be ineligible as potential beneficiaries. The MST has been careful to make sure that occupations take place on public lands, outside the boundaries of private property, as they began to do in the latter years of the Cardoso government.

Another important change is that the rural social movements and the segment of civil society championing agrarian reform are recognised by the Lula government as important actors and even partners in defining state policies with respect to the reform. There is an ongoing dialogue between the state and the social movements on such issues as credit, technical assistance, and the content of adult education.[20] Nonetheless, a number of important issues still remain to be resolved.

Pending issues

Gender and land rights

In the mid-1990s women comprised only 12.6 per cent of agrarian reform beneficiaries (INCRA/CRUB/UnB, 1998). While women were often active in the land takeovers and played an important role in the encampments, once the settlements were constituted, women tended to retreat into traditional gender roles with low rates of participation in the *assentamento* organisations (Neto and Bamat, 1998). This lack of participation was increasingly linked to women's lack of direct land rights, particularly the failure of the reform to grant joint titles to couples (Deere, 2003).

In his campaign platform, Lula pledged to end the discrimination against women in the agrarian reform program through the use of affirmative action (Coligação, 2002). Even before the PNRA-II was adopted, in October 2003, an INCRA norm made the joint adjudication and titling of land to couples mandatory, irrespective of their marital status.[21] Moreover, the norm also established that in the case of separation or divorce, wives and female partners who maintained custody of the children be given priority in terms of retaining their land rights. In such cases their husbands or male partners would be given priority as potential beneficiaries in another *assentamento*. These innovative principles were reaffirmed in the PNRA-II (MDA, 2003).

The Cardoso government had also endorsed the mandatory joint adjudication and titling of land to couples and a resolution of the National Council for Sustainable Rural Development had established the principle of non-discrimination in order to encourage the incorporation of women as beneficiaries of the reform. While the 2001 norm was less explicit than that adopted in 2003 by the Lula government, under Cardoso the newly created Affirmative Action Office of the MDA had begun revising the various beneficiary application forms to ensure that when a couple applied for and received land it was in the name of both adults in the family. All the forms were revised in that period except for the most crucial one – entering the beneficiary in the *assentamento* cadastre (the *Relação de Beneficiários*) – and thus joint titling remained illusive (Deere, 2003).

The Lula government's Office for the Promotion of Gender, Race and Ethnic Equality in the MDA faces a similar problem: resistance within INCRA to changing the current practice of entering only one name in the information system of agrarian reform beneficiaries. Thus, it remains impossible to ascertain if couples are indeed the joint beneficiaries; moreover, the system still does not even generate data on the sex of the beneficiaries.

Another challenge in ending the discrimination against women in the agrarian reform is that the Lula government has yet to give attention to the situation of female household heads. They have been considerably under-represented among the agrarian reform beneficiaries thus far (Deere, 2002) and it will probably take strong affirmative action measures – such as giving them priority over other applicants – to significantly increase their numbers.[22] The incorporation of female household heads as beneficiaries is currently one of the demands of CONTAG (CONTAG, 2004).

The Lula government has taken steps to address one of the long-standing demands of the rural women's movement – their lack of official documentation – which constitutes a precondition for greater numbers of women to be incorporated into the reform as direct beneficiaries since personal and/or work documents are necessary to receive land or credit. Finally, the Lula government seeks to increase rural women's access to credit. Thus far a new credit line has been set up for them through PRONAF which can be used for agricultural or non-agricultural activities related to food processing.

Land titling and the cadastre

Two major components of the PNRA-II involve a land titling program to benefit squatters and the development of a national land cadastre and registration system.[23] Inter-American Development Bank financing was sought for the national land cadastre and registration system (a US$260 million project), to be initiated as a three-year pilot programme in five states (MDA/INCRA, 2004).[24] A much scaled-down programme (a US$18 million project, with an $10.8 million IADB loan) was finally approved in late 2005. It will be coordinated by the MDA's Secretariat of Agrarian Reordering in cooperation with INCRA and the state governments. Current targets include surveying and registering 144,000 farms, and titling an additional 44,500 between 2005 and 2007 in five states (MDA/Crédito Fundiário, 2006).

Both programmes are supported by the rural social movements since they are seen as important in potentially reducing the degree of rural violence (often associated with the dispossession of squatters) and, in the case of the cadastre, in establishing the basis for a more ample agrarian reform.[25] In contrast to other Latin American countries, the cadastre may not be in the interest of the landholding class, given the large extensions of land in Brazil that have been usurped illegally over the centuries and continue to be so with the rapid expansion of soya production on the agrarian frontier.

There is general agreement that both programmes will be difficult to implement, given the lack of a trained cadre within the state. This makes it likely that the programmes will be decentralised and potentially carried out by private contractors. This possibility is of concern to PT officials, since they worry about the power of the landlord class at the local level and its ability to manipulate the local judges and land registries to serve its interests.[26]

The cost of land

One of the achievements of the Cardoso regime was the return of relative price stability as the Plan Real of 1995 reduced double-digit inflation. This had the expected impact on land prices, reducing them by 60 per cent in some regions, as it became less attractive to hold unproductive land as a hedge against inflation (Reydon and Plata, 2002). Even though the Lula government has continued Cardoso's macro-economic policies, there are indications that the price of land is rising again in many regions, partly related to the soya boom in the central and central-west area of the country. The average price of land paid by INCRA increased sharply in 2003 and more than doubled in the first half of 2004 (to $R1,231 per hectare).[27] While this figure obscures wide variation in the price of land by region and state, it clearly has increased the cost per family settled on the *assentamentos*, which tripled between 2001 and 2004. This trend does not bode well for the future of the agrarian reform.

Revising the productivity index

A major constraint in expanding the scope of agrarian reform is that under current criteria there is a dwindling number of farms, particularly in desirable agricultural regions, which can be potentially expropriated for not meeting productivity criteria. The current index is woefully out of date, having been constructed on the basis of the 1975 Agricultural Census at a time when the process of modernisation of Brazilian agriculture was only commencing. The Lula government's proposal is to revise these criteria in accordance with the 1996 Agricultural Census, which is already out of date. Notwithstanding, this proposal has been strongly contested by landowners and the Ministry of Agriculture and the Lula government has not demonstrated the political will to overcome their opposition.

The inability to implement this revision has exacerbated the tensions between the government and the rural social movements, since the lands that the government has been able to expropriate are often severely degraded, with minimal infrastructure and poor access to markets in regions with low agricultural potential. This has increased the costs of creating viable agrarian reform settlements and meant that increasingly, the lands made available for new settlements are not the ones that have been occupied by the social movements and where their encampments have been located.

Conclusion

Viewed historically, one of the main lessons of the Brazilian agrarian reform is that its pace has largely depended on the intensity of the struggle for land combined with the degree of repression that any particular government was willing to tolerate. In the context of redemocratisation of the country, a window of opportunity was created for a new form of struggle, the land occupations. There is little question but that the refinement of this form of land struggle by the MST in the 1980s and 1990s was the compelling force behind the land reform efforts of the Cardoso government, leading to the largest redistribution of land in favour of the landless in Brazilian history to that moment. Moreover, even under the Lula government, the pace of agrarian reform has largely depended on the degree of pressure from below.

Notwithstanding the significant land redistribution efforts of the past two decades, these have been insufficient either to meet the effective demand for land or to change Brazil's agrarian structure. Moreover, even if Lula had adopted the target of one million beneficiaries under his agrarian reform plan, this would also have been insufficient to make a significant dent on the concentration of land in this huge country. It would take a truly massive effort to change the distribution of land ownership and in particular, the model of development. The more immediate problem is that the Lula government has been unable to satisfactorily meet its own modest targets.

There are significant constraints on the agrarian reform moving forward in the current period, not the least of which is the correlation of forces between those favouring and opposing agrarian reform. The key role of agri-business to the health of the Brazilian economy has created an impasse in terms of broadening the scope of the reform in two ways. On the one hand, it has led to the commitment by the Lula government to maintain neoliberal economic policies even though the impact of these policies run counter to the PT's professed programme of social inclusion and land and income redistribution. On the other hand, favourable policies and high international prices have strengthened the agro-export sector in ways that make it less disposed toward agrarian reform than in the past. To the extent that the agro-export sector and the landless compete for the lands of the unproductive *latifundia*, the correlation of forces moves against agrarian reform. This unfavourable correlation means that the government's hands are often tied or that it would take much greater political will (such as in the case of the productivity indices) in terms of enacting legislation to facilitate a broader reform or even greater efficiency in its actions.

Another major constraint has been the state's incapacity to undertake an integral agrarian reform. The Brazilian case shows that it is not an easy matter to rebuild the state after a period of neoliberal governance, given the propensity of the latter to privatise and strip away state functions. Moreover, the Lula government has an ambitious land policy agenda, in many ways trying to do everything at once: social inclusion and an integral reform, redistributive and market-led agrarian reform, land titling and a national land registry, all of which require substantial human and financial resources. The government has found it difficult, for example, to move forward on planned territorial development, with most potential expropriations still being the result of the actions of the rural social movements.

But the Lula government can point to a number of accomplishments. In the international arena, Lula has effectively lobbied for the opening of international agricultural markets to favour Brazil's agro-exports; his discourse and actions, however, have been different from those of his predecessor. For example, the MDA now participates in international trade delegations and negotiations and incorporates themes relevant to family agriculture. Moreover, reflecting the importance that he places on supporting a strong domestically oriented agricultural sector, Lula has argued for the right of Third World countries to maintain control over their domestic agricultural policies in order to favour those sectors potentially harmed by trade agreements and free trade.[28] And he has put this into practice in Brazil by significantly increasing the amount of subsidised agricultural credit made available to family farmers.

With respect to the *assentamentos*, the Lula government has also made progress in meeting the deficit with respect to promised infrastructure and installation credits inherited from the previous government. Along with increasing the level of production and investment credit made available to agrarian reform beneficiaries and other family farmers, he has revamped the system of technical assistance – the latter a necessary measure to assure that credit is utilised effectively. And he has increased the role of the state in the marketing of basic foodstuffs, measures that have favoured the family farming sector.

Since Brazil is one of the few countries carrying out both redistributive as well as market-led agrarian reform (see Moyo for Zimbabwe and Borras *et al.* for the Philippines, this volume), it provides a unique setting to analyse the potential of these competing approaches through a poverty reduction and gender equity lens. Can these in fact be complementary, resulting in more land being available for redistribution and in a greater number of beneficiaries than would otherwise be the case?

A rigorous comparative framework is needed to be able to assess the relative efficacy of redistributive versus market-led agrarian reform. As a minimum, such a study requires the selection of settlements under similar productive conditions in the same municipality, with controls for the age of the settlement and the level and timing of state assistance. Such a study would be useful in answering the question of whether beneficiaries of the market-led programme will be able to repay their land debts and the impact of doing so on the welfare of beneficiary households. A comparative framework would also be useful in studying the problem of abandonment on the various types of settlements, a topic that requires much further analysis, particularly as it relates to the different forms of indebtedness and the lack of provision of adequate infrastructure.

Brazil also offers a unique opportunity to study different kinds of agrarian reform settlements according to the manner in which they were formed and how this relates to their social cohesiveness and sustainability.[29] First, how do settlements formed via encampments under the leadership of the MST, CONTAG, the CPT and other land rights organisations differ among themselves due to the specific characteristics of these organisations? Second, how do those settlements characterised by strong grassroots participation in the struggle for land differ from those organised for the purpose of purchasing land at the behest of either local-level elites or NGOs (the *Cédula da Terra*) or CONTAG (the CFCP). Advocates of the decentralised, market-led reform argue that one of its benefits is 'self-selection' since only those with the skills and dedication for farming will come forward to buy land and take on a mortgage, but have given little attention to the process through which these associations are formed and whether they have the internal cohesiveness to function as a community.

Little research has been done comparing welfare outcomes on settlements constituted as production cooperatives with those characterised by individual family farming. What makes the Brazilian case particularly interesting is that the decision to form a production cooperative has not been imposed by agrarian reform planners 'from above' as in the Latin American agrarian reforms of the past. Rather, their promotion has been at the behest of the MST with relatively little special assistance from the state. Moreover, besides facilitating the provision of infrastructure and other public goods, a number of production cooperatives have successfully developed agro-industrial activities, thus diversifying incomes and generating employment opportunities for family members such as women and youths. A more systematic study is also needed of the various forms of potential cooperation, ranging from loosely organised associations, to credit and service and marketing cooperatives.

The fact that joint titling of couples as beneficiaries of the reform is just being implemented provides a unique moment to study the impact of this policy on women's participation within the *assentamentos*. The sharp drop in women's participation from the encampment stage to when the land settlements are constituted and their associations formed has frequently been noted. Will joint titling and the legal right to be a member of the association, with voice and vote, make a difference, not only in terms of women's participation in the community but also in the outcomes on the *assentamento*? What kinds of mechanisms or policies enhance women's greater participation? Will women's enhanced land rights impact upon household decision-making, bringing about positive changes in gender relations and in the welfare of women and children?

Rural standards of living in Brazil continue to remain abysmally low. It is in this context where agrarian reform can be a successful poverty reduction strategy, particularly in terms of raising rural standards of living, if not income levels across the board. In the context of a lack of alternative labour market opportunities, the land reform settlements provide a place to live and raise a few animals, and through organisation, the possibility of obtaining some minimal state services. It is notable that the great majority of agrarian reform beneficiaries consider that they are better off, even when the state has been slow to deliver on its promises. The dilemma is that generating the conditions for self-sustaining rural communities is not cheap and will continue to require a significant state role, a challenge for any government pursuing neoliberal policies.

Notes

1 In the Land Statute landholdings were defined as follows: *minifundios* (farms less than one rural module) and, hence, by definition incapable of generating the average level of subsistence necessary for a rural family; *latifundios* by utilisation (properties between 1 and 600 rural modules whose level of productivity was less than the regional average); *latifundios* by size (properties larger than 600 modules, irrespective of type or productive characteristics); and enterprises (farms between 1 and 600 modules), with the module defined regionally taking into account land quality, climate and the prevailing technology (Campagnole, 1969).

2 Brazilian legislation requires beneficiaries to pay for their land, but over a lengthy period and only once the state has provided them with the necessary infrastructure to be able to do so, including schools, health facilities, physical infrastructure, etc.

3 This programme allows for individual land mortgages, but individuals are not eligible for the grant component of the programme. For groups, as in the *Cédula da Terra* programme, there is a flexible grant/loan financing mechanism, with the funds not used to purchase land constituting a grant for

infrastructure and other costs. It is this latter portion that is funded through the US$200 million World Bank loan. The state's US$200 million share of the programme finances the 20-year mortgages of the beneficiaries at an interest rate of 6 per cent.

4 In addition to the 580,000 families that gained land through redistributionary agrarian reform, 51,608 gained land through the Land Bank and 3,694 through the Land Credit and Poverty Reduction Programme (MDA/INCRA, 2002).

5 The PROCERA programme provided subsidised credit to the *assentamentos* for the purchase of inputs and implements. While coverage of the *assentamentos* was quite spotty, it was due to the persistent demands of the settlers that the government slowly increased the total amount of resources made available through this program. The downside of the programme is that even subsidised credit proved too expensive for many of the precarious *assentamentos*, and in other cases there was over-borrowing with respect to repayment possibilities, leading to growing levels of indebtedness.

6 In 2000 the rural poor in Brazil made up 47.5 per cent of the total poor (Banco Mundial, 2001).

7 The official evaluations of the *Cédula da Terra* programme were carried out by a team at the State University of Campinas, led by economist Antonio Márcio Buainain. The results are summarised in Buainain *et al.* (2000), a very laudatory report.

8 Authors' interviews. Also, for the critiques from the Left, see Carvalho (2004) and Canuto and Balduíno (2004).

9 Interview with João Pedro Stedile, MST, São Paulo, 28 September 2004.

10 See Stedile (2004) and Sampaio (2004) on this point.

11 Interview with José Vaz Parente, president of the INCRA Workers' Union, 21 July 2004.

12 In March 2003 there were 171,288 families in encampments, a figure that rose to approximately 200,000 in the first half of 2004.

13 This target was considered ambitious enough since it would involve settling an average 100,000 families per year, a higher rate than the number of families settled annually (65,547) during the eight years of the Cardoso government.

14 The record was set in 1999, when 265 land occupations were reported (MDA/INCRA 2004a).

15 See de Oliveira (2006) for a flavour of this controversy.

16 FETRAF-SUL is made up of small farmers organised by the progressive union forces once affiliated with the rural department of the CUT. Their social origins are similar to those in the MST in this region, being pauperised family farmers whose political formation was at the behest of the Catholic Church. In 2005 FETRAF became a national-level organisation and began challenging CONTAG in many regions.

17 On the different credit lines made available through PRONAF, which have been expanded under the Lula government, see PRONAF (2003).

18 Figures differ in the various studies, however, on by how much ((MDA, 2005; Christoffoli, 2006). Christoffoli argues that, while PRONAF credit overall has increased under Lula, the share going to agrarian reform beneficiaries has decreased. Moreover, the lion's share of credit (both state and private) continues to go to agro-business.

19 As put to us by one MST leader, the dilemma is 'how to be against the model without being against the government'. Interview with Gerardo Flores, MST National Office, São Paulo, 27 July 2004.

20 Interviews with Gilberto Portes, National Forum for Agrarian Reform, Brasilia, 20 July 2004, and Manoel dos Santos, president of CONTAG, Brasilia, 20 July 2004.

21 Portaria INCRA No. 981 of 3 October 2003 in Portal NEAD de Estudos Agrários, '*Notícias Agrárias*', No. 205, 6–12 October, 2003, www.nead.org.br.

22 Moreover, the new guidelines for the selection of agrarian reform beneficiaries leave in place two criteria that in other countries have tended to discriminate against female household heads since these households are usually missing an adult male (Deere and León, 2001): the granting of more points to candidates with large families and those with the largest number of working members. See INCRA, '*Norma de Execução*', No. 38, 30 March 2004 in *Diário Oficial da União*, No. 85, 5 May 2004: 53.

23 See Teófilo *et al.* (2002) on the efforts under the Cardoso government and the problems in consolidating the various state registries into a national land registration system and developing a modern cadastre. The Cardoso government did make progress in identifying illegally held as well as abandoned lands. In 1999 INCRA issued Portaria 558 which required large properties to re-register their properties in the INCRA land registry. Some 3,065 large properties were notified of this requirement and 1,899 did not respond; as a result 62.7 million hectares reverted to the state. Law No. 10.267 of 2001 created the new, unified National Land Registry System, to be based on a modern cadastre (MDA/INCRA, 2004).

24 Interview with João Leonel dos Anjos, Secretariat of Agrarian Reorganisation, MDA, Brasília, 26 July 2004.

25 Interview with Gerardo Flores, MST, São Paulo, 28 July 2004. Also see CONTAG (2004: pt. 11–13).

26 Interview with Rolf Hackbart, president of INCRA, Brasilia, 21 July 2004.

27 Data made available to the authors by INCRA, November 2004.

28 This point was made by Caio França, director of NEAD, at the Seminar on Public Policies held at CPDA/UFRRJ, 24 November 2004.

29 Carvalho (1998) offers an insightful conceptual framework for analysing different forms of associations under the Brazilian agrarian reform, emphasising the factors that contribute to their social cohesiveness.

References

Assunção, J. (2006). 'Land Reform and Landholdings in Brazil.' Paper prepared for the WIDER-UN Conference on Personal Assets from a Global Perspective, Helsinki, May 4–6.

Banco Mundial (2001). *O Combate a Pobreza no Brasil*. Vol. I. Washington, DC: Departamento do Brasil, Setor de Redução da Pobreza e Manejo Econômico, Região da América Latina e do Caribe.

Brasil, Governo Federal (2006). *Relatório de 36 Meses de Governo: Reforma Agrária.* www.brazil.gov.br/noticias/publicacoes/publicac_teste (downloaded 22 March 2006).

Bruno, R. and L. Medeiros (2001). 'Índices e causas da evasão nos assentamentos.' Brasilia: FAO/INCRA.

Buainain, A. M. *et al.* (1999). 'Relatório Preliminar de Avaliação do Projeto Cédula da Terra.' Brasília: NEAD.

Buainain, A. M., J. M. da Silveira and E. Teófilo (2000). 'O Programa Cédula da Terra no Contexto das Novas Políticas de Reforma Agrária, Desenvolvimento e Participação: Uma Discussão das Transformações Necessárias e Possíveis,' in Ministério do Desenvolvimento Agrário, ed., *Reforma Agrária e Desenvolvimento Sustentável*, pp. 157–174. Brasília: Ministério do Desenvolvimento Agrária.

Campanhole, A. (1969). *Legislação Agrária*, 3rd edn. Sao Paulo: Atlas.

Canuto, A. and T. Balduíno (2004). 'Reforma Agrária Ontem e Hoje.' Comissão Pastoral da Terra. www.cptnac.com (downloaded 10 June 2004).

Cardoso, F. H. (1994). *Mãos à Obra, Brasil: Proposta de Governo.* Brasilia: Cardoso 2004 presidential campaign document.

Carvalho F. J. Juliano (2004). 'Reforma Agrária: A Proposta e uma Coisa, o Plano do Governo e Outra.' Interview, *Revista Sem Terra*, January–February, pp. 23–28.

Carvalho, M. de (1998). 'Formas de Associativísmo Vivenciadas pelos Trabalhadores Rurais nas Áreas Oficias de Reforma Agrária no Brasil,' Instituto Interamericano de Cooperação para a Agricultura y Ministério Extraordinário de Política Fundiária. August 1998, in www.incra.gov.br/projetos/nead (downloaded 28 March 2003).

Christoffoli, P. I. (2006). 'A Evolução Recente da Questão Agrária e os Limites das Políticas Públicas do Governo Lula para o Meio Rural.' Mimeo, Sustainable Development Department, University of Brasilia.

Coligação Lula Presidente (2002). *Vida Digna no Campo. Programa de Governo 2002 Coligação Lula Presidente.* Sao Paulo: Coligação Lula Presidente.

CONTAG-FETAGs-STRs (2004). *Pauta do Grito da Terra Brasil 2004.* Brasilia: CONTAG.

CPT (Comissão Pastoral da Terra) (2003). 'Nota da XVI Assembléia da CPT' (3 April 2003). www.cpt.org.br.

de Oliveira, A. U. (2006). 'A "Não Reforma Agrária do" MDA/INCRA no Governo Lula.' Paper presented to the parallel meeting of Vía Campesina at the FAO International Conference on Agrarian Reform and Rural Development, Porto Alegre, 7–10 March.

Deere, C. D. (2002). 'Diferenças Regionais na Reforma Agrária Brasileira: Gênero, Direitos à Terra e Movimientos Sociais Rurais," Estudos Sociedade e Agricultura (Rio de Janeiro), No. 18, pp. 112–146.

Deere, C. D. (2003). 'Women's Land Rights and Rural Social Movements in the Brazilian Agrarian Reform,' *Journal of Agrarian Change*, vol. 3, nos 1 and 2, pp. 257–288.

Deere, C. D. and M. León (2001). *Empowering Women: Land and Property Rights in Latin America.* Pittsburgh: University of Pittsburgh Press.

Dias Victor, A. and S. Sauer (2002). *Estudo Sobre a Política do Banco Mundial para o Setor Agrário Brasileiro com Base no Caso do Projeto Cédula da Terra.* Research report. CPT/MST/Rede Brasil sobre Instituições Financeiras Multilaterais/FIAN-Brazil.

Equipe Técnica (2003). *Proposta de Plano Nacional de Reforma Agrária. Apresentada ao MDA pela equipe técnica encarregada da sua formulação.* Brasilia: MDA, October.

Fox, J. (2001). 'O Painel de Inspeção do Banco Mundial: Lições dos Cinco Primeiros Anos', in F. Barros, org., *Banco Mundial, Participação, Transparência e Responsabilização. A Experiência Brasileira com o Painel de Inspeção.* Brasilia: Rede Brasil.

Grzybowski, C. (1987). *Caminhos e Descaminhos dos Movimientos Sociais no Campo.* Petrópolis: Vozes.

INCRA/CRUB/UnB (1998). 'Primeiro Censo da Reforma Agrária do Brasil.' Brasilia: Ministério Extraordinário de Política Fundiaria.

Leite, S. *et al.* (2004). *Impactos dos Assentamentos. Um Estudo Sobre o Meio Rural Brasileiro.* Sao Paulo: Edunesp e Nead.

MDA (Ministério do Desenvolvimento Agrário) (2003). *Plano Nacional de Reforma Agrária. Proposta. (PNRA-II).* Photocopy. Brasilia: MDA, November.

MDA (2005). 'O Maior Plano Safra da História,' Noticias. Artigos do Ministro, 6 June 2005. www.mda.gov.br (downloaded 2 August 2005).

MDA/INCRA (2001). 'Balanço da Reforma Agrária e da Agricultura Familiar 2001.' www.incra.gov.br (downloaded 29 July 2003).

MDA/INCRA (2002). 'Balanço da Reforma Agrária e da Agricultura Familiar 2002.' www.incra.gov.br (downloaded 29 July 2003).

MDA/INCRA (2004). 'A Lei 10.267/01 e Seus Reflexos na Gestão Fundiária Brasileira.' Internal report. Brasilia: INCRA, July 2004.

MDA/INCRA (2005a). 'Em Dois Anos, Governo Criou Projetos de Assentamentos em 9 Milhões de Hectares.' *Boletim da Terra*, n.d., p. 1. www.incra.gov.br (downloaded 2 August 2005).

MDA/INCRA (2005b). 'Saneamento e Moradia Digna Fortalecem a Reforma Agrária.' *Boletim da Terra*, n.d., p. 4. www.incra.gov.br (downloaded 2 August 2005).

MDA/INCRA (2005c). 'Maioria dos Assentamentos Já Tem Assistencia Técnica.' *Boletim da Terra*, n.d., p. 3. www.incra.gov.br (downloaded 2 August 2005).

MDA/INCRA (2005d). 'Energia Elétrica Leva Inclusão Social para os Assentados.' *Boletim da Terra*, n.d., p. 4. www.incra.gov.br (downloaded 2 August 2005).

MDA/Program Nacional de Credito Fundiário (2006). 'Cadastro e regularização fundiária.' www.creditofundiario.org.br/principal/pcrf (downloaded 8 April 2006).

MDA/SDT (2006). 'Territórios Apoiados Pelo MDA.' www.mda.gov.br/sdt (downloaded 22 March 2006).

Medeiros, L. S. de (1989). *História dos Movimentos Sociais no Campo*. Rio de Janeiro: FASE.

Medeiros, L. S. de (2002). *Movimientos Sociais, Disputas Políticas e Reforma Agrária de Mercado no Brasil*. Rio de Janeiro: Editora da Universidade Rural and UNRISD.

Medeiros, L. S. de and S. Leite (2004). *Assentamentos Rurais. Mudança Social e Dinâmica Regional*. Rio de Janeiro: Mauad.

MEPF (1999). 'Agricultura Familiar, Reforma Agrária e Desenvolvimento Local para um Novo Mundo rural. Política de Desenvolvimento Rural com Base na Expansão da Agricultura Familiar e Sua Inserção no Mercado.' Brasilia: MEPF, mimeo.

NEAD (Nucleo de Estudios Agrários) (2004). 'Noticias Agrárias,' Portal NEAD de Estudos Agrários, various issues. www.nead.gov.br (downloaded 22 March 2006)

Neto, G. I. and T. Bamat (cords) (1998). *Qualidade de Vida e Reforma Agrária na Paraíba*. João Pessoa, Paraiba: UNITRABALHO/UFPb.

Pereira, J. M. (2004). 'O Modelo de Reforma Agrária de Mercado do Banco Mundial em Questão: O Debate Internacional e o Caso Brasileiro.' Masters thesis, Postgraduate course in Development, Agriculture and Society (CPDA), Federal Rural University of Rio de Janeiro, August.

PRONAF (2003). 'Plano Safra para a Agricultura Familiar 2003/2004.' www.contag.org.br/PL 2003 4.doc (downloaded 11 August 2003).

Reydon, B. P. and L. A. Plata (2002). 'Intervenção Estatal no Mercado de Terras: A Experiência Recente no Brasil.' Série Pesquisa. NEA-IE/UNICAMP and INCRA [2002]. www.nead.org.br (downloaded 12 August 2003).

Sampaio, P. A. (2004). 'A Necessária Pressão Social Pela Reforma Agrária.' MST Biblioteca. April, in www.mst.org.br/biblioteca/textos/reformagr/plinio2004.htm. (downloaded 17 June 2004).

Spavrorvek, G. (2003). *A Qualidade dos Assentamentos da Reforma Agrária Brasileira.* Sao Paulo: Páginas e Letras Editora e Gráfica.

Stedile, J. P. (2004). 'Carta del MST.' Letter distributed through Minga Informativa de Movimientos Sociales to email distribution list of pasavoz@movimientos.org, 7 April 2004.

Teixeira, G. and Coletivo petista para reflexões sobre as políticas agrícola e agrária (2006). 'Um Balanço do Programa de Reforma Agrária no Governo Lula. Subsídios para o Debate Interno no PT.' Draft mimeo, March 2005.

Teófilo, E., A. G. de Matos *et al.* (2002). 'Políticas e Instrumentos para Fomentar el Mercado de Tierras: Lecciones Aprendidas.' Paper prepared for the conference on Desarrollo de las Economías Rurales en América Latina y el Caribe: Manejo Sostenible de Recursos Naturales, Acceso a Tierras y Finanzas Rurales, Asamblea de Gobernadores del BID, Fortaleza, March.

Vinot, T. (2005). 'Uma Experiência de Sucesso,' in *Raízes da Terra*, SRA/MDA, April www.creditofundiario.org.br (downloaded 14 August 2005).

Wolff, L. and S. Sauer (2001). 'O Painel de Inspeção e o Caso da Cédula da Terra,' in F. Barros, org., *Banco Mundial, Participação, Transparência e Responsabilização. A Experiência Brasileira com o Painel de Inspeção.* Brasilia: Rede Brasil.

Wright, A. and W. Wolford (2003). *To Inherit the Earth: The Landless Movement and the Struggle for a New Brazil.* Oakland: Food First.

Zibechi, R. (2003). 'Brasil y la Reforma Agraria,' Servicio Informativo ALAI-América Latina, 18 July 2003, distributed by info@alainet.org to list serve.

4 Land, poverty and state–society interaction in the Philippines

Saturnino M. Borras Jr, Danilo Carranza and Ricardo Reyes

1 Introduction[1]

Land reform policies are heterogeneous in character and their relationship to and timing in the context of national development strategies and poverty eradication has been varied between and within countries.[2] In the conventional literature, land reform means redistributing landed property rights in large private landholdings from rich landlords to poor landless and near-landless peasants. This policy is coercive; the state expropriates and redistributes landed property rights.[3] As explained by Borras, Kay and Akram-Lodhi in the introductory chapter of this book, not all purported land reform policies are the same and conform to this ideal concept. The contemporary Philippine land reform, for example, is close to the conventional type, but it has components that are closely similar to the pro-market land reform model that has been developed since the 1990s: the voluntary, market-led 'willing seller, willing buyer' formula – making it similar to Brazil's (see Deere and Medeiros, this volume). It is a policy that calls for a non-coercive approach in land reform based on the belief that landlord opposition to reform is one of the key reasons for the 'failure' of past land reforms. In analysing land reform and how it impacts on poverty, it is crucial to take a critical and differentiated view between the traditional state-led and the market-based land distribution mechanisms that exist either within a single land reform policy, as in the case of the Philippines, or separately, as in the case of Brazil.[4]

Moreover, in this chapter, landed property rights are considered not as things but as 'social relationships'.[5] Thus land reform means reforming social relationships, and necessarily the structure and pre-existing distribution of power in society among different groups linked together to the common issue of land resource use and control. These relationships are mediated by a variety of formal and informal institutions, including the state and state laws and rules. It is in this context that it is important to look into the dynamics of state–society relations. Land laws are neither 'self-interpreting nor self-implementing' so that actual political dynamics within the state, in society, and in state–society relationships become

crucial processes in determining the course of political-legal interpretation and implementation of land policies (Houtzager and Franco, 2003;
Franco, 2005).

The rest of this chapter is organised as follows: Section 2 briefly
explores the context and object of current land policies, i.e. the agrarian
structure and national rural development strategies and their relationship
to the distribution of wealth and power in society. Section 3 is devoted to a
critical examination of the contemporary land reform policy, while
Section 4 analyses the impact of land reform on rural poverty. Section 5
examines the socio-political actors and institutions responsible for the
actual interpretation and implementation of land reform laws. Section 6
offers brief concluding remarks.

2 Land, social relationships and poverty

The Philippine agriculture sector's importance to the economy has been
declining although it has retained its significance. The distribution of
GDP shares is highly skewed in favour of the service sector that grew from
44 per cent in 1990 to 52 per cent in 1999. For the same period, the industrial sector remained somewhere in the low 30s. The agricultural sector's
share of GDP contracted from 27 per cent in 1988 (Putzel, 1992: 17) to 22
per cent in 1990 down to 20 per cent in 2003. Yet, as Balisacan and Hill
(2003: 25) have explained, when 'a broader definition that encompasses
agricultural processing and related activities is adopted, the indirect share
[of agriculture] rises to about 40 per cent and 67 per cent' in GDP and
employment shares, respectively.

Poverty and inequality have remained important features in Philippine
society. The poverty incidence was 44.2 per cent in 1985 and 33.7 per cent
in 2000 (ADB, 2005: xiii). Moreover, according to the ADB (Asian Development Bank) (ibid.) poverty report: 'The Gini coefficient [for income
distribution] fell slightly from 0.49 in 1997 to 0.47 in 2003, but this still
represents a worse income distribution than the 0.45 level observed in
1985, 1988, and 1994.' Finally, the same report explained that,

> income poverty in the Philippines is a dynamic phenomenon: people
> move in and out of poverty over time. A first attempt to gauge chronic
> and transient poverty found that over a three-year period about one-
> fifth of the surveyed households were chronically poor ... whereas
> nearly one-third of the households moved into and out of poverty
> during the period.
>
> (ibid: xiv)

And poverty in the Philippines is a rural phenomenon. According to the
ADB report, 'of the 26.5 million poor people in the country in 2000 ...
7.1 million were urban and 19.4 million live in rural areas. In other words,
nearly 75% of the poor are rural poor' (ibid: 64). And the poverty

incidence among farming households during 1985–2000 has remained almost unchanged. It was 56.7 per cent and 55.8 per cent, in 1985 and 2000, respectively (ibid: 98).

Philippine agriculture is diverse in terms of products and production systems but can be broadly differentiated into two types. The 'small farmer' sector,[6] or the 'traditional sector' – rice, corn, coconut and sugarcane – continues to predominate in terms of nationally aggregated monetary value and land use. Around nine out of every ten hectares of farmland are devoted to this type of crops. Characterised by high-volume, low-value crops, this sector is dominated by traditional landed elites who generally own the land that small farmers work under varying types of tenurial relations, although the small family farms that have been created through land reform are emerging as an important section of this sector. In contrast, the 'capitalist farmer and corporate plantation sector' or, the 'non-traditional sector', produces low-volume, high-value crops and products such as banana, mango, pineapple and aquatic products, and has seen expansion, although less than expected, in recent years. Marked by production and exchange relations different from the traditional sector, such as contract growing schemes and wage relations, this sector is where non-traditional landed elites, including urban-based entrepreneurs and multinational corporations, have gained the most ground,[7] although a small section of this sector is comprised by (land) reformed farms whose farming system generally maintains the pre-reform farming operational method. Modern technology and equipment, as well as a capitalist management system, also characterise these modern farm enclaves. However, the 'traditional-modern' dichotomy represents ideal types. In reality many farms have features of both, as peasants construct and defend their livelihoods, and as the elites diversify their sources and strategies of capital accumulation, from one location to the next over time.[8]

Landlessness and share tenancy emerged in the country during the Spanish colonial period, heightened during the American occupation during the first half of the twentieth century, and persisted after the Second World War and up to the present. But this history of landlessness is also a history of peasant upheavals, where hundreds of peasant revolts marked the colonial times. These violent peasant-based revolts persisted in the 1930s to 1950s (Kerkvliet, 1977) and up to the present. All throughout, the reaction of the Philippine state was more of the same: a settlement programme in addition to promises of limited tenancy reform and state repression. Again, the state failed to solve the growing land-based political and economic problems during this period. It was in the early 1960s when a redistributive land reform was first introduced by the state. But the law that called for redistribution of tenanted rice and corn lands had a very high land ownership 'ceiling' that effectively exempted most farms (Putzel, 1992; Wurfel, 1983), and, although the law declared share tenancy illegal, it was not implemented on any significant scale.

As part of the process of national state-building and the state's effort to manage peasant unrest, various land policies were promulgated, as for example resettlement programmes were introduced as early as the first quarter of the past century (Abinales, 2000; Putzel, 1992). But state-organised settlement programmes failed to achieve their goals of developing family farms, citing expense as the main reason (Lichauco, 1956). These various forms of entry into the land frontier had a profound impact on the pre-existing agrarian structure in these communities, with the general effect leading to the concentration of control over land resources in the hands of the few. These series of settlements altered pre-existing agrarian structures, creating webs of complex social relationships that would prove difficult to untangle and resolve in the decades to come.

President Ferdinand Marcos introduced a land reform in 1972 (Presidential Decree or PD No. 27), but it was limited to tenanted rice and corn lands. This land reform had various overlapping intentions: to legitimise the authoritarian regime, to debase the then-fledgling peasant-based communist guerrilla movement and to crush some of Marcos's land-based elite political opponents (Kerkvliet, 1979; Putzel, 1992: 127–156). At the time when Marcos was overthrown in 1986, the land redistribution accomplishment of the programme was below the level of its promises: 444,277 peasant beneficiaries covering 766,630 hectares of distributed land, and 690,207 leasehold contracts were awarded to 645,808 tenants (Putzel, 1992: 138–139; Wurfel, 1983). While limited in its accomplishment, the land reform nevertheless contributed to the general weakening of the political power of landlords of rice and corn farms (Riedinger, 1995).

The unresolved landlessness persisted into the post-authoritarian era. In 1988 (the year the current land reform law was passed) roughly 70 per cent of the total agricultural population were landless or near-landless households (Putzel, 1992: 24–26). The landless and near-landless agricultural population are, in turn, categorised as tenants (fixed-cash rent or variations of sharecropping), owner-cultivators below subsistence, cultivators of land without secure property rights, seasonal and plantation (more or less permanent) farm workers, and part-time subsistence fisherfolk. It is again very difficult to estimate how many households belonged to which category, although it is widely assumed that the seasonal farm workers (rural semi-proletariat) were the most numerous. Meanwhile, share tenancy relations were widespread, and were marked by onerous terms, such as *tersyuhan* – one-third/two-thirds sharing in favour of the landlord wherein the tenant-peasants usually shoulder most of the production costs. Moreover, the rural population continued to increase at the current rate of 2.6 per cent per year (ADB, 2005), pointing to a rising number of potential claim-makers for land reform from 1988 onwards, amid a marginal increase in the area of farmland, irrigated land, and land/labour productivity gains between 1980 and 2004.

Before the implementation of the land reform law in 1988, the land ownership distribution was highly skewed: small farms, or those 2.99 hectares and less, accounted for some two-thirds of the total number of farms but for less than one-third of the total hectares of agricultural land; farms five hectares or more, which as the potentially expropriable farms (those above the land size ceiling of five hectares) accounted for almost 14 per cent of the total number of farms but less than half of the total hectares of agricultural land. Most estimates place the total farmland area at 10.3 million hectares. Based on the 1988 data, Putzel (1992: 29) calculated the Gini coefficient in land ownership in 1988 to be 0.647, showing a high degree of inequality.

Meanwhile, a glance at the economic indicators in agriculture helps to partly explain the persistence of rural poverty. There has been a generally low level of productivity in agriculture since the 1980s. The gross value added (GVA) of agriculture was a low 1.0 in 1980–1990 and 1.8 in 1990–2000 in the Philippines. Meanwhile, the real value added per worker during the period 1970–2000 also showed the dismal performance of the agriculture sector: it was almost stagnant for this sector at PhP15,800 in 1970 to PhP17,100 in 2000 – in contrast to the industry sector's PhP62,300 and PhP72,000, respectively, and the service sector's PhP36,600 and PhP32,400, respectively (Balisacan and Hill, 2003: 13). Furthermore, contrary to the goals of and earlier claims by agricultural trade reformers about growth and progress in the agricultural sector, the initial results seem to indicate the opposite: the country has been transformed from a net agricultural exporting country to a net agricultural importing country, beginning in the early 1990s, with the average annual deficit steadily increasing (David, 2003; Borras, forthcoming).

3 Land policies

The 1988 land reform law (Comprehensive Agrarian Reform Programme, CARP) declares that all farmlands, both private and public, and regardless of tenurial and productivity conditions, be subject to agrarian reform. Based on the original 1988 scope, CARP intends to reform tenure relations on 10.3 million hectares of the country's farmland via land redistribution; the estimated number of beneficiaries could reach some five million landless and land-poor peasant households, comprising close to 80 per cent of the agricultural population. This was however reduced in early 1996 to eight million hectares of private and public lands through a highly questionable process where significant quantities of private lands disappeared from the official working scope of the land reform programme (Borras, 2003b). In addition, some two million hectares of farms smaller than 5 hectares (including the farms legally retained by landlords) were made subject to leasehold reform that would benefit an estimated one million tenant households.[9] The implementation of CARP in private lands and some government-owned lands is handled by the Department of

Agrarian Reform (DAR), while all alienable and disposable (A&D) lands as well as publicly owned 'forested' lands are to be distributed by the Department of Environment and Natural Resources (DENR).

The political conflict marked by pro- and anti-reform maneuvers internalised within CARP is reflected in the various CARP land acquisition modalities for private lands: i) Operation Land Transfer (OLT) was the mechanism used for tenanted rice and corn lands under the Marcos-era land reform programme and later was integrated within CARP; ii) aims to reduce landlord resistance, the Voluntary Offer-to-Sell (VOS) increases the cash portion in landlord's compensation by 5 per cent with a corresponding 5 per cent decrease in the bonds portion; iii) the Voluntary Land Transfer (VLT) aspires to attract landlord cooperation to the programme as it provides for the direct transfer of land to peasants under terms mutually agreed between peasants and landlords with the government's role confined to information provision. A landlord who is interested in the scheme is expected to agree with the buyers about the transaction terms: land price, mode of payment and set of beneficiaries, before submitting the VLT proposal to the DAR which approves or disapproves the plan. The difference between VOS and VLT is that in the former the landlord sells land to the state, while in the latter the landlord sells directly to the peasants. Both VOS and VLT operate in the context of expropriation; that is, if landlords refuse VOS or VLT, their estates could nonetheless be acquired by the state. Finally, CARP's last acquisition mode is Compulsory Acquisition or CA, through which land is expropriated with or without the landlord's cooperation. OLT is akin to CA. These latter two, and arguably VOS under certain conditions, are land acquisition methods that are most straightforwardly expropriationary and redistributive.

By 2005, the partial outcomes of CARP demonstrate a relatively significant achievement. Official records show that the government has been able to redistribute 5.9 million hectares of private and public lands, accounting for a little over half of the total farmland in the country. These lands were redistributed to three million peasant households, accounting for a little over two-fifths of the total agricultural households in the country. In addition, official records show that 1.5 million hectares of land were subjected to share tenancy leasehold reform, benefiting a million tenant households (see Table 4.1). These statistics put the Philippine land reform outcomes in comparable level vis-à-vis major land reforms elsewhere historically. But in reality, the actual accomplishment is lower, and this will be explained below.

Land distribution under DAR

The CARP components under DAR consist of three broad reform clusters. First is redistribution of private agricultural lands.[10] Second is the implementation of leasehold reform. The third component is the redistribution

Table 4.1 Number of beneficiaries of land reform programme, 1972–2000

Programme	Number of beneficiary households
Land transfer under DAR	1,697,566
Land transfer under DENR	1,273,845
Leasehold operations	1,098,948
Stock Distribution Option (SDO)	8,975
Total	4,079,334

Source: Reyes (2002: 15).

of some government-owned lands.[11] Official claims about the land reform accomplishment under DAR are shown in Table 4.2 where by early 2005, 3.56 million hectares of (private and government-owned) farmlands were redistributed by DAR to nearly two million peasant households, accounting for about three-quarters of the total DAR working scope in land redistribution.

Some critics argue that the 'reality' in CARP implementation outcome is far below the level of official claims, and they point out some anomalies in accounting, e.g. lands declared as land reform accomplishments despite peasant beneficiaries being unable to occupy them due to continued landlord opposition, previously awarded lands that were later recalled due to so-called erroneous technical processes, and so on. However, while such problems certainly do occur, the scale of these remains relatively small compared to the entirety of CARP's land redistribution outcomes. For example, the total number of households affected by the problem of 'non-installation' (formal land award was made but the beneficiary could not take possession due to landlord opposition) only around 20,000 by 2003. Hence, the dominant critique of the official claims about land reform outcome under DAR has been correct to point out that the government statistics are not reliable – but in what way and to what extent, the critique offers only partial and at times problematic evidence.

An alternative critical evaluation of these outcomes therefore becomes necessary. In general terms, what is missed in most critical analysis of CARP outcomes is the issue of lands that were 'mysteriously' taken out of the CARP scope – a problem that possibly affects around two million households, and the non-redistributive nature of transactions carried out through the voluntary schemes, especially SDO and VLT – a problem that affects at least a third of a million households (Borras, 2003b, 2005). In addition, most critics and scholars on Philippine land reform tend to also dismiss the possibility that real pro-poor redistributive reform can actually occur through leasehold reform and in public lands (Borras, 2006a). Thus in effect and in total, these observers omit from their land reform accounting three to four million households.

Table 4.2 CARP's land redistribution accomplishment, in hectares (1972–2005)

	Land area (in hectares)
*Total land redistribution by land type, under the Department of Agrarian Reform (DAR)**	
Private lands	2,036,201
OLT	576,556
CA	289,250
VOS	494,133
VLT	514,277
GFI	161,985
Government-owned lands	1,530,790
KKK	737,512
LE	70,658
Settlement	722,620
Sub-total	3,566,991
*Total land redistribution by land type under the Department of Environment and Natural Resources (DENR)***	
Public/state lands	
A&D	1,295,559
CBFM	1,042,088
Sub-Total	2,337,647
Total	5,904,638

Sources: Borras (2006b); DENR (2004).

Notes
CARP = Comprehensive Agrarian Reform Program; LAD = Land Acquisition and Distribution; OLT = Operation Land Transfer; CA = Compulsory Acquisition; VOS = Voluntary Offer-to-Sell; VLT = Voluntary Land Transfer; GFI = Government Financial Institution; KKK = Kilusang Kabuhayan at Kaunlaran; LE = Landed Estate; A&D = Alienable and Disposable Land; CBFM = Community-based Forest Management.
* DAR data = 1972 to 31 March 2005. ** DENR data = beginning 1987 to 31 December 2004.

Meanwhile, DAR was able to redistribute a total of 1.53 million hectares of government-owned lands.[12] As mentioned earlier, most of these lands are in fact highly productive crop lands where tenurial relations occur. Thus, the implementation of CARP in these lands, contrary to popular belief, has been almost always politically contentious. The reported implementation and land redistribution accomplishment must be taken with extreme caution because it is likely that many reported accomplishments may in fact not constitute truly pro-poor redistributive reform (e.g. beneficiaries were non-poor, but rather landed elite who bribed or connived with government officials, etc.). The reason for this is not because reform in such types of land inherently does not result in pro-poor redistributive reform, because in fact it can, and did. The caution is required because some DAR officials approached the issue of land redistribution of these types of land from a very technically oriented perspective. Specifically, many officials, driven by the desire to be able to come up with a good annual accomplishment report, simply took out big parcels of government-owned lands, formalising the existing land claims therein by declaring the pre-existing claimants as beneficiaries of land reform, and reported the whole process as land redistribution accomplishment. Such a simplified process resulted in formalising the land claims by elites inside these government-owned lands, and thus perpetuated pre-existing tenurial relationships. It is this type of outcome that one should be wary of; it is this type of outcome that should be counted out of the CARP land redistribution outcome (Borras, 2006a).

Furthermore, there are CARP land reform modalities most likely to result in outcomes that do not constitute pro-poor redistributive reform, and may even provide important ammunition to those wishing to undermine the land reform process to a greater degree. These CARP land acquisition modalities are the Stock Distribution Option (SDO) and the Voluntary Land Transfer (VLT), both very much like the contemporary World Bank's 'willing seller, willing buyer' formula. And because the World Bank is actually pushing for such types of 'alternative' modality in approaching the land reform issue in private lands in the Philippines as elsewhere, it is relevant to analyse these two related schemes that are ongoing in the country.

In the SDO, corporate farms are spared from land redistribution if the landlords opt to redistribute corporate stocks equivalent to the value of the land. The workers, who would then become co-owners, would get their earnings from their daily work, but would get extra income from corporate dividends if the corporation realised a net profit. By 2004, only a few SDO contracts were approved, involving not more than 20,000 hectares nationwide. The best example of SDO is the 6,400-hectare sugarcane hacienda owned by former president Corazon Cojuangco-Aquino and her family (Cojuangco). It effectively evaded redistributive land reform by maintaining control over majority stocks of the corporation through simple accounting manipulation (Putzel, 1992; Carranza, 1994, 2004).

On the other hand, the VLT scheme is the ideal voluntary-nonredistributive modality, as opposed to the more expropriationary modes of OLT and CA.[13] A brief background is warranted: The anti-land reform lobby within the state and in society has escalated in recent years. Congress has consistently cut annual budget allocations for CARP's land acquisition component. Using the issue of insufficient funds as an excuse, conservative forces have increasingly employed the VLT scheme as a way to undermine redistributive land reform. For the government, a VLT-based CARP implementation strategy appears to have become a politically convenient means to effectively drop redistributive land reform from the state policy agenda. Since recently, while the government has not admitted as much in official statements, it has not continued to expropriate to any significant extent the private landholdings of landlords and rich peasants.

The VLT scheme has been used to an increasing extent to 'transfer' land, although past administrations preferred not to talk about these transactions in formal policy discourse. A policy shift occurred in early 2002 when the Macapagal-Arroyo administration announced its adoption of VLT as the main strategy to 'redistribute' land.

By 2003, a significant portion of DAR official land redistribution figures in private lands is made up of aggregate VLT output, at around 0.5 million hectares of land, affecting perhaps up to 300,000 peasant households. Closer analysis of the VLT transactions reveals their nonredistributive nature. This is done by analysing evidence from the annual CARP internal programme audit and other cases directly examined for this study. There are at least three ways in which VLT was used to serve the interest of anti-reform forces. First, evasions of expropriation via VLT have occurred in two general ways. The first type is declaring children, relatives and other dummies as beneficiaries of the VLT land reform process. This arises from the CARP law that allows children and other relatives to become 'preferred' beneficiaries but only if they were at least 15 years of age as of 1988 and actually tilling or willing to till the land. Many of the VLT 'transfers' sampled in the government programme audit reports were not only made in favour of family members, but in favour of family members not legally qualified to become beneficiaries because they were minors and/or not working on the farm. The other type is where peasants are tricked, cajoled or coerced to agree to become 'on-paper beneficiaries'. In this case, the landlord is deemed to have complied with the land reform law, while the old tenancy sharing arrangement between landlord and tenants/farmworkers continues. It can be surmised that the landlord anticipates an on-paper resale after the ten-year rental/sales prohibition. The CARP law prohibits the sale or renting of awarded land within a period of ten years after such an award has been made.

Second, the VLT scheme has also become a favourite scam for corrupt petty officials. It is public knowledge within the internal circles of the agencies associated with land reform that some government officials coach the landlords on how to evade land reform via VLT. This is done on the condition that a set of beneficiaries that the government official provides, in addition to the landlord's preferred and paper beneficiaries are included in the final set of beneficiaries. Third, there is also a variety of arrangement where VLT becomes a key component in other nonredistributive schemes. Many of these schemes involve powerful landlords, multinational companies and huge plantations. This has been the case, for example, for the Danding Cojuangco estate in Negros Occidental (see Feranil, 2005) and the banana plantations controlled by Don Antonio Floirendo in Davao (see de la Rosa, 2005; Franco, 2005; Borras and Franco, 2005; Hawes, 1987). The bottom line for these landlords is to use VLT to comply with the land reform law, and then cancel out whatever potential there is for redistributive reform by imposing a variety of joint venture agreements ensuring the landlord's perpetual control over the farm and the surplus generated from its production. In short, there was no real transfer of wealth and power.

Market-led agrarian reform

The World Bank and the Philippine government have started to experiment on market-led agrarian reform (MLAR). They explained that it is meant to be a programme that will be complementary to CARP's more expropriationary features. The World Bank first attempted to recruit government officials to adopt its MLAR in 1996 when it insinuated that the Philippine government must halt CARP's land distribution implementation especially in the 5–24 hectare farm size category, because it was said to be 'distorting' the land market and is financially expensive. DAR rejected the WB proposal and subsequent protest from agrarian reform activist circles stopped the WB initiative. They came back in 1999 with greater persistence, gaining some initial ground (Franco, 1999b).

In early 1999, WB officials lobbied for the adoption of a small pilot MLAR project in the context of exploring other 'complementary approaches' in land reform. The DAR leadership expressed an interest in exploring the possibilities of MLAR, based on expectations that it would bring in fresh grants.[14] It was agreed that a feasibility study would be carried out. It got started in October that year (WB, 2000a: 3).[15] All through this period, most rural NGOs and peasant organisations campaigned against MLAR believing that it was not real land reform and that it would undermine, not support, existing state-led land reform (see Franco, 1999b; Reyes, 1999; UNORKA, 2000). This sustained anti-MLAR campaign forced the WB to re-label MLAR in the Philippines the 'Community-Managed Agrarian Reform Programme' or CMARP.

The feasibility study involved two community-based test cases. The first case in the southern Philippines involved a tenanted 178 hectares of government-owned land, a significant portion of which lay idle and uncultivated, while the rest was devoted to subsistence crops. The DAR chose and enlisted 178 potential buyer-beneficiaries. The government, owner of the land, was selling the land for PhP31,000/ha, a price the potential buyers did not agree. They eventually agreed on a price tag of PhP16,000/ha (UPSARDFI, 2001: 94–95), with the buyers paying full cost for the land (MUCEP, 2001). The other case in Luzon island involved a tenanted 48 hectares of private marginal farmland planted with subsistence crops. The landlord originally set the land price at PhP35,000/ha. The DAR chose 19 potential buyers with assistance from an NGO. The relatively organised potential beneficiary households rejected the landlord's asking price and bargained for a much lower price. The final price was set at PhP6,000/ha. The buyers will have to pay full cost for the land to be paid through a loan from the Land Bank at commercial interest rates (UPSARDFI, 2001: 94). Both test cases used VLT as the legal mechanism to execute the transactions.

After completion of the feasibility study, the bank expanded the project into a pilot programme. Called the Community-Managed Agrarian Reform and Poverty Reduction Program (CMARPRP), the pilot started in mid-2003. It aimed to facilitate the sale of 1,000 hectares to 1,000 rural poor households in ten provinces across the country. Its basic operational method does not differ much from the feasibility study, i.e. it is technically and legally anchored on the use of the VLT scheme.[16] The MLAR pilot programme has been integrated into the ongoing World Bank-funded Agrarian Reform Community Development Program, a support programme for agrarian reform beneficiaries heavily oriented toward infrastructure building.[17] The pilot programme is supposed to be completed within two years.[18] The short period of implementation was used by the programme managers to justify dropping the supposedly required component of civil society (NGO) involvement in the project as its inclusion would most likely result in extended project implementation processes.[19] While this may be true, another more likely reason is the fact that almost all autonomous NGOs and peasant organisations in the Philippines are opposed to the WB's MLAR concept and any form of pilot-testing.

Little insight can be deduced from the cases in the two villages of the MLAR feasibility study, except that even a government entity can be tempted to overprice land slated for sale to peasants under the direct sale process. The second case, at a glance, seems interesting, especially in how the land price was bargained down. But this case may not be representative of the country because the balance of power was overwhelmingly in favour of the peasants due to the direct assistance of national-provincial-local government and NGO actors in the process. It is unlikely that anything substantive or meaningful can develop from the ongoing pilot programme because a market-led agrarian reform land transaction does not constitute truly pro-poor redistributive reform. The VLT experience in the Philippines provides lessons about what is likely to happen when voluntary market-led mechanisms are carried out in agrarian settings like those of the Philippine countryside – it will not result in redistributive reform, and it will undermine existing potentially redistributive state-led land reform (see Borras, 2005).

Leasehold

The CARP's leasehold programme invloves formal, secure long-term lease contracts between landlord and tenants. It can lead to improvement in the livelihood and social well-being of leaseholders (in fact, it did, as shown in the empirical study of Reyes (2002) discussed in the next section). Under CARP, leasehold is also used as a transitory scheme to quickly break the nexus between landlords and peasants; later, expropriation can be carried out. The achievement of leasehold within the official CARP process has been modest but relatively significant. Between 1972 and 1986, or during the Marcos regime, leasehold reform (in rice and corn lands) covered nearly 600,000 hectares of land benefiting about 300,000 tenant households. From 1987 to 2003, the government reported an additional 800,000 hectares of land involving about 400,000 tenant households to have been subjected to leasehold.

At first glance, the official statistics speak of significant achievement through leaseholds. But on closer inspection, it is revealed that the real extent of reform achieved through this process is much less. The main reason is that, wittingly or unwittingly, DAR entered erroneous data into its leasehold data bank with the effect of incorrectly jacking-up the quantity of lands subjected to leasehold by as much as 500,000 hectares. The leasehold accomplishment report should be limited to 'permanent leasehold' and should not include the 'transitory type'. The problem was that the data for 1990 to 1995 included all transitory leaseholds in the national data, leading to the ballooning of the leasehold statistics, and it is extremely difficult to uncover the current status of the lands officially claimed to have been subjected to temporary leasehold. Thus, a reasonable estimate of the real leasehold accomplishment is somewhere around 900,000 hectares involving more or less 450,000 tenant households – much fewer than in the official claims, but still not altogether insignificant (Borras, 2006b).

Land distribution under DENR

There are two subprogrammes for public lands under the DENR, namely, the alienable and disposable (A&D) lands and the Community-Based Forest Management (CBFM) programmes. The former provides 'free patents' to peasant beneficiaries. The latter is the programme carried out in lands formally classified as 'forested lands', and a CBFM stewardship contract of 50 years is awarded to a community organisation of beneficiaries, although actual occupancy and land rights remain individualised within the CBFM areas. The post-Marcos constitution classifies lands of the public domain into agricultural, timber, mineral lands and national parks. Of these, only agricultural lands are subject to disposition/ alienation. While only alienable and disposable lands can be titled, a tenurial instrument that guarantees security is also issued among occupants of forest and/or timberlands. Thus, the A&D lands were officially made subject of the CARP law notwithstanding the provision which states that forest lands or timber lands are excluded from CARP coverage. In its 3.7 million hectares distribution target, the DENR placed 2.5 million hectares under the A&D land, and 1.2 million hectares under the CBFM programmes. By 2003, substantial outcomes for these two programmes were reported by the DENR (see Table 4.2). Many of these lands are actually productive croplands where tenurial relationships already exist, meaning that these are officially classified public lands, but many of them had actually been appropriated privately. There is thus a great potential for real redistributive reform to occur in these lands (Borras, 2006a).

In its 2004 report, the DENR claimed that from 1987 to June 2004, it had distributed a total of lands equivalent to 61 per cent of its target scope to around 600,000 peasant households. The remaining balance on A&D land distribution is thus only 1.1 million hectares. The government has admitted that it is moving slowly in completing this programme, citing the reason as 'lack of funds'. No funds were provided for the development of the farms distributed through this programme either (DENR, 2004).

Critical examination is warranted. For one, even for the reported partial accomplishment of CARP's A&D land programme, there are serious grounds to doubt the official government claims. The annual reports of the internal programme audit of the government have discovered numerous anomalous practices whereby land beneficiaries were actually nonpoor, but rather middle and upper classes based in town centers and cities or government officials or their relatives. It could be surmised that one reason for this was because autonomous civil society organisations, in general, have not engaged the state on this particular programme. Another critical issue revolves around the reliability of the government's reported accomplishment and of the official working scope for A&D land programmes. In many instances, however, the actual farmer occupants are not aware of the law and the process of application to acquire title on the land. Likewise, many big landowners gain control of lands applied for by others, so that, even though another name appears in the title application, that applicant does not actually control the land. Instead a more powerful landowner holds control, with tenants working the land, unaware that the land is not titled to their landlord or of the actual applicant for title.

In lands officially classified as 'public forest', the Community-Based Forest Management (CBFM) programme applies. This involves allowing community organisations to use and manage land resources in forest/timber zones for 25 years, renewable for another 25 years. Active and transparent community participation and security of tenure shall be among the key strategies for achieving success. According to the 2004 official report, the DENR has already completed implementation of CBFM, benefiting around 700,000 peasant households (DENR, 2004). Since 2001, the DENR has not targeted other areas for CBFM, although data suggest that more areas should be subjected to CBFM and there are increasing demands from farmers who have occupied and tilled timber/forest lands. Many of these lands are believed to be occupied by landless settlers without land security, much less social services from the government. Many of these lands are actually farmed by peasants, with coconut, corn and fruit trees the dominant crops.

Again, a critical view is necessary for a better understanding of the CBFM programme. Just like in the A&D lands programme, the internal programme audit of the government discovered numerous anomalous cases in the implementation of CBFM, mainly that beneficiaries were nonpoor, from the middle and upper classes in the town centres and faraway cities, as well as government officials and their relatives. In such cases, truly redistributive reform was not achieved. Moreover, despite the official claims that the programme was completed a few years ago, ample evidence from the ground shows that many huge parcels of 'forested lands' are not being declared subject to CBFM. While the government's explanation is that no funds are available to further expand CBFM coverage, it is also likely that many public lands eligible for CBFM are in the hands of the powerful landed elite, especially those lands officially classified as 'timber lands' and with ongoing or expired 'timber lease agreements'. Another issue with regard to 'forest lands' concerns the growing cases of lands that have been titled to private individuals even if officially they are part of the 'inalienable' domains of the state. Therefore, the potential of CBFM as a poverty alleviation programme needs to be tapped fully for the benefit of landless occupants in forest lands. Available data suggest that there is enormous potential for the expansion of land reform in timber land areas. There are likely to be a few million hectares of land that should be subject to CBFM.

4 Land policies and their impact on rural poverty

In general, agrarian reform has impacted positively on the income of beneficiary households, as shown by empirical studies (e.g. Reyes, 2002; Reyes, 2000; Deininger *et al.*, 2000). Even the highly productive modern farms, like banana and pineapple, subjected to land reform have, in general, been able to maintain productivity levels. And there are no significant divestments in agriculture due to agrarian reform. However, the reported level of improvements in the livelihoods of agrarian reform beneficiaries is very similar to that in Brazil (see Deere and Medeiros, this volume), that is, not that radical and dramatic in terms of scale systemwide. And the reason for this may be found in the broader character of the agrarian transformation process taking place in the country, where generally small family farms are in a constant precarious condition, due to lack of state support services, problematic public investment in rural infrastructure, disadvantageous national and international policies on credit and trade, among other factors. Finally, the interaction of state–society actors has also influence to support or undermine the pro-poor impact of land redistribution. These issues will be addressed in this section.

The central state's general policy toward agriculture (implicitly) stands on a 'tripod'. First, it actively supports medium- to large-scale modern agriculture – the so-called non-traditional agricultural exports sector dominated by corporate agribusiness and capitalist farmers – which are already relatively economically and commercially efficient and competitive in the global trade. Second, the state actively encourages agricultural sectors that it believes to be 'inherently' economically inefficient and commercially non-competitive to get out of that sector or get out of farming altogether. These farms come from the ranks of small family concerns, and chiefly targeted are upland rice, coconut and corn family farmers engaged in (sub)subsistence farming. Those who cannot get out of this sector for various reasons, such as the numerous members of indigenous people's communities, the central state treats in the context of 'social welfare', not in the context of 'economics', and as such they fall into social safety nets, such as subsidised food support. In fact the government anti-poverty programmes have been directed toward this subsector. This has been the case in what has been purported to be a 'super presidential commission' and 'super state–society partnership body' in the anti-poverty campaign, the National Anti-Poverty Commission (NAPC). When viewed from this broader perspective, in fact NAPC is miniscule in scope and conservative in orientation. But the concept of NAPC per se is not altogether useless and irrelevant because it has the potential to become a staging ground for citizens to hold the state accountable to its mandate and promises. Unfortunately, efforts to transform NAPC into a vibrant platform of civil society organisations have not achieved significant or sustained success.

Third, in two politically sensitive agricultural sectors, the central state oscillates back and forth between the first and second 'legs of the tripod', so to speak: sugarcane and irrigated rice. The sugarcane sector has been extremely inefficient economically and non-competitive commercially, but the central state nevertheless has continued to maintain various indirect subsidies, including trade protection. It must be noted that this sector is controlled by landlords who are historically powerful economically and politically. Meanwhile, being the staple grain of the people, rice is inherently politically sensitive, and the government's policy has historically been partly marked by an urban bias – meaning, it gives important consideration to maintaining abundant supplies of cheap rice in the burgeoning urban centers, especially Metro Manila, where the urban population and the media readily react to rice supply and price fluctuations. It is in this context that the central state could not decisively abandon its support for the necessary physical and social infrastructures (e.g. road, irrigation, marketing channels) for the rice sector, at least just to maintain the status quo. For example, the irrigation facilities meant mainly for the purpose of rice cultivation have only been maintained by the state in their status quo over the past decades, but that means they are unable to match the rate that the population and rice farmland area expanded during the same period. Yet its principal policy to ensure sufficient supply of rice at cheap prices especially in urban centers pushed the government to cultivate a habit of importing rice in excessive quantities from sources abroad.

It is within this context that one should analyse and understand why, how and to what extent the government has also provided a distinct programme to support the post-land transfer farm and beneficiary development of land reform beneficiaries. The main strategy in farm and beneficiary development is through the Agrarian Reform Community or ARC. The ARC strategy is defined by DAR as a barangay (village) at the minimum or a cluster of contiguous barangays where there is a critical mass of farmers who benefited from land reform. Aware of its limited funds for rural development, DAR decided to focus resources on strategic target communities that had potential for 'spill-over' effect.

By 2004, DAR was able to launch about 1,200 ARCs nationwide covering close to one million hectares of largely reformed lands. The bulk of the funds came from multilateral and bilateral aid agencies. The target coverage of the ARC strategy is thus inherently limited. Aggravating its problem is the financial limitation of DAR. After more than seven years of implementation, this strategy failed to actually allot funds to a majority of the communities officially declared as ARCs. In fact by 2000, the effective reach of the ARC programme was only 16 per cent – meaning less than one out of every five land reform communities were able to receive actual funds from DAR. Overall, the government reported that by 2004, only 20 per cent of the entire population of land reform beneficiaries had received some form of government support service (NEDA, 2004). Meanwhile, it was also later discovered that many of the communities declared as ARCs in fact have significant pending land redistribution problems (Franco, 2000, 1999c, 1998).

Despite its inherent limitations, the ARC strategy has contributed to the cause of agrarian reform in a number of ways. First, the ARC concept was partly responsible for reinvigorating the foreign donor community's interest in CARP, mobilising about PhP22.5 billion (or, $500 million, current dollar exchange rate) in foreign development assistance between 1993 and 1997 alone. Second, the ARC concept partly shielded CARP from the attacks of the anti-reform forces that contended that lands awarded to peasants had become unproductive. Finally, with the renewed interest of the foreign donor community, other anti-CARP state actors hesitated to attack the programme. Peasant organisations and NGOs have remained critical of the ARC concept and strategy largely because only a fraction of redistributed lands and beneficiaries can actually be covered by the programme. Lately, many other NGOs have realised, however, that defaulting on any post-land reform development undertaking may only give ammunition to those seeking ways to edge land reform out of the state agenda. Thus despite their critical views on ARC, some peasant organisations and NGOs have begun interfacing with DAR in this regard.

The above discussion prompts some observations. First, the ARC strategy does not contradict, but rather supports, the broader paradigm of the state on agricultural and national development. In fact, many of the funded projects in ARCs are those types that provide large-scale physical infrastructure (roads, bridges) to communities with the potential to become, or already are, commercially competitive, and many of the so-called institutional support projects, such as 'market-matching' (having land reform beneficiaries find their match in the market) are in fact processes where the government technocrats essentially act as marketing agents of transnational companies (e.g. looking for supply and demand for their cocoa, coffee and bananas). Second, the ARC strategy in fact implements the overarching 'triad policies' of the government in agriculture. This is reflected in many of the funded and non-funded projects in ARCs. For example, after a very brief period of modestly funded projects in the early 1990s, the government allotted no funds (not even overseas development assistance) for the post-land transfer farm development programmes in the A&D and CBFM areas.

Third, the ARC strategy is also opportunistic in the sense that it provides projects in land reform communities because either there were actual offers from international agencies to fund these types of project, or there were calculated opportunities for funds from the international aid community for particular types of project – especially when packaged as 'anti-poverty' projects. This is for example how the market-led agrarian reform invented and promoted by the World Bank ended up being one of the ARC-funded projects, and packaged as an 'anti-poverty' programme. Finally, the limited scale of ARC in terms of funds mobilised for its programme suggests that it serves the political legitimacy needs of the central state more than its developmental goals. In short, while the ARC strategy has contributed in the post-land transfer farm and beneficiary development, the broader agricultural context may prove more strategically important. And, as discussed earlier, developments on the agricultural front reveal extremely problematic conditions for small family farms.

Despite the relatively hostile overarching agricultural and national development framework and strategies adopted and promoted by the national government and supported by mainstream international development agencies, some improvements in the lives and livelihoods of land reform beneficiaries are observable. By the year 2000, official statistics showed that 4.1 million peasant households had directly benefited from the combined land and leasehold reform programmes. Yet, as discussed earlier, in reality the number of actual beneficiaries of truly redistributive reform is lower than this figure and is most likely to be somewhere just around three million. Yet, three million peasant households – involving close to 20 million individuals – is a significant number, equivalent to more or less two-fifths of the current rural household population. It is in this context that land reform, to a relatively significant extent, did deliver part of its promise (see also Putzel, 2002).

Two recent, quite rigorous, longitudinal empirical studies are important and are relevant to this paper, namely, Deininger *et al.* (2000) and Reyes (2002).[20] The first set of study, i.e. Deininger *et al.*, examines a set of data surveyed in 1985, 1989 and 1998 by teams from the IRRI and IFPRI (International Rice Research Institute and International Food and Population Research Institute) from a number of municipalities in two provinces.[21] This study is limited to rice and corn farms, the sector where the Marcos land reform started in 1972, a programme continued by CARP beyond 1988. The other empirical study, i.e. Reyes (2002), builds on a previous set of survey data in 1990 and 2000. This study is broader in scope in terms of provinces covered in the country. But like the first study, it also focuses on rice and corn farmers.

The Deininger *et al.* study finds that land reform has impacted positively on the income and welfare of beneficiary households (see Table 4.3), i.e. those of rice and corn farmers. The average farm income of the beneficiary household during the wet season doubled: from a daily average of PhP98 to PhP219 (there was no data for the 1998 dry season). This dramatic increase in income is largely accounted for by the increases in productivity that will be discussed below. Two other household categories with more secure access to land, namely, 'owner' and 'leaseholder', have posted net increases in their average income during the wet seasons of 1985 and 1998, though the increases were not as radical as those of the land reform beneficiaries.

On the flipside, the average farm income of share tenants was nearly cut by half during the same period. The average farm income of land reform beneficiaries was also substantially superior compared to the income of their counterparts among the leaseholders, share tenants and even owners (except for the wet season in 1985 when the average incomes of beneficiaries and owners were almost at the same level). Obviously, share tenants have the lowest level of incomes at any given point in time and in any season.

The income increases among land reform beneficiaries observed in

Table 4.3 Household income by tenure status (in rice and corn lands), 1985 and 1998 (in pesos)

Year	Income	Owner	Land reform beneficiaries of the OLT	Leaseholders	Share tenants
1998	Rice farm income (wet season)	161	219	111	12
1985	Rice farm income (wet season)2	103	98	82	2
1985	Rice farm income (dry season)	76	237	137	20

Source: Deininger *et al.* (2000: 32).

Note

Figures are rounded off.

Table 4.4 and their superiority to other households' in other tenure categories could be explained by the net improvement in the value of production and efficiency per hectare in the beneficiaries' farms as demonstrated in Table 4.4. The average value of production per hectare among the beneficiaries more or less doubled from 1985 to 1998 for both wet and dry seasons. As to the net profit per hectare during the same period, it doubled during the dry season, but more than quadrupled during the wet season.

Of course these dramatic improvements could be accounted for by many factors, including the introduction of modern farming technology, more widespread use of certified seeds, construction of better rural physical infrastructures, among others. But these same improved objective farming conditions could also have benefited other households in other tenure categories. What differentiated the land reform beneficiaries from the rest was the improvement in tenure status. While leaseholders and owners also posted net increases in average incomes during the same period of time and seasons, the amount of net increases were below those

Table 4.4 Farm production characteristics by tenure status, 1985 and 1998 (in Philippine pesos)

Year/season	Owner	Land reform beneficiaries of the OLT	Leaseholders	Share tenants
1998 wet season				
Farm size (in hectares)	1.27	1.49	1.07	1.37
Value of production per hectare	800	1,064	995	430
Net profit per hectares				
(excluding family labor)	361	483	359	43
1998 dry season				
Farm size (in hectares)	1.16	1.44	1.12	1.05
Value of production per hectare	1,36	1,611	1,402	594
Net profit per hectare				
(excluding family labor)	787	876	676	62
1985 wet season				
Farm size (in hectares)	1.41	2.31	1.79	1.15
Value of production per hectare	531	516	534	409
Net profit per hectare				
(excluding family labor)	232	105	132	43
1985 dry season				
Farm size (in hectares)	1.15	1.98	1.58	1.05
Value of production per hectare	663	936	836	665
Net profit per hectare				
(excluding family labor)	323	405	316	103

Source: Deininger *et al.* (2000: 34).

Note
Figures are rounded off.

gained by the beneficiaries; and in absolute terms at every period in time and in both seasons, the average income of land reform beneficiaries was much better than the average income of their counterparts among the leaseholders and owners. Again, share tenants failed to make any net increase in income at all times and seasons.

Meanwhile, the findings of the Reyes (2002) study convey more or less the same conclusions as those presented in the Deininger *et al.* (2000) inquiry. The average annual income of the surveyed beneficiary households doubled during 1990–2000, from nearly PhP50,000 to almost PhP100,000 (see Tables 4.5a and 4.5b). During the same period, the bene-

Table 4.5a Average annual income of households by source in 2000 (Agrarian reform beneficiary and non-beneficiary households)

Source of income	Average income	Share (%)
Total	86,608	100.0
Non-beneficiary	76,156	100.0
Beneficiary	98,653	100.0
Farm	57,407	53.8
Non-beneficiary	46,508	45.1
Beneficiary	67,761	61.5
Off-farm	6,591	2.0
Non-beneficiary	6,370	2.4
Beneficiary	6,878	1.7
Non-farm	50,324	44.2
Non-beneficiary	51,057	52.7
Beneficiary	49,419	36.7

Source: Reyes (2002: 24).

Table 4.5b Average income of households by source in 1990 (Agrarian reform beneficiary and non-beneficiary households)

Source of income	Average income	Share (%)
Total	43,997	100.0
Non-beneficiary	39,142	100.0
Beneficiary	49,594	100.0
Farm	32,008	70.6
Non-beneficiary	28,213	68.9
Beneficiary	36,246	72.1
Off-farm	6,898	3.9
Non-beneficiary	6,442	4.5
Beneficiary	7,555	3.4
Non-farm	25,181	25.5
Non-beneficiary	22,348	26.6
Beneficiary	28,780	24.5

ficiaries' average income derived from farm and non-farm sources nearly doubled. The average total income of land reform beneficiaries was PhP10,000 higher than the non-beneficiaries' in 1990; this gap increased even more in 2000 to PhP22,000, despite similar increasing trends in the farm and non-farm incomes of non-beneficiary households. It is also observable that, while the income of beneficiaries from farm activities declined during the same period from 72 to 61.5 per cent shares of the total income, the extent of this decrease is lower than that of the non-beneficiaries' – which was from a 69 per cent share of the income down to 45 per cent. Finding farm activities less attractive, and/or perhaps finding off-farm and non-farm economic activities more rewarding, non-beneficiary households seemed to have engaged more in livelihood activities outside their farms than their counterparts among the ranks of the beneficiaries. The shares of non-farm and off-farm incomes in the income of non-beneficiaries doubled from 1990 to 2000, compared to the less dramatic increases in the same income shares among the beneficiaries.

Moreover, although both the average real incomes (in 1994 prices) of beneficiary and non-beneficiary households posted net decreases from 1990 to 2000, as shown in Table 4.6, the net real income of beneficiaries remained greater than the non-beneficiaries'. Furthermore, the poverty incidence among the land reform beneficiaries was lower than among the non-beneficiaries, both in 1990 and 2000, even when both groups posted modest decreases in poverty incidence (see Table 4.7). Finally, the general social conditions of land reform beneficiaries, in terms of education, health and sanitation are much better than those of the non-beneficiaries, according to the Reyes (2002) study. The better performance of land reform beneficiaries in income and social well-being compared to non-beneficiaries could be partly explained by the substantial difference in their land productivity in 2000 when on average a beneficiary household

Table 4.6 Average real income in 1994 prices

Status	1990	2000
Total	65,093	56,938
Non-beneficiary	57,802	50,258
Beneficiary	73,488	64,626

Source: Reyes (2002: 25).

Table 4.7 Poverty incidence in 1990 and 2000

	1990	2000
Non-beneficiary	55.1	56.4
Beneficiary	47.6	45.2

Source: Reyes (2002: 28).

Table 4.8 Land productivity (Philippine peso/hectare)

Status	Average
Non-beneficiary	8,032.36
Beneficiary	20,429.87

Source: Reyes (2002: 41).

had a productivity level at PhP20,400 per hectare compared to non-beneficiaries' PhP8,000 per hectare (see Table 4.8) – meaning that the average land productivity of agrarian reform beneficiaries is more than double that of non-beneficiaries.

In sum, what this data tells us is that land reform beneficiaries are doing better in terms of production, productivity gains, and net income improvement in their farms as well as in their social conditions, than those who are not beneficiaries of land reform.

The findings of the two studies cited here, which are the most thorough and most systematic empirical studies to date, validate the assumption and conventional belief that improvement in the tenure status of peasants results in the reduction of poverty and improvement of social well-being in land reform beneficiaries. It also validates, in comparative perspective, the predicament of non-beneficiaries (share tenants and farmworkers) in sharp contrast to their counterparts who have more secure control over land resources.

However, caution is advised for two reasons. On the one hand, while the studies cited here are so far the most systematic existing, still, they are only two survey-based studies. On the other hand and closely related to the first reason, like most studies on the correlation between land reform and poverty reduction in the Philippines and elsewhere, the two cited here suffer some conceptual and methodological flaws, two of which merit further discussion.

First, both studies have a lopsided distribution of respondents, with the overwhelming majority coming from the ranks of rice and corn farmers. While these sectors are significant both economically and demographically, those in the coconut, sugarcane and root crop sectors may even be far more significant economically and more numerous in number. These latter sectors are also the ones that face tremendous obstacles and difficulties in post-land transfer development undertaking for various reasons connected with the pre-existing structure of production, processing and trade. In sugarcane production for example, the milling centrals remain in the hands of landlords despite land reform. The coconut and root crop sectors are usually located in upland communities where the physical infrastructures for entry–exit movements of farm input–output goods and services are quite poor, leading to perennially low farm and labour productivity levels – with the latter partly due to the inaccessibility of non-farm employment sources in these geographically remote communities.

Second, the selection of the survey respondents in the Reyes (2002) study was not based on the various modalities of land transfer within the CARP law. It did not specify whether a survey respondent beneficiary is a beneficiary through a Compulsory Acquisition mode, or Operation Land Transfer for rice and corn farms, or Voluntary Land Transfer, or a Stock Distribution Option, or the various mechanisms for non-private lands (KKK, LE, Settlement, A&D, and CBFM). The non-disaggregation of respondents based on land transfer modality renders the study unable to tell us whether or not those interviewed had actually, and not just formally and nominally, gained control over which type of 'awarded' land and the subsequent farm surplus produced and extracted from the said farm.

Nevertheless, these serious flaws do not negate the studies' findings, showing that land reform, under certain conditions, leads to improvements in the lives and livelihoods of peasant beneficiaries, and, on the flipside, that continued unreformed tenurial relationships perpetuate or even worsen the pre-existing poverty and social exclusion of affected households – certainly for rice and corn farmers. It can also be deduced from the same studies that in situations where poverty conditions do not improve significantly in nationally aggregated terms despite significant national accomplishment in land reform, it is not that land reform failed the central state in its development campaign. But rather it is that the state failed land reform: urgent and necessary complementary support services and policy frameworks were not delivered by the state.

5 Social and political actors and institutions

Whether the land reform law is interpreted and implemented in favour of poor peasants depends on how and to what extent political conflicts over land resources are fought between anti- and pro-reform forces within the state and society (Franco, 2005). Because of this, it is relevant and important to examine closely actual state–society interactions around land reform implementation. Such analysis should neither be state-centred nor society-centered (Borras, 2001; Franco, 1999a). Fox's (1993; see also 1996) 'interactive' state–society perspective is more relevant in analysing public policies such as land reform.

The CARP implementation during the Aquino administration (1986–1992) resulted in less significant outcomes in land distribution. This was due to a number of factors including several public scandals (land-related corruption) that marked this period, and several changes in DAR leadership (four secretaries in six years). The DAR bureaucracy remained in the hands of conservative politicians and technocrats. The situation changed during the administration of President Fidel Ramos

(1992–1998), when the DAR leadership was given to Ernesto Garilao, a former NGO bureaucrat. The encouraging performance during this period can be explained by a number of factors, including the fact that the Ramos administration was able to stabilise the country's political situation and invigorate the national economy, and that Secretary Garilao brought a number of NGO and political activists into the DAR bureaucracy, undermining the hold of conservative forces while reinforcing the emerging small reformist enclave within the department. Moreover, the Garilao DAR identified the importance of working closely with autonomous peasant groups and NGOs. It was at this point that the Garilao DAR became an active player in the reformist state–society alliance in land reform implementation – of combining initiatives by state reformists 'from above' with pressures from social mobilisations 'from below' (see Borras, 1999; 2001; Garilao, 1999: xxi).

The Horacio Morales Jr. DAR administration under the presidency of Joseph Estrada (1998–2000) pursued the strategies of his predecessor, but with some limitations and alterations. First and foremost, the Morales administration had been affected in a negative way by the kind of governance practiced by the national administration of Joseph Estrada. But perhaps most importantly, the subsequent re-alignment of forces within the state during the Estrada administration caused significant shifts in the alignments within the rural social movements. These had created problems between different pro-reform groups because they took different positions with regard to the location of the agrarian reform struggle in the context of the overall call to oust Estrada. Some contended that the struggles for land reform should wait until Estrada was ousted; others argued that land reform struggles should be made an important component of the broader political fight for deeper social reforms (see Franco, 2004). This disunity relatively weakened the pro-agrarian reform civil society groups. The subsequent social and political context within which the Morales leadership was embedded put enormous constraints on it. The Morales DAR was able to deliver a relatively significant outcome in land reform, but not what had been promised.

Gloria Macapagal-Arroyo (2001–present) took over the presidential seat in January 2001 after the Estrada administration was overthrown by a popular people's mobilisation on charges of corruption (Reyes, 2001). The president's husband comes from a big landed family, but her Cabinet has included agrarian reform activists. The Macapagal-Arroyo administration proved to have no serious agenda on agrarian reform, and the president appointed DAR secretaries based on electoral-political considerations, rather than from a social reform angle. Unsurprisingly, the secretaries did not deliver the promised reform, instigating popular protests from the ranks of militant but pragmatic rural social movements. The latter were able to oust from office two secretaries. Between 2001 and 2005, there were four DAR secretaries. This period has been marked by what appears to be widespread corruption by top DAR officials and the Office of the President (see Franco and Borras, 2005).

Meanwhile, the rural social movements have been highly differentiated. Based on their political strategy and strategic vision, there are three broad types of peasant movements and civil society organisations in the Philippines today in the context of the struggles for land and agrarian justice, namely,

i   those pursuing outright opposition to the reformist land reform policy of the state and calling for a more revolutionary reform, i.e. land confiscation without compensation to landlords and free land distribution to peasants;

ii   those engaged in 'conflict-free partnership' with the state in implementing the official reformist land reform programme; and

iii   those trying to maximise the reformist potential of the current state land reform law but without losing sight of a broader and deeper notion of agrarian justice outside the official parameters of the state policy, and using militant but pragmatic political strategies and forms of action in an attempt to stretch the limits of the official policy.

The three types of rural social movements are ideal types. In reality, many of the different groups identified here, especially their local affiliates, actually travel back and forth between the different types through time, spaces and issues. The emergence of these broad formations of autonomous peasant organisations and their allies among the ranks of civil society organisations ushered in an era marked by militant but pragmatic rural people's movements in the country. The willingness and capacity of these groups to engage the state, or more specifically forge alliances with reformists within the state while remaining autonomous, have made a difference in land reform implementation, resulting in significant positive outcomes as far as land redistribution is concerned.

In short, passing a progressive land reform law and having it implemented in favour of the landless and near-landless rural poor has been extremely difficult in the context of the Philippines where the central state is heavily influenced by the landed elite. However, this already problematic setting has become even more difficult for land reform amid far-reaching neoliberal reforms where the traditional obligations of the state to its rural citizens, including its responsibility to implement its land reform law, have increasingly been marginalised in the official policy agendas in favour of more market-friendly policies. But as said earlier, policy outcomes are not necessarily automatically reflective of the intentions of different state and societal actors. Policy outcomes are the results of politically conflict-ridden interactions between different contending groups and classes within the state and society. Thus, the interpretation and implementation of the land reform law and how it actually impacts on poverty remain a contested terrain between different actors within the state and society.

6 Concluding remarks

The land redistribution and leasehold reform programmes in the country have not fully delivered their promise in terms of land redistribution and socio-economic development in the countryside. But substantial partial reforms have been achieved. However, a relatively sizeable portion of this accomplishment data must be taken out of the achievement accounting because it does not constitute truly redistributive reform – it includes the market-based land transfers, particularly those through the Voluntary Land Transfer (VLT, a variant of the current model of Market-Led Agrarian Reform), Stock Distribution Option (SDO), some actual practices of the Voluntary Offer-to-Sell (VOS), padded reports on leasehold, and anomalous transactions in public lands. It was also shown not only that these voluntary, market-driven schemes do not constitute redistributive reform, but that they also undermine the potentially redistributive state-led modalities within the land reform programme. Nevertheless, the possible net accomplishment data remain significant. Land redistribution and leasehold reform have also directly resulted in a significant reduction of poverty among beneficiary peasant households, at least in the rice and corn sectors.

However, despite the relatively high degree of land redistribution and leasehold reform during the recent past, poverty in the country continues to be significant, and it has remained a rural phenomenon. The reasons why the significant partial land and leasehold reform accomplishment has not been translated into an equally significant degree of rural poverty reduction and agricultural development are precisely because land redistribution has remained partial and because the dominant overarching development strategies of successive national governments in the country have been quite hostile to small family farms. These development strategies have focused their attention (i.e. state package of support including necessary policy frameworks) on the elite section of agriculture, namely, the capitalist farmer and corporate agribusiness sectors (for 'developmental' reasons) and some landed elite in the 'traditional sector', particularly sugarcane (for 'political' reasons), who represent a minority in the countryside in terms of the number of people having livelihoods or employment. Land reform, despite its formal legal mandate to cover all farm types regardless of productivity conditions, has been generally kept out of this sector (or voluntary market-based land transfer schemes were employed here).

In short, indeed land reform leads to poverty reduction as well as land and labour productivity gains. These gains could have been greater and

could have been sustained with sufficient state support and service programmes for land reform beneficiaries. In this regard, the Philippine state
has, to a large extent, failed to deliver. Finally, the experience in land
reform in the Philippines shows that it is the conflict-ridden pro-reform
interaction between state reformists and autonomous rural social movements that accounted for the positive outcomes in land redistribution. It is
also the relative absence of this type of pro-reform state–society alliance
and interaction in post-land transfer farm and beneficiary development
processes that has partly contributed to the contemporary predicament in
many land reform communities.

Notes

1 The authors are grateful to the participants in the 'ISS–UNDP land and
poverty workshop' held in February 2005 in The Hague, as well as to Haroon
Akram Lodhi, Cris Kay and Terry McKinley for their critical and very constructive comments to earlier versions of this chapter.

2 See for example Byres (1974), as well as the comparative analysis offered by
Kay (2002) on the East Asian and Latin American experiences.

3 For related historical comparative discussions about the causes and consequences
of some classic land reform cases, see Byres (2004) and Bernstein (2004).

4 For general background material, refer to Borras (2003a); for the Philippine
case, see Borras (2005).

5 This follows Tsing (2002) in her conceptual argument about the nature of
property rights in the historical context of Indonesia.

6 The small farmers in this sector are in different tenurial status. The only
significant exception in this sector is the category of some sugarcane plantations operated under a variety of wage labour-based production relations.

7 Refer to the scholarly works of Ofreneo (1980), Tadem *et al.* (1984) and
Vellema (2002).

8 Refer to the various analyses by Angeles (1999), Rivera (1994) and Rutten
(1993).

9 It should be noted that the average farm size in the country is two hectares,
while the land reform award ceiling is fixed at three hectares. For redistributed
private lands, a Certificate of Land Ownership Award (CLOA) is issued to beneficiaries. Beneficiaries have the option to stay either in a collective or individual land title.

10 The CA, VOS, VLT, GFI (Government Financial Institution) land transfer
modes, including the Marcos land reform, i.e. OLT, in tenanted rice and corn
lands that was subsumed by the CARP law.

11 These are: *Kilusang Kabuhayan at Kaunlaran* or KKK lands which are lands
segregated for the livelihood programme by the Marcos regime, landed estates
(LE) which are the remnants of the 'friar lands', and settlement lands previously identified and segregated for purposes of the resettlement programme.
Many of these government-owned lands are cultivated farmlands, most of
which are hosts to a variety of tenurial relationships between elite and subaltern social groups.

12 Under the landed estates (LE), settlement lands, and the KKK lands.

13 The succeeding discussion about VLT draws from Borras (2005).

14 Based on various discussions between Borras and DAR secretary Horacio
Morales in 1999 and 2001.

15 With a total of US$398,000 funding.
16 The estimated cost of this project is US$5.24 million, or $5,240 (PhP262,000) per beneficiary.
17 For details of this programme, see World Bank (2000a).
18 Contained in the letter dated 30 October 2001 from DAR's assistant secretary Jose Mari Ponce to WB country director Robert Vance Pulley. The money will come from the Japan Social Development Fund (JSDF) grant. The paper also benefited from an interview with DAR (acting) secretary Jose Mari Ponce in August 2004, Quezon City. Refer also to Fox and Gershman (2000) for a good background on the World Bank agrarian reform programme in the Philippines into which the expanded MLAR or CMARPRP was later inserted.
19 Informal discussion with Karlo de Asis, a staff within the programme, 2004.
20 Another interesting empirical (longitudinal) study about the impact of agrarian reform on peasants' lives and livelihoods at the household level is the one carried out by Ricardo Reyes (2000).
21 These are the rice-producing provinces of Iloilo and Nueva Ecija.

References

Abinales, P. (2000). *Making Mindanao: Cotabato and Davao in the Formation of the Philippine Nation-State*. Quezon City: Ateneo de Manila University Press.

ADB (2005). *Poverty in the Philippines: Income, Assets and Access*. Manila: Asian Development Bank.

Angeles, L. (1999). 'The Political Dimension in the Agrarian Question: Strategies of Resilience and Political Entrepreneurship of Agrarian Elite Families in a Philippine Province', *Rural Sociology*, vol. 64, no. 4, pp. 667–692.

Balisacan, A. and H. Hill (2003). 'An Introduction to the Key Issues', in A. Balisacan and H. Hill, eds, *The Philippine Economy: Development, Policies, and Challenges*, pp. 3–44. Quezon City: Ateneo de Manila University Press.

Bernstein, H. (2004). 'Changing before Our Very Eyes: Agrarian Questions and the Politics of Land in Capitalism Today', *Journal of Agrarian Change*, vol. 4, nos 1 and 2, pp. 190–225.

Borras, S. Jr (forthcoming). '"Free Market", Export-led Development Strategy and its Impact on Rural Livelihoods, Poverty and Inequality: The Philippines Experience Seen from a Southeast Asian Perspective,' *Review of International Political Economy*.

Borras, S. Jr (2006a). 'Redistributive Land Reform in "Public" (Forest) Lands? Lessons from the Philippines and their Implications to Land Reform Theory and Practice', *Progress in Development Studies*, vol. 6, no. 2, pp. 123–145.

Borras, S. Jr (2006b). 'The Philippine Land Reform in Comparative Perspective: Some Conceptual and Methodological Implications', *Journal of Agrarian Change*, vol. 6, no. 1, pp. 69–101.

Borras, S. Jr (2005). 'Can Redistributive Reform Be Achieved via Market-based Land Transfer Schemes? Lessons and Evidence from the Philippines', *Journal of Development Studies*, vol. 41, no. 1, pp. 90–134.

Borras, S. Jr (2003a). 'Questioning Market-led Agrarian Reform: Experiences from Brazil, Colombia and South Africa', *Journal of Agrarian Change*, vol. 3, no. 3, pp. 367–394.

Borras, S. Jr (2003b). 'Inclusion-Exclusion in Public Policies and Policy Analyses: The Case of Philippine Land Reform, 1972–2002', *Journal of International Development*, vol. 15, no. 8, pp. 1049–1065.

Borras, S. Jr (2001). 'State–Society Relations in Land Reform Implementation in the Philippines', *Development and Change*, vol. 32, no. 3, pp. 545–575.

Borras, S. Jr (1999). *The Bibingka Strategy in Land Reform Implementation: Autonomous Peasant Movements and State Reformists in the Philippines*. Quezon City: Institute for Popular Democracy.

Borras, S. Jr and J. Franco (2005). 'Struggles for Land and Livelihood: Redistributive Reform in Agribusiness Plantations in the Philippines', *Critical Asian Studies*, vol. 37, no. 3, pp. 331–361.

Byres, T. (2004). 'Neo-classical Neo-populism 25 Years On: Déjà vu and Déjà Passé: Towards a Critique', *Journal of Agrarian Change*, vol. 4, no. 1 and 2, pp. 17–44.

Byres, T. (1974). 'Land Reform, Industrialization and the Marketed Surplus in India: An Essay on the Power of Rural Bias', in D. Lehmann, ed., *Peasants, Landlords and Governments: Agrarian Reform in the Third World*, pp. 221–261. New York: Holmes and Meier Publishers.

Caouette, D. (2004). 'Persevering Revolutionaries: Armed Struggle in the 21st Century, Exploring the Revolution of the Communist Party of the Philippines'. PhD Dissertation, Cornell University.

Carranza, D. (2004). 'Hacienda Luisita Massacre: A Tragedy Waiting to Happen: A Briefing Paper', December 2004, Quezon City: PEACE Foundation (www.peace.net.ph, downloaded 18 May 2006)

Carranza, D. (2000). 'Case Study No. 1: Barangay Cambuga, Bondoc Peninsula', in J. Franco, ed., *Agrarian Reform Communities and Rural Democratization in Quezon*. Quezon City: UNDP/Institute for Popular Democracy.

Carranza, D. (1994). 'Failing a Reform: The Hacienda Luisita Formula', SENTRA Monograph 1, Series of 1992, pp. 1–35. Quezon City: SENTRA.

David, C. (2003). 'Agriculture', in A. Balisacan and H. Hill, eds, *The Philippine Economy: Development, Policies, and Challenges*, pp. 175–218. Quezon City: Ateneo de Manila University Press.

de la Rosa, R. (2005). 'Agrarian Reform Movement in Commercial Plantations: The Experience of the Banana Sector in Davao del Norte', in J. Franco and S. Borras, eds, *On Just Grounds: Struggling for Agrarian Justice and Exercising Citizenship Rights in the Rural Philippines*, pp. 45–114. Quezon City: Institute for Popular Democracy; Amsterdam: Transnational Institute.

Deininger, K., F. Lara Jr., M. Maertens and A. Quisumbing (2000). 'Agrarian Reform in the Philippines: Past Impact and Future Challenges'. World Bank document, Unpublished.

DENR (2004). 'Land Distribution Accomplishment for A&D Lands and CBFM Program, as of June 2004'. Quezon City: DENR CARP-Secretariat, photocopy version.

Feranil, S. (2005). 'Evolving Peasant Movement in Negros Occidental: Stretching the Limits of Official Land Reform Policy', in J. Franco and S. Borras, eds, *On Just Grounds: Struggling for Agrarian Justice and Exercising Citizenship Rights in the Rural Philippines*, pp. 199–262. Quezon City: Institute for Popular Democracy; Amsterdam: Transnational Institute.

Fox, J. (1996). 'Does Civil Society Thicken? The Political Construction of Social Capital in Rural Mexico', *World Development*, vol. 24, no. 6, pp. 1089–1103.

Fox, J. (1993). *The Politics of Food in Mexico: State Power and Social Mobilization*. Ithaca: Cornell University Press.

Fox, J. and J. Gershman (2000). 'The World Bank and Social Capital: Lessons from

Ten Rural Development Projects in the Philippines and Mexico', *Policy Sciences*, vol. 33, nos 3 and 4, pp. 399–419.

Franco, J. (2005). 'Making Property Rights Accessible: Movement Innovation in the Political-Legal Struggle to Claim Land Rights in the Philippines,' *IDS Working Paper Series* No. 244 (www.ids.ac.uk/ids/bookshop/wp/wp244.pdf, downloaded 18 May 2006).

Franco, J. (2004). 'Philippines: Fractious Civil Society, Competing Visions of Democracy', in M. Alagappa, ed., *Civil Society and Political Change in Asia*, pp. 97–137, Stanford: Stanford University Press.

Franco, J. (2001). *Elections and Democratization in the Philippines*. New York: Routledge; Quezon City: Institute for Popular Democracy.

Franco, J. (2000). 'Agrarian Reform Communities and Rural Democratization in Quezon Province'. Quezon City: Institute for Popular Democracy (IPD) /United Nations Development Programme (UNDP) – SARDIC Programme.

Franco, J. (1999a). 'Between Uncritical Collaboration and Outright Opposition: An Evaluative Report on the Partnership for Agrarian Reform and Rural Development Services, PARRDS', *IPD Occasional Papers* No 12. Quezon City: Institute for Popular Democracy (www.ipd.org.ph).

Franco, J. (1999b). 'Market-assisted Land Reform in the Philippines: Round Two – Where Have All the Critics Gone', *Conjuncture*, vol. 11, no. 2, pp. 1–6. Quezon City: Institute for Popular Democracy (online version, www.ipd.org.ph).

Franco, J. (1999c). 'Organizational Strength Appraisal of Organizations in Top Agrarian Reform Communities (ARCs)'. Food and Agriculture Organization (FAO) – SARC-TSARRD Programme: Quezon City.

Franco, J. (1998). 'Problems-Needs Assessment of Agrarian Reform Communities (ARC) Organizations in the Least Developed ARCs'. Quezon City: Food and Agriculture Organization – SARC-TSARRD Programme.

Franco, J. and S. Borras Jr (eds) (2005). *On Just Grounds: Struggling for Agrarian Justice and Exercising Citizenship Rights in the Rural Philippines*. Quezon City: Institute for Popular Democracy; Amsterdam: Transnational Institute.

Garilao, E. (1999). 'Foreword', in S. Borras, *The Bibibgka Strategy in Land Reform Implementation*, pp. xix–xxi. Quezon City: Institute for Popular Democracy.

Hawes, G. (1987). *The Philippine State and the Marcos Regime: The Politics of Export*. Ithaca: Cornell University Press.

Houtzager, P. and J. Franco (2003). 'When the Poor Make Law: Comparisons across Brazil and the Philippines'. Research Note. Law, Democracy, and Development Program, Sussex: Institute of Development Studies.

Kay, C. (2002). 'Why East Asia Overtook Latin America: Agrarian Reform, Industrialization and Development', *Third World Quarterly*, vol. 23, no. 6, pp. 1073–1102.

Kerkvliet, B. (1979). 'Land Reform: Emancipation or Counterinsurgency?', in D. A. Rosenberg, ed., *Marcos and Martial Law in the Philippines*, pp. 113–144. Berkeley: University of California Press.

Kerkvliet, B. (1977). *The Huk Rebellion: A Study of Peasant Revolt in the Philippines*. Quezon City: New Day Publishers (and 1977, Berkeley: University of California Press).

Lichauco, L. (1956). 'Land Settlement in the Philippines', in K. Parsons *et al.*, eds, *Land Tenure – Proceedings of the International Conference on Land Tenure and Related Problems in World Agriculture*, held in Madison, Wisconsin, 1951, pp. 188–197. Madison: University of Wisconsin Press.

MUCEP (2001). 'Proposal for the Preparation of Area Development Plan and Household Level Farm Business Plans for World Bank–DAR–CMARP Project in Sibula, Lopez Jaena, Misamis Occidental'. A project proposal by the Misamis University Community Extension Program (MUCEP) submitted to the ARCDP–DAR. Misamis Occidental: MUCEP; Quezon City: DAR–ARCDP.

NEDA (2004). 'Medium-term Philippine Development Plan, 2004–2010'. Manila: National Economic Development Authority (NEDA).

Ofreneo, R. (1980). *Capitalism in Philippine Agriculture.* Quezon City: Foundation for Nationalist Studies.

Putzel, J. (2002). 'The Politics of Partial Reform in the Philippines', in V. K. Ramachandran and M. Swaminathan, eds, *Agrarian Studies: Essays on Agrarian Relations in Less-developed Countries*, pp. 213–229. New Delhi: Tulika Books (2003, London: Zed)

Putzel, J. (1992). *A Captive Land: The Politics of Agrarian Reform in the Philippines.* London: Catholic Institute for International Relations; New York: Monthly Review Press; Quezon City: Ateneo de Manila University Press.

Reyes, C. (2002). 'Impact of Agrarian Reform on Poverty', in *PIDS Discussion Paper Series* No. 2002–02. Manila: Philippine Institute for Development Studies.

Reyes, R. (2001). 'People Power Comes into the New Millennium', *IPD Political Brief*, vol. 9, no. 2, pp. 1–30. Quezon City: Institute for Popular Democracy.

Reyes, R. (2000). 'CARP Past the Deadline: Where's the Beef?', in 'The Impact of Agrarian Reform and Changing Market on Rural Households', *MODE Research Papers*, vol. 1, no. 4, pp. 7–56. Quezon City: MODE.

Reyes, R. (1999). 'Market-assisted Land Reform: An Indecent Proposal'. www.philsol.nl (downloaded 18 May 2006).

Riedinger, J. (1995). *Agrarian Reform in the Philippines: Democratic Transitions and Redistributive Reform.* Stanford: Stanford University Press.

Rivera, T. (1994). *Landlords and Capitalists: Class, Family, and State in Philippine Manufacturing.* Quezon City: University of the Philippines Press.

Rutten, R. (1993). *Artisans and Entrepreneurs in the Rural Philippines: Making a Living and Gaining Wealth in Two Commercialized Crafts.* Quezon City: New Day Publishers.

Tadem, E., J. Reyes and L. S. Magno (1984). *Showcases of Underdevelopment in Mindanao: Fishes, Forests, and Fruits.* Davao: Alternate Forum for Research in Mindanao (AFRIM).

Tsing, A. (2002). 'Land as Law: Negotiating the meaning of Property in Indonesia', in F. Richards, ed., *Land, Property, and the Environment*, pp. 94–137. Oakland: Institute for Contemporary Studies.

UNORKA (2000). 'No to the World Bank's Market-assisted Land Reform', Statement circulated during the International Conference on Agrarian Reform and Rural Development, Tagaytay City, Philippines, December. Mimeo.

UPSARDFI (2001). 'Families and Households in the ARC: Focusing ARCDP II for Greater and Lasting Impact in the Rural Countryside – A Final Report on the Social Assessment for the Second Phase of the Agrarian Reform Communities Development Project', prepared by the University of the Philippines Action and Research for Development Foundation, Inc. (UPSARDFI) for the ARCDP–DAR. Quezon City: UPSARDFI, College of Social Work and Community Development, U.P.-Diliman; DAR.

Vellema, Sietze (2002). *Making Contract Farming Work?: Society and Technology in*

Philippine Transnational Agribusiness', PhD dissertation. Wageningen: Wageningen University, Maastricht: Shaker Publishing.

World Bank (2001). *World Development Report 2000/01: Attacking Poverty*. Oxford: Oxford University Press.

World Bank (2000a). 'Philippines – Second Agrarian Reform Communities Development Project, or ARCDP-2, Project Concept Document'. Manila: World Bank, East Asia and Pacific Region Office, Philippine Country Department.

World Bank (2000b). 'World Bank Report No. 20755-PH – Land Administration and Management Project'. Washington, DC: World Bank.

Wurfel, D. (1983). 'The Development of Post-war Philippine Land Reform: Political and Sociological Explanations', in A. Ledesma, S. J., P. Makil and V. Miralao, eds, *Second View from the Paddy*, pp. 1–14. Quezon City: Institute of Philippine Culture, Ateneo de Manila University Press.

5 Land markets and rural livelihoods in Vietnam

A. Haroon Akram-Lodhi

Introduction

Over the course of the past 20 years Vietnam has demonstrated impressive rates of growth, poverty reduction and social development.[1] These trends are illustrated in Table 5.1, which shows that constant per capita gross domestic product (GDP) almost doubled between 1985 and 2000, that poverty was reduced significantly in both urban and rural areas, that literacy and life expectancy both notably improved, and that gender gaps in literacy were reduced. In light of these figures, it is not an overstatement to suggest that 'Vietnam's performance in terms of poverty reduction has been spectacular' (Joint Donor Report to the Vietnam Consultative Group (henceforth Joint Donor Report), 2004: 118).

Nonetheless, poverty remains a pivotal issue in Vietnam. The rate of poverty reduction fell from 4 per cent per annum between 1993 and 1998, to 2 per cent per annum between 1998 and 2002 (Joint Donor Report, 2003: 9), and the numbers of those living in poverty remain great. In rural areas in particular, where 75 per cent of the population continues to earn

Table 5.1 Growth, poverty and social development in Vietnam, 1985–2000

	1985	1990	1995	2000
Constant GDP per capita, US$	188.0	211.2	284.1	369.5
Average annual rate of growth of constant GDP per capita*	–	2.3	6.1	5.4
Urban poverty rate**	–	25.1	9.2	6.6
Rural poverty rate**	–	66.4	45.5	35.6
Female literacy rate, %***	85.1	87.1	89.0	90.7
Male literacy rate, %***	93.8	94.0	94.2	94.5
Female life expectancy	64.6	66.8	69.4	71.5
Male life expectancy	60.7	62.8	65.0	66.7
Under five infant mortality rate	60.0	50.0	43.0	34.4

Source: World Bank (2004); Joint Donor Report (2003).

Notes
* 5 year average; ** 1993, 1998 and 2002, respectively; *** Over 15 years.

their livelihood, more than a third of the population in 2002 lived below the poverty line, and almost 14 per cent of the population were food inse-cure.[2] Thus, the social and economic performance of the rural economy remains central to poverty reduction strategies. A key issue in this regard is that of access to land. Following the decollectivisation of agriculture in 1988, the principal mechanism used by the government to manage rural land access has been the land market. Thus, it is through the more effect-ive and efficient use of land markets that the government hopes to achieve key elements of its rural poverty reduction and growth strategy. It is in this light that recent suggestions that 'the tendency towards the concentration of land is clearly visible' (Joint Donor Report, 2003: 38), that 'differences in landholdings ... show a link with poverty' (Government of Vietnam-Donor-NGO Poverty Working Group (henceforth PWG), 1999: 28; Oxfam (GB), 1999), and that 'a rural proletariat is emerging' (Haughton, 2000) must generate concern regarding the capacity of land markets to con-tribute to the achievement of an equitable, pro-poor pattern of rural development in Vietnam. Therefore, this chapter aims to examine how the emergence of the land market in Vietnam has affected rural liveli-hoods, growth and poverty reduction.

Beginning with a review of government policy since the mid-1980s and its impact on agricultural production, the chapter next examines possible relationships between market-led land access and rural poverty reduction, identifying, as the critical transmission mechanism, the relationship between the structure of access to land and non-land assets and agricul-tural productivity. The chapter demonstrates that the emergence of land markets has fostered inequality in rural access to land, non-land assets, working capital, income and expenditure. There are gender dimensions to this inequality. It also demonstrates that this inequality is reflected in differences in agricultural productivity and market integration across farms, with relatively wealthier households being more productive and more market-oriented than relatively poorer households. In this light, it is suggested that Vietnam is witnessing the emergence of a small group of commercial farmers that can be set beside a dominant group of subsis-tence farmers and the landless, with the latter being the poorest group in Vietnam. The chapter continues by looking at the current policy frame-work of the government and the donor community, emphasising that both actors seek to deepen the resource allocation role of the market and thus market-led socio-economic security, promote rural diversification and non-farm employment, and construct social safety nets to assist those whom these policies do not benefit. The impact of market-led land con-centration on civil society activism is also discussed. The conclusion draws together the central thrust of the argument presented.

Land markets in Vietnam

Decollectivisation and the establishment of private property rights

In the latter half of the 1970s, a precipitous decline in farm productivity in Vietnam resulted in a sharp fall in per capita foodgrain availability despite increased foodgrain imports, and led to peasant unrest and food riots (Akram-Lodhi, 2001a; Tuan, 2005). This fall is illustrated in Figure 5.1. The reasons for this foodgrain productivity and availability crisis were twofold. The first cause was the incentive structure of collective agriculture, offering low prices for farm output produced in excess of government quotas, consumer subsidies that devalued work, and an overvalued exchange rate that encouraged imports (Men, 1995: 39). The second cause was the inadequate amount of investment in agriculture (Akram-Lodhi, 2001a), which was in large part due to the heavy industry bias of the State Planning Commission.

The Vietnamese government had long recognised the weaknesses of collective agriculture, having permitted localised experiments in the late 1960s and early 1970s designed to increase rural productivity (Akram-Lodhi, 2001a). The success of these experiments encouraged the government to begin a process of agrarian restructuring in the wake of the agrarian crisis. The 'first wave' of agrarian reform took place between 1981 and 1987 (Men, 1995: 42), during which time household contracts spread throughout the country, under the aegis of Directive 100 of 1981. These contracts allocated land to farms based principally but not exclusively upon the size of their adult workforce in exchange for the delivery of an output quota at a fixed price to the cooperative. Any output produced in excess of the contract could be retained by the farm household for

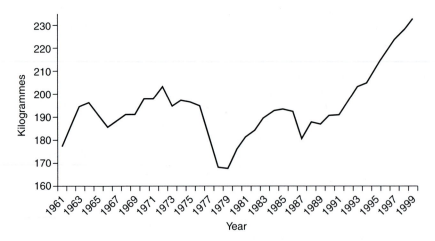

Figure 5.1 Per capita net cereal availability, 1961–1999 (source: interpolated from Akram-Lodhi (2005)).

consumption, or could be sold to private traders. Directive 100 thus restructured incentives, so that aggregate output, and more especially yields, started to play a bigger role in farm decision-making. However, Directive 100 did not supplant the role of the cooperative, or move toward market-based prices.

The result of Directive 100, as demonstrated in Figure 5.1, was an initial boost to production, and an attendant increase in real incomes. However, once these one-off static efficiency gains were achieved, another sharp drop in per capita foodgrain availability in the mid-1980s followed. Further piecemeal reforms failed to yield improvements in farm production and productivity, and the widespread recognition of this within the government served as the precondition to the decision to abandon collective agriculture. This was undertaken in the wake of the sixth Congress of the Communist Party in 1986, which paved the way for Resolution 10 in 1988.

Resolution 10 restructured agriculture by recognising, for the first time, the primacy of the farm household as the basic economic unit of the rural economy and relegating cooperatives into the role of supporting farm households. Cooperatives were obliged to fully contract out land to farm households for 15 years for annual crops and 40 years for perennial crops. In most instances land was allocated on the basis of the size of the family, although it was subject to a ceiling. As a consequence of Resolution 10, a remarkably egalitarian distribution of land was quickly introduced across the country as peasant family farming emerged from within central planning. What Resolution 10 did not do, however, was to create a formally institutionalised land market. Land remained the responsibility of the government; transactions in land remained heavily restricted; and the government resumed control of land when necessary so that it could be reallocated when households moved or stopped farming.

With decollectivisation, capital stock, working capital and other productive assets were no longer controlled by the cooperatives, and they became obliged to rent them out. Farm households were thus allowed to buy and sell animals, equipment and machinery. Output quotas were retained, but significantly reduced, allowing farm households to keep a minimum of 40 per cent of average output, and the quota was fixed for five years. In terms of markets, private sector activity in food marketing was formally accepted. Finally, input, production and output directives from higher administrative levels could no longer be issued to cooperatives. Instead, responsibility for the implementation of Resolution 10 was passed to the communes, in effect decentralising land management within an overarching indicative planning framework. Thus ended central planning in the rural economy.

The 1993 Land Law built on Resolution 10 by extending land tenure to 20 years for annual crops and 50 years for perennial crops. While households were limited to three hectares per farm for annual crops in the Red

River Delta and five hectares per farm for annual crops in the Mekong River Delta, for the first time the exchange, transfer, lease, inheritance and mortgaging of land use rights were permitted. These became known as the 'five rights'. The government also became obliged to compensate holders of land in the event of repossession by the government. This deepening of rural property rights was a necessary response to changes on the ground, where, following Resolution 10, an illegal informal land market quickly developed in secret in much of the country (Akram-Lodhi, 2004). In order to facilitate the development of the formal land market in the wake of the 1993 Land Law, a process began of issuing farm households with land use certificates, known as Red Books. By 2003 91 per cent of agricultural households using land had received their Red Book (Joint Donor Report, 2004: 21).

Revisions to the Land Law in 1998 made the operation of the embryonic land market clearer, with provisions governing the lease, transfer and accumulation of land in excess of previous legal ceilings, depending on particular local conditions, being enacted. These revisions cleared the way for the legal creation of so-called 'large-scale farms' of more than five hectares. Indeed, it quickly became government policy to promote so-called 'average' and 'large-scale' farms, to the seeming detriment of 'small-scale' farms. With regards to non-agricultural land, the 1998 revisions to the Land Law created the capacity to re-lend land and the capacity to use land as capital in a joint venture.

In 2003 a further revision to the Land Law was introduced, and implemented in 2004, which clarified the format and content of the 1993 Land Law, but also introduced substantive reforms regarding land utilisation and transfer. Primarily in response to the demands of domestic and foreign urban businesses in Vietnam, but with important implications for the rural economy, the revisions formally recognised the land market as a legal and institutional reality. The 2003 Land Law did this by significantly simplifying the procedure by which land use certificate holders could buy and sell their usufruct rights or change the functional assignation of their land, within the overall indicative planning framework of the government. This is expressed in the addition of five more 'rights', bringing the total to ten: the right to re-rent land use rights; the right to grant land use rights; the right to use land use rights as collateral, which had previously been the practice even if it was not formally recognised; the right to use land use rights with others to generate capital; and the right to be compensated at market prices if land use rights were repossessed by the government, although new regulations weakened the impact of this right by granting local government the right to determine the parameters of the 'administrative price', which did not have to be the same as the market price. It should be noted that in addition to these rights, the 2003 Land Law also recognised, for the first time, the possibility of communities holding land use rights, as opposed to individuals, institutions and enterprises holding land use rights. This therefore opened up the possibility of legally recognising local land tenure arrangements by assigning the responsibility for them to the community. Finally, and significantly, it should be noted that, as a result of pressure from Vietnamese women's groups, the 2003 Land Law mandated that both the husband and the wife's name be placed on the land use certificate, and that both parties had to consent to land transfers. In addition to enhancing women's bargaining power within the household, this also had the effect of bestowing on women the right to use land as collateral (Mekong Economics, 2004a: 21).

The simplification of buying and selling procedures in the 2003 Land Law was explicitly designed to make the land market operate more efficiently, and in so doing 'deepen' the market. The right to change the functional classification of land was significant in light of the reallocation of the responsibility for large amounts of forest, communal and waste land away from higher tiers of government to communes, which were expected, in turn, to allocate such land to households for their use (*Vietnam News*, 20 January 2005). This effectively placed more land onto the land market as those households allocated land sought to change the functional assignation of the use of their land. As such, the land market was 'broadened'. Communes were also expected to promote voluntary reallocation of land from landed to landless households, although the practical capacity of communes to implement this reform or households to take part in this objective, given that the current value of unirrigated land in current Vietnamese dong[3] (VND) is 30 million per hectare and that of irrigated land of VND 85 million per hectare, is open to question (Joint Donor Report, 2004).

There can be little doubt that Vietnam now has the most active land market in the country's history as policy changes have sought to accommodate and integrate informal practices that had been established by rural households across the country. However, the land market remains highly partial, with continued administrative and regulatory oversight by the effective owner of the land, the government; with the continued capacity of local government officials, operating for the most part in a particularly weak formal institutional environment, to interfere in market operations in arbitrary ways, especially when the legal status of the land is unclear; with significant transactions costs involved in matching supply and demand beyond social networks; and with the continuing role of informal, non-market, social networks to affect the terms and conditions under which land is accessed and utilised, especially when the local formal institutional environment is weak and when, as a consequence, transactions costs in informal activities may be significantly less than those invlolved in formal activities. Thus, activity within the land market bears significant economic, social and political transactions costs, resulting in a market that is segmented. Moreover, there is spatial fragmentation over comparatively short distances. In this light, it is not surprising that there remains a strong residual element of personalised transactions in the emerging land market. Thus, in a recent study, while the formal land market dominated land market transactions, some 32 per cent of all land market transactions were informal (Mekong Economics, 2004b: 2). Finally, there is another factor deeply affecting the operation of the land market, and that factor is a legacy of Vietnamese history. Rural households continue to believe in the need to retain land, for the purposes of food security, a hedge against inflation, and insurance, even in circumstances where their income-earning activities and standard of living remove the need to maintain land.

Land markets and poverty reduction

Recent research has suggested that the land market that has emerged in Vietnam is pro-poor. This is so in the sense that land sales are not concentrated among the poor, and that demand for land to rent comes principally from those with lower levels of assets, most particularly land (Deininger and Jin, 2003; Ravallion and van de Walle, 2003), so that they can fully utilise their labour resources, and in so doing increase their incomes. The basis of this research is tabular and econometric, based upon the Vietnam Living Standards Surveys (VLSS) undertaken in 1993 and 1998 (General Statistical Office (GSO), 1994, 1999) and the Vietnam Household Living Standards Survey (VHLSS) undertaken in 2001 and 2002 (GSO, 2004) by the GSO, with financial and technical assistance from donors. The first VLSS, which is nationally representative, in a statistical sense, surveyed 4,800 households, while the second VLSS surveyed 6,000 households, including 4,300 that had been surveyed during the first VLSS. Thus, Vietnam has a panel data set, even though the 1998 VLSS is, for technical reasons, 'not a true random sample of Vietnamese households' (Desai, 2000: i) and is thus not statistically representative. The VHLSS is also, in a statistical sense, a nationally representative living standards survey, but with a much larger sample size than the VLSS, using a shorter survey protocol, and without interviewing households already surveyed by the VLSS (Joint Donor Report, 2003).

The quality of Vietnam's Living Standards Measurement Surveys (LSMS) remains open to question, for four reasons. The first reason is that the sampling frame upon which the surveys have been carried out may not be fully representative of the population. In particular, the high degree of labour mobility in Vietnam has resulted in a sampling frame that has excluded an important segment of the population, namely unregistered migrant labour. The second reason is that the sampling units used in a conventional LSMS must typically reside in a permanent structure. It can be argued that this underrepresents those who live in temporary structures, substandard housing or institutional housing, all of which are important in Vietnam. The third reason is that the labour force surveys built into the LSMS are often inadequately completed because of the time spent on the lengthy and detailed expenditure component of the surveys. This reduces the reliability of the labour market data contained in the LSMS. The fourth, and perhaps most disturbing, reason lies in the implementation protocols governing the surveys. In 2001, when the VHLSS was being implemented, the survey protocols were distributed to local authorities, which were given the responsibility for implementing the survey. There have been reports that, after receiving training, the authorities distributed the surveys to senior members within the community, who completed them. According to these reports, households themselves were not, by and large, interviewed. The surveys were then returned to the local authorities and the results reviewed in order to ensure consistency with data that is, as a matter of course, relayed to provincial statistical offices. In the process, some quite significant irregularities in the results may have been generated; for example, some observers have suggested that the extent of rural diversification and rural non-farm employment was significantly overstated. Of course, it must be stressed that these reports may be examples of isolated incidents, which would not, then, undermine the validity of the LSMS results overall. However, it should be noted that, although the LSMS evidence suggests that most land is rented out at no charge, this phenomenon has *never* been witnessed in my fieldwork over the past seven years. Land that is rented, whether it is for short- or long-term periods, and whether it is within or between households, is always paid for in some way, whether in cash or in kind. In addition, it should be stressed that it is widely known that there were extensive informal discussions within both the government and the donor community of problems in the design, implementation and analysis of the LSMS in both 1993 and 2002, and that, with regards to the former, if such is indeed the case, it suggests that similar problems plague the 1998 LSMS. Finally, it can be noted that the summary of findings of the VHLSS contains far more limited amounts of data than those contained in the summary of the 1998 VLSS. If these suggestions are indeed accurate, many of the policy recommendations that have been made, based upon LSMS results, by the government, the donor community, and academic observers should be considered very carefully, because it would suggest that possible methodological errors mean that Vietnam has in fact a very narrow evidential base upon which to develop policy recommendations.

Nonetheless, the LSMS results remain, for the moment, the only national descriptive data available on rural Vietnamese economic conditions. For this reason, these data are extensively used in this chapter, although it is important to remain cautious regarding the inferences that can be drawn based upon them. With this caveat in mind, Table 5.2 collates some of the data, arraying cropland and perennial land per household and, in the case of cropland, per worker, by per capita expenditure quintiles. Table 5.2 also contains data on crop area in three important

Table 5.2 Agrarian structure in Vietnam

1 All Vietnam

	1993			1998					2002				Elasticity of perennials with respect to crop land	
	Crop area per household	Perennial area per household	Cropped to perennials (%)	Crop area per worker	Crop area per household	Perennial area per household	Cropped to perennials (%)	Crop area per worker	Crop area per household	Perennial area per household	Cropped to perennials (%)	Per worker	Per worker 1993–1998	Per household 1993–2002
Poorest	3,808	362	9.5	1,719	4,052	654	16.1	1,468	4,778	1,114	23.3	2.1	2.5
Near poor	4,042	539	13.3	1,713	4,508	1,002	22.2	1,598	3,898	1,189	30.5	2.0	2.3
Middle	4,583	956	20.9	1,910	5,130	1,188	23.2	1,788	4,333	1,427	32.9	1.3	1.6
Near rich	5,534	952	17.2	2,233	5,366	1,668	31.1	1,724	4,610	2,239	48.6	2.3	2.8
Rich	7,373	1,488	20.2	3,207	5,079	3,740	73.6	1,770	4,867	2,649	54.4	4.6	2.7

2 Regions

	Mekong Delta Crop area per household			Red River Delta Crop area per household			Central Highlands Crop area per household		
	1993	1998	Percentage change	1993	1998	Percentage change	1993	1998	Percentage change
Poorest	5,355	5,699	106.4	2,482	2,451	98.8	4,892	4,842	99.0
Near poo	6,361	8,057	126.7	2,639	2,731	103.5	6,883	6,889	100.1
Middle	8,680	8,997	103.7	2,522	2,710	107.5	5,607	6,242	111.3
Near rich	9,681	8,756	90.4	2,186	2,444	111.8	7,177	3,643	50.8
Rich	11,828	9,930	84.0	1,711	1,702	99.5	11,009	1,564	14.2

Sources: GSO (1994: Tables 5.1.1, 5.1.5, 5.1.8, 5.1.13); GSO (1999: Tables 5.1.1, 5.1.4, 5.1.5); Joint Donor Report (2003: Table 3.2).

agricultural regions of Vietnam, the Mekong River Delta, the Red River Delta, and the Central Highlands. Cumulatively, then, Table 5.2 provides an overview of broad trends in agrarian structure across all of Vietnam and in selected regions of Vietnam between 1993 and 2002. Per capita expenditure quintiles are used as a proxy for wealth and, while their use is far from ideal, they can be justified on the basis that consumption expenditure data tend to be more accurate than income data and are, moreover, a better illustration of household welfare (Glewwe *et al.*, 2000), which has implications for the assessment of the impact of poverty. However, to this point it should be added that expenditure-based wealth proxies may not be appropriate in evaluating the position of female-led rural households, because female expenditure patterns may systematically differ from those of men (Scott, 2003: 248). Certainly, expenditures in female-led households appear to be higher than those in male-led households (Desai, 2000: Table 3.1).

Several important points seem to emerge from Table 5.2. First, it is apparent that farms in rural Vietnam are on average small, and thus for many farmers land held under land use certificates is likely to be insufficient to meet the subsistence needs of the household. In this sense, then, land rental and sales markets possess the potential to have a significant effect on the welfare of rural households. Second, when examining crop area per household across Vietnam, it seems apparent that land distribution has improved in favour of those households in the relatively poorer per capita expenditure quintiles. This is true on the basis of both per household and per worker. Thus, whereas in 1993 the average cropped area for the relatively richer households was almost double that of the relatively poorest, by 2002 there was no significant difference between the cropped area of the relatively richer households and the relatively poorer.[4] Third, the data demonstrate a significant shift in how land is used. There have been, across all per capita expenditure quintiles, increases in the share of the cropped area devoted to perennial crops such as coffee, cashews and citrus fruits. There may well be, however, gender-based differences in shifts in cropping patterns, if data from the 1998 VLSS is correct (Desai, 2000: Table 4.2.4).

Examining the elasticity of perennials with respect to crop area, on a per worker basis between 1993 and 1998 the elasticity is smallest for those households in the middle of the per capita expenditure distribution, and greatest for those in the relatively richer households. On a per household basis, between 1993 and 2002 the data indicate again that the shift to perennials is weakest among households in the middle of the per capita expenditure distribution and fairly uniform across the other per capita expenditure quintiles. The figures for perennial crops are important in understanding patterns of agricultural accumulation in rural Vietnam, and will therefore be explored in more detail later in the chapter.

In part, the data in Table 5.2 may reflect the increasing use of freshly cleared land in upland areas as well as the administrative reallocation of land previously retained by local government following decollectivisation to individual households, trends that have been well documented (Joint Donor Report, 2003; Marsh and MacAulay, n.d.; Asian Development Bank (ADB), 2002). Notwithstanding this, however, it might be inferred from the all-Vietnam data in Table 5.2 that the emergence of partially complete land markets during the 1990s served to redistribute land towards those households in relatively poorer per capita expenditure quintiles.

This finding seems to have been confirmed in a number of econometric studies of the land market in Vietnam examining the panel data in the VLSS. Thus, Schipper (2003: Table 2) reports changes in landholdings between 1993 and 1998 by form of ownership and by landholding quintiles as a percentage of the land area in 1993. The evidence indicates that the distribution of land became more equal over the 1990s, with the most land-poor landholding quintile increasing its control of land by 265 per cent between 1993 and 1998. Supporting this finding, Ravallion and van de Walle (2003) argue that over the 1990s the land market served to iron out some of the inefficiencies in land allocation generated by initial administrative decisions. Rural households with too little land after decollectivisation used the emerging market to acquire additional land, and witnessed the largest increase in holdings, while those with too much land disposed of it through the market. Deininger and Jin (2003) reinforce this finding, and argue that in addition to the equity enhancements generated by the land market, land transfers have improved efficiency because the demand for land, either to buy or to rent, was driven by the more productive households with lower endowments. This is consistent with the much earlier findings of Chung (1994), who argued that farmers leased land to supplement operational holdings, boost income, and fully utilise available assets, principally labour. Land is leased out for a variety of reasons, including a lack of capacity to invest in productivity enhancements, fragmentation of holdings, lack of access to labour, economic shocks at the household level such as illness, and because of income and asset diversification into rural non-farm household enterprises (Deininger and Jin, 2003; Ravallion and van de Walle, 2003; Vijverberg and Haughton, 2004; Mekong Economics, 2004b) – a condition that is also observed in Armenia (see Spoor, this volume).

In this light it is not surprising that the number of households in the 1998 VLSS selling land was five times the number selling land in the 1993 VLSS and that the number of households buying land in the 1998 VLSS was seven times the number buying in the 1993 VLSS (Deininger and Jin, 2003: Table 2). Clearly, land markets, even if only partially complete, are operating in rural Vietnam. It should be noted that these data cover the period before women and men were both listed on land use certificates, and thus land sales might have been gender-differentiated in terms of their pattern and impact. Outright land sales are less common in the north and central regions of Vietnam, but more common in the southern part of the country. Moreover, of that land which is purchased in the north, the seller is often the government (Mekong Economics, 2004a: 21). Land that is purchased or sold from outside the government is typically bought from within the extended family or social networks established within communes, or from the commune itself, which serves to reduce transactions costs. While they do take place, informal land sales are not a preferred mode of transaction because, while they avoid fees, charges and taxes, they do not result in the formal transfer of the name on the land use certificate (Mekong Economics, 2004b).

In terms of land rental, estimates from the 2002 VHLSS suggest that the 15 per cent of rural households that currently lease in or lease out land represents a threefold increase in land market participation since 1993 (Joint Donor Report, 2003: 38) and, for this to make sense in the context of the data contained in Table 5.1 it would have to be the case that land rentals are principally the provenance of relatively poorer per capita expenditure quintiles.[5] Short-term rental agreements are often informal, and can last as little as a season, whereas formal agreements are often longer in duration, suggesting that households rent because they cannot afford the costs involved in the purchase of land when it is available (Mekong Economics, 2004a: 24; Mekong Economics, 2004b: 54–55). Again, land rental is often from the extended family or from social networks established within communes. The relationship between land rental and gender is currently not known, but the role of social networks in gaining access to land to rent might suggest that gender-based differentiation is operating. Fixed rents are the most common form of land rental, with payment established in terms of volumes of rice and then paid in the current cash equivalent. At the same time, though, the survey data clearly show that some sharecropping has returned. However, perhaps the most interesting aspect of the land rental market in the survey data is that in terms of both renting in and renting out it is most common for land to be leased for free.[6] One possible explanation of this that is consistent with the LSMS data is that this may be a consequence of the enhanced power of local officials to intervene in the land market as a consequence of land market legislation (Ravallion and van de Walle, 2003). This would help explain, for example, why Ravallion and van de Walle (2003) find that, despite continuing administrative obstacles in some regions with the potential to restrict land markets in many circumstances, non-market land administration is 'cooperant' with the market forces that are operating, albeit unevenly and partially. Alternatively, this could be a consequence of households simply giving up farming and migrating to urban areas as a result of strong economic growth, particularly in neighbouring provinces, without bothering to liquidate their assets because of ongoing bureaucratic obstacles, a phenomenon which has been well documented in several areas of Vietnam.

Vietnam is a spatially diverse country, and it could be the case that pooling national data obscures significant inter- and intra-regional differences. Therefore, the second part of Table 5.2 examines the distribution of crop area by per capita expenditure quintiles for three important agricultural regions between 1993 and 1998. Consistent with the all-Vietnam data, a redistribution of crop area that is not in favour of relatively richer per capita expenditure quintiles is confirmed in all three regions, most starkly in the Central Highlands. Thus, both the survey data and econometric analysis based upon it appear to suggest that the land market, while developing, has been operating to the benefit of the relatively poorer per capita expenditure quintiles in Vietnam in that it redistributes land to those who are relatively poorer, allowing them to more fully utilise their scarce available assets and increase their incomes, and in this sense the land market is pro-poor.

Land markets, rural productivity and rural inequality

Property rights, productivity and poverty

The activities of rural producers and the succession of reforms in Vietnam since 1988 have together created a functioning land market. A key issue, then, is the relationship between the land market and poverty. Conceptualising the link between land markets and poverty reduction is straightforward, although several mitigating factors surround these linkages. The relationship would take the following form: increased security of tenure is predicated upon enforceable property rights that cut transactions costs. With enforceable property rights comes the possibility of the establishment of a formal institutional framework governing land allocation through markets. As the land market then becomes formalised, there is an increase in the efficiency of land allocation between competing users, as the marginal benefits from the acquisition or disposal of land are compared to the marginal costs of acquiring or disposing of land. One key aspect of increased efficiency should be increased investment to boost productivity, competitiveness, farm profits and farm incomes, as holders of land seek to maximise the benefits accruing from their available resources. This can be done by both collateralising land so as to generate the financial liquidity necessary to boost investment and by reinvesting farm profits in the farm enterprise. In this sense, then, land markets should increase incomes and reduce rural poverty.

Nonetheless, real, mitigating factors surround these linkages. A precondition of a well-functioning land market is that product, labour and financial markets also function well. This condition is unlikely to hold in many economies. In such circumstances, the 'theory of the second best' suggests that the welfare effect of a removal of market distortions in the land market cannot be foreseen. A second mitigating factor is that, in circumstances of missing or incomplete markets, the emergence of personalised transactions may preclude the ability to take advantage of improvements in the operation of the land market. A third factor is that improved land markets will, in and of themselves, have no impact on the landless poor. A fourth factor is that it cannot be assumed that the poverty reduction benefits of more efficient land markets are equitably distributed between men and women within the household (Johnston and le Roux, 2005).

It is apparent that a first, necessary, step in substantiating whether linkages between land markets and poverty reduction can be found in Vietnam is to establish whether there have been improvements in farm productivity, as a precondition of improvements in farm incomes. In this regard, the growth in per capita foodgrain availability illustrated in Figure 5.1 was a direct function of two factors in the farm production process: intensity and yields. In terms of intensity, between 1985 and 1998 the rate of growth of rice cropping intensity was 2.1 per cent per year (ANZDEC, 2000: 7). In terms of yields, in 1979–1981 cereal yields per hectare amounted to 2,049 kilograms. By 2000, this had risen to 4,048 kilograms per hectare (World Bank, 2004). This dramatic improvement in productivity is illustrated in Figure 5.2, which displays indexed data on constant agricultural value added per worker and per hectare, using 1986 as the base of the index. Figure 5.2 demonstrates that a moderate upward trend in productivity halted in 1988, when decollectivisation occurred, giving way to an impressive improvement in trend productivity growth in both per worker and per hectare terms.[7] The inference is indeed suggestive: that from the time that individualised usufruct rights in land began to be established, productivity substantially improved. This was especially the case with regard to total factor productivity, which strongly influenced

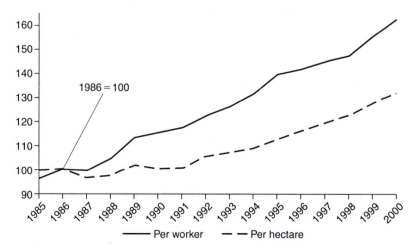

Figure 5.2 Constant agricultural value added (source: interpolated from Akram-Lodhi (2005)).

agricultural growth overall, and which increased as a direct consequence of changes in the incentive structure and in the agricultural institutional environment (Tuan, 2005: 24). Cumulatively, it might be suggested that the establishment of land markets laid the foundation for the improved productivity that underpins the impressive poverty reduction performance of Vietnam's economy illustrated in Table 5.1.

Land markets and poverty: an alternative view

There are, however, strong reasons to question the legitimacy of this analysis of the impact of land markets on Vietnam's rural poor and near-poor. To start off with, consider the price of land in the 1990s. The average price of cropland per hectare, in current prices, jumped from VND 11.9 million in 1993 to VND 26.1 million in 1998. As already noted, in 2004 the average price of a hectare of unirrigated cropland was VND 30 million, while a hectare of irrigated cropland cost an average price of VND 85 million, an astounding 14 times the value of average per capita GDP (Joint Donor Report, 2004). It should be stressed that during most of this period inflation was low, very low or negative. This increase is significantly faster than the growth in either per capita income or per capita expenditure, and calls into question how rural households were able to finance land purchases. In this light, the general finding that female-led households have higher levels of expenditure offers a different angle on the issue of which type of household can finance land purchases, although, it must be admitted, recent research has sought to unpack the category of female-led household, and in so doing opens up the possibility of previously unrecognised vulnerability dynamics (Scott, 2003). Deininger and Jin (2003) find that asset endowments and access to credit are important determinants of land purchases, but there are clear inequities in access to credit (Akram-Lodhi, 2004), while the non-labour asset endowments of the rural poor and near-poor are, as will be seen, also low. Moreover, inequities in access to credit would reinforce inequities in asset endowments, and these, together with price levels, suggest that relatively poorer rural households would not be likely to be able to finance the purchase of land. Whether they could finance the long-term leasing of additional land is an open question. As a result, the land market, in its sales, mortgaging or leasing components might well be segmented on the basis of wealth. In this light, the finding that in 1998 some 9.8 per cent of agricultural households sold land but only 2.5 per cent of agricultural households bought land (GSO, 1999: Table 5.1.10) might be possible evidence of a land sales market that was generating differential access to land.[8]

In addition to the issue of price, it should also be noted that the quality of land held by relatively wealthier households is improving. In 1993, some 16 per cent of land held by the wealthiest quintile was classified as good, and 41.5 per cent of their land was irrigated. By 1998 the former figure had risen to 21 per cent, while the proportion of land irrigated among wealthier households stood at 82 per cent (GSO, 1994: Table 5.1.11; GSO, 1999: Table 5.1.7), as households either established irrigation facilities where none had previously existed or acquired land to use through purchase or rental that was irrigated. It is worth recalling, in this regard, the already noted value of irrigated land compared to unirrigated land. By way of contrast, the relatively poorer households are more likely to have a significant proportion of their total holding forested, which is far less remunerative (Joint Donor Report, 2003: Table 3.2). It is not known whether there are differences in land quality between male-led and female-led farms.

There is clear evidence of gender differentiation in access to land contained with the 1998 VLSS. Thus, the average amount of land per adult on female-led farms was 2,036 m^2 and the average size of a female-led farm was 4,940 m^2. On male-led farms, the average amount of land per adult was 3,166 m^2 and the average size of a male-led farm was 8,834 m^2 (Desai, 2000: Figure 4.9, Table 4.17). The factors driving gender-based differential access to land are not understood, and clearly require further research.

One important indicator seeming to support the possibility that the operation of the land market has been fostering the emergence of divergent access to land and a gradual concentration of land control and ownership in some parts of the country, is the rise of marginal holdings and landlessness. It is important to stress, in making this point, that increasing landlessness is not *de facto* evidence of increasing concentration. Rather, it might be said that increasing landlessness may be indicative of increasing concentration. In this light, consider the case of the Mekong River Delta, the 'rice bowl' of Vietnam. Whereas 28 per cent of rural households in the Mekong River Delta in 1994 had less than 0.2 hectares of land, by 1997 the figure had risen to 37 per cent (World Bank and ADB, 2002: 49). Similarly, whereas 16.9 per cent of rural households in the Mekong River Delta were landless in 1993, by 2002 that figure had risen to 28.9 per cent (Joint Donor Report, 2003: Table 3.1). Moreover, the rise in landlessness in the Mekong River Delta is both concentrated among the poorest and is very rapidly increasing. Thus, whereas in 1998 the poorest per capita expenditure quintile in the Mekong River Delta contained 26 per cent of all landless rural households, by 2002 this figure had increased to 39 per cent (Joint Donor Report, 2003: 39). The relationship between increasing landlessness and gender in the Mekong River Delta is currently not known, but is an important area for further research.

The growth in rural landlessness is not however restricted to the Mekong Delta; landlessness in rural Vietnam as a whole is increasing. In 1993, some 8.2 per cent of rural households had no land. By 1998, this figure had increased to 9.2 per cent. In the four years between 1998 and 2002 it doubled, to 18.9 per cent (Joint Donor Report, 2003: Table 3.1). This rapid acceleration in landlessness is found across all regions of Vietnam. Admittedly, significant factors in the rise of landlessness, discussed below, are the diversification of relatively richer rural farm households into, in the first instance, rural non-farm household enterprises and, second, wage labour, as a means of raising household living standards and welfare (Vijverberg and Haughton, 2004), processes that have been confirmed in participatory poverty assessments (Poverty Task Force, 2003b: 21). The finding that female-led households are relatively better off would have to be placed within this context when evaluating the relationship between landlessness, poverty and gender because female-led households have less reliance on crop production as a principal source of income than have male-led households (Desai, 2000: Table 3.11). In addition, population pressures can, in certain areas of the country, contribute to processes that foster marginalisation and landlessness, even if such pressures are rarely the direct cause of landlessness. Nonetheless, given the continuing importance of on-farm activity in sustaining rural livelihoods and building diverse asset portfolios (Deininger and Jin, 2003) the apparent fact that 'a rural proletariat is emerging' (Haughton, 2000) is a significant issue in rural Vietnam, especially given the fact that agricultural employment in farm and off-farm activities are, over time, contracting, even as the female share of agricultural employment in farm and off-farm work is, over time, slowly increasing (GSO, 2004: Table 14). This is not only because, as Haughton (2000) notes, agricultural labour is the poorest occupational category in the country, with 55 per cent falling below the poverty line, and where, as a consequence, it is significant that there are clear gender-based differentials in rural wages, with females being consistently paid less than men (GSO, 2004: Table 143). In the Mekong River Delta, for example, agricultural labour is highly seasonal, with employment available for only 110 to 150 days a year, very low paid, and it offers women daily wage rates that are often a quarter less than those received by men (Joint Donor Report, 2003: 111–112; GSO, 2004: Table 143; An, 2005). Labour contracts are most typically casual, although relatively wealthier rural households are, while still in a minority of cases, more like to engage hired labour under permanent contracts (Mekong Economics, 2004a: 52). It should be noted, however, that the majority of rural households hiring permanent labour do so for non-farm work. Casual labour is typically hired from family and social networks, in order to ease transactions costs. The growth of casual labour is also driven by a deepseated material and cultural reticence on the part of poor households to sell land. Rural people in general and, given gender-based differences in consumption patterns (Desai, 2000: Table 3.6), rural women in particular know only too well that the difficulties in securing stable, well-paid employment with reasonable terms and conditions make it a livelihood imperative that land be retained. For the majority of the poor and the near-poor in rural Vietnam, land is the principal social safety net. Thus, the rapid growth in landlessness between 1998 and 2002 might be taken as circumstantial evidence that rural livelihoods are coming under increasing stress, as well as the fact that divergent access to land is deepening in rural Vietnam.

Thus, in contrast to the conventional view that emergent land markets in rural Vietnam are pro-poor, it might be the case that the emergence of land markets is promoting a relative concentration of land. This perspective is supported by two pieces of evidence. The first can be derived from the LSMS results that form the basis of the conventional view. For this chapter, farm households have been extracted from the LSMS data sets; individual farm economics profiles for a number of variables have been constructed from across the entire data set; and the resulting individual household-based variable sets have been grouped according to land ownership. Table 5.3 presents the all-Vietnam data. The results are quite striking in the way they differ from the conventional analysis.

The relationships demonstrated in Table 5.3 show a remarkable degree of linearity when considered in light of those offered by conventional analysis of the VLSS and VHLSS. When grouped according to land ownership, as a reasonable proxy for rural wealth, there is a clear positive linear relationship between land ownership, total non-land assets, working capital expenditures, the value of total farm output, total income from all sources, and household expenditure. It can be noted, in this regard, that recent participatory poverty assessments have also found that, when ranked by wealth, relatively wealthier rural households can have more than ten times the total assets of the poor; for example, a well-off household in the Red River Delta might have four or five buffalo or cattle, while the poor household will have none (Poverty Task Force, 2003b: 18). It should also be mentioned that the correlation presented in Table 5.3 has been found to hold in a recent, thorough, statistically representative survey of parts of the Mekong River Delta, where land size was correlated with productive assets, non-productive assets, income, food consumption and poverty status (An, 2005). There are, in short, clear correlations between land assets, non-land assets, output, income expenditure, as well as understandable degrees of association with total incomes. Unfortunately, it has not been established whether female-led households and male-led households display variance in their pattern, although it is known that female-led households, which have smaller farms than male-led households, also have lower stocks of animals (Desai, 2000: Table 4.25).

The second piece of evidence to question the conventional view is that generated from fieldwork. Published results from four field surveys (Akram-Lodhi, 2005) and unpublished observations from other field visits conducted, principally in the south of Vietnam but also in central Vietnam, the Central Highlands, the northern uplands and the Red River

Table 5.3 Assets, inputs, output and income on Vietnam's farms, 1993–2002

Size	Percentage of farms	Average area (hectares)	Value of non-land assets	Family labour	Working capital costs	Gross farm output	Total household income	Total household expenditure
1993								
>0–0.5	87.4	0.1	1,599.2	2,972.8	1,105.9	4,036.4	8,120.7	3,678.0
>0.5–1	7.2	0.7	2,535.4	4,126.7	1,640.9	6,352.7	7,008.8	4,499.7
>1–3	4.9	1.5	4,294.6	4,117.4	3,300.1	9,123.8	8,944.5	6,262.9
>3	0.5	4.9	6,942.1	3,555.5	7,160.5	23,242.0	16,945.5	10,740.0
Average	–	0.2	1,701.3	2,906.2	1,227.8	4,143.7	7,794.2	3,793.5
2002								
>0–0.5	58.3	0.3	2,238.9	3,026.9	3,678.3	8,770.1	14,974.0	9,683.4
>0.5–1	17.8	0.7	3,505.9	3,728.1	5,685.2	14,736.1	18,975.5	12,247.6
>1–3	18.5	1.7	4,452.3	4,189.9	7,890.3	20,835.9	21,937.3	13,590.0
>3	5.4	5.8	8,990.1	5,191.8	12,469.5	32,116.5	30,846.7	17,706.5
Average	–	0.8	3,103.7	3,319.7	5,075.4	12,681.3	17,917.6	11,363.7
Change, 1993–2002								
>0–0.5	–29.1	0.2	639.7	54.1	2,572.4	4,733.8	6,853.3	6,005.4
>0.5–1	10.6	0.0	970.5	–398.6	4,044.3	8,383.4	11,966.7	7,747.9
>1–3	13.6	0.2	157.7	72.5	4,590.3	11,712.1	12,992.8	7,327.1
>3	4.9	0.9	2,048.0	1,636.3	5,308.9	8,874.5	13,901.2	6,966.6
Average	–	0.6	1,402.4	413.5	3,847.7	8,537.7	10,123.4	7,570.2

Source: Interpolated from GSO (1994) and GSO (2002).

Notes

All monetary values in thousands of current Vietnamese dong; labour is hours per year.

Delta all consistently demonstrate that the emergence of land markets fosters unequal access to land. This can be witnessed both between and within communities and households, with relatively wealthier rural households using land markets as a mechanism to reallocate land to their advantage, with the consequence that they have relatively larger holdings of land compared to relatively poorer households. There is, moreover, a high degree of correlation between unequal control of land and gender. A male-led household is more likely to have more land. Those with a better education are more likely to have more land, and those with a better education are more likely to be men. Those who have been established in rural communities for a long period of time are more likely to have more land, and long-established social networks in Vietnam, as elsewhere in Asia, demonstrate a male bias (Mekong Economics, 2004a: 14). These findings, it can be noted, are quite consistent with the all-Vietnam data presented in Table 5.2 if the processes at work are spatially specific and are, moreover, relative. Thus, farms that have acquired land through land markets within specific villages and communes in the Red River Delta may have doubled the size of their holding relative to their neighbours but still have farms that are, on average, smaller than those in the Mekong River Delta.

If land markets are fostering processes which lead to increased inequality in access to land, an important issue in terms of their impact on poverty and social equity is the impact of land acquisition on the production of agricultural surplus. In the Red River Delta the land allocation following decollectivisation was predicated upon assigning an amount of land per person that was sufficient to meet subsistence. If a farm, then, is, through the use of land markets, able to double its size, all additional production is surplus, indicating the emergence of a stronger capacity to generate the income increases that serve as a precondition of improvements in welfare. If, at the same time, the farm's consumer–worker ratio declines, because of the emergence of rural non-farm employment, this capacity is but reinforced. This would occur even as those households unable to acquire more land remain at a subsistence production level.

The following example, from fieldwork, can illustrate the processes at work. Consider a farm in the Red River Delta which had five family members in 1988. With decollectivisation, the household was allocated seven *sao*. Each *sao* in northern Vietnam is equal to 362 m², so the family farm in 1988 comprised about 0.25 hectares. Improvements in farm productivity over the 1990s allowed the farm to produce five tonnes a hectare in 2004. Assume for the moment that each person needs 250 kilogrammes of rice per year for subsistence, which is, it should be noted, below World Health Organisation norms but not below Vietnamese government norms. This means that farm production, at 1.25 tonnes, matched household subsistence requirements of 1.25 tonnes. This is not surprising; it was an explicit objective of decollectivisation. Now assume that, in a short period of time, two family members leave, one by death, and one by migration, which results in cash remittances. The family retains 0.25 hectares, but now only needs 0.75 tonnes a year. This means that 0.5 tonnes is surplus; with rice prices from traders of VND2,400 per kilo in the village, the family now earns US$80 a year along with any remittances from migration. Following the example of other households in the village, the household decides to reallocate the non-subsistence part of their production to producing flowers, which can be sold once a year during *Tet*. Two *sao* are allocated, and generate the average of that produced by other flower producers, VND6,000,000 per *sao*. On its two *sao* the farm now produces VND12,000,000, or US$800 a year, along with remittances from migration, while still maintaining food security. It is relatively easy to see how the security of the subsistence production allows the household to begin to consider strategies to further enhance income growth, such as, for example, renting an additional *sao* of land for flower production. It is also relatively easy to see how this household might, in the course of a few years, occupy economic circumstances quite different from a household with identical land endowments but which had retained all its members. Thus, processes of inter-household inequality in rural livelihoods are engendered.

In addition to field evidence indicating processes fostering unequal access to limited amounts of land, whether it be within particular communes or villages or by gender, field studies and econometric analysis of survey data clearly demonstrate that the technical coefficients of production and yields per hectare can be differentiated on the basis of scale of production, in that reasonably consistent findings show that a statistically significant positive relationship between farm size, modern equipment and machinery and yields per hectare (Akram-Lodhi, 2001b, 2005; An, 2005). These findings support the hypothesis that farms with larger landholdings also have larger amounts of capital stock, use larger quantities of hired labour, and are thus large scale. They are, as a consequence, more productive. Farms with smaller landholdings are associated with smaller amounts of capital stock, and lesser use of hired labour, and are thus small scale. They are, as a consequence, less productive. This analysis is but reinforced by Table 5.4, which arrays paddy productivity per hectare in 1993 and 1998 by expenditure quintiles. The results are quite striking. In 1993 the difference between the least productive expenditure quintile and the most productive expenditure quintile was 325 kilos per hectare. Although expenditure, as a proxy for wealth in this case, was correlated with productivity, the relationship was not linear. By 1998, circumstances had dramatically changed. The difference between the least productive expenditure quintile and the most productive expenditure quintile was 740 kilos per hectare. Whereas productivity for the poorest wealth expenditure quintile increased by just over 15 per cent, productivity for the wealthiest expenditure quintile increased by 31.6 per cent. Moreover, the wealthier the household, the more productive it was. In a sense, this is hardly surprising; relatively wealthier farms have

Table 5.4 Paddy productivity by expenditure quintiles

Expenditure quintiles	Total output, 00s of kilos per hectare	
	1993	1998
Poorest	29.28	33.7
Near poor	30.89	38.4
Middle	31.91	39.2
Near rich	32.53	40.9
Richest	31.24	41.1

Sources: GSO (1999: Table 5.2.4); GSO (1994: Table 5.2.5).

both the resources and the motivation to invest more in productive purposes, thus fostering the emergence of scale economies. Indeed, in the 1993
VLSS Wiens (1998: 87) calculated that smaller farms, defined as those of
less than 0.25 hectares, had only 40 per cent of the total factor productivity
of larger farms, defined as those of more than two hectares. The finding
that there are total factor productivity differences between farms of relatively narrow differences in size clearly indicates that there are, indeed,
economies of scale in farm production in rural Vietnam.

This finding, however, does not come as a surprise. Although scarce,
land is still the principal agrarian asset, but the effective use of this asset
requires other, complementary assets such as farm equipment, machinery,
livestock and labour, whether it be owned or hired, and which are therefore acquired through partially complete asset, product and factor
markets. Many complementary assets are neither scale- nor resource-
neutral. Non-labour factor input markets in particular remain partially
complete, with farmers complaining about the price of inputs and about
monopoly practices in the provision of non-labour factor inputs (Mekong
Economics, 2004b). Indeed, the mutually reinforcing character of these
processes should be stressed: that increasingly unequal access to relatively
limited amounts of land is reinforced by and reinforces increasingly
unequal access to complementary assets and factor inputs. Thus, while it is
theoretically possible for land distribution to become more equitable even
as the distribution of total farm assets becomes more inequitable, it should
be stressed that, in counterpoint to the conventional view, there is strong
evidence to question whether this is in fact the case in rural Vietnam.

Eight final points can be made about the apparent characteristics of
market-led land concentration in rural Vietnam. The first, important, point
is that the process is spatially specific, being located within and between
particular communes and households in different parts of the country.
Second, and also importantly, land holdings remain relatively small
throughout the country and, as a consequence, land must be considered
in light of the control of other productive assets. Third, market-led land
concentration appears to be correlated with concentration of non-land

assets and factor inputs. Fourth, while LSMS evidence clearly shows that tenancy relations, including sharecropping, returned to rural Vietnam during the 1990s, as the land market became increasingly active, it has not been able to capture all aspects of these relations, such as the nature of payment. Fifth, it must be reiterated that landlessness in rural Vietnam is increasing dramatically, and not just among relatively richer rural house-holds that have diversified into rural non-farm activities. Sixth, although it has not yet been discussed, fragmentation of landholdings has increased significantly since decollectivisation despite the emergence of the land market. Thus, it has been estimated that 11 million farming households operate 100 million plots (World Bank and ADB, 2000: 47), which undoubt-edly generate important diseconomies in small-scale agriculture. Seventh, there is reason to believe that these processes may be gender-differentiated. Finally, the geographical specificity of market-led land concentration may help explain the 2003 Land Law, with its attendant easing of restrictions on the operation of the rural land market within localities. Although the 1993 Land Law stipulated a maximum farm size of five hectares, by 1995 there were already 113,700 farms in excess of this limit and 1,900 farms in excess of ten hectares. While these farms constituted only 1.1 per cent of farm households, it is worth stressing that 66 per cent of them were in the Mekong River Delta. In a sense then the 2003 Land Law is simply an *ex post* recognition of changes in the agrarian structure that had already occurred as the emerging land market had developed. Indeed, in February 2000 it was revealed that these so-called 'large-scale' farms, which have been the explicit object of public policy, generated an average household income of US$7,500 per year, well above the average per capita national income of US$350 (*Vietnam Investment Review*, 14 February 2000).

It thus appears to be the case that the emergence of partially complete land markets in rural Vietnam has fostered a process of market-led land concentration, and that this process reinforces and is reinforced by a complex process of market-led non-land asset concentration in the coun-tryside. While the process is an all-Vietnam phenomenon, it is a process that is witnessed within particular provinces, and, more specifically, within particular districts, communes and households and which, as such, will display significant variation, not least in its gender dimensions, across the spatial diversity of Vietnam.

Market integration, agrarian structure and social equity

Differential access to land, differential technical coefficients of production and differential productivity suggest that farms may be pursuing different production purposes. This is supported in Figure 5.3, which demonstrates that poorer quintiles retain the bulk of their paddy, and market propor-tionally less, being, at best, only partially integrated into markets. By way of contrast, the wealthier quintiles market the bulk of their paddy, and

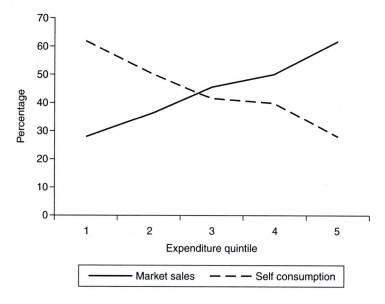

Figure 5.3 Market integration in Vietnamese agriculture, 1998 (source: GSO (1999)).

retain a much smaller fraction of output. Moreover, these farms are becoming increasingly commercialised.

Thus, there has been a shift to higher value perennials concentrated in relatively richer per capita expenditure quintiles, as demonstrated in Table 5.2. That an increasing absolute share of output can be accounted for by higher-value crops among relatively richer per capita expenditure quintiles, while relatively poorer per capita expenditure quintiles continue to devote significant proportions of their cropped area to paddy, could promote further divergence between increasingly commercialised farmers and those that produce for subsistence.

The evidence thus shows the development of a bifurcated agrarian structure. There is an emergent group of commercial farmers with, perhaps, relatively larger landholdings, greater total assets, and, although the data has not been presented, larger use of hired labour (Akram-Lodhi, 2005; Mekong Economics, 2004a). This can be set alongside a quantitatively larger group of subsistence farmers with smaller landhold-ings, fewer total assets, and, although the data has not been presented, a heavier reliance on family labour. Farm productivity in commercial farms is apparently linked to the scale of production, and this capacity of com-mercial farmers to shift the purpose of production from subsistence to commercial activities is made possible by the ability to deploy and benefit from more productive agricultural technology. By way of contrast, subsis-tence farms produce to survive.

If the process of bifurcation is an accurate characterisation of the rural economy, it might be thought that it would explain an important proportion of the increase in the Gini coefficient for expenditures for Vietnam from 0.34 in 1993 to 0.37 in 2002 (Joint Donor Report, 2003: 14). Such figures as are available are displayed in Table 5.5, which suggest that since 1978 it is possible that inequality has increased by almost 50 per cent in the Red River Delta, although it should be stressed that inequality remains, by international standards, moderate.

However, trends in the evolution of inequality in Vietnam are not clear, as Tuan (1997) demonstrates. Formal analysis of the data usually produces the finding that the key dimension to inequality in Vietnam is the urban–rural divide (Government of Vietnam–Donor–NGO Poverty Working Group, 1999). Most commentators, on the other hand, accept that inequality is increasing both within and between urban and rural areas. Thus, as one poor woman has recently said, 'I have not seen people getting poorer, but some people got richer quite remarkably. If our income increased by one or two times, the rich would have their income increased ten times' (Poverty Task Force, 2003b: 18). The factor of ten was also repeated in another participatory poverty assessment in a different part of the country (Poverty Task Force, 2003a: 15). A similar figure also appears in the introduction to the summary of the 2002 VHLSS (GSO, 2004). The driving factors behind these – admittedly at times empirically unsupported – views are the increasing commercialisation of some parts of agriculture, a process that has already been examined in this chapter, as well as the increasing availability of wage-labour opportunities, which is, it should be stressed, spatially specific, driven in particular by rapid expansion of labour markets in Ho Chi Minh City, Hanoi, Da Nang and Haiphong.

Responses to market-led land concentration: government, donors and civil society

Government and donors

The emergence of market-led land and non-land asset concentration has led to a remarkable uniformity of views between the government and the donor community as to what constitutes an appropriate response. The

Table 5.5 Gini coefficients for Vietnam, 1978–2000

	1978	*1981*	*1984*	*1990*	*1993*	*1998*	*2002*
All Vietnam	–	–	0.30	–	0.34	0.35	0.37
Mekong Delta	–	0.30	–	0.35	0.33	0.30	0.30
Red River Delta	0.25	–	–	0.25	0.32	0.32	0.36

Sources: Tuan (1997: Table 5.5); Dollar and Litvack (1998); Joint Donor Report (2003).

analysis of both senior figures in government and the donor community remains that well-functioning markets promote pro-poor growth by improving resource allocation and enhancing the interrelationships between market participants. In other words, market-led welfare is prioritised over support-led welfare. This applies, particularly so, to the land market. Thus, the successive versions of the Land Law have sought to establish land as property, through changes to legal and institutional arrangements. They have sought to establish the parameters whereby land sales, transfers, mortgaging, leasing, renting and collateralisation can be facilitated. Finally, they have sought to successively reduce the regulatory burden facing households wanting to transfer or acquire transfers of land. In so doing, and consistent with the overarching approach of both the government and the donor community, they have sought to facilitate the operation of even a partially complete land market as a means of enhancing equity.

Thus, the view of the government and donor community has been that those who witness an increase in their incomes should 'follow the market' by eventually diversifying agricultural production out of staples, as well as promoting the development of rural non-farm employment (World Bank, 1998). This view has percolated right down to the local government level, with officials suggesting that crop diversification and the promotion of rural non-farm employment is the second most important factor contributing to poverty reduction at the commune level (Poverty Task Force, 2003b).[9] Diversification should occur within the context of ongoing specialisation, in order to sustain comparative advantage and generate the capacity of farms to shift to 'average'-scale and 'large'-scale production, which has been an explicit goal of government policy for some years. Indeed, it is widely believed within government that ongoing specialisation, combined with continuing liberalisation, offers important opportunities to integrate into global agro-food value chains. However, both the government and donors understand that the deepening commercialisation of agriculture would have major implications for the pattern of rural employment. As stated by the World Bank, ADB, and United Nations Development Programme (2000: 12), 'Vietnam needs to adopt the seemingly paradoxical stance of giving a high priority to raising agricultural productivity while recognising that success can come only as agriculture declines as an employer of labour.' Granted, for those farmers who are in a position to make a conscious choice it is indeed the case that diversification can offer significant rewards. Thus, two people working a specialised flower-producing enterprise in the Red River Delta in 2004 had an annual income of US$1,300 per person on a holding of 6.5 *sao*, half of which they rented to sustain improvements in their livelihoods. These sorts of farmers are the object of government and donor policy. However, in their village, they were a clear minority. Moreover, this approach is predicated on an assumption that diversification can be made as a conscious choice among those who face limits to the continued growth of their incomes, and who diversify within the context of specialisation as a way of offsetting those limits. Such an assumption may be tenuous.

At the same time, the emphasis on rural diversification and the creation of non-farm employment by the government and the donor community remains speculative. Tuan (2005: 24–28) has argued that crop diversification has occurred very slowly, in part, perhaps, because the goal of diversification among subsistence farmers, at least, is the maintenance of income levels in the face of falling prices for their principal output, rice. Moreover, diversification requires investment, which has not been forthcoming from within agriculture (Tuan, 2005: 24), while rural non-farm incomes have been used to fuel resource flows into the agricultural sector that sustain a consumption boom (Tuan, 2005: 28). There may also be, moreover, significant obstacles to diversification put in place by local government, which has sought in certain localities to maintain rice production, and which has also restricted farmers in certain places from exercising their land use rights such as buying, renting or bequeathing land (Mekong Economics, 2004a: 18).

Concurrently, the emphasis on rural diversification and the creation of non-farm employment fails to explicitly address the implications of policy for intra-household relations, subsistence farmers and the landless poor. With regard to intra-household relations, there is an assumption that the gains of diversification and specialisation will be pooled within the household. There is evidence to question this assumption in Vietnam. With regard to subsistence farmers there is an implicit policy perspective: if they fail to reap scale economies they will, over time, shift out of farming, joining the landless in specialising as a source of wage labour. Indeed, one member of the Politbureau stated some years ago that farmers who work on the land of others make more money than if they only work their own plots (*Far Eastern Economic Review*, 10 December 1998). This labour can be in the countryside, working for the rural non-farm enterprises established by diversifying commercial farmers. It could also be in the city. In either instance, then, the implicit view of the donor community and the government is that specialisation in wage labour offers the best means of raising the less efficient asset-poor rural poor out of poverty. Whether this is the case, however, remains to be seen. Certainly, this view assumes that those who must shift out of farming have the skills that potential employers require, and this appears to rarely be the case.

For those households that face difficulties coping with the market, the government has introduced two key targeted safety nets. The first is the Hunger Eradication and Poverty Reduction (HEPR) Programme, launched in 1998 and renewed in 2001. The HEPR Programme targets those households identified by commune officials as poor, which in turn are exempted from school fees, receive subsidised healthcare, receive subsidised credit, and are exempted from a range of local taxes, fees and compulsory contributions (Joint Donor Report, 2004: 24). The second was Programme 135, which was also launched in 1998, and which is designed to provide resources for investment in local infrastructure for individual communes or clusters of communes, as well as provide assistance for agricultural extension, training of commune officials, and the transformation of communities relying on shifting agriculture into sedentary agricultural communities. It has been argued recently that these programmes 'have performed quite well' (Joint Donor Report, 2004: 24). However, if the total spending on these two programmes were evenly distributed among the poor, a beneficiary household would receive only 7 per cent of the expenditure needed to meet the poverty line (Joint Donor Report, 2004: 25), clearly indicating the lack of resources available through the programmes. There is, moreover, significant mistargeting in both programmes. Thus, although poor people who receive benefits under the government's two principle safety nets do claim that the benefits are, for them, important, it is also clear that the programmes are not able to adequately fulfil their mandate.

Civil society

Within civil society the increasing reliance on markets served to galvanise the re-emergence of local rural politics in Vietnam in the 1990s. However, the dynamics of rural politics in Vietnam are complex. On the one hand, as Ravallion and van de Walle (2001: 6) argue, 'reforms were only possible through an implicit coalition between the peasants and reformers at the center', a point first stressed by van Donge *et al.* (1999). On the other hand, Vietnam has quite a decentralised political system, with local government officials drawn from within the communities where they live, and with such officials having the capacity to shape livelihoods, for better or worse, in a variety of ways. Thus, peasants seeking to improve their resource base through the land market must interact with local government functionaries who, despite explicit laws to the contrary, have the capacity, if they so wish, to use their powers for the purposes of rent seeking and the maintenance of their relative affluence, and this, in some ways, may help explain part of the rationale behind the central government's 2003 Land Law.

At the local level, market-led land concentration has intersected with other rural complaints, including unresolved land claims, the appropriation of public and communal lands, corruption, and the fact that local communities have no voice in local government land politics (Kerkvliet, 1995; Akram-Lodhi, 2004; Suu, 2004). There are a number of spatial and social specificities to these complaints, but the procedures whereby communities seek to have input are remarkably similar. In seeking to have their concerns addressed, individuals, households and communities have consistently tried to use official channels, and have been careful, when they have felt the need to be critical, to criticise individuals rather than political institutions in an effort to stretch the limits of official policies through the use of 'everyday forms of resistance.'[10] However, when complaints are, as they often are, unsuccessful, they have mutated into disputes. Often these disputes are between villagers, rather than being aimed at political institutions. Such disputes can turn quite violent (Kerkvliet, 1995). Rural disputes do not however solely take the form of interpersonal conflicts. Collective grievances have, over the 1990s through to 2004, resulted in collective action designed to confront local government and press for changes to government policy at the local, provincial and central level. Moreover, there are numerous examples of collective action becoming violent when communities have felt that their voices are not being heard (Akram-Lodhi, 2004). This is especially the case when specific complaints about land issues, including encroachment, appropriation without consultation, or local government abuse of land allocation, have festered into wider discontent regarding the abuse of authority and corruption by local government officials, most notably with regards to the diversion of locally paid fees and contributions that have become, over the last decade, increasingly onerous to rural communities. The latter aspect, for example, was a motivating factor behind conflicts in Thai Binh in the late 1990s (Akram-Lodhi, 2004). The former aspect is demonstrated in some of the circumstances surrounding the most recent rural conflicts, between communities and local government in the Central Highlands in 2001 and 2003 (Akram-Lodhi, 2004). In this latter unrest, two processes appear to be at work that mutually reinforce each other. On the one hand, the appropriation of land by the government clashed with local customary laws and institutions as well as farming systems and thus appeared to challenge communal values, culture and lifestyles that, as elsewhere in Vietnam, are often rooted in land (Baluch et al., 2004). On the other hand, the issuance of legal rights to land by the local government did not result in changes in actual land rights and practices, based as they were on customary law, and the application of actual land rights remained the objective of negotiation among rural actors. Property rights thus remained highly contested, which set the stage for possible conflict when, for example, those with formal title sought to exclude those who would have rights under customary practice. Thus, those without formal title cleared land to farm, confident that the local authorities, important members of which came from the clearing community, would side with them. That this was not always the case demonstrates the highly contingent nature of the emergence of possible conflicts over tenure, rooted as they can be in differing relations of economic, political and cultural power, and the need for formal tenure rights to correspond to customary tenure practices (Thanh and Sikor, forthcoming).

Clearly, market-led land and non-land asset concentration could have potentially serious implications for social stability in rural Vietnam. If previous experience of rural politics in Vietnam in the last 15 years is any example, rural communities are more than prepared to go beyond official channels and 'everyday forms of resistance' to voice their discontent with the way land market policies and local government corruption are affecting their livelihoods. Indeed, given the current policy environment in Vietnam, with its emphasis on enhancing the role of the market in rural resource allocation decisions, it is probable that ongoing processes of market-led land concentration, emerging landlessness, and the creation of an underemployed rural wage labour force in Vietnam have generated ample scope for rural unrest, especially if governance strategies toward rural livelihoods do not recognise the realities faced by farmers in Vietnam and respond to them.

Conclusion

In 1988 Vietnam decollectivised agriculture and established an egalitarian peasant family farming system across the country. In 1993 the Land Law solidified the property rights of the peasant farm economy, and a rudimentary land market began to emerge, as farms were conferred five rights in land. In 2003 the new Land Law was designed to further solidify land markets, by offering five additional rights, and establish land markets as important mechanisms of asset distribution in rural Vietnam. The existing land market in Vietnam is, however, only partially 'complete', being constrained in its operation by the government regulatory framework, by the capacity of newly emergent rural economic and political elites to shape the operation of the market to their advantage, and by social networks and norms which, being rooted in local communities and cultures, restrict the institutional development of the land market.

The establishment of partially complete land markets within an egalitarian peasant farm sector has led to a process of restructuring in the peasant farm economy. Farmers generating surpluses have been able to use the land market to access additional land, particularly through renting but also, in some cases, through purchase, further reinforcing their capacity to generate surpluses and increase their incomes. Increased incomes have allowed some investment in farm equipment, machinery and non-family labour, enhancing yet again the capacity to generate surpluses and further increase incomes. To maintain income growth, these farms have begun to diversify their livelihood activities into both higher-value-added agricultural activities as well as into rural non-farm activities. They have become commercialised, specialised and diversified rural enterprises. Farmers unable to generate surpluses on an increasing scale remain predominantly subordinated to the market, in that they produce a large share of their product for self-consumption and use the rest on markets to generate cash to purchase essential inputs and non-produced consumption items. They are not, however, able to use land and other markets to enter a virtuous cycle of productive expansion, and remain caught as predominantly subsistence farmers supplementing their income from a variety of farm and non-farm activities. Subsistence farmers are far more likely to either be poor or, in the event of shocks to the household, fall into poverty. Finally, there are the landless, who have lost their land either due to government repossession or a household economic situation forcing them to sell their most valuable non-labour resource. These households face the strong probability that they will either be poor or will fall into poverty. The land market, then, along with the operation of other product and labour markets, has facilitated a process of deepening rural inequality and market-led land and non-land asset concentration. It should be stressed that there are clear gender dimensions to these processes.

The policy solution of the government and the donor community in Vietnam to these processes is to promote the further diversification of agricultural production and the development of rural non-farm employment opportunities for the poor, the landless and the functionally landless. These policy solutions are, however, unlikely to solve the problem of rural Vietnam, because they reinforce the market-led processes underpinning what appears to be deepening rural inequality. Commercial farmers diversify out of choice, using markets to promote cycles of productive expansion and income growth. Subsistence farmers diversify out of necessity, hoping that such a move will obviate pressures upon household livelihoods. However, being weaker in the asset, product and labour markets in which they operate, their livelihood options continue to be constrained by more powerful rural actors, including emerging commercial farmers, who are able to use the mechanisms of government and partially complete land, labour and capital markets to reinforce the strength of their livelihood portfolio. The response of the government to these ongoing processes has been to create a social safety net, but it is poorly resourced and frequently targets the non-poor at the expense of the poor and the near-poor.

The following observations can thus be made about the operation of the rural land market in Vietnam in the mid-2000s. First, there is a clear lack of consistency between the analysis generated from the econometric analysis of LSMS data and the evidence that has accumulated as a result of fieldwork and a household-based analysis of nationally representative data. There is, in contrast to the conventional view offered by the government and the donor community, clear variation in access to land, particularly as regards certain districts and communes, in the Mekong River Delta, where evidence of increasingly divergent access to land remains reasonably strong, but also in other parts of the country where government appropriation or shocks to rural livelihoods have served to foster landlessness. Second, tenancy relations, including sharecropping, have returned to rural Vietnam as the land market has become increasingly active. There is, across the country, an active market in land use rights certificates, in some cases in the short term but often over longer periods. Land sales also occur, but on a comparatively smaller scale. Third, landlessness in rural Vietnam is increasing dramatically. Land sales and mortgage losses, government appropriation, along with the growth of the rural non-farm household economy among relatively richer rural households appear to have a major role to play in explaining landlessness. Fourth, fragmentation of landholdings has increased significantly since decollectivisation despite the emergence of the land market. The land market deepens, rather than obviates, this source of rural inefficiency. Fifth, farms that are large, in both the size of their operational holding and their scale of production, can increasingly be witnessed in rural Vietnam. This phenomenon is however restricted to southern areas of the country. Sixth, while some of its aspects are not clear, there are good reasons to believe that processes of market-led land and non-land asset concentration have gender-differentiated effects. Finally, the government and the donor community, in their emphasis on social safety nets, rural diversification, rural non-farm employment, and the continued stress of deepening market relations and making markets work for the poor, demonstrate that they are not prepared to take seriously the possible impact of the emergence of the land market on worsening access to land and social inequality. Thus, while Vietnam's major donors have recently written, in a report that was accepted by the government, that 'the tendency towards the concentration of land is clearly visible' (Joint Donor Report, 2003: 38), the resulting policy prescription is clear: more of the same.

There are, however, alternative possibilities for public action that would enhance the livelihood opportunities of male and female subsistence farmers and the landless poor, and which would thus be much more concretely pro-poor. Existing safety nets, while worthwhile, do not provide adequate transfers of resources to the rural poor and near-poor, who require improved access to assets and improved returns on their labour. There is a need, in this context, to examine once more agricultural price policy, agricultural taxation, and the possible ways in which rural financial markets could better serve the needs of the rural poor and the near-poor. There is also, however, the need to reassess the failure of the private sector in facilitating the promotion of growth-enhancing investment in the rural economy. Government-led investment has the potential to increase the income-earning possibilities of both subsistence farmers and the landless if it is directed towards necessary improvements in rural infrastructure and if it seeks to undertake those in a labour-intensive manner utilising the labour of the poor and near-poor landless. Indeed, the promotion of substantial increases in government-led investment has the potential to facilitate the entrance of hundreds of thousands of rural households into a virtuous cycle of increased income and productive expansion. In evaluating the potential of these policy options, it is important to remain aware of gender-based differences within and between rural households. At the same time, however, it must be stressed that these possibilities for public action are predicated upon challenging the prevailing dominance of the market in rural resource allocation decisions. In this sense, then, possible public action to improve the capabilities and livelihoods of the rural poor and near-poor would require the government and the donor community to rethink their policy analysis from the starting point of how rural markets operate in practice, rather than how they should operate in principle. This would require a paradigm shift on the parts of the government and the donor community. It would not, however, require a paradigm shift within rural Vietnam, for, as Ho Chi Minh once said, 'peasants believe in facts, not theories' (Langguth, 2000: 36).

Notes

1 The author is grateful for the inputs of Nguyen Van Suu, Aparna Nyampalli and John Sawdon in the preparation of this chapter, as well as for incisive comments from Saturnino Borras, Jr. and the participants in the ISS/UNDP Workshop on Land Reform and Poverty Reduction, held in The Hague on 17–19 February 2005. The usual disclaimers apply.
2 Participatory poverty assessments suggest that this might be an understatement (Poverty Task Force, 2003a).
3 US$1 = VND15,770 in 2006.
4 As both the 1993 VLSS and the VHLSS are statistically representative, this finding cannot be explained by the fact that the surveys do not form a panel.
5 Fieldwork would suggest that this is an underestimate of land rental.
6 See, however, above, where this finding is questioned. I must confess a strong view here: I do not believe it.
7 Boxplots of Dfbeta statistics for foodgrain availability and per capita foodgrain availability confirm that 1987 is indeed a point of influence.
8 Interestingly, Deininger and Jin's (2003) econometric analysis finds that the proportions of agricultural households buying and selling land are the reverse of those reported by the GSO. Clearly, further research is required here.
9 'Reform policy' was the most important factor.
10 I am grateful to Saturnino Borras Jr for making this point to me.

References

Akram-Lodhi, A. H. (2001a). '"Landlords Are Taking Back the Land": The Agrarian Transition in Vietnam', Institute of Social Studies *Working Paper Series*, no. 353, November.

Akram-Lodhi, A. H. (2001b). 'Vietnam's Agriculture: Is There an Inverse Relationship?', Institute of Social Studies *Working Paper Series*, no. 348, September.

Akram-Lodhi, A. H. (2004). 'Are "Landlords Taking Back the Land"? An Essay on the Agrarian Transition in Vietnam', *European Journal of Development Research*, vol. 16, no. 4, pp. 757–789.

Akram-Lodhi, A. H. (2005). 'Vietnam's Agriculture: Processes of Rich Peasant Accumulation and Mechanisms of Social Differentiation'. *Journal of Agrarian Change*, vol. 5, no. 1, pp. 73–116.

An, N. T. S. (2005). 'Hunger in the Land of Plenty? Household Food Security in the Mekong Delta of Vietnam'. songan@hcm.vnn.vn.

ANZDEC (2000). 'Vietnam Agricultural Sector Program (ADB TA 3223-VIE): Phase I Technical Report'. www.ifpri.org.

Asian Development Bank (2002). 'Indigenous Peoples/Ethnic Minorities and Poverty Reduction in Vietnam'. Manila: Environmental and Social Safeguard Division, Asian Development Bank.

Baluch, B., T. T. K. Chuyen, D. Haughton and J. Haughton (2004). 'Ethnic Minority Development in Vietnam: a Socioeconomic Perspective', in P. Glewwe, N. Agrawal and D. Dollar, eds, *Economic Growth, Poverty and Household Welfare in Vietnam.* Washington, DC: World Bank.

Chung, D. K. (1994). 'Resurgence of Rural Land Markets after Decollectivization in Vietnam: Empirical Findings and Policy Implications'. Chapter presented at the International Workshop on Social Research Methods in Agricultural Systems: Coping with Increasing Resource Competition in Asia, Chang Mai, Thailand, 2–4 November.

Deininger, K. and S. Jin (2003). 'Land Sales and Rental Markets in Transition: Evidence from Rural Vietnam', World Bank *Policy Research Working Paper* no. 3013.

Desai, J. (2000). *Vietnam through the Lens of Gender: Five Years Later.* Hanoi: Food and Agriculture Organization of the United Nations.

Dollar, D. and J. Litvack (1998). 'Macroeconomic Reform and Poverty Reduction in Vietnam', in D. Dollar, P. Glewwe and J. Litvack, eds, *Household Welfare and Vietnam's Transition.* Washington, DC: World Bank.

Donge, J. K. van, H. White. and L. X. Nghia (1999). *Fostering High Growth in a Low Income Country: Programme Aid to Vietnam.* Stockholm: Swedish International Development Agency.

Far Eastern Economic Review. Various issues.

General Statistical Office (GSO) (1994). *Vietnam Living Standards Survey 1992–93.* Hanoi: General Statistical Office.

General Statistical Office (GSO) (1999). *Vietnam Living Standards Survey 1997–98.* Hanoi: General Statistical Office.

General Statistical Office (GSO) (2004). *Results of the Survey on Households Living Standards 2002.* Hanoi: Statistical Publishing House.

Glewwe, P., M. Gragnolati and H. Zaman (2000). 'Who Gained from Vietnam's Boom in the 1990s? An Analysis of Poverty and Inequality Trends', World Bank *Policy Research Working Paper* no. 2275.

Government of Vietnam–Donor–NGO Poverty Working Group (1999). *Vietnam: Attacking Poverty.* Hanoi: World Bank.

Haughton, J. (2000). 'Ten Puzzles and Surprises: Economic and Social Change in Vietnam, 1993–1889', *Comparative Economic Studies,* vol. XLII, no. 4, pp. 67–92.

Johnston, D. and H. le Roux (2005). 'On Shaky Foundations? The Implications for Land Reform of Unreconstructed Thinking about Households'. dj3@soas.ac.uk.

Joint Donor Report to the Vietnam Consultative Group Meeting (2003). *Vietnam Development Report 2004: Poverty.* Hanoi: Vietnam Development Information Center.

Joint Donor Report to the Vietnam Consultative Group Meeting (2004). *Vietnam Development Report 2005: Governance.* Hanoi: Vietnam Development Information Center.

Kerkvliet, B. J. T. (1995). 'Rural Society and State Relations', in B. J. T. Kerkvliet and D. J. Porter, eds, *Vietnam's Rural Transformation*, pp. 65–96. Boulder: Westview Press.

Langguth, A. J. (2000). *Our Vietnam: The War, 1954–1975*. New York: Simon and Schuster.

Marsh, S. P. and T. G. MacAulay (no date). 'Land Reform and the Development of Commercial Agriculture in Vietnam: policy and issues'. Mimeo, Department of Agricultural Economics, University of Sydney.

Mekong Economics Ltd (2004a). *Access to Resources: The Case of Rural Households in Vietnam – Final Report*. Hanoi: Mekong Economics Ltd.

Mekong Economics Ltd (2004b). *The Impact of Land Market Processes on the Poor – 'Implementing de Soto': The Case in North Vietnam*. Hanoi: Mekong Economics Ltd.

Men, N. T. (1995). 'Vietnamese Agriculture in a Centrally Planned Economy and in the Transition to a Market Economy', Institute of Social Studies *Working Papers* no. 197.

Oxfam (GB) (1999). *Tra Vinh: A Participatory Poverty Assessment*. Hanoi: World Bank.

Poverty Task Force (2003a). *Ninh Thuan: Participatory Poverty Assessment*. Hanoi: Center for Rural Progress and the World Bank in Vietnam.

Poverty Task Force (2003b). *Red River Delta – Ha Tay and Hai Duong: Participatory Poverty Assessment*. Hanoi: Rural Development Services Centre and the World Bank in Vietnam.

Ravallion, M. and D. van de Walle (2001). 'Breaking Up the Collective Farm: Welfare Outcomes of Vietnam's Massive Land Privatization', World Bank *Policy Research Working Paper* no. 2710.

Ravallion, M. and D. van de Walle (2003). 'Land Allocation in Vietnam's Agrarian Transition', World Bank *Policy Research Working Paper* no. 2951.

Schipper, Y. (2003). 'Case Study: Land Ownership in Vietnam'. Vietnamese–Dutch Project for MA Programme in Development Economics, University of Economics, Ho Chi Minh City.

Scott, S. (2003). 'Gender, Household Headship and Entitlements to Land: New Vulnerabilities in Vietnam's Decollectivization', *Gender, Technology and Development*, vol. 7, no. 2, pp. 233–263.

Suu, N. V. (2004). 'The Politics of Land: Inequality in Land Access and Local Conflicts in the Red River Delta since Decollectivization', in P. Taylor, ed., *Inequality in Vietnam: Challenges to Reform*. Singapore: Institute for Southeast Asian Studies.

Thanh, T. N. and T. Sikor (forthcoming). 'From Legal Acts to Actual Powers: Devolution and Property Rights in the Central Highlands of Vietnam', *International Journal of Forestry Research*.

Tuan, D. T. (1997). 'The Agrarian Transition in Vietnam: Institutional Change, Privatization and Liberalization', in M. Spoor, ed., *The 'Market Panacea': Agrarian Transformation in Developing Countries and Former Socialist Economies*, pp. 156–169. London: Intermediate Technology Press.

Tuan, N. D. A. (2005). 'Agricultural Surplus and Industrialization in Vietnam since the Country's Reunification,' PhD Final Seminar Chapter presented at the Institute of Social Studies, The Hague, 6 January.

Vietnam Investment Review. Various issues.

Vietnam News. Various issues.

Vijverberg, W. J. M. and J. Haughton (2004). 'Household Enterprises in Vietnam: survival, Growth and Living Standards', in P. Glewwe, N. Agrawal and D. Dollar, eds, *Economic Growth, Poverty and Household Welfare in Vietnam*, pp. 95–132. Washington, DC: The World Bank.

Wiens, T. (1998). 'Agriculture and Rural Poverty in Vietnam,' in P. Glewwe, J. Litvack and D. Dollar, eds, *Household Welfare and Vietnam's Transition*, pp. 61–98. Washington, DC: The World Bank.

World Bank (1998). *Vietnam. Advancing Rural Development from Vision to Action.* Chapter prepared for the Consultative Group Meeting, Haiphong, 7–8 December.

World Bank (2004). *World Development Indicators 2004.* Washington, DC: World Bank.

World Bank and Asian Development Bank (ADB) (2002). 'Vietnam: Delivering on Its Promise.' Hanoi: Vietnam Development Information Center.

World Bank/Asian Development Bank (ADB)/United Nations Development Programme (2000). *Vietnam 2010. Entering the 21st century – Vietnam Development Report 2001* (in 3 volumes). Hanoi: Vietnam Development Information Center.

6 Land reform, rural poverty and inequality in Armenia

A pro-poor approach to land policies

Max Spoor

Introduction

The following analysis intends to contribute to the development of 'pro-poor land policies' in Armenia, and is focused primarily on improving the position of peasant farms and their poor and vulnerable households, for which land is still the main 'safety network'.[1] The agricultural sector in Armenia has been dominated by small-scale landholdings since a redistributive land reform in the early 1990s. Land policies are highly relevant in Armenia today, as the country has entered a new phase (or wave) of land reform, through the massive transfer of remaining state-owned land to the jurisdiction of the communities and by finalising the formal registration of private land titles in the period 2003–2005. Taking into account the interlocking roles of land, credit, services, output and input markets, the institutional framework, and the appropriateness of some forms of intervention in these markets, the analysis directs itself to the following questions: What can the state do to improve the growth of agricultural output, without worsening already high rural unemployment and weakening the safety net that land has represented for the rural poor? Does it leave everything to the market, apart from providing public goods, and create a facilitative institutional framework, or can it go beyond this role of the 'minimal state', steering as it were the development of markets, and safeguarding the interests of those in the weakest positions? The latter – in rural Armenia – are without any doubt those who have little or no land. Therefore, while many factors are important in analysing the success and failures of the agricultural sector's economy of Armenia, land and the access to it, are indeed of crucial importance.

The chapter is structured as follows. The following section provides a brief overview of the Armenian land reform. The emerging agrarian structure is analysed more from a regional perspective,[2] parting from the initially relatively equal land allocation during the land reform, later to be influenced by increased rural out-migration and the land lease and sales markets, which are growing in importance – a process and condition similar to that observed in Vietnam (see Akram-Lodhi, this volume). Rural poverty is looked upon from the perspective of land access, which could provide a cushion against the impact of the dramatic economic crisis, and represents the ultimate refuge for food self-sufficiency of households as well as partial employment generation, as agriculture absorbed superfluous labour from other sectors. Rural poverty indeed reduced at first, but since 1996 has stagnated while urban poverty rapidly declined.

The third section scrutinises the performance of the agricultural sector, also using *mars* data.[3] This disaggregated analysis offers insights as to why agricultural production is developing relatively slowly. The product mix changed, in particular reflecting the 'risk-averse' behaviour of peasant farms. However, agriculture in terms of volume has done better than the (value-based) growth figures suggest, in particular due to the 'price scissors' of the immediate post-Russian crisis years. However, rural incomes did not grow, although the domestic terms of trade have improved somewhat since 2000. Although the data is not detailed enough to be able to provide a definitive analysis, it seems that there is a certain dynamism and regional specialisation in the changing agrarian structure, which reflects the fact that somewhat larger farms produce the bulk crops, such as grain (Aragatsotn, Shirak and Gegharkunik) and potatoes (Gegharkunik and Lori), while other *marses* specialise more in fruits (Ararat, Armavir and Kotayk) or vegetables and melons (Ararat and Armavir) produced in much smaller farms, although this is not always the case, because of the risk-averse behaviour of peasant farms.

The fourth section is fully dedicated to the operation of land (lease and sales) markets. Detailed data are not (yet) available on who buys or leases land, from whom and for what reason. However, aggregate data, in particular from the State Cadastre Committee, show an increasing number of land transactions, in particular since 2001. The main push factor for land sales is poverty and destitution (and the strategy to migrate, which in the case of Armenia means the last step, cutting very important roots). Pull factors include the demand for land from neighbouring farms which do better and expand, but also from absentee financial groups which invest (or speculate) in land,[4] or the emerging agro-industry (of wine and canned fruit) which seeks vertical integration. The chapter presents an overview of the current land distribution at *mars* level, in which nascent forms of land concentration can be seen to be emerging.[5] The land structure in Armenia still shows a large number of very small farms, which at the same time possess fragmented landholdings, with an average of three plots. Therefore, land consolidation – understood as a process of 'consolidating' these plots into unified land areas of farms, and distinct from the concept of land concentration – is needed. However, in the absence of trust in each other and in existing institutions to handle these issues, this process seems to be highly complicated and costly.

The fifth section analyses the current new phase (or wave) of land reform occurring at this very moment. Although going on rather unnoticed, the state is transferring a substantial amount of land, mostly hay land, pastures and meadows to the jurisdiction of the communities, only keeping the land that is outside their *de jure* borders.[6] This gives communities the chance to decide about the allocation of this land, its privatisation, leasing, or sales through public auctions. Around one-third of the rural communities have by now received full control over this part of the State Reserve Fund of land. There is some anecdotal evidence that first sales were done in a rather non-transparent manner and that even some large land transactions took place.[7] Nevertheless, the rural communities have been granted a powerful instrument with which to improve the weak position and meagre landholdings of poor and vulnerable farm households through land allocations, supported by a combination of private and public finance. Communal pastures should furthermore be carefully handled, and access to these 'commons' has to be regulated through collective property rights and leasing rather than selling to private farmers, as the latter action is neither efficient (except for specific cases) nor equitable.

The sixth section will attempt to broaden the focus of this chapter beyond issues of 'land, rural poverty and inequality', towards rural markets and the institutional environment surrounding peasant farms in the transition economy of Armenia. There are three crucial issues defining this 'environment', which is still largely characterised by 'missing' markets and institutions, i.e. inefficient, fragmented (just as in the case of land) and with high transaction costs. Following the initial land reform, agricultural and rural development policies have been minimal, to say the least, reflecting a rather strong urban bias in the political economy of Armenia. In the absence of cooperative or associative institutions, lack of credit and investment resources, and asymmetrical information problems, the rural producers are often in substantial disadvantage in commodity chains. Furthermore, the quality of land, along with irrigation, are indicated as the main bottlenecks to improving agricultural production, or even fully using the available (albeit scarce) land resources.

The concluding section seven returns to the original question 'what can the state do' in terms of pro-poor land and rural development policies, discussing a number of possible policy interventions that should be considered in order to improve production and efficiency on the one hand (perhaps through land consolidation and increased differentiation of farm size), while safeguarding as much as possible access to land because of its high propensity to reduce poverty levels. Several institutional issues will be brought forward regarding pro-poor land policies: regulated and transparent forms of using transferred state reserve land by the communities (allocations directed to the poor and vulnerable peasant farm households, leasing, sales and proper management of community land, such as pastures); promotion of cooperative or associative forms of production and/or marketing; completion of the property title registration (which is in full swing at the moment); further development of land markets (and the institutional capacity to manage this process); and improvement of institutional cooperation, with the main objective the strengthening of institutional capacity for (rural) policy analysis, development and implementation of rural (land and development) policies, which is currently rather weak (at central, regional and local levels).

Finally, the chapter discusses a number of rural economy growth scenarios based on our current knowledge of the agrarian structure and the development of the Armenian agricultural sector.

Redistributive and egalitarian land reform

In only a few countries of the former Soviet Union has a redistributive land reform taken place, particularly in the smallest newly independent states; namely first in the early 1990s Armenia and Georgia, later on in Kyrgyzstan (mid-1990s), and finally in Moldova (late 1990s). Actually, some of the required institutional framework for Armenia's land reform was already in place in early 1991, even before the Soviet Union fell apart. Soon after independence the land reform started, and 70 per cent of arable land came into the hands of individual peasant farms.[8]

Outcomes of land reform

The redistributive land reform in Armenia created a large number of peasant farms (see Table 6.1) with an average size of 1.3–1.4 hectares (and less than 0.5 ha per rural capita), divided into several parcels. Primarily arable land (with in addition most of the orchards and vineyards) was privatised, while an important part of the hayfields and all pasture land remained in the hands of the state. This meant that by the mid-1990s one-third of agricultural land had been privatised.[9] According to the official 'Land Balance' of 1997, around 330,000 individual peasant farms had been formed, remaining fairly stable since.

While access to land was in principle egalitarian in nature, the standard allocation of land to members of eligible families depended on the available amount of land in the community, and the density of the eligible population at that moment. Hence, regional differences emerged. This is clear from the Land Balance of 1997, and further data that are available for the year 2000.

The average farm size in the *marses* such as Ararat and Armavir was much smaller than in for example the *marses* of Shirak and Syunik.[10] However, this comparison still misses important variables, namely the altitude, the availability of water (irrigation) and the soil quality, but it provides some indications for the somewhat unequal endowments for peasant farms in the country, at least in terms of size. A similar conclusion can be drawn from a recent household survey (Table 6.3), which also shows these different averages per region, close to the data presented by the NSS for the year 2000.

Table 6.1 Number and acreage of peasant farms (1998–2003)

	1992	1993	1996	1998	2000	2002	2003
Number of peasant farms	165.20	238.30	316.40	333.80	332.60	334.70	337.90
Land area of peasant farms (×1,000 ha)	214.90	310.40	429.20	447.00	460.10	453.10*	461.30
Average size of peasant farms (ha)	1.30	1.30	1.36	1.34	1.38	1.35	1.37

	Agricultural land	Arable land	Perennial grass	Fallow land	Hay land	Pasture
Land Balance (1997) (% of Agricultural Land)	100.00	35.53	4.59	0.03	9.98	49.88

Sources: NSS (2003a, 2004d); StatKom SNG (2002), *Eshegodnik SNG* (2001).

Note
* NSS (2003a) did provide another figure, namely 471.9, suggesting an increase in acreage.

Table 6.2 Land inventory (private and state-owned) for the year 2000

	Number of farms*	Total private land (Ha)	Average private land area	Arable land	Orchard	Vineyard	Hayfield	Fallow and other	Total state land	Arable	Orchard	Vineyard	Without use	Hayfield	Pasture
Aragatsotn	37,139	–	1.51	41,219	1,875	2,164	1,705	9,006	61,549	12,051	266	121	426	1,233	47,452
Ararat	52,482	33,728	0.64	18,366	1,886	3,711	874	8,891	31,045	10,697	289	316	0	1,459	18,284
Armavir	50,332	45,876	0.91	27,773	2,813	3,782	30	11,478	25,020	12,777	795	434	580	121	10,313
Gegharkunik	46,133	74,578	1.62	48,769	27	0	15,655	10,127	97,847	27,701	89	0	5,350	6,272	58,435
Kotayk	37,611	45,731	1.22	27,060	2,428	749	7,734	7,760	41,932	9,316	788	13	79	2,525	29,211
Lori	32,549	64,659	1.99	33,258	885	74	21,483	8,959	87,826	9,889	745	3	707	12,690	63,792
Shirak	28,153	68,858	2.45	57,944	22	0	2,875	8,017	76,014	19,110	119	0	242	7,819	48,724
Syunik	12,707	38,330	3.02	30,231	750	81	3,806	3,462	95,302	12,237	319	26	1,216	3,256	78,248
Tavush	24,492	29,222	1.19	19,470	493	1,258	3,524	4,477	39,932	7,411	1,006	39	107	7,168	24,201
Vayots Dsor	11,010	16,748	1.52	10,924	291	472	2,814	2,247	40,320	4,602	52	7	2,016	2,122	31,521
Yerevan	2,478	3,443	1.39	198	68	127	0	3,050	2,970	1,308	337	389	0	37	899
Within the community boundary	335,086	477,142	1.59	315,212	11,538	12,418	60,500	77,474	599,757	127,099	4,805	1,348	10,723	44,702	411,080
Outside the community boundary	–	–	–	–	–	–	–	–	324,868	6,540	44	3	0	30,740	287,541
Total agricultural land in Armenia	–	477,142	–	315,212	11,538	12,418	60,500	77,474	924,625	133,639	4,849	1,351	10,723	75,442	698,621

Sources: NSS (2003b) and data provided by the State Cadastre Committee.

Note
* These include 335,086 (individual) peasant farms and ten collective peasant farms. From 2002 the latter category was renamed 'commercial organisations'. In 2003 there were, according to the NSS, 334,789 peasant farms and 110 commercial organisations.

Table 6.3 Owned and leased land by peasant farms, distribution by region (2003) (hectares)

	Agricultural land in use	Of which is owned	Of which is rented*
Aragatsotn	1.79	1.73	0.07
Ararat	0.57	0.51	0.07
Armavir	1.16	1.01	0.16
Gegharkunik	1.77	1.54	0.25
Kotayk	1.58	1.53	0.05
Lori	2.13	1.68	0.49
Shirak	2.83	2.79	0.05
Syunik	2.48	2.03	0.52
Tavush	1.18	1.14	0.07
Vayots Dsor	1.34	1.21	0.14
Total average	1.53	1.37	0.16

Source: Center for Economic Reforms (2004), based on a survey of 6,000 households.

Note
* Most of this land was rented from the State.

According to Table 6.3, individual peasant farms were leasing (again on average) small plots of land (0.16 ha), to increase the meagre average landholdings they owned (1.37 ha).[11]

The original land reform has only touched upon a relatively small part of the total agricultural land area of Armenia. In the year 2000 (since then there has only been gradual change, as we will see in the section on land markets) 477,141 ha were private land,[12] while 924,625 ha were still state-owned (with 599,757 ha within the boundaries of the communities, and 324,868 ha beyond these boundaries). The latter distinction is important as currently, during the period 2003–2005, state land 'within the boundaries of the communities' is being transferred (free of charge) to these administrative units, giving them a variety of options to privatise, lease or manage them (see below). Most of that still state-owned land is pasture (75.5 per cent), while further arable land, and in addition orchards and vineyards in the hands of the state, represent 15.1 per cent of the state-owned 'land fund'.

Land as a 'cushion' against poverty

The Armenian land reform has functioned as an important buffer or cushion against the impact of the negative supply shock that has struck the Armenian economy during the first years of transition. By the mid-1990s, when economic growth started to regain positive momentum, after years of extremely severe contraction, poverty had become a widespread phenomenon in the country, with urban poverty more severe than its rural counterpart (World Bank, 2002). Widespread access to land, providing the capability to produce food for household consumption (or crop/animal-based output to increase cash income), has definitely improved the lot of many rural dwellers, and also for the influx from urban centres, and other economic sectors that had largely collapsed (see the section on agricultural employment).

In Table 6.4 one can see the development of poverty (distinguishing urban and rural poverty) between 1996 and 2003. The income gap between rural and urban areas is widening and, during the past years, urban poverty is rapidly diminishing (going down from 59.8 per cent in 1996 to 39.7 per cent in 2003), while rural poverty remains stagnant (fluctuating around the level of 48.0 per cent in 1996 to 47.5 per cent in 2003). Even worse, as poverty is measured by using only monetary-based indicators or the level of nutrition, it does not take into account the severe deterioration of social (and other public) services in rural areas. Altogether this means that the 'poverty reduction elasticity' of land ownership seems to have somewhat diminished over the years, mainly, as will be seen below, because of the weak bargaining position of peasant farmers in markets. Primary producers have been suffering price discrimination, and incomes for agricultural producers have stagnated or even dropped. This has led to the perseverance of similar levels of rural poverty since the mid-1990s, while urban poverty is rapidly diminishing.

Performance of the agricultural sector

Rural incomes are largely dependent on the agricultural sector. Hence, its performance is of crucial importance for the sustainable reduction of rural poverty in Armenia. In the following section we will look at issues of agricultural employment, gross agricultural output development, the deterioration of the domestic terms of trade, and the development in output specialisation and farm size.

Agricultural employment

The importance of the agricultural sector in the transition to a market economy has grown substantially in Armenia. This is mainly because sectors other than agriculture largely collapsed in the early 1990s, in particular in industry. The agricultural sector henceforth absorbed a substantial volume of redundant labour, shed by other sectors. Agricultural employment increased from an estimated 389,000 workers in 1991 to 586,000 in 1996, thereafter stabilising at a level of around 565,000 during the late 1990s (StatKom SNG, 2002: 211).[13] This process instigated a form of 're-peasantisation' of the economy, which can also be noted in countries such as Georgia, Moldova, Kyrgyzstan and Uzbekistan. As could be expected, agricultural labour productivity declined during the first half of

Table 6.4 Rural and urban poverty compared (1996–2003) (percentage shares of total)

| | Urban areas | | | | | | Rural areas | | | | | |
	1996	1999	2001	2002	2003		1996	1999	2001	2002	2003
Total population	100.0	100.0	100.0	100.0	100.0		100.0	100.0	100.0	100.0	100.0
Not poor	41.2	41.7	48.1	47.4	60.3		52.0	49.2	51.3	54.7	52.5
Poor	29.2	35.1	33.6	37.6	–		23.6	28.2	37.4	35.1	–
Extreme poor	29.6	23.2	18.3	15.0	–		24.4	22.6	11.3	10.2	–

Source: NSS (2003c).

the 1990s, with a value added per worker decreasing to a level of 69.6 per cent of the 1990 level in 1995 (with the entire economy being at 58.3 per cent). It continued to reduce until the year 2000 (when value added per worker stood at 52.4 per cent of the 1990 level), while the entire economy was recovering, and overall labour productivity had recovered to 86.6 per cent of its original pre-transition level.[14]

Gross agricultural output

Gross agricultural output (GAO), with relatively small fluctuations, shows a smaller decline during the 1990s than GDP. For example, it dropped 16.3 per cent between 1991 and 1993, and in comparison with 1990 only 2.0 per cent (Griffin *et al.*, 2002: 55). In the past decade, 1998 was a good year for agriculture, but in the aftermath of the Russian crisis, another more severe dip in GAO followed (see Table 6.5),

The negative trend in GAO between 1998 and 2000 can only be partially explained by the trends in physical output. According to official numbers, in this period, physical output (measured in equivalents) from the crop sector decreased by 12.6 per cent, while subsectoral GAO decreased by 44.5 per cent. Its counterpart, the animal husbandry sector, increased its physical output by 17.4 per cent, while the corresponding GAO dropped by 8.3 per cent.[15] This is a clear indication that prices for primary agricultural products were decreasing in real terms and that profits were shifting towards other parts of the value chain (such as the food and agro-processing sector). On the whole, agricultural output (in volume) has done relatively well during the whole period, at least better than one would expect, when keeping in mind the deep economic crisis Armenia went through in the early 1990s (see Figures 6.1 and 6.2).

What is very important to note from these data, is that 'low value, high volume' crop output (such as is represented by wheat and potatoes), indicates an increasing trend throughout the 1990s and 2000s, in particular during the latter. In the case of grain the expansion of output can be

Table 6.5 Gross agricultural output (1998–2003) (billion AMD current prices)

	1998	1999	2000	2001	2002	2003
Total GAO	402.1	311.7	281.2	351.0	377.6	410.1
Plant-growing GAO	245.6	180.0	136.2	208.0	226.6	228.7
Animal husbandry GAO	156.5	131.7	145.0	143.0	151.0	181.4

Source: NSS (2003a, 2004d).

Note
The NSS makes a differentiation between two sectors, namely 'household plots' (or sometimes even 'people's enterprises') and commercial enterprises. The latter represents only a very tiny share of production. No other data than GAO at current prices (in billions of AMDs, or Armenian drams) are available at aggregate levels for Armenia.

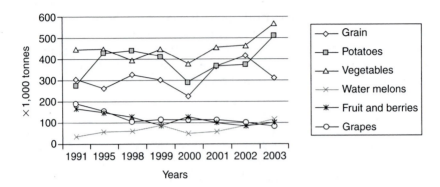

Figure 6.1 Main crop indicators (1991–2003) (source: NSS (2003a 2004d)).

Note
The data for 1999 were substantially lower in NSS (2003a), than in NSS (2004d).

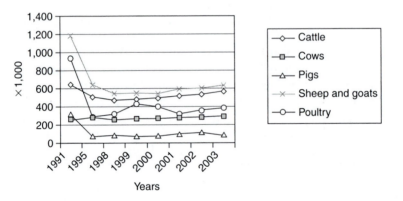

Figure 6.2 Main livestock indicators (1991–2003) (source: NSS (2003a, 2004d).

Note
Per 1 January following year. For poultry the unit of measurement is (×10,000).

largely attributed to a bigger sown area, which expanded from 152,500 ha (1991) to 200,800 ha (2003) (NSS, 2001, 2002a, 2004d).

This shows the food self-sufficiency strategy of many small peasant farms. Grain yields have fluctuated wildly, as output is very much dependent on stable rainfall, and in its absence, of functioning irrigation systems. Production of 'high value, low volume' crop output follows a more complex trend. Low-investment crops, such as vegetables and fruits, have substantially expanded in terms of output, adding cash income for the peasant farms. High-investment crops such as grapes, have substantially suffered. Anecdotal evidence from a field visit to the Vayots Dsor *mars* in October 2004 also revealed that individual peasant farms had sometimes cut (sic) vineyards in favour of planting wheat, because credit, inputs and outlets were 'missing', and hence food self-sufficiency was preferred instead. This also happened in other *marses*, such as Ararat and Armavir.

The livestock sector in Armenia, again similar to other transition countries of the Former Soviet Union (FSU), suffered a severe contraction (although much less than for example in Russia and Kazakhstan). This was particularly strong in the sub-sectors of pigs, sheep and goats, beef cattle, and poultry, although this last category has been picking up substantially throughout the first years of this decade. Interestingly enough, the herd of cows has gradually expanded (to be expected with the large number of individual peasant farms), just as has the production of milk and eggs (the latter after a substantial trough in the early 1990s, when specialised large-scale livestock and poultry complexes collapsed and the centralised production of fodder practically vanished). Finally, wool production dropped to about half of its previous production level, which reflects the sudden drop in subsidised and centralised fodder provisioning.

Deteriorating domestic terms of trade

Another depressing effect for agricultural incomes, in spite of the reasonable performance when looking to physical indicators, was the negative development of the domestic (agriculture *versus* industry) terms of trade. Although the data are insufficient to be able to calculate this important indicator with a solid degree of confidence, the overall trend can be clearly discerned, in particular for the period 1998–2003, with 1997 as base year (when the statistical system was substantially improved): the overall trend for the domestic terms of trade (ToT_D) was negative (see Figure 6.3). The producer price index (PPI_A) for agricultural production declined between 1997 and 1999 by 19.5 per cent, followed by fluctuations and an increasing trend until 2003. Overall the PPI_A index in the latter year compared with 1997 was 96.7. However, the PPI_I index for industrial production grew to 132.8 (compared to 1997 = 100), which means a deterioration of the ToT_D by −27.2 per cent!

Although there was a small relative improvement of the ToT_D during the years 2000 and 2001, by late 2003 the deterioration of the ToT_D for agriculture was still at the same level as at the end of 1999. One explanatory factor is that, while Armenia became a relatively open economy during the 1990s, the trade blockade at its borders with Turkey and Azerbaijan, and the continuous internal upheavals in neighbouring Georgia, made Armenia *de facto* landlocked. Surplus production could therefore most often not be sold externally, depressing domestic prices of agricultural products (Griffin *et al.*, 2002). However, other important factors are also negatively influencing the ToT_D, namely the insufficient bargaining power (towards traders and processors) of large numbers of unorganised and individually operating peasant farmers; insufficient access to finance; poor infrastructure (including storage facilities); and the change in crop mix.

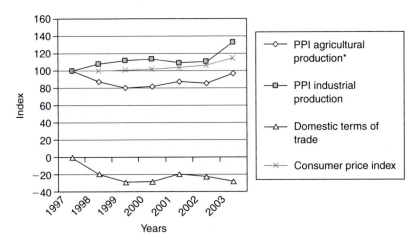

Figure 6.3 Domestic terms of trade (1997–2003) (source: NSS (2002b, 2003a).

Notes
The domestic terms of trade between agriculture and industry worsened during the period 1997–2003 by 27.2 per cent, going down to the level of 1999–2000, after some recovery in 2001–2002.
* Measured by the sales prices of agricultural products (a weighted index of crop and animal production).

While volume trends for agricultural production during the same period were largely positive, with the above shown negative relative price development (depressing farm gate prices in relative and sometimes even in absolute terms), the impact on agricultural incomes was negative.

Output specialisation and farm size

As stated in the introduction, Armenian agriculture shows very specific regional differences, reflecting natural endowments (the Ararat valley versus pre-mountain and mountainous areas); land allocation during the land reform (available land in combination with population density, causing the individual peasant farms in Ararat and Armavir to be relatively small); and crop/livestock specialisation.

In Table 6.6 the estimated GAO per *mars* is given, which clearly shows a much higher GAO/ha for Ararat and Armavir, followed (at quite some distance) by Lori, Kotayk and Vayots Dsor. From the data on physical output, this can be simply explained by the fact that the first two *marses* produce a large portion of vegetables, fruits and grapes, while the other regions produce more grain, potatoes (representing a lower value of output/ha), or specialise in livestock production.[16] However, as mentioned before, there is also a problematic tendency in the most important (in terms of GAO) agricultural *marses* to diminish the acreage of vine-

Table 6.6 Gao per *mars* (1999–2002), per hectare (1,000 AMD/hectare)

	1999	2000	2001	2002
Aragatsotn	489.7	310.8	422.7	503.1
Ararat	1,271.4	1,251.0	1,289.4	1,445.7
Armavir	1,246.1	1,117.5	1,262.6	1,208.1
Gegharkunik	477.6	445.8	563.1	630.6
Kotayk	570.8	538.2	678.5	761.1
Lori	690.3	630.9	786.5	857.1
Shirak	432.9	343.2	428.8	472.5
Syunik	441.4	540.9	677.0	640.8
Tavush	541.7	424.9	724.9	689.5
Vayots Dsor	427.0	417.8	669.8	745.5

Source: NSS (2003b).

yards, while the grain area (for food security reasons) increases at the same time. If we compare the data of Table 6.6 (GAO/hectare) with the average size of farms given in Table 6.2 (for the year 2000), we can see that there is a clear inverse relationship between the two variables (see Figure 6.4). Even so, these data combined with data on regional averages of farms indicate that the initial unequal distribution of land has indeed produced differences in production of GAO, not compensated for by crop/livestock specialisation.

However, from the above discussion it remains unclear whether a more efficient and high-value producing farm sector is emerging in which individual farms tend to own more land (see further discussion below on this topic, examining in detail an emerging change in the distribution of land in Armenia).

Emerging land sales and lease markets

In the early 1990s a new agrarian structure emerged in Armenia, with a large number of small peasant farms privately owning most of the arable

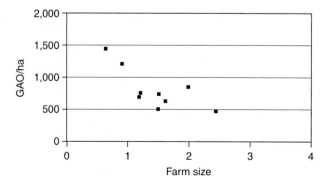

Figure 6.4 Gross agricultural output versus farm size (source: NSS (2003b).

land, orchards and vineyards, and part of the hayfields, while all pasture land remained state-owned. Agricultural land was managed under formal, informal and customary arrangements, and only by the late 1990s land markets for the sale and lease of land emerged in Armenia. As is generally the case in agricultural land markets, there are 'push' and 'pull' factors that provoke land transactions.[17] One 'push' factor for land sales in particular is obviously the emergence of rural poverty and destitution. Poor families might in the end be forced to migrate to urban areas or even abroad, and therefore have to sell their land in a form of a 'distress sale'. According to Armenian tradition, this is indeed the last step of uprooting, as the sale of land really means cutting the umbilical cord with the place of birth or traditional residence. Other 'push' factors include the low capacity to cultivate the land (such as within the growing group of pensioners), and the need for cash income that can be derived from the sale (or renting) of land. A 'pull' factor for the sale of land (or in this case, the buying), is the demand for land by those neighbouring peasant farms doing well, and wishing to expand in size. Agro-industry (in the cases of wine/cognac production, or fruit and vegetable canning/processing) is trying to integrate vertically, in order to be able to guarantee sufficient quality and quantity of supplied raw materials and therefore invest in land (and infrastructure). Land purchase can also be 'pulled' by capital groups or rich individuals who speculate with agricultural land (which is expected to have a higher value in the future), while only having to pay low land taxes.

As can be seen from Table 6.7, the official data provided by the State

Table 6.7 The agricultural land market in Armenia (1998–2004) (agricultural land alienation) (number)[a]

	1998	1999	2000	2001	2002	2003	Total
Aragatsotn	29	51	80	78	250	379	867
Ararat	132	272	364	618	675	950	3,011
Armavir	42	141	318	270	341	588	1,700
Gegharkunik	37	12	8	17	63	216	353
Kotayk	10	121	118	131	327	559	1,266
Lori	3	29	23	45	73	181	354
Shirak	10	32	47	69	171	282	611
Syunik	2	0	2	14	15	66	99
Tavush	2	7	15	29	6	27	86
Vayots Dsor	1	11	48	16	12	64	152
Total number	268	676	1,023	1,287	1,933	3,312	–
Total number of land lease transactions	–	127	103	4,355	3,915	2,110	–

Source: State Cadastre Committee (2004).

Note
a 'Alienation' means sales, donations, and inheritance. No. = Number of transactions.

Cadastre Committee show the emerging (formal) agricultural land sales and land lease markets in Armenia. From a level of only 268 land sales transactions in 1998, the land market developed relatively quickly, to a level of 3,312 transactions in 2003.

Land lease transactions numbered only 127 (in 1999) and 103 (in 2000), while in the following years their numbers grew to respectively 4,355 (2001) and 3,915 (2002). Interestingly enough, in the following year the registered number of leasing transactions reduced again substantially, although the exact reason is unknown. However, it might well be that many lease operations are done without formal registration, avoiding substantial transaction costs.[18] Regional differences are fairly large, with the *marses* of Ararat, Armavir and Kotayk representing 70.3 per cent of all sales of agricultural land. Although there are slight discrepancies in the data, in comparison with the previous table, Table 6.8 provides insights about the amount of agricultural land that has been transferred in terms of sales. For 2003, this was only 296.2 hectares of land in 145 transactions (which is 2.0 ha on average) of state land to private owners, and 2,175 hectares of land in 3,057 transactions between private landowners (0.7 ha on average). This is most likely because the former are pastures, and the latter is largely arable land. In the first half of 2004, the first category grew to 815.9 hectares of land in 261 transactions (increasing the average), and the latter to 1,232 hectares in 2,145 transactions (lower in comparison with 2003).

These data indicate a rapid growth in sales transactions, albeit starting from a near-zero level, but the total area of agricultural land subject of sales

Table 6.8 Land sales of private and state land (2003–2004)

| | 2003 | | | | 2004 (First Half) | | | |
| | State Land | | Private Land | | State Land | | Private Land | |
	Number	*Hectares*	*Number*	*Hectares*	*Number*	*Hectares*	*Number*	*Hectares*
Aragatsotn	72	69.7	301	197.2	7	49.3	226	131.8
Ararat	12	47.5	903	298.5	190	412.9	543	204.7
Armavir	0	0.0	581	630.8	7	225.8	353	326.3
Gegharkunik	23	160.8	192	326.6	0	0.0	27	26.2
Kotayk	37	17.2	508	192.2	50	101.4	648	245.4
Lori	0	0.0	164	136.2	0	0.0	101	82.2
Shirak	0	0.0	280	295.0	0	0.0	139	132.3
Syunik	1	1.0	48	37.2	1	0.1	32	35.2
Tavush	0	0.0	23	11.2	1	1.2	41	38.5
Vayots Dsor	0	0.0	57	50.3	5	25.2	35	9.1
Total	145	296.2	3,057	2,175.2	261	815.9	2,145	1,231.7

Sources: State Cadastre Committee (2003a), (2004).

in the past six years is still relatively insignificant, namely less than 2 per cent of privately owned land in Armenia. This means that the land sales market is still nearly non-existent or 'missing', at least the formal market. There is some anecdotal evidence that informal land renting, in view of migration to urban areas and abroad, has become more popular, leading to a slightly higher degree of land concentration than before. Finally, the land sales market is expected to expand rapidly (with larger areas of agricultural land to be sold or leased), in particular because the government is pushing forward the process of (first) property title registration. At this moment this registration has started or has even been completed in 778 of the 929 communities, and is expected to be completed by late 2005.

Land concentration?

There is an emerging diversity in the size of Armenian farms. This differentiation in landholdings is mostly caused by renting (leasing) land in (or out), as there are some small farm householders who do not have the capital, or even knowledge to farm, and have moved into off-farm employment or migrated. Although no hard data exist, this explanation is more likely, in that land concentration is emerging through purchasing and selling. Even in terms of official data on land distribution (ownership titles and formally leased land) there is a serious data problem. The State Cadastre Committee gathers this type of data at a disaggregate level in the regional and sub-regional offices, but no nationwide land distribution data are (as yet) available.[19] At the moment it is working at an updated Land Balance, which was to be published in 2005 (the last one is from 1997). Therefore, in this chapter we reverted to recent data produced for the publication *Armenian Social Trends* (No. 6, November 2004), based on a survey including 6,000 households.

Table 6.9 presents these data (in accumulated form), using categories of landholdings with intervals of <0.0–1.0, <1.0–3.0, and >3.0 hectares, and comparing the ranking of the survey-based regional average of landholdings and the one produced for the 1997 Land Balance of the State Cadastre Committee.

At a slightly more disaggregated level the original survey measured land distribution within the following categories: <0.0–0.5, <0.5–1.0, <1.0–2.0, <2.0–3.0, <3.0–5.0, <5.0–10.0 and >10.0 hectares. For example, in Shirak 4.5 per cent of the farms were larger than ten hectares, while in Lori and Syunik these only accounted for 2.1 per cent.

There is, however, some anecdotal evidence that much larger farms are being formed through informal leasing arrangements. In the above-mentioned *mars* of Suynik, for example a recent field study found entrepreneurial farmers, cultivating between 15 and 500 (sic) hectares of mostly rented land (ICRA, 2004: 42). This study introduced a farm household typology, which is possibly useful for the *marses* that are outside the

Table 6.9 Land distribution, by region (2003) (percentage hectares)

	<0.0–1.0	<1.0–3.0	>3.0	Average farm size[1]	Average farm size[2]
Shirak	22.3	41.4	36.3	2.83	2.28
Syunik	36.4	37.2	26.4	2.48	2.87
Lori	42.6	28.3	29.1	2.13	1.72
Aragatsotn	44.0	40.0	16.0	1.79	1.26
Gegharkunik	49.0	36.1	14.9	1.77	1.42
Tavush	50.5	46.0	3.5	1.18	1.01
Armavir	52.4	43.7	3.9	1.16	0.68
Kotayk	54.6	25.4	20.0	1.58	1.03
Vayots Dsor	62.3	24.9	12.8	1.34	1.18
Ararat	82.8	16.3	0.9	0.57	0.48

Source: AST, No. 6 (2004).

Notes
1 Center for Economic Reforms (2004).
2 NSS (1997) (owned land).

Ararat valley, distinguishing between entrepreneurial, subsistence and vulnerable farm households (see Box 6.1). However, this is a very crude differentiation, unfit for other *marses* such as Ararat, Kotayk and Vayots Dsor, which show large numbers of very small farms. It is likely that the latter category also presents substantial differentiation, which is not measured through the degree of land concentration, but through the involvement in remunerative off-farm employment or business activities. Nevertheless, the proposed farm household typology does help to understand the emerging differentiation that is taking place in rural areas in Armenia.[20]

Box 6.1 Categorizing farm households

Entrepreneurial farmers: They have sufficient capital, own machinery, processing equipment; they rent out equipment and often produce seeds; rent in land (15–500 ha); own livestock (5–50 heads of cattle); hire workers, and have good access to credit and market outlets; they sell >50% of output.

Subsistence farmers: They have limited capital, little or no owned machinery. They have their own land (1.5–5 ha), do not rent in other land, but rent out or leave it fallow. They have limited access to credit and markets; sell around 20–50% of output.

Vulnerable farmers: They have no capital, and often no working capital. They rent out land, leave their land fallow, or are landless. They have no access to credit, and limited market access. They sell/barter <20% of farm produce, and are involved in mostly off-farm activities.

When sorting the data according to the number of farms in the first category of between nought and one hectares, the survey results tell us that (in ascending order), the following *marses* have more than 50 per cent of their peasant farms in this category: Tavush, Armavir, Kotayk, Vayots Dsor and Ararat. The latter is a (well-known) extreme case of land fragmentation, namely 82.8 per cent of the peasant farms are smaller than one hectare (Table 6.9), and 54.2 per cent of the farms are even smaller than 0.5 hectare (UNDP and Government of Armenia, 2004, No. 6).[21] If we combine this particular order of *marses* with the average size of the peasant farms, it is clear that the order is the inverse one (with only small exceptions in the ranking), as the smaller share of very small peasant farms will also produce a higher overall farm size at *mars* level. However, returning to the discussion on land markets, it seems that most differentiation has been initially defined by the land reform of the early 1990s. To a lesser extent it can be explained by the follow-up process of (market-led) land concentration, although data on the informal land rental market are lacking, which – if available – could highlight its importance in the changing agrarian structure.

Completing the current process of property title registration will certainly lead to more sales/purchases of land and a gradual concentration of land in the hands of more dynamic farms. The extremely small peasant farms will struggle to be competitive in an open economy as Armenia is at the moment, but land for them will remain the main source of income, and a continued 'cushion' against worsening poverty. The future size of farms is of course completely dependent on the type of crop mix, the available technology and the capital/labour ratio. Land concentration should furthermore not be confused with land consolidation, which is the process of interchange (through purchasing and selling, barter and the use of public compensation funds) of fragmented plots of land belonging to one peasant farm, with the objectives of reducing transportation costs, and removing technological bottlenecks, such as not being able to work the land with machinery. This need is still fairly urgent in the Armenian agricultural economy, as most owners have on average three plots of land, which are often quite distant from each other. The plots (especially in the Ararat valley) are often of awkward size, such as 5–10 metres wide and 1,000 metres in length.[22]

The government, through the State Cadastre Committee (SCC) and through its Land Use Planning Institute (*Giprosem*), has developed a pilot project for land consolidation in eight communities in the *marses* of Ararat, Armavir and Kotayk.[23] Furthermore, one of the most recent initiatives is a pilot project financed by the FAO, which focuses on land consolidation and improved land management schemes.[24] Unfortunately, this project was initially incorrectly portrayed as a project that would force peasants to sell, and therefore in the interest of land concentration. This shows how politically and socially sensitive land consolidation is. The government has also made some steps towards avoiding further fragmentation of land, by prohibiting the division of land in case of inheritance.

Land transfer: a new phase (or wave) of land reform

It is crucial to note, as part and parcel of an analysis of land policies in Armenia, that the new institutional transformation underway in terms of property rights of land involves a large-scale transfer of state-owned land to the jurisdiction of the communities. This transfer also means that these communities will have discretion to dispose of the land as they please, to sell it, to lease it, or to manage it (or even establish systems of communal 'use rights'). The impact of this fundamental change in property rights might well be deeper than it seems at the surface. Going back to the detailed Table 6.2, a total of 599,757 hectares of agricultural land (with as main categories 127,099 hectares of arable land and 411,080 hectares of pastures), i.e. all state-owned land that falls within the boundaries of the communities, was to be transferred to the communities themselves between 2003 and 2005. Before this transfer, this land could be (and was also) used by and leased to individual peasant farms.[25]

The rent and the taxes paid had to be transferred to the central authorities, and could not be retained by the local administrations, although they were already very short in revenues. The current transfer within the realm of 'public ownership' means that fiscal and other revenues (such as from renting and sales) from land that is legally controlled by local administrations will be fully retained by them, and these proceeds can be used at that level. The State Cadastre Committee would like to see the proceeds being earmarked for expenditure needed for land development and area management plans, which are now occasionally financed at the central level, while other parts of the government voice different ideas for the use of this income. No specific rulings seem to have been developed for this purpose, although central government direction and guidance of this crucial process is badly needed.

Clearly, this represents a strong incentive to the community administrations to sell land, as they can retain the revenue raised. This might well be contrary to other priorities, namely the search for improved institutional arrangements of land management at local level, in particular when it concerns communal pastures. The land transfer program should be used in order to strengthen the weak position of the extremely small peasant farms, as a primary tool of pro-poor land policies. Furthermore, the communal pastures – in case of their privatisation – would provide only limited access for many peasant households who will have not gained private ownership, leading to rapidly increasing inequality of access to such important rural resources as grazing grounds and water resources. Interestingly enough, this issue was already raised in the World Bank survey of 1998. As Lerman and Mirsakhanyan (2001: 31) stated: 'Farmers express an overwhelmingly negative opinion of the privatisation of pastures: 74 per cent of respondents are opposed and only 9 per cent support the suggestion.'

Table 6.10 shows the current state of this land transfer programme. By October 2004 it had been completed in 309 of the total 929 (urban and rural) communities, including a total amount of 288,898 hectares of land being transferred from the state to the jurisdiction of the community. Only a small share of this land has actually been privatised through land markets, as shown in the previous section.

This observation will also be confirmed when we analyse detailed local data from a sample of 20 rural communities which was provided by the SCC in November 2004 (see Annex 6.1).[26] There were only incidental sales in this sample between 2001 and 2004, some of them representing very tiny plots (that look more like household or *dacha* plots), and some larger ones (such as one case with only one transaction of 38 hectares).[27] The problem is not that the situation has changed dramatically, but that neither clear regulations nor transparency (in terms of access to auctions and other instruments of sales or leasing practices) exist, which might well lead to undesired practices of land concentration or speculation with this very scarce resource. From the detailed data provided for these 20 communities (two for each *mars*), which can only be used to provide some trends and indications, and should in no way be generalised for the whole country, we can see a few other important variables. Communities only (or still) own 17.9 per cent of total arable land within their boundaries. In some communities all arable land is irrigated, in some none, while on

Table 6.10 Land transfer programme (2003–2005) from the State Reserve Fund, completed in 309 rural communities (hectares)

	Total agricultural land	*Private*	*Community*	*State*	*Other*
Aragatsotn	69,801.3	18,682.6	48,874.7	2,244.0	0.0
Ararat	56,448.6	21,900.8	32,030.5	2,388.9	128.4
Armavir	81,874.8	35,348.0	43,194.2	3,332.6	0.0
Gegharkunik	46,345.0	18,523.1	26,706.3	1,115.6	0.0
Kotayk	32,454.8	10,689.8	18,797.1	2,961.1	6.9
Lori	42,596.3	9,887.8	22,377.6	10,331.4	0.0
Shirak	82,186.6	32,243.3	43,444.0	6,478.8	20.5
Syunik	74,646.9	15,660.2	53,473.1	5,513.5	0.0
Tavush	–	–	–	–	–
Vayots Dsor	–	–	–	–	–
Total	486,354.3	162,935.6	288,897.5	34,365.9	155.8

Sources: Data provided by the State Cadastre Committee.

Note
The category 'private land' has been the outcome of the land reform of the early 1990s. 'State land' will remain as such, as this is 'outside the boundaries of the communities'.

average (although this 'mean' does not mean much) around one-third of arable land is irrigated (see Annex 6.1). Pasture land, which is most of the land to be transferred to the communities – in the sample – accounts for around 58 per cent of the total land (while total pastures in Armenia comprise around 50 per cent of agricultural land, see Table 6.2).

As mentioned before, the land transfer programme can – in the absence of a regulatory framework – lead to rapid and uncontrolled land concentration, which is inefficient and anti-poor. It can also have an important positive impact on the Armenian agrarian structure in the immediate future, especially if clearly defined land policies are in place. Moreover, this new stage (or wave) of land reform could be used to provide allocations of scarce land (finance by mixed public/private funds and even loans) to those poor households currently in dire need of land for their basic survival (primarily food), in view of a rural non-farm economy in Armenia that is still poorly developed (Besemer and Davis, 2003), with urban jobs in short supply. It is also a crucial moment in time to promote more actively different associative and cooperative forms of labour exchange in production, joint marketing of output and purchasing of inputs (i.e. the so-called 'single purpose cooperatives'). Important bottlenecks for land policy are, furthermore, the management of communal pastures, the land consolidation of already established peasant farms (resolving existing extreme fragmentation), and the development of locally managed sustainable land management plans (such as developed on an experimental basis by the SCC), which will facilitate efforts to modernise agricultural production.

Rural markets 'beyond land'

After more than a decade of transition, any visitor to Armenia would be impressed by the relative wealth encountered in the city centre of Yerevan. However, if he or she would take the trouble to travel only a short distance beyond the borders of the capital, this impression would be suddenly replaced by the observation of an amazing gap between the 'rest of the country,' in particular the more remote rural areas, and the capital. This enormous gap can be seen in the standard of living, infrastructure, and quality of services. Areas struck by the earthquake of 1988 (the northwest), and those that have absorbed large numbers of Armenian refugees, originating in the conflict around Nagorno-Karabakh, have particularly high indices of poverty and destitution (World Bank, 2002). Rural poverty used to be lower than urban poverty, and access to land has been important in explaining this phenomenon. However, as shown above, rural poverty in 2003 has surpassed its urban counterpart, stagnating at a level similar to 1996 (Table 6.4). While access to land is still widespread in rural Armenia, among farm households, the poor and extreme poor are those who own very little land, or the landless. It can be shown (for example in the *mars*

Ararat) that a small addition to the private landholding substantially reduces the risk of poverty. Nevertheless, for peasant farm households land is important, but not land alone. This would indicate that (the lack of) across-the-board development of rural areas (including the small towns) and particularly rural markets has become the real Achilles' heel of the Armenian transition, in its quest for sustainable (and equitable) development strategy. The current growth pattern is clearly '*urban-b(i)ased*', and the fruits of growth equally so. Therefore, in this section we will analyse some of these markets (and corresponding institutions) 'beyond land', in order to properly frame land policies in the broader rural development context of Armenia. The most important of these contexts are: irrigation, credit, farm services and output markets, while one of the cross-cutting bottlenecks is the problematic state of rural infrastructure (such as roads, communication).

Irrigation: the 'kingpin' of agricultural development

Irrigation is without any doubt the most important aspect of agricultural (crop-based) production in Armenia.[28] Reliable data on the current state of the irrigation system in Armenia are scarce. In their 1998 household survey, Lerman and Mirsakhanyan (2001) found that only an estimated 18 per cent of all agricultural land was irrigated. This would correspond with 252,000 ha. The FAO (in its FAOSTAT data base) presents a near constant level of irrigated land of around 283,000 ha. The latter is hard to believe, as in most of the FSU there was a rapid process of deterioration of these large-scale, energy-intensive irrigation systems.[29] We therefore assume that the current irrigated acreage is substantially smaller. This is confirmed by micro-data in the most recent household survey of UNDP (AST, No. 6, November 2004). In total 44.2 of the surveyed households indicated that they did not utilise, partially or totally, their owned and rented land.[30] It is clear that irrigation is a crucial issue in (successful) agricultural production, and substantial investments are needed, hand in hand with institutional changes regarding subsidies for, rights to and pricing of water.[31]

Rural financial markets and access to credit

Lack of financial means is the second major factor preventing farm households from using all their agricultural land. According to the quoted UNDP household survey, in total 20.7 per cent indicated that they had 'no [financial] means for cultivation', and therefore left fallow part or all of their land, or rented it out. The access to financial services for the majority of small peasant farms in Armenia (and in many other countries) is quite problematic. A large part of state financial institutions have been dismantled, and most (new) commercial banks do not lend to the agricultural sector, except to those farms that are sufficiently large, and integrated into the High Value Agriculture (HVA) value chain. The only bank seriously lending to the agricultural sector is the ACBA Bank, which in 2003 claimed to have 61 per cent of the total commercial bank portfolio in agriculture. This seems a lot but, as the overall level is problematically low, it is no surprise that in 2003 (ACBA, 2004: 14) the agricultural loan portfolio was only US$8.8 million (or just above 1 per cent of GAO for that same year). Some progress has been made in terms of microcredit, as in total 596 agricultural cooperative village associations have been set up, with a total of 20,491 members. However, all in all, credit remains a crucial bottleneck (and equally so the absence of financial institutions in the regions able to combine the savings and credit function in one) and, if compared with countries such as Kyrgyzstan and Moldova, much more needs to be accomplished in establishing savings and credit associations. Finally, also relating to finance, in Armenia peasant producers still face insecurity as to which kind of tax regime will be introduced in order to comply with Armenia's obligations under the WTO agreement on agriculture. A timely resolution of this problem, for example, by the implementation of a comprehensive lump sum tax below a certain ceiling of turnover (avoiding complicated VAT payments and administration for small-scale producers) would be very helpful in this respect.

Inputs, technology and land use

With the collapse of the planned economic system, the redistributive land reform, and the formation of a large number of small-scale peasant farms, the declining purchasing power and the alignment of (all imported) input and machinery prices, the use of the latter reduced dramatically. Although there seems to have been a slight recovery in input use in the past few years, in the 1990s only limited amounts of nitrogen fertilisers were used, while others were practically abandoned, being too expensive. According to the FAO (FAOSTAT, 2004), the volume of N-fertiliser consumed in Armenian agriculture, went down from 25,000 tonnes in 1992 to 5,000 in 2001, only to grow again to a level of 8,200 tonnes in 2002. This is comparable with many other countries in the FSU, where most often the fertiliser use dropped to levels of 10–20 per cent of what it had been in the Soviet era.[32] Although in many cases there had been over- (and mis)-use of fertilisers, the extreme drop now causes land quality to degrade.[33] Most trade in inputs is being executed by private traders, sometimes operating as commissioners of international companies active in Armenia. Prices are relatively high (see previous discussion of the ToT$_D$) and, as credit is most often unavailable (even for working capital), the intensity of input use is low (with negative consequences for yields). Machinery services suffer a similar problem as elsewhere in the FSU, as the deterioration of the stock (of tractors, harvesters, etc.) is enormous, many machines having passed their useful lifespan, but there are no funds to buy new machinery.[34] Better-off farmers, who had (or bought) machinery, currently rent out machinery services to neighbouring peasant farms. Still, the problem of land fragmentation can often prohibit machine use, as the plots are scattered or even geographically unsuitable for machine operation.

Output markets for agricultural produce

Output markets are exemplary for their 'asymmetrical information' problems for small peasant farms. The latter produce directly for the open market, hence not using any form of supply contracts with agro-industry (except for some canning works and wineries). Producers bring their produce to the market as soon as they harvest, and many with them do the same, depressing local market and farm gate prices. There are few (mostly donor-supported) marketing cooperatives to improve the bargaining power of the peasant farmers. These are badly needed (such as the already mentioned labour exchange groups, and 'single purpose cooperatives' for marketing of output of purchasing of inputs). In Armenia the main market is Yerevan, in the absence of sufficiently important regional wholesale markets. Distances are substantial, especially if one takes into account the dreadful state of roads in many of the more remote areas. Intermediaries often behave in non-competitive ways, operating with high marketing margins. Finally, the country is not only physically landlocked but, with the trade blockade imposed by its neighbours Turkey and Azerbaijan, and the complications of trade through Georgia (which might improve in the near future, enabling penetration of the Russian market), export possibilities are limited. This causes domestic prices to be lowered, as domestic demand is limited (and cross-regional trade as well). It is therefore not surprising that the sale of agricultural produce does not provide a large share of income for peasant farms, and many small farmers are part-time agricultural producers, forced to find other employment in the rural non-farm economy, temporarily move to urban areas or even migrate altogether, in order to complement their meagre household incomes by other earnings or remittances.

Pro-poor land (and rural development) policies

This chapter has highlighted a number of critical phenomena related to agricultural land in Armenia. First, as in Vietnam (see Akram-Lodhi, this volume), land concentration seems to emerge, although it is very difficult to judge how rapidly this is proceeding. According to cadastral data, this is not even the case, but informal rental markets might well escape the eye of official measurement, and anecdotal evidence suggests that the 'push' factors in renting out land (namely poverty, insufficient land, and absence of capital to work the land productively) are important in combination with various 'pull' factors. The completion of the (formal) property title registration will contribute to a better working of land markets and hence, to a further 'natural' process of land concentration, and economically more viable farms. In the medium and long run, this scenario will certainly be relevant for Armenia but, in the short run, it may simply lead to more poverty and destitution, with land rapidly becoming concentrated in the hands of a few powerful buyers, without the expected investment drive needed to modernise (and capitalise) the agricultural sector, and to the detriment of many small landowners, who will become poorer than they already are.

Second, the current second stage (or wave) of land reform, which includes the massive transfer of the remaining arable land, hayfields and most of the pastures, to the jurisdiction of the communities, is much more than just an administrative operation. Community administrations, which have substantial independence in terms of 'local governance', will have the chance to privatise, rent or manage land resources. Therefore, they could use these scarce land resources as an important tool for safeguarding (and improving) the livelihood of vulnerable farm households, which would benefit substantially from small allocations of land, rather than for promoting the sales of land to individual (more 'entrepreneurial') farmers. The first (preferred) option will need central finance, while the second is attractive to local authorities, as it will bring in badly needed revenue. Third, land policies cannot be seen in isolation, and actually land is not important in Armenia if not irrigated and if there is no market and institutional development 'beyond land', i.e. in terms of inputs and machinery services, infrastructure and farm produce market outlets, rural public investment and pro-poor rural tax policies. Departing from these three main observations, the following land-related policies would need to be addressed in order to promote pro-poor rural development.

• The new phase (or wave) of land reform, concerning the transfer of much of the remaining state-owned agricultural land to the jurisdiction of the communities, can be used to promote four targets. The most important one is that part of the transferred arable land resources needs to be used to improve the livelihood of those vulnerable peasant farmers, through directed land allocations (to be financed by a mix of public/private funds, and loans). Land consolidation has to be facilitated (through exchange and merging, using the physical land reserve), using donor-financed land consolidation projects executed in pilot areas, providing 'best practices'. Equal (and transparent) access is needed at auctions of land to be privatised. Through the use of land ceilings, the (most often 'distress') sales of large tracts of land to a small elite have to be prohibited. Finally, land policies (and local institutions) are needed to safeguard the communal pastures where this is appropriate for equity reasons in terms of access (using joined group rights of access, leasing arrangements, etc).

- The formation of cooperative, associative, and group-based institutions is warranted. These should dedicate themselves to selling and buying of inputs and output in agricultural markets (and labour exchange in productive activities), in order to break through the current deadlock or squeeze, in which many small peasant farms are caught. Public awareness campaigns should emphasise that these kind of cooperative or associative institutions bear no resemblance to the Soviet-type collectives, and that, in many developed countries, they have been at the heart of the success of agricultural development. This mentioned 'deadlock' is not primarily an inefficiency problem, but one that requires market integration and some degree of 'market power', which peasant farms now completely lack. These institutional changes at local level can also have direct positive impacts on the production side, as it will be possible to prepare and harvest land with machinery through cooperation or rental arrangements.

- The rental market of land needs further formalisation, promoting the official registration of land rent transactions (by lowering the notaries' fees and taxes to be paid), as otherwise this market will begin functioning largely underground, and no sensible land policies will be possible (as insufficient knowledge of the emerging reality exists). Proper lease payment enforcement is also badly needed, as are awareness campaigns about the rights and obligations for both parties in a lease agreement. Finally, a nationwide land lease market study should be undertaken in order to make an inventory of the various informal and formal arrangements (as has recently been done in the Republic of Moldova).

- The completion of the formal property title registration of all agricultural landowners will lead to the facilitation of selling and buying of land, or the increasing use of land as collateral (currently planned to be completed by the end of 2005). Central and local institutions would need to become more actively involved in sustainable land management planning, taking into account agro-ecological specificities, land fragmentation and actual land use, in order to support the local transformation of agrarian structures, leading to more economically viable peasant farms. For this the Armenian government should give more importance to decentralisation (and local institutional capacity building), stimulating regional and local economic development, while similarly undertaking sufficient public investment to support the latter.

- The institutional capacity at central, *mars* and community administration levels needs strengthening in Armenia, in order to improve their institutional policy analysis and policy development capacity *versus* the rural sector, with particular regard to the livelihood of farm households. After first having been the focal point of attention in the transition (with the land reform in the early 1990s), it seems that in the past years they have been somewhat lost in the government's 'priority agenda'. Possibly there was at least some belief that the 'spontaneous' emergence of markets (and institutions) would provide an environment in which small peasant farms would quickly become economically viable. However, reality has shown a different outcome: rural poverty is stagnating (at a fairly high level) and 'missing' markets and institutions are the rule rather than the exception.

In conclusion, in terms of possible rural economy growth scenarios, analysed from a perspective of poverty reduction and inequality, three possible future paths can be distinguished. The first one is somewhat of a doom-scenario, involving the increased (including temporary) migration of the most important part of the rural population, namely workers between 15 and 50 years of age, leaving behind increasingly socially (and economically) unviable villages. This scenario might well go hand in hand with 'distress sales' of land, but not necessarily with the development of economically viable farms. The second (limited growth) scenario will be more equivalent to a status quo path, in which there will be some spillover of the rapid growth in the urban areas, externally financed investment in infrastructure and communication (shifting some of the observed extreme 'urban bias'), but no real boost to agricultural production, except in some agro-industry connected subsectors. This would be a 'muddling through' scenario. The third scenario would focus more on integrating rural and urban economies, counteracting the rapidly growing gap in terms of income and human development. This scenario would be the outcome of a concerted effort of institutional change, together with the introduction of a countervailing 'rural bias', a gradual concentration of land corresponding with the absorption of surplus labour into the emerging rural non-farm economy (RNFE) and other – urban-based – economic sectors. This more optimistic scenario would be based on sustainable agricultural growth, with the emergence of cooperatives and small peasant farmers' associations, able to improve the bargaining position of their members in various markets, next to individual (more capitalised) medium-sized farms, both having linkages to an innovative agro-industry (and export opportunities). Meanwhile, an expanded and strengthened household economy (using the momentum of new allocations proposed under the current state land transfer) would be able to improve food and income poverty levels in rural (and indirectly in urban) areas. This scenario would require a full-scale regional development strategy and a coherent institutional and policy framework to become realistic.

Annex 6.1 Private and community-owned agricultural land in 20 communities (October 2004)

Marses	Aragasotn		Ararat		Armavir		Gegharkunik		Lori		Kotayk		Shirak		Syunik		Vayots Dsor		Tavush	
Name of community	Vardenul	Artashavan	Darakert	Arevshat	Hushakert	Aragats	Gandsak	Haravanh	Vahagni	Debet	Hankavan	Aghavnadsor	Arevshat	Megrashen	Khot	Brnakot	Arpi	Rind	Achajur	N.K. Aghbiur
Arable land (AL)																				
Private	361	283	216	82	265	226	868	300	269	62	0	192	506	780	504	1,581	173	259	636	544
Community	71	59	43	63	48	58	191	28	37	53	63	38	112	198	28	230	50	111	103	188
Orchard/Vineyard																				
Private	79	1	4	112	42	37	0	0	19	0	0	0	0	0	49	5	0	32	118	29
Community	9	0	0	2	0	11	0	0	0	0	0	0	0	0	0	0	0	0	0	0
Irrigated AL (%)	7	137	286	122	313	284	97	17	19	30	0	113	54	0	16	557	163	67	300	74
Hayfields																				
Private	79	71	0	2	0	0	392	178	42	141	0	110	0	0	30	0	0	50	183	0
Community	9	99	0	0	0	0	11	1	224	29	132	34	7	0	3	30	0	0	5	61
Pastures/Others																				
Private	0	0	4	0	0	0	0	0	0	0	0	0	0	0	0	0	0	0	0	0
Community	1,178	2,125	59	124	510	304	1,503	528	1,179	340	1,317	1,009	796	435	999	2,825	722	2712	1,177	727
Land sales from community	0	2.7	12.1	38	0	66.8	8.36	19.8	0	0	0	10.1	0	0	0	0	0	0	0.13	0
(number)		(1)	(85)	(1)		(5)	(7)	(18)				(23)							(2)	–

Source: Data provided by the State Cadastre Committee. This was a specially commissioned study. It should be noted that in the communities of the marses Vayots Dsor and Tavush no land had been transferred to the community level as yet (see also Table 13).

Notes

1 This chapter was originally written as a UNDP report, produced with the assistance of two Armenian national consultants, Gagik Gabrielyan (agricultural economist) and Vahagn Grigoryan (real estate property specialist). Furthermore the author was supported, particularly in establishing contacts with members of government, by Aghassi Mkrtchyan, UNDP country economist. The draft version of the paper benefited from comments from the national consultants, Astghik Mirsakhanyan (UNDP, Yerevan), Terry McKinley (Bureau for Development Policy, UNDP New York), and one of the book editors. Finally, during the field mission that took place 5–15 October 2004, the team received excellent support from the UN resident coordinator and UNDP resident representative, Lise Grande, and her office staff. A similar reception was encountered in visiting various government agencies (among others the State Cadastre Committee and the Ministry of Agriculture). All this support is hereby gratefully acknowledged. Nevertheless, only the author is responsible for the opinions expressed, and of course, for any remaining mistakes.

2 Armenia is a country with large geographical differences (valleys, pre-mountain areas and high mountains).

3 The *mars* is the Armenian name for the main regional administrative unit.

4 With the expectation that agricultural land will soon increase in value.

5 Although we will show that only a very small share of land has been subject to sales, and most land concentration is effectuated by informal or formal leases.

6 This had been on the agenda since the late 1990s, but was only recently concretised (see first reference in Lerman and Mirsakhanyan, 2001: 8).

7 There were some reports of sales (of state land by communities) that were between 100 and 300 hectares, as was confirmed by a high official of the SCC. In response the government has installed restrictions on such land sales (Interview, 7 October 2004, Yerevan).

8 Lerman and Mirsakhanyan (2001: 6–7).

9 Hay land and pastures were mostly held by state farms during the Soviet period, most often with communal (informal) grazing rights for households. Comparable with countries such as Kyrgyzstan and Mongolia, the Armenian government also decided to keep the communal access arrangements (in combination with leasing to individual producers), and did not privatise substantial areas of this land.

10 'Private land' excludes land that is rented from other individuals or the community.

11 These data are somewhat lower than those of the World Bank-sponsored farm survey of 1997. See Lerman and Mirsakhanyan (2001: 16), where the authors present an average size of 2.17 ha for all surveyed farms, including 1.99 ha for owned and 0.18 ha for leased land. However, only a small share of all farms lease land, and for those who do, the lease land plot was on average 1.16 ha. The legislative changes implemented since 2001, which concerned the privatisation of reserved lands transferred to the vulnerable population (mostly to refugees and internally displaced persons, which was done free of charge), and the emerging land sales and lease market might explain some of these differences.

12 This includes land in the form of household ('subsidiary') plots, estimated at around 70,000 hectares.

13 It seems that relatively minor re-migration has occurred into the urban sectors, during the second half of the 1990s. There is, however, substantial temporal migration into Russia, in search of employment.

14 Griffin *et al.* (2002: 85).

15 See StatKom SNG (2002), and Table 6.5.

16 See NSS (2003b: 31–33).

17 In the Armenian legislation, 'land alienation' is generally used, rather than transaction. Alienation includes the sale, inheritance or donation of land, and excludes leasing. Land transactions also include leasing and mortgaging of land.

18 Although registration costs are low (US$5), red tape and therefore time investment are substantial. Furthermore, peasants want to avoid the 10 per cent of income tax on rental income.

19 As we will present later in this chapter, on special request of the mission, the State Cadastre Committee produced a special set of data, with 20 communities, on their land distribution and operations on the land market. This effort is highly appreciated.

20 Lerman and Mirsakhanyan (2001) distinguish between sellers and non-sellers, in which probably the last category would include the 'vulnerable farm households'.

21 From Figure 6.2 it can be noted that the *marses* of Ararat, Kotayk and Vayots Dsor have the largest share of very small peasant farms (<0.0–0.5 hectares).

22 Interview with an official of an Armenian agrarian NGO, 8 October 2004, Yerevan.

23 CFOA (2003).

24 FAO project (TCP/ARM/3004), to be executed during the period 2004–2006, with as counterpart the State Cadastre Committee.

25 In some cases, it seems that even land which was leased for very long periods of time was included (in a sense illegally) in the most recent formal land titling process.

26 It is not known on what methodological basis these communities were chosen by the SCC.

27 A recent government decree establishes a ceiling for community land that can be alienated at 20 has.

28 The Armenian government has successfully applied for support for irrigation rehabilitation from the so-called Millennium Challenge Account, financed by the Bush administration.

29 The draft 'Agricultural Sustainable Development Strategy' document published by the Ministry of Agriculture of the Republic of Armenia (MOA, 2004: 5) states that, of the 274,000 hectares of potentially irrigated acreage, only between 200,000 and 210,000 hectares were actually irrigated.

30 MOA (2004: 11) notes that in 2001 a total of 35.9 per cent of arable land was not used for cultivation. The most important reason was 'no irrigation or limited irrigation' (26.3 per cent of the farm households). Another 14.3 per cent stated that it was poor-quality land that was the main factor for this decision. On the other hand, the same household survey data tell us that 28.6 per cent of agricultural land was irrigated, and that even this was substantially less than the previous year.

31 'If land is not irrigated, it does not make sense to add it to your property. The land value of an irrigated versus a non-irrigated plot of land has a ratio of 10:1.' Interview with an official of the SCC (12 October 2004).

32 MOA (2004: 5) notes that 'in the last decade, the use of mineral fertilisers was reduced by 10 times, organic by 18 times and plant protection means by 10 times' (sic!).

33 In many conversations, the issue of producing ecological products was discussed, sometimes suggesting that not using fertilisers and pesticides is enough. The fact that this niche market needs substantial investments in certification, packaging and advertising was most often ignored.

34 MOA (2004: 5): '93 per cent of present agricultural machinery and equipment is worn out'.

References

ACBA Bank (2004). 'Annual Report'. Yerevan.

ArmGov (2003). 'Sustainable Economic Development Policy for Armenia: The Concept Paper'. Ministry of Trade and Economic Development, Yerevan.

Besemer, D. J. and J. R. Davis (2003). 'The Rural Non-farm Economy in Transition Countries: Findings from Armenia', in M. Spoor, ed., *Transition, Institutions and the Rural Sector*, pp. 163–184. Lanham and Oxford: Lexington Books, Rowman and Littlefield.

Center for Economic Reforms (2004). *Armenia Social Trends*, no. 6 (November), Center for Economic Reforms, Yerevan.

CFOA (2003). 'Armenia Country Paper: Land Policy'. Paper prepared for the South Caucasus Regional Land Policy Conference in Tbilisi, 22–26 February 2003. www.aplr.org/conference/en/country_papers/countrypaper_armenia_eng. htm (downloaded 18 May 2006).

EDRC (2004). *Economic Policy and Poverty*. Periodical Publication of the Economic Development and Research Centre, Yerevan, nos 3 and 8.

FAO (2003). 'What Is Land Consolidation?'. www.fao.org/docrep/006/Y4954E/ y495e06.htm (downloaded 18 May 2006).

FAOSTAT (2004). *Statistical Databases*. Rome: Food and Agricultural Organization.

Gabrielyan, G. (2004). 'Armenia Chapters on Pro-Poor Policies'. Notes and Considerations for the Land Reform, Rural Poverty and Inequality Paper'. Yerevan, October.

Glinkina, S. and D. Rosenberg (2003). 'Social and Economic Decline as Factors in Conflict in the Caucasus'. Helsinki: WIDER Discussion Paper 2003/18.

GovArm (2003). *Anti-Corruption Strategy and Implementation Action Plan*. Yerevan.

GovArm (2004). *Agricultural Sustainable Development Strategy*. Yerevan.

Griffin, K. (2002). *Growth, Inequality and Poverty in Armenia*. Mimeo. Yerevan: UNDP.

ICRA (2004). 'Cooperating to Reconstruct Rurality: A Study of Institutional Support Needs for Agricultural Livelihoods in Sisian and Goris Regions of Syunik Mars, Armenia'. Wageningen: Wageningen Agricultural University.

IMF (2003). 'Republic of Armenia: Fourth Review under the Poverty Reduction and Growth Facility and Request for Waiver of Performance Criterion'. Washington, DC: IMF.

IMF (2003). *Republic of Armenia: Poverty Reduction Strategy Paper*. Washington, DC: IMF Country Report No. 03/362.

Information-Analytical Center for Economic Reforms of Armenia and UN Armenia Office (2002). 'Armenia Social Trends', nos 3–5. Yerevan.

Lerman, S. and A. Mirsakhanyan (2001). *Private Agriculture in Armenia*. Lanham and Oxford: Lexington Books.

Lerman, S. and D. J. Besemer (2002). 'Rural Livelihoods in Armenia'. Mimeo.

MOA (2004). 'Agricultural Sustainable Development Strategy'. Mimeo. Yerevan: Ministry of Agriculture of the Republic of Armenia.

NSS (2001). *Agriculture in Armenia 1991–1999*. Yerevan: National Statistical Service.

NSS (2002a). *Agricultural Data 2001–2003*. Yerevan.

NSS (2002b). *Data on Agricultural Sector and Prices/Tariffs* www.armstat.am.

NSS (2003a). *Data on Agricultural Sector and Prices/Tariffs* www.armstat.am.

NSS (2003b). *Regions of the Republic of Armenia in Figures, 1998–2002.* Yerevan.

NSS (2003c). *Social Snapshot and Poverty in the Republic of Armenia.* www.armstat.am.

NSS (2004a). *General Information Census 2001.* Yerevan.

NSS (2004b). *Population Data 1998–2002.* Yerevan.

NSS (2004c). *Results of Census 2001.* www.armstat.am.

NSS (2004d). *Statistical Data 2003.* Yerevan.

Riddell, J. and F. Rembold (2000). 'Farm Land Rationalisation and Land Consolidation: Strategies for Improved Land Management in Eastern and Central Europe'. Mimeo, www.fig.net/pub/proceedings/prague-final-papers/riddell-rembold.htm (downloaded 18 May 2006).

State Cadastre Committee of the Republic of Armenia (2003a). 'Agricultural Land Market in 2003.' Mimeo. Yerevan: Cadastre.

State Cadastre Committee of the Republic of Armenia (2003b). 'Real Property Market in 1998–2003.' Yerevan: Cadastre.

State Cadastre Committee of the Republic of Armenia (2004). 'Agricultural Land Market in the First Six Months of 2004'. Mimeo. Yerevan: Cadastre.

StatKom SNG (2002). *Eshegodnik SNG 2001.* Moscow.

UNDP and Government of Armenia (2002–2004). 'Armenian Social Trends, Information-Analytical Bulletin, nos. 3–6', Yerevan: UNDP/Government of Armenia. www.undp.am /?page=publications (downloaded 18 May 2006).

World Bank (2002). *Armenia Poverty Update.* Report No. 24339-AM. Washington, DC: World Bank.

World Bank (2003). *Land Policies for Growth and Poverty Reduction.* World Bank Policy Research Report. Washington, DC: World Bank; Oxford: Oxford University Press.

7   The land system, agriculture and poverty in Uzbekistan

Azizur Rahman Khan[1]

Introduction[2]

At the time of its emergence as an independent state at the end of 1991, Uzbekistan had been under the typical Soviet system of collectivised agriculture for about six decades, thereby erasing all experience of individual farming from the agricultural population at the time. While agricultural institutions in Uzbekistan during the Soviet period were similar to those prevailing in the rest of the Soviet Union, the outcome, in terms of rural development, was different from the typical Soviet case in several important ways.

Like the rest of former Soviet Central Asia, Uzbekistan was rapidly transformed during the decades after the mid-1930s. By 1976 per capita income in Uzbekistan was above US$1,300 at current prices, at the official rate of exchange. Even allowing for the inappropriateness of the official rate of exchange and differences in the systems of accounting in comparing income in Uzbekistan with incomes in other countries, this is indicative of a relatively high material standard of living in Uzbekistan in comparison, for example, with its South Asian neighbours. By the early 1960s virtually universal literacy was achieved for both males and females, compared to 20 per cent in the Indian subcontinent, and there were seven times as many doctors per person as the average for Asia.[3]

While industrial progress was quite substantial, the rapid growth of agriculture and the continued predominance of the rural economy was the key element in this progress. Uzbekistan was ahead of the rest of the USSR in terms of urbanisation immediately before the Soviet revolution. By the time of the dissolution of the USSR, the proportion of the population living in urban areas was far lower in Uzbekistan (40 per cent) than in the rest of the USSR. The continued predominance of the rural society and the low rate of urbanisation were not the outcome of inadequate economic growth. What Uzbekistan experienced was a pattern of growth that was very unusual, both historically and in contemporary experience; namely, rapid agricultural growth leading to a rise in living standards in rural areas and a relatively low urban–rural income differential, which weakened the incentive to emigrate from the rural areas.

The principal vehicle for the rapid material progress of rural society was the state policy of promoting cotton specialisation. By 1976 official Soviet sources claimed that output of raw cotton per hectare in Uzbekistan had reached three tons, the highest yield among all major producers at the time.[4] High price incentives were a major instrument in promoting cotton specialisation within the institution of collective agriculture, which otherwise suffered from the usual distortions of a command system. While collectivisation in much of the USSR was an institutional vehicle for extracting resources from agriculture, cotton, the principal marketed crop of Uzbekistan, was granted extraordinarily favourable terms of trade compared to the other major products of Soviet agriculture. For a period after collectivisation, the policy towards cotton was the same as the policy towards the rest of agriculture: officially dictated output targets and compulsory procurement at very low prices, resulting in falling yield per hectare. In 1935 the Soviet authorities initiated a major shift in policy by nearly quadrupling the procurement price of cotton. The result was dramatic: by 1937 the production of raw cotton in Uzbekistan was nearly three times the pre-revolution peak and yield per hectare was at an all-time high of 1.6 tons.

For the next two decades this discrimination in favour of cotton continued to be the central element of agricultural development strategy in Uzbekistan and the rest of Soviet Central Asia. The extent of this positive discrimination is illustrated by the fact that in 1952 the procurement price per ton of cotton was nearly 37 times the procurement price for grains while the average cost of production per ton of cotton was probably less than four times the cost of grain for Uzbekistan.[5] Another way to look at the relative prices is to compare them with the prevailing international prices. For grains and meat the average procurement prices paid to producers in the USSR in 1952 was less than one-seventh of the international prices. For cotton the procurement price was nearly a third above the international price.[6]

The exceptionally favourable terms of trade for cotton led to a sharp shift of the area sown – especially in irrigated land – away from grain into cotton. Labour requirement per hectare of cotton in Uzbekistan in the mid-1970s was six times as much as for grains for the *kolkhozy* (the plural of *kolkhoz*, meaning collective farms) and 11.5 times for the *sovkhozy* (the plural of *sovkhoz*, meaning state farms). Thus, increased specialisation in cotton led to a much greater demand for labour in agriculture than would otherwise have been the case. The payment of a sufficiently high income, to make the increased demand for labour effective and to weaken the attraction of wages offered by urban industries, was made possible by the favourable terms of trade for cotton. Unfortunately, the earliest year for which sectoral earnings differentials can be documented is 1965, after the beginning of the reversal of the favourable treatment of cotton. In that year earnings in industries were only 14 per cent higher than earnings in *kolkhozy* in Uzbekistan. The difference was 56 per cent for the USSR as a whole! Without doubt the sectoral earnings differential was even more favourable for agriculture in Uzbekistan relative to the USSR in the years prior to the post-Stalinist relaxation of the strategy of 'primitive socialist accumulation'.

The primary motivation behind this policy of favourable terms of trade for cotton was to ensure quick Soviet self-sufficiency in this basic commodity. This was achieved with singular success. It is uncertain if the spectacular increase in specialisation in cotton was in excess of what would be dictated by the criterion of the comparative advantage of Uzbek agriculture. Furthermore, cotton production and agriculture, like the rest of the economy, suffered from numerous inefficiencies of resource use, which are characteristic of central planning.

Starting in the 1950s the highly discriminatory procurement pricing for Soviet agriculture came gradually to an end. During this period cotton lost much of its extraordinarily advantageous position and for a period the price–cost ratio for cotton fell well below that for grain, with a consequent decline in the growth of cotton output and yields and a rather severe decline in peasant earnings. By 1963 the procurement price of cotton was adjusted upwards and from then onwards price policy was carefully balanced to keep the price–cost ratio higher for cotton than for grain. Thus, in 1976 the ratio of the procurement price of cotton to the procurement price of grains was 3.73, while the ratio of the costs of production on Uzbek *kolkhozy* was 3.53. The ratios of procurement prices to international prices, converted at the official exchange rate, were 1.32 for cotton, 1.01 for grain and 2.02 for meat in the same year. Unless the exchange rate at the time was grossly overvalued, cotton was subjected to a relatively modest 'concealed' taxation; in any case it was subjected to a far smaller concealed taxation than grain.[7] The difference between industrial and agricultural earnings became wider than in the years of greater positive discrimination in favour of cotton, but the differential was still lower than for the USSR as a whole.[8] The procurement price of cotton continued to rise in real terms throughout the 1980s until the eve of independence. It is therefore reasonable to assume that the overall system of incentives described above continued throughout the 1980s.

The performance of Uzbek agriculture since independence

Table 7.1 contains estimates of growth in GDP and agricultural output in the period since 1990. Following independence, GDP and agricultural value added both declined for a period. The annual rate of decline in GDP until 1995, the year in which it bottomed out, was 4.1 per cent. The rate of decline in per capita GDP over the same period was 6.1 per cent per year.

The rate of decline in agricultural value added, which bottomed out a year later, was slower, 1.7 per cent in aggregate value added and 4.3 per

Table 7.1 Indices of GDP and agricultural value added (1991=100)

Year	Agricultural		Population		Per capita GDP	Agricultural value added per rural population
	GDP	Value added	Total	Rural		
1990	100.5	97.8	97.9	97.3	102.7	100.5
1991	100.0	100.0	100.0	100.0	100.0	100.0
1992	88.9	93.5	102.4	103.0	86.8	90.8
1993	86.8	94.9	104.7	105.9	82.9	89.6
1994	82.2	91.7	106.8	108.6	77.0	84.4
1995	81.5	93.5	108.7	111.2	75.0	84.1
1996	82.9	88.2	110.8	114.0	74.8	77.4
1997	87.2	93.3	113.0	116.8	77.2	79.9
1998	90.9	97.2	114.8	119.3	79.2	81.5
1999	94.9	102.5	116.5	121.7	81.5	84.2
2000	98.5	105.8	117.6	123.5	83.8	85.7
2001	102.6	110.1	119.2	125.1	86.1	88.0
2002	106.9	116.8	120.6	126.6	88.6	92.3
2003	107.3	123.7	122.1	128.1	87.9	96.6

Source: These indices have been calculated from the time series data shown in World Bank (2004) for all years until 2002. Updating for 2003 was made on the basis of data from the IMF and official Uzbek sources. Indices of GDP and value added are those for constant price values.

cent in value added per rural person. Thus, in the aftermath of independence the decline in agriculture took place at a much slower rate than the decline in the rest of the economy. Notice, however, the far greater gap between the rates of decline in per capita value added than in aggregate value added for agriculture than for the economy as a whole. This was due to a much faster rate of increase in rural population than aggregate population.

After 1995 GDP started growing and during the next eight years it achieved an annual average growth rate of 3.5 per cent, or 2 per cent per annum in per capita terms. Agricultural recovery was steady after 1996, when it achieved an annual average growth rate of 5 per cent, or 3.2 per cent per capita. Thus, agriculture performed better than the rest of the economy taken together: its rate of decline in the aftermath of independence was slower and its rate of recovery since the mid-1990s was faster as compared to the rest of the economy.

By 2003 per capita GDP was still 12 per cent below what it was on the eve of independence. Agricultural value added per rural person was also lower in 2003 than on the eve of independence, but only by about 4 per cent. Since GDP includes agricultural value added, it can easily be gauged that per capita value added for the non-agricultural population has fallen at an almost catastrophic rate since independence.

Change in output and income

The fall in agricultural income per capita since independence has almost certainly been greater than the fall in output per capita. This is because there is strong evidence that the terms of trade for agriculture have declined since independence. An example of such evidence is provided by the ratio of the value-added deflator for agriculture to the GDP deflator. Between 1990 and 2002 this ratio fell by more than 17 per cent.[9] Most of the decline in the terms of trade appears to have taken place in the earlier years: between 1990 and 1997 the above ratio actually fell by 22 per cent, while it rose by 6 per cent between 1997 and 2002. Support for this is also provided by the recent World Bank estimate showing that net implicit taxation of cotton and grain by compulsory procurement at low prices fell from 3–5 per cent of GDP during 1996–1998 to 2.6 per cent of GDP in 2000.[10]

Change in employment

Table 7.2 contains information on rural employment in agriculture and other activities. Employment in agriculture increased initially, until 1994, though falling as a proportion of the rural population. Thereafter, absolute employment in agriculture fell steadily, despite a faster rise in rural population than national population.[11]

Growth in agricultural employment in the early 1990s was perverse in view of the decline in agricultural output. Almost certainly this period was characterised by increased concealed unemployment in agriculture. The fall in agricultural employment after 1996 is also perverse since this period was characterised by the resumption of agricultural growth. One important cause of this is the change in cropping pattern and the shift of sown

Table 7.2 Rural employment (numbers in million)

	1991	1994	1995	1996	2000	2003
Population	12.48	13.63	–	14.30	15.46	16.21
Agricultural employment	3.45	3.62	–	3.50	3.09	3.03
Shirkats, etc.	2.08	2.18	–	2.03	1.63	1.25
Private commercial farms –	–	–	0.19	0.28	0.58	–
Dehkan farmers	1.38	1.44	–	1.28	1.18	1.21
Distribution of rural employment (% of total)						
Agriculture	–	–	81.9	–	70.3	66.8
Industry	–	–	3.1	–	4.3	5.5
Services	–	–	15.0	–	25.5	27.7

Note
The source of the data is the State Statistical Committee, and is available from the author. There is a slight discrepancy between these official population estimates and the ones from the World Bank, which have been used to calculate the indices in Table 7.1.

land from cotton to grain crops. Between 1990 and 2003 there was a shift of about 0.6 million hectares of land from cotton to grain. Estimates from the Soviet period show that a hectare of land under cotton required 908 hours of labour more than a hectare of land under grain.[12] Assuming that the labour requirement per hectare of cotton now exceeds the labour requirement per hectare of grain by two-thirds of the above figure (608 hours more per hectare), eight hours of work per day and 220 days of work per worker per year, this represents a loss per hectare of 0.35 person years of employment due to the shift from cotton to grain, or an aggregate loss of employment of 207,000 person years, nearly half the total fall in agricultural employment. Much of the remainder of the fall in agricultural employment was due to institutional restructuring: the privatisation of *shirkat* (cooperative organisations that succeeded the *kolkhozy*) land reduced aggregate employment in farming because private farms employ fewer workers per hectare than *shirkats*. This is seen largely as the elimination of concealed unemployment that collective agriculture was made to carry.[13] This may also partly be due to the adoption of more capital-intensive technology by the larger farms, which have become increasingly dominant in terms of the share of total land. This is an issue to which this chapter will return later.

To gauge the impact of the decline in employment on rural income and its distribution, one needs to know the change in alternative sources of rural employment. First, if the figures in Table 7.2 are correct, then total rural employment in Uzbekistan, as a proportion of rural population, fell from an estimated 32.4 per cent in 1994 to 28 per cent in 2003.[14] This means that the annual rate of growth in total rural employment during this period was insignificant, a rather puzzling phenomenon since the significantly faster increase in rural population than in urban population suggests the possibility that net emigration out of urban areas was higher than net emigration out of rural areas, or even that there might have been net immigration into rural areas. Be that as it may, there was a remarkable change in the composition of rural employment away from agriculture to rural non-farm (RNF) occupations. Most of the expansion of RNF employment took place in services, a category that official statistics still calls the 'non-production sphere'. The rate of expansion of rural industrial employment was relatively lower. It is hard to know the exact nature of these employment categories in terms of productivity and earnings. Given declining overall labour demand, it however seems likely that the growth of RNF employment was largely a residual category, driven by the influx of labourers pushed out of agriculture. It would be most unusual for these residual employment categories to provide earnings in excess of, or even equivalent to, the earnings of the workers employed in agriculture.

Rural poverty

The World Bank estimates that 30.5 per cent of Uzbekistan's rural population were in poverty with reference to a poverty line that represents an
expenditure consistent with 2,100 kilocalories of food energy consumption
per person per day in 2000/2001. This compares with an urban poverty incidence of 22.5 per cent for a similar poverty line. For a more stringent
poverty line, representing extreme poverty that allows just 1,500 kilocalories
per person per day, the incidence of rural and urban poverty were respectively 11.2 per cent and 7.1 per cent.[15] It is worth noting that, despite the
possible pull of the rural society to induce immigration from (or at least the
absence of a push to induce emigration to) urban areas, the incidence of
poverty is higher in rural areas for a similar poverty threshold. Furthermore,
relative to urban areas, the incidence of extreme poverty is proportionately
greater in rural areas than the incidence of less extreme poverty.

The draft Interim Poverty Reduction Strategy Paper (IPRSP) recently
prepared by the government[16] estimates, using similar data sources as the
World Bank, that in 2003 poverty in rural areas fell to 28.7 per cent while
urban poverty fell less perceptibly. It is noteworthy that during this period
agricultural value added per rural person went up quite rapidly, by about
4.5 per cent a year. Compared to this the fall in the poverty incidence
ratio, by just 2.5 per cent per year, would appear to have been very
modest. A number of researchers have argued that this is due to rising
inequality in the distribution of income.[17]

No information is available on the change in poverty over time prior to
2000.[18] It is however clear from Table 7.1 that agricultural value added per
rural person fell by 4 per cent between 1990, the immediate pre-
independence year, and 2003. It has been surmised that over the same
period agriculture's terms of trade may have fallen by about 15 per cent or
more. Thus, per capita rural income from agriculture probably fell by
something between 15 and 20 per cent. Nothing is known about the earnings in the RNF activities into which rural labour shifted in large proportions. There is, however, little evidence of dynamic growth in that sector,
though value added in services has obviously gone up with the spread of

Table 7.3 Incidence of rural poverty (per cent of population)

Year	Rural		Urban	
	Poverty	*Extreme poverty*	*Poverty*	*Extreme poverty*
2000/2001	30.5	11.2	22.5	7.1
2003	28.7	–	22.0	–

Note
Estimates for 2000/2001 are from World Bank (2003) and those for 2003 from Government
of Uzbekistan (2004a).

the market economy. Even under the most optimistic assumptions about the RNF activities, the conclusion that average rural income fell during the period under review seems inescapable.

Poverty outcomes are determined by the change in average income and the change in the distribution of income, or, more specifically, the change in the bottom range of income distribution. Once again, direct estimates of change in the distribution of income are not available. On the whole, decollectivisation and the transition to a market economy are by and large believed to have unleashed forces of inequality, with loss of agricultural employment being a major source of this. And yet two opposing forces need to be considered. As discussed below, universal access to land, albeit of an amount that is generally inadequate to ensure an income above the poverty threshold, has provided a cushion to offset the consequences of the removal of the safety net that prevailed during the Soviet period. But the promotion of larger commercial farms since the late 1990s must have, at the same time, led to greater differentiation in rural society. On balance, income distribution appears to have worsened and the share of the poor in total income fallen though, almost certainly, not at anything like the catastrophic rates at which these changes took place in most other former Soviet republics. It thus seems certain that rural poverty has increased in Uzbekistan since independence though, again, perhaps not as rapidly as in most other former Soviet societies. The most likely scenario seems to suggest that the incidence of poverty increased until at least the middle of the 1990s and since the late 1990s there has been a slow reduction in the incidence of rural poverty.

Institutional reform in agriculture[19]

Table 7.4 provides a broad overview of the evolution of agricultural institutions in Uzbekistan since independence. At the time of independence Uzbekistan's agriculture was organised into *kolkhozy* and *sovkhozy*, with a tiny proportion of the total sown land allocated to workers as personal plots (the residual category 'others' represented different mixed state/collective forms, including experimental farms). The principal difference between the two main forms of ownership was that a *sovkhoz* was

Table 7.4 Distribution of sown land among different forms of organisation (per cent of total)

Year	Kolkhozy/shirkats	Sovkhozy Commercial	Private (Dehkan)	Individual	Others
1990	34.9	58.7	–	0.1	6.3
1994	75.3	1.0	–	2.1	21.6
2004	48.6	–	34.5	10.4	6.5

Source: State Committee on Statistics.

a state enterprise in which the workers were employed at fixed wages whereas *kolkhoz* workers – in principle, the cooperative members – received the residual earnings of the collectively operated enterprise after the deduction of all costs and provision for investment and welfare from gross revenue. The trend before independence was towards an increase in the proportion of *sovkhozy*. State ownership was considered to be 'ownership by the entire population,' a superior form of ownership in the 'transition towards a communist society,' as compared to the cooperative ownership that characterised the *kolkhozy*.

By 2004 the institutional form of agriculture had been transformed completely. At one extreme were large cooperative enterprises called *shirkats*, successors to the collective farms of the past. At the other extreme, the former personal plots of households had been substantially increased by endowing them with more land. This category is known as *dehkan* farmers (smallholders). In between these two a category of private farmers had emerged, who, unlike the *dehkan* farmers, operate relatively large, commercially oriented farms.

The evolution of agrarian institutions has taken place through a number of stages, and the process is still evolving. The following are the three principal stages through which changes have occurred so far.

The first phase, 1989–1997/1998

During the first phase of reform, arguably beginning before independence and continuing through 1997/1998, three principal changes took place: increased land endowment for what used to be the personal plots of the rural households during the Soviet period; the abolition of the *sovkhoz*; and the institution of greater flexibility within the *kolkhoz*, allowing its evolution into *shirkats*, variously described as associations of cooperatives or joint stock companies of farmers.

Dehkan *farmers*

Starting in 1989 the land endowment of the *dehkan* farmers began to increase. This appears to have led to a simultaneous sharp increase in the number of *dehkan* farmers, growing far faster than rural population. There has, however, been no appreciable effect on the size of an average *dehkan* holding in the period since 1991. The average size of a *dehkan* farm is 0.12 hectares, although the legal limit is said to be higher: 0.35 hectares of irrigated land, 0.5 hectares of unirrigated land and one hectare of pasture. Access to this source of land seems to be universal, and extends beyond rural areas. More than half the urban households and 98 per cent of the rural households have access to *dehkan* plots, endowing 82 per cent of all Uzbek households with this source of basic insurance for a minimal standard of livelihood.[20]

Dehkan families have lifelong heritable tenure. They can use land for any agricultural and residential purpose. While the holding size is too small to permit production beyond subsistence income, they are free to sell their product in the market and not subject to procurement quotas. They are subject to land tax after an initial two-year tax holiday. Their labour force must consist only of family members.

The abolition of the sovkhozy

The most visible of the early changes in agricultural institutions consists of the abolition of the *sovkhozy* and their conversion into *shirkats* (see below). One reason for this was the practical consideration of relieving the state budget of the burden of wage payments to the large *sovkhozy* workforce in a period in which agriculture was subjected to a high rate of resource extraction (see below). In addition, the abolition of the *sovkhozy* can almost certainly be defended on efficiency considerations.[21] By 1994 the only remaining state farms in agriculture were those engaged in experimental work, such as the development of improved seed varieties. All others had been converted into cooperative farms or enterprises under other forms of ownership.

Evolution of kolkhozy into shirkats

Perhaps the most important change that occurred during this first phase of transition is the institution of the system of contracting between the *kolkhoz* and its individual members or groups of members. Under this system, production is managed and organised by individual farmers while the *kolkhoz* provides certain services and inputs and receives a share of revenues. A typical arrangement was for the contracting *kolkhoz* member to meet the state procurement order at a fraction of the price received by the *kolkhoz* and to share with the *kolkhoz* according to agreed proportions the revenue for above quota sales. This system of contracting strongly resembles the household contracting that characterised the early phase of transition of the Chinese communes to individual farming. The objective was to create stable individual responsibility for land. The duration and terms of contracts were mutually agreed upon by the two parties. Land was allocated in proportion to the available family labour after making allowance for the ability to work. Every household was guaranteed a minimum amount of land. The practice of household contracting has spread rapidly since the early 1990s even before a legal framework was enacted for its formalisation. A convergence of former systems took place in so far as the *sovkhozy* were also transformed into similar cooperatives. Gradually these cooperatives assumed the nomenclature of *shirkat* in place of *kolkhoz.*

The system is essentially individual family farming. A much reduced administrative structure of the former *kolkhoz* or *sovkhoz* continued to exist to facilitate the transformation itself, to provide some common services and, most importantly, to intermediate in the implementation of state procurement. In many other respects, elements of the old system were retained. Thus procurement quotas on cotton and grain, at very low prices, were continued as was control over supply of inputs and credit.

Much of the change during this first phase is captured by the land distribution for 1994 shown in Table 7.4. *Sovkhozy* virtually ceased to exist, the proportion of land under *dehkan* farming increased at a very rapid rate, and *shirkats* came to dominate landholding. The rather large residual category for that year actually represents large enterprises of some type of cooperatives, perhaps not qualitatively different from *shirkats.*

The second phase, 1997/1998–2003

Among important changes during this phase was the legal recognition of the emergence of a new track of individual farms, distinct from the *dehkan* farms in so far as they are much larger and commercially oriented. During this phase the system of contracting in *shirkats* was also formalised; and further strengthening of *dehkan* farming took place.

Private commercial farm enterprises

Independent commercial farms[22] had started developing within *shirkats* under contract with the latter in the early 1990s. Indeed, it is hard to trace their origin. It is possible that they grew out of the system of contracting that *shirkats* began practising with *dehkan* households, some of which were able to take on more than the usual amount of *dehkan* holding through special contractual arrangement. These arrangements were initially not favourable for the growth of commercial private farming: they were not legally recognised entities; they were subjected to compulsory procurement by the *shirkat* at a price which was substantially lower than the state procurement price that they received; and many of the farms initially set up did not survive. However, a decree in March 1997 granted these farms independent juridical status by separating them from the *shirkats* and making it possible for them to enter into transactions with buyers of outputs and sellers of inputs independently of the *shirkats*. Next, the 1998 Land Code made a clear distinction between the independent commercial farms and *dehkan* farms. Commercial farms were recognised as legal entities with leasehold tenure for a minimum of ten years and a maximum of 49 years, with the possibility of renewal. They were allowed to employ hired labourers. Their minimum size was to be ten hectares for cotton and wheat farms, one hectare for horticulture and orchard crops, and 30 heads of animals for livestock farms. There was no stipulation of the maximum size. Their establishment was to be approved by the *shirkat* and the district administration on the basis of a business plan that specified agricultural activities to be undertaken. They were subject to land tax and compulsory procurement at state-determined prices.

Dehkan *farms*

In comparison, the *dehkan* farmers held indefinite heritable right to land use; were subject to a ceiling of 0.35 hectares of irrigated land and 0.5 hectares of unirrigated land; were not within the state procurement net; were limited to the employment of family members as workers; and were free to produce anything. Their establishment was also subject to approval by the *shirkat* and the district administration, and they were also subject to land tax. The share of *dehkan* farmers in total land went up further during this period.

Formalisation of the transformation of collectives into shirkats

Simultaneous with the promotion of individual farming, the trans-formation of the former collective enterprises into *shirkats* was formalised during this phase. *Shirkats* remained dominant in terms of the share of total land. Their cooperative character was emphasised by the require-ment that all members must work in them. Members, as owners, had the right and responsibility to share costs and returns to the enterprises. In practice, however, few *shirkats* were successful enough to pay dividends to their members. Family and small-team contracts were recognised as the basis for the organisation of production in a *shirkat*. A variety of systems of lease contracts, with families, small teams and collectives, emerged during this period. Usually a minimum of five years as the period of such con-tracts was stipulated, although annual revisions appear to have been common.

Formal transformation of the former collective farms into *shirkats* was implemented in stages, beginning with the more profitable collectives. By 2002 90 per cent of the former collectives had been transformed into *shirkats*. Unprofitable collectives were subjected to a period of readjust-ment. Successful readjustment led to their transformation into *shirkats*. Those which failed to readjust successfully into profitable enterprises were converted into private commercial farms.[23]

The third phase, 2004–

The restructuring of the *shirkats*, permitting household and small-team contracting, was aimed at promoting incentives, the lack of which had been the principal problem with collective agriculture in the past. In this the inspiration might have been derived from the Chinese experience of instituting a similar organisation of agriculture in the late 1970s, which had made agriculture the leading sector in ushering in an era of unprecedented economic growth. This hope was not realised in the case of Uzbekistan. Overall agricultural growth, though stable, showed little improvement in productivity and an ever-increasing proportion of *shirkats* came to be afflicted with financial difficulty. Gradually the decision to convert the poorly performing *shirkats* into private farms emerged and the Presidential Decree of October 2003 made private farms the principal form of agricultural enterprise for the foreseeable future. A cabinet decision at the same time outlined the plan to redistribute the land of 55 per cent of the 1,840 *shirkats* to create new private commercial farms during 2004–2006.

An outline of the emerging land system and agricultural institutions

By the time of the field visit for this study, in March 2005, it had become clear that the process of transforming *shirkats* into private farms was accelerating and that it would go beyond the 55 per cent of the so-called unprofitable *shirkats*. According to indications given by the senior officials of the government, a wholesale conversion of *shirkats* into private farms is currently taking place. This is likely to be completed by the year 2007, when *shirkats*, large cooperatives and state enterprises will cease to be significant forms of organisation in Uzbek agriculture. Thus, the experimentation with agricultural institutions in Uzbekistan since independence appears to be culminating into a structure that in the very near future will be characterised by the following features: First, private commercial farms, with the modal size group ranging between 30 and 50 hectares, will emerge as the dominant form by claiming anything close to 85 per cent of total sown land. Second, *dehkan* farms, encompassing the entire rural population and a sizable proportion of urban population, would claim approximately 12 per cent of sown land, with an average size of just over a tenth of a hectare. Third, large cooperative and state enterprises will become a rarity, limited to experimental research or special activities, and claiming an insignificant proportion of total land. Fourth, land will continue to be owned by the state with leaseholds granted to private farms and indefinite heritable usufruct right to *dehkan* farmers. Consequently, a firm decision has been made to avoid the creation of a private market for land. All are subject to land tax (after an initial tax holiday for two years for *dehkan* and private farmers) and all except the *dehkan* farmers are subject to compulsory procurement of cotton and grain at state-determined prices.

Thus the emerging system will consist of two parallel tracks of private farming, *dehkan* farms and larger commercial farms. In this Uzbekistan will resemble several of its Central Asian neighbours, notably Kazakhstan. Even in Tajikistan the original drive towards the creation of private farming was halted in the early 2000s in favour of a two-track system: private farms and large-scale cooperatives and collectives operating a *de facto* system of individual farming under household contracting. The Kyrgyz Republic is the only country in the region to have adopted a uniform system of redistributive land reform leading to a universal and egalitarian access to land (but see also related discussion on Armenia by Spoor, this volume).[24]

In creating commercial private farms, the emphasis is on ensuring a large average size. The law specifies lower limits for the size of such farms but no upper limit. As Table 7.5 shows, though, through time the average size of the newly created farms has been increasing.

The creation of a bi-modal distribution of scarce land, with the over-whelming majority of households having very small holdings and a small minority endowed with landholdings averaging 200 times or more of the holding size of the masses, involves a difficult and complex process of rationing. The country has a maximum of 4.5 million hectares of 'sown' land for cropping. Deducting *dehkan* plots, there remain four million hectares to be distributed among private farmers. Over the years the average parcel of land distributed to the newly created private farms has been rising. The number of new private farms created in 2004 is reported to be 103,921, with an average size of 28.2 hectares of agricultural land, of which 17 hectares is sown land. The current posture of public policy is to promote even larger farms. If the average size of a private farm turns out to be 20 hectares of sown land – which is well below what the policy makers appear to believe to be the optimum size to exploit economies of scale[25] – then only 200,000 farms can be created. This means that only one out of 14 rural households will be selected for the endowment of land for private commercial farming. If the pool of potential private farmers includes urban households (see Annex 7.1 for the indication that this is likely), then one out of 16 or more of the potential candidates will be chosen. How is this difficult process of rationing being implemented? Land being scarce in Uzbekistan and agriculture being the principal form of livelihood for the population, it is clear that competition for private land is intense. In the absence of a private land market, administrative decision making, rather than price, is the rationing device. This inevitably means that there is a tendency for land to go to those with connections,

Table 7.5 Newly created private farms in 2003 and 2004

Year	Number	Average size in hectares	
		Agricultural land	*Sown land*
2003	87,552	24.5	16.0
2004	103,921	28.2	17.0

Note
Source of the data is the State Statistical Committee. Agricultural land includes pasture and other land, in addition to land sown to crops.

power and resources. Official briefings by policy makers emphasise that great care is taken to make sure that land goes to those who are potentially the ablest farmers. Decisions are made by open 'tenders',[26] a process in which both the members of the *shirkat* and outsiders participate. Applicants are asked to provide information on such matters as education, experience in agriculture and management, and the amount of starting capital and creditworthiness for bank borrowing. Arbitrariness in decision making is unavoidable in these circumstances (see Annex 7.2 for a case study).

Official justification for the emerging system can be pieced together from routine policy pronouncements. The creation of *dehkan* farms was driven by the objective of ensuring some minimum level of food and income security for all rural (and many urban) households, although admittedly the current average *dehkan* holding does not ensure a living standard above any meaningful poverty threshold. There is an official distrust in the ability of these farms to provide a framework for agricultural progress that is consistent with the official view of national development. This distrust arises out of an inherent belief, inherited from Soviet times, in the virtue of large-scale farming. This is further reinforced by the knowledge that *dehkan* farms do not produce any cotton, the vital cash crop earning foreign exchange, which is considered a second, independent, limitation of the *dehkan* farms in leading agricultural growth. A third problem of a *dehkan*-based development strategy as officially perceived is that it is impossible to create a system of compulsory procurement for millions of smallholding farmers.[27] Thus, policy makers visualised the need for larger-scale enterprises as the vehicle for efficient agricultural growth and surplus extraction through compulsory procurement. Yet another reason cited in official justifications for large-scale farming is the presumed difficulty of efficiently delivering irrigation water to small *dehkan* farmers. During the earlier years of transition it was hoped that the restructured collectives – *shirkats* – would be such large agricultural enterprises. Over the years this hope was belied by the poor performance of the *shirkats*, leading to the decision to opt for larger private farms as the principal vehicle of agricultural growth on the evidence of what is claimed to be the indicators of their superior performance to that of the *shirkats*. By now a policy decision has been made to eliminate the *shirkats*, with just a handful of exceptions, and split them up into private farms.

An examination of the case for the emerging land system

To judge the efficacy of the emerging system from the standpoint of poverty reduction it is necessary to have one or more alternatives as the counterfactual. The one that Uzbekistan has clearly foregone is that of a uniform system of egalitarian access to land. This might have evolved in several alternative ways of which two, from recent experience, deserve to be highlighted. The first is the Chinese strategy of a household contract system under which all members of a commune received usufruct right to an amount of land that was proportional to the size of the family under terms that *de facto* were synonymous with fixed-rent farming. For a period the former commune continued to provide services and procure state quota output. Gradually these roles became minimal and the system became one of permanent heritable tenure, periodically readjusted to take into account demographic changes. Land continues to be under state ownership and there is no private land market. The success of this path in ushering in a period of rapid poverty-alleviating growth after the beginning of reforms is well documented. It was only after public policy in China reversed the improvement in the terms of trade for agriculture and reduced investment in agriculture in the mid-1980s that growth slowed down. To this day however agriculture in China remains an island of equality in a sea of surging inequality of distribution of income from other sources.[28]

The second path is the one chosen by Kyrgyzstan, which redistributed most of the formerly collective land among rural families in the form of land shares, ensuring that pretty much every household resident in rural areas ended up with land entitlement. Initially this was in the form of leasehold for 49 years, which was soon extended to 99 years. In 1998 the national parliament legislated to grant full ownership rights to the peasant households, including the right to sell land. Simultaneously, a moratorium on the right to sell was declared for five years, which was rescinded in 2001. In Kyrgyzstan land reform was not accompanied by complementary policies of improved incentives and input delivery. Indeed, the terms of trade for agriculture deteriorated and the system of input delivery faced disruptions. Despite this, Kyrgyz agriculture achieved decent and egalitarian growth to an extent that rural poverty declined in the late 1990s.[29]

If Uzbekistan opted for one of the above paths, and distributed land to all rural households, an average household would have ended up with 1.62 hectares of sown land as compared with a *dehkan* household now having just 0.12 hectares.[30] If peasant farms were created only for those who are employed in agriculture, while giving a subsistence plot of an existing average *dehkan* holding to the rest, an average peasant farm would have 2.36 hectares of sown land.[31] There would of course be regional variation in average size, depending on regional difference in land endowment. But the average farm size would be several times higher than what it is in China.[32] How would this counterfactual stand up to the concerns implicit in the justification of the present land system?

There is no serious argument about the superiority of this counterfactual over the existing one on grounds of equity. Moreover, while precise projections cannot be made about the unequal distribution of landholding characterised in Uzbek agriculture once the transition is concluded, it appears that there will be a great deal of inequality. This would be the case even if private farms were equally distributed because of the bi-modality of the overall distribution: at one extreme about 12 per cent of the land would be distributed among *dehkan* farmers with limited inequality among themselves and a very low average holding. At the other end there would be the commercial private farms commanding around 85 per cent land with an average holding of approximately 150 to 200 times the average holding of the *dehkans*! In reality, though, it appears that inequality among the commercial private farms will be substantial.

Table 7.6 shows the size distribution of the new farms created in 2003 in terms of agricultural land. The inequality is very considerable: assuming that the average size for each group is at the midpoint of the class interval and the average size of the largest, open-ended group is 72.5 hectares, the Gini ratio of the distribution for these 87,552 farms turns out to be 0.441! Given that there has been a steady upward drift in the average size of these farms through time and that ultimately the smallest 90 per cent or more of holdings, representing the *dehkan* farmers, will end up with only about 12 per cent of the land, Uzbekistan is clearly heading for an extremely unequal distribution of land. This is the system that policy makers, so completely won over by the doctrine of the paramount import-ance of economies of scale, are consciously promoting.

This emerging system will undoubtedly provide a worse distributional outcome than the counterfactual. This will come from at least two sources. First, the great inequality in the distribution of land will mean a very unequal distribution of factor returns to land. In Uzbek agriculture land's factor share in value added must be high due to the relative scarcity of land as a factor of production. This high share of income will become increasingly more unequally distributed as the distribution of land gets unequal. A second source of increased inequality, perhaps with an even more serious consequence for the poverty outcome, is the adverse effect

Table 7.6 The size distribution of private farms created in 2003 (hectares of agri-cultural land)

Size group	Number of farms	Percentage of farms
Below 5	12,662	14.5
Above 5–10	13,738	15.7
Above 10–15	10,722	12.2
Above 15–20	10,898	12.5
Above 20–25	9,806	11.2
Above 25–30	8,902	10.2
Above 30–40	8,179	9.3
Above 40–60	5,950	6.8
Above 60	6,695	7.6
All	87,552	100.0

Source: State Statistical Committee.

on employment. Private farms appear to employ far fewer workers per hectare than either the *shirkats* do or the peasant farmers in the counterfactual would. Consider the cases reported in Annexes 7.2 and 7.3. In the large-scale Said Ovul farm only 74 persons are employed at a 0.75 rate of employment intensity (nine months in a year) on 245 hectares of sown land. In a location under the same former *shirkat* the peasant farmer with two hectares of land employs five family workers. Even after allowing for the possibility that these family workers are employed at only a 0.75 rate of intensity (although no such point was made by the farmer interviewed), the large farm employs a mere 12 per cent of the labour that small farms sharing the same amount of land would have absorbed. Arguably the workers employed at the large farm enjoy higher earnings than the members of the peasant household, although a direct comparison is not possible. According to the owner of Said Ovul farm, an average worker currently receives a wage of 60,000 *sum* per month, or a total of approximately US$540 for a nine-month year. Annual cash income per worker in the peasant farm was US$260. Information on the earnings of the Said Ovul workers during the remaining three months and the consumption of self-produced goods and services of the peasant farm is not available though it seems that the latter is substantially larger than the former, making the difference in 'total earning' per worker lower than the difference in cash earning. The principal difference between the large farm and the counterfactual of many small two-hectare peasant farms on the same area of land is that up to eight times the number of workers might be employed in the latter scenario, each with a somewhat smaller income than the workers employed in the large farm, but their total income would be far greater than the total income of the workers in the large farm because the fabulous income of the owner of the latter would have been shared among many more peasant-household workers. As a consequence, many more workers and their dependents would have been lifted out of poverty.[33]

As noted earlier in this chapter, there has been a sharp reduction in agricultural employment, far in excess of what might have been caused by the change in cropping pattern. The anecdotal evidence above, together with the Ministry of Labour data quoted earlier, that employment per hectare in private farms is about 36 per cent lower than in *shirkats*, suggests that a large part of the decline in agricultural employment may have been caused by the ongoing shift of land to large private farms.[34] Under the counterfactual of egalitarian peasant farming the employment outcome would have been vastly more favourable.

The question is whether the counterfactual would be at least as efficient as the path that current policy has charted. To look for an answer, one might begin by considering how each of the usual limitations attributed to *dehkan* farming would apply to this uniform system of egalitarian peasant farming.

According to certain simple indicators of static productive efficiency, *dehkan* farmers appear to have easily outperformed the other forms of agriculture. One frequently quoted indicator is presented in Table 7.7, which shows that the ratio of the proportion of the value of crop output to the proportion of land is a staggering 3.58 for *dehkan* farmers and far below one for both private farms and *shirkats*. This indicator of efficiency is often countered by the defendants of the larger enterprises by arguing that *dehkan* farmers, not being subject to procurement, are free to produce the most valuable crops. As a result they end up with much higher aggregate output value per unit of land. An answer to this is provided by Table 7.8, which shows that *dehkan* farmers have achieved far higher yields in wheat as well and that this advantage appears to be improving over time.[35]

Table 7.8 shows that private farms' yield of wheat in recent years has been lower than the yield of the *shirkats*! This is the case for cotton as well.[36] Once again, the defenders of private farms have often argued that this is largely due to the privatisation of unprofitable *shirkats* in recent years. One might wonder if this argument does not imply that the poor performance of these *shirkats* was caused not just by bad management but also by agro-climatic or other material disadvantages that privatisation has been unable to overcome.

One need not emphasise the evidence in Tables 7.7 and 7.8 too much because the egalitarian peasant farmers visualised in the counterfactual would be qualitatively different from the *dehkan* farmers.[37] Thus, they would on average have more than 15 times the land that the *dehkan* farmers have today. Peasants of this size group, or even smaller, have spearheaded agricultural growth and economic transformation in many countries, notably in Asia. They have the inherent advantage of family

Table 7.7 Relative productivity levels, 2000 (percentage of total)

	(a) Value of crop	*(b) Land*	*Ratio (a)/(b)*
Dehkan farms	43	12	3.58
Private farms	9	16	0.56
Shirkats	48	72	0.67

Source: World Bank (2003), which says that the estimates are based on official data from the Ministry of Agriculture and Water Resources (MAWR).

Table 7.8 Index of yield per hectare of wheat with yield in *shirkat* = 100

	1998	*1999*	*2000*	*2001*
Dehkan farms	137	132	137	151
Private farms	110	101	98	98

Source: World Bank (2003) based on official government data.

labour, whose opportunity cost is much lower than the market price that commercial farms need to pay for hired labour. There is consequently far more use of labour, the relatively abundant factor, on land, the scarce factor. Moreover, the argument that these farmers cannot take advantage of economies of scale is vastly exaggerated. Many of the critically import-ant technological components, seed and fertiliser, are sufficiently divisible in any case. The use of large machines for land preparation and harvest-ing, where desirable, could be purchased from others who can produce those services more efficiently than individual farmers. Even now this is widely practised by *dehkan* and small farmers (see Annex 7.3). What is important is for policy makers to promote competition among the providers of these services so that their delivery can be efficient and economical.[38]

Next, it is necessary to consider the argument that *dehkan* farmers do not produce cotton, a vital cash crop without whose exports Uzbekistan cannot do. The answer, simply, is that cotton was made relatively unprof-itable by state policy (see next section) so that its production declined across all forms of agriculture. Indeed, but for compulsory quotas, it would have gone down even more, given the relative price disincentive. However, there is nothing in its production technology that makes it any more difficult to be produced under peasant farming than most other crops. Furthermore, the peasant farms in the counterfactual would not be the minuscule *dehkan* farms of today. In many countries, notably China, with the largest cotton production in the world, small-scale peasant agri-culture is the pervasive form of organisation. Annex 7.2 illustrates a *dehkan* farmer's plan to devote all his land to producing cotton in the next two years, now that relative incentives have improved.

Finally, one needs to deal with the argument that small-scale farmers are hard to bring under the net of procurement. There are two impera-tives that drove the system of procurement in Uzbekistan: extraction of surplus from agriculture; and ensuring a cropping pattern that conforms to the target of the policy makers. The first of the two arguments has already become obsolete at least in principle: government policy at present is to set procurement prices at international prices. This issue is further discussed in the next section. The second justification for procure-ment is simply inefficient. The composition of output should be a matter of relative incentives. Once incentives are appropriate, the socially desir-able composition of output would be produced without any direct regula-tion such as procurement quotas, whose presence would only distort production.

Incentives and inputs

The creation of a suitable land system and agricultural organisation will by itself not satisfy the preconditions for rapid agricultural growth. It must be complemented by appropriate incentives and an infrastructure for the supply of inputs and the marketing of outputs. Successful cases of agricultural growth following agrarian reforms are all characterised by the simultaneous institution of these complementary policies. There is an extensive literature on how land reforms in Taiwan and the Republic of Korea were complemented by such measures and, as a more contemporary example, one can refer to the well-known argument that the remarkable development of China, initially spearheaded by agricultural growth since the late 1970s, owes as much to the institutional reform in agriculture as to the sharp improvement in terms of trade in 1979.[39] In Uzbekistan problems with incentives and input supply have been a very serious impediment to agricultural development. They need to be set in order if institutional changes are to have the desired outcome, in the form of higher growth.

The two far-reaching changes in the incentive structure of Uzbekistan's agriculture after independence were: (i) a sharp decline in agriculture's terms of trade; and (ii) a major shift in relative incentives against cotton and in favour of grains. The motivations behind both changes are closely related to the circumstances of Uzbekistan's independence. Independent Uzbekistan was cut off from the budgetary grant that it used to receive from the USSR.[40] The government had to find new sources of revenue. Extraction of surplus from agriculture, by driving a wedge between the procurement price and export price of cotton, was an attractive and readily available choice. Indeed, the extraction of surplus from agriculture was extended to grain crops (and indeed other agricultural produce for a short period) by reducing their procurement prices to well below market prices.

The policy of shifting relative incentives against cotton and in favour of grains reflected concern about Uzbekistan's dependence on grain imports. Quick self-sufficiency in grain was accepted as a goal of economic policy. To achieve self-sufficiency it was decided to transfer land from cotton to grain. A shift in incentives against cotton and in favour of grain was one of the instruments to bring about a shift in the area under cultivation.

A minimum estimate of the rate of 'concealed taxation' through cotton procurement for the year 1995 showed that a staggering 12 per cent of the GDP originating in the agricultural sector as a whole was extracted. Grain was also subject to resource extraction, though to a much smaller extent.[41]

With the passage of time, the severity of 'concealed taxation' of agriculture declined. World Bank estimates show that in 2000 net concealed tax on agriculture through the procurement of cotton and grains amounted to 8.5 per cent of value added in agriculture, or 2.6 per cent of total GDP. These estimates also show that in 2000 the rate of concealed taxation was much higher on cotton than on grain.[42] Government policy statements claim that since 2003 'concealed taxation' of cotton and grain have been abolished, at least in principle, in so far as procurement prices have closely followed world prices. It does appear that procurement prices are still lower than 'market prices' (see Annex 7.1) and that the difference between the two prices is greater for cotton than for grain. The government claims that whatever difference between the two prices exists is due to the problem of forecasting world prices at the time procurement prices are decided. A recent study has confirmed that systematic downward bias in the forecasting of the world cotton price was a source of significant concealed taxation of cotton through procurement in 2003.[43]

The effect of strong discrimination against cotton relative to grain has been not only to reduce the area under cotton cultivation but also its yield per hectare. Clearly, resources other than land have also been moved out of cotton. The area devoted to grains has increased sharply. The far-reaching effect of this change on agricultural employment, with its possible consequence for poverty, has been discussed above.

Since the imperative of extracting surplus from agriculture has lessened due to the availability of new sources of revenue during the phase of recovery, no useful purpose is served by retaining the system of procurement. The ostensible justification for it is that it allows the government to ensure a desirable composition of output. As said above, this is best done by appropriate adjustments in the system of incentives. The system of procurement can easily have the unintended consequence of distorting the system of incentives due to the difficulties of forecasting world prices and other errors in calculation. It is an unnecessary bureaucratic tentacle on agricultural enterprise that harms production incentives.

Uzbekistan's agriculture has faced an acute problem of input supply. The use of fertiliser per hectare has fallen since independence. Transition to individual farming has not been adequately backed by the creation of a system of credit, extension and services delivery. The system of irrigation and the budgetary subsidy towards it is in need of urgent review, and the irrigation infrastructure is in need of proper maintenance. Detailed discussion of these issues is outside the scope of this chapter. It only wants to underline the importance of the creation of an efficient network of supply of these inputs and services as a precondition to the success of any agrarian system, especially of egalitarian small-scale peasant farming, which is the clearly preferred alternative suggested by this chapter.

A guiding principle for the organisation of the system of distribution of inputs should be to establish the right combination of the role of the market and the state. Among the delivery of inputs which should be primarily left to the market are: fertiliser and the services of tractors, harvesters and large machines. Some optimistic news heard by this author came from the *dehkan* farmer he interviewed who reported that he had bought fertiliser from the local mini-market. It is not known how extensive or competitive this distribution network is. The peasantry, long oppressed by the system of bureaucracy, would benefit from distribution networks free from official interference and regulation. This does not mean that the government should withdraw from these areas completely. It should make necessary investments in the infrastructure for transport, distribution and dissemination of information. It should also remove impediments to competition among delivery networks.

A second set of services – notably extension and credit – should be an area of collaboration between the government, NGOs and the private sector. Credit for small farmers, including a system of micro-credit, is of high priority. Extension services, with enormous externalities, are a natural area for the government to invest resources in; but their delivery can be facilitated by the participation of NGOs, which can also have a central role in the delivery of micro-credit as amply demonstrated by the experience of countries like Bangladesh. Irrigation, arterial transport and power supply should primarily be government responsibility because of the indivisibility of investment in these activities.

This chapter does not have a problem with the government decision to avoid the creation of a private land market. As the Chinese experience has demonstrated, in a system of small peasant farming the absence of a land market can protect small farmers. The absence of a land market did not prove an impediment to agricultural development in China, especially because the local community and administration have made periodic adjustment to land distribution in response to changes in the demographic characteristics of individual households. The need to permit the use of land as collateral for credit may emerge as an important issue, and this can be allowed with clearly outlined limitations and safeguards.

Concluding comments

After experimenting for a decade and a half to find an alternative to the collectivised agriculture that characterised the Soviet period, Uzbekistan has finally opted for a two-track system of individual farming. At one end virtually all rural households and approximately half the urban households have been given small pieces of land, averaging 0.12 hectares each, as a source of insurance for the satisfaction of the very basic food needs. The rest of the land is being allocated to a small proportion of households in parcels that are very large by the standard of the overall land/person ratio for the country. The objective is to create a class of commercial farmers, with a modal size group of 30–50 hectares, a minimum size of ten hectares for cotton and grain, and often allowing much larger farms. The selection of private farmers, constituting something like one in 15 rural households, is necessarily arbitrary. By all available indications, those with power, influence and resources are succeeding in getting allocations of commercial farm land. The ostensible justification for this transformation is that only large farms are able to operate efficiently by deriving the advantage of economies of scale that are inherent in mechanisation, which is seen as the path to modernisation and the progress of agriculture. For a period Uzbekistan experimented with reformed collective institutions, the *shirkats*, as the large-scale institutional vehicle for agricultural growth. By 2004 the decision was finally made to abandon that path and privatise *shirkat* land.

The case for this system is far from convincing. The near-universal access to land for *dehkan* farmers does not protect an average *dehkan* household from poverty. Even if an average household received the ceiling of land allowed the *dehkan* farmers – 0.35 irrigated hectares – it would not ensure a living standard above poverty. Something like twice that amount would be needed.[44] But an average household now has only 0.12 hectares, just about a sixth of the land that would make it free of poverty – assuming of course that produce from land is the sole source of income.

The expectation that large private farms constitute the best vehicle for agricultural growth is more a matter of faith than a judgment supported by facts. On the evidence of available indicators, the average productivity of large farms does not appear to be any higher than the productivity of the discredited *shirkats*. An agrarian structure dominated by them would be characterised by a great deal of inequality. Given the employment aversion of these farms and the meagre land endowment of the *dehkan* farms, poverty alleviation would be very difficult under this system. International evidence and *a priori* reasoning lead one to expect that a system of egalitarian peasant farming, properly supported by an infrastructure of services and appropriate incentives, would probably be more efficient than the large-scale commercial farms. They would undoubtedly provide a far more egalitarian distribution of income. Rural poverty would be virtually eliminated.

In terms of making a choice between alternatives, Uzbekistan has by all indications crossed the point of no return. Arguing in favour of the counterfactual would thus appear pointless. Given the inexorable march towards large-scale private farming, what can one recommend to improve Uzbekistan's ability to cope with the problem of poverty?

First, it needs to be emphasised that what would have made perfect sense in the counterfactual case is not necessarily the best policy under the unfolding scenario. The avoidance of creating a land market could be justified for the protection of small peasants. Under large-scale farming it could be an impediment to efficiency. While continuing to guarantee heritable usufruct right to *dehkan* farmers, it would be desirable to sell land to the large farmers by competitive bidding rather than continuing with the non-transparent system of distribution by administrative decision. Indeed it would be desirable to open up all the land thus far distributed for re-bidding. An alternative, in the event that the creation of a private land market is not politically feasible, would be to auction the lease to the highest bidder.[45] Free irrigation water should be replaced by a system of appropriate water charges. Revenues from these sources would finance public goods and services in rural areas.

Wherever possible, the land endowment of the *dehkan* farmers should be increased to at least the present ceiling. Wherever possible, the ceiling should be raised to a level that would enable the *dehkan* farmer to produce an income equivalent to a reasonable poverty threshold. There may be some scope for this in the *shirkats* yet to be privatised, although it seems unlikely that the existing distribution of political power would permit this to be realised.

Private capitalist farming should be free of policy distortions that promote inefficiency. Thus, the system of procurement, artificially distorting incentives against the labour-intensive crop, should be discarded and other similar distortions prevented and/or eliminated. Policies outlined in the previous section for improved and competitive access to inputs and credit would be just as important under this scenario.

Simultaneously, it must be realised that private capitalist farming will not absorb nearly as much labour as would be absorbed in the counterfactual. Thus, *dehkan* farmers would need to be helped and protected by granting them access to micro-credit and inputs and services at competitive prices, freeing them from the power of the large farmers, who would want to take advantage of interlinked markets to get the *dehkan* farmers to accept monopsonistic wages. Remunerative employment opportunities must be created in RNF activities and indeed in the urban economy. The conversion of agriculture into a system of predominantly capitalist farming will take away the hospitality that the rural society provided for the last decade and a half to an ever-increasing proportion of the national population. The country must begin to tread the more conventional path of gradual urbanisation of the population and the labour force.

Annex 7.1 Korasuv Shirkat

Kolkhoz Karl Marx in Urtachirkik *raion* in the outskirts of Tashkent was renamed Korasuv *Kolkhoz* in 1991 and converted into a *shirkat* in March 1999. It has 837 members and 1,551 hectares of land. Its main products are cotton and wheat, with the remaining land devoted to vegetables and other grains. The *shirkat* carries out all production activities through contracting with member households. Last year it signed contracts with 38 households for the production of cotton and 39 households for the production of wheat. There were an additional 189 household contracts for the production of rice and vegetables. The present writer examined an individual contract which was written in a two-page standard format which specified the product (cotton in this case), area of land (22.3 hectares), target yield (2.7 tons/hectare, a higher figure than the national average), total target output (60.2 tons), total value of output (15,052,000 *sum*), the amount to be paid to the contracting household as a 'wage' (4,816,800 *sum* or 32 per cent of the total value). Seventy per cent of the wage is paid at the end of the production cycle and the remainder is paid after the crop is available, with adjustment for the shortfall in or exceeding of the target output. All inputs are provided and costs borne by the *shirkat*. The contract is much more limited than the kind of household contracting that China practised in the initial stage of restructuring. The present contract is not much more than a labour contract with the output and inputs fixed. The contracting household has the very limited entrepreneurial role of day-to-day care of the field and the work of the co-workers. The *shirkat* is the main entrepreneur in the sense that it decides the crop mix (which in turn is dictated by the state procurement quota) and inputs.

An interesting feature of the above contract (pulled out randomly from a sheaf of documents by this author) is that a single contractor was being given such a large tract of land (more than 22 hectares) when the amount of land available per member was less than two hectares. The contracting individual no doubt used other workers, perhaps others from the *shirkat* itself, both from his own family and from others'. Why this was done, instead of contracting with a larger number of members each for smaller tracts of land, was not a matter that was discussed with the *shirkat* management. But the practice is consistent with an abiding faith in the efficiency of the large scale that is so pervasive in this economy, despite a resource endowment that strongly indicates small-scale farming as the natural outcome.

Government quota consists of 50 per cent of the target output of grain and cotton and is invariant in the event of a shortfall from or the exceeding of the target output. For grain the above-target output was sold at market prices to members of the *shirkat,* and in the open market. This market price last year was no more than 10 per cent higher than the state procurement price. For cotton the above-quota output was sold to the state at 20 per cent more than the procurement price.

All intra-*shirkat* irrigation costs are borne by the *shirkat* while the cost of the irrigation system outside the *shirkat* border is borne by the state budget and managed by the Regional Department of the Ministry of Water and Agriculture. Irrigation water itself is provided free of charge. Fertiliser and other chemical products are purchased – over and above what is received from the government under procurement agreement – from the warehouse run by the Uzbek Chemical Trading Company, in which the government holds a 25 per cent share. As compared to the pre-independence period, the use per hectare of pesticides, herbicides and certain fertilisers has fallen, while the use of biological nutrients has increased. Without a great deal of additional information, it is impossible to determine if the *shirkat* suffers under any concealed taxation: it cannot be determined if the resources extracted through procurement are in excess of the subsidies paid in the form of irrigation water and fertiliser for quota output. It is clear, however, that the *shirkat*'s production plan is strongly controlled by the government through the procurement quotas.

The *shirkat* earned a profit of 30 million *sum* last year after all costs including land tax, which was 300,000 *sum*. Its chairman and a committee of 11 others, including technical and managerial personnel, are elected by the members for a period of three years. The remaining 11of its 23 employees are appointed by the chairman and the committee. The *shirkat* chairman expressed the hope that they would escape privatisation because they had been consistently profitable.

Annex 7.2: Said Ovul Farm

Mamatkul Salamov was a deputy minister in the Uzbekistan Ministry of Building and Construction until 2000, when he retired at the age of 63. In the same year he, along with his three sons, submitted a 'tender' for land for private farming from Kimpen Hwa *shirkat* in Urtachirchik *raion*. The *shirkat* was unprofitable and was going out of business by distributing land to be privately farmed. On the standard criteria indicated in the tender application, Salamov claimed that he was highly educated, with management experience in building and construction (though none in farming), and with enough starting capital and proof of worthiness for bank loans. He hired a highly qualified agronomist as a deputy. He was granted 200 hectares of land on a 49-year lease. This land was not indivisible in any sense; it consisted of eight distinct contours which could have been allocated to different applicants, but it was given to him because he persuaded the decision makers that he would manage it well and derive large-scale benefits. The land was of medium to good quality. In 2004 he added another 50 hectares of land by successfully bidding for the land of a private farmer who had become bankrupt. Together with about ten hectares of building land and road surface, he has a total of 260 hectares, of which 245 hectares are sown land. In 2001 he bought four hectares of land from a *shirkat* for industrial use – farm land can only be leased – and set up a livestock farm and plants for processing grain. This was financed by a bank loan which has since been paid off.

Last year he produced cotton on 86 hectares, achieving a yield of four tons/hectare, way above the national average. For wheat, on 105 hectares he achieved a yield of six tons/hectare, also far above the national average. Of wheat 2.5 tons/hectare was the procurement quota. For cotton the quota was 50 per cent of output. He received a much higher procurement price for wheat because he was able to provide processed grain, thanks to his processing plant. His livestock farm produces milk and meat in addition to processed manure, which satisfies much of his fertilisation requirements. He maintains the intra-farm irrigation system with 20 kilometres of channels. Irrigation water is provided free of charge by the government department. He paid 3.3 million *sum* of land tax on the 200 hectares originally obtained from the *shirkat*. The additional 50 hectares is still under tax holiday.

His farms are highly mechanised, with a variety of large machinery. He claimed to have built the processing plant by using scrap metal. He employs 74 workers, who work for about nine months a year on his farm. Most of his workers are *dehkan* farmers with small plots on which they work for the remaining time. His mechanised farm operates with far fewer workers than would be employed under the old *shirkat* or by smaller farmers (see the next Annex describing a farm of two hectares which 'fully' employs five family workers).

His office displays a chart showing comparative performance during the *shirkat* years and under his management. It is hard to know to what extent the indicators, many of the absolute ones being in current value, are comparable. The 'rate of profit', defined as profit as the ratio of the value of sales, was just 4 per cent in the last year of the *shirkat* and 36 per cent under his management in 2002 on the initial 200 hectares. In 2004 his net profit from all farm operations was 85 million *sum*, approximately US$85,000.

Clearly he is a great entrepreneur. But it is also clear that without his status and influence as a former deputy minister, he would not have succeeded in getting such a huge amount of land in a country starved of land resources. The practice of creating such huge private farms out of former *shirkats* with low land endowment per member (see Annex 7.1 which shows that the nearby functioning *shirkat* Korasuv has just 1.85 hectares of land per worker) has undoubtedly led to an enormous inequality in the distribution of land, the vital resource for the vast rural population. Employment on the land has declined although wages per employed worker has risen. He is very much a gentleman capitalist farmer who lives in Tashkent and has access to financial and technological resources beyond the reach of an average private farmer, not to mention the *dehkan* farmers.

Annex 7.3: Mukhidinov Tashkhodja, a *Dehkan* farmer

Mukhidinov Tashkhodja has worked in Kimpen Hwa *shirkat* (previously *kolkhoz*), the same former collective out of whose demise emerged the huge capitalist farm described in Annex 7.2, since 1975. His family consists of his mother, wife, two sons, a daughter, a daughter-in-law and a granddaughter – altogether, eight members. He was an ordinary *kolkhoz/shirkat* worker. Currently his household consists of five working members; all except his mother, wife and the infant granddaughter.

During the period of collectivised agriculture he had a personal plot of only 0.14 hectares of which 0.07 hectares was a garden plot with his homestead on the remainder. In 2002 he received 0.5 hectares of land for himself and 0.7 hectares each for his two sons, making the total sown land for the entire household just under two hectares. He absolutely insisted that the land he received was *dehkan* land. If this is true then this contradicts officially provided information that there is an upper ceiling of 0.35 hectares of irrigated and 0.5 hectares of unirrigated *dehkan* land per household, even if one allows for the fact that his sons are counted as separate households, which by itself would be an odd practice in the case of his second son, who is single and just 18, 16 when the land was allocated. The case suggests that the official rule is perhaps not always rigidly applied.

All five working members of the household work on the family farm. Apparently this farm of approximately two hectares provides labour for all five of them; none has worked outside the farm. During the last two years his farm produced wheat, achieving a yield of 4.5 ton per hectare, higher than the national average, though well below what Said Ovul, a farm with a large investment in capital equipment and superior technology, achieved. In the next two years he plans to produce cotton, again contradicting the well-known argument that *dehkan* farmers do not produce cotton. Besides wheat, he allocates a small part of his land to other grains and he also produces vegetables and other products after the wheat harvest. The family has a cow whose milk is consumed by the family members.

He gets free irrigation water, has enjoyed land tax holiday so far, buys fertiliser from the mini-market and also buys tractor services for land preparation from others for payment in cash.

His net cash income from the sale of 6.5 tons of grain and certain minor products, after deducting all production cost, was 1.3 million *sum*, which alone makes the per capita income of the household approximately US$163 per year or PPP$862 (using the ratio of PPP$ income to 'Atlas' $ income for Uzbekistan for 2002 from the *World Development Indicators*), thereby placing the household far above international and national poverty thresholds on the basis of cash income alone. Once allowance is made for self-consumed food and services, per capita family income would be higher still.

He did not apply for land as a private farmer when Kimpen Hwa *shirkat's* land was privatised. Asked why not, he replied that he thought he would be rejected because he did not have the necessary starting capital.

Notes

1 The author is grateful to Muzaffar Kasimov of the Center for Economic Research, Tashkent, who provided all the logistical assistance in carrying out the field research in March 2005 on which much of the chapter is based. Galina Saidova and Aktam Khaitov of the Ministry of Economy were of immense help in clarifying issues and data on a variety of aspects of the economy. Uktam Abdurrakhmanov of the Center for Economic Research and numerous others in Tashkent helped in many ways. Keith Griffin, Max Spoor and the editors of the present volume made many useful suggestions on an earlier draft. To all of them the author is deeply grateful.

2 This introductory section draws on the author's previous work, Khan and Ghai (1979) and Khan (1995).

3 For references to these and other historical data for the region see Khan and Ghai (1979).

4 Compared to this contemporary Soviet estimate, the yield was officially estimated to be 2.76 tons per hectare in 1990 and 2.56 tons per hectare in 1994. Whether the lower 1990 estimate is due to a reduction in yield over time or to an overstatement of output estimates in the past, or both, is an open question. It is also important to emphasise that the high yields per hectare in the Soviet period do not by themselves represent high efficiency in the production of cotton. Output per worker was very low and there are indications that the use of water and other inputs in cotton cultivation was inefficient.

5 The cost estimates are for the 1970s. They are not available for the 1950s.

6 See Khan and Ghai (1979) for details.

7 The question of 'concealed' taxation is complex and an accurate estimate would require information on the pricing of all inputs as well as outputs of the goods that the agricultural sector sold and purchased. See Khan and Ghai (1979) for a discussion of the issues involved.

8 In 1975 earnings in industries were 32 per cent higher than the earnings in *kolkhozy* in Uzbekistan. The difference for the USSR was 43 per cent.

9 The GDP deflator is from World Bank (2004). The agricultural value-added deflator has been calculated by dividing the current price value added by the constant price value added, both shown in the same source.

10 See World Bank (2003: 64).

11 Employment data, which are from official sources, imply that rural employment has been falling as a proportion of total employment. This is hard to explain since official data also claim that rural population, as a proportion of total population, has been rising. Whether the faster rise in rural population was due to a faster rate of natural growth than for urban areas is a question on which Uzbek analysts do not have a consensus. In any case, the pattern is perverse, in so far as in most developing countries where the natural rate of population growth is higher in rural areas, emigration usually ensures that over time rural population as a proportion of total population falls.

12 This dated estimate, referring to the mid-1970s (see Khan and Ghai, 1979), is for the collective farms existing at that time. It is, however, not obvious if this has changed and, if so, in which direction.

13 The Ministry of Labour, during a briefing, stated that their estimates show that a *shirkat* employs a worker for every 2.5 hectares of land while a private commercial farm employs one worker for every 3.9 hectares of land. Thus employment per unit of land is 36 per cent lower in commercial farms than in *shirkats*.

14 For 1994 estimated rural employment is obtained by dividing agricultural employment for that year by the ratio of agricultural to total rural employment for 1995, because the ratio is not available for 1994.

15 See World Bank (2003) for these estimates, which are based on the 2000/2001 Household Budget Survey (HBS).

16 Government of Uzbekistan (2004a).

17 Government of Uzbekistan (2004) claims that the Gini ratio went up from 0.28 in the late 1980s to 0.389 in 2001. It argues that this rising inequality is the principal reason why the reduction in poverty in the period of recovery was far less than what it could have been with unchanged distribution of income. Note that the phenomenon could also be explained by a very slow growth in income in RNF employment.

18 A Soviet period estimate for 1989 shows that 44 per cent of Uzbek population were in poverty with reference to a poverty line of 75 rubles (reported in World

Bank (1993: 98)). The Soviet period poverty line of 75 rubles cannot be compared with the national poverty line or the PPP$1 poverty line for 2000. It is well known, however, that poverty thresholds in the Soviet period were rather high in relation to the usual standards of subsistence used to calculate national poverty thresholds elsewhere.

19 Kandiyoti (2004), besides providing a useful analysis of the first two phases of reform, also discusses the writings of other authors who have contributed to an analysis of these reforms.

20 World Bank (2003).

21 Output per unit of land, the scarce factor of production, has been higher in *kolkhozy* than in *sovkhozy*. In addition, the overall unit cost was lower in *kolkhozy* than in *sovkhozy*. Output per worker has been higher in *sovkhozy* than in *kolkhozy* but this has been due to much larger amounts of capital and complementary resources per unit of labour in the *sovkhozy*. See Khan and Ghai (1979).

22 It is customary to refer to these entities simply as farms. This paper frequently uses the term commercial farms to distinguish them from smallholding *dehkan* farms.

23 Starting in 2001 a small number of unprofitable collectives began to be converted into private farms without the interregnum of a readjustment process.

24 The actual implementation of redistributive reforms in Kyrgyzstan, along with the subsequent modification of laws on land ceilings and the prevention of private land sales, is alleged to have robbed the reform of a good deal of its initial egalitarian focus.

25 During a recent meeting the First Deputy Minister in the Ministry of Economy told the author that the government considers 30 to 50 hectares to be the optimum range of holdings for private farms. In discussions with the senior officials of the State Committee on Land and the State Committee on Property, the author was left in no doubt that the official view was strongly in favour of creating very large farms.

26 The original word in Uzbek, *tanlov*, more accurately translates as 'selection' or 'contest' although in official English translation the term 'tender' is used. Since tender indicates competitive bids in terms of price or cost, the use of this term is somewhat odd in a situation in which no such bidding is involved for the simple reason that land is not being sold to the highest bidder or to one who is willing to pay the highest 'rent', in the form of land tax, which is periodically fixed by the government.

27 One might be reminded that the true reason for the imposition of collectivisation by Stalin in 1930 was his miserable failure to attain the procurement target implied by the First Five Year Plan in an agriculture 'fragmented' into millions of household farms.

28 See Khan and Riskin (2001).

29 See World Bank (2001). Recent modifications of land laws, especially those permitting the creation of a private land market, have led to serious concern about the egalitarian focus of land reform in Kyrgyzstan.

30 This is based on close to 16 million rural people, an average household size of 5.8 and arable crop land – not 'agricultural land', which is much more – of 4.47 million hectares.

31 This is on the assumption that a third of the rural labour force is employed in RNF activities, meaning that a third of the households would not have farming as the principal occupation. Since these households would employ members outside agriculture, they would need, or be able to care for, smaller landholdings than the other rural households.

32 In China arable land per rural family in 2001 was 0.64 hectares. Furthermore, while in China only 36 per cent of agricultural land is irrigated, in Uzbekistan the ratio is 88 per cent.

33 Is it plausible to argue that total output would have been smaller on this land under peasant farming than under the large farms? Once again, a direct comparison of the output of the two farms is neither possible nor relevant. It is not possible because information on output is available for the small peasant farm for only the marketed major crop. That yield in this crop is lower in the small farm than the large farm does not necessarily indicate that total output per hectare is lower, or lower to the same extent. More importantly, the comparison is not relevant because the large farm has a very large capital investment and is vertically integrated with some processing activities, for which there is nothing comparable in the small farm.

34 What about the argument that the excess labour in *shirkats* simply produced nothing, so that their removal by the private farms was a good thing? First, the evidence in Tables 7.7 and 7.8 do not suggest anything so unambiguous. Second, even if that were the case, the distributional consequence of privatisation would be adverse.

35 The writer has heard critics suggest that the *dehkan* yield in wheat is inflated because *shirkats*, in trying to avoid procurement, have shown their wheat output as belonging to *dehkan* farmers. These critics have not claimed or cited any hard evidence for this conjecture. One might note that, if true, this would further improve this indicator of performance for the *shirkats* which is already better than the performance of the private farmers according to this index.

36 According to official sources yield per hectare of cotton was 3.5 tons in *shirkats* and 3.38 tons in private farms in 2003.

37 Indeed, the indicators in Tables 7.7 and 7.8 are too partial and incomplete to serve as the basis of an evaluation of relative performance of the three systems. Furthermore, they are based on the historical performance of the three forms, which do not represent well what their performance would be under more ideal circumstances. *Shirkats* in the past were under arbitrary government control and distorted incentives to such an extent that their performance can hardly be taken as an indicator of how they might have performed in the absence of those controls and distortions.

38 Ironically the vehemence of the ongoing argument among officials in Uzbekistan that economies of scale, leading to large-scale mechanisation, are of paramount importance for agricultural progress reminds one of the similar arguments that Stalin made in order to justify collectivisation. Stalin of course complemented his position by arguing that collectivisation was also essential for equity because, in the absence of it, the small and weak peasants would be devoured by the stronger and bigger ones. In today's Uzbekistan the equity argument has been completely ignored; but the economies of scale argument has become the central focus for policy.

39 See Griffin *et al.* (2002) and references therein.

40 In the late 1980s the budgetary grant from the USSR amounted to 7 to 10 per cent of the grant was a net transfer to Uzbekistan from the rest of the USSR. The complexity of real and monetary flows between Uzbekistan and the rest of the USSR is beyond the scope of this chapter.

41 See Khan (1995).

42 World Bank (2003: chapter 4).

43 Center for Economic Research (2004).

44 This extremely rough guess is based on the following assumptions. If a person is to obtain the entire food energy of 2,100 kilocalories from grain, one would need 0.6 kilograms per day, or 1.27 tons for an average family of 5.8 per year. Assuming that food energy is 60 per cent of expenditure at the poverty threshold, this means that the grain equivalent of income to raise an average house-

hold above poverty is 2.12 tons, which, on the assumption of an average yield per hectare of 3 tons, would require 0.71 hectares of land.

45 The author is under no illusion that either of these would be politically feasible.

References

*Center for Economic Research (2004). *Reorganization of Cooperative Agricultural Enterprises (Shirkats) into Farming Business Entities.* Tashkent.

*Government of Uzbekistan (2004). *Living Standard Strategy for 2004–2006 and Period up to 2010.* Tashkent.

*Government of Uzbekistan (2004a). *Welfare Improvement Strategy Paper of the Republic of Uzbekistan for 2005–2010 (Interim Document).* Tashkent.

Griffin, K. (ed.) (1996). *Social Policy and Economic Transformation in Uzbekistan.* Geneva: UNDP-ILO.

Griffin, K., A. R. Khan and A. Ickowitz (2002). 'Poverty and Land Distribution,' *Journal of Agrarian Change,* vol. 2, no. 3, pp. 279–330.

Kandiyoti, D. (2004). *Post-Soviet Institutional Design, NGOs and Rural Livelihoods in Uzbekistan.* Geneva: UNRISD; Rome: FAO.

Khan, A. R. (1995). 'The Transition to a Market Economy in Agriculture,' in K. Griffin, ed., (1996). *Social Policy and Economic Transformation in Uzbekistan.* Geneva: UNDP-ILO.

Khan, A. R. and D. P. Ghai (1979). *Collective Agriculture and Rural Development in Soviet Central Asia.* London: Macmillan.

Khan, A. R. and C. Riskin (2001). *Inequality and Poverty in China in the Age of Globalization.* New York: Oxford University Press.

World Bank (1993). *Uzbekistan: An Agenda for Economic Reform.* Washington, DC: World Bank.

World Bank (2001). *Kyrgyz Republic: Poverty in the 1990s in the Kyrgyz Republic.* Washington, DC: World Bank.

World Bank (2003). *Uzbekistan Living Standard Assessment, Vol. II,* January. Washington, DC: World Bank.

World Bank (2004). *World Development Indicators 2004 CD ROM Version.* Washington, DC: World Bank.

* These references are available in the form of manuscripts in the respective organisations.

8 Mubarak's legacy for Egypt's rural poor

Returning land to the landlords

Ray Bush

Introduction

This chapter explores the continuities and discontinuities in land and tenure reform in Egypt.[1] It does so by examining the historical record of land ownership and the implications for poverty in rural Egypt, focusing on the impact of Law 96 of 1992 which reversed the momentous Nasserist land reforms of the 1950s and 1960s. Gamal Abdel Nasser had tried to break the economic and political power of the landowning Pasha class. He did that by limiting land ownership and for the first time securing legal rights for tenants, enabling them to inherit tenancies in perpetuity and to farm tenancies with secure fixed rents. Under the guise of regulating relations between owners and tenants, Law 96 became the most significant element in a long process of de-Nasserisation: reversing security of tenure, ending fixed rents and rights of inheritance. President Mubarak completed the policy of rewarding land ownership that began with Anwar Sadat's influence even before Nasser's death in 1970. Sadat later, in 1974 and 1981, restored about 150,000 feddans[2] of tenanted land to pre-1952 owners, and improved the representation of large landowners in agrarian reform cooperatives.

This chapter explores the counter-revolution in Egypt's countryside that Law 96 promoted (Bush, 2002a). I examine how the change in land tenure legislation emerged and what the impact of it has been for tenants and the *fellahin*[3] more generally in rural Egypt. I set this debate against policy rhetoric of declared expectations from land reform and the failure to understand links between land access and poverty as well as the need to develop an understanding of poverty that looks at the structures and processes of poverty creation and the relationships that sustain it. There is also an added dimension that can perhaps only be hinted at here. There is the suggestion that 2005 would witness a major political turning point in Egypt's history. The constitutional amendments allowing a competitive presidential election, rather than a referendum to confirm a single candidate nominated by the parliament, are viewed as an historic step toward political liberalisation. Yet already by mid-2005 the euphoria or limited optimism had turned to despair for many Egypt watchers. That despair resulted from the awareness of increased restrictions placed upon political parties and organisations aiming to challenge the aging Hosni Mubarak, who was standing for a fifth term (HRW, 2005).

Monitoring the political debate about regime continuity is important. As we will see, one persistent issue in the debate about the *fellahin* and rural development more generally is that the countryside has been deprived of possibilities to become fully engaged in the political reform and debate. Egyptian peasants have repeatedly challenged the practice of successive regimes to treat them as malleable supporters of the status quo (Cuno, 1992). Yet until the *fellahin* are actively engaged in dialogue about land and agricultural reform more generally, there is little hope that Cairo-based 'initiatives', which have generally emanated from USAID, will meet the stated policy agenda of improving productivity and delivering poverty reduction. There is a significant disjuncture between the rhetoric of globalisation and its implied pressure for democratisation, rural empowerment and rural development and a rural reality of accelerating poverty and the enhanced economic and political power of landowners, many of whom are absentee.

Contrary to the view that political reform is providing opportunities for rural dwellers to voice their concerns, repression in Egypt has actually tightened. Deliberalisation has included the prevention of participation from the grassroots: 'umdas' or village headmen, and university deans have become government appointments rather than elected positions, and syndicate elections have been regularly postponed when it became clear that islamists would win (Kienle, 2001).

An interesting analogy has recently been made comparing the Nasserist period of army cadres in 1952, in khaki fatigues busying themselves telling Egyptians about the need to reform the 'rottenness of palace politics' with today's modernising technophiles in trim suits telling Egyptians about the need 'to wait until the economy is liberalised' and the people (*sic*) are democratic *before* beginning any democratic experiments (El Ghobashy, 2005).

Linking urban debate about political reform with developments in the countryside is important. This is because there were promises that tenure reform would promote greater farmer representation and that the new agricultural modernisation would stem rural poverty by driving export-led growth. The outcome has been very different. Higher levels of rural poverty have been evident since the early agricultural reforms began in 1987. Instead of agricultural modernisation driven by tenure reform and higher rental values for owners leading to sustained levels of productivity and farmer security, increased rural debt, displacement and dispossession – especially of female-headed households – have led to a return of indentured labour and the power of the blue *gelabiya* – a revamped landlord class.

Nasser's revolution

Nasser's agrarian reform Law 178 of 1952 was the first large-scale land reform in the Middle East and probably the most influential in the region. The first agrarian reform law was rushed in by the Free Army Officers only one and a half months after seizing power. It was the first of four land reform laws, the others following in 1961, 1963 and 1969 and distributing land and other resources representing 12 per cent of the total cultivated land. It indicated the importance to the revolutionary regime of the need to rid Egypt of what were effectively a rentier privileged class. Although the legislation preserved the sanctity of private property and individual family farms remained the centrepiece for rural development, significant redistribution of land took place and the welfare of poor *fellahin* improved. In the words of the Land Reform Act, the legislation had the intention to 'build Egyptian Society on a new basis by providing free life and dignity to each peasant and by abolishing the wide gap between classes and by removing an important cause of social and political instability' (cited in El-Ghonemy, 1990: 228).

Limited attempts at land reform since 1924 had all been successively opposed by the rural elite of landowners and high-ranked officials. The essentially feudal structures that had been created by the Sultan Mohemad Ali and his heirs between 1805 and 1952 coupled by the influence of land grants and dispossessions imposed by French and British colonial policy, created a strong and robust class of landowners. That class had developed urban industrial and financial interests too failing to have concerns with redressing worsening rural poverty and increasing landlessness.

The social and economic livelihoods of Egypt's *fellahin* had got worse in the years leading to the seizure of power by the Free Officers. 'Statistically Egypt stood still in the 40 years before 1950' (Yapp, 1996: 62); economic growth in the period had been about 1.5 per cent per annum. The average Egyptian was as well off in 1950 as in 1910.

Two sources of rural poverty were extreme inequality in landholdings and insecurity of income-earning opportunity. Table 8.1 indicates that, before the agrarian reform of 1952, about 0.1 per cent of landowners owned 20 per cent of the cultivated area. Some 199 out of a total of 2,000 large landowners owned 7.3 per cent of the agricultural land. This contrasted with about three million *fellahin* who owned less than one feddan. The near-landless represented about 75 per cent of landowners but they only cultivated 13 per cent of the land. Between 1931 and 1950 rental values increased fourfold, access to rural credit was sparse and tightly controlled by two banks; and rural poverty intensified. As one commentator has noted, 'The pre-1952 land based power structure obstructed rural development and stratified the rural society into an upper class minority of rich landlords and cotton merchants and a mass of very low income and poor *fellaheen*' (El-Ghonemy, 1990: 226–227).

Table 8.1 Distribution of land ownership before promulgation of agrarian reform laws

Feddans	Landowners	Holding size	Landowners percentage	Area owned percentage
<5	2,642,000	2,122,000	94.3	35.4
5–	79,000	526,000	2.8	8.8
10–	47,000	638,000	1.7	10.7
20–	22,000	654,000	0.8	10.9
50–	6,000	430,000	0.2	7.2
100–	3,000	437,000	0.1	7.3
200–	2,000	1,177,000	0.1	19.7
Total	2,801,000	5,984,000	100.0	100.0

Source: Adapted from Sallam (1998: 2).

Nasser's reforms gave the state the authority to seize privately held land over 200 feddan, a ceiling reduced to 100 feddan in 1961 – although families could still hold up to 300 feddan and the amount a landlord could rent out was limited to 50 feddan. Exemptions also existed for families with more than two children; to *wagf* (religiously endowed) land, desert land or land owned by industrial or scientific organisations. Landowners (except the royal family who lost 170,000 feddan) received compensation for assets like buildings and irrigation equipment.

There were four dimensions to Nasser's agrarian reforms of 1952 and 1961. Nasser wanted to distribute land to the landless and near-landless, improve rural incomes and increase agricultural production. Table 8.2 indicates that after the 1962 reforms there were 300,000 new landowners in the important category of five feddan and less compared with the situation pre-1952. The reforms also had an important political dimension as they were intended to break any political opposition to the revolution from the *ancien regime*'s 'Pasha' class. Nasser wanted to shift the balance of

Table 8.2 Distribution of land ownership after 1952–1961 agrarian reform (upper level of holding set at 100 feddan)

Feddans	Landowners	Holding size	Landowners percentage	Area owned percentage
<5	2,919,000	3,172,000	94.1	52.1
5–	80,000	516,000	2.6	8.5
10–	65,000	648,000	2.1	10.6
20–	26,000	818,000	0.8	13.5
50–	6,000	430,000	0.2	7.1
100–	5,000	500,000	0.2	8.2
Total	3,101,000	6,084,000	100.0	100.0

Source: Adapted from Sallam (1998: 4).

political power in the countryside away from landowners and if not to the *fellahin* at least to the state so that the military could call upon the support of farmers when it was deemed necessary.

Overall, however, underpinning the agrarian reforms was a desire to improve the efficiency of Egyptian agriculture. Nasser wanted, especially after 1961 and his increased turn to the left, to drain increases in rural surplus away from the countryside to subsidise urbanisation and a strategy of rapid industrialisation (Radwan and Lee, 1986).

Seized land was distributed to agricultural labourers, tenants, and those with holdings of less than five feddan. The recipients on average received 2.4 feddan and had to pay for the land in instalments over a 40-year period. The new owners paid probably less than half the rent they had done before the reforms (King, 1977: 382–383) and almost two million benefited from the reforms. Smallholders also benefited from an increase in land sales as landowners feared sequestration of their estates. The act made it illegal for landowners to evict tenants unless rent was not paid. Crucially too, as Saad has noted, 'tenants were registered in the agricultural co-operatives as holders, the same as landowners who farmed their own land' (2002: 105).

There has long been a contentious debate about just how effective Nasser's land reforms were and who benefited the most from them. Landowners certainly seemed adept at finding ways of maintaining access to landholdings in some form, often by parcelling land to relatives. Exact figures for the numbers that benefited are difficult to ascertain although Table 8.3 indicates official evidence of beneficiary families. For a long time it was also assumed that the biggest impact of the reforms was felt by the largest and the smallest landholders. Those with less than five feddan may have increased this by up to 13 per cent and the land they owned by 74 per cent. The biggest estates of more than 200 feddan disappeared. In 1952 *fellahin* who owned five feddan or less represented 94 per cent of all owners and controlled 35 per cent of the cultivated area. After the first reforms they owned 52 per cent of cultivated acreage. Yet it is also evident

Table 8.3 Beneficiary families of Nasser's agrarian reforms

Year of agrarian reform law	Area, feddans	Number of beneficiary families
1952	388,831	186,009
1961	110,581	56,262
1963	21,850	10,658
1969	32,525	17,399
Awkaf (religious endowed) land	105,322	51,484
Herasa (state custody) land	22,574	11,550
Others	32,525	13,107
Total	714,208	346,469

Source: Sallam (1998: 4).

that middle peasants were significant beneficiaries from Nasser's agrarian reform – those owning 11–50 feddan. The reforms enabled this class that represented 3 per cent of all landowners to own 24 per cent of the cultivated area. This class was able to bolster their position by buying land sold as a result of the 1952 reforms. They also managed to take advantage of the system of agricultural cooperatives that emerged after 1952 (Abdel Fadil, 1975).

Prior to 1952, landlords had dominated agricultural cooperatives but the new reforms revamped and increased their role and activities. The system of coops began to dominate the lives of farmers providing inputs and tractors, supplies of credit and the purchase of crops through marketing agencies. Coops were run by a board dominated by a government-appointed chairman and they became an added dimension to the legal and institutional framework within which farmers were required to operate after 1952.

Tenure relations became a key factor in promoting security for Egyptian farmers. About 60 per cent of total cultivated land was worked by tenants and the rental values were set at seven times the agricultural land tax. A lease was issued, where in most cases none had previously existed. This security of tenure provided a contract for three years unless the tenant decided otherwise. And the new laws gave the tenants rights of inheritance in perpetuity, effectively transforming the reality of land ownership.

Despite these successes, wide disparity remained. There was an *increase* in the numbers of landless labourers as the breakup of estates led to an increase in smallholders that only employed family labour.

While there may be disagreement about the number of beneficiaries and the form that the benefits from Nasser's agrarian reforms took, one general issue seems clear: the reforms reduced rural poverty and promoted agricultural growth (El-Ghonemy, 1993, 1999). Egypt moreover benefited generally from improvements in the opportunities for labour migrancy of its rural workforce nationally and in the region that accompanied increases in the price of crude oil and general improvement in rural welfare (Toth, 1999). The rural poor gained from land redistribution, new tenure relations, improved welfare security and price and crop guarantees. The land reforms and the improved rural incomes for beneficiaries improved living conditions across the countryside as demand for locally produced items like foodstuffs and household goods rose.

Reform, however, did not prevent a decline in agricultural investment. Investment in agriculture across the Arab world slumped in the 1970s and 1980s as regimes preferred to import food and consumer goods rather than produce them nationally. Gross investment in agriculture between 1980–1992 fell in Egypt from 31 per cent to 23 per cent. The 1970s were crucial in rolling back Nasser's legacy, accelerated by the humiliation of defeat against Israel in the 1967 war. The counter-revolution began with

Anwar Sadat, who sought to reverse the gains of the smallholders and tenants. Despite the intense rhetoric of support for Egypt's rural poor, it is more accurate to describe the series of agrarian reform legislation measures as being only partial and fragmentary in the onslaught against the identified excesses of the large landholders. By 1980, for example, only 13.9 per cent of the total cultivated land was redistributed to 9.6 per cent of total agricultural households. The partial character of the reforms did not entirely break the stranglehold on land and farmers that large landowners and financiers had in Egypt's countryside. The provision of compensation to the dispossessed, the maintenance of private property, the differential limits on landholding size at different times as previous limits were frustrated, and the continued disparity and inequality in landholdings, especially those with less than five feddan, failed to irreversibly transform the character of power and politics in Egypt. That failure ensured the continued politicisation of land and added to the myth of land as being at the core of Egyptian culture and the president, like the perception of the Pharoah in history, as having responsibility for the country's citizens (Frankfort, 1948). Although the imperfect agrarian reform that Nasser had promoted excluded two-thirds of tenants and most landless wage labourers, these groups did benefit from the stability in Egypt's countryside that accompanied legal protections and lower rents – that changed in 1992.

Counter-revolution

Agricultural reform in Egypt pre-dated economic adjustment in 1991 and culminated in Law 96 of 1992. While there seems to be little explicit requirement from the IFIs that Egypt should reform its land tenure and raise rental values, it is clear that external pressure, including neoliberal economic hegemony, gave the green light for Mubarak to do what had been mooted many times since 1970. Market relaxation, removal of price controls and cropping targets, together with gradual increases in rents, led to Law 96 of 1992 providing for the hitherto unthinkable: the removal of rights of inheritance in perpetuity, the introduction of annual contracts (although contracts of any duration are rarely issued) all underpinned by the rhetoric of market reform for land rent.

Market reform

Egypt's agricultural crises characterised in 1991 by academic commentators and IFIs alike had been a long time in the making. The 'boom' years of oil-led growth, of Sadat's economic opening or *infitah* were also years when the state neglected agriculture. Oil-led growth in the 1970s meant an under-development of agriculture or, in short, and perhaps a little crudely, 'dutch disease' – an overvalued exchange rate driven by increases in rent accruing to the state and its political and military class. In Egypt, the government's relative ease of access to rents from oil sales, migrant remittances and transits through the Suez Canal led the state to neglect agriculture.

Agriculture in Egypt accounts for about 17 per cent of GDP (industry 34 per cent, services 49 per cent), 36 per cent of overall employment and 22 per cent of commodity exports. More than half of Egypt's population of in excess of 70 million live in the countryside. Farming is limited to about 4 per cent of the total land area with 90 per cent of farming centred in the Nile delta, the banks of the Nile and in Lower Egypt along the Mediterranean. This limited area of farming has recently been expanded by land reclamation in desert areas and along the northern coast. A doubling of Egypt's cultivable land is projected by the development of Toshka in the western Desert at a cost of up to US$100 billion, some provided by private Gulf and Saudi entrepreneurs (Mitchell, 2002). By the end of the 1980s Egypt imported more than half of the country's food consumption and food imports accounted for 25 per cent of all imports. Between 1981 and 1992 the average rate of real growth in agriculture was about 2 per cent compared with GoE targets of 5 per cent.

International agencies, especially USAID (United States Agency for International Development), as well as academic commentators put Egypt's agricultural underachievement down to the legacy of the Nasserist state. Public sector control of pricing, marketing and state ownership of major agricultural industries, were seen as undermining the greater efficiency of the market. By the early 1980s the GoE, with USAID, initiated a reform programme that had at its core the importance of liberalising markets and input provision and the promotion of high-value, low-nutritious food, and flowers, to Europe (World Bank, 1992; USAID, 1998; USAID and GoE, 1995; USAID, 2000; Richards, 1993).

The economic reforms of market relaxation were driven by the zealous, pro-business, long-standing, now erstwhile, Minister of Agriculture, Deputy Prime Minister and General Secretary of the ruling National Democratic Party, Yusif Wali. A large landlord, Wali was stripped of his official positions in 2004 after becoming mired in accusations of corruption.

The characterisation of Egypt's agricultural crisis as caused by state monopoly is replicated in IFI neoliberal explanations for low productivity across the Middle East and elsewhere in Africa. An interesting phenomenon, however, is that in Egypt there is a long history of USAID involvement associated with reform and its continued underachievement. Since the mid-1980s USAID has provided more than US$1.26 billion for the development and reform of the agricultural sector. Yet the advances in the areas concerned have been slow. USAID focused on persistent inappropriate pricing policies, bureaucratic governance and decision-making structures, technological innovation and improved use of land and water. As shown in the reports and publications of the World Bank and FAO,

USAID advisors have consistently pushed for the GoE to liberalise markets. For USAID:

> Freeing prices will encourage farmers, buyers and processors of agricultural commodities to invest in productivity enhancing capital and technological improvements, and over time should shift the sector toward the production of commodities for which Egypt has a comparative advantage. Increases in income in the agricultural sector will provide a significant and broad-based contribution to the enhancement of Egypt's long term prosperity.
>
> (USAID, 1992: 15)

The influence of USAID on GoE agricultural reform strategy cannot be overemphasised. And such emphasis does not reduce the significance of the Mubarak regime's go ahead, accelerating a return to private land ownership and the political class that has benefited from it. It is instead to recognise that the many years of USAID influence, its financial support, and since 2000, link with at least five GoE ministries, reflects a pervasive influence of agenda setting as well as policy implementation. Since the mid-1990s, following the 1991 structural adjustment package (Fritchak and Atiyas, 1996; Bromley and Bush, 1995; Abdel-Khalek, 2001), USAID has stressed the importance of putting in place a US farm-type model of extensive capital intensive agriculture driven by market liberalisation, export-led growth and tenure reform. The withdrawal of state intervention has been key to that strategy, although at different moments the GoE has been unable and reluctant to comply with that aspect.

The successes of the agricultural reform programmes have been trumpeted long and hard (Nassar, 1993; Fletcher, 1996). The reported GoE improvements in the sector include dramatic reductions in government agricultural subsidies and changes in cropping patterns, productivity and improved farm-gate prices. Egypt's cultivated area increased from 6.2 million feddans in 1981 to 7.6 million feddans in 1993. In the same period there were productivity increases in the main food crops of wheat, maize and rice (FAO, 2000). Reformers hail the shifts in pricing policy of Egypt's 23 major crops between 1980 and 1990, an increase in farmer incomes – although exactly which group of farmers is not identified – and the doubling of wheat production between 1986 and 1992 (Faris and Khan, 1993).

I have dealt elsewhere with the critique of the IFI and GoE strategy of agricultural market reform (Bush, 1999; see also Mitchell, 1998, 1999). It is nevertheless important to note here that there are significant areas where the reforms of agriculture have been less successful than the protagonists assert. This critique is important because it gainsays the rationale for the introduction of Law 96 of 1992 and the subsequent impoverishment of many of Egypt's tenants that has accompanied tenure reforms.

Underneath the rhetoric of reform success lie several caveats. They are important as a context for understanding the ways in which the liveli-hoods of tenants have dramatically declined since 1992. And, despite the volume of assistance, USAID admits that, while production increases seemed evident in the mid-1980s, production has slowed since 1990. But instead of concluding from this that the policies are at best inappropriate or at worst have further undermined the sector, USAID argues that 'con-tinued USAID support for the sector is essential' (USAID, 2000).

Market failure

There are four major clusters of concern when exploring whether Egypt's agricultural reforms have had a positive effect. The first shortcoming is that the evidence used by reformers is questionable as regards to its accu-racy. Reformers use evidence to support reform success that refers back to productivity growth in the 1980s (Faris and Khan, 1993; Fletcher, 1996). While the capacity of the Ministry of Agriculture and Land Reclamation (MALR) has improved, it is still very much dependent upon 'guestimates' of actual production and cropping patterns. The emphasis placed by MALR and USAID on early productivity increases is notable. They stress production improvements as prices for agricultural products improved from 1986 to 1992. Yet it is uncertain that those recorded productivity improvements were the result of market reforms. Mitchell (1998) has noted that the farmers were just very good at hiding from state officials what they were producing during the years of state controls. Since 1990 the rate of agricultural growth has been less than between 1980 and 1987 (an exceptional year it seems was 1996/1997 when growth was recorded at 4.3 per cent). USAID notes that agricultural production peaked in the early 1990s, but has continued to be less than was expected following lib-eralisation of prices, inputs and marketing, and we might add, tenure reform (USAID, 1998; World Bank, 2000).

The second major shortcoming of the recent policies for agricultural modernisation is that Egypt is unable to benefit from the export-oriented strategy consistently stressed by the policy makers. The simple fact is that most agricultural imports in Egypt have a low elasticity of demand, like wheat, edible oils and sugar – the value of wheat imports alone increased from US$94 million to US$215 million 2002/2003 to 2003/2004 (Central Bank of Egypt, n.d.: 186). Yet most of Egypt's export commodities are renowned for high elasticity – rice, vegetables and cotton. The value of cotton yarn fell by over 3 per cent from 2002/2003–2003/2004 and rice fell by 8 per cent for the same period (Central Bank of Egypt, n.d.: 184). It seems disingenuous that Egypt will, in the words of one official, become 'another Mexico' (quoted by Sami, 2000) in its drive to promote horticul-tural export-driven growth. This major plank of USAID's programme of Agricultural Technology Utilisation and Transfer has encouraged the pro-duction and export of strawberries for European out-of-season dinner

Table 8.4 Changes in cropping pattern between 1995 and 2003 (area in feddans)

Change (in feddans)	1995	2003	Crop
−5,636	2,511,814	2,506,178	Wheat
107,614	1,400,020	1,507,634	Summer rice
162	701	863	Nili rice
−175,117	710,207	535,090	Seed cotton
−1,247	2,041	794	Composite fibres nili
−6,436	37,400	30,964	Fibrous flax composite
−6,436	37,400	30,964	Composite flax seed
−50,664	623,580	572,916	Short clover
36,795	18,630	55,425	Alfalfa
−22,153	152,830	130,677	Clover
38,249	351,518	389,767	Summer sorghum
−2,460	10,706	8,246	Nili sorghum
−93,580	1,751,379	1,657,799	Summer maize
−746	328,112	327,366	Nili maize
−331,139	447,780	116,641	Barley
−42,104	294,662	252,558	Dry beans
4,158	25,018	29,176	Green beans
−42,276	62,012	19,736	Soya beans
20,737	306,478	327,215	Sugarcane
81,261	50,062	131,323	Sugar beet
41,114	106,097	147,211	Summer peanut
−6,794	10,945	4,151	Lentil
−10,015	23,219	13,204	Dry fenugreek
836	14,582	15,418	Dry chickpeas

Source: Crop production tables of the Government of Egypt, available from the author.

tables but this fruit and the export of vegetables do not seem to offer Egypt an escape route from its persistent agricultural underachievement. In promoting Egypt's comparative advantage as a 'natural greenhouse', little regard seems to have been given to factors such as its regional competitors; its poor and bureaucratic port and transport systems; and the vulnerability to global markets while promoting export of high-value, low-nutritious foodstuffs. Export revenue to compensate for low staple food production does not seem a useful way forward for Egyptian agriculture.

The third major shortcoming is that agricultural reform and structural adjustment since 1991 have had a disastrous impact on employment. Job losses in agriculture for 1990/1995 alone numbered at least 700,000 (Fergany, 2002). Reform was premised upon high levels of national economic growth to create urban jobs to absorb displaced rural labour, with these jobs to be created by the private sector: there is little evidence of either. Linked to this extraordinary growth in unemployment has been a dramatic, catastrophic escalation in rural poverty.

Fergany (2002) has argued that the most used poverty line measure, the cost of a minimum basket of commodities, underestimates the extent of poverty in Egypt and elsewhere in the Middle East. Using that measure, poverty in Egypt doubled between 1990 and 1996 to 44 per cent – about 30 million people. Using the crude US$1 a day measure, he demonstrated that from the 1991 Egyptian official Household Income and Expenditure Survey (HIES) survey, 88 per cent of the population would be considered poor – levels of 94 per cent in the countryside and 80 per cent in the towns. He actually estimates that a majority of the population lived on less than half the measure of US$1 a day. Using the 1995 survey in constant 1990 prices, he estimated that 90 per cent of Egyptians were poor with rural poverty pervasive with a greater relative rise in urban poverty (Fergany, 2002: 213–214, 1995). These figures are at odds with those presented by the Government of Egypt's statistical office, CAPMAS and FAO that consistently seem to downplay the country's level of poverty (FAO, 2003).

Law 96 of 1992 – land to the 'owners'

The law and its context

An understanding of the broader economic and reform context helps explain why and how the reform of land tenure emerged on the statute books in 1992. Law 96 of 1992 introduced a counter-revolution into Egypt's agricultural sector. It extended the power and confidence of landowners, reiterating the totem of the centrality of neoliberal orthodoxy, market reform, sanctity of private property and price-driven incentive structures to shift the agricultural production function in the strategy to raise productivity. In passing the law, the GoE managed a most careful sleight of hand: they managed to mask the naked return of power, money and authority to landowners while insisting no change had been made to the Nasserist revolutionary inheritance that secured tenant rights.[4] President Mubarak presented himself as the defender of Egypt's tenants and most tenants simply did not believe that he would allow the legislation to dispossess them. The GoE deceit is captured well by the prime minister of the time, Atef Sidki, as he closed the parliamentary debate that confirmed the new law:

> I hope that some people would not think that the purpose of this law is to give the landlords a sword to hit the tenants' necks with, for the law has come to achieve balance and justice between the two parties. We should not forget that we are a compassionate and supportive society, that it is inconceivable that an owner would expel a tenant just because a law was issued.
>
> (*Al Ahram*, 25 June 1992, cited in Saad, 2002: 104)

Law 96 revoked Nasser's Agrarian Reform Law no. 178 of 1952 that gave tenants rights of security of tenure and legal rights of tenancy. After the five-year transition period, on 1 October 1997, all landowners could retake their land and charge tenants market-based rent. The explanation for the tenancy reform was that it sought to redress an imbalance that had emerged since the mid-1960s between rental values and market rates for land. The land act was therefore intended to introduce a new, market-based regulation of owner–tenant relations and to allow owners to realise their property ownership rights. Absentee landowners in particular had been unable to realise the value of their property.

Nasser's reforms had given permanent contracts to Egypt's tenants who in 1992 numbered about one million and who therefore probably accounted for no less than five million Egyptians. The tenants farmed between 25 and 30 per cent of the cultivated area. These figures are only approximations, however, as the new law was passed without any accurate tenancy maps indicating landholdings or evidence of who owned what land and where it was located. The Shura Council, for example, Egypt's upper house estimated that there were about 2.5 million tenants. Probably as many as 90 per cent of Egypt's one million tenants rented in five feddans or less. Justification for the new act took three different and inter-related forms. The first was the clear demand from landowners that rents were much less than they would be if the market was allowed to determine them. Second, the political context within which the legislation was promoted built upon Sadat's inheritance that had accelerated de-Nasserisation. This was namely that the epoch of revolutionary change was replaced by contemporary realities of constitutional legitimacy. Finally, the promotion of the reforms was accomplished with a programme to defame the character and lifestyle of Egypt's peasants. The stereotyping of peasants by urban-biased (and government-controlled) media helped reinforce the way the ruling elites legitimated their authority. This is captured by an article in *El-Gumhurriyya* on Farmers Day September 1988. The article was entitled 'The *fellah*: is he the oppressor or the oppressed?'

> [In the village] there are cafes everywhere and secret video clubs that show forbidden films which *fellah* youths watch until dawn. They thus wake up the day after unable to work and produce. I think there is a link between agrarian reform law and these negative phenomena. For the low rents make the tenant lazy and he does not exert any effort to increase his production, since the very least of produce will suffice to pay the rent and there will still be a reasonable amount that he spends on his own enjoyment [*mezag*]. And no doubt if the *fellah* knew that he has to pay a reasonable rent for the land he will certainly exert an effort to increase his production, and no doubt this increase will be beneficial for society as a whole.
>
> (*El-Gumhuriyya*, 2 September 1988, cited in Saad, 2002: 109;
> see also Saad, 1999, 2000)

Implementation and its outcomes

Law 96 was fully implemented in October 1997 after a five-year transitional period. Until 1992 rents for tenants were fixed at seven times the land tax, revised every ten years and were on average E£20 per feddan. After 1997 rents in most locations rose to and often exceeded 22 times the land tax. Rents in some cases increased to E£1,200–1,800 per feddan, depending on location and productivity, and in some cases jumped as far as E£2,400 from E£240. Tenancies became annual tenancies but seldom involved an actual contract held by tenants. Landowners became legally able to dispose of land as they saw fit, without notifying tenants who might have been farming a piece of land for 40 years. Those who renewed contracts were often threatened with expulsion if they became troublesome. And despite the five-year transition many farmers simply did not think the legislation would be enacted. Farmers lost crops in the ground especially in Upper Egypt where the major crop, sugar, matures for 12 months.

At the time of the legislation it was feared that there would be a massive opposition to the act – but this did not emerge. What did take place, however, was an often piecemeal, spontaneous and uncoordinated opposition that involved the security forces using considerable violence to quell any hint of protest about landlords' resumption of their property rights. While data are sometimes difficult to confirm, an indication of the scale of violence used by security forces and also the level of violence promoted by conflicts between owners and tenants, is given by a centre, based in Cairo, that focuses on human rights issues of farmers. The Land Centre for Human Rights (LCHR) calculated, from unprecedented access to wide areas of Egypt that between January 1998 and December 2000 there were a total of 119 deaths, 846 injuries and 1,409 arrests related to Law 96 and related land conflicts (LCHR, 2002: 127).

Although organised opposition seems to have been uncommon, the implementation of the act led to an escalation of rural violence and confirmed the view that such violence was systemic. The act gave landowners a green light to retake land and to shift tenancies in the way that they thought suitable to meet their perceived legitimate rights. For the IFIs, notably USAID and FAO, Law 96 was 'consistent with the privatisation and economic liberalisation policies of the GoE. . . . [providing] the basis for the development of land market' (USAID, 1997: 1). FAO noted that the act would provide for greater 'equity, security and efficiency in the holding and utilising of agricultural land (FAO, 1999: 4).

The IFIs may not have driven the need for a reform of tenure but they certainly saw the efficacy in the policy and quickly supported the GoE in its actions. The support extended to what can only properly be seen as a cover-up of rural violence. Belatedly, the GoE recognised the need to introduce the idea of reconciliation committees to smooth over disagreements between landlords and tenants regarding rents, dispossession of

land and dwellings on the land. USAID noted the absence of rural conflict, implying that this was due to local officials' actions in reconciliation
committees, which were used to foster consensus and agreement about
changes in landholdings after October 1997. In contrast the Land Centre
for Human Rights argued repeatedly that rural relations were far from
cordial. Where the committees were established, and this was very seldom,
they were viewed by tenants as arenas in which local powerholder's
exacted retribution for years of low rent. The proceedings were usually,
moreover, held in the presence of police and security services, mobilised
by landowners to enforce the law. That enforcement of the law was often
at the barrel of a gun, late at night and after farmers had been tortured,
wounded and imprisoned without *habeas corpus* (LCHR, 2002).

The reform of tenure gave USAID a chance to establish a market in land.
The ignorance of IFIs, even of those whose representatives had been 'on
the ground' for many years ensured that land tenure reform was approved
at any cost. Law 96 provided the opportunity to create a land market, yet it
was assumed that none had previously existed. Before the act a seller could
only agree a sale if the tenant had approved it and received a third or half
of the sale price. Security of tenure also ensured that, if the tenant had not
approved the sale, he/she could continue to farm part of the land even
after its sale. After the five-year transition period a landlord could dispose of
the land in whichever way they wanted. Yet this revamped landlord power
did not create a land market and neither did it lead to land consolidation as
the IFI representatives imagined it would. Land fragmentation has for a
long time been seen to undermine agricultural productivity in Egypt and
Law 96 was thought to remove the obstacle to consolidation. Although
some landlords did sell land after October 1997, making a financial killing
in the process, land sales did not dramatically increase. Moreover, family
consolidation within landlord families did not take place. Fragmentation of
holdings continued where siblings in landowner households saw an
opportunity to access land where none had existed before. Yet where large
landowners clawed land back from experienced tenants, new holders often
lacked farming knowledge. Landowner relatives who had often never previously farmed, jeopardised, with their inexperience, agricultural productivity
and decades of tenant investment in the soil.

The GoE and USAID might lament the slow pace of a land market and
land sales, asserting that it is still difficult to prove ownership and thus they
call for a programme of land registration. Much land remains registered in
the names of the first cadastre in the early twentieth century. Landowners
are often unable to prove ownership with a deed but instead do so by
showing a tenancy agreement. USAID argues, therefore, that a programme
of up-to-date registration will smooth the development of a land market
(MALR and USAID, 1999: 9). Underpinning this concern with proof of
land ownership is the view that it will facilitate security of tenure, legal
rights and collateral for borrowing that can be used to invest in land devel-

opment. It might be argued in fact, that the concern with this particular aspect of policy confirms USAID's role of promoting a regulatory frame-work to secure the interests of private capital and land alienation.

It is without question the case that land registration in Egypt is a bureaucratic and expensive process. Yet this does not mean that no land market existed before 1996. Neither does it mean that the introduction of a resource-costly and conflict-high registration process would free up land through easier processes of alienation and raise (rich) farmer incentives. USAID's preoccupation with land registration and alienation lags behind IFI policy suggestions elsewhere, namely for southern Africa. In many con-texts outside Egypt IFIs have argued the need to promote flexibility and local understanding of tenure structures to help promote local agricul-tural production systems (Adams, 2000). In short, USAID in Egypt, and FAO and the World Bank seem to set to one side the importance of tenure reform, land alienation and security of rights for investors while sidestepping the more important issues of security of *access* to land, land-lessness and the opportunity for the rural poor to find employment. The IFI's have also in Egypt sidestepped the importance of developing rural infrastructure and availability and high production costs that can only be met by a minority of farmers.

Recent evidence would indicate that there has indeed been a concen-tration in land holdings towards the category of 'fully owned' compared with 'fully cash paid' tenancies. Table 8.5 indicates that the increase in year 2000 of the fully owned category compared with 1990 was a full 20 per cent of holders representing an increase of 18.2 per cent of the total landholding area. Table 8.5 also indicates a significant reduction in the number of tenancies where farmers have a myriad of different forms of access to land like sharecropping.

Evidence from Tables 8.5 and 8.6 must be encouraging for Egyptian policy makers. If the evidence is accurate, it indicates in broad terms a reduction in the number of different holding categories and an increase in the category of land being fully owned. Table 8.6 also shows how the concentration since 1990 confirms an increase in the well-being in formal terms of those farmers with 5–10 feddan (large farmers in a context where 74 per cent of holders have less than five feddan). The table also indicates an increase in the absolute and relative numbers of landless and a skewing of landholdings towards larger landowners. Less than 0.9 per cent of holders in 2000 held 24.85 per cent of the land while 74 per cent held 47 per cent.

A consequence of the formulation of Egypt's agricultural crisis being one of land ownership rather than access, security of property rights for owners rather than security of rights for tenants and employment opportunities for landless and near-landless is that Law 96 has accelerated rural social differentiation, marginalising especially female-headed house-holds and promoted a return to indentured child and adult labour.

Table 8.5 Legal status of land tenure in 1990 compared with 2000

Tenure category	1990				2000			
	Number of holders	Percentage	Area in feddan	Percentage	Number of holders	Percentage	Area in feddan	Percentage
Fully owned	1,968,371	67.6	5,089,851	64.8	3,256,384	87.6	7,325,493	82.0
Fully cash paid rental	387,160	13.3	177,069	2.3	189,355	5.1	313,800	3.5
Shareholding, non-cash rental	44,473	1.5	103,660	1.3	33,763	0.9	66,925	0.7
Invested fully in other ways*	37,648	1.3	488,198	6.2	46,409	1.2	574,712	6.4
Shareholding including ownership, cash rental,and other forms**	472,627	16.2	1,490,392	19.0	192,080	5.2	647,605	7.3
Total	2,910,279	100.0	7,849,173	100.0	3,717,991	100	8,928,535	100.0

Source: Ministry of Agriculture, 1990 and 2000.

Notes
* Includes those who may own land or who have inherited it; renting in land; and non cash rental.
** Includes those with a single form of tenure whatever that may be including private sector investors.

Table 8.6 Individual landholders in 1989/1990 compared with 1999/2000

Size of landholding feddans	1989/1990				1999/2000			
	Number of holders	Percentage of total	Landholding	Percentage of total	Number of holders	Percentage of total	Landholding	Percentage of total
Landless	562,695	16.2	–	–	821,188	18.09	–	–
<1	1,050,156	30.25	508,144	6.47	1,615,267	35.59	722,310	8.08
<5	2,615,944	75.3	3,837,634	48.89	3,359,445	74.04	4,215,970	47.21
5–10	198,758	5.7	234,225	2.98	234,225	5.16	1,441,642	16.14
10–20	20,698	0.59	793,706	10.11	81,326	1.79	1,049,554	11.75
21–50	27,050	0.77	770,402	9.81	33,326	0.73	923,186	10.33
51–100	4,373	0.12	287,585	3.66	5,528	0.12	357,119	3.99
>100	1,223	0.03	909,803	11.59	2,281	0.05	941,056	10.53
Total	3,470,813	–	7,849,173	–	4,537,319	–	8,928,535	–

Source: Ministry of Agriculture, 1990 and 2000.

Poverty and violence in the countryside

There were two main clusters of impact relating to the imposition of Law 96 of 1992. One was the increase in level of impoverishment of tenants and the other was the confirmation of a systematisation of violence both direct and indirect. Both of these impacts have transformed rural livelihoods.

Impoverishing the farmers

Egyptian agriculture has for a long time been viewed as a sector of the economy that can function without support for poor farmers. Smallholders have simply been neglected in the strategies of the policy makers. Egypt's rural poor have got poorer since economic reform began in the sector in 1987 and that poverty has been a function of the increased wealth and political power of a landlord class that received an extra fillip with Law 96 of 1992.

I am using the term poverty to refer to 'a deprivation of human capability of essential opportunities and choices needed for the well being of an individual, household or community' (UNDP, 2002: 94). And while common international criteria for poverty, like lack of income and purchasing power parity of local currencies, standardised in relation to the US dollar, remain important guides, they seldom provide anything more than a glimpse at crude measures of poverty (Bush, 2004). These are both measures used extensively in discussions of poverty in Egypt. They usually lead commentators to discuss the need to incorporate the poor into the local and national economies more efficiently. GoE policy and that of the IFI's can be summarised as a strategy to incorporate into 'the market' rural dwellers to combat their poverty, raise incomes and reduce inequality – although frankly the extent of inequality is seldom on any policy maker's agenda. An alternative view, however, is to argue that poverty is created precisely in the *type* of incorporation of Egypt's small farmers rather than their non-incorporation. Adverse incorporation has, among other things, led to the emergence of hugely exploitative labour regimes. In some cases it has led to the extension of child indentured labour as foremen visiting villages round up the young to work in neighbouring farms for large landowners. A full account of poverty thus requires more than a simple summation of farmer and tenant access to assets, land and livestock. Other aspects need to be factored into an assessment of what is understood by poverty, including social and individual rights, knowledge and levels of education and the extent to which households can participate in political processes. Indeed, one major area neglected when assessing poverty in Egypt, and certainly in understanding its relation to landholdings, is that little is said about the processes and dynamics of political and economic power that *generate* poverty and inequality skewing income distribution towards the rich. We need to try and develop a way of understanding how changes in landholdings impact on rural livelihoods and wealth to create and reproduce poverty. The GoE and IFIs have singularly neglected this in their collusion to promote neoliberal panaceas to perceived agricultural underachievement and to meet GoE concerns of rewarding the powerful with greater economic assets.

The absence of research or assessments of the kind necessary to understand the impact of Law 96 of 1992 is lamentable in a country that rhetorically prides itself upon its agricultural heritage and future. A failure to understand rural livelihoods in general and strategies for livelihoods coping with economic crisis are the more galling as the levels of poverty already noted, even accepting the conservative GoE estimates, suggest a major crisis of rural production and social reproduction. In the cases of two villages that I examined in the Delta, for instance (Bush, 2002c), it was clear that tenants displaced following large rent increases were seldom re-employed as labourers on the lands that they had been forced to vacate or even in many cases locally at all. Higher rents meant that new tenants had less cash to hire labour. If land was farmed by owners then it was not uncommon for them to use family labour or hire labour from neighbouring villages. Landowners seemed to be fearful that local villagers would effectively become de facto owners if rehired.

The slide into poverty seems to have been worse for female-headed households, with landowners reluctant to renew tenancies for these households. This was the case even where women had proven successful farmers following the loss of their husbands and had managed to access sufficient funds to pay higher rents. It is thus difficult to identify the reasons why landowners were so reluctant to renew contracts with women farmers who had a successful track record and paid their rents. It is also difficult to establish the numbers of women who lost tenancies although evidence from village studies in the Delta recognised this as an obvious outcome of the law, with the women suffering rapid impoverishment as a result. In one case a 55-year-old woman with four sons in a Delta village could not afford the post-1997 rent. Before 1992 rent for the 12 qirats that she farmed was E£10. This went up to E£30 after 1992 rent and E£100 after 1997. Although she managed to negotiate the rent down to E£80, she could not afford to pay it. She had no means to pay the rent from the returns of her farming, even if she only farmed cash crops; and her sons had already begun waged work on reclaimed lands to improve the household's cash income.

The woman's slide into poverty began quickly after 1997 and the loss of land. Her survival strategy was to begin, for the first time in her life, work as an agricultural labourer picking vegetables but this paid poorly and was literally backbreaking labour for a woman of her age who was already working longer and harder than ever before in her adult life. She began to try and sell small quantities of vegetables from outside her house.

Trying to survive by reducing her food consumption, she ate less meat and more carbohydrates and spent longer in the *souk* trying to find foodstuffs at prices she could afford. She began to sell assets, including her only live-stock, a cow that she had used for milk; she borrowed wherever possible from her relatives; and worked longer hours with a feeling of less auto-nomy and greater insecurity than she had ever previously experienced. Her biggest challenge, however, was to try to keep her youngest child in school and she very much regretted the increased prevalence of labour-hiring foremen who recruited children to work in neighbouring fields. This labour hire took on the form of indentured labour as parents accessed cash set against the labour time of their children.

Additional findings from a series of studies indicate that smallholder and tenant households experienced an increase in rural debt and an inability to generate sufficient collateral funding to secure revised tenancy agreements. Many at the time of full implementation of the act in 1997 lost crops in the ground as landowners dispossessed farmers. Before the land tenancy legislation there seemed to be a consensus among many village respondents that the most pressing perceived difficulties of farmer households focused around access to credit, transport, health and educa-tion facilities. During the transition period of 1992–1997 concern was sin-gularly focused around fear of losing land, the uncertainty that President Mubarak would countenance such legislation, many thinking that he would become their saviour at the last hour, and increased debt. After the land act respondents became concerned with how to cope without access to land and fulfil what they saw as basic needs: access to food, education and health at a time when their income base had been severed. The inter-esting issue here is that, although tenant households are not the poorest in rural Egypt, as the period since 1997 extends it is likely that, if new sources of income are not accessed, the inevitable decline in stocks of income that families may have had during previous tenancies will expire along with other livestock and asset sales.[5] An obvious consequence of the challenge to households to replenish assets and access to other livelihoods is to be further ratcheted down into poverty and to increase feelings of powerlessness (see Table 8.7).

For the tenants who were able to *renew* contracts, it seems that their cropping calculations have led them to increase cash crops of vegetables and rice and to move away from berseem and cotton. But this should not necessarily mean that more will be available for the market and therefore be seen as a positive result of the economic reforms. Farmers also increase their own household consumption to reduce the burden of purchase. Cotton and berseem production, it seems, have either become irrelevant for farmers who no longer own cattle or too expensive to cultivate for resource-poor peasants. Only larger landowners, those with more than five feddan, are now seen to have the necessary resources of labour and cash to cultivate cotton. Shifts in cropping patterns were shaped more and

Table 8.7 Farmer survival and livelihood strategies in response to Law 96 of 1992

Strategies for increasing resources	Strategies for increasing resource efficiency
Longer working day	Change in diets
More women in the labour force	Fewer visits to health centre and reduction in number of children in school
Increased petty commodity production	
Asset sales	Change in overall consumption patterns and reduced cultural association and travel
Migration	
Theft	Increased pressure on women's time

more by short-term considerations of access to land and the new insecurity of tenancy that has become dependent, as one respondent noted, 'on the mood of the owner'.

The impact of the law has been felt in other, more intangible ways too. For instance, small farmers have suffered insecurity and uncertainty so that it is more and more disingenuous for policy makers to view the way that farmers make decisions as primarily shaped by market considerations. Farmer choices have been more dominated by a world of tenancy struggles rather than the demands of everyday life. The insecurity generated by the new law was considerable. The flexibility given to landowners by the law, their ability to move tenants during contract periods, led to a perception by tenants that they should no longer make soil enrichment calculations that exceeded a calendar year.

Endemic rural violence

A linked impact of the law was the further institutionalisation of rural violence. This has been documented extensively (LCHR, 1999a, 1999b, 2000, 2002; Ismail, 1998). In both the build-up to the full implementation of the act in 1997 and subsequently, a wide range of abuses of tenants' human rights, including wrongful imprisonment, arrest and torture, took place. These abuses exacerbated smallholder and tenant mistrust of government and local administrators. The mistrust extended to recognition among some tenants that, given the *fait accompli* with which they were presented with Law 96 and the insurmountable obstacles to preventing its implementation, because many agricultural areas especially in the Delta had been overrun with security forces, opposition to the act had necessarily been non-confrontational. In the teeth of naked aggression from the police, other security forces and hired thugs, the consequences of openly resisting dispossession or challenging the authority of the landowner were dire. When tenants refused to comply and move from the land, often with no compensation for the loss of crops still in the fields and eviction from their dwellings, security officials seized farmers, bullied them and tortured them in the village or in neighbouring police stations (LCHR, 1999b).

There were, nevertheless, incidents of organised opposition to the tenancy reform; and many rallies promoted by the leftist political party, Tagamu', especially in Dakhalia and Cairo attracted large numbers of *fellahin*. In April 1997 about 7,000 farmers took part in a rally in the capital city that also coincided with the anniversary of the infamous assassination of peasant activist Saleh Hussein on 30 April 1966 in the village of Kamsheesh. The murder had been organised by a large landowning family in the village who objected to Hussein's rallying cry to dispossess the land-lords and that criminal act, motivated by political conflict and challenges to the landowning class, continues to have resonance in the contemporary period. The largest collective opposition to the law, however, took the form of the attempt by opponents to submit a petition opposing the legis-lation. Yet the Minister of Agriculture refused to accept the petition of 350,000 names (collected over eight months) asserting that opposition to the act could not be so strong. We know too that a consequence of the act was the politicisation of land in the countryside. This was revealed by the mushrooming of incidents relating to land boundaries, irrigation and rights of access.

Many of the disputes were promoted by large landowners. They used the premise of the legislation and the confusion surrounding its detail and implementation, and the lack of knowledge about it among large sec-tions of the *fellahin*, to reclaim land that was not covered. They moreover colluded with security forces to dispossess tenants at the barrel of a gun. Agrarian reform land and agricultural lands from the *Awqaf* (the authority that manages religiously endowed land) were excluded from the 1992 act. Yet landowners took the opportunity to contest established legal provi-sions even though these lands were explicitly excluded from the 1992 leg-islation. Additionally, it seems that local administrative authorities used the expediency of implementation of the act and subsequent confusion to seize land that was important for expanding city boundaries (LCHR, 1999b: 5).

The violent incidents created by the implementation of Law 96 were seldom dealt with openly by the GoE. And, if referred to, they were explained as a consequence of the activities of Islamic extremists. For while the *fatwa* committee of Al-Azhar headed by the Grand Sheikh con-firmed that it was indeed an Islamic act to confirm the security of property rights upon the legal owners, the radical Islamic group Gamaa el Islamia disagreed. It opposed any government act that would further impoverish Egypt's poor farmers.

While there has been some critical understanding of the way in which political opposition during Mubarak's authoritarian rule has been prob-lematised (Bayat, 2002), there has only recently been an attempt to explore dimensions of rural opposition. Tingay (2004) has developed an interesting and provocative interpretation of the consequences of the act as extending the idea of power and politics in Egypt's countryside. She has argued that the reform of tenancy has dramatically promoted agrarian transformation and radically affected forms of village coexistence. Tingay (2004) has argued that village norms and values of rights and duties, *inter alia*, good neighbourliness, care of the land, financial obligation, consideration for neighbours has been rendered problematic by the 1992 legislation. Careful not to stray into a romanticised view of harmonious rural coexistence, she has also been very clear on how structures of ownership and control of land impacted on rural livelihoods. Detailing a case study in the Delta Governorate of Dakahlia, Tingay has explored many types of conflict over land that emerged after 1992. Her work supports other cases in the Delta and Upper Egypt (Bush, 1999; Abdel Aal, 2003).

Tingay has argued that farmers have responded in particular ways to the changes in tenancy since tenants were dispossessed or threatened with dispossession after 1997. She believed that enormous hikes in rental values led villagers to be verbally critical of landowners who were identified as upsetting village norms of reciprocity, rights and duties. These obligations were universal but it was especially incumbent upon villagers who were relatively wealthy to safeguard these customs, rights and duties. Village conflicts have often taken the form of struggles over land and water but violent opposition, as noted and confirmed by Tingay, was never a realistic option for smallholders who were relatively powerless in relation to landlords. She has also argued that the complex structure of landholdings where farmers may simultaneously own a tiny plot of land, rent land in and out and also sharecrop (what Abdel Aal (2003) has called the 'tenancy web') made the identification of a single landowner opponent against whom to fight over the new law) very difficult. At times village pressure was brought to bear on landowners not to raise rents as high as had sometimes been threatened. In these types of case the role of the market determining prices and rents needed to be set alongside the logics of village life. This is an argument taken further by Mitchell (2002). He has argued, for instance, that it is important to understand economic transactions do not always take place in 'the market'. They take place through networks and kinship and marriage and ties of affection. Crucially for Mitchell who offers a penetrating critique of the destructive force of neoliberalism, and the reification of economics in general, the non-market relationships are not 'backward' and they certainly do not necessarily inhibit growth.

The lack of overt violent conflict after 1992 and in particular after the full implementation of the act in 1997 did not mean that there was no opposition to the legislation. On the contrary. Tenant farmers were very aware that overt opposition would have been met with state terror. And it is clear that this did occur in many cases (LCHR, 2002). Instead, tenants and smallholders more generally, affronted by the new economic power of landlords, opposed them through verbal criticism and whisper, by challenging village notables to hold landlords to account for the disrespect that they seemed to demonstrate in their failure to live up to the expectations of villagers in relation to rights and duties. Villagers were angry that landlords did not seem to respect the conventions of the village whereby rights to land were safeguarded by custom and mores rather than solely by access to cash to afford the new high rents. While there had not been an appreciable increase in returns from farming, for example remaining at one village in the Delta at between E£1,000 and E£2,000 per feddan depending on crop rotation, the rents rose dramatically. In one village where I had collected extensive data, rents had increased from E£600 to between E£1,500 and E£2,000 (Bush, 2002c).

Thinking the unthinkable – land to the tillers?

Law 96 of 1992 was successful in two major ways. The first was to return economic and increased political power to large landowners. The second was to politicise land in a way that had not happened since the 1950s. The increased power and control over land by larger landowners was remarked upon by all informants in my studies of four villages in the Delta and they featured prominently in the comments made by villagers in the Delta and Upper Egypt to authors like Abdel Aal (2003) and Kirsten Bach (2002). And the politicisation of land was at the heart of the ways in which the ruling National Democratic Party was able to put in place legislation in 1992 that had fallen at early hurdles in previous decades. The green light for reform came with economic adjustment in 1991 and subsequently with increased pressure for market liberalisation by USAID and the World Bank. At no time during the process of the counter-revolution was the need for owners to receive higher levels of rent from their tenants questioned. At stake for opposition parties, particularly the leftist Tagamu', was the need to maintain the tenancy relationship to ensure rural stability and continuity and for there not to be the naked reward to landowners that would accompany an undermining of tenancy. Moreover, there was a concern that the years of hard labour and investment by tenants in the land would be lost as new tenants or owners cut a dash for cash crops rather than strategic crops. Yet the GoE was not prepared to even listen to calls made from the Tagamu' that a fund should be established to pay landowners full costs for the immediate sale of their land and for tenants to then repay the GoE in instalments. The leadership of the Tagamu' seems to have been hijacked by GoE rhetoric that a discussion about tenant rights would take place. The leadership moreover seems to have been at odds with its rank-and-file membership and readers of the leftist newspaper *Al-Ahali* over the fact that sales could proceed without *prior* guarantee of available funds to prevent tenant destitution or compensation to those lacking the means to establish themselves on new land or in other employment.[6]

The importance of challenging property rights was therefore never articulated and it thus seemed inevitable, despite Tagamu's rhetoric that a radicalised countryside was emerging, that the law would be fully implemented and it would represent reinstatement of landowner interests. In those circumstances the emergence of an alternative to Law 96 was extremely problematic. What has emerged has been a call for a greater understanding of the extent of rural poverty and the investment that rural non-governmental organisations might be able to make to help facilitate poverty reduction (CARE, 2000). UNDP has constructed an interesting and provocative shopping list for sustainable rural livelihoods (UNDP, n.d.). Noting that agriculture 'itself is unlikely to provide sufficient jobs for the rural poor [w]hat is required is a broader vision of rural development which extends both beyond markets and beyond agriculture' (UNDP, 1997: 49). Importantly the UNDP authors have noted that creating rural employment is crucial for livelihoods as well as a stronger role for the poor themselves in creating schemes for work and decentralising decision making in the Middle East's countryside. UNDP notes that food security is crucial in the region and that this might be promoted by 'more equal smallholdings' (UNDP, 1997: 49). But on this important point, and on several others that follow a series of reports on human development and eradicating poverty in the region, the authors are out of sync with authoritarian governments and IFIs that see issues in crude terms of market policy ('good') versus non-market policy ('bad'). To calls for government intervention, gender targeting for poverty relief, and research and action to help pro-poor (staple) crop production the Egyptian government has been deaf.

In understanding this deafness two issues are important. The first is the way in which GoE policy since the initiation of economic liberalisation in the mid-1980s in the agriculture sector has been a strategy to reinforce the power of officeholders and their clients. The second is that there has been an absence of strong and sustained critique beyond merely criticising the policies of the GoE and the IFIs, directed at the underpinnings of those policies. On the issue of land, for example, the overriding underpinning of policy makers has been always to talk about and formulate policy in relation to 'the farm' and the 'market', rather than the household as a unit of analysis. As such, there has been a complete failure to recognise the importance of understanding the dynamics of rural Egypt and how the market, so much stressed by neoliberal agencies, is only a small part of how it is that households take decisions and do what they do at times of adversity.[7]

The policy failures are accounted for by the dominance of self-interest among the GoE but also, and as importantly by the institutional self-interest and arrogance of USAID. The two biases defend the political realities of authoritarian Egypt. Despite, or perhaps because of, rhetoric of political reform in Cairo, there is only a very limited and constrained space for agrarian transformation. Despite the hype regarding political liberalisation in 2005, there is an absence of concern with rural democracy or opportunity for smallholders to express their anxiety regarding agricultural strategy.[8] Egyptian politics in the twenty-first century still seems to be a long way from answering the plea made by the authors of the Arab Human Development Report in 2003 for the promotion of an Arab renaissance through democratic values (UNDP, 2003: 143).

Notes

1 I am grateful to Abdel Moula Ismail for data collection and material for the compilation of tables. Thanks also to Amal Sabri.
2 1 feddan = 1.038 acres or 0.42 hectares; 24 qirats = 1 feddan
3 *Fellahin* (plural of *fellah*) means 'tiller of the soil'. The term is often also used to mean someone who lives in the countryside as opposed to the town.
4 The detail of how the bill became law is dealt with by Saad (2002).
5 This was confirmed to me in a series of follow-up interviews with female-headed households between 1999 and 2003 as savings and asset sales expired and desperation with failure to improve access to cash mounted.
6 This debate is dealt with further by Saad (2002).
7 Exceptions to this debate are Hopkins (1993) and Mitchell (2002).
8 A confirmation of the limited character of political liberalisation might be read into the sacking of Hani Shukrallah as executive chief editor of the liberal *Al Ahram Weekly* in July 2005. It seems that his critical analysis of domestic politics and the clarity of perspectives for reform offered by several articles during 2005 were too much for the political establishment. See, *inter alia*, Hani Shukrallah, 'Enter the Absent Actor?' *Al Ahram Weekly*, 3–9 March 2005, available on the internet as www.weekly.ahram.org.eg/2005/732/op17.htm.

References

Abdel Aal, M. (2003). 'Agrarian Relations in Transition: The Impact of the Change in Tenancy Law on Agricultural Work and Production in Qena and Aswan', Final Report, Mimeo, Social Research Centre Cairo, July.

Abdel Fadil, M. (1975). *Development, Income Distribution and Social Change in Rural Egypt 1952–1970: A Study in the Political Economy of Agrarian Transition*. Cambridge: Cambridge University Press.

Abdel-Khalek, G. (2001). *Stabilization and Adjustment in Egypt: Reform or De-industrialization*. Cheltenham: Edward Elgar.

Adams, M. (2000). *Breaking Ground: Development Aid for Land Reform*. London: Overseas Development Institute.

Bayat, A. (2002). 'Activism and Social Development in the Middle East', *International Journal of Middle East Studies*, Winter, no. 1.

Bayat, A. (1997). 'Cairo's Poor: Dilemmas of Survival and Solidarity', *Middle East Report*, Spring, no. 202.

Bianchi, B. (1989). *Unruly Corporatism: Associational Life in Twentieth Century Egypt*. New York: Oxford University Press.

Bromley, S. and R. Bush (1995). 'Adjustment in Egypt? The Political Economy of Reform', *Review of African Political Economy*, vol. 22, no. 65, pp. 339–348.

Brown, N. (1990). *Peasant Politics in Modern Egypt: The Struggle against the State.* New Haven and London: Yale University Press.

Bush, R. (ed.) (2002a). *Counter Revolution in the Egyptian Countryside.* London: Zed Books.

Bush, R. (2002b). 'Land Reform and Counter Revolution,' in R. Bush, ed., *Counter Revolution in the Egyptian Countryside.* London: Zed Books.

Bush, R. (2002c). 'More Losers than Winners in Egypt's Countryside: The Impact of Changes in Land Tenure', in R. Bush, ed., *Counter Revolution in the Egyptian Countryside.* London: Zed Books.

Bush, R. (2000). 'An Agricultural Strategy without Farmers: Egypt's Countryside in the New Millennium', *Review of African Political Economy*, vol. 27, no. 84, pp. 235–250.

Bush, R. (1999). *Economic Crisis and the Politics of Reform in Egypt.* Boulder and Oxford: Westview Press.

CARE Egypt (2000). 'Capability Enhancement through Citizen Action (CAP) Project, Amendment of CAP Project Grant Agreement (ESDF 015) in View of Rresults of Pilot Phase Assessment July 1999–June 2000, Final Draft 25 October'. Cairo: CARE-Egypt, unpublished Mimeo.

Central Bank of Egypt (n.d.) *Economic Review.* www.cbe.org.eg.

Deininger, K. and H. Binswanger (1999). 'The Evolution of the World Bank's Land Policy: Principles, Experience, and Future Challenges', *The World Bank Research Observer*, vol. 14, no. 2, pp. 247–276.

El-Ghobashy, M. (2005). 'Egypt Looks Ahead to Portentous Year', *Middle East Report Online*, 2 February (www.merip.org; downloaded 2 February 2005).

El-Ghonemy, M. R. (1999). 'Recent Changes in Agrarian Reform and Rural Development Strategies in the Near East', *Land Reform*, vols 1 and 2, pp. 9–20.

El-Ghonemy, M. R. (1993). 'Food Security and Rural Development in North Africa', *Middle Eastern Studies*, vol. 29, no. 3, pp. 445–466.

El-Ghonemy, M. R. (1990). *The Political Economy of Rural Poverty: The Case for Land Reform.* London and New York: Routledge.

Faris, M. A. and M. H. Khan (eds) (1993). *Sustainable Agriculture in Egypt.* Boulder and London: Lynne Reiner.

Fergany, N. (2002). 'Poverty and Unemployment in Rural Egypt', in R. Bush, ed., *Counter Revolution in the Egyptian Countryside.* London: Zed Books.

Fletcher, L. B. (ed.) (1996). *Egypt's Agriculture in a Reform Era.* Ames: Iowa State University Press.

Food and Agricultural Organisation of the United Nations (FAO) (2003). *Nutrition Country Profiles: Egypt.* Rome: FAO.

Frankfort, H. (1948). *Kingship and the Gods.* Chicago: University of Chicago Press.

Friscak, L. and I. Atiyas (eds) (1996). *Governance, Leadership, and Communication.* Washington, DC: World Bank.

Ismail, A. M. (ed.) (1998). *The Liberalisation of Egypt's Agricultural Sector and the Peasants' Movement.* Cairo: LCHR.

Khedr, H., R. Ehrich and L. B. Fletcher (1996). 'Nature, Rationale and Accomplishments of the Agricultural Policy Reforms, 1987–1994', in L. B. Fletcher (ed.), *Egypt's Agriculture in a Reform Era.* Ames: Iowa State University Press.

Kienle, E. (2001). *A Grand Delusion: Democracy and Economic Reform in Egypt.* London: I. B. Tauris.

King, R. (1977). *Land Reform: A World Survey.* London: G. Bell and Sons Ltd.

LCHR (2002). 'Farmer Struggles against Law 96 of 1992', in R. Bush, ed., *Counter Revolution in the Egyptian Countryside*. London: Zed Books.

LCHR (2000). 'The Impact of Implementing the Land Law in Egypt: Collapsing of Farmers' Income – Violating Their Rights', in *Land and the Fellahin*. Cairo: LCHR.

LCHR (1999a). 'Violence in the Egyptian Countryside 1998–1999', in *Land and the Fellahin*. Cairo: LCHR.

LCHR (1999b). 'Agricultural Land Disputes in Egypt's Rural Community', in *Land and Fellahin*. Cairo: LCHR.

Ministry of Agriculture (2000). *Agricultural Census 2000*. Cairo: Ministry of Agriculture.

Ministry of Agriculture (1990). *Agricultural Census 1990*. Cairo: Minsitry of Agriculture.

Mitchell, T. (2002). *Rule of Experts. Egypt, Techno-Politics, Modernity*. Berkeley: University of California Press.

Mitchell, T. (1999). 'No Factories, No Problems: The Logic of Neo-Liberalism in Egypt', *Review of African Political Economy*, vol. 26, no. 82, pp. 455–468.

Mitchell, T. (1998). 'The Market's Place' in Nicholas Hopkins and Kirsten Westergaard, eds, *Directions of Change in Rural Egypt*. Cairo: American University in Cairo Press.

Nassar, S. (1993). 'The Economic Impact of Reform Programs in the Agricultural Sector in Egypt'. Cairo: Ministry of Agriculture, Livestock and Fishery Wealth and Land Reclamation, Economic Affairs Section, Mimeo.

Radwan, S. and E. Lee (1986). *Agrarian Change in Egypt: Anatomy of Rural Poverty*. London: Croom Helm.

Richards, A. (1993). 'Economic Imperatives and Political Systems', *Middle East Journal*, vol. 47, no. 2.

Richards, A. and J. Waterbury (eds) (1990). *A Political Economy of the Middle East: State, Class and Economic Development*. Boulder: Westview Press.

Saad, R. (2002). 'Egyptian Politics and the Tenancy Law', in R. Bush, ed., *Counter Revolution in the Egyptian Countryside*. London: Zed Books.

Saad, R. (n.d.). 'Community and Community Development in Egypt'. Unpublished mimeo, Social Research Center, American University in Cairo.

Saad, R. (1999). 'State, Landlord, Parliament and Peasant: The Story of the 1992 Tenancy Law in Egypt', in A. Bowman and E. Rogan, eds, *Agriculture in Egypt from Pharaonic to Modern Times*. Oxford: Oxford University Press.

Sallam, M. S. (1998). 'Agrarian Reform in Egypt'. Paper presented to Land Reform Conference, Cascavel, Brazil, April, Mimeo.

Sami, A. (2000). 'Strawberry take-off?', *Al Ahram Weekly*, 16–22 March, issue no. 473.

Sfakianakis, J. (2000). 'Crony Capitalism, the State, the Characteristics of Egyptian Business and the Business Elite'. Paper presented to the First Mediterranean Social and Political Research Meeting of the Robert Schuman Center for Advanced Studies, European University Institute, Florence, 22–26 March

Toth, J. (1999). *Rural Labor Movements in Egypt and Their Impact on the State, 1961–1992*. Cairo: American University Press in Cairo.

Toulmin, C. and J. Quan (eds) (2000). *Evolving Land Rights, Policy and Tenure in Africa*. London: Department for International Development/DFID and IIED; Norwich: Natural Resources Institute.

UNDP (2003). *Arab Human Development Report: Building a Knowledge Society*. New York: UNDP and Arab Fund for Economic and Social Development.

UNDP (1997). *Preventing and Eradicating Poverty*. New York: UNDP and UN Department for Development Support and Management Services, UNDP Regional Bureau for Arab States.

USAID (2001). 'PVO Development in Egypt'. www.usaid.gov/regions/ane/new-pages/perspectives/egypt/egpvo.htm (downloaded 14 June 2001).

USAID (2000). 'Congressional Presentation Financial Year 2000'. www.usaid.gov/pubs/cp2000/ane/egypt.html (downloaded 6 June 2001).

USAID (1999a). 'Agriculture – Vision for 2003', RDI *Policy Brief*, issue no. 12, November.

USAID and GoE (1999b). *Land Tenure Study Phase II* APRP, RDI Unit, March, Cairo.

USAID (1999c). 'The Impact of Liberalization and Role of Rural Organizations: Policy Issues', October, APRP, RDI Report no. 78.

USAID (1998). *Horticultural Sub-sector Map*. Cairo: USAID Agricultural Policy Reform Program, Reform Design and Implementation, Report no. 39, June.

USAID (1997). *A Study on Developing Revised, Integrated Land and Water Plan*. Cairo: USAID, Agricultural Policy Reform Program Reform Design and Implementation Unit, B. B. Attia *et al.*, December.

USAID (1995). 'The Egyptian Agricultural Policy Reforms: An Overview'. Paper presented at Agricultural Policy Conference, Taking Stock, Eight Years of Egyptian Agricultural Policy Reforms, 26–28 March, Mimeo.

Waterbury, J. (1983). *The Egypt of Nasser and Sadat: The Political Economy of Two Regimes*. Princeton: Princeton University Press.

World Bank (2000). *Can Africa Claim the 21st Century?* Washington, DC: World Bank.

World Bank and GoE (2000). *Towards Agricultural Competitiveness in the 21st Century, Egypt Agricultural Export-oriented Strategy*. Cairo. Draft unpublished mimeo, July.

9 Land reform in Namibia
Issues of equity and poverty

*Jan Kees van Donge with George Eiseb and
Alfons Mosimane*

Introduction

Land is a central issue in Namibian politics and, in order to grasp this, two
basic facts about Namibia need to be explained: the first is that about 40
per cent of land in Namibia is commercial, surveyed and fenced land and
is overwhelmingly in the hands of a white minority. Second, 45 per cent of
the Namibian population lives on about 7 per cent of the territory's
surface, situated mostly in the north of the country. Most land there is
not surveyed and fenced and is held by individuals with large residual
communal rights.

   This situation reflects a pattern of incorporation in the imperialist
world that has to be seen against the background of the physical geo-
graphy of Namibia. A large part of the area is covered by desert, arid and
semi-arid regions. As a rule, the further south and west one goes in
Namibia, the more desertlike the conditions. It is thus in the northeast
that climatic conditions are best and where one finds a large concentration of population. Some commercial land is suitable for crop production:
first, the maize triangle Otavi-Grootfontein-Tsumeb in the north and,
second, some irrigated arable areas throughout the country, mostly along
the Orange river on Namibia's southern borders. However, virtually all
commercial land in the hands of the white minority is in the semi-arid and
arid areas. This sets the scene for land reform in Namibia: large tracts of
land are in the hands of the Namibians of European descent, but this land
is only marginally suitable for commercial agriculture because water is
scarce.

   This pattern of population[1] and land distribution results from
Namibia's colonial history. Namibia was declared a German colony in the
latter half of the nineteenth century. Early on, the Germans established a
survey department and gave out massive tracts of land, expropriated
mainly from the Herero population, to white settlers in the centre and
south of the country. The mainly Oshivambo-speaking people in the north
living in the basins of the Kunene and Zambesi rivers were colonised in
the way that is familiar further north: treaty making and subordinating

indigenous authorities to colonial overrule. The northern part became a native reserve, and land ownership remained in the control of indigenous authorities that administered individual ownership with strong residual communal rights. The distinction between the two areas was firmly established by what was called the 'police line' and is nowadays called the 'veterinary cordon fence' that keeps cattle from the communal areas of the north out of the commercial farming area. Its official rationale is the control of veterinary diseases.

After the Second World War, the Germans lost authority over the territory and it was given in trust to South Africa by the United Nations. The system as it had evolved of course fitted the apartheid ideology that came to dominate South African politics. The apartheid formally implemented by the Odendaal commission in 1962 affected the centre and south of the country especially. White farmers moved out of black areas and 'tribal' groups were concentrated in homelands. The administration of land tenure in the homelands was given to 'traditional authorities' who administered again on the principle of individual ownership with strong residual communal rights. Ultimately, the land belongs to the descent group of the farmer.

The Odendaal commission did not, however, merely create a white commercial sector and a black traditional sector. For those defined as black, it also opened the way for European-style individual ownership on fenced and surveyed land. This gained government support towards the end of the colonial period. The government then bought white-owned land in order to turn this into settlement schemes for Africans on individual titles (Harring and Odendaal, 2002: 26–27).

Against this background, two land questions have emerged in Namibia. On the one hand, individual claims are emerging in communal areas as richer farmers fence land. This threatens access to land by the poor. The Namibian government relies on the vote in those areas, and it is thus not surprising that it removed powers over land administration from the traditional authorities. A formal procedure for registering the fencing of land is administered by land boards appointed by the government. This, however, is not politically divisive in Namibia.[2] The second issue is the distribution of white-owned land among the non-white population. This is politically a very sensitive matter and needs to be understood against the background of the emergence of African politics in Namibia.

The basic division between north and south of the police fence is also central in the growth of nationalism (Saunders, 2004). There were many proto-nationalist movements in Namibia, but the first nationalist party to emerge was the South West African People's Organisation (SWAPO), which originated mainly in the north. There also the guerrilla war erupted and was most intense. At independence in 1990, SWAPO won the elections overwhelmingly. It found almost universal support among the Oshivambo-speaking population. They comprise 51 per cent of the Namibian population and are concentrated in the north (RON, 1994: 65). The other African political parties had grown into an alliance with white parties that aimed at a very gradual movement towards independence in an apartheid (federal) framework (Democratic Turnhalle Alliance, DTA).

One of the first initiatives undertaken by SWAPO after independence was the organisation of a national conference on land. There, a policy of market-led land reform – willing buyer/willing seller – was agreed upon. However, more importantly, it was decided that historical claims would not be entertained (Harring and Odendaal, 2002: 31–32), broadly similar to the key features of the 1980 Lancaster Agreement in Zimbabwe (see Moyo, this volume).

Historical claims on land were of course not an issue in the north, because land had not been alienated in colonial times. South of the police line, the situation was very different. The decision not to entertain historical claims was especially directed against the Herero, who dominate the central part of Namibia. They claim not only land that was expropriated by the Germans but also compensation because of the attempted genocide by the German colonisers. A mere stress on the obvious lack of interest in the recognition of historical rights does no justice, however, to SWAPO's stance, because it is extremely difficult to establish the exact historical rights of the Herero.

At the end of the nineteenth and the beginning of the twentieth century, the part of Namibia that is now commercial farmland was a cauldron of African, migrating, cattle-keeping people, mainly European traders, and German settlers. Groups of Afrikaans-speaking black people were dominant in the south, Herero-speaking people were migrating with cattle in the centre and towards the north of the country and German settlers were mainly found in the central belt of the country. There was relatively little centralisation and there were many conflicts between the various parties. This seemed to change as centralising forces emerged among the Herero and built upon an alliance with the German occupational power. Contrary to what one would expect, however, and fuelled by blind racism, the Germans started a war against their Herero allies. This was a brutal war in which the Herero were chased to certain death in the Kalahari Desert. It was therefore tantamount to genocide: the virtual destruction of the Herero as a people was the result (Gewald, 1999).

In pre-colonial times, there were no fixed tribal territories in most of Namibia. There were territories through which certain groups moved, but this movement was mainly motivated by local, temporary, climatological conditions. There was no fixed seasonal migration pattern as is the case in transhumance. Different ethnic groups identify with certain areas, but these claims are for that reason less unambiguous than is desirable when allocating land. Among these identities there was little centralisation. Centralisation under indigenous authorities is a product of colonialism. Although it is true that Hereroland was an artificial creation under the apartheid ideology, any other designation would be artificial as well. Herero claims are very extensive: they claim about one-third of Namibia, while only about 8 per cent of the Namibian people speak Herero at home (RON, 1994: 65). Recognition of these claims would mean a massive relocation of people because it would involve not only white farms but also the Damara people. The questions that would arise are illustrated in a comparison of the two maps presented in Figure 9.1: one indicating the present communal areas in Namibia and the other reflecting Herero claims on an historical basis taken from a PhD dissertation on a Herero communal area by a Herero author (Kakujaha-Matundu, 2002). Such an operation would resemble an apartheid-style operation based on an assumed indivisible link between land and a certain ethnic designation.

Herero demands for land and reparation payments from the Germans were quite muted while they were in the coalition with European parties: the DTA. The DTA brought together all parties that were accommodating to apartheid but nationalistic during South African rule. However, the political party that represents most of the Herero, the National Union of Democrats (NUDO) broke away from the DTA in February 2004. Their leader, the Herero chief Khoime Rikuraka, voiced radical demands for Herero compensation and land claims. SWAPO accepts that there is a case for the payment of compensation but says that this should not be specifically paid to the Herero. According to SWAPO, there is a just case for compensation for the suffering in colonial times to be paid to the whole nation. Similarly, there is support in SWAPO for land redistribution, but this should be done on the basis of need and not on the basis of historical claims.

The white section of the Namibian polity has paradoxically moved closer to SWAPO. One would expect the opposite: Nujoma is a ferocious defender of Zimbabwe's president Robert Mugabe on controversial matters such as the condemnation of homosexuality and the land seizures from white farmers, but the German community in Namibia came to the support of Nujoma when he was attacked in the German weekly, *Der Spiegel*:

> It is true that Nujoma and SWAPO are loyal to their allies from the times of liberation struggle (Castro and Mugabe) and express gratitude rendered to them also in the renaming of the streets. But does somebody live in the past because he did not drop his old friends like a hot potato when the tide turns against them? Above all, Namibia's Head of State and government has been elected democratically – by a majority (almost 77%) of which US presidents can only dream.
> (*Windhoek Observer*, 24/7/04: 18)[3]

Land reform is supported from within the white farming community, for example:

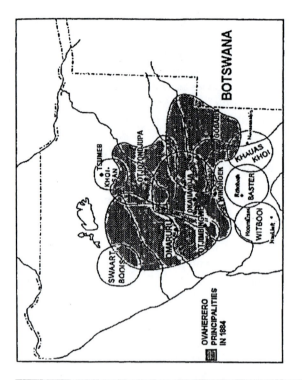

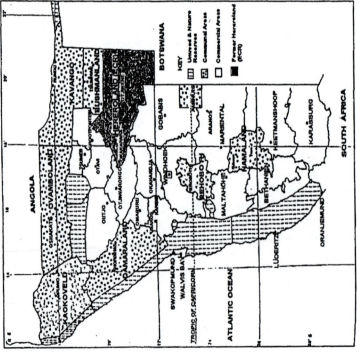

Figure 9.1 Map of present communal areas and map of Herero claims on land (source: Kakujaha-Matundu (2002)).

If Namibians do not own the land, the surface, the soil itself, the country does not belong to them. Thus, because commercial farmers own a substantial part of the country's land surface, the country is still perceived as belonging to the 'colonialists'... we should at least try to understand and have sympathy with the compatriots.

(Mudge, 2004: 100)[4]

The events in Zimbabwe (see Moyo, this volume) and renewed Herero nationalism have brought land reform onto the political agenda with a new urgency. This was obvious, for example, when Nujoma directly seized a number of farms in 2003 because of a labour dispute. This led to unrest in the white farming community, because a labour dispute is seen as a distinctly different issue from equitable distribution of land among the various population groups (Leithead, 2004). The Minister of Lands, Resettlement and Rehabilitation later suspended the expropriation order, but the order was not reversed. The policy stance of the white farming communities is an acceptance of the need for land reform, but they strongly stress the need for a clear strategy. The insecurity of property is paralysing for economic enterprise (*Allgemeine Zeitung*, 30/7/04: 1).

As a result of the instability generated around resettlement policy, in August 2003 the government instituted a paradoxically named Permanent Technical Team (PTT) on Land Reform in the Ministry of Land, Resettlement and Rehabilitation that was to report within nine months on an Action Plan for land reform. It reported, however, only in the last quarter of 2004.

The economy, agriculture and land[5]

The Namibian economy is unusual by African standards. It is a relatively rich country: GNP per capita is estimated at an average of US$2,334 in the period 1995–2003 as compared to an African average of US$681. Poverty is widespread, however, and the headcount of the 1999 Namibian levels of living survey concluded that 75.9 per cent of the Namibian population lives in poverty (RON, 2001). Great inequality is a logical conclusion that follows from being a relatively rich country containing a large poor population. Income is concentrated in a very small group of people. The Gini coefficient is a staggering 0.80 in Namibia (World Bank, 2004).

For example, the richest 5 per cent of the population control 71% of GDP, with an average income of US$14,000 per year which is comparable with the middle stratum of developed countries in Europe. The poorest 55 per cent account for merely 3% of GDP, with a per capita income of less than US$100 a year.

(RON, 1995: 20)

Namibia's wealth derives mainly from natural resources. Diamond mining is a declining activity but is still at the heart of the Namibian economy:

> Diamond mining makes a contribution of around 10% to Namibia's Gross Domestic Product. The overall contribution of the diamond mining industry to government tax and non tax revenues has almost tripled to 14.7% in 2002/03 from 5.7% in 1990/91. Another indicator of the economic importance of the industry to Namibia is the balance of payments which shows that in 2002 rough diamonds comprised 50% of all merchandise exports by value. It is therefore also Namibia's principal generator of foreign exchange.
>
> (Boer and Sherbourne, 2004: 7)

The mining sector is diversified, however. Metal mining is less significant but nonetheless contributes 19 per cent to exports.

Other important sectors have developed since independence. Fishing is one of these, albeit that most income is derived from fishing rights rather than from actual fishing on the part of the Namibian fleet. Tourism is another area that has developed in a big way since independence in 1990. Annual tourism receipts amount to about US$290 million.

In Namibia, employment is concentrated in services, which comprise government as well as the tourism industry (47.4 per cent). Manufacturing (including mining and quarrying) contributes far less to employment (18 per cent). Commercial agriculture does not employ much labour. The sector employs 36,000 people, that is, about 8 per cent of the labour force. Commercial agriculture is very extensive. An average commercial farm employs about six people on an average area of 8,620 hectares (RON, 1995: 3).

In other respects, commercial agriculture is more important. Livestock products rank third in the contribution to exports behind minerals and fish/fish products. The agricultural sector contributes 10 per cent to GDP, a figure comparable to mining's contribution. Beef is by far the largest sector of agricultural production, and income from beef is estimated at about 87 per cent of Namibia's gross non-fishing agricultural income. Namibia has to import food. For example, Namibian farmers produce merely up to 55 per cent of the country's grain consumption in good years, which occur roughly four years in ten.

The dualistic nature of Namibia's economy is evident in government statistics. The contribution of the communal farming sub-sector to GDP is much lower (about 2.5 per cent) than the commercial sub-sector, which contributes about 7.5 per cent, yet the communal sector employs about 20 per cent of the workforce as compared to 8 per cent in the commercial sector.

The majority of the Namibian population (67 per cent) live in rural areas (RON, 2003). Most poverty is found there, and this has a gender dimension as well:

Urban male- and female-headed households generate average incomes of N$1,047 and N$678 respectively. Rural females were worse off compared to their male counter-parts as they earned N$210 per month while the latter were earning N$328 per month.

(RON, 2003: 4)

Within Namibia there are also important geographical dimensions to poverty: 'average expenditure was lowest in all the northern regions. In contrast, expenditure was reported to be the highest in the Khomas, Erongo and Omaheke regions' (RON, 2001: vii).

A similar pattern emerges from the poverty headcounts. The lowest were found in the regions with relatively large urban populations: Khomas (0.491), Erongo (0.612) and Omaheke (0.751). The highest headcounts were reported from Omusati (0.979), Ohangwena (0.947) and Oshikoto (0.910) in the north where agriculture on communal lands is concentrated. In the Khomas, Erongo and Omaheke regions there is also much commercial land. In rural Namibia, agriculture is not as important a source of cash as the statistics suggest. For example, for 20 per cent of rural households, cash remittances and pensions are the main cash income according to the 2001 census (RON, 2003: 18). Much more dependency on the urban sector would have appeared if the enquiry had singled out crucial supplementary income.

Poverty reduction is thus an urgent matter in rural Namibia. The question is whether redistribution of land can play a role.

Market-led voluntary land reform: the Affirmative Action Loans Scheme (AALS)[6]

The changeover of commercial land from white into African hands is a slow process (Table 9.1). In 1991 there were about 6,000 commercial farms in Namibia covering about 36 million hectares. About one-seventh (five million hectares) had passed into African hands in 2005. Sherbourne (2004a) calculated that about 1 per cent of this commercial land was redistributed to black farmers yearly in the period 1990–2002. The table also shows that most land was transferred through AALS, which is a voluntary, non-redistributive programme.

AALS was established soon after independence and the scheme has been implemented since 1992. It provides targeted subsidised credit to formerly racially disadvantaged groups to assist in buying farms from Namibians of European descent. The parastatal Agribank administers the scheme. It is emancipatory in design, but not particularly redistributive. Its main official rationale is to give emerging large-scale farmers the chance to develop into full-scale commercial farmers and in this way to relieve land pressure in commercial areas.[7] Applicants need to have a track record of farming in communal areas, evidenced by ownership of at least

Table 9.1 Distribution of agricultural land in Namibia (2004)

Type of land	Area in hectares
Commercial land	36,000,000
Communal land	34,000,000
Total agricultural land	70,000,000
Commercial land in African hands	
Individual smallholder resettlement	530,500
Group smallholder resettlement	195,400
Affirmative Action Loans Scheme	3,470,700
Total redistributed since 1990 (independence)	4,196,600
Estimated additional transfers	
State land (commercial) acquired before 1990	500,000
Commercial land bought by black people on market	300,000
Estimated total in African hands but not redistributed	800,000
Total commercial land in African hands	±5,000,000

Source: Permanent Technical Team on Land Reform, 2004.

150 head of cattle or 800 small livestock, or a combination of the two that is equivalent. Many urban Africans of managerial rank can make that claim. AALS is in practice an elite–elite transfer. The scheme functions primarily as an instrument of black empowerment.

The duration of AALS loans is 25 years at subsidised rates, but the scheme provides incentives to pay off the debt early. Full-time farmers are exempted from both interest and redemption payments for three years. Thereafter, the interest rate increases progressively from 2 per cent to a maximum of 13.5 per cent from the tenth year onwards. Part-time farmers do not benefit from the initial exemption, but pay interest from the first year. The interest rate can vary, depending upon the farmer's income, between 1 per cent and 13.5 per cent a year. Part-time farmers, similar to full-time farmers, pay 13.5 per cent a year interest on the remaining loan amount after ten years.

AALS is a prime example of market-led land reform based on the principle of willing buyer/willing seller. In the words of Sherbourne (2004a: 2): 'the policy is very much a market-based mechanism in much the same way as a bank loan, associated as it is with clear property rights and incentives to perform'.

The government is not a particularly active party in the land market as such, albeit that the procedure of land sales gives ample opportunity for intervention. If a farm is put on the market, it has first to be offered to the government on the basis of willing buyer/willing seller. A waiver is given when the government is not interested and the farm can be sold on the open market. In the period 1999–2003 a waiver was given in most cases (88 per cent) and the government only bought 69 of the 652 farms offered on the market (Sherbourne, 2004a). The Land Tribunal decides on the price if the government and seller cannot agree on the market price. A sale under AALS automatically gets a waiver. AALS applicants usually enter into dialogue with Agribank before an actual transaction is at stake. The bank asks them to indicate the area where they would like to buy land and what price they would consider paying. Buyer and seller must first reach an agreement in principle that has to be endorsed by the bank's evaluators; the evaluators also have the right to veto sales. It is striking that there has not been one appeal to the Land Tribunal yet.

Yet government intervention is crucial in the working of the land market, as it intervenes through the credit system. The government provides the funds to Agribank to lend the money under AALS, and it subsidises Agribank to cover the difference between an AALS loan and an operation on the commercial market. Lastly, the government guarantees the loan to Agribank. Average prices paid by those who receive AALS loans have been higher than when a sale did not involve the loan scheme (Motinga, 2003). This suggests that the subsidy on AALS pushes prices up: farms would not have been bought, or would have been purchased at lower prices, if the scheme did not exist. The market-led reform of the AALS scheme may thus actually distort markets.

The factors that drive prices are, however, subject to intensive debate in Namibia. It may be that demand from abroad has played a role. Sale of land to non-Namibians is not possible, but there was a loophole if land was in the hands of a company – in Namibia mostly a closed corporation. Change of individual ownership has to be recorded in the deeds registry, but if land is in the hands of a company, then a change of ownership is not recorded. Shares in such companies may well be in foreign hands. Fuller and Eiseb (2002) found a significant move from individual to corporate ownership, especially in 1995. Motinga (2003: 2) has elaborated on these findings and noted that land sales peaked in 1995: 'Of the over 2 million hectare of land that changed hands in 1995, approximately 45 per cent was transferred from white males to corporate entities, and 48 per cent of the latter transactions were designated as an inheritance or gift.' There is now also legislation limiting this route: individual land ownership may no longer be converted into corporate ownership. However, this does not affect land already in the hands of a closed corporation.

It may be that acquiring a commercial farm is attractive as a purely strategic investment. At present, losses on the farm can be written off against tax on income earned elsewhere, although government is preparing legislation to prevent losses on farming being offset against gains in other businesses.

The explanation for burgeoning demand for land may, however, be found elsewhere than in profitability as such. The productivity of Namibian farming has remained stagnant: 'Real growth in commercial farming value added has been a mere 1 per cent since 1994, less than half the rate of the overall Namibian economy' (Sherbourne, 2004b: 17). The cost of farming has risen because subsidies have been abolished since independence. During the apartheid days there were substantial subsidies – most notably a subsidy on diesel for water supply to keep rural Namibia populated for strategic reasons. The only significant subsidy nowadays is the subsidy on AALS loans. It is not surprising that the production structure of commercial farming has also changed drastically. The commercial herds have declined in numbers by about a third in the period 1990–2001. Farms are increasingly stocked with game that is kept for incoming trophy hunters to shoot. The amount of trophy-hunted game tripled between 1994 and 2002. Farmhouses have become lodges for game viewers and hunters. Commercial farmers have to a large part changed their profession to become managers of a tourist enterprise.

Sherbourne (2004b) has made a powerful argument that farming has become a rich man's hobby in Namibia. This is primarily evident in the AALS scheme, where 41 per cent of the applicants buying 41 per cent of the land under the scheme in the period 1994–2003 were part-time farmers. The number of part-time farmers would, according to Sherbourne, be greater if it were transparent when there were backers behind those taking up AALS loans.

The desire to own a farm as an auxiliary economic activity would also explain the segmented nature of the land market in Namibia. Average prices per year were relatively stable at N$100 per hectare until 2000 if 'smallholdings' (less than 100 ha) are excluded. Average prices increased, however, from N$900 per hectare in 1990 to over N$11,000 per ha by 2002 (Motinga, 2003).[8] There is considerable pent-up demand among black Namibians who cannot afford to buy a large farm, but who desire to have land of about 1,000 ha on which to keep cattle. Such farms are scarce on commercial farmland, as there is a law against subdivision of such farmland. That law was passed in the last years before independence and is seen by those desiring small farms as an attempt to keep black people out of commercial farming.

The manifest rationale of the law is to protect commercial farming, as ranching in small units is seen as incompatible with economic farming, given that one needs on average 12 to 15 ha to carry one head of livestock in Namibia. The minimal economic unit for livestock farming was therefore usually seen as 6,000 ha. This calculation is bitterly debated and readjusted. A recent analysis by the Permanent Technical Team on Land Reform noted:

> Given our analysis, one can reasonably recommend that high rainfall areas can achieve net returns with farm sizes of about 1000 hectares. Equivalent numbers for medium, low and very low areas are about 2000, 3000 and over 3000 hectares respectively.
>
> (Stephanus and Sumaila, 2004: 14)

However, farming in Namibia on small units requires considerable capital. Livestock farming is always capital-intensive, as it has a long-term cash flow. In the ranching that is common in Namibia, small units need more capital than large units because of risk management. The calculation of an economic unit usually implies a large component for risk because of drought. Size is one way to protect against risks. One needs a surfeit of land in order to be secure in a year when grazing is poor. In a big unit, the farmer is also able to fall back upon small microclimates in the event of drought. Livestock farming on small units requires an infrastructure that gives reliable access to water all year round. This often requires more investment in boreholes, etc. than on a large unit where there are more water sources. In a small unit, grazing is limited and one needs to buy supplementary feed if grazing is poor. Third, as land is scarce, one has to invest more in containing bush encroachment.

The proponents of farming in small units argue that they base their calculations on spreading risks through time: if one has on average two good seasons in six years, then in those two years sufficient cash has to be generated to carry one through the others. Those who favour small farms argue also that a farm yields many more products than just livestock: the tradition of hunting and gathering has also persisted through the years.

A loophole in the law against subdivision allows it if tourism is given as the reason. Yet that does not fulfil the demand. Subdivision is also cumbersome and expensive because it requires surveying the land and registering it in parcels. The skills necessary for this are in short supply in Namibia. Even if subdivision were allowed, it is not certain that large farmers would take the opportunity to subdivide. The desire to farm relatively small herds on a relatively small acreage results also in significant demand to rent land. Renting out is an attractive alternative to selling land that is not in use.

The situation changes if large farmers are faced with big debts that have to be repaid, as is the case with a substantial number of AALS beneficiaries. Then it becomes attractive to sell land to raise enough cash to repay the loan and perhaps make a profit as well. It is also possible that AALS farmers are interested in retaining only a part of the farm. Originally, AALS farmers were not allowed to sell their farm or subdivide it in the first ten years after acquisition. Agribank has changed the conditions of the loan by asking for 10 per cent of the capital to be paid upfront by the buyer so that cash-strapped buyers cannot enter the scheme. It has also allowed farms to be sold. It is further proposed that the law will be suspended in the case of AALS farmers so that they can subdivide at will. Subdivision may be a hassle, but it may be a way to sanitise the financial situation.

The profitability of farming remains a pertinent question, however. Agribank does not publish figures on the servicing of AALS loans. One is dependent upon impressions gleaned from Agribank by researchers. For example, according to Chiari:

To date, Agribank considers as financially viable only 50–60 per cent of the farms purchased through AALS. In many cases the minimum stock required to AALS buyers is not sufficient to make the farm viable, especially if large. Another alarming indicator is represented by the growing demand for extending the grace period during which full-time farmers are exempted from the payment of the interest rate.

(Chiari, 2004: 34)

On the other hand, a survey undertaken for the PTT concludes that only a minority are in difficulty. Their major indicator for the viability of the farm was an increase in size of herds: 'sixty-two out of 83 farmers had increased their herd sizes from the time they purchased the farm. By the same measure only 22 farmers had smaller herds than when they purchased the farm' (Fuller and van Zyl, 2005: i).

Farmers got into difficulty for reasons outside the normal run of farming operation: divorce or death; shocks such as drought, a breakdown of water equipment; or theft of assets from the farm prior to occupation. Providing loans for post-settlement operations are, according to Fuller and van Zyl, the main mechanism to improve the viability of the farm.

Fuller and van Zyl's results can be contested however. The survey suffered from organisational difficulties and the sample comprised only 83 instead of the projected 180 farmers. There is no indication as to whether this led to bias in selection. The herd size may be a poor indicator of progress on the farm, as ownership of animals is often ambiguous: relatives may have claims on the livestock or there may be loan arrangements of various types. Third, it is doubtful whether one can see drought or breakdown of water equipment as external shocks: investment in water infrastructure and provision for drought are essential in ranching in Namibia.

Similarly, the cost–benefit analysis by Stephanus and Sumaila (2004) can be questioned. Their main methodological device is to extend the period over which returns are calculated as, according to them, farms have a value beyond one generation. This leads to higher net present values (NPV) on sensible grounds. Much more questionable is their assumption that much commercial farmland is unused: 'it should be noted that these values (NPV of unchanged ownership) depict production levels at lower capacity. Therefore the cost to the economy is the opportunity cost of the non-utilized capacity' (p. 14).

Unused land can be considered reserve land in marginal farming areas such as those found in Namibia. It is difficult to regard land as unused if it can also be seen as reserve land for grazing in the event of drought. It assumes that the smaller farms that will result from land reform will be more intensively farmed, and that also requires more capital.

Second, according to their calculations, over 55 per cent of total income is derived from off-farm sources. Farms can in many cases only be considered viable if there is off-farm income: 'this means that without off-farm income most beneficiaries will have very low incomes overall and thereby lowering net present values to possibly negative levels' (Stephanus and Sumaila, 2004: 15).

Both the survey of AALS farms and the cost–benefit analysis recommend post-settlement support in the form of loans or grants. This position comes close to arguing that farming is only profitable if there is a subsidy on capital.

The actual findings of the research commissioned by the PTT indicate therefore that farming can be profitable under paradoxical conditions: in propitious circumstances in a high-risk environment. Sherbourne's conclusion that farming is a secondary economic activity is actually born out by Stephanus and Sumaila when they mention the importance of off-farm income. Sherbourne (2004b: 9–10) argues that, even with a subsidised AALS loan, farming is not profitable: 'clearly the biggest cost to the investing farmer is the purchase of land. Thus profitability is only possible if the farm is inherited and the land does not need to be purchased.'

This comes close to a rule of the thumb that is used by Namibians who want to break into farming: you should get either the land or the stock for free. The perceived profitability of farming in Namibia depends in the first place on what is perceived as a cost.

Land reform for poverty alleviation: non-compulsory land purchase with distribution according to need

Land reform in Namibia is driven more by the wish for black empowerment than by concerns about economic inequality. The practice of land reform in Namibia primarily supports the transfer of large-scale farms from owners of European descent to African owners. This is evident in a comparison of AALS with programmes designed to redistribute land and that have an explicit aim of poverty alleviation. The latter are usually designated with the word 'resettlement' and are market-led in the sense that they do not involve compulsory purchase, but the land is either distributed free of charge to a community of farmers (resettlement projects) or subdivided into individual plots (resettlement farms).

It is not only from the amount of land transferred under AALS as compared to resettlement projects (Table 9.1) that the priority given to elite–elite transfers is evident. The budget for AALS has also consistently been over-spent (in the period 1996–2003 by 35.8 per cent), while the budget for resettlement is consequently under-spent (in the period 1996–2003 by 20 per cent). The budget for resettlement was bigger in the same period (N$111.28 million for resettlement as compared to N$92.8 million for AALS), but that does not mean that more land could be purchased. It is also more than three times more expensive to transfer land under a resettlement programme than under AALS (Sherbourne, 2004b). It is even cheaper per beneficiary to transfer a large AALS farm than to transfer to a smallholder a farm that is much smaller in hectarage (Table 9.2).

AALS is thus far more effective than resettlement from the point of view of black empowerment. AALS is also more market-based than the other schemes and it suggests therefore a greater efficacy of market-led land reform. However, as argued above, that is a simplification: in reality this market-led land reform distorts markets. Resettlement is totally state-led on the demand side: the government determines who will get a farm. Landlessness and poverty should be the criteria for allocation. However, the resettlement programmes have not been effective in poverty alleviation.

Resettlement projects[9]

SWAPO was inspired by socialist ideals while the nationalists were in exile (Werner, 2001). Little is found of these ideals in the actual land reform policies that have been implemented since independence. However, in the immediate post-independence period, resettlement projects were initiated that had a weak collective property model: communal income-generating and farming practices were designed in the schemes. Common fields were provided with the aim of generating income. These projects had a strong social welfare character, as is evident from the target groups for resettlement: ex-combatants, people who were disabled in the war and the minority San community.[10]

There was some expansion of this communal approach beyond the immediate aftermath of the war. The largest proportion of land designated for communal resettlement in the second half of the 1990s – 21,102 hectares – is on farms donated to the state by Carl List, one of Namibia's biggest landowners. The Namibian government bought only one farm in that period for this purpose. The total area allocated for communal resettlement covered less than 200,000 ha in 2004. This is less than 5 per cent of all land redistributed. Communal resettlement has thus no priority in government policy.

Table 9.2 Different types of land reform: cost structure to government

Type of resettlement	Average size per beneficiary (hectare)	Average cost/hectare (N$)	
		Per beneficiary	Per hectare
Individual smallholder	1,768	272,002	154
Group smallholder	159	17,226	108
AALS	5,553	257,041	48

Source: Permanent Technical Team for Land Reform, 2004.

Resettlement projects are located in areas that, by Namibian standards, have high economic potential. Nevertheless, the accounts given of life in these settlement schemes are invariably bleak. Chiari likened the situation to refugee camps. Settlers were allocated individual plots that are very small by Namibian standards (5–35 ha) and communal ranching has not been realised. Very little farming is taking place.

> Another problem is the involvement in resettlement of unmotivated farmers as well as beneficiaries losing interest in farming. The rate of abandonment is considered very high, especially among ex-combatants who show a marked preference for non-farming jobs.
>
> (Chiari, 2004: 30)

The schemes provide pools of labour for neighbouring commercial farms: 'it is easy for men, one woman said, they can get work on neighbouring farms to get an additional income which is for women very difficult' (Harring and Odendaal, 2002: 65).

As the schemes are situated in relatively good farmland, they are close to farms where there is a demand for labour. Recruitment from the resettlement scheme allows commercial farmers to employ labour on a casual basis without having to provide housing and other amenities. Resettlement projects have thus become pools of stagnant poverty instead of instruments for poverty alleviation.

Resettlement farms[11]

Whereas immediately after independence communal resettlement was a government priority, this changed rapidly to a priority for individual resettlement of landless people. The 1994 SWAPO manifesto promised to commit N\$20 million a year over a five-year period for land purchase. These intentions were backed up by the Agricultural (Commercial) Land Reform Act of 1995. The effects of this legislation and the resulting National Resettlement Policy have been modest. Individual resettlement is a much bigger programme (0.531 million ha in the period 1992–2004) than group resettlement (0.196 million ha), but it is small as compared to AALS (3.12 million ha).[12]

The allocations are made to individuals and there is no collective element in these schemes. The individual allocations of plots – designated by the Afrikaans word *kampe* – are also much bigger than in resettlement projects. In the central and northern cattle-ranching regions, the minimum allocation should be 1,000 ha of grazing land. In the southern part of the country the equivalent figure is 3,000 ha, as that is supposed to be the minimal size for an economically viable unit in these ecological zones. Allocations were supposed to be made on priority following these categories:

000 No land, no income, no livestock
001 No land, no income, some livestock
011 No land; however, there is income and livestock

People in the first category are obviously the most urgently in need of land.

These categories are so broad that they gave rise to a mass of applications. In practice they are ignored, and applications are considered when an actual farm is purchased for resettlement. The official procedure is that the Regional Resettlement Committee advertises for applications. The regional committee then makes recommendations to the National Resettlement Committee. The actual application procedure for resettlement is extremely cumbersome (Harring and Odendaal, 2002: 42–47).

People interested in resettlement thus watch carefully if the government purchases a farm. These are often not the best farms, as those are snapped up by elite AALS applicants. The actual allocation of plots is highly informal. Politicians dominate the resettlement boards selecting the beneficiaries, and political influence is thus a major determinant in allocation. Allocations are also made to people who manage to turn themselves into a political problem, for example, farm labourers or squatters who camp on the road because they are evicted from farms. Farmers may be allocated temporary grazing on farms purchased for resettlement and remain on them. Illegal settlers are a problem in all resettlement programmes and most do not come under an official cover such as drought relief. People who are not officially selected can easily claim land, because plots are usually not properly surveyed. The Ministry of Land, Resettlement and Rehabilitation lacks the surveying and legal capacity and thus legal uncertainty surrounding the farms is considerable (Harring and Odendaal, 2002: 58–59).

There is a clear image among those concerned with individual resettlement that there is a big discrepancy between actual social practices and the aims of the policy. However – unlike in the case of AALS and group resettlement – no secondary material is available on it. Therefore we collected material on individual resettlement during a field visit to the Omaheke region.[13]

The Omaheke region is good ranching country. It is situated in the east of central Namibia close to the Botswana border. Its landscape is extremely monotonous: fenced grassland dominated by small shrubs. Occasionally the land is covered by more substantial mopane or acacia trees. It is the landscape of the Kalahari Desert,[14] dominated by vast fenced farms covering sometimes tens of thousands of hectares on which herds of livestock roam. From this perspective it is a suitable area for land reform.

Our visit confirmed that centrally designed policy plays only a limited role in the actual process of resettlement. Land reform has a comparatively long history in the region. One of the three settlement farms we visited, Tsjaka, dated from before independence. Its origin is associated with the droughts in the 1980s. Farmers then moved their cattle out of the communal areas into the so-called corridor areas. These corridors are meant to allow cattle herds to migrate; they are not intended for permanent settlement. Migration to cope with local droughts is a recurrent phenomenon among all farmers. Unavoidably, sometimes cattle become stranded in these corridors. When such cases occur, they lead to clashes between Herero and Tswana farmers. Tsjaka is designed to relieve the pressure in these corridors resulting from pressure on land in Aminuis, the Tswana homeland area. Although Tsjaka is claimed to be a Tswana settlement, one finds Herero households there as well as San people.

The plots at Tsjaka were well designed however, and property rights were secure. Such was not the case in the second scheme composed of two purchased farms: Vaalpos and Almapos. These are emergency resettlements. The farms were mainly given to those who claimed they had been chased off commercial land at Witvlei in the late 1990s. However, the link between those who live on the plots and those who were at Witvlei is often tenuous. We even found a cluster of three farms that were managed by employees of people who live in Windhoek. Similarly, we found one farm where an old lady was living with hardly any livestock (six goats) but was obviously guarding the land in the company of some grandchildren. The plots were allocated in 1997/1998 as temporary, but in 2003 there was little prospect of a more permanent solution. In the words of a civil servant, in such cases: 'Where there was room for five farmers, there are then fifty'. People are desperate for a more permanent solution, because fields are too small. Overgrazing, with its consequent ecological degradation, is rampant. Plots are not surveyed and people have no certificate of leasehold. The tenuous claim on land is also apparent in the case of two families (Herero and Damara from further north) that moved into Almapos with their cattle. They graze on other people's land: their cattle are said to open gates with their horns. The intruders refuse to go, claiming also to be landless. In contrast to Tsjaka and Rembrant/Samile (see below), there are no clear links with the Aminuis Tswana communal area and, more so than in other cases, the background of the settlers is on commercial farms or in town.

Rembrandt/Samile is the third farm we visited. These are two resettlement farms that had quite recently been made available by the government. Settlers had arrived about two to three years previously. When one drives around these farms, it is apparent that the old infrastructure – roads, fences, boreholes – is still intact but, apart from building houses on the plots allocated, the settlers do not appear to have engaged in further development. Farms are still not big by Namibian standards, but slightly bigger than in Tsjaka: 1,000–1,500 ha and much bigger than in Vaalpos/Almapos. The plots are given on a 99-year leasehold and people claim to have a certificate entitling them to the plot, although the farms do not seem to have been surveyed for that purpose. Settlers usually come here also from Aminuis, the Tswana communal area. However, here as well there is a mixture of Tswana and Herero households. The households that are resettled are not strikingly poor, and links with educated children in urban areas are common. Retirement pensions seem to be an important ingredient in the livelihoods of the settlers.

Settlement on resettlement farms is driven by processes from below. This is true in some cases more than in others, but it was to be found on all farms. In Tsjaka, a group of workers were managing a group of farms that had been bought by businessmen in Windhoek. On Rembrandt/ Samile, besides the old farmer's house, there was a neat row of brightly painted Herero-style houses. A lady answered piously to an enquiry about who lived there: 'We are not allowed to admit other people to live on our farm.' This kind of occupation was, however, most striking at Vaalpos/ Almapos as illustrated below.

Second, farming in most cases represents only one strand in people's livelihoods. This is clear in the case of Wilhelmina below. Some farms are primarily places for retirement while depending upon outside sources of

---

Wilhelmina

Wilhelmina was born on a commercial farm in the Windhoek area. She herself also worked on a commercial farm. Her parents were among those who were camping along the road with their livestock at Witvlei. The police tried to chase them away. Her father was even jailed. The issue got so much exposure that the president intervened and they were allocated their plot. The parents are not staying at the plot however, but are working on a commercial farm near Geelpos. Her grandparents live close by and her household has to share the little land with them. She lives at Almapos with her husband, a car mechanic who left his job when he became disabled. Nevertheless, the husband was at the time in Windhoek working as a car mechanic. Their herd has declined drastically since coming to Almapos: from 54 head of cattle, 28 goats and 15 sheep to eight head of cattle, 11 goats, eight donkeys and 17 chickens.

- The people who are now occupying the plot are thus different from the ones to whom it was allocated, albeit with a kinship link. However, the whole community is much more geared to wage labour than to farming. This farm seems to be more integrated with livelihoods based on wage labour than on farming.

cash: pensions, remittances, or renting out urban real estate. However, even when people claim to have purely rural livelihoods, the links to the urban sector are obvious.

Redistributed farmland can become a means to sustain, rather than alleviate, poverty. As stated above, outside sources of income are important in livelihoods on the redistributed land. If outside income falls away, impoverishment can set in. For example: old age pensions provision in Namibia is wide-ranging and, in quite a number of cases, people who had settled in a rural environment were drawing pensions. The death of a person drawing a pension can undermine the livelihood of those living on

---

Headman Arnold

Arnold is a Tswana headman on the Tsjaka scheme, and this government position gives him an income of N$1,200 (US$150) a month. He used to work in a uranium mine near Swakopmund and also had cattle at that time in Aminuis, the communal area. Arnold's farm is relatively small – two paddocks – and on it he has about 30 or 40 head of cattle and about 110 goats. His farm enterprise is interwoven with his extended family. At present, most of the cattle on his farm are owned by relatives. All his own children are at school elsewhere, but children of relatives are at school in Gobabis/Omaheke and they help him on the farm. In return, his relatives remit money that is an important part of his income. He does not sell much livestock. When there is an immediate emergency, he sells small livestock. Cattle are sold at the auction in Gobabis when school fees have to be raised. He does not sell more than a maximum of three at a time.

Being a headman fits Arnold's social, gregarious nature. He was organising the collection of devil's claw at the time we met him. Devil's claw is a weed used in homeopathic medicines. He was also a spokesman for the smaller farmers in our interview. Arnold was unusual: he maintained that poor people could farm profitably because there is much more to land use – hunting and gathering – than cattle keeping.

- In this example, farming is a minor source of the income constituting Arnold's livelihood: his salary and remittances are the mainstay.
- However, the livestock are essential in maintaining his base of solidarity among his relatives. Their children help him on the farm; they are the source of his remittances. He also needs a base among his relatives to maintain his claim on the headmanship.

the farm. For destitute people, life in a rural setting is slightly less difficult than in town, as hunting and gathering provides some free resources. Emergency expenditure can force people to sell their herds and a downward spiral can set in, although not in the case on the previous page.

Redistribution of farmland obviously serves the purpose of making Namibia a more just society. There is a need for black empowerment and there is a need to redress the inequity of colonialism, but that is quite another question from: will resettlement lift poor people out of poverty? The evidence we found suggests that land redistribution may help people in poverty to ameliorate their condition, but not to alleviate it. The reason

---

A Herero household

Herero households in resettlement schemes look different from Tswana ones: whereas the latter will limit the number of households and relatives living on the farm, the Herero usually settle with heterogeneous communities. An old lady is at the centre of this settlement. Her husband had been given the plot as 'a reward for looking after government cattle'. A link with the Department of Agriculture thus appeared fortuitous in this case. The husband also had a pension, but this payment stopped after his death. The children have moved away: three are working in urban areas. There are children around, but these belong to the other households. On the plot are a total of eight houses that are to a certain degree independent. Some claim to be relatives, but that may be putative. For example, one lady said she had returned to her grandfather's land, which in a strict sense can never be the case in a resettlement scheme. The grandfather was a classificatory brother of an original settler. She never married and had been chased away from her previous place of residence. She has no land, but brought children. Another single male lost his job in town and was happy to be received there. He obviously brings labour power. Some households are old, but they bring in some cash from pensions. Finally, there are two San households. The old lady claims to have only 19 head of cattle, but an outsider was also mentioned who came to graze 46 head. The herd had been severely diminished as cattle sales had financed a new engine for the pump. Water is a big problem for the large settlement. She claims there are very few remittances from town.

- This hardly seems to be a farming household at all, but a collection of households that is not bound together by a farm. The tie to the land is no longer an unambiguous principle of settlement.

is that it is impossible to earn an income from farming in Namibia without a considerable capital outlay.

The arid and semi-arid conditions in most of Namibia mean that ranching on big tracts is the only farming option. Any form of ranching is capital-intensive for the following reasons:[15] First, land may be cheap but, by any standards, one needs a big unit to farm. Second, the major constraint in farming in Namibia is probably not land, but water. Drilling boreholes requires capital and the recurrent cost of diesel requires a large capital outlay. Third, in order to get good grazing, farmers have to work continuously to stop bush encroachment; this implies a continuous drain on resources. Fourth, it takes at the minimum one year before a heifer can be sold. In Namibia one needs to breed as well in order to protect oneself against massive loss in the event of drought. Cashflow is thus not even to be counted in annual terms, and the demands on capital are evident. Sixth, small farmers are often dependent upon commercial farmers for their cashflow. Small farmers often do not have the capital to buy supplementary feed stuffs. They are not able to fatten cattle to the minimum standard required by the Namibian Meat Corporation (MEATCO) and their cattle thus have to be fattened on a commercial farm. If small farmers do manage to fatten their cattle, then they often have difficulty getting them to market.

In Namibian farming, the mode of production militates against the emergence of a peasantry in which wealth is spread widely. Only some form of collective farming supported by government finance could overcome this, but such alternatives are not entertained.

In the Namibian political arena only two options for poverty reduction through land reform are proposed. First, there is the argument that commercial livestock farming is not appropriate for large areas of Namibia. Exotic species, such as improved cattle, do not do well if rainfall drops below a certain level. At that level it is much more profitable to farm indigenous species in an environment of biodiversity. These can then be managed communally by self-governing bodies that are called conservancies. It is, on the one hand, a plea to retain the hunting/gathering elements of African farming. On the other hand, it is a plea for subsidies as a reward for environmental conservancy. It is hoped that cash incomes can be raised from field produce as well as tourism. Conservancies have been pioneered in the communal areas, but they are also seen as applicable to ranching land redistributed to African farmers (Brown, 2004). Second, there is an argument advocating land reform through the distribution of land to farmworkers. Namibian farmworkers usually operate in a culture where ties with the communal area of 'origin' are becoming weaker and weaker. They become proletarians in a very weak position, as they have no rights to the land on which they live and work. On the other hand, ranches that consist of large areas of marginal land with few water sources cannot be broken up into smaller economic units. If farmworkers could gain equity on the farm where they work, land would be transferred without the need to break up farms. Collective ownership by farmworkers in this or in other manners would maintain expertise and lead to poverty reduction through land redistribution (Werner, 2002). Both these ideas are propagated outside the government.

Conclusion and policy alternatives

The consensus in Namibia is that land reform is needed. Ownership of commercial farmland should not be a white prerogative. Large-scale land redistribution is also necessary to redress the grievances and desires felt by the Herero community. Similarly, everyone concedes that the effects of land reform policies since the early 1990s have been disappointing.

It was therefore expected that the taskforce on land reform would recommend a more state-led process in order to make progress. However, the actual action plan that resulted is above all inconclusive: First, the plan covers a 15-year time span. Second, in that period, 15 million hectares of farmland is expected to be redistributed. Third, ten million hectares is supposed to be distributed through AALS and five million hectares through resettlement projects. Fourth, the cost of the plan is budgeted at N$6 billion, which is equivalent to about US$1 billion. Fifth, the availability of credit for post-settlement expenses and investment is central. The government is expected to provide credit guarantee schemes so that banks will be interested in lending. Sixth, capacity building within government (law and surveying) is integral to the plan. Seventh, government acquisition will not be outright compulsory. However, the government will target farms for acquisition, and expropriation is not excluded. Finally, the plan is considered to be pro-poor. Half a million US dollars are to be spent on capacity building in the communal areas. There is a proposed quota for the poor of land in the commercial areas. There will be grants for post-settlement support for the poor (PTT, 2004).

The plan boasts little in the way of innovation, except in two aspects. One is that attention is to be paid to post-settlement support in terms of provision of finance; this may be construed as a renewed subsidy for the farming sector. A second innovation is that attention is to be directed at capacity building in the government; this is necessary for effecting the subdivisions into the smaller farms. This is an inconclusive rather than an innovative plan, however, as it avoids two crucial questions. First, it is silent on how finance for the plan should be raised. Second, the question remains as to whether government will compulsorily purchase land and, if so, at what price. Lastly, the plan promises poverty alleviation through land reform, but it is not clear whether that is possible. Capacity building for the administration of land in communal areas will benefit first and foremost the biggest farmers on communal land: they will want to have individual title for land that they fence.

The proposal to reserve a quota for poor farmers will, unless there is innovative policy thinking, result in situations where the land is part of an urban livelihood or farms become places for sustaining poverty. More land will become available and, as mentioned above, there are powerful forces urging that this should be in small units. Most probably there will be elite capture. In such a situation, it may exacerbate inequalities if land is distributed as a free resource. Funds spent on the purchase of land will not be pro-poor. There is of course the argument for compulsory purchase on the grounds of historical redress. However, that brings us back to land reform for black empowerment rather than land reform to counter inequality in income and property.[16]

Notes

1 Namibians can be of African descent or of European (German) descent. For convenience in this article, the former are referred to as Africans or black, or by their tribal name, the latter as of European (or German) descent, or white.
2 Chiari (2004) gives an elaborate overview of land tenure problems in communal areas. According to him: 'There is a general consensus in the development arena on considering communal areas as the real challenge that the country is facing in terms of land policy reform, poverty reduction and development' (p. 16). The development arena in Namibia has then to be distinguished from the national political arena. In the latter, land reform of commercial land is the major issue. Kakujaha-Matundu (2002) provides a highly informative account of land issues in communal areas.
3 The response appeared in all Namibian newspapers. It is of particular interest that it appeared in the *Windhoek Observer*, the newspaper voicing anti-SWAPO white feeling.
4 Dirk Mudge wrote this as a member of the Kalkveld Farmers' Association. The significance of his opinions stems, however, not from that position but from the fact that he was the leader of white politics before independence.
5 Unless otherwise indicated, statistical information quoted in this section is obtained from 'Namibia' in *Africa South of the Sahara 2004*.
6 This section could not have been written without the research assistance of George Eiseb.
7 Beneficiaries of AALS are not supposed to give up their land in the communal areas. Resettlement is meant to relieve pressure there. In practice, resettled people keep stock there 'to keep the hearth warm'. The same is applicable to resettlement farms discussed below.
8 This figure may not reflect a desire for farmland only, as it probably comprises also many peri-urban plots.
9 This section is based mainly on Harring and Odendaal (2002) and Chiari (2004).
10 The San were also deeply implicated in the war. They had been recruited as trackers by the South African Army. Apart from that they are, as hunter gatherers, a marginalised community.
11 This section is especially based on Sherbourne (2004a) and Chiari (2004).
12 These figures are provided by the Permanent Technical Team on Land Reform.
13 This section is based on field visits and could not have been written without the research assistance of Alfons Mosimane.
14 The Kalahari Desert does not qualify officially as a desert because it receives on

average more then 100mm rain in a year. Rainfall is highly unpredictable, however, and the soil is extremely porous sand. There is thus virtually no surface water.

15 In making the following points I benefited greatly from the insights of George Eiseb and Alfons Mosimane.

16 This view was expressed by Dr. Ben Fuller, NEPRU/UNAM.

References

Boer, M. and R. Sherbourne (2004). *Managing Diamond Dependency: Should Namibia Risk More to Gain More?* Windhoek: Institute for Public Policy Research, Report No. 6.

Brown, C. (2004). 'Namibia's Conservation Paradigm; Use to Conserve versus Protect to Conserve' in *Conservation and the Environment in Namibia 2004/5.* Windhoek: Ministry of the Environment and Tourism.

Chiari, G. P. (2004). *Draft Report: UNDP Mission on Rural Livelihoods and Poverty in Namibia.* Windhoek: United Nations Development Programme.

Fuller, B. and G. Eiseb (2002). *The Commercial Farm Market in Namibia: Evidence from the First Eleven Years.* Windhoek: Institute for Public Policy Research, IPPR Briefing Paper No. 15.

Fuller, B. and D. van Zyl (2005). *A Socio-Economic Survey of the Affirmative Action Loan Scheme Farmers; prepared for the Permanent Technical Team on Land Reform.* Windhoek: Namibian Economic Policy Research Unit.

Gewald, J.-B. (1999). *Herero Heroes; a Socio-Political History of the Herero of Namibia 1890–1923.* Oxford: James Currey.

Harring, S. L. and W. Odendaal (2002). *'One Day We Will All Be Equal . . .' A Socio-Legal Perspective on the Namibia Land Reform and Resettlement Process.* Windhoek: Legal Assistance Centre.

Kakujaha-Matundu, O. (2002). *Common Pool Resource Management: the Case of the Eastern Communal Rangelands in Semi-Arid Namibia.* Maastricht: Shaker Publishing.

Leithead, A. (2004). *Namibia's worried white farmers* http://newsvote.bbc.uk accessed on 12/07/04.

Motinga, D. (2003). *A Summary of Key Trends in Farm Transactions between 1990 and 2002.* Windhoek: Institute for Public Policy Research, IPPR Briefing Paper No. 29.

Mudge, D. (2004). 'Land reform in perspective' in Justine Hunter, ed., *Who Should Own the Land: Analysis and Views on Land Reform and the Land Question in Namibia and South Africa.* Windhoek: Konrad Adenauer Stiftung and Namibian Institute for Democracy, pp. 100–104.

'Namibia' in *Africa South of the Sahara 2004.* London: Europa Publications/Francis & Taylor, pp. 726–740.

Permanent Technical Team (PTT) on Land Reform, Republic of Namibia (2004). *Recommendations, Strategic Options and Action Plan on Land Reform in Namibia.* Windhoek: Ministry of Land, Resettlement and Rehabilitation.

RON [Republic of Namibia] (1994). *1991 Population and Housing Census.* Windhoek: Central Statistics Office, National Planning Commission.

RON (1995). *National Agricultural Policy; Presented as a White Paper to Parliament.* Windhoek: Ministry of Agriculture, Water and Rural Development.

RON (2001). *Levels of Living Survey 1999; Main Report.* Windhoek: National Planning Commission; Central Bureau of Statistics.

RON (2003). *2001 Population and Housing Census; National Report; Basic Analysis with Highlights.* Windhoek: National Planning Commission; Central Bureau of Statistics.

Saunders, C. (2004). 'Namibia, Recent History' in *Africa South of the Sahara.* London: Europa Publications.

Sherbourne, R. (2004a). *Rethinking Land Reform in Namibia: Any Room for Economics?* Windhoek: Institute for Public Policy Research, IPPR Briefing Paper No. 29.

Sherbourne, R. (2004b). 'A rich man's hobby,' in J. Hunter, ed., *Who Should Own the Land; Analysis and Views on Land Reform and the Land Question in Namibia and South Africa,* pp. 8–19. Windhoek: Konrad Adenauer Stiftung and Namibian Institute for Democracy.

Stephanus, K. and U. R. Sumaila (2004). *Intergenerational Cost Benefit Analysis of Smallholder Farming Models in Namibia.* Windhoek: Ministry of Land, Resettlement and Rehabilitation; Permanent Technical Team on Land Reform.

Werner, W. (2001). *Land Reform and Poverty Alleviation: Experiences from Namibia.* Windhoek: The Namibian Economic Policy Research Unit, NEPRU Working Paper No. 78.

Werner, W. (2002). *Promoting Development Among Farm Workers: Some Options in Namibia.* Windhoek: The Namibian Economic Policy Research Unit, NEPRU Research Report No. 24.

World Bank (2004). *African Development Indicators.* Washington, DC: World Bank.

10 Untying the Gordian knot

The question of land reform in Ethiopia

Mwangi wa Gĩthĩnji and Gebru Mersha

Introduction

Issues related to land, as to any other form of property, have always and everywhere been both political and economic in any society. The patterns and rights of ownership or possession of land, the various forms of access to and control over it, the organization of agriculture and distribution of its products are decided both by political exigency and economic interests – both in the narrow sense of individual and class interests and in the broader sense of a selection of the most productive pattern of institutions under the given constraints. Access to and control over land are issues of major competing interests, representing diverse social forces, individuals and institutions, such as landlords, peasants, commercial farmers, pastoralists, the state, and multinational corporations. This becomes more complex in a multi-ethnic and multi-nation state where nationality and culture are intimately tied to place and thus questions of land ownership become a Gordian knot of rivaling political and economic interests. This is the case in Ethiopia where the challenge to transform the agricultural sector and make it an engine of growth must take into account at every turn the very political nature of land ownership in the country.

Historically, and as partly explained by Borras *et al.* in the introductory chapter (this volume), the land question and the fate of agriculture in general in any country has never been decided solely in agriculture or by the farmers. Strong social forces, internal and external, have been and still are the ones which determine who should own land and the uses of this vital resource. In this case, what is decisive is the interplay between the various forces, such as the most powerful international financial institutions representing the interests of multinational corporations (MNCs), particularly food MNCs, and the Western states that work hand in glove with those corporations, and relatively weaker institutions, the local state, domestic capital and the rural population. Increasingly African governments are under pressure to privatize resources of production, particularly land. Despite the reluctance of some African states to privatizing land, the

World Bank/IMF and the international community 'advise' that it is in the best interests of these economies as privatization will lead to increases in efficiency. What is unsaid but is also clear is that failure to comply with the wishes of the international community could result in a restriction of aid flows which so many of these governments depend on for basic budgetary purposes. This is the quandary in which the present government of Ethiopia finds itself. On one side are the international community and parts of the local elite advocating the privatization of land while on the other are a significant proportion of the rural population, different sections of the elite and regionally based parties. The regime is challenged to find a middle ground between a policy that could result in political instability and inaction which could result in a severe diminution of government revenues, as well as slow economic growth.

In this chapter we will examine the question of land in Ethiopia, taking into account both the political reality on the ground and the economic necessity for agrarian transformation. We shall do this by first laying out the history of the Ethiopian state and the relationship between politics, economic interest and land over the last century. We shall follow this with an examination of the present land distribution patterns in Ethiopia and their relationship to income generation and poverty, and we shall conclude by exploring the possibility of an agrarian transition in Ethiopia and the nature of land reform in the context of our prior findings.

The socio-historical context of the politics of the land question in Ethiopia

Ethiopia, as a multinational state, came into existence towards the end of the nineteenth century. It was constructed by the Shoan[1] expansion and occupation in the second half of that century, of the southern, southeastern, and southwestern[2] parts of the present-day Ethiopia.[3] At the same time, the various states and regional dynastic rulers in Abyssinia[4] came under the direct political control of Shoa. By the end of the century, it had established its hegemony both in the rest of Abyssinia and the conquered territories. Consequently, there evolved a multinational empire-state set firmly in a composite type of social formation (see Markakis, 1974; Hiwot, 1975; Zewede, 2002; Crummy, 1980; and Mersha, 1985).[5]

The major consequences of Shoan conquest other than the political subjugation were the alienation of land from peasant producers, especially in the south of the country, and the creation of a feudal order of agrarian relations. From the 1870s under Menelik to the 1970s under Haile Selassie, the crown alienated land which was then distributed to members of the imperial family, the clergy, members of the nobility, Menelik's generals, soldiers, his royal retinues, and the local agents of the state (for more details see, for example, Hiwot, 1975; Markakis, 1974). After the Ethiopian–Italian war Haile Selassie continued this process of land grants to those who mattered to him socially and politically. The actual process was done under a pretext of tenure reform, ostensibly designed to provide land to the poor and landless. The emperor, like his predecessor, emperor Menelik, made extensive land grants to members of the royal family, the loyal members of the nobility, members of the armed forces and the police, top government officials and civil servants, and notable businessmen. The land grant in the south, in the period between the early 1940s and early 1970s, was about five million hectares; just a tiny fraction of that was distributed to poor and landless peasants. In the earlier period, grant of land referred mainly to temporary rights but after the war the emperor started giving freehold status to the grants. Even those who had held land under various guises were now permitted to convert their holdings into freehold private property (Ståhl, 1974; Zewede, 2002: 191). This privatization of land in the south continued at renewed great speed and force in the period of 35 years leading to the 1974 revolution.

The immediate three most important consequences of land privatization were the eviction of a large number of peasants, the spread of tenancy and the emergence of absentee landlordism (Markakis, 1974: 125–127), and the displacement of pastoralists (Markakis and Ayele, 1978: 56–59). The rate of tenancy was very high in the southern parts of the country where intensive land privatization was carried out. Although tenancy existed in the northern parts of the country, it was not as widespread as in the central and southern parts because land was not privatized in the former. Similarly, the rate of absentee landlordism, a phenomenon characteristic to the members of the nobility, high government (civilian and military officials), and civil servants was also high. A large amount of the operated holdings in the south were rented, that is, the uprooted peasants had to rent their former land from the feudal lord who owned it (Markakis, 1974: 126–127). This made the social and economic conditions of the peasantry extremely miserable and led to the people in those areas to rise up in revolt against the government and, in most cases, the social system that reduced them to tenant status. In most instances, because of the overwhelming military superiority of the conquering forces, it took the withdrawal of the imperial forces and state during the Italian occupation (1936–1941) for the beginning of organized resistance to appear.

As stated earlier, the land question everywhere is both political and economic. In an agrarian country, this is especially the case. Various social groups, whether directly involved in agriculture or not, are often connected to the land question because of the overwhelming importance of agriculture in the country. In Ethiopia, in addition to peasants, other prominent social groups that participated in the politics of land were members of the new national elite who themselves were often landowners though based in urban areas; urban residents who were often only one generation removed from the land or who had family still living and working in rural areas; and the student movement which, though urban-based as this is where the universities were located, was made up of students whose families still lived in rural areas. The fact that agriculture was the major source of production in and itself made the land question a national question.

A number of movements challenged the alienation of land that took place. Because the nature of land alienation had created both a land question and a national question, these movements took both these forms. Three exemplar movements were the Weyane movement of 1943, the peasant movement in Gedeo district in 1960 and the Bale peasant rebellion of 1963–1970. In all these movements the alienation of land and the high taxation imposed by feudal overlords were central issues of concern. These often overlapped with issues of national and or religious identity and sovereignty. Because of the overlapping concerns, these movements, while dominated by peasants, were also composed of other elements of society such as local elites.

Resistance to the land policies of the central government was not only waged in the countryside by peasant-dominated movements but also in the cities by the university student movement. The introduction of modern education, in Ethiopia was intended primarily to train young Ethiopians to serve the monarchy and to prolong its existence. It produced, however, two contradictory social forces. On the one hand, it gave rise to the emergence of the bureaucratic bourgeoisie which formed a class alliance with the aristocracy; on the other, it created a social force (students, young intellectuals, etc.) that gradually eroded and finally destroyed the basis of the feudal system. The students were organically connected to the land question in a number of ways. One, many of the students were not from urban areas but from rural areas. The land question was therefore not an abstract issue of justice but an issue that directly affected them and their immediate families. Two, national universities, as in most Third World countries, are one of the few places where individuals from different regions and nationalities come together. In this space a realization was built that some of the issues previously thought of as being local or regional were actually common across the country. In many ways the student movement helped transform the land question into a national question. Lastly, the students played important roles in the agitation for land reform and for the overthrow of the feudal order.

The university became the melting pot for students, who came from different social, nationality and religious backgrounds, for new ideas and beliefs, and for social interactions of a diverse nature. This process led to students questioning the status quo as they became more aware of the situation countrywide (Markakis, 1974: 357–361). The radicalization process emerged publicly in February 1965 when the university students staged a demonstration in the street of Addis Ababa, raising the slogan 'Land to the Tiller' (for this and more information on the subject, see Balsvik,

1985: 150–152). The impetus for this was a series of land and tax 'reforms' that had taken place from 1942 to 1964. This had culminated in the formation of the Ministry of Land Tenure and the presentation to parliament of a bill on tenancy. This bill was rejected by a landlord-dominated parliament and it was this rejection that led to students taking to the streets (Zewde, 2001: 195). The slogan remained to reverberate for a decade, promising hope for the oppressed and causing an ominous nightmare for the regime. However, the profound significance of the slogan and its serious implications were neither realized at the time nor were they discussed and understood by the Ethiopian 'left' and/or the political organizations that evolved in the subsequent years.

In the Ethiopian context, the slogan 'Land to the Tiller' encapsulated two equally explosive yet complementary elements – class and nationality – combined in one. In the southern provinces, the alienation of the land from the peasantry and oppression based on their nationality were symbiotically related. In other words, in the south, the 'peasant question' involved also the question of nationality. In the northern provinces, where landholding was communal, the intended import of the slogan was less significant as it would not have any meaning to mobilize the northern peasantry either on a class or a nationality basis as there was no land alienation and hence no national oppression based on that.

The land question being one of the burning political issues of the period, the slogan underscored a number of gains. First, it was a direct challenge aimed at eroding the foundation of the feudal social order, and second, it set in motion a process that brought together students and other progressive forces in society to challenge the imperial regime.

The land question and the question of nationalities under the military regime (1974–1991)

In 1974, after a series of military mutinies, strikes by teachers, taxi drivers and eventually the Confederation of Ethiopian Trade Unions, followed by demonstrations by both Muslim and Christian religious orders, the military took power in a creeping coup that culminated in its full control of the state at the beginning of September 1974 (Zewde, 2001: 195). They remained in the saddle as the Provisional Military Administrative Council (PMAC), alternatively called *Derg*[6], for 17 years, starting from June 1974. The Derg immediately laid out a plan to tackle three intimately linked structural problems, which underlay the 1974 revolution. These were the question of nationalities, the land question and the social and economic backwardness of the Ethiopian society.

As noted earlier, the question of radical land reform had been raised by students a decade before the revolution. Also mentioned earlier, in 1965, university students had demonstrated in the streets of Addis Ababa under the slogan 'Land to the Tiller.' It remained, until March 1975, one of the burning political issues. Besides this historical factor, there was a set of historical circumstances and conjunctures which put the land question at the top of the political agendas of the day. First, the two opposition democratic left groups recognised that a radical land reform was necessary for the future development of the country. Second, the reform was believed to be essential for resolving the nationality question. These groups and students exerted great pressure on the junta to come up with a radical land reform (Zewede, 2002: 239–243). Third, the junta realized the need for a radical policy measure regarding land in order to uproot the landed aristocracy from the rural areas, to appease the left opposition, and to win over the support of peasants, thereby consolidating its power. Fourth, within the Derg, there were some forward-looking elements, who then had significant influence. Fifth, in the early days of the popular uprising, peasants in the central and southern parts of the country – in areas where earlier package programmes and large-scale mechanized farming were introduced – directly seized land 'belonging' to the landlords, using violent measures such as killing or expelling landlords. There were also other forms of resistance such as withholding rent or the burning of landlords' property. This gave great urgency to the land question and was a constant reminder to the military that it was on the agenda of the day.

Except for the land reform, the other two parts of the regime's plans were a total failure. The regime's policy to solve the question of nationality was to use brute force to make the multinational/multiethnic organizations and nationalist/peasant movements bend to its will.[7] The faulty policy of the regime drove the country into internecine civil war and hastened the end of the Derg. On the land question, the regime's policy was quite radical: with a single stroke in 1975, all land was nationalized, largely eliminating the politico-economic basis of the *ancien régime*. The land reform bill abolished all private ownership of land by individuals or organizations and declared that 'all rural lands shall be the collective property of the Ethiopian people.' More specifically, it stated that, 'without differentiation of the sexes, any person who is willing to personally cultivate land shall be allotted rural land sufficient for his/her maintenance and that of their family.' The use of hired labor was prohibited (PMAC, 1975). Large-scale mechanized farms were expropriated without compensation except for movable property and permanent works on such farms. These farms were to be converted into state farms or cooperatives, or broken into smaller plots and distributed to peasants (ibid.).

The 1975 land reform transformed Ethiopian agriculture in a number of major ways. First and foremost, it gave land to the tiller as had been demanded by the students and other sections of Ethiopian society since the 1960s; in so doing it also destroyed the basis of the feudal regime. Second, it gave the peasants some sense of security over their land and reduced the need for devotion of resources to protecting individual access to land (Pausewang *et al.* 1990). Third, and probably most importantly for rural consumption, it released the peasants from the obligations to the landlords. This meant that the peasants now had more to consume and invest. Fourth, it introduced new institutions into the countryside, such as peasant associations, state farms and producer and service cooperatives.

Some of the changes, particularly the first three mentioned, impacted positively on the lives of the rural population. In the initial period and up to 1982, there was a small increase in total agricultural output as peasants took advantage of their new freedoms to plan and control their farming activities and expand the area cultivated (Griffin, 1992: 24). This initial increase was, however, soon lost due to a number of factors that can be directly tied to state policy on agriculture. Initially, the Derg undertook the land reform due to popular pressure and so was unenthusiastic about placing any demands on the peasantry. However, it soon realized that, as the peasantry accounted for the majority of the population and production, it would have to tax the peasantry in order to raise government revenues. Within a short period of time, the obligations that the peasantry had formerly had to landlords were replaced by obligations to the central government, which were collected via pricing and tax schemes that were biased against peasant agriculture.

We have noted that new forms of institutions were introduced into the countryside. The 1975 land reform reorganized Ethiopian agriculture into three forms (modes) of production. The vast majority of households and farms became individually run peasant enterprises. A number of former large estates became state farms, and a few cooperative farms also came into existence. Throughout the period of the Derg, peasant farms dominated agriculture. In 1982, for example, only 3 percent of the land was in producer cooperatives' land and only 0.7 percent of the households participated in this form of production. The rest were organized as peasant farmers: the state sector at this time accounted for no more than 5 percent of all landholdings (Griffin, 1992: 57). By 1987, despite the government's efforts, the situation had not changed much. At this time producer cooperatives accounted for 2 percent of the land while state farms accounted for 4 percent of land use. While these two sectors remained small, government policy was consistently biased toward them. They received priority for inputs such as fertilizers, subsidies for the purchase of animal draft power or mechanized power and favorable prices in comparison to the peasant sector. Lastly, they were established on more fertile land (Brune, 1990).

These biases against peasant agriculture mean that the 1975 land reform, while important in giving peasants control over resources on their land, did not necessarily lead to greater support in material inputs, nor did it necessarily reduce the level of surplus extraction from this sector. As one might expect, the net result was that there was little improvement in agricultural production. This is not to suggest that the land reform was not positive, but rather that its impact on productivity improvement was limited by other measures carried out by the government. As Kebret (1998) points out, agricultural production would not necessarily have been higher without the land reform.

It was, however, not only the anti-peasantry policy that denied resources to the agricultural sector. During the late part of the Derg's regime it used a fair amount of its resources to retain its power via military means. Not only was it engaged in war against Eritrean nationalists, but at home it had to engage with nationalists in Oromo and Tigray. Compared to surrounding East African countries[8] during the period of the Derg's rule for which data is available (1985–1991), only Uganda's military expenditures were as large a part of central government expenditure as Ethiopia's. However, even in this case they were a much smaller part of gross national income. Compared to Kenya and Tanzania, Ethiopia was spending approximately three times as much. This drops off in the post-Derg period (1992–1997) when Ethiopia's average expenditures are comparable to both Kenya and Tanzania. The same kind of trend is visible in the amount of military personnel employed as a percentage of the laborforce. Here again Ethiopia in the early period has a military at least three times the size of Tanzania's and close to six times the size of Kenya's. Even if we were to correct for land size and population, the military is still substantially larger than its neighbors. While diversion of government revenues to military expenditures obviously do not deny the agricultural sector alone, given this sector's size in Ethiopia compared to the other countries in its neighborhood, it is likely that the negative impact on agriculture would actually be greater in Ethiopia.

From the beginning, the Derg was confronted with the problem of how to deal with popular demands without losing control. Unable to balance the demands against individual members' desire to remain in power, it turned early on to assassination –including that of its own members – and repression of all forms of opposition. One of the effects of this was the creation of new, and the revitalization of old, ethno-nationalist organizations such as the Tigrian Peoples Liberation Front (TPLF), *Ich'at* (Ethiopian Oppressed Peoples' Revolutionary Struggle), the Oromo Liberation Front (OLF), Eritrean Liberation Front (ELF) and Eritrean People's Liberation Forces (EPLF). Forced to fight on many fronts, the Derg finally collapsed and was replaced by the Ethiopian Peoples Revolutionary Democratic Front (EPRDF) in 1991.

The land policy of EPRDF

EPRDF, realizing the political sensitivity of the land question and also as a matter of practical political purpose, decided to retain the public ownership of rural land. The ethno-nationalist groups that made up EPRDF when it seized power in 1991, particularly the OLF, were and still are totally against land privatization and the same was true for the other member organizations of the Transitional Government. The apprehension comes from the fear that privatization of land could possibly lead to land accumulating in a few hands, and inevitably, once again, to a massive eviction of peasants, but also from the memories of the pre-1974 revolution period, when peasant eviction and the displacement of pastoralists were common phenomena in areas where privatization of land was followed by the formation of large-scale commercial farms and plantations (see, for instance, Ståhl, 1974).

The Charter of the Transitional Government (1991–1994) declared that public ownership of land of the former regime would be retained and that was an important aspect of government's overall socio-economic development policy and its political agenda in addressing the question of nationalities. After a long and intense deliberation in the constituent assembly, the existing public ownership of land was narrowly upheld. The votes were 495 in favor of privatization against 499 for the retention of public ownership. It is now Article 40 (3) of the Constitution of the Federal Democratic Republic of Ethiopia (FDRE). It reads

> The right to ownership of rural and urban land, as well as of all natural resources, is exclusively vested in the State and in the peoples of Ethiopia. Land is a common property of the Nations, Nationalities and Peoples of Ethiopia and shall not be subjected to sale or to other means of exchange.

A concession or qualification was made, however, to accommodate the interests of private investors. Article 40 (6) states: 'Without prejudice to the right of Ethiopian Nations, Nationalities, and Peoples to the ownership of land, the government shall ensure the right of private investors to the use of land on the basis of payment arrangements established by law.'

The government therefore finds itself in a position where politically its hands are tied on the land question, but where the failed economics of agricultural production in Ethiopia demand a transformation of agrarian production. We turn in the next section to analyzing the present status of land distribution in Ethiopia before taking up the question of what kind of reform needs to take place.

Relating poverty to land distribution in Ethiopia

Compared to most developing countries and particularly to other sub-Saharan African countries, the land question in Ethiopia is rather unique. The 1975 land redistribution was particularly extensive both in terms of its impact across a broad swath of the rural population, and the amount of land redistributed. Of 22 developing countries identified by El-Ghonemy (1999) as having accomplished redistributive land reform between 1915 and 1990, Ethiopia ranks in the top group along with China, South Korea and Cuba for the extensiveness of the reform. This is clearly illustrated by plotting these countries on a chart that maps the beneficiary households from the land reform as a percentage of agricultural population onto the X-axis against the percentage of land redistributed as a proportion of total agricultural land (See Figure 10.1).

As is clear from the figure, only five countries during this period have implemented a land reform that covered more than 50 percent of agricultural households and holdings; and only three of these were more extensive than in the Ethiopian case. In two of these cases, namely China and Cuba, the redistribution took place over a fairly long time period. In the Chinese case the distribution took place from 1949 to 1956, while in the Cuban case it took place over six years from 1959 to 1965. Compared to these two cases, the distribution in Ethiopia was fairly cataclysmic, taking place in one large instance in 1975 under the Derg. Only the distribution in South Korea (1945 and 1950) is comparable. Given how extensive, both in terms of percentage of land area covered and proportion of rural population affected, the reforms in Ethiopia were, most economic discussion of the land question in Ethiopia has begun from the supposition that land is relatively equally distributed. It is then natural to turn to issues of how to transform Ethiopian agriculture from small-scale subsistence farming into a more productive form of agricultural system.

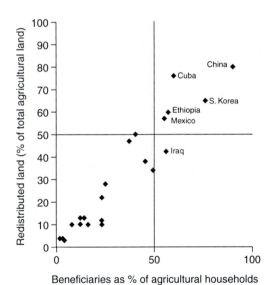

Figure 10.1 Extent of redistributive land reform in 22 developing countries (1915–1990) (source: El-Ghonemy, 1999: 8).

Note
For full list of countries please see Table 10.6: Appendix.

We would like to begin our discussion by revisiting the issue of actual distribution of land in Ethiopia and examining the relationship between present distribution and both income and poverty. Using a fairly new national land tenure data set collected in 2001 by the Ethiopian Economic Association and the Ethiopian Economic and Policy Research Institute (EEA/EEPRI, 2001; Deininger *et al.*, 2003), we analyze the distribution of land at the national level in Ethiopia and its relationship to both income generation and poverty. The data collected in 2001 were national in coverage, including 8,540 rural households and all states of the Federal republic as well as the different agro-ecological zones. The data are representative at both the national and regional levels. The purpose of collection of this data was threefold: one, to provide good, national-level data on land to inform the growing debate on the question; two, to gather new information on output, income and activities of farming households; and three, to solicit the opinions of rural households on the existing land tenure arrangements.

As noted earlier, much of the discussion on land distribution has assumed a fairly equal distribution. Based on the information available from four major agricultural regions, Khan (1998) showed that the top two quintiles had only twice as much land as the bottom two quintiles. Teklu (2003) reports a Gini coefficient of 0.399 for a sample of households in southern Ethiopia that rent in land. To examine what the present distribution of land is in Ethiopia, we used the data to calculate Gini coefficients and Lorenz curves of land farmed by households. Our results at the national level are presented in Table 10.1.

Contrary to what is generally reported, there is a fair amount of inequality in land distribution. We caution here that this does not necessarily mean that there is a need for additional redistribution in and of itself. The Gini coefficient at the household level we calculate to be 0.499. While probably not very high by African standards, it does suggest that, while land distribution was extensive, it did not equalize holdings as much as had been presupposed. Take, for example, two other cases reported on by El-Ghonemy (1999). In South Korea the redistribution covered 76 percent of rural households and 65 percent of agricultural land and resulted in a change of the Gini coefficient from 0.729 to 0.303 at the time of measurement in 1980. In a less extensive land reform in Egypt the Gini coefficient dropped from 0.740 to 0.384. In this case only

Table 10.1 Gini coefficients for land distribution in Ethiopia, 2001

	Household	*Per capita*	*Adult equivalent*
GINI coefficient	0.499	0.541	0.538

Source: Calculated from EEA/EEPRI Land Tenure Survey of 2001. Unless otherwise stated all tables and charts that follow have been calculated from this database.

14 percent of the population was involved and 13 percent of the agricultural land (for in-depth discussion, see Bush, this volume). Additionally the land ceiling was set at a high level of 42 hectares while in the Ethiopian case it was set at ten hectares. Both of these redistributions resulted in much lower inequality probably because the distribution resulted in the break-up of the largest holdings and their distribution to people with the least land or no land at all.

A more useful measure of the actual access to land is a per capita or per adult equivalent measure of land size (See Table 10.1). As is the case with most measures of distribution, the distribution is more unequal at the individual level than at the household level. Both measures of the Gini coefficient get larger. The per capita measure is 0.541 while the adult equivalent measure is 0.538. The fact that both these measures go up substantially suggests that even less attention has been paid to family size in the allocation of land than to equalizing holdings between families. Given that a drastic redistribution took place, it is also surprising that this measure of inequality is not substantially lower than that of neighboring Kenya which, with a land Gini of around 0.615, is considered to have a fairly unequal distribution of land (Gĩthĩnji, 2000). For the sake of comparability with other work that has used this data set, we will use the adult equivalent measures in the rest of the text.

Why is it the case that such an extensive redistribution did not lead to much lower measures of inequality? While part of the answer has to do with the total amount of land actually available for redistribution, part also has to do with who got left out. In Table 10.2 we present the Lorenz distributions for land distribution by household, per capita, and adult equivalent measures. What is immediately noticeable is that the lowest deciles (most land-poor) have no land. That is to say that, either at the time of redistribution or subsequently, land redistribution in parts of Ethiopia has not addressed the problems of the actual landless but rather has tended to redistribute between those already owning land. We should also note that a fair amount of the redistribution that took place in 1975 was from the landlord to the tenant. So, rather than a change in the actual amount of land that tenants had, what changed were their rights and obligations.

In comparison to Khan (1998), our measure of the ratio of the top quintile to the bottom gives us a ratio of 36, which is 18 times what we reported earlier from Khan (1998). Another possibility that we are unable to explore at this time is that inequality may have increased more recently as the government has made it easier for individuals to lease in land. In an examination of the informal land markets in central Ethiopia, Gabriel (2001) finds that during the 1990s richer households increased in the amount of land they farmed. Gabriel finds that richer families with more access to animal draught power were able to cultivate more land by leasing in land from poor families that have less access to animal draught power.

Table 10.2 Distribution of land in Ethiopia by land deciles, 2001

Percentage of population population ranked by land size	Cumulative share household	Decile share	Cumulative share per capita	Decile share	Cumulative share per adult equivalent	Decile share
10	0.00	0.00	0.00	0.00	0.00	0.00
20	1.83	1.83	1.53	1.53	1.54	1.54
30	5.17	3.34	4.52	2.99	4.52	2.99
40	10.18	5.00	9.04	4.52	8.91	4.39
50	16.78	6.61	14.62	5.57	14.73	5.82
60	24.38	7.59	21.96	7.34	22.02	7.29
70	34.80	10.42	32.11	10.15	32.37	10.36
80	48.01	13.21	43.99	11.89	44.57	12.20
90	65.63	17.62	60.25	16.26	60.93	16.36
100	100.00	34.37	100.00	39.75	100.00	39.07

The result in this limited case has been an increase in land inequality, the poorer households having to work as laborers on very low wages.

Ethiopia is a large country inhabited by a number of different nationalities, and with varied agro-ecological zones. A fairly unequal distribution may be due to differences in land potential between different regions rather than one between households or individuals across the nation. To examine this possibility, we looked at the regional distribution of land using the same measurements. Our findings are reported in Table 10.3.

As is clear from the Table 10.3, there is a fair amount of variation in distribution across the country. While land is fairly equally distributed in the regions of Affar and Somalia which have adult equivalent Gini coefficients of 0.38, it is highly unequally distributed in the SNNPR region and in Benishangul. Both latter regions have coefficients above 0.6. In the SNNPR, the most unequal state, the ratio between the richest quintile in land and the poorest is a staggering 175. Tigray and Amhara have fairly moderate inequality with Gini coefficients of between 0.45 and 0.46, while Oromiya, the largest state, has a Gini slightly higher at 0.51. What is interesting in the regional variation is the potential overlap between distributional issues and political questions on land. In both Oromiya and the SNNPR, both of which show a fair amount of inequality, the question of land not only concerns the distribution of land between locals, but the distribution between both locals and more recently settled migrants into the area who came in the last century with the expansion of the feudal Ethiopian state into these areas.

The problem of landlessness is also different between the regions. While Benishangul and the SNNPR are characterized by fairly large amounts of landless – around 20 percent in Benishangul and 10 percent

Table 10.3 Gini coefficients and decile shares of land at the regional level, 2001

	Tigray	Affar	Amhara	Oromiya	Somalia	Benishangul	SNNPR
Gini	0.45	0.38	0.46	0.51	0.38	0.62	0.65
Decile	Decile share	Decile share	Decile share	Decile share	Decile share	Decile share	Decile share
10	1.93	2.43	0.07	0.05	1.97	0.00	0.00
20	3.34	3.58	2.95	1.92	4.61	0.00	0.38
30	3.97	5.87	4.24	3.45	6.10	0.18	2.15
40	4.89	5.55	5.56	4.60	6.70	4.15	3.06
50	6.07	6.33	7.26	6.28	7.29	5.25	4.26
60	7.11	9.03	7.95	8.03	7.87	5.98	5.78
70	8.85	9.41	10.05	10.05	9.22	5.65	7.54
80	12.48	13.24	12.19	12.46	9.33	13.47	10.04
90	15.67	15.42	15.20	16.70	10.77	21.94	16.26
100	35.69	29.13	34.52	36.47	36.15	43.39	50.52

in SNNPR, this is much less of a problem in the northern states of Tigray and Affar. In Oromiya and Amhara the problem is more moderate. This regional variation in distribution suggests that land redistribution issues have a clearly local context that should be taken into account in any discussion of the possible policy approaches to the problem. We shall return to this in our discussion of policy.

While it is the case that land is more than an economic asset, in this part of our discussion we focus on the economic implications of the differences in landholding. To do this we examine at both the national and regional levels the relationship between landholding, land fragmentation and income, both total household and farm income per adult equivalent. Our aim here is to start understanding the relationships between the physical asset of land and income in the Ethiopian case. The reason why this is important is that arguments for or against land redistribution are closely tied to the impact land distribution itself has on the distribution and generation of income.

In Table 10.4 we present the averages of different variables for each decile of the population based on the land distribution. For example in Table 10.4 under the 'Number in household' variable for the decile 10 is an average of 4.96, this means that the average number of people (in adult equivalents) for the poorest 10 percent of households in terms of land have 4.96 individuals. The first thing that is clear from the table is that while, as we have argued, there is still a fair amount of inequality in landholdings, the actual size of the landholdings is not very large. For example the ratio of the average land size held by the richest (in land terms) quintile to the poorest quintile is 19. While this is still higher than has been reported from smaller regional studies, it is still lower than when you compare quintiles in terms of the overall percentage of land con-

Table 10.4 Average land size, household size and number of parcels farmed by per adult equivalent land decile for Ethiopia, 2001

Decile	Holding size	Land per capita	Number in household	Parcels of land
10	0.00	0.00	4.96	2.37
20	0.34	0.06	5.96	1.54
30	0.62	0.11	5.77	1.93
40	0.81	0.15	5.51	2.26
50	1.00	0.19	5.32	2.27
60	1.25	0.24	5.23	2.47
70	1.46	0.30	4.80	2.61
80	1.96	0.39	5.11	2.83
90	2.52	0.50	5.01	2.67
100	4.25	1.02	4.23	2.78

Note
For the first decile the holding sizes are so small that rounded off to two decimals they appear as zero.

trolled. The key here is the relatively low ceiling of ten hectares per house-hold that was put on the total amount of land could be held. Since then, based on the data we have available, it is clear that there are households that have amassed larger tracts of land.

The small size of the holdings is clearly brought out by an examination of the land per capita averages for each decile. The richest households have average landholdings that are only 1.02 hectares large per adult equivalent. Due to the increase in rural population this is an expected result. Jayne *et al.* (2003) report that the land-to-person ratio in hectares dropped from 0.508 in the 1960s to 0.252 in the 1990s. The other salient feature of this distribution is that for the poorest 10 percent the average holding size is zero. We must also treat this figure as an underestimate of the degree of landless because the collectors of the data were assisted by the peasant associations. As these are actually farmer associations, one would expect that they would be predisposed to leading enumerators to landholding families rather than landless ones.

What is of particular interest to us is actually the trend of the averages as you move from land-poor households to, in Ethiopian terms, land-rich households. To illustrate this we put the figures from Table 10.4 above into Figure 10.2.

As expected, both average sizes per capita and per household go up. We should note here, however, that the increase in land size both in per capita and household size terms is relatively steep over the last three deciles as compared to the first seven. In this same chart we present the parcels of land held and the number of people in each household in adult equivalent terms. We present this data for a variety of reasons. First, both

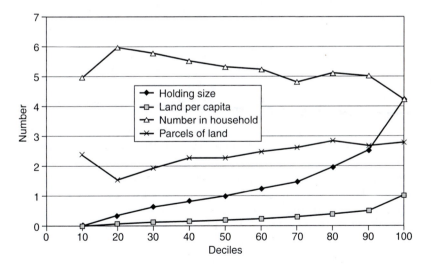

Figure 10.2 Trends in average land size, household size and number of parcels farmed per adult for Ethiopia, 2001.

in Ethiopia and many parts of Africa, there has long been a discussion about the fragmentation of holdings and its relationship to both total holding size and also to household income. Two opposing views are often presented. One is that fragmentation leads to loss of efficiency as returns to scale do not apply and extra resources are used in tending multiple fragments. Those arguing this position often see agrarian reform as an opportunity to consolidate multiple small fragments into larger single farms that are more amenable to the application of machinery. Others argue that in highly variable environments such as much of sub-Saharan Africa, fragments which often lie in somewhat different local agro-ecological areas represent a way of spreading risk.

At this descriptive level of analysis it does seem that the increase in frag-ments is associated with an increase in farm size. In a situation where indi-viduals might be able to consolidate their holdings through a market easily, this might be prima facie evidence of the desirability of fragments for possible risk-spreading strategies. However, because we know in this case that most consolidation or redistribution occurs through administra-tive procedures, this may not necessarily be the case. This trend may simply be an artifact of the administrative procedure. We shall return to this question in our econometric examination to follow. The next trend that we examine is that of household size. We examine this for two reasons. The first is that household size in a rural society with low levels of techno-logy is an important indicator of the potential of the household to exploit landholdings. The second is that it is now well established that richer households (in income) tend to have smaller families due to the relatively high opportunity cost of children. Our findings suggest that household size decreases with land size, an indication that income may increase with land size. We turn our attention to this facet of the question below.[9]

In Figure 10.3 we present the relationship of two variables to land dis-tribution. The first is the net farm income per capita, with the second the net household income per capita. In an agricultural economy one would expect these to be fairly highly correlated. However the degree to which they are correlated in the Ethiopian case is extreme. This is due to the fact that not only is agriculture important as a primary means of production, but there are also very few alternative employment opportunities in rural Ethiopia (Khan, 1998). With the exception of a drop in income between the most land-poor households and the second most land-poor decile, the relationship between landholdings and both net incomes is positive.[10] In a country in which a rural transformation is occurring one would expect and one normally finds that higher-income households tend to have lower proportions of the income from agriculture, especially when the form of agriculture is fairly low in productivity.

From a visual examination of Figure 10.3 it is not clear if there is a trend in the ratio of the two incomes. We therefore present in Figure 10.4 a graph of the ratio of the two incomes by land deciles.

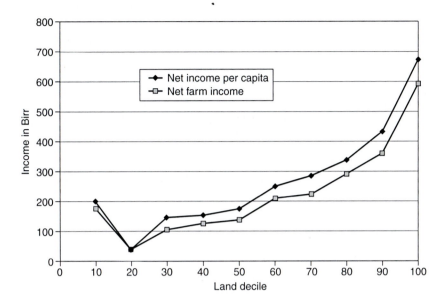

Figure 10.3 Net farm and household income in Ethiopia, 2001.

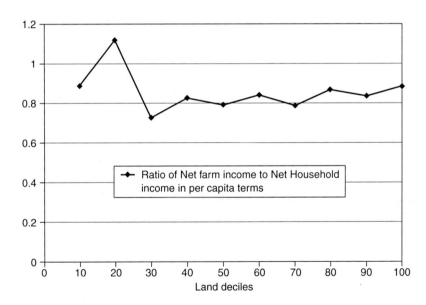

Figure 10.4 Ratio of net farm income to total household income per capita (adult equivalent terms) in Ethiopia, 2001.

While it is not a very strong trend, it is clear that above the third deciles there is somewhat of an upward movement in the ratio of the two incomes. This suggests that our rich households are slightly more dependent on farm income than our poorer households. This tends to confirm our observations about the lack of employment or entrepreneurial alternatives in the Ethiopian countryside. At the regional level we find that there is great variability between states. In the northern states of Tigray and Amhara the relationship between income and land size does not seem as clear-cut as it is at the national level. This is also the case for Somalia and Benishangul. In all the cases, however, the relationship between land size and number of parcels holds. These regional differences suggest that we need to undertake a more rigorous analytical examination of the relationships before we can make any strong claims.

The previous section described the actual state of land distribution in rural Ethiopia, and explored the relationships between land distribution and income. In general we find the following. One, land is not as equally distributed at the national level as one would expect, given the history of land reform in Ethiopia. Two, there is significant variation in land distribution between different states in the Federal republic. Three, despite the somewhat unequal distribution, the size of landholdings is relatively small. Four, there is a clear positive relationship between size of landholdings and income. Finally, the dependence on agriculture and farm income tends to increase with the increase in size of holding at the national level. At the regional level the relationship is not as strong and is varied across the different states.

The determinants of poverty and their relationship to land distribution in rural Ethiopia

While there is general agreement that poverty is pervasive in rural Ethiopia, its exact measurement and trend over time are difficult to establish due to the incomparability of surveys over time. The World Bank reports headcount ratios of 83, 76 and 77 in 1981, 1995 and 2000 based on the moderate poverty line of US$2 per day purchasing power parity and 46 percent in 2000 based on a national poverty line (World Bank, 2005). In our sample and that of Deininger *et al.*, 53 percent of the households are poor based on the national poverty line. In order to more carefully analyze the relationship between land and specifically poverty in the following pages, we present the results of a logistic model of poverty. Our model is a fairly basic and standard one. Our dependent variable is a dummy variable that represents whether the household is poor or non-poor based on the national poverty line. We regress this on a number of household and head of household characteristics that represent the resources the households have for production. We can divide the variables that we use into five distinct categories. The first represents the human capital of the head of the household plus a measure of the amount of labour available to the household for farming. The second category is one that captures the land characteristics such as size and number of parcels. The third is the type of farming in terms of the major crop, plus the land management practices of the farmer. The fourth category is a series of regional and geographic categories, such as state, agro-ecological zones,[11] population density. The penultimate category includes variables that proxy for the impact of prior redistributions. These include the change in the number of parcels and size of the farm over time. The final category is the external resources that the farmer has access to, including the quality of access to markets, non-farm employment and extension services. A full description of the variables and the results are found in Table 10.5.

Our logistic model is robust. The proportion of observations that are concordant is 80 percent and Mcfadden's r-square for logit analysis is 0.21. Our results from the regression confirm many of our earlier suppositions. First there is a statistically significant relationship between land per capita (at 1 percent level of significance) and poverty. In the case of farm size an increase in overall land size in and of itself does not reduce the likelihood of poverty. That is to say, it is likely large farms are correlated with larger families which tend to be poorer. It is also likely to be the case that areas which have poor farming conditions will also have large farms. Increases in the land per capita however have the opposite effect which is to decrease the likelihood of poverty. In fact an increase of 1 hectare of land per capita is likely to reduce the probability of poverty by 43 percent.

Interestingly, the number of parcels a household farm has positively affects income or, to put it in terms of poverty, reduces the likelihood of poverty. This is interesting because we have controlled for size, so we are not capturing an increase in size here. The benefits and costs of extra separate parcels of land may be considered in the following ways in the African context. Extra parcels are more costly because they require additional time to go to and to set up as farms. They may, however, have the benefit of being in slightly different local agro-ecological zones and therefore may be risk-reducing especially in a shock-prone system such as is most sub-Saharan subsistence farming and particularly Ethiopia. Our results suggest that the benefits of extra parcels outweigh the costs.

With respect to the household characteristics, only two of them were statistically significant, namely the degree of education (at the 1 percent level) and the size of the household in adult equivalents (at the 1 percent level). In the case of education, increases in education lead to a fall in the probability that the household will be poor. In our sample over 53 percent of the individual heads of household are illiterate and fewer than 75 percent have up to four years of primary education. This suggests that there might be fairly high rates of return to productivity from a basic education campaign. As one would expect, large households tend to be poorer. It is well established that larger households are also associated

Table 10.5 Determinants of poverty – logistic model

Type	Parameter	Estimate	Standard error	Chi-square	Pr > ChiSq	Marginal effects
	Intercept	0.729	0.327	4.98	0.0256	–
Household	Education	−0.053	0.015	12.22	0.0005	−0.0131
	Household size	0.107	0.021	27.05	<0.0001	0.0264
	Years farmed	0.000	0.000	0.49	0.484	−0.0001
	Age	−0.002	0.002	0.82	0.3649	−0.0004
	Sex of head	0.023	0.113	0.04	0.8419	0.0056
Land	Farm size	0.075	0.053	2.01	0.1561	0.0187
	Parcels	−0.065	0.018	13.29	0.0003	−0.0162
	Land per capita	−1.734	0.267	42.06	<0.0001	−0.4302
Main crop	Coffee	−0.623	0.099	39.71	<0.0001	−0.1546
	Teff	−1.510	0.172	77.18	<0.0001	−0.3748
	Enset	2.392	0.723	10.96	0.0009	0.5936
	Maize	0.535	0.220	5.94	0.0148	0.1328
	Wheat	−1.634	0.184	78.67	<0.0001	−0.4055
Farming Practices	Soil maintenance	−0.098	0.158	0.38	0.5374	−0.0242
	Crop rotation	0.292	0.073	15.91	<0.0001	0.0723
	Terracing	−0.111	0.063	3.11	0.0778	−0.0276
	Fallow	0.126	0.067	3.53	0.0602	0.0313
	Intercropping	0.052	0.068	0.60	0.4404	0.0130
	Tree planting	−0.026	0.054	0.23	0.6321	−0.0065
Geography	Tigray	−0.324	0.282	1.33	0.2494	−0.0804
	Amhara	0.361	0.264	1.88	0.1703	0.0897
	Oromiya	0.705	0.254	7.73	0.0054	0.1749
	Somalia	−0.970	0.357	7.38	0.0066	−0.2408
	SNNPR	1.457	0.268	29.49	<0.0001	0.3616
	Population density	−0.143	0.053	7.32	0.0068	−0.0355
Land changes	Change in parcels	−0.010	0.018	0.29	0.5902	−0.0024
	Change in farm size	0.000	0.001	0.44	0.5088	−0.0001
Access to external resources	Extension	−0.189	0.138	1.87	0.1719	−0.0469
	Infrastructure	−0.770	0.155	24.72	<0.0001	−0.1911
	Ratio of incomes	−1.340	0.075	322.31	<0.0001	−0.3325

with low levels of education and opportunity for women. Thus an education campaign in this context would not only affect production directly but would also lead to smaller households. Our other two household characteristics, namely sex of the head of the household and length of period that the head of the household has been in position do not show up as statistically significant. While it is a little surprising that those female-headed households are not statistically significantly poorer than male-headed households, it may be the case that administrative redistributions have not been strongly biased against women. We should also note that the number of female-headed households is also substantially lower than is generally found in sub-Saharan Africa. These results on female-headed households are similar to what Bigsten *et al.* (2003) find for per capita expenditure. That is, there is no significant difference between the expenditures of female-headed households and those of male-headed households. These findings on female-headed households should not be treated as conclusive, but should lead to caution in the generalization on the nature of differences between female-headed and male-headed households in Africa.

One would expect that the type of crops that a farmer plants and their management of farm resources would have an effect on income and therefore poverty. We have created dummy variables for all households where farming is dominated by a single crop, such as coffee, wheat, teff,[12] maize or enset.[13] The comparative category in this case are farmers whose farms are not dominated by a single crop type. Households that concentrate on coffee, wheat and teff are all less likely to be poor (statistically significant at the 1 percent level). These crops tend to be commercial crops with coffee being an important export crop and teff being an important commercial crop locally. Bigsten and colleagues (2003) also find the same thing in their examination of poverty in Ethiopia. Their study, which includes a new export crop, chat, which is now produced in a few parts of Somalia and Oromiya finds that chat farmers are less likely to be poor. On the other hand, farmers who concentrate on enset and maize are more likely to be poor. Our findings here suggest that maize and enset farmers tend to be low-productivity farmers and some attention should be paid towards improving their productivity. In the case of enset particularly there should be an exploration of whether it has been ignored by extension services as is often the case with indigenous crops.

Beyond the type of crop planted, we also looked at actual farm practices, including terracing, planting of trees, crop rotation, land fallowing and use of manure for maintenance of soil fertility. We found that crop rotation (at 1 percent level) and terracing and fallowing (at 10 percent level) are all statistically significant. Increases in terracing are associated with reductions in poverty. The practice of terracing decreases the probability of poverty by 11 percent. Surprisingly, the other two practices are associated with increases in poverty. It may be the case that these practices are more common where land has already been substantially degraded and therefore, rather then being associated with improvements in productivity, they are associated with maintaining rather lower-level production equilibriums.

As noted in our earlier discussions, there is a fair amount of regional variation in the relationship between income and land. To explore the impacts of regional variations, we included each state as a dummy variable and also included the agro-ecological zones. Our omitted state which also serves as the comparison state is Benishangul. In this case the probability of being poor is statistically significantly different in three states (at 1 percent level). Households in Oromiya and SNNPR are 17 percent and 36 percent more likely to be poor then residents of Benishangul. On the other hand, residents in Somalia are 24 percent less likely to be poor. We also find that increases in population density are associated with decreases in the probability of poverty. This conforms with what we might call a Boserupian view of agrarian change after Esther Boserup's (1965) work. Boserup postulated that, as population density increases and land becomes scarce, its value increases. Because of the increase in value farmers practice more intensive and efficient techniques leading to higher productivity and output and thus lower levels of poverty.

Some of the regional variation is going to be explained by differences in climate and basic land endowment. To explore this, we used dummy variables for different agro-ecological zones. As one would expect in an agricultural economy that is completely dominated by rain-fed agriculture, it is the moist and humid areas where people are less likely to be poor. Three of the four areas are in the highlands while one is in the lowlands. All these areas are classified as either moist or humid. For example, households in the hot to warm moist lowlands are 2.8 times less likely to be poor than the other households. On the other hand agro-ecological zones where people are more like to be poor are more varied including both humid and dry areas.

Elsewhere (Kebret, 1998) there have been discussions of the productivity effects of previous land reform. We were interested in whether the administrative process of reallocating land had had either positive or negative effects on the households in our sample. We were able to examine this through two variables. One was the change in land size since the head of household started farming and the second was the increase or decrease in the number of parcels during the same period. Both increases in size and number of parcels over the life of the farm are associated with a decreased probability of poverty though neither variable is statistically significant.

The last set of variables we examined were those that represented the access to external resources. These included access to infrastructure such as roads which improved access to markets, access to extension services and lastly access to non-farm jobs as measured by the ratio of total net farm income to total net household income. While both access to extension and access to infrastructure decreased the probability of poverty, only access to infrastructure was significant (1 percent level). A surprising finding was the result for access to non-farm jobs. In this case as the ratio increased, that is to say as household income became more dependent on farm income, the probability of poverty decreased. This would suggest that farm jobs actually have a higher productivity than the available non-farm employment. Normally it is the case that, as a country develops, the non-subsistence agricultural sector and the non-agricultural sector have higher productivity and thus higher income. One would then expect individuals to leave the labour-rich subsistence sector and enter the other sectors, forcing the subsistence sector to adapt by improvements in productivity. Since this is not the case in rural Ethiopia, one can only assume that the agrarian sector is extremely rudimentary. This has important implications for how we view land reform and the agrarian transformation taking place. In the next section we turn our attention to the debate on land reform in Ethiopia in the context of what we have established in the last few pages.

Twists of the Gordian knot

Ethiopia, or, more correctly, the Ethiopian government finds itself at a crossroads. Increases in income and development will only take place if there are huge improvements in the agricultural sector, which employs over 85 percent of the population and produces over 50 percent of GDP and practically all its exports (Khan, 1998). While the agricultural sector has recovered since the fall of the Derg and grown, the amount of growth has not been enough to sustain a transformation of the rural areas, let alone become the engine of development as a whole as envisaged by the government's development policy which calls for agricultural demand-led industrialization.

Figure 10.5 presents a number of agricultural indices in per capita terms. As is plainly evident, production has recovered from 1993 when the index for total production was just under 90 and since 1998 has averaged around 100. The total growth per capita for the period 1993–2003 has therefore been only slightly over 11 percent. Most estimates for substantially reducing poverty and allowing growth of income call for growth rates of GDP of at least 7 percent per annum. Clearly, given its heavy dependence on agriculture, Ethiopia falls drastically short of this. The question is how one achieves a rapid transformation of this sector while still ensuring that the vast majority of people dependent on it have a secure livelihood and do not fall deeper into poverty. This is complicated by the question of nationality which is intimately tied to the land question in Ethiopia. To put this differently, the question in Ethiopia cannot and

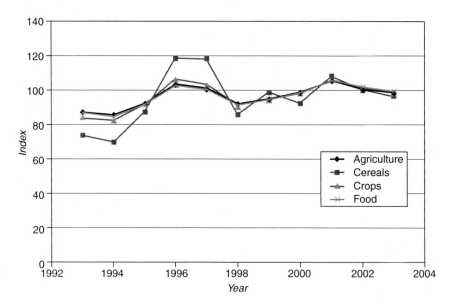

Figure 10.5 Agricultural per capita indices of production in Ethiopia, 1993–2003 (source: FAO, (2005).

should not be treated simply as one of land reform but rather as a question of political and agrarian transformation and transition.

This question has provoked discussion in Ethiopia on how to transform the agricultural sector. While the government's approach has been an attempt to improve productivity through improvements in extension services, debate has increasingly centered on the nature of land tenure and its impact on the efficiency of the rural sector. Studies on tenure and investment have begun to appear in Ethiopian research journals and our data were collected specifically to provide good data for this discussion. Prior to this collection of data, many of the studies were limited to Amhara and Tigray.

In the initial discussions immediately after the EPRDF took power, the debate was one between proponents of standard privatization of land and those who advocated the continued public ownership. In the short term that question has been settled, as we have noted, by the constitutional act that entrenches the continued public ownership of all land. This has not, however, stopped the proponents of privatization from a continued assault on the present tenure system. Over time the discussion has become a little more nuanced. We can group the arguments into three categories. The first are the arguments for the full privatization of land. The second are the more subtle arguments for security of tenure, which can mean a number of different things, including the ability to sell land or simply the promise that the government will take no more redistributive actions. The third are those who argue for the continued public owner-ship of land.

Those in favour of privatization of rural land argue that the con-solidation of land into the hands of what, one of them, Rahmato (1997: 10), refers to as 'efficient and enterprising farmers' will lead to an increase in output. The ability to buy and sell land will therefore lead to the allocation of land to the most efficient and able farmers. Those who argue for the security of tenure insist that investment on land in the form of terraces, trees, or irrigation systems depends on the tenure status of individuals. Gebremedhin *et al.* (2003) and Deininger *et al.* (2003) show this using Tigrian data and national data respectively. Those arguing for continued public ownership are most concerned about the possibility of distress sales that may occur with privatization and the possible removal of tenants from farms. They also argue that privatiza-tion, as shown in other African countries (Migot-Adholla *et al.*, 1991) and in Ethiopia (Gebeyehu, 2000; Holden and Yohannes, 2002; Shiferaw and Holden, 2001), does not necessarily lead to an increase in credit or investment. Gebeyehu finds that there is not a statistically significant difference between owner-occupied land and tenanted land. In both cases what he finds to be more important is the fact that both groups of farmers hugely underutilize their resources and that huge gains in production could result from more efficient utilization of existing resources. He also notes that the larger farms (over two hectares) are in general less efficient than the small farms, probably due to the lack of complementary capital as the farm size increases. Work by Shiferaw and Holden and Holden and Yohannes points to resource poverty rather than tenure regime as the main determinant of investments in terracing and the use of manufactured inputs. This work also identifies the low returns to investment for farmers, as being a determinant of the low rates of investment.

In addition to the arguments marshaled against privatization above, one may also note that privatization, in the absence of the development of fairly sophisticated financial markets that provide other savings instru-ments, may lead to the use of land as such an instrument. Since in an agrarian country land is likely to hold its value against inflation, indi-viduals may choose to hold land not to farm but as a hedge against infla-tion. In countries like Kenya this has led to fairly large landholdings with low productivity existing side by side with large numbers of landless individuals.

The arguments for and against privatization are not, however, only simple objective scientific discussions but are clearly influenced by class and regional interests. For example the EEA/EEPRI survey included both a survey of professionals and a survey of farmers. In the survey of mostly urban professionals, the investigators found that a majority of them favored the privatization of land (EEA/EEPRI, 2002: 92). On the other hand, 61 percent of the rural population favored the continuance of public ownership. This varied regionally from a low of 37.7 percent in Benishangul to a high of 77.5 percent in SNNPR. With the exception of Benishangul, all regions reported a majority (slim in Amhara at 52 percent and Oromiya at 56 percent) in favor of public ownership (EEA/EEPRI, 2002: 40). In a smaller survey we carried out that included members of parliament, academics and NGO professionals, all the members of parliament from southern areas, namely Oromiya and SNNPR, were clear that from their perspective privatization was not a viable option.

A further investigation of the EEA/EEPRI data suggests that, not only are there regional differences, but there also exist differences based on income. It is clear that higher-income households tend to favor the present system as compared to the poor. At the regional level this same trend is obvious in Amhara, Tigray and Benishangul. In Benishangul, for example, which overall had the lowest proportion of its population supporting the present land tenure, only approximately 23 percent of the poorest three deciles support the system while approximately 50 percent of the richest third of the population support it. In the other regions there is no discernible relationship between income and the desirability of the present tenure system. Surprisingly, both at the national and the regional level there seems to be very little relationship between landholdings by deciles and the desirability of the present tenure system. Our last two points on attitudes to land reform reinforce the connection between issues of nationality and issues of land ownership. This should caution us not to treat land reform simply as an economic question but also as a political question.

Untying the Gordian knot: a path for agrarian transformation

Where does this leave the question of land reform in Ethiopia? The first thing to acknowledge is that one cannot separate land reform from the entire process of agrarian change and continued political evolution. The continuation of the present tenure regime or a change to privatization must be considered in the broad context of what happens in the rural sector. Because of the experience under the imperial state, many fear changes in the tenure system may lead to the loss of livelihoods for a section of the population. We also have evidence that allowing markets to allocate land leads to increased inequality of land and the impoverishment of landless peasants, who are forced to work as wage laborers for extremely low remuneration (Gabriel, 2001). It is also clear from other countries that market-led attempts to transform agriculture while decreasing poverty have not had the desired results (see, e.g. Borras, 2003; and Borras, Kay and Akram-Lodhi, this volume). At the same time, the existing system in Ethiopia is clearly reaching its limit and must be transformed. As population continues to grow, plot size will continue to decrease, making it more difficult for rural households to support themselves on their own agricultural production.

To transform agriculture without increases in poverty, the rural population must have alternatives to farming. We would suggest that the government needs to rethink its approach to rural development: rather than expecting surplus produced in the rural sector to drive the demand for industrial products, it must first start by transforming the rural sector, providing alternative employment and increasing the productivity of agricultural holdings. In some ways what we propose is similar to Abegaz (2004) and focuses on the sequencing of agrarian reform. Our basic position and that of Abegaz is that, for land reform to be successful, a group of complementary reforms must take place. In our estimation these reforms are necessary before a tenure regime change if part of the reason for land reform is the eradication or at least alleviation of poverty. Where we part with Abegaz is in his advocation of a freehold tenure system. We are agnostic on the final form that land tenure systems should take and would prefer a 'natural' evolution to occur through local experimentation.

We suggest that the government engage in four tasks to achieve this, namely: (i) labor-intensive public investment, (ii) a national campaign for literacy and education, (iii) intensify and extensify the use of animal draught power and other inputs in farming, and (iv) where possible, consider the introduction of new commercial crops.

First, the government should engage in substantial labor-intensive public investment. This would be geared towards the provision of rural infrastructure that increases the productivity of agriculture. As shown in our logistic model earlier, access to infrastructure and markets is key in decreasing the probability of poverty. The infrastructure would include, but not be limited to, roads, irrigation facilities, rural electrification and environmental reclamation such as the building of terraces, gabions and reforestation projects. In fact, as these improvements lower the cost of farming and increase returns, one might expect a fair amount of private on-farm investment to take place. Not only would these projects by themselves increase productivity, but they would also in the short run provide alternative jobs plus training for rural individuals, thus relieving some of the population pressure on land. These projects would also lower the cost of locating small industry in the rural areas, thus beginning to make the permanent provision of off-farm employment sustainable. Further, while off-farm employment is often disequalizing, public works tend to attract the poorest of farmers and are thus also directly poverty-reducing (Wolde-hanna and Oskam, 2000). In organizing local public investment projects, the role that local peasants associations could play in choosing and organizing such projects should be critically examined. Lastly, we should note that improvement of rural infrastructure will improve the value of land

and thus the asset wealth of rural populations. If at any time in the future these populations had to sell or lease out their land, they would be able to do it at higher prices.

Second, one of the key variables in improving productivity is education. Both in our study and numerous others, low levels of education were highly correlated with poverty and low productivity. The low level of literacy in the rural areas of Ethiopia provides another opportunity for employment in a productivity-improving venture. The government should engage in a national literacy campaign that specifically seeks to use rural individuals to bring literacy to their local community. Again, like the creation of infrastructure, this would both improve productivity and create jobs.

Third, the government should continue improving agricultural productivity by intensifying and making more widely available extension services and inputs such as fertilizer. While not conclusive, the EEA/EEPRI (2002: 60) rural survey found that farmers with access to extension services and modern inputs had 26 percent higher income than those that did not. Those who received extension services, however, were only 35 percent of the sample. In addition, a key determinant in ensuring that poorer households can cultivate all their land in some areas is the availability of animal draught power in the form of oxen (Gabriel, 2001). Wherever possible, the government should improve the availability of this to poor farmers. In providing extension services and inputs, the government should make sure that it does not have a bias against traditional food crops such as enset.

Fourth, the government should consider assisting wherever possible in the introduction of new commercial agricultural products. Our evidence and that of other studies suggest that farmers growing commercial crops do better than those who are dependent on subsistence food production. These crops could include the traditional commercial crops such as coffee, wheat or teff, or new commercial crops such as flowers for export and chat. We should note here that consideration of the backward and forward linkages that may be created with the project of rural industrialization should be an important component in deciding what crops should be chosen. Although no real data are available, the government should carefully study the livestock and leather industry in the country. A casual walk around in the urban areas of Ethiopia quickly exposes one to what seems a fairly large and vibrant leather industry for local production. The role this industry could play in the transformation of rural Ethiopia should be carefully considered.

In implementing all of the above policies, the government should involve the peasants associations in identification, planning and carrying out of projects. This will give the efforts local ownership and increase the probability of success. Only after substantial progress has been made in both increasing farming productivity and providing sufficient off-farm employment can there then be an honest discussion of tenure reform taking the question of poverty alleviation seriously.

Assuming that the government was successful in implementing the programme outlined above, where does this leave us on land reform as part of the agrarian transition? Two questions need to be addressed in an Ethiopian context. One is the question of nationality, ownership and culture and the second is how to allow for flexibility in the use of land so that the most productive institutional arrangements can evolve. The first thing that the government and proponents of the various position vis-à-vis privatization must accept is that a 'one size fits all' policy is not practical or desirable. In formulating agrarian policy, the government must allow for regional variation which takes into account local concerns and culture.

The second issue is how to allow the most productive pattern of agriculture to emerge. In the absence of complete markets, there is no compelling reason to believe that privatization in and of itself will increase investment and thus production as well as ameliorate poverty. However, an increase in the options of what individuals can do with the land they control would allow for the emergence of new and potentially more productive institutional arrangements. One way of realizing some of the perceived benefits of privatization, while ensuring that individuals are not cast landless on the market without an alternative source of income, is to legally allow for the leasing in and out of land. While this will allow for the more efficient former to increase the acreage under their control and thus increase production, it will also ensure an income stream for the farmer who has given up their land. Such a system would also enable the gradual evolution of the tenure system. We cannot overemphasize the importance of local experimentation and the evolution of land tenure systems that are locally acceptable and also improve productivity. Too often it has been the case in African 'development' discussions and planning that grand plans for whole-scale change are imposed from either outside the country or by the central government only to fail because of local disaffection. To guard against this, an approach that takes local conditions seriously is preferable, allowing the rural population to consider a flexible and gradual land reform as described without being haunted by the feudal past or worried by the very real possibility of landlessness and its attendant poverty in the globalised present.

Appendix

Table 10.6 Results of redistributive land reform in vairous countries

Country and years of land reform	Beneficiary households (% of total agricultural households)	Redistributed land (% of total agricultural land)
China (1949–1956)	90	80
South Korea (1945, 1950)	76	65
Cuba (1959–1965)	60	76
Ethiopia (1975)	57	60
Iraq (1958, 1971)	56	42
Mexico (1915, 1934, 1949, 1971)	55	57
Tunisia (1956, 1957, 1958, 1964)	49	34
Iran (1962, 1967, 1989)	45	38
Peru (1969, 1970)	40	50
Algeria (1962, 1971)	37	47
South Yemen (1969, 1970)	25	28
Nicaragua (1979, 1984, 1986)	23	12
Sri Lanka (1972, 1973)	23	22
El Salvador (1980)	23	10
Syria (1958, 1963, 1980)	16	10
Egypt (1952, 1961)	14	13
Libya (1970–1975)	12	13
Chile (1967–1973)	12	10
Philippines (1972, 1988, 1994)	8	10
India (1953–1979)	4	3
Pakistan (1959, 1972)	3	4
Morocco (1956, 1963, 1973)	2	4

Source: El-Ghonemy (1999).

Notes

1 Shoa or Shewa was the southernmost fringe of Abyssinia. In the eighteenth, nineteenth and twentieth centuries, it changed its territorial and political configurations and since the late nineteenth century, it became the center of the Ethiopian empire.

2 For convenience, we shall use the term 'south' or 'southern' to refer to all conquered territories and peoples.

3 This expansion and occupation of those territories was, for Emperor Menelik, the architect of the modern Ethiopia, regaining the lost territories of his forefathers, whereas for the Oromo Liberation Front (OLF) it was colonialism.

4 The name Abyssinia is used here to refer to the highland Ethiopia. Before World War II, it was used interchangeably with Ethiopia but since then the name Ethiopia has been officially adopted (see Crummy, 1980: 119).

5 Although Ethiopians and for that matter many other African groups do not conform to a Western naming structure of family names, for the sake of consistency we have used it in our references. The full names of the cited authors are found in the bibliography.

6 The term 'Derg' or 'Darg' in Amharic means 'committee,' in reference to the fact that the members came from different branches and units of the armed forces, police and the Territorial Army. Here it thus refers to that small contin-

gent of the armed forces that seized state power after deposing emperor Haile Selassie in 1975.

7 Incidentally, the Tigrain Peoples Liberation Front (TPLF), the dominant nationalist organization in the current government, EPRDF (Ethiopian Peoples Revolutionary Democratic Front), was established after the Derg seized power. It was under the military hegemony of TPLF that the EPRDF defeated the Derg and came to power. The same was true for other nationalist movements that were formed in the central, southern and eastern parts of the country. The Oromo Liberation Front (OLF), the most important one, socially and politically, was established in 1974.

8 Namely Kenya, Sudan, Uganda, and Tanzania. Data are from the World Bank's World Development Indicators 2001.

9 Please note for any discussion involving income we have dropped the Affar region from our calculations. We have done this because the average incomes reported in the data tend to be ten times the average of any other region. This has not however resulted in any substantive differences in the nature of our findings. The trends we report tend to hold even with the inclusion of this region.

10 We should also note here the possible error in some calculation of net income that results in a ratio of greater than one for the second decile. This is theoretically possible in cases where a loss-making enterprise is actually being subsidized by the farming enterprise.

11 For ease of reporting we have not presented the 13 agro-ecological zones in the table that are simply described as agro-ecological zone 1 and so on to 13.

12 Teff is a traditional grain that is native to Ethiopia and is a staple.

13 Enset is a traditional cultivar related to the banana which is a traditional staple in southern Ethiopia.

References

Abegaz, B. (2004). 'Escaping Ethiopia's Poverty Trap: The Case for a Second Agrarian Reform,' *Journal of Modern African Studies*, vol. 42, no. 3, pp. 313–342.

Balsvik, R. R. (1985). *Haile Selassie's Students: The Intellectual and Social Background, 1952–1977*. East Lansing: African Studies Center, Michigan State University, East Lansing, Michigan.

Bigsten, A., B. Kebede, A. Shimeles and M. Taddesse (2003). 'Growth and Poverty Reduction in Ethiopia Evidence from Household Panel Surveys,' *World Development*, vol. 31, no. 1, pp. 87–106.

Borras, S. Jr (2003). 'Questioning Market Led Agrarian Reform: Experiences from Brazil, Columbia and South Africa,' *Journal of Agrarian Change*, vol. 3, no. 3, pp. 376–394.

Boserup, E. (1965). *The Conditions of Agricultural Growth; the Economics of Agrarian Change under Population Pressure*. Chicago: Aldine Publishing Co.

Brune, S. (1990). 'The Agricultural Sector,' in S. Pausewang *et al.* (eds) (1990) *Ethiopia: Rural Development Options*. London: Zed Books.

Crummy, D. (1980). 'Abyssinian Feudalism,' *Past and Present*, no. 89.

Deininger, K. *et al.* (2003). 'Tenure Security and Land Related Investment: Evidence from Ethiopia,' *World Bank Discussion Paper*, Washington, DC: World Bank.

Ege, S. (2002). 'Peasant Participation in Land Reform: The Amhara Land Distribution of 1997,' in Z. Zewede and S. Pausewang (eds) *Ethiopia: The Challenges of Democracy from Below*, pp. 71–86. Stockholm: Elders Gotab.

El-Ghonemy, M. R. (1999). 'The Political Economy of Market Based Land Reform', *UNRISD Discussion Paper No. 10*. Geneva: UNRISD.

Endashaw, A. (2002). *Ethiopia: Perspectives for Change and Renewal*. Singapore: Seng Lee Press.

Ethiopian Economic Association/Ethiopian Economic Policy Research Institute (EEA/EEPRI) (2001). 'Land Tenure and Agricultural Development.' Addis Ababa: EEA/EEPRI.

FAO (2005). FAOSTATS-Agriculture www.fao.org/waicent/portal/statistics_en.asp.

FDRE (1995). *The Constitution of the Federal Democratic Republic of Ethiopia. 1st Year No. 1*. Addis Ababa, 21 August 1995.

Gabriel, A. H. (2001). 'Peasant Endowment and the Redistributive Function of Informal Rural Land Markets,' *Ethiopian Journal of Development Research*, vol. 23, no. 2, pp. 1–34.

Gebeyehu, W. (2000). 'Does Type of Tenure Impact on Technical Efficiency of Farmers,' *Ethiopian Journal of Economics*, vol. IX, no. 1, pp. 58–92.

Gebremehdin, B. *et al.* (2003). 'Land Tenure and Land Management in the Highlands of Northern Ethiopia,' *ILRI Working Paper*, Addis Ababa: ILRI.

Gilkes, P. (1975). *The Dying Lion: Feudalism and Modernisation in Ethiopia*. New York: St Martin's Press.

Gīthīnji, M. wa (2000). *Ten Millionaires and Ten Million Beggars*. Aldershot: Ashgate Press.

Griffin, K. (ed.) (1992). *The Economy of Ethiopia*. London: St Martin Press.

Gudina, M. (2003). *Ethiopia: Competing Ethnic Nationalism and the Quest for Democracy, 1960–2000*. Addis Ababa: Chamber Printing House.

Hiwot, A. (1975). 'Ethiopia: From Autocracy to Revolution,' Occasional Publication no. 1, *Review of African Political Economy*, London.

Hiwot, A. (1987). 'From Autocracy to Revolution: Reflections on the Intelligentsia,' in *Proceedings: Second International Conference on the Horn of Africa: The Ethiopian Revolution and Its Impact on the Politics of the Horn of Africa*. New School, New York, 29–30 May 1987, pp. 41–64.

Holden, S. and H. Yohannes (2002). 'Land Redistribution, Tenure Insecurity and Intensity of Production: A Study of Farm Households in Southern Ethiopia,' *Land Economics*, vol. 78, no. 4, pp. 573–590.

Jayne, T. S. *et al.* (2003). 'Smallholder Income and Land Distribution in Africa,' *Food Policy*, vol. 28, pp. 253–275.

Jemma, H. (2001). 'The Debate over Rural Land Tenure Policy Options in Ethiopia: Review of the Post-1991 Contending Views,' *Ethiopian Journal of Development Research*, vol. 23, no. 2, pp. 35–84.

Kebret, H. (1998). 'Land Reform: Revisiting the Public versus Private Ownership Controversy,' *Ethiopian Journal of Economics*, vol. 7, no. 2, pp. 46–64.

Khan, A. (1998). 'The Development of Ethiopia's Rural Economy'. Mimeo.

Lipsky, G. A. (1962). *Ethiopia*. New Haven: HRAF Press.

Markakis, J. (1974) *Ethiopia: Anatomy of a Traditional Polity*. Addis Ababa: Addis Ababa University Press.

Markakis, J. and N. Ayele (1978). *Class and Revolution in Ethiopia*. Nottingham: Spokesman.

Mersha, G. (1985). 'The Formation of the Ethiopian Empire-State and the Attendant National and Class Oppression: An Essay in Historical and Socio-Economic Analysis.' M. Phil Thesis, ISS, The Hague.

Mersha, G. (1987). 'The Emergence of the Ethiopian "Left" in the Period 1960–1970: An Aspect of the Formation of the "Organic Intellectuals."'in *Proceedings: Second International Conference on the Horn of Africa: The Ethiopian Revolution and Its Impact on the Politics of the Horn of Africa, New School for Social Research.* New York, 29–30 May, 1987.

Migott, A. *et al.* (1991). 'Indigenous Land Rights in Sub Saharan Africa: Constraint on Productivity?' *World Bank Economic Review,* vol. 5, pp. 155–175.

Pausewang, S. *et al.* (eds) (1990) *Ethiopia: Rural Development Options.* London: Zed Books.

PMAC (Provisional Military Administrative Council) (1975). 'Proclamation No. 31/75: A Proclamation to Provide for Public Ownership of Rural Lands', Negarit Gazeta 34th Year no. 26.

Rahmato, D. (1994). 'Land Policy in Ethiopa at the Crossroads,' in *Land Tenure and Land Policy after the Derg. Proceedings of the Second Workshop of the Land Tenure Project,* Land Tenure Project, IDR, Addis Ababa University, pp. 1–20.

Rahmato, D. (1997). 'Land, Poverty and Food Insecurity,' in *Economic Focus: Bulletin of the Ethiopian Economic Association,* pp. 2–5, Addis Ababa.

Shiferaw, B. and S. T. Holden (2001). 'Farm Level Benefits to Investment for Mitigating Land Degradation Empirical Evidence from Ethiopia,' *Environment and Development Economics,* vol. 6, pp. 335–358.

Ståhl, M. (1974). *Ethiopia: Political Conditions in Agricultural Development.* Stockholm: Liber Tryck.

Tareke, G. (1968). 'Rural Protest in Ethiopia, 1941–1970: A Study of the Three Rebellions,' PhD Thesis, University of Wisconsin, Madison.

Tareke, G. (1996). *Ethiopia: Power and Protest, Peasant Revolts in the Twentieth Century.* Lawrenceville, NJ: Red Sea Press.

Teklu,T. (2003). 'Rural Lands and Evolving Tenure Arrangements in Ethiopia,' *FSS Discussion Paper No. 10.* Addis Ababa.

Woldehanna, T. and A. Oskam (2000). 'Off-farm Employment and Income Inequality: The Implication for Poverty Reduction Strategies,' *Ethiopian Journal of Economics,* vol. IX, no. 1, pp. 40–57.

World Bank (2005) *World Development Indicators Database.* Washington, DC: World Bank

Zewde, B. (2001). *History of Modern Ethiopia, 1855–1991* (second edition). Oxford: James Currey.

11 Land policy, poverty reduction and public action in Zimbabwe

Sam Moyo

Introduction

A 'fast-track', state-driven approach to land reform was introduced during 1997 in Zimbabwe, culminating in extensive land transfers by 2004. Land reform took centre stage in Zimbabwe's politics and economy, and polarised land policy discourses nationally and internationally. The earlier period of 1980–1996 represented a relatively 'slow-track' land redistribution programme, characterised by a market-driven approach to land reform. The effects these land reforms have had on poverty reduction have not been adequately discussed so far.

Current discourses eschew rigorous analysis of the relationship between land reform policy and public action, and its longer-term effects on poverty reduction, development and democratisation. They focus on short-term manifestations, such as the land disputes, agricultural decline and the electoral (mis)fortunes of competing political parties. Zimbabwe's fast-track land reform has been considered to be an odd aberration (Bernstein, 2001), contrived for political electoral advantage (Sachikonye, 2005), or for black elite interests (Davies, 2004). This discourse subordinates the land issue to 'good governance' procedural questions (Raftopolous, 2003), to be condemned for their human rights transgressions (Hellum and Derman, 2004). The place of land rights in this perspective is not adequately conceptualised or empirically defined, given the contested nature of land rights (Hunzwi,[1] Sadomba, 2005). The tendency has been to reduce complex and diverse social actions or processes of civil society–state interactions over land to the atavistic manipulations of a 'pre-modernist' (Worby, 2004), 'authoritarian nationalist' regime, using the modern institutions of the state, political parties and 'uncivil' associations.

In general Zimbabwe land redistribution policy envisioned a changing racial composition of access, of landholding sizes, land use norms (exports versus food) and of tenure systems, given the entrenchment of racially structured land access, tenures and production systems. Poverty benefits tended to be defined in general terms of more equitable land and natural resources ownership and de-racialised 'commercial' farming.

The main controversy in the land reform debate today concerns the efficacy of market-led reforms in delivering racially equitable land distribution, vis-à-vis the physical violence and the violation of property rights of landowners and of farmworkers, which the militant and state-led approach pursued, having suspended certain land and related laws and 'rights' in order to reverse past injustices. Demands for a poverty-oriented land reform grew in 1997, when the international community rejected land expropriation and the deracialisation of commercial farming, in favour of support for small-scale settlers and a slow redistributive pace (ODA, 1996).

This chapter assesses the evolution of land policy and social action for reform, in relation to issues of poverty reduction in Zimbabwe, based on three key arguments. First, that Zimbabwe's pursuit of variants of a market-led approach to land reform, during 17 of its 25 years of independence, between 1980 and 1996, and then between 1998 and 1999, rather than the lack of political will per se, led to less land redistribution than was promised or expected. This outcome limited the potential scope for poverty reduction at the national and farm household level. The reigning neoliberal development policy framework then further limited the prospect of wider poverty gains from land. This induced expanding social agitation for radical reforms.

Second, the chapter argues that the radicalisation of the land reform approach in 1997, and then between 2000 and 2004, towards state-driven land transfers, was significantly induced, in terms of land acquisition and allocation, by popular mobilisations of land occupations. This led to extensive land redistribution over five years, but yielded mixed poverty-reduction gains in the short term (five years). The potential positive impacts of this non-market approach to land transfers on poverty reduction at farm household and national level were however limited, not only by the rapid 'loss' of substantial agricultural (food and export) production by former landowners and farmworker job losses, but also by the wider effects of economic collapse and weak policies, internal opposition to land reform and international isolation.

Third, the chapter argues that the shifts in Zimbabwe's land reform and development policy approaches over 25 years, and the nature of the redistributive outcome, as well as their impacts on poverty reduction, can be explained by complex changes in state–society interactions and relations, occasioned by the negative effects of economic liberalisation and unfulfilled land redistribution. Issues such as 'political will', 'electoral instrumentalisation' and 'weak governance' were symptomatic effects of wider social (including economic) effects, which played a subordinate part in influencing the pace and nature of land reform, given that the role of social movements was more fundamental in radicalising land policy formation.

These three propositions suggest the need to consider the various direct and indirect effects of land reform on poverty, at the micro-household and economy-wide level, including the political conflicts that arose from the dramatic shifts in the correlation of social forces that emerged as a result of the contradictions of neoliberalism, and from Zimbabwe's 'dissidence' against the hegemonic models of market-based and internationally supported approaches to land reform and economic management (see Borras, Kay and Akram-Lodhi, this volume, for elaboration). This complex interaction of factors suggests that the land and poverty relationship can easily be confounded, in terms of causes and effects, particularly when the long-term structural effects of unequal agrarian structures and an extroverted development strategy are not properly taken into account.

The next section outlines the nature of poverty in relation to land access and development policy. The evolution of land reform approaches and their effects on poverty are then discussed, followed by an assessment of the changing public actions and institutional settings of land reform advocacy. The last section draws some conclusions and outlines some elements of pro-poor land policy options.

Land, development strategy and poverty

The poverty and land relationship in Zimbabwe

According to a national human development report (ZHDR, 1999), 60 per cent of Zimbabwe's population was earning less than US$1 a day, 80 per cent of these living in the rural areas, while 25 per cent was unable to meet basic needs, mainly as a result of the Economic Structural Adjustment Programme (ESAP). Due to frequent droughts, between 1.5 and five million people require food relief every three to five years. Zimbabwe ranks 130th on the Human Development Index.[2] Rural poverty was exacerbated by reduced remittances to the rural areas from urban relatives due to retrenchment of urban workers. Still categorised as a medium-income country, Zimbabwe is among 16 sub-Saharan African countries that experienced reversals in human development since 1990 (Economist Intelligence Unit, 1999).[3]

Poverty is predominantly rural, given that 70 per cent of Zimbabwe's population resides in the countryside (CSO, 2002). Rural livelihoods are mainly agricultural and depend on access to land and related resources (e.g. water, woodlands, etc). About 65 per cent of the population lives in 'communal areas', as a differentiated peasantry, facing the second highest poverty levels, surpassed only by rural farm labourers (comprising 12 per cent of the population) until 2000. This labouring class (now reduced to about 5 per cent of the population) depended heavily on smaller-scale food crop cultivation in both communal and commercial areas, given their low wages and insecure land rights. But a large part of the urban population, mostly with incomes below the poverty datum line, straddles the rural–urban divide, and also depends on land for its livelihood within the rural, peri-urban and urban areas. Rural–urban income and food transfers define livelihood strategies intended to secure precarious social conditions.

Thus, over 80 per cent of Zimbabwe's rural and urban populations have continued since 1980 to depend on farming and therefore access to increasingly overcrowded land in communal areas, given the stagnation and decline of employment in the secondary and tertiary sectors, and the slow land redistribution process. Farming incomes for small farms remained low as a result of low productivity and poor returns to sold outputs, reflecting a long legacy of biased allocations of economic incentives towards large farmers. Land policies since 1980 had failed to redress the need among the poor for the effective control of productive assets, such as fertile land and related access to public irrigation water infrastructures, and of natural resources for consumptive and productive use. This relationship between landholding structures and poverty in a predominantly agrarian economy was shaped by racially unequal (agricultural) landholdings in terms of area allocated and farm sizes, until 2004 (Table 11.1).

Considerable differentiation in the size of land holdings has been typical. At the upper extreme are the transnationals and 'landed gentry', mainly comprising whites (Moyo, 1998), holding large estates and multiple farms with sizes of between 10,000 and over 100,000 hectares, pitted against black 'kulaks', holding between over ten and 100 hectares depending on the agro-ecological region potential. At the lower extreme were the black landless and land-poor, with dryland holdings of below three hectares, pitted against their relatively fewer large-scale white landowners holding on average between 500 and 2,000 hectares. On the margins, numerous 'squatters' in various rural and peri-urban areas tended to occupy small plots of less than one hectare, including former farmworkers with informal access to land, at the mercy of landowners. About 25 per cent of the 1.2 million rural households were short of land (Sukume and Moyo, 2003). The urban poor and unemployed required at least one million residential land plots, while farmworkers, amounting to over 150,000 farmworker households, required access to residential land. Land reform since 1980 gradually shifted the land distribution and holdings size patterns over time, as the comparative figures of 1980, 1996 and 2004 show.

The share of the incomes of the smallholder farmers and of investments into rural social services, infrastructure and credit has consistently been the lowest. Rural communities' capacities to reverse poverty and improve their livelihoods have tended to be precarious and dependent on small-scale external welfare transfers from the state, urban workers' remittances, and aid-dependent NGOs.

Table 11.1 Land distribution and holdings size (million ha) patterns (1980–2004)

Farm class	1980		1996		2004	
	Number of families/farms	*Hectares (million)*	*Number of families/farms*	*Hectares (million)*	*Number of families/farms*	*Hectares (million)*
Smallholder	700,000	14.4	1,000,000	16.4	1,312,866	24.34
Small to medium-scale commercial	8,000	1.4	8,000	1.4	21,000	2.83
Large-scale commercial	6,000	15.5	4,500	7.7	4,317	3.00
Corporate estates	–	–	960	2.04	960	2.04

Source: Moyo (forthcoming).

Development strategy and land policy

Settler colonial rule from 1890 to 1979 was characterized by racial land dispossession and political and economic discrimination (see Mlambo, 2000; Moyana, 2002), which defined Zimbabwe's land question and mass nationalism. The settler colonial state sought to turn most of the peasantry into full-time industrial workers disconnected from the land (Yeros, 2002). The development strategy was structurally imbalanced and discriminatory, seeking to secure mainly the domestic markets of the white minority and exports, while providing minimum incomes for the subsistence of the black poor and the reproduction of migrant labour. The uneven allocation of economic infrastructures in rural areas was integral to this strategy, which emphasised import-substituting industrialisation. Under these conditions, nationalist struggles mobilised extensive militancy in the rural areas. The United States and Britain facilitated a negotiated settlement towards 'majority rule' in 1979 (the Lancaster House agreement and constitution). This provided critical parameters to protect property rights, proscribing land reform within a market-oriented, liberal, democratic governance framework, and brought unequal parliamentary power-sharing with the white minority.

At independence, a key development policy challenge was to promote redistributive strategies to reduce racial inequality and poverty, and broadly based economic growth, focused on the domestic needs, particularly of the poor (GoZ, 1982). Land reform and agrarian reform policy was vested in a development strategy still focused on import-substituting industrialisation within a heterodox macro-economic policy framework. The expansion of agricultural production envisioned land reform leading rural development and poverty reduction. The development strategy activities of Zimbabwean civil society organisations (CSOs) during the 1980s focused on welfare projects, with little emphasis on land reform (see Moyo, 2001). From the mid-1990s, their focus tilted towards demands for accelerated democratisation, and limited interrogation of the failure of neoliberal economic policies to deliver development. The Zimbabwean Congress of Trade Unions (ZCTU) had been calling for proactive land reform within a more developmentalist economic strategy for some time. The underlying land conflict which limited the productive use of land and access by the poor was underplayed.

Between 1980 and 1989 major political change occurred in the context of maintaining in general terms the pre-independence 'heterodox' and 'dirigiste' macro-economic strategy, based on a legacy of sanctions-induced economic introversion and industrialisation. Social services (health and education) and infrastructure were extended to the small-holder farm sector, alongside policies in support of monopoly capital and state enterprise growth. Rapid growth followed the lifting of sanctions, the influx of aid and good rains. This accompanied increased social spending, minimum-wage legislation and the inception of an 'accelerated resettle-ment' programme. A balance of payments crisis in 1982 saw the govern-ment engage the International Monetary Fund (IMF), leading to currency devaluation by half, increased interest rates, and reduced maize subsidies, through a 'homegrown' SAP programme. This undercut the 'growth with equity' programme. By 1984, however, the government had disengaged the IMF by repaying its outstanding debts, and 'went alone', rejecting the austerity measures (Yeros, 2002). Yet after 1984, a gradualist market-based land reform programme was pursued, while unemployment hovered between 30 and 40 per cent right into the early 1990s.

As the budget deficit mounted, due to its increasing social policy and security expenditures, borrowing from the World Bank in 1991 grew, espe-cially when the ESAP was adopted, in the absence of economic crisis (Stoneman, 2000). Significantly, this coincided with the expiry of the Lan-caster House provisions pertaining to land. The IMF 'rescue mission' of January 1992, due to the ESAP and drought-induced effects on Zim-babwe's external balances, demanded reduction of the budget deficit, trimming of the public sector, cutting back of social services; and the lib-eralisation of currency, prices, interest rates, trade, capital flows, and the labour market (Yeros, 2002).

The adverse effects of droughts in 1991/1992 and 1994/1995, and the negative effects on export revenues arising from the expiry in 1992 of the 1964 preferential trade agreement with South Africa (renewed in 1996), saw the withdrawal of agricultural subsidies and foreign exchange depreci-ation to increase competitiveness (Yeros, 2002). Inflation grew to 42 per cent in 1992 from an average of 14 per cent in the 1980s and high interest rates choked the economy, while financial liberalisation pushed interest rates even higher (ibid.). From 1993 foreign dealing on the Zimbabwe Stock Exchange (ZSE) was introduced and money supply, interest rates and currency became highly exposed to global financial instability (ibid.). Between 1990 and 1996 there was significant de-industralisation, reduc-tion of social expenditures and subsidies in general, liberalisation of agri-cultural markets and trade, and erosion of working-class wages and incomes. These factors were accompanied by escalating strike actions, while the least amount of land was distributed during the period.

The period between 1997 and 2004 saw the gradual return to a dirigiste and heterodox macro-economic policy framework, alongside the execu-tion of extensive land reforms, in a context of increasing the economic decline and international isolation. Policy immediately after the ESAP had continued with an export-oriented strategy, through the deepening of the Export Processing Zones (EPZ) Act. A new international financial institution (IFI)-sponsored programme, the Zimbabwe Programme for Economic and Social Transformation (ZIMPREST) was designed to restructure public enterprises, reform the financial sector, and proposed market-oriented land reform, focusing on land taxes and subdivision.

But the government contradicted the IFI demands in 1997 by making unbudgeted pension disbursements to disaffected war veterans, and by designating about 40 per cent of the large-scale commercial farms (LSCF) for compulsory acquisition. ZIMPREST collapsed, as the currency crashed, losing 74 per cent of its value on 14 November 1997. This led to price hikes and job losses, followed by food riots and serial industrial actions led by the ZCTU, which the state forcefully suppressed. Meanwhile, the international financial institutions withheld balance-of-payments funding and demanded a return to SAP. Instead, in 1998 price controls were reintroduced on staple goods and tariffs were reimposed on luxury goods.

In the same year, the government (with Namibia and Angola) intervened militarily in the Democratic Republic of Congo (DRC) at the invitation of the Kabila government. This put a further strain on the national budget and led to harsher criticism from western donors. The IMF and World Bank withdrew support to Zimbabwe from 1999, following the government's default on its debt obligations. However, they admitted that ESAP could not have been successful in an environment with extreme disparities and where land reform would need to be undertaken before economic reforms could have had their intended impact in the economy (Yeros, 2002).

The radicalisation of land reform (through expropriation) between 1997 and 2002 and the economic management strategy brought about increased economic isolation and restricted access to external credit and aid in general. Further control of prices, markets and the foreign exchange was introduced during 2000, and the indigenisation of banks, mines and industries was mooted more forcefully. A decrease in LSCF agricultural production and repeated droughts up to 2004 introduced additional imbalances. By 2003, inflation had risen to 600 per cent, forex earnings had declined by at least 50 per cent, and cumulative gross domestic product (GDP) declined by about 30 per cent. A more formally pronounced heterodox stabilisation and state interventionist development strategy was introduced in late 2003, albeit in a plan with limited coherence and backing by capital and various social forces. This led to a reduction of inflation to 132 per cent by December 2004. The flows of forex into official instead of parallel channels increased to a small extent as a result of tighter regulation and anti-corruption measures. A somewhat slower rate of GDP decline was seen but the cost of living for the poor continued to be unbearably high. Forex shortages persisted, although the essentials (fuel, critical imported inputs, etc.) become more regular in supply at higher prices until early 2005. But food security remained precarious and agricultural exports declined as inputs shortages and loss of farm production grew.

Official development strategy emphasised equitable land distribution, agrarian reform, agricultural inputs and food price subsidies, nurturing of small business enterprises, the promotion of value-added industrial production, and the indigenisation of mining and agri-business concerns. This thrust found support from a nationalist cross-class alliance of social forces around Zimbabwe African National Union Patriotic Front (Zanu PF) and selected CSOs, while the main opposition party opposed it, as did international finance. Symbolic resumption of repayment of international loans in 2004 suggested the re-forging of IFI relations,[4] and the IMF/World Bank publicly pronounced cautious approval of the direction of macro-economic policy during 2004.[5] The political opposition and IFIs oppose current controls on the capital account, the foreign exchange management system and the dual interest rate system (IMF, 2004; Ndlela, 2004). It is improbable that there is likely to be a 'reversal' of the fast-track land reforms, nor would it be feasible without large-scale violent evictions of new landholders. However, the accommodation of some more former white farmers on smaller farms and of bilateral investors (on less than 5 per cent of the land) is under consideration.

Significantly, this period was characterised by an enduring violent political conflict between the ruling Zanu PF party and the main opposition (Movement for Democratic Change (MDC) party, as well as by international economic isolation, largely because the election results of 2000 and 2002 were contested. The MDC–CSO alliance movement pushed for governance reforms and challenged the government's legitimacy. However, by late 2003 they were giving out mixed signals over not reversing the fast-track land reforms (see MDC, 2004). Zanu PF had shifted its policy thrust towards the rural electoral constituency, and remobilised the liberation and nationalist forces around land reform, through extensive land occupations led by war veterans (see Moyo and Yeros, 2005) and statist interventionism. The narrowing of democratic space for political parties and for a proliferated new wave of governance and human rights NGO activism, which had mushroomed from the mid-1990s, polarised politics and land reform processes to an extent not seen since independence (Moyo, 2000).

Market-driven land reform and poverty (1980–1996)

The market-driven land reform process limited the potential poverty-reduction gains in Zimbabwe in a number of ways. The mechanisms of land transfer, including land acquisition, land prices and the quality of land redistributed limited the scale of access to land by new beneficiaries, while land concentration persisted. The agricultural support system under the ESAP policy framework limited the benefits of resettlement and of communal farming in general, while raising the urban demand for unavailable land. Even those smallholders with land realised limited productivity and income gains.

Mechanisms of the market-driven land redistribution approach

Land reform in Zimbabwe between 1980 and 1996 was pursued with a 'predominantly market-based' approach, whose main mechanism of land transfer was a willing seller–willing buyer process, agreed to at Lancaster House. The state played a dominant role in acquiring the land for the poor and supported resettlement schemes. Private agricultural land market transfers reallocated land to various new large farmers (white and black), while land concentration among a few existing large landholders proceeded (see Moyo, 1998).

The GoZ had placed emphasis on agricultural and rural development within the peasant sector during the 1980s, based largely on raising productivity, improving inputs and commodity markets. Agricultural research, extension services, roads and marketing depots, education and health became a focus (Bratton, 1987), rather than the extensive redistribution of land and national agrarian restructuring. Yet, when the Lancaster House constitutional safeguards for market-based land transfers expired in 1990, legal instruments for state land expropriation were introduced but not fully used. The implementation of the ESAP instead reinforced the market-based character of land reform, reduced state interventions in support of small farmers and perpetuated the unequal agrarian economy.

Market mechanisms for land transfer limited the redistributive efforts in various ways. First, landowners led the identification and supply of land available for resettlement, while central government was a reactive buyer choosing land on offer (Moyo, 1995). Until 1996, the amount, quality, location and cost of land acquired for redistribution was driven by landholders rather than by the state or the beneficiaries in accordance with their needs and demands. The lowest-quality land was redistributed (ibid.). Land prices increased dramatically throughout the period, spurred also by the growth of demand for land the by growing black elite.

The UK provided grants worth approximately £33 million (US$44 million) during the 1980s for market land acquisition as well as for various resettlement inputs. This money, conceptualised as 'aid' rather than reparations, was provided as a matching grant to GoZ's own financial inputs, and was disbursed as reimbursements for GoZ land purchases approved by the Overseas Development Administration (ODA). This financing mechanism experienced various bottlenecks and aroused conflicts between the donor and the GoZ (personal communication).[6] Blacks also purchased farms on the market, some using credit offered by the Agricultural Finance Corporation. Not surprisingly, few peasants or poor working-class families and women could afford land (see Rugube *et al.*, 2004).

The market-led land redistribution outcome

About 70 per cent of the land acquired on the market was procured during the 1980s, through the 'Normal Intensive Resettlement' programme. The rest was purchased on the market, following its 'illegal' occupation by peasants (see Tshuma, 1997; Moyo, 2000; Alexander, 2003), through an official 'Accelerated Land Resettlement Programme', complementing the 'normal' programme. Thus, land occupations significantly challenged the market-driven land transfers during the early 1980s, although these were regularised into the market procedure.

From the middle of the 1980s, the state increasingly evicted, often in violent fashion, those deemed to be occupying land illegally in commercial farms (Herbst, 1990). This violence, carried out by both the police and farmers, mirrored colonial evictions. During the 1990s land occupations expanded in content and form, ranging from illegal access to land to the widespread poaching of natural resources, targeting not only private lands but also state lands, some 'communally' owned lands and urban land (Moyo, 1998, 2000, 2003). The severe drought during the 1991/1992 farming season also led to extensive commercial farm labour retrenchments, and increased the pressure on communal area land and natural resources (Moyo, 2000, 2003). Wider ESAP retrenchments in mining fuelled land occupations (Yeros, 2002) and 'illegal' land occupations expanded, especially in the Mashonaland provinces, culminating in more intense occupations from 1998 (Moyo, 2001).

As a result, the pace of land reform between 1980 and 1996 was slow. Between 1980 and 1985 about 430,000 hectares were acquired each year. Between 1985 and 1992, the pace of acquisition fell to about 75,000 hectares per year, while between 1992 and 1997, approximately 158,000 hectares were acquired per year. Thus by 1996 about 3.4 million hectares of land had been transferred, reducing the white commercial farming area to 11 million hectares or by 29 per cent, leaving the large landholdings with approximately 35 per cent of the total agricultural land, most of which was prime land.

About 70,000 families were resettled, far short of the targeted 162,000 families (Moyo, 1995). Moreover those on official waiting lists for land far exceeded this target. The government provided land to beneficiaries selected mainly by its district officials under the direct supervision of central government officials. This meant that congested communal areas stood little chance of getting relief from land assets, as those districts not near these commercial lands received less land.

By the end of the market-based land reform in the late 1990s, about 9,000 black capitalist farmers had established themselves in the former small-scale and new large-scale commercial farming areas, through land purchases, leases and inheritance, on about 19 per cent of former large-scale commercial farmland. New private land bidding patterns had emerged, as the prime lands were now a source of intra-capitalist (black and white) competition and inter-class conflicts. Aspiring black capital called for the state to 'set aside' commercial land for them in the interest of 'indigenisation', even as they were being directly co-opted by local white and transnational capital, including through linkages promoted by donor-funded enterprise development programmes. While these pressures unfolded, a squatter control policy continued to be implemented (Moyo, 1995).

Poverty impacts of market-driven land reform and agrarian policy

Scepticism reigned among key policy makers, stakeholders and CSOs about the desirability of extensive land redistribution and the efficacy of non-market approaches during the 1980s. But the adoption of the ESAP reined in the official drive for land redistribution and reduced agricultural support to small farmers, yielding negative effects for poverty reduction through land reform.

Some have argued that the Zimbabwean state lacked the political will or capacity to implement land reform prior to 2000, suggesting that constitutional and market constraints were not important. Yet the various administrative constraints imposed by the willing transactor principle had significantly affected the quality and pace of land redistributed, while imposing high financial costs on land reform (Moyo, 1995). The potential negative impacts of extensive redistribution on development and agriculture (see, e.g. World Bank, 1991) was the mantra touted by many policy analysts, to the neglect of the potential benefits of redistribution (Moyo, 1998).

Empirical evidence (Kinsey, 2004; Moyo, 1995; Deininger *et al.*, 2000) suggests that the majority of the few poor rural households who gained access to new land and related natural resource assets tended in the medium term to realise increased farm and woodland resources production, incomes and consumption benefits. For example, resettlement households had over 20 years tripled their livestock wealth, while their productivity increased substantially, and their overall incomes were five times higher than those in communal areas with similar agricultural potential (Moyo, 1995). While they represented less than 5 per cent of the peasant population, they produced over 15 per cent of marketed maize and cotton outputs, and satisfied their own consumption needs (Moyo, 1995). Moreover, redistribution had not negatively affected the large-scale farm outputs, although this sector retained its high land underutilisation rates of over 40 per cent (ibid.; World Bank, 1991).

This evidence contradicts the assertion (CSO, 1999) that resettlement farmers had the highest prevalence of poverty, largely because the survey data used had numerous computation problems and it reflected the immediate effects of the drought in the previous year, in a resettlement situation where households rely less on non-farm employment than in communal areas (Deininger *et al.*, 2000). Moreover, the evidence suggests that resettled farmers' livelihoods improved after a five-year transitional period of low output (Kinsey, 2004) during stable macro-economic conditions.

Such conditions were eventually reversed by the negative effects of ESAP macro-economic policy, wider economic decline and repeated droughts, which had the effect of limiting wider socio-economic and poverty-reduction gains in general, and of reducing state support to farm households to reduce poverty. And landlessness had grown to around 30 per cent by 1994 (Rukuni Commission, 1994; Chasi *et al.*, 1994)

Agrarian policies were dramatically redirected by ESAP, with far-reaching anti-poor effects on land use, land markets and the demand for land redistribution. The state retreat from subsidising agriculture was supported by the Commercial Farmers Union (CFU), which was a lesser target for many subsidies (see Toye, 1993; Moyo, 2000). Marketing boards were commercialised or privatised and converted to purchasers of last resort, while private traders were allowed to compete, partly reversing the late 1980s' trends of increased smallholder profitability and relatively affordable food. Higher real prices for some crops such as maize and wheat were seen, but not for beef and cotton (see also Yeros, 2002). Generally, incentives mainly benefited the large farms able to switch and expand production flexibility. Budget contraction led to reduced extension services, inputs support and credit for smallholders which, along with the depreciation of the dollar, eroded farm incomes. Smallholder market sales did not increase in the 1990s (with this share in 1998 equal to that of 1984), and they were regionally and socially differentiated, having been effectively confined to 20 per cent of the 'better-off' households in communal and resettlement areas (see also Maast, 2000). A notable agrarian change was the integration of smallholders into seed and fertiliser markets now more controlled by transnational corporations.

Significantly, these developments dovetailed with job losses in the formal sector and the erosion of wages to reduce remittances from urban workers to their relatives in the rural areas. Many of the urban poor turned back to the land and illegal occupations ('squatting') increased. The extension of peasant farming on marginal grazing lands increased, as did the intensification of women's casual farm labour, reflecting limited access to land among other problems. The upsurge of demand for land, the deepening of land markets, and further social differentiation in communal areas led to the undermining of local government institutions (Moyo, 2000).

But the most significant agrarian change, with regard to its effect on land rights and land use, to occur was the expansion of non-traditional export activities, specifically wildlife management, ostrich husbandry and horticulture. This reinforced the division of labour and income distribution between smallholders and large-scale farmers (Moyo, 2000), while limiting the expansion of food production and undermining national food security. The larger farmers expanded export operations while the smallholders remained in maize and cotton production, given that historical constraints (such as access to land, water, credit and infrastructure), compounded by retrenched extension services, limited their responsiveness to the ESAP agricultural market incentives. About 300 large-scale farmers had embraced ostrich husbandry, 31 per cent of LSCF had come under wildlife, and 36 per cent of the LSCF were engaged in horticulture. In communal areas, on the other hand, it is estimated that less than 10 per cent of households became marginally involved in these new exports, thus limiting their income gains from ESAP, and other poverty-reducing potentials.

Critically, the expansion of wildlife land use amounted to the compulsory conversion of some communal lands to exclusive commercial exploitation by private leasees, reducing the access by some poor rural households to natural resources used for various consumption needs. This was sacrificed in return for cash invested in social services with limited capacities vis-à-vis demand. In commercial areas, this trend justified pre-existing large-scale landholding in terms of export and environmentalist values. Agricultural land use conversion to wildlife enterprises created new relationships between local agrarian and transnational capital, whereby conservancies created private companies which held and managed groups of farms in one block, further restructuring by concentrating and depersonalising land ownership. This institution consolidated the land and development policy lobby power of large landowners which, together with the increasing demands of black elites to enter the LSCF, generated important contradictions in land reform policy and poverty-reduction strategies.

The ESAP therefore reinforced the direct market approach to land reform by promoting the deregulation of land markets, including through increased land subdivisions and private sales, benefiting the elite, while initiating policy discourses on communal area land titling (World Bank, 1991; Land Tenure Commission, 1994). Improving exports within the existing land ownership structure was the preoccupation (Moyo, 2000). This affected the agricultural markets of the poor, deepened national and agricultural income and wealth inequalities. De-industrialisation (including in the agro-industrial sector) led to drastic employment and wage declines. These effects on the labour market not only strained urban workers' incomes and consumption, but also limited the beneficial rural–urban linkages based on urban remittances used to boost rural investment capacities and the latter's supply of cheap foods.[7]

Yet land-based livelihoods which could have emerged through land reform were blocked. The ESAP thus had extensive negative effects on land reform per se, as well as on poverty in general. But one unintended consequence was the increased scale and sources of demand for land, in all farming areas, among the urban retrenched and poor, and among land-seeking indigenous elites (Moyo, 2000).

Furthermore, since a significant share of rural incomes, especially from petty agricultural sales, is absorbed by direct and indirect expenditures on education and health services, the introduction under ESAP of cost-recovery systems for social services increased the financial strain on the rural poor. The Social Development Fund, did not ameliorate the situation adequately, since providing safety-nets for the poor through social and agricultural facilities was fraught with bureaucratic bottlenecks and failed to reach most of the vulnerable rural poor. In addition, direct government support to small-scale agricultural producers through crop pack subsidies had been phased out in the mid-1980s, only to be reintroduced during the 1991/1992 droughts. These programmes were inadequate and did not reach most of the rural poor. Thus the poverty-reducing potential of the market-driven land reform programme was limited in general.

State-driven land reform and poverty (1997–2004)

The state-driven land reform approach began in earnest in 1997, based on state expropriation of land directed by widespread and nationally organised land occupations. Both the state and land seekers allocated land to beneficiaries on a large scale. While the poor gained extensive access to land, natural resources and infrastructure, the effects on poverty reduction of this approach to land reform has been mixed, and limited during the short term.

The process entailed numerous political and land conflicts, aroused by worker strikes and illegal land occupations, in a context of economic decline. By 1997 the Zimbabwean state faced political challenges from within and externally. In a racially divided wealth and agrarian structure, facing an economic crisis, nationalistic land policies were remobilised and state-led land reform strategies gained significance. The land question also grew in significance in intra-ruling party succession politics and social discourses. Zimbabwe's development strategy and macro-economic policy context had shifted, a new correlation of social forces emerged to mobilise the rural and urban poor into two movements aligned with the two main political parties, Zanu PF and the MDC. A deepening conflict between the international community and the Zimbabwean state had emerged from 1998. In effect a wide set of conflictual state–society interactions and domestic–external relations had radicalised land reform, economic policy and the state (see Moyo and Yeros, 2005).

Mechanisms of state-driven land transfer

In 1990, a new bifurcated land policy which sought to redistribute land to the poor and to create more commercial indigenous farmers was introduced, alongside constitutional amendments to the property rights clause. This was followed by a new Land Acquisition Act introduced in 1992 to enable the state to expropriate land. The government started acquiring land compulsorily on a small scale (targeting only 130 out of 7,000 properties), from then until 1995, but without renouncing the market land acquisition method, which it continued to use. The new compensation formula obliged the government to pay a fair compensation within reasonable time (rather than on a prompt and adequate basis) and in local currency (not forex), as pertained in the 1980s. A crafted compromise on non-justiciability was also sought by the government to deny the courts the power to declare land acquisition unconstitutional, only for it to accept the principle of legal recourse. In 1993 the government appointed a Land Tenure Commission (LTC), which produced inadequate alternatives on land redistribution.

State-driven land redistribution was instigated by popular land occupations, led by war veterans from 1998, building upon scattered and loosely organised 'illegal' land occupations, which persisted between 1980 and 1996 (Moyo, 2001). This community-led approach to land transfer entails groups of households leading the identification of land for redistribution by squatting on it, with the expectation that the government would regularise the transfer, either by purchasing such land at market prices or by expropriating it. Local squatter communities self-selected themselves as beneficiaries for redistribution, often supplanting official beneficiary waiting lists. Abandoned and underutilised lands, most of which were in the liberation war frontier zone of the eastern highlands, as well as state lands and sparse communal lands in the Zambezi valley, had been prime targets for land occupation, as were some black-owned LSCF farms by 1997. Whereas the GoZ had, up to 1998, restrained occupations, there is evidence of direct complicity in them among some Zanu PF, GoZ officials, and war veterans during the first 17 years (Tshuma, 1997; Alexander, 2003; Sadomba, 2005).

Land occupations highlighted the land restitution approach (see Marongwe, 2003), which had driven the land reform agenda since independence (see Moyo, 2001). The land occupation movements, however, had varied over time in an unclear relationship with the pace and form of official land redistribution, given their repression during ESAP. The phase of low profile high-intensity land occupations, had occurred, from 1980 to 1985, parallel to the official land resettlement programme. The period between 1985 and 1996 witnessed growing occupations, in what I have termed a 'normal profile low intensity land occupation' process (Moyo, 2001, 2003). While the former occupations reflected the residual militancy of landless communities in liberated zones and districts where chiefs, war veterans and war collaborators had been highly mobilised and/or disgruntled by progress with land reform, the latter movements were more broadly based. High profile intensive land occupations, occurred on a national scale from 1997, after the GoZ had acceded to the war veteran demands to expropriate land (Moyo, 2001, 2003). In these occupations, a vanguard of war veterans, numerous rural peasants, some traditional leaders and spirit mediums, and elements of the urban working class and elites, including largely Zanu PF and GoZ officials, were gradually mobilised towards direct action for land reform, challenging the entire state apparatus and its land reform instruments.

Interestingly, between 1995 and 1996, the government and Zanu PF had initiated provincial land committees to begin an extensive process of identifying land which could be compulsorily acquired, suggesting that the legal bureaucratic-technocratic route to state-led land reform was getting ensconced in the dominant state and political institutions. Parallel to this, negotiations with the UK ODA to fund land redistribution had been stalled by various differences.

The full-scale, state-driven approach thus started with the designation of 1,471 farms (about four million hectares) for expropriation in 1997, using the new compensation rules. About 641 farms were delisted by the state from its acquisition agenda in 1998, while the rest were never acquired because of court challenges in 1998 and 1999. Revisions to the constitution and land act in 2000 led to new land expropriations and numerous court challenges, but these were now backed by extensive 'illegal' occupations condoned by the state during 2000 and 2001.

The outcome of state-driven redistribution

The state-driven redistribution of land was low during its inception between 1990 and 1999. By 1993, only 90 farms had been designated, the bulk of which were in the less fertile regions (71 per cent in Natural Regions III, IV, and V), while 36 of these farms became undesignated through the stipulated legal challenges. The government proceeded to allocate land to 600 peasant families displaced by the construction of the Osborne Dam in Makoni District and thereafter, on a leasehold basis, to black capitalist farmers.

The land redistribution outcome from 2000 was extensive. By November 2004, smallholder allocations were granted to 140,866 families, while new commercial beneficiaries amounted to 14,500[8] new farmers, on 4.2 and 2.3 million hectares respectively (Table 11.1). The number of commercial farm units (including old and new units) increased by 64 per cent, although their area dropped by 42 per cent. Smallholder land increased from 56 per cent of the total land area to 70 per cent. The quality of land redistributed varied across the provinces depending on agro-ecological potential and the distribution of water and irrigation resources. About 2.5 million more hectares were still under expropriation procedures and unallocated. Some irrigated land went to small farmers (7,618 hectares or 6 per cent of national irrigable land), while the commercial beneficiaries received 12,448 hectares (10 per cent) (Manzungu, 2004) and communal area smallholder irrigation schemes retained 11,861 hectares (10 per cent). By 2003, the rest remained in the unacquired large-scale commercial farms. Thus, peasant farmers mostly accessed land nearer the communal areas, with fewer physical advantages, such as being nearer markets and infrastructure.

The patterns of land distribution, in terms of wealth, gender and class were diverse. Urban households gained access to about 34 per cent of the land allocated by 2003. These included working-class groups and rich and influential rural people. The latter included rural businesspeople, teachers, civil servants, political leaders and chiefs among others, and constituted about 10 per cent of the urban beneficiaries. About 400 influential individuals had allocated themselves more than one A2 plot, while about 145 black and white farmers still owned multiple farms which had been acquired on the open markets (Buka Report, 2002; PLRC, 2003).

The rural poor, including communal area farmers and some former farmworkers, as well as a number of the urban poor, constituted about 87 per cent of all beneficiaries, and they had access to 66 per cent of the land so far redistributed, mainly through the A1 scheme intended for the landless, land-short and congested rural households. This degree of inequality in landholdings meant that the decongestion of densely populated communal areas was inadequate (Moyo and Sukume, 2004). Some needy communal farmers, women and former farmworkers did not adequately benefit. Women (as individuals) gained an average of between 12 and 24 per cent of the smallholder land allocations and an average of between 5 and 21 per cent of the commercial land allocated, across the provinces. War veterans on average gained about 20 per cent of the land.

Most farmworkers lost homes and employment, and received little land, as they were largely perceived to have been against the Fast-Track Land Reform Programme (FTLRP) (Chambati and Moyo, 2004), and tended to be relegated to being potential farm labourers by new beneficiaries (ibid.). Out of 175,000 full-time farmworkers prior to the FTLRP (Magaramombe, 2003a; Chambati and Moyo, 2004), about 80,000 retained their employment in the unacquired large-scale commercial and parastatal farms and on large-scale plantations. The remaining 95,000 full-time workers were dispersed into communal areas, re-employed in A1/A2, and resettled, to live on informal settlements or former compounds. The 170,000 part-time workers tended to relocate to communal areas, while only 5 per cent (4,600) of the resettlement beneficiaries were former farmworkers. Some provide casual labour to new farmers and live with informal rights in farmworkers' compounds. Close to 30,000 were displaced into informal settlements, while more than 20,000 joined the expanding informal gold panning industry. Thus, close to 90,000 former farmworker families at present do not enjoy secure tenure in the rural areas.

Redistribution broadened the access to land among various social segments, while raising questions about security of some rights and access to land by some who claim rights to land. Excluded were many farm-workers who lost jobs and security of residential tenure; many single women; some people who did not receive land allegedly because of their support for the MDC; some youth, given their limited social and political influence; and peasants in communal areas remote from the LSCF areas. Some white LSCF owners, who claimed to accept smaller units, also alleged exclusion. Tenure insecurity is evident in the new landholding arrangements, since lease title or permits for the redistributed land have not yet been provided.

The state-driven approach's implications for poverty reduction

Zimbabwe's agrarian structure has thus changed in terms of the differential farm size allocations and the inferred class character and nationality of beneficiaries, as well as the demography of the farming population, in terms of its racial and gender composition (see Table 11.1). This has also generated adjustments in the character of agro-services providers and services, just as it has changed the character of the rural labour market and labour process. Indeed, the fast-track process has reconfigured Zimbabwe's agrarian question, reflecting new problems for the transformation of agriculture and industrialisation, including the trajectories for technical change, productivity, labour utilisation, mechanisation and support institutions in the public and private sphere. These demand an agrarian reform strategy that addresses rural poverty, a policy which has not yet been adequately crafted.

The downsized LSCF sector is dominated by the small- to medium-scale plots, largely comprising farms with average landholdings of 135 hectares, with an upper end averaging 695 hectares, while the remaining white LSCF farms average 871 hectares. At the top end of the new LSCF farm sector are the agro-industrial/company farms with average landholdings of 2,126 hectares. However, the latter are being downsized through acquisition during 2004. Small to middle capitalist farmers now comprise about 21,000 units, holding 9 per cent of the total agricultural land, on farms of between 30 to 150 hectares, and employing non-family labour. There is likely to be ongoing reconfiguration of these competing classes, while the middle capitalist farms, including the remaining large units, have great advantage in the land bidding and accumulation process, by virtue of their better access to other means of production (credit and technology), to contacts and information, and to the policy-making process itself. This differentiation can potentially trigger new agrarian class formation processes, based upon uneven control of access to land, capital, labour and policy influence.

Land redistribution has reduced land pressure in crowded communal areas, by increasing the smallholder land areas by 21 per cent (Moyo and

Sukume, 2004), although only 9 per cent of households in communal areas was resettled. The proportion of landless households was reduced from around 30 per cent prior to 2000 (Moyo, 1995; Chasi *et al.*, 1994) to below 20 per cent, except in Manicaland where only about 2.4 per cent of the households remain landless. In general, resettlement left a significant numbers of households in communal areas with relatively more arable land per family, as more remaining land-short families gained extra land, increasing smallholder household access to an average of about 1.5 hectares.

The new agrarian structure gains analytic significance for poverty reduction when examined in relation to the shift in agrarian labour processes, including the changing demand for and utilisation of farm labour, recruitment processes, wage and income patterns and the power of organised farm labour to influence their interests. The emerging agricultural labour and employment structure reflects the increased number of potential agricultural and non-farm employers in a context of increased numbers of the rural unemployed since 2000. This represents a total of 3,339,143 farm jobs comprising owner operators and employees, with the new farms accounting for 356,040 jobs. Estimates suggest that in the medium term, an additional 40,000 farm jobs could be created by the new resettlement schemes, while the new commercial A2 farms could create 150,000 more (Chambati and Moyo, 2004; Magaramombe, 2003b). New employers include new commercial farmers, expanding state farms (the Agricultural Rural Development Authority), the remaining black and white large-scale commercial and indigenous farmers, the better-off communal farmers, as well as small-scale gold miners and other informal non-farm enterprises. These entities re-engaged former farmworkers on a limited basis and employed new farmworkers from communal and urban areas (Chambati and Moyo, 2004), reflecting new rural power relations, agrarian labour structures and relations.

The social relationship between the predominantly black agrarian employer and farm employee, under changing residential and local government conditions, has shifted partially from the landlord–labour tenant relationship of the former LSCF (see Rutherford, 2000, cited in Moyo, 2003) towards a new social patronage system, alongside lingering animosities between new farmers and former farmworkers. However, new farm jobs in resettled areas tend to be low-paying and less secure, while the variability of farm wages is very high within and across farms, and even higher between districts. Some former farmworkers refuse to be employed under these new conditions, allegedly even where better wages are paid. Farmworkers' residential rights in farm compounds have become more precarious. Indeed, low farm wages have created a huge demand for alternative income sources such as mining (e.g. gold panning and chrome mining), petty trading and prostitution among female former farmworkers. New employers evict such workers from their compounds.

Employment conditions have tended to deteriorate on the new farms, with high variability in the wages and benefits paid to farmworkers by new farmers, with some paying more than the official wages and others less. Wage levels seem to be better where high-value commodities (e.g. tobacco) and mechanisation are established, as these require skilled operators. Some new farmers do not provide employment contracts, and the provision of social services to workers by employers has greatly diminished. It is reported that in some newly resettled areas, arbitrary firing of workers, lack of protective clothing, lack of leave days and lack of consideration for the special needs of female workers prevail (Parliament of Zimbabwe, 2003).

Even before the FTLRP, former farmworkers, especially those employed on a part-time basis, always relied on alternative sources of income to supplement their wages. Since the land redistribution and the deterioration of the rural economy and other speculative activities, new rural labour options have emerged. More former farmworkers rely entirely on alternative sources of income for their livelihood, such as gold panning, fishing, animal poaching, fuel wood selling, construction of new homesteads[9] and petty trading among others (see Magaramombe, 2003a; Sachikonye, 2003). Under new and transitional land tenure relations, greater opportunities to pan gold, poach and sell wood have emerged, given the overstretched security system.

These structural trends potentially indicate a significantly broadened home market, founded upon a larger peasantry and its predominantly rural population, as well as a larger black agrarian capitalist class based on smaller farms compared to the pre-2000 situation (Moyo and Yeros, 2005). If the combined commercial farms succeed in re-entrenching a disarticulated pattern of accumulation, there could be negative implications for poverty reduction.

Moreover, in an agrarian economy dependent on foreign input supplies and markets, the weak performance of the wider economy and negative reactions of external markets following the land redistribution, even if transitional, have become a key constraint to the realisation of the potential poverty-reduction benefits that the land reform might otherwise have yielded in the medium term.

Agricultural production declined in volume and value terms since 2000 when compared to average output during the 1990s, but this was confined to eight of the 15 key commodities produced in Zimbabwe, and these exhibited varied rates of decline. This type of transitional production decline has not been uncommon where extensive land reforms were effected, although in Zimbabwe the transition has been longer for various reasons. Agricultural production fell because of the interrelated decline of the macro-economic conditions and their constraints on agricultural inputs supplies, the reduced production from LSCF land transfers, sustained droughts, economic isolation and the unwillingness of some LSCFs to produce under downsized landholdings.

Complex sets of domestic policy constraints, some arising from inter-national isolation, economy-wide dislocation and a negative balance of domestic political forces, have limited the potential of the rural and urban poor to benefit from the productive use of redistributed land assets since 2000.

While a wider potential economic base has emerged for the poor, the failure of policy to rapidly promote the productive use of land by all small farmers has, alongside the effect of droughts, led to the persistence of rural food insecurity and poverty. Humanitarian aid has been provided alongside counter-accusations between donors and government over the politicisation of food. The promotion of food security, including agricultural recovery among the poor, as opposed to short-term feeding, has been limited.

The endogenous factors which affected agricultural production include the macro-economic conditions which affected the supply and use of inputs during the period, the land reallocation process itself and the limited productive capacities of the new LSCF farming in the short term. Weak macro-economic conditions and policy (including agricultural policy) during this period grossly affected the profitability of farming and of agribusiness and agricultural support agents, especially because forex shortages limited the entire range of inputs available to all farmers, while inflation and price controls resulted in a cost-price squeeze that weighed heavily against agricultural investment. In 2004, these conditions improved marginally. However, these internal factors were exacerbated, if not triggered off in some instances, by exogenous factors, whose real effects had commenced prior to the fast-track programme in 1997/1998, including reduced external credit and aid (i.e. economic isolation) and political conflict, and later the protracted droughts (see also Moyo and Sukume, 2004; Moyo, 2005).

The capacity of new and communal area farmers in terms of skills, own savings and credit to produce the crops formerly dominated by the LSCF have been limited. Access to investment resources (credit) has been limited partly due to the insecurity of their land tenure, as well as the poor political and economic conditions and policy environment. This has limited the potential gains of the land reform.

Thus, the long-run trend of growing poverty levels in Zimbabwe, espe-cially since the ESAP period, has been compounded by the recent eco-nomic decline, including the loss of agricultural export revenues, inputs shortages in communal areas, increased staple food insecurity, reduced national capacity (including of the urban poor) to invest in agricultural recovery, and the debilitating effects on household labour of HIV/AIDS, which has affected smallholder agricultural production. The extent to which state policy and civil society advocacy promote the land reforms and poverty-reducing farm production, rural employment and rural, off-farm, income-earning opportunities could determine the longer-term benefits to poverty reduction of the fast-track land reform.

The institutional context of land reform and poverty policies

The recent macro policy and structural context of land reform was shaped by Zimbabwe's swing to a new heterodox economic policy and dirigiste political management framework after 1997. The Zimbabwe Congress for Trade unions (ZCTU) successfully coordinated growing urban social protest in the face of economic decline, setting up the opposition MDC party. By 1999, local and international support for increased NGO governance and human rights activism had grown under the ZCTU-National Constitutional Assembly (NCA) coordination.

A new setting and conjuncture of civil society activism emerged after this. The government had challenged the international financial institutions and was being weaned off IFI loans, now based on broader conditionalities. Reduced external financial flows, forex shortages, and economic instability created a new context for policy formation.

Zanu PF and the government of Zimbabwe became radicalised in terms of their nationalist and anti-imperialist ideology and rhetoric, as well as land reform policy, by the war veteran-led land occupations and challenges to their powers, by the emergent opposition, and the external conflict (Moyo and Yeros, 2005). Zanu PF remobilised the rural and other liberationist constituencies around land reform first in 2000, and then around economic indigenisation and statist development strategies from mid-2000, emphasising their sovereign right to choose the governance system. Public action on land reform and development policy advocacy in this situation, particularly from the perspective of the subjectively dominant, largely urban-based CSOs (NGOs and trade unions, business associations and farmers' unions became polarised and viscous. Contradictory alliances in class and wider social and political terms emerged. Some fractions of the minority black capital aligned with white capital, external capital, labour and middle-class elements (including those in NGOs, the professions and academia) around the NCA–MDC formation. The other factions of indigenous capital aligned with government policy elites, the peasantry and elements of the middle class.

This suggests that, apart from national influences on development and land policies, external influences on development and land policy are critical to explaining domestic state–civil society policy interactions. Understanding the institutional framework in which the interests of local capital, workers and peasants, policy elites, CSO elites, as well as international finance are mediated is critical.

This raises some important questions. What were the main actions of key state and CSO institutions in advancing pro-poor land reform and development policies? What land policy alternatives were proffered? And, what was the role of international interests in the land reform, development and governance agenda of Zimbabwe?

Zimbabwe's land policy framework in the international context

The intellectual and financial role of the international community in influencing Zimbabwe's land, economic and governance problems has been understated in current research (see for instance Raftopoulos, 2004; Phimister, 2004; Davies, 2004; Sachikonye, 2004), largely because undue weight is given to state-centric, internal causes of the problem, neglecting the roles of international capital and civil society oppositional forces.

Zimbabwe's market-led land reform was embraced by the World Bank, which had focused on raising peasant productivity (World Bank, 1982) and promoting freer land markets (World Bank, 1991). A modified market-assisted and community-based approach to land reform was proposed during 1997–1999 (World Bank, 1999). This sought a curtailed role of the state in land reform, increased NGO participation, and it challenged rapid land expropriation and the administrative pricing of land compensation as initiated by GoZ in 1997 and in policy statements at the 1998 donors' conference (GoZ, 1998). Zimbabwe's demands for British colonial responsibility to fund land acquisition were opposed by the latter, who allegedly sponsored the internationalisation of the land question, focusing instead on a poverty-oriented aid framework to land reform. This led to bilateral conflict and the politicisation of land reform policy (see also Short, 1997).

The international community had increased its funding of land NGOs by 1998 in support of community and demand-led market-assisted land reform. Meanwhile, popular pressures on the state to get on with land expropriation, regardless of market principles and property law restrictions in the constitution, were in 1998 stoked by war veteran demands for land reform to be sped up, countervailing the market-friendly proposals in favour of land expropriation and 'illegal' land seizures.

A compromise was reached at the 1998 donors' conference where a two-pronged approach to land reform was proposed in the ill-fated two-year Inception Phase Land Reform Programme (GoZ, 1999). It intended to acquire less than 10 per cent of LSCF land in two years, combining land expropriation with market purchases, including self-selected land transactions between landowners and potential beneficiaries, with NGO support assisted by external finance. Public credit and small subsidies were to be granted to new farmers. But the lack of external finance and mutual mistrust between the GoZ and donors killed this learning project in its tracks, reflecting their differences over sustainability issues, defined in terms of an orthodox macro-economic strategy, transparency and the rule of law. Failure also reflected the reluctance of landowners to transfer land outside the market mechanism, and their litigations.

GoZ officials interpreted this impasse as a tactic of delaying land reform until the post-2000 election period, and larger political and economic interests had enveloped the land policy process by 1999. Numerous conflicts over land seizures between former and new farmers emerged, and political conflict and governance problems expanded, the latter expressed through struggles over the rule of law, elections and human rights. The international isolation of Zimbabwe grew incrementally in various ways (Elich, 2002), including through condemnation of Zimbabwe, aid withdrawal such as the US Zimbabwe Democracy Act, and trade and credit restrictions. Donors went as far as to discriminatorily apply humanitarian aid for food and social services against poor land beneficiaries (HRW, 2004; Amnesty International, 2004), as well as from the Global Fund for HIV/AIDS, on the grounds that they were on stolen land, and that the aid would legitimise the land reform and the government. Donors even funded the resettlement of white farmers in countries such as Zambia, Mozambique and Nigeria. By 2003, most of the European donor country offices had refocused their visible dialogue with the GoZ over land to pursuing exemption from land expropriation for their citizens' farms protected by Bilateral Investment Protection Agreements.[10]

These domestic–international contradictions in land policy dialogue have proven a critical source of the failure to find an agreed approach to land reform in Zimbabwe. The emergence of domestic political confrontations in general, and specifically over land reform, among the heterogeneous CSO formations was as much part of these contradictions, as they were based on the sharp class, racial and ideological polarisations that emerged after 1997. The legal-bureaucratic and technocratic land policy formation and implementation process became subordinated to the wider dimensions of internal and external politics. The social mobilisation to gain access to land and opposition to dispossession, within complex, class-based land struggles and competing demands for land, had overtaken technocracy in shaping land policy and its poverty orientation. A different redistributive focus challenged the conservatism of official programme design, while the responses by those opposed to the radical land reforms in turn shaped policy responses. Indeed, since state policy elites now had direct and indirect material interests in land, just as had some leaderships in opposition parties and CSOs, care is required in interpreting the origin and motives of public action over land reform processes and the nature of opposition to it.

The CSO institutional landscape and land reform

Zimbabwe has over 1,000 formal NGOs, a few thousand CSOs, two federations of trade unions representing over 50 trade unions, one major agricultural workers' union (GAPWUZ), and various unregistered associations focused on a variety of social issues. These institutions include local and national-level NGOs, which encompass teachers' associations, youths' and women's groups, church-affiliated welfare organisations, farmers' groups, village associations, burial and credit societies, advocacy and research institutions, human rights organisations, rural development institutions, and professional and cultural groups (Moyo *et al.*, 2000). It is estimated that at least 300 other NGOs, largely those which emerged in the last ten years, are registered under trust laws with the Registrar of Deeds and the High Court.

In Zimbabwe the NGO institution as an organisational form has developed the greatest visibility and weight in terms of resources (skills, finances and connections in the CSO landscape and society in general. However, its members and those it represents are much fewer than the CSO formations which in rural areas mainly represents peasants. The CSOs and other informal associations are the dominant institutions in terms of members and constituency, although these tend not to be well coordinated nationally and exist mostly as regional groupings, coordinated by intermediary NGOs. While they are less visible nationally, they have great weight in micro-localities. The NGO formation has increased its impact on the national policy and political arena in selected fields.

The ZCTU, the main federation of labour unions, has generally played a peripheral role in advocacy for land reform, although it played a more critical part in the ESAP policy re-design debates, especially around 1995 (ZCTU, 1996; Yeros, 2002). It aligned with the opposition MDC, in alliance with NGOs, students, professional and businesspeople, initially under the umbrella of the NCA in 1998. By 1999, through its joint campaigns with the NCA and the MDC for constitutional reform and the electoral campaign of 2000, the union seemed increasingly subsumed into the MDC, whose political strategy became focused on elections and delegitimising the government of Zanu PF, on grounds of alleged electoral improprieties, the breakdown of the rule of law, and human rights violations. The ZCTU tactic included mobilising the MDC membership, articulating a general critique of government economic policies and governance and human rights records, coupled with disengagement from GoZ-labour negotiation forums (such as the National Economic Consultative Forum and the Tripartite Negotiating Forum. It allegedly campaigns for Zimbabwe's international isolation including the mobilisation of regional trade unions to this effect.

In the context of polarisation around political parties, the false bimodal trade off between governance and development issues, and the Zimbabwe state vis-à-vis the donor community, there have been critical constraints on engaging CSOs, particularly around resolving the land question. The CSOs' lobby on macro-economic policy reform became weakened after 1999, unlike their more coherent stance during the 1980s around the nationalist nation-building agenda, focusing on the reformation of racially discriminatory policies and unequal employment opportunities. Then

CSOs exhibited a more ideologically common front of collaborating with a stronger state, whose growing fiscal resources ensured expanding social services provisions and some worker protection.

During the ESAP era (1990–1996), the political environment for policy reform advocacy was slightly more liberalised. This period witnessed the emergence of stronger CSO indigenisation lobby groups, the expansion of women's advocacy groups, new environmental CSOs, many HIV/AIDS service and lobby CSOs, and, to a lesser extent, a few CSOs (e.g. the SAPRI network, ZIMCORD) focused on economic policy. Governance issues found greater scope as a handful of new CSOs turned towards elections and human rights advocacy to supplement the Catholic Commission for Justice and Peace effort. The ZCTU increasingly expanded its economic policy advocacy, tending towards qualified support for ESAP, following a rapprochement with government in 1995, providing a mild critique of it, but not outrightly rejecting it. From 1996 the ZCTU's mobilisation of numerous labour strikes, and the increased militancy of civil servants, teachers and medical workers, with which the former were loosely aligned, heralded a stronger critique of ESAP. Yet at this stage, as NGOs grew and the effects of economic liberalisation were hurting urban workers the most, the ZCTU remained largely workerist. It slowly evolved towards a political movement agenda as it gained autonomy from the ruling political party and its international aid increased. It has been suggested that this international alliance softened the ZCTU stance on the economic liberalisation policy (Yeros, 2002).

The dramatic loss of jobs, erosion of wages, and increased cost of living during the early 1990s created the social basis for a more political but largely urban-based mobilisation of CSO alliances within the ZCTU. But this was muted until the cracks emerged within Zanu PF in 1997, as a result of declining economic conditions and social difficulties, the evident accumulation of wealth by a few indigenous elites alongside dominant white capital and large farmers, and increased incidences of corruption. The increased political challenge and interest group activism of the reorganised and consolidated Zimbabwe National Liberation War Veterans Association (ZNLWVA) was critical in opening the political space for militant activism in general, beyond the strike mechanism, and in generating a new edge of radical demands around economic policy and leadership succession. They called for social welfare benefits (pensions, etc.) financial support for their economic projects and more land redistribution, claiming their promised 20 per cent share. Also demanded was a greater representation within Zanu PF and the government structures to counter the 'fat cats'.

This upsurge of war veteran influence into the economic policy-making process, land reform policy, regime maintenance and the political succession issue had crept in around 1995, but it took a sharp organisational and strategic turn in 1997, when the war veterans held street marches, and in

1998 when they invaded rural land. This internal critique of Zanu PF and government set a new framework for political activism. Their pension demands aggravated workers for its tax effects, angered the landowners whose lands faced expropriation, upset businesses reeling from the forex rate collapse and price instabilities, affected the urban poor by inflation, and upset the donors because their actions gave weight to the abrogation of neoliberalism. The reaction all round was an uproar, with the media turning to frenzied calls for stabilisation and a slow down on land expropriation.

Thus, from 1997 a new era of policy influence and contestation of political power and land and development policy emerged, characterised by the opening of political space for CSO advocacy. This space was created by both the war veterans and labour unions, and provided a conjunctural opportunity for new forms of alliance building, such as the 1998 ZCTU–NCA–MDC alliance. This alliance exploited the political divide or rupture within Zanu PF by attempting to recruit members of the latter and by expanding their mobilisation of the increasing urban protest and workerist activism.

This dramatic realignment of socio-political forces was conjunctural and rapid. It emerged from the dramatic economic effects of the sudden devaluation and the flight of forex, and from the market jitters created by these events and the land occupations and expropriation moves. Increased external displeasure at these trends, and the DRC interventions' cost and international political ramifications, led to reduced international aid and credit, generating further instability in the financial markets. Meanwhile, increased external aid to CSOs and the ZCTU strengthened the ZCTU–NCA–MDC alliance from 1998/1999. In parallel to this largely urban alliance, Zanu PF co-opted the war veterans and remobilised some nationalist capitalists and peasants during 2000 around the liberationist ideal against the interests of white farmers and of domestic and foreign capital into an anti-imperialist, pan-Africanist, and nationalist ideology.

The NGO community became paradoxically divided over the land issue, posed as a governance issue (Interviews, 2004). The broader agenda for redistributive development policies, was now increasingly usurped by a focus on the symptoms of poverty in their reduction strategies and on 'process rather than content' (see NCA, 1999) in all policy matters. Land reform policy discourses became reductionist and polarised, with less emphasis on social redistributive justice.

During 1998, for the first time since independence, a national land movement emerged, from combining scattered, sporadic and local land occupations (Moyo, 2001; Alexander, 2003; Sadomba, 2005). The ZNLWVA was the only CSO to truly build peasant capacity to demand land compared to the micro-level welfarist and environmentalist land use interventions of most NGOs. Initially, war veterans joined the peasant occupations led by spirit mediums and traditional leaders, with the support of their urban-based offspring, notably in Svosve and Hwedza (Sadomba, 2005). Then, independently of Zanu PF, they mobilised 30 similar peasant-led land occupations across the country. In 2000, after the referendum rejected drafted constitutional reforms, including a clause to expropriate with payment only for improvements, nationwide occupations were led initially by war veterans. They were soon supported by Zanu PF and state officials, and were joined from 2001 by urban, working-class and elite occupiers, building a cross-class land movement (Moyo, 2001). The recent attention directed towards war veterans, through the urban evictions and demolitions of 2005, is a response to the tactic of land occupation having been used in towns, against the elite's wishes. The war veterans had fast become influential political actors, and a strong organisation, especially once it took a less entryist tactic and autonomous protest strategy vis-à-vis Zanu PF and the state during 1992–2000.[11]

Academic and public debate has tended to conflate the ZNLWVA membership, which was organically born from Zanu PF membership, with Zanu PF organs and strategies as a party (see also Moore, 2004; and Kriger, 2003), neglecting the empirical evidence of the changing social and political relations of the two organisations, and the nuanced shifts in the alliance. A complex evolution of autonomy (full and/or partial) and co-optation or control of the ZNLWVA by Zanu PF and the state at its national and provincial branches was evident. It entailed a multiplicity of locally independent actions, mostly by the middle-class and poor war veterans, challenging the local and central state and Zanu PF structures. These initiated processes such as land expropriation; they invaded urban land factories; and later exposed corruption in land and agrarian resource allocations. However faulty the execution and the poverty outcome, the reform was essentially led by war veterans, in a cause that Zanu PF and the state coopted and gave direction, long after the elections of 2000 and 2002 had transpired.

Various other CSOs were later mobilised by Zanu PF and the government in support of fast track. These included the organisation of war collaborators, and ex-detainees, associations representing emerging indigenous business, farming and professional class interests, such as the ZFU and the Indigenous Commercial Farmers Union (now the Zimbabwe Commercial Farmers Union) and various district level new farmers associations such as the Mazoe/Nyabira farmers' association and the Marondera association. Their advocacy for land, agrarian inputs and other services were critical in shaping the land reform and economic policy over dual interest rates, subsidies, and import regulations, and served to strengthen this alliance. In urban areas, housing cooperatives, informal traders and other interests were also mobilised around the provision of land. Together this organisational network consolidated a rural (and small urban) land movement which shaped much of the direction of the fast-track land reform and the emergent heterodox economic policy and development strategy.

The Zanu PF-war veterans nationalist movement alliance that this triggered exhibited important social and political differentiation in terms of ideology, tactics and material interests. The land occupations and state expropriation process was not a uniform and hegemonic structure, and was riddled by numerous internal conflicts and contradictions (Moyo, 2001). Some sought the total restitution of all land and displacement of all white ('settler') farmers, while others sought to negotiate with and accommodate them on downsized farms. Some promoted physical confrontation in the invasions but most did not, and instead sought the more effective use of the legal instrument of land expropriation. Some engaged in corrupt land-grabbing of large and multiple farms and equipment, but the majority did not, preferring to be formally allocated land and subsidised credit according to policy. These competing currents took four years to harmonise, and pervaded the the political succession battles of Zanu PF. Landowners and farmworkers opposed the land occupations or GoZ allocations through physical scuffles which led to the death of six landowners and 11 farmworkers, through legal challenges of the expropriation, and through internet protest advocacy. These fuelled the advocacy of various CSO organisations, and financed the mobilisation of legal defence structures.

By the end of 2004, the allocation of land and potential tenurial rights to peasants, various elites and lower-tier urban workers evoked a new agrarian and economic policy constituency, which included policy elites and CSO agents. Many white farmers had left after their eviction while some remained and splintered into three tendencies: a coopted, independent and non-confrontationists thread; a radical confrontationist group led by Justice for Agriculture, and the moderate Commercial Farmers' Union led by a mainstream group in favour of engagement with the state and donors. Landowners retained their extensive legal challenges of the expropriation, while negotiating without pre-prejudice. This unfolding reconfiguration of agrarian civil society structures and interests gradually shifted land policy discourses, the state's policy attitudes and the role of the international community. Even the MDC was reorienting its land policy by 2004 (MDC, 2004).

Local government and land administration institutions

Rural local authorities, including elected councillors, local government officials and traditional leaders also interacted with civil society organisations and the land movement. Local government structures had experienced declining fiscal capacities to cover administrative, logistical and other implementation responsibilities by 1999. Yet the fast-track land reform gave them substance at a relatively low direct budgetary cost, given that payment for land was not the constraint, and that only rudimentary support services and infrastructures were being provided by the state to some new settlers. Various government and ruling party task forces were established to monitor the land reform process. The district land committees, which had been initiated in 1996, were restructured, around a command centre concept in 2000, comprising almost all local ministry officials and traditional leaders, war veterans, the ruling party and the security organs. They reported to similarly constituted provincial land committees, coordinated by provincial governors, and these in turn reported to the central ministry of land. For at least three years (2000–2002), the authority of local state structures tended to be subordinated to the war veterans' structures, which tended to influence the identification of land and beneficiaries.

These structures regulated the land occupations, identifying land to be expropriated, selected land beneficiaries, negotiated the former farmers' retained landholdings, resolved land conflicts and prevented 'crime'. They also coordinated the distribution of state-subsidised agricultural inputs and machinery for tillage and harvesting. Their advocacy spurred two GoZ land audits during 2002 and 2003 period (Buka Report, 2002; PLRC, 2003), and led to the restructuring of the Ministry of Land and the initiation of land reform corrections from 2003.

However, structure and policy consistency in the land reform process took almost four years to emerge, when the institutions responsible for implementation stabilised through incrementally completing various procedures (e.g. court confirmations of acquisition, tenure certificates offered, compensation, support services, etc.), building on the rudimentary allocation of land. It relegated to the longer-term the costly implementation processes (e.g. land subdivision surveying, infrastructure investments, etc.). The first 18 months of the fast-track process entailed two parallel actions: coordinated and uncoordinated land occupations by groups of occupiers and individuals on about 20 per cent of the large farmers' land; the state-led expropriation of 80 per cent of the large farmers land, comprising invaded ('occupied') and unoccupied land, and the formal allocation to selected beneficiaries, including the initial occupiers. Both processes entailed elements of chaotic process, at the beginning, including incidences of violence on the farms, although disorder gradually receded as state administrative and legal structures gained greater countrywide control of the process from late 2001. This process was mediated by the district land committees, and monitored technical audits and security monitoring task forces. But sporadic land invasions and violence on a few farms persisted into 2004.

However, although the scale of land eventually transferred was almost double that proposed in the land reform plans of 1998 (GoZ, 1998), some of the principles of that policy guided implementation (see GoZ, 2001), while the correction exercises attempted to sustain many of the principles (see PLRC, 2003). Inconsistent implementation of some principles reflected social demands, which forced the government to acquire more land and reduce the original farm size ceilings to accommodate more people. Yet opportunistic groups, which sought larger and multiple plots or used land as patronage among beneficiaries, also pressured the state to acquire more land or to evict more former landowners and some newly settled peasants. The media propaganda against corrections, which vilified the return of land to some 'whites' was also used to check corrections.

Traditional peasant leadership structures

Traversing the rural structures of the local state and rural civil society, the institution of traditional leaders had a pervasive influence over the peasant land movements, besides their control of critical levers of local power (traditional courts, etc.) as well as over land policy and local state actions. They led some land occupations, lobbied for more formal powers over the regulation of land allocation, land use and natural resource management, and mediated competing land demands.

They competed among themselves over jurisdictions to allocate new land, and with local government structures, and against outsiders, to get as much land for their subjects. Their displeasure received wide media coverage, such that their advocacy influenced central land policy elites and local land committees in the land acquisition and allocation processes. Their position on land committees was strengthened but their relative influence over other members was shaky.

Their influence led to equity-inducing or potential poverty-reducing land policy responses from the state at times, highlighting the importance of various sources of internal critique alongside the external, especially media, critique, which seized the opportunity of exposing oppositional grievances to the fast-track process. Yet some chiefs gained larger pieces of prime land and homesteads, as did their elite counterparts in the state and private sector. This support for the larger commercial landholdings was an inequity-inducing form of interest and policy influence, justified on grounds of royalty. This trend extended to their access to electricity, vehicles and farming inputs, co-opting them into the agrarian bourgeois.

A few chiefs in Matabeleland (an MDC stronghold) had not cooperated in the land occupations or in supplying waiting lists of potential beneficiaries in the earlier formal process, limiting the land gains of their peasantry, relative to their counterparts and new commercial farmers. This was inequity-inducing and extended the redistribution exercise.

These various public interactions, including the key efforts of political parties, were critical to the mobilisation of land reform and/or opposition to it, and thus in shaping land policy. More systematic research on the events and context of the incidences of violence related to the land occupations, and expropriation vis-à-vis the elections, which engulfed Zanu PF and the MDC, and landowner opposition to land takeovers, is required, for these struggles influenced key shifts in land policy, especially as to the scale of takeover and the aggression involved.

These state–civil society interactions generated what could be called an expanded redistributionism and equity inducement, tied to both an internal self correcting mechanism within the government and ruling party, and influence by an external critique of elite land and equipment grabbing, led by the MDC and its allies. But it did not entirely eliminate the uneven land allocation tendency. Nor did it ameliorate the wider economic problems and poverty effects in relation to land reform.

Conclusions

Zimbabwe's land reform process changed from a market framework under neoliberal policy conditions towards a statist tendency, led by popular demands for land, which arose from growing poverty and in response to rekindled grievances over colonial injustices, associated with external influences on the recent political economy. Public advocacy and social demands for land were shaped by both the inequities of pre-existing socio-economic structures and institutions and the conjunctural turn in Zimbabwe's economic and political conditions, as induced by both international forces and by internal struggles for accumulation and political succession.

Land policy approaches changed in relation to the changing strategies of non-state actors such as peasants, war veterans, chiefs and NGOs, as well as of the landowners and international community. These ranged from direct actions such as land occupations and street action, to collaborative or corporatist engagement in the implementation of official land reform programmes. Different tactics of policy dialogue, negotiation and publicised confrontations were adopted at different times. These processes varied as the ideological and material conditions and interests of key actors changed in relation to economic decline and growing poverty.

The influence on land policy is a more complex phenomenon than is often recognised. The shaping of the fast-track policy came from varied sources, including internal and external pressures mobilised by political parties and CSOs, local structures of the state, traditional authorities, and peasants' movements. The negative impacts of neoliberalism mobilised greater demand for land among the poor and nascent black elites. The growth of formal political opposition ignited land politics, given the racial dimension of land inequality and legacy of the colonial responsibility. This reinforced the nationalist ideology of the land movement, while international opposition to a smaller scale mixed land reform, and economic isolation, radicalised central policy elites.

The internal critique (supportive of the reform) and the external critique opposing the reform had their greatest effect on the commercial component of the land reform programme, in which elite access to land, inputs and credit exhibited tendencies of cronyism, corruption and ineffective use of allocated land. These pressures sustained rural demands for greater equity in land allocations, and diverted the initial emphasis that had been placed on blaming the purported failure of land reform on the allocation of land to poor subsistence farmers, especially by landowners and some middle-class political party and CSO actors (see Tsvangirai, 2002),[12] and decrying the method of mass expropriation of large farms. These advocacy processes reflected unintended and intended, entryist and oppositional, confrontational and constructive, processes of state–civil society interactions to influence the poverty and land policy nexus.

Both the ruling and opposition political parties and CSOs aligned to them had various forms of influence on land policy. The government's dramatic turn to co-opt the land movements and later to effect policy changes for extensive redistribution was fomented both by the advocacy of war veterans and scattered peasant movements, and by the emergence of the ZCTU–MDC alliance as a political force, supported by middle-class NGO formations, as well as capital, including landowners. This reconfigured the correlation of social forces and the balance of power in general. The 'pro-democracy' alliance between the MDC and some local CSOs, local and international capital, international donors and northern NGOs, was presented with the dilemma of apparently rejecting redistributive policies and their potential to reduce inequality and poverty. The redistributionist and nationalist alliance faced the dilemma of being associated with democratic governance deficiencies, despite a strong statist reform agenda.

The focus by some of these CSOs on governance and human rights advocacy had the positive effect of highlighting Zimbabwe's democracy deficit and creating civil society capacities to influence policy in general. But they neglected to promote redistributive land reform after 1980, and again when the opportunity arose in 1997, following years of devastating ESAP policies and the economic decline, and this remains their main enigmatic contradiction. The rural populations' land rights thus became a neglected basic human right, until recent land beneficiary evictions, given their focus on the shortcomings in governance by the state and ruling party.

The Zimbabwean experience suggests the need to examine carefully how national and international policy (macro-economic, governance and land) interacts and evolves, in relation to their competing objectives and conceptualisations, within the wider context of political and economic agendas. It suggests that the wide range of public actions, including elect-oral matters, land policy, wider economic policy, and direct actions over land, as well as social institutions, compete under state and international orchestration, and that these mediate and shape policies and public actions in struggles to protect existing property rights against struggles to gain access to land, as explained by Borras, Kay and Akram-Lodhi in the introductory chapter of this book. The dynamics of land policy and public action thus reflected the changing political and economic fortunes of various classes, social groups and political formations, in relation to the progressively unsustainable economic performance and development of neoliberal Zimbabwe and in relation to changes in the political organisation and landscape of civil society formations.

Notes

1 Hunzwi, public statement on RBZ/ZTC May 2000.
2 This measures quality of life, using real GDP per head, the adult literacy rate and life expectancy (which in Zimbabwe dropped due to HIV/AIDS related deaths).
3 www.eiu.com.
4 In October 2004, the MDC also expressed the desire for Zimbabwe not to be suspended from the IMF, on grounds that on winning the 2005 elections they would not want to start reapplying for membership (MDC, 2004).
5 The MDC has called upon the IMF not to make positive pronouncements on policy as these delay 'reform' and give government a propaganda advantage (ibid.).
6 Sam Geza, former director of resettlement.
7 By 1995 20,000 workers had lost their jobs in the public sector and 25,000 in the private sector. Real wages also declined, such that by 1993 real average total wages stood at 61.9 per cent of their 1980 level, down from 103 per cent in 1990 (Yeros, 2002). In addition the share of wages and salaries in national income stood at 40 per cent in 1996, down from 64 per cent a decade earlier, while the share of profits accruing to capital was at 60 per cent, up from 37 per cent over the same period (ibid.).
8 Internal land reform and resettlement progress reports, Ministry of Lands and Rural Resettlement, Government of Zimbabwe.
9 There is huge demand among new farmers for labour to build houses and other farm structures, especially for former farmworkers who possess construction skills.
10 See Moyo (forthcoming) on details of such farms.
11 Urban discourses tend to emphasise a perceived 'uncivil' character of the war veterans, based on their military or guerrilla formation, rather than the civil associational basis of their organisational cohesion.
12 Newspaper statements.

References

Alexander, J. (2003). '"Squatters," Veterans and the State in Zimbabwe', in A. Hammar, B. Raftopoulos and S. Jensen, eds, *Zimbabwe's Unfinished Business: Rethinking Land, State and Nation in the Context of Crisis.* Harare: Weaver Press.

Amnesty International (2004). 'Zimbabwe: Power and Hunger – Violations of the Right to Food'. www.amnesty.org/library/print/ENGFR460262004.

Bernstein, H. (2001). 'Agrarian Reform after Developmentalism?'. Presentation at the Conference on Agrarian Reform and Rural Development: Taking Stock. Social Research Centre of the American University in Cairo, 14–15 October.

Bratton, M. (1987). 'The Comrades and the Countryside: The Politics of Agricultural Policy in Zimbabwe', *World Politics*, vol. 39, no. 2, pp. 174–202.

Buka Report (2002). A Preliminary Audit Report of Land Reform Programme. Mimeo.

Chambati, W. and S. Moyo (2004). *Land Reform and the Political Economy of Agricultural Labour*. Harare: African Institute for Agrarian Studies.

Chasi, M., F. Chinembiri, C. Mudiwa, G. Mudimu and P. Johnson (1994). 'Land fragmentation', Study Number 3, the Commission of Enquiry into Land Tenure Systems in Zimbabwe, Government of Zimbabwe, September.

CSO (1999). 'Poverty in Zimbabwe'. Harare: Central Statistical Office.

CSO (2002). 'Census 2002: Zimbabwe's Preliminary Report'. Harare: Central Statistical Office.

Davies, R. (2004). 'Memories of Underdevelopment: A Personal Interpretation of Zimbabwe's Economic Decline', in B. Raftopoulos and T. Savage, eds, *Zimbabwe: Injustice and Political Reconciliation*. Cape Town: Institute for Justice and Reconciliation.

Deininger, K., R. van den Brink and S. Moyo (2000). 'How Land Reform Can Contribute to Poverty Reduction – Empirical Evidence from International and Zimbabwean Experience'. Mimeo.

Elich, G. (2002). 'Zimbabwe under Siege'. www.swan.com/library/art8/elich004.html.

Government of Zimbabwe (1982). 'Transitional National Development Plan (1982–85)', vol. 1. Harare: Government of Zimbabwe.

Government of Zimbabwe (1998). 'Zimbabwe: Programme for Economic and Social Transformation'. Harare: Government of Zimbabwe.

Government of Zimbabwe (1999). *The Inception Phase Framework Plan of the Second Phase of Land Reform and Resettlement Programme*. Harare: Ministry of Land and Agriculture.

Government of Zimbabwe (GoZ) (2001). *Fast Track Land Reform Programme*. Harare: Government Printers.

Hellum, A and B. Derman (2004). 'Land Reform and Human Rights in Contemporary Zimbabwe: Balancing Individual and Social Justice through an Integrated Human Rights Framework', *World Development*, vol. 32, no. 10, pp. 1785–1805.

Herbst, J. (1990). *State Politics in Zimbabwe*. Harare: University of Zimbabwe Press.

Human Rights Watch (HRW) (2004). 'The Politics of Food Assistance in Zimbabwe', Human Rights Watch *Briefing Paper* August 2004.

IMF (2004). *Zimbabwe: 2004 Article IV Consultation*. IMF Country Report No. 04/297. www.imf.org.

Kinsey, B. (2004). 'Zimbabwe's Land Reform Program: Underinvestment in Post Conflict Transformation', *World Development*, vol. 32, no. 10, pp. 1669–1696.

Kriger, N. (2003). *Guerrilla Veterans in Post-War Zimbabwe: Symbolic and Violent Politics*. Cambridge: Cambridge University Press.

Land Tenure Commission (1994). 'Report of the Commission of Inquiry into

Appropriate Agricultural Land Tenure Systems', vols 1 and 2. Harare: Government Printers.

Maast, M. (1996). *The Harvest of Independence: Commodity Boom and Socio-economic Differentiation Among Peasants in Zimbabwe.* Unpublished Ph.D dissertation, Roskilde University, Roskilde, Denmark.

Magaramombe, G. (2003a). 'Resource Base and Farm Production: Farm Labour Relations Use and Needs', African Institute for Agrarian Studies Discussion Series Paper, Harare.

Magaramombe, G. (2003b). 'An Overview of Vulnerability within the Newly Resettled Former Commercial Farming Areas', Draft Report, United Nations Humanitarian Coordinator, Harare.

Manzungu, E. (2004). 'Towards Sustainable Water Resources and Irrigation Development in the Post Fast Track Land Reform Era in Zimbabwe', Mimeo.

Marongwe, N. (2003). 'Farm Occupations and Occupiers in the New Politics of Land in Zimbabwe', in A. Hammar, B. Raftopoulos and S. Jensen, eds, *Zimbabwe's Unfinished Business: Rethinking Land, State and Nation in the Context of Crisis.* Harare: Weaver Press.

Mlambo, A. S. (2000). 'Manufacturing in Zimbabwe, 1980–90', in A. S. Mlambo, E. S. Pangeti and I. Phimister, eds, *Zimbabwe: A History of Manufacturing, 1890–1995.* Harare: University of Zimbabwe Publications.

Moore, D. (2004). 'Marxism and Marxist Intellectuals in Schizophrenic Zimbabwe: How Many Rights for Zimbabwe's Left? A Comment', *Historical Materialism*, vol. 12, no. 4, pp. 405–425.

Movement for Democratic Change (MDC) (2004). *RESTART: Our Path to Social Justice. The MDC's Economic Programme for Reconstruction, Stabilisation, Recovery and Transformation.* Harare: MDC.

Moyana, H. V. (2002). *The Political Economy of Land in Zimbabwe.* Gweru, Zimbabwe: Mambo Press.

Moyo, S. (1995). *The Land Question in Zimbabwe.* Harare: SAPES Books.

Moyo, S. (1998). *The Land Acquisition Process in Zimbabwe (1997/8).* Harare: United Nations Development Programme (UNDP).

Moyo, S. (2000). *Land Reform under Structural Adjustment in Zimbabwe: Land Use Change in Mashonaland Provinces.* Uppsala: Nordiska Afrika Institutet Uppsala.

Moyo, S. (2001). 'The Land Occupation Movement and Democratization in Zimbabwe: Contradictions of Neo-liberalism', *Millennium: Journal of International Studies*, vol. 30, no. 2, pp. 311–330.

Moyo, S. (2003). 'The Interaction of Market and Compulsory Land Acquisition Processes with Social Action in Zimbabwe's Land Reform', in I. Mandaza and D. Nabudere, eds, *Pan-Africanism and Integration in Africa.* Harare: SAPES Books.

Moyo, S. (2004). 'The Land and Agrarian Question in Zimbabwe'. Paper presented at the first annual colloquium, at the University of Fort Hare, 30 September.

Moyo, S. (2005). 'Land Policy, Poverty Reduction and Public Action in Zimbabwe'. Paper presented at the ISS/UNDP conference on Land Reform and Poverty Reduction, The Hague, Netherlands 17–19 February.

Moyo, S. (forthcoming), 'Fast-Track Land and Agrarian Reform in Zimbabwe: Contradictions of Neoliberalism'.

Moyo, S. and C. Sukume (2004). 'Agricultural Sector and Agrarian Development Strategy'. Paper prepared for World Bank.

Moyo, S. and P. Yeros (2005). 'Land Occupations and Land Reform in Zimbabwe: Towards the National Democratic Revolution', in S. Moyo and P. Yeros, eds, *Reclaiming the Land: The Resurgence of Rural Movements in Africa, Asia and Latin America*. London: Zed Books.

Moyo, S. J. Makumbe and B. Raftopoulos (2000). *NGOs, the State and Politics in Zimbabwe*. Harare: SAPES Books.

National Constitutional Assembly (NCA) (1999). 'Task Force Report, June–December 1999'. Harare: Government Printers.

Ndlela, D. (2004). 'Economic Policy and Its Consequences in Zimbabwe in 2004'. Harare: Movement for Democratic Change.

Overseas Development Administration (ODA) (1996). 'Report of ODA Land Appraisal Mission to Zimbabwe: 23 September–4 October'. Harare: British Development Division in Central Africa.

Parliament of Zimbabwe (2003). 'Second Report of the Portfolio Committee on Public Service, Labour and Social Welfare on the Plight of Farm Workers and Newly Resettled Farmers'. Harare: Government Printers.

Phimister, I. (2004). 'South Africa Diplomacy and the Crisis in Zimbabwe: Liberation Solidarity in the 21st Century', in B. Raftopoulos and T. Savage, eds, *Zimbabwe: Injustice and Political Reconciliation*. Cape Town: Institute for Justice and Reconciliation.

Presidential Land Review Committee (PLRC) (2003). 'Report of the Presidential Land Review Committee', vols 1 and 2. Harare: Government Printers.

Raftopoulos, B. (2003). 'The State in Crisis: Authoritarian Nationalism, Selective Citizenship and Distortions of Democracy in Zimbabwe', in A. Hammar, B. Raftopoulos and S. Jensen, eds, *Zimbabwe's Unfinished Business: Rethinking Land, State and Nation in the Context of Crisis*. Harare: Weaver Press.

Raftopoulos, B. (2004). 'Nation, Race and History in Zimbabwean Politics', in B. Raftopoulos and T. Savage, eds, *Zimbabwe: Injustice and Political Reconciliation*. Cape Town: Institute for Justice and Reconciliation.

Rugube, L., S. Zhou, M. Roth and W. Chambati (2003). *Government Assisted and Market Driven Land Reform: Evaluationg Public and Private Land Markets in Redistribution of Land in Zimbabwe*. Centre for Applied Social Sciences, University of Zimbabwe and Land Tenure Center, University of Wisconsin-Madison.

Sachikonye, L. M. (2003). 'The Situation of Commercial Farmers after Land Reform in Zimbabwe', report prepared for the Farm Community Trust of Zimbabwe. Mimeo.

Sachikonye, L. M. (2004). 'The Promised land: From Expropriation to Reconciliation and Jambanja', in B. Raftopoulos and T. Savage, eds, *Zimbabwe: Injustice and Political Reconciliation*, pp. 1–18. Cape Town: Institute for Justice and Reconciliation.

Sadomba, W. (2005). 'Chefs, You Forget Where We Came From, Why? The Role of War Veterans in the Land Occupations'. Mimeo.

Short, C. (1997). www.publications.parliament.uk/pa/cm199899/cmhansrd/vo981201/text/81201w05.htm.

Stoneman, C. (2000). 'Zimbabwe Land Policy and the Land Reform Programme', in T. A. S. Bowyer-Bower and C. Stoneman, eds, *Land Reform in Zimbabwe: Constraints and Prospects*, pp. 47–58. London: Ashgate Publishing Ltd.

Sukume, C. and S. Moyo (2003). 'Farm Sizes, Decongestion and Land use:

Implications of the Fast Track Land Redistribution Programme in Zimbabwe'. Mimeo.

Toye, J. (1993) *Dilemmas of Development: Reflections on the Counter-Revolution in Development Economics*, 2nd edn. Oxford: Basil Blackwell.

Tshuma, L. (1997). *A Matter of (In)Justice: Law, State and the Agrarian Question in Zimbabwe*. Harare: SAPES Books.

Worby, E. (2004). 'The End of Modernity in Zimbabwe? Passages from Development to Sovereignty', in A. Hammar, B. Raftopoulos and S. Jensen, eds, *Zimbabwe's Unfinished Business: Rethinking Land, State and Nation in the Context of Crisis*. Harare: Weaver Press.

World Bank (1982). 'Zimbabwe: Small Farm Credit Project, Staff Appraisal Report No. 3888', Southern Agriculture Division, Eastern Africa Projects Department, World Bank, Washington, DC.

World Bank (1991). 'Zimbabwe: Agriculture Sector Memorandum: Vol. 1 and Vol. 2'. No. 9429-Zim. Washington: The World Bank.

World Bank (1999). 'Project Appraisal Document on Zimbabwe Land Reform Support Project', Report No. 19618-Zw, July, Washington: The World Bank.

Yeros, P. (2002). 'Zimbabwe and the Dilemmas of the Left', *Historical Materialism*, vol. 10, no. 2, pp. 3-15.

Zimbabwe Confederation of Trade Unions (ZCTU) (1996). 'Beyond ESAP: Framework for a Long Term Development Strategy in Zimbabwe beyond the Economic Structural Adjustment Programme'. Harare: ZCTU.

Zimbabwe Human Development Report (ZHDR) (1999). 'Zimbabwe Human Development Report 1998 Poverty Reduction Forum', Harare: ZHDR.

12 Neoliberal globalisation, land and poverty

Implications for public action

A. Haroon Akram-Lodhi, Saturnino M. Borras Jr, Cristóbal Kay and Terry McKinley

Introduction

This volume has provided a rich set of empirical evidence from ten countries on the impact of land reform policies on poverty reduction and social exclusion. The ten countries examined were: Armenia, Bolivia, Brazil, Egypt, Ethiopia, Namibia, the Philippines, Uzbekistan, Vietnam and Zimbabwe. The purpose of this concluding chapter is twofold. On the one hand, it seeks to synthesise the principal findings from the case studies in order to develop a critical assessment that highlights areas of commonality and difference between country case studies and that demonstrates how complex social relationships predicated upon access to and use of land impact on growth, poverty and social exclusion among the rural population. On the other hand, it seeks to demonstrate how the country case studies show that the state, civil society and the character of production are not separate analytical categories but rather factors that are inherently linked to each other by their association with the politics and economics of land resources. As such, it is argued, the relationship between production, the state and society offers a useful framework from which to evaluate the conditions necessary for a successful land reform, when it is placed within the underlying structural context of the distribution of property, power and privilege which, in this instance, is predicated upon the control of land and other non-land productive assets. In undertaking this dual purpose, then, this conclusion shall provide comparative evidence and analytical implications on the strengths and weaknesses of current land reform policy strategies and implementation approaches, which are, of course, embedded within the broader development strategies of governments.

A comparative assessment of the experience of land reform

In many settings across the rural world today, land remains the most important input in agricultural production. However, in all the cases studied in this book restricted access to land has occurred as a result of a historical process of enclosure, which resulted in small segments of the rural population controlling a large proportion of the land. In Bolivia, Brazil and the Philippines (see Kay and Urioste, Deere and Medeiros, and Borras *et al.*, this volume), this historical process was rooted in colonialism, and resulted in the creation of a class of landlords that dominated rural social relations and cultural life. In Namibia and Zimbabwe (see van Donge *et al.*, and Moyo, this volume), the historical process of enclosure was similarly rooted in colonialism, but with a strong ethnic character, resulting in the creation of a class of large-scale farms controlled by European settlers. In Egypt, Ethiopia and Vietnam (see Bush, Mersha and Gĩthĩnji, and Akram-Lodhi, this volume), the historical process of enclosure predated colonialism, and reflected the continued sustenance of country-specific varieties of feudalism that fostered, in the first two, a class of landlords that shaped the operation of the rural economy and, in the last, a class of rentier bureaucrats that dominated rural culture and society. In Uzbekistan (see Khan, this volume) the historical process of enclosure reflected the wholesale incorporation of Central Asia into the Russian Empire and the introduction of a form of 'neo-feudalism' predicated on the creation of a class of landlords. Only in Armenia (see Spoor, this volume) did the process of incorporation into the Russian Empire not result in a set of enclosures; the rugged terrain of the country, along with its relative underpopulation, helped determine the fact that independent petty peasant production remained the norm until well after the foundation of the Soviet Union.

In all countries bar Armenia, then, enclosure shaped the rural production process by establishing a set of social relations that witnessed the systematic transfer of agricultural surpluses to the land-controlling elite. In each country, this gave rise to a set of political struggles between landlords and subaltern peasant and agricultural labouring classes trying to reshape rural society. As a consequence of these struggles over land, production, surpluses and social power, during the course of the twentieth century, the countries undertook, to varying and differential degrees, a process of agrarian reform (see, e.g. Griffin *et al.*, 2002; Ghimire, 2001; King, 1977; Tuma, 1965; Bernstein, 2002). In Armenia, Ethiopia, Uzbekistan and Vietnam this reform witnessed the collectivisation of land, which could be considered, arguably, a later form of 'socialist enclosure' that had the objective of facilitating structural transformation of the economy and society. In Bolivia, Brazil, Egypt and the Philippines restructuring took the shape of a redistributive land reform that could be considered a form of 'peasant enclosure' that was, in principal, designed to be reasonably equitable, but whose impact in terms of access to land and livelihoods varied substantially across the four countries. Finally, in Namibia and Zimbabwe highly tentative efforts at agrarian reform occurred in the immediate post-independence period; the effect of such reform on the distribution of land and livelihoods was derisory, and the vestiges of what could be termed 'colonial enclosure' have, to a significant extent, remained.

Poverty and inequality in the wake of current land reform policy

The implications of changes in access to land for poverty and inequality have been complex and diverse between and within the countries examined in this volume. Despite such complex diversity, however, it can be suggested that the impact of changing access to land *on poverty* should be examined separately from that of the impact of changing access to land *on inequality*. The reason for this is straightforward: in all the country case studies described rural inequality has, at best, experienced no change or has, at worst, deepened during the current wave of neoliberal globalisation. There is not a single case where rural equality has improved. This suggests that neoliberal globalisation does not improve equality. On the contrary: it fosters inequality.

In contrast to inequality, in terms of poverty reduction it is, in general, possible to identify four very broad experiences within the country case studies in this book. The first case is that of Vietnam, which has witnessed a rapid reduction in poverty that may indeed be historically unprecedented (see, e.g. Akram-Lodhi, 2005). The case of Vietnam demonstrates very clearly that initially equitable distributions of income and assets, and in particular of land, at the beginning of the period of neoliberal globalisation can, in the context of complementary forward-and-backward linkages between the export and peasant production subsectors, foster rapid rates of poverty reduction. This relative success can be set beside the cases of Bolivia, Brazil, Egypt, Namibia and the Philippines, where poverty reduction has been at best limited and at worst stagnant. Each of these five cases are notable for the counterpoint that they provide to the Vietnamese example, in that, contrary to Vietnam's experience, each of them commenced the latest wave of neoliberal globalisation subject to extremely skewed income and asset distribution. It should be noted that in Bolivia, Brazil and Namibia this skewed distribution had a strong ethnic dimension. The impact of initially inequitable income and asset distributions was similar in all six cases: the benefits that accrued to the rural economy from integration into the global economy were skewed in favour of those that initially controlled assets. In this way, the impact of neoliberal globalisation on rural society has been to reinforce the social power of the dominant elite.

The third broad set of experiences witnessed in the case studies are those of Armenia, Uzbekistan and Zimbabwe, which have witnessed increased poverty during the current wave of neoliberal globalisation. Clearly, increased poverty in Armenia and Uzbekistan can be traced back to the collapse of the Soviet Union, the economic shock that accompanied the independence of both countries, and the effective seizure of large parts of the state-owned economy by private interests with ties to the political elites running the countries both before and after independence (see also Spoor, 2003). As a consequence of economic decline and deepening poverty, in Armenia many who had previously worked in cities, for the government or for state-owned enterprises, found that their ability to construct a livelihood came under sustained pressure. They commenced smallholder farming as a means of coping, with the result that a widespread re-agrarianisation took place in Armenia during the 1990s. By way of contrast, in Uzbekistan the large collectives and state farms that dominated cash crop production prior to the collapse of the Soviet Union were effectively privatised during the 1990s, and increasingly sought to operate along the lines of capitalist agriculture. One outcome of this process was massive shedding of labour in a rural economy with limited labour absorption. As a consequence, poverty worsened. Finally, in the case of Zimbabwe, the increase in agricultural staple exports decreed by the international financial institutions accompanied the partial re-enclosure of former settler farms by rent-seeking members of the political elite with strong ties to the ruling party. The result, in terms of farm productivity and eventually production, was a massive decline, even as agricultural staple exports meant that per capita food availability in the country declined. The resulting food crisis pushed much of rural Zimbabwe into chronic poverty for the first time in the country's history, from which it has yet to recover, and which formed the backdrop to the land seizure movement of the early 2000s.

The outlier, in terms of poverty reduction, in the country case studies has been Ethiopia. There, a record of stagnant poverty reduction cannot be laid at the door of an initial maldistribution of income and assets, as was the case in Bolivia, Brazil, Egypt, Namibia and the Philippines. There was inequality, to be sure, as explained by Mersha and Gĩthĩnji (this volume); but the key factor inhibiting poverty reduction in Ethiopia since the collapse of the Derg has been the inability to technologically transform agriculture, through the provision of water, appropriate biotechnologies, and stable prices, which has had the consequence of sustaining the seasonality of Ethiopian agriculture and thus its poor productivity performance. Although Ethiopia pursues an agriculture-led development strategy, it is precisely the underdevelopment of agriculture that constrains the rural economy and its ability to foster sustainable poverty reduction.

Notwithstanding this outlier, however, the evidence emerging from a comprehensive overview of the country case studies contained in this volume demonstrates some broad similarities that can help us understand some of the processes at work in the rural economies. Shifting access to land during the latest wave of neoliberal globalisation had the effect of restructuring rural production processes in relatively more capital- or more labour-intensive patterns, altering the nature and rate of capital accumulation in both the export and peasant production subsectors – which, in turn, affected both inequality and poverty. An important variable in this process has been the extent of forward and backward linkages between the export and peasant production subsectors, as demonstrated by Brazil and Vietnam. However, the critical variable in this process, in terms of its impact on poverty, appears to be the degree of equality in the distribution of assets, income and resources at the start of the restructuring process (see also Borras, forthcoming, in the context of Southeast Asia). Vietnam was without doubt the most relatively egalitatarian economy at the start of the process of rural transformation. It is, as a direct consequence, also the economy that has witnessed far and away the best performance in poverty reduction during the process of rural transformation.

Rural politics and the state

Changing access to land, alterations in the rural production process, and shifts in rates of rural accumulation and poverty reduction could be expected to have an effect on rural politics, because the fulcrum of rural politics is precisely the rural production process and rural capital accumulation. The country case studies in this volume do indeed demonstrate that understanding the relationship between these variables is very important in helping to understand rural politics.

In examining the impact of changing access to land on rural politics in an era of neoliberal globalisation, two central and interrelated issues need to be examined. The first is the character of rural politics. Here, the focal issue is whether rural politics are dominated by highly individualistic, often indirect, covert engagement with the formal rules and informal norms governing the production and allocation of resources, or what Kerkvliet (2005) calls 'everyday forms of peasant resistance' (also referred to as the 'weapons of the weak' by Scott, 1986), or by the more 'organised' and overt collective engagement with dominant social actors. Of course, the distinction between these two types is often less than clear. Nonetheless, such a distinction is useful in understanding the substantive diversity demonstrated within the country case studies. However, two important factors have to be integrated into a discussion of the character of rural politics. The first is whether ethnicity is used as a means of mobilising everyday politics into collective action. There is extensive historical evidence that the use of ethnicity as a means of mobilising collective action allows dominant elites to sustain their social control over communities. The second is whether migration serves to constrict the capacity of civil society to transform everyday politics into collective action, by both reducing the binding character of economic constraints on households and by intensifying workloads among those who do not migrate.

The second key issue that needs to be examined is the character of the state and its relationship to civil society. The processes and mechanisms by which the state formally and informally constructs, implements, transforms and avoids its interventions, which affect the production and distribution of resources, will have a profound impact upon the character of rural politics and, in turn, on the terms and conditions by which the state interacts with civil society. There is thus a need to understand the specific articulation of consent and coercion by which the state and civil society collaborate or conflict with each other, in order to comprehend the trajectories of variation demonstrated in the country case studies.

All the countries examined in this book of course witness 'everyday politics'. The issue here is whether everyday politics is the predominant form of rural political expression and, if so, why. Here, it is possible to identify Armenia, Egypt, Ethiopia, Namibia, Uzbekistan, Vietnam and Zimbabwe as countries where 'the weapons of the weak' are the principal, but not exclusive, means by which dissent is expressed. The reason why rural political discourse is dominated by everyday politics has to do with the nature of dominant social actors. Each of these countries witnesses dominant social actors controlling political parties, popular mass organisations, and the state. These actors use their control of politics to tightly restrict political activity, if necessary coercively, and thus control the activities of civil society actors. In most instances the state is capacity-constrained and this does allow limited amounts of political space for autonomous organisation. Nonetheless, rural politics remains by and large 'everyday'.

However, in these circumstances, it is necessary to unravel the character of politics within dominant social actors. Here, some diversity emerges. Armenia, Egypt, Uzbekistan and Vietnam possess strongly cohesive elites that dominate social relations in politics, economics and society. In Vietnam, however, this domination operates through diverse mechanisms designed to build and maintain reasonably consensual relations between the governing and the governed. By way of contrast, Ethiopia, Namibia and Zimbabwe have, on the surface, reasonably cohesive political and economic elites, but beneath this lies fractional divergence rooted in both political and ethnic differences. These differences remain submerged, however, under the political authority associated with liberation movements.

Bolivia, Brazil and the Philippines offer a stark contrast. In all three cases, the use of everyday politics remains widespread. However, in all three, everyday politics has been forged, through a long and diverse set of processes, into more explicit collective action by social movements. These actions seek to alter the terms and conditions governing the production and distribution of rural resources by engaging with both dominant social actors and the state. Brazil offers the starkest example, with the *O Movimiento dos Trabalhadores Rurais sem Terra* (Landless Worker's Movement, or MST) being the best known of a host of rural advocacy and action groups that collectively challenge rural elites and the state (Deere and Medeiros, this volume; Wright and Wolford, 2003). However, in Bolivia as well, everyday politics has been welded, collectively, into the *Movimiento al Socialismo* (Movement toward Socialism) which is, again, one of a number of rural peasant movements that has moved beyond its peasant base, having established a political party to contest national elections and which saw its leader elected to the presidency by an unexpectedly large margin in 2005 (Kay and Urioste, this volume). Finally, the Philippines has a long history of rural-based collective struggle and armed insurgency, involving various rural social movement organisations, of which the most important is currently the National Coordination of Autonomous Local Rural People's Organisations, or UNORKA (*Pambansang Ugnayan ng Nagsasariling Lokal na mga Samahang Mamamayan sa Kanayunan*) (see Franco and Borras, 2005). Collective action has witnessed rural elites being confronted and the state challenged using both peaceful and non-peaceful tactics.

The diversity demonstrated in these three cases stem from the character of the rural elite. In Brazil, the elite is reasonably cohesive, with a clear vision of how the economy and society should be structured. In Bolivia and the Philippines, by way of contrast, the elites are subject to fractional faultlines. In the Philippines, these faultlines revolve around differential rent-seeking interests within the elite and its relationship to the state. They also include the differences witnessed between a modernising, economically motivated, export-oriented rural elite interested in promoting higher value agro-exports and an export-oriented rural elite that produces less valuable agro-exports and which is, through its use of patron–client relations in rural society, more, for lack of a better word, 'traditional' in its social, political and economic outlook. In Bolivia, fractional faultlines are spatially oriented, with an export-oriented modernising fraction based in Santa Cruz engaged in conflictual relations with the non-resource-rich highlands whose peasants are less interested in the economic possibilities offered by neoliberal globalisation.

Rural peasant movements, by entering into what Tarrow (1998) calls 'contentious politics' vis-à-vis the state and dominant classes, have had an impact on the state. This impact differs between and within the three countries, in part because of the nature of the response of the elites. In Brazil, the cohesive character of the dominant elite means that while rural social movements are able to contest the state, it remains, despite the election of the Worker's Party, dominated by the elite, which continues to use the state to pursue a project of 'conservative modernisation'. Nonetheless, the role of the Worker's Party, along with rural social movements, means that the dominant social elite is struggling to exercise a degree of hegemony over society. In the Philippines, a long-standing history of rural social organisation and struggle, along with fractional faultlines within the dominant elite, has allowed civil society to seek to contest the state from within. This is witnessed, for example, in the internal struggles played out in the Department for Agrarian Reform between social activists and conservative modernisers. Once again, the ability to contest the state has meant that the rural elite has been unable to exercise an adequate degree of hegemony over society so as to shape the process of social and political change. Finally, in Bolivia, fractional faultlines within the dominant elite have been exploited by strong rural social movements undertaking consistent and coherent collective action, with the result that the capacity of the state to govern civil society has been challenged. The state itself is thus the subject of contestation between rural civil society and the dominant social elite.

Implications of the country case studies

There have been modest but significant achievements in redistributive land reform in Brazil, the Philippines and Zimbabwe, as well as the establishment of peasant family farming in Armenia and Vietnam, in the past 15 years. These achievements have been obtained as a result of diverse strategies by state and civil society actors. They can be set beside a comparative stasis in Bolivia, Ethiopia and Namibia, and, if anything, a comparative retreat from the gains of redistributive land reform in Egypt and Uzbekistan, again partly as a result of diverse strategies by state and civil society actors. Thus, the country case studies in this book clearly demonstrate substantive diversity. Nonetheless, as demonstrated in the previous section, a number of common themes have been established, in which deviation from common processes assists in explaining the differential trajectories of variation witnessed. Therefore, a number of comparative conclusions can be derived from the case studies.

First, neoliberal globalisation has facilitated a process of 'partial re-enclosure' in the agrarian production systems. This alteration in the character of the agrarian structure has reshaped the rural production process and facilitated the expanded commodification of rural economic activity. Partial re-enclosure has been witnessed in access to land. However, it has also been witnessed in access to other natural resources such as water and forests. However, there are substantial differences in how this process has taken place in the countries examined in this book.

Second, transformations in the rural production process, while different, have nonetheless had, in all the country case studies, an impact on the potential capacity of the rural economy to create productive resources surplus to its reproductive requirements. This has, in turn, affected the processes of accumulation, poverty reduction and structural change. In particular, the process of accumulation has been, once again, affected by the overarching process of globalisation, the entry of agro-food-based profitseeking transnationals into national economies, and by the emphasis on agricultural exports as the motor of accumulation. Nonetheless, the countries studied demonstrate that there are no uniform lessons to be learned about how to enhance the production of agricultural surplus. Rather, in each country, the historically specific path of change demonstrated means that it is necessary to undertake a historically informed and country-specific analysis of the capacity of a rural economy to supply in a sustainable fashion an agricultural surplus.

Third, country-specific changes in rural production and accumulation invariably have an impact on rural politics. The way in which this plays out will be, in part, a function of the relationships within and between the peasantry, the rural elite and the state. The country case studies in this volume demonstrate that, when countries with large peasant populations are able to transcend everyday politics and create and sustain collective alliances within the peasantry itself and with other sectors, the dominant social elite and the state can be seriously challenged. This can lead to the point where the capacity of the state to govern in the interests of the elite is itself challenged and, in a very real sense, the peasantry seeks to strike back.

The case studies thus demonstrate that land-linked social and economic relationships, which are both causes and consequences of the various prevailing landed property rights regimes, are in many agrarian settings economically inefficient, socially exclusionary, culturally alienating and politically disempowering. Therefore, if land policies are intended partly to reform these conditions, they must by definition reform land-based social relationships in a multidimensional manner, taking into account the plurality and diversity of these relationships. Granted it is important to reform and improve the relationship between people and land in the context of economic activities. Nonetheless, the basis for and imperatives of truly transformational land policies are the urgent and necessary reforms of relationships within and between households, communities, and different social classes and groups, that often have competing political-economic and socio-cultural interests linked together in a variety of ways by their association to land.

In this context, and given the impact of access to land on a diverse set of relationships, reforming landed property rights should be explicitly linked to efforts to eliminate poverty, social exclusion and the political disenfranchisement of poor people in the countryside. Moreover, the conceptual and practical strengths and weaknesses of various land reform frameworks and approaches should be critically assessed from the impact of reform on the social relationships that are supposed to be reformed, as has been attempted in the country case studies. In other words, land reforms must remain firmly embedded within the broader structure and goals of strategies for capital accumulation and national development, poverty elimination and social transformation (see, e.g. Kay, 2002). However, the ability to embed land reform within national development strategy is located within the global setting, in which trans-national corporations seek to use the international markets that they operate in to allocate resources, including capital and technological innovation. While this process can improve the capability to implement a pro-poor social development strategy, as was demonstrated in the case of Vietnam, it is more likely to constrain such capabilities, as shown in many of the country case studies in this volume. This necessitates a creative analysis of ways in which transformational land reform might be attempted. In particular, it is necessary to exploit the possibilities offered by globalisation, just as South Korea and Taiwan did in the past in order to achieve national development and the modernisation of agriculture.

The analytical themes that emerge out of the country studies and which have been addressed in this conclusion suggest that the convergence of four broadly distinct but interlinked factors or conditions can facilitate a land reform that transforms social relationships. These interlinked conditions are grounded in agrarian production systems, the process of accumulation, and the character of rural politics. These four conditions are that the agrarian reform process should be part of a growth-oriented development strategy that is productivity-enhancing, state-supported, and beneficiaries-led.

'Beneficiaries-led'

The autonomy and capacity of peasants and of their organisations, as well as of their societal allies, to mobilise for their legitimate claims before the state is of paramount importance in effecting successful land reform (see, e.g. Petras, 1998; Petras and Veltmeyer, 2001), as can be inferred from some of the country case studies. This insight is different from other dominant views that consider peasant organisations important but in the context of being necessary administrative adjuncts of the state bureaucracy, or from conventional views that see participation by or partnership with peasant associations only in the context of a lack of conflict between the state and civil society. Moreover, as some of the country case studies demonstrate, it is not enough to investigate the mere presence or absence of such groups in given spaces, but rather necessary to go deeper into the questions of mobilising structures, political strategies, identity formation and solidarity.

Most fundamentally, the studies described in this book support the proposition that peasant movements that are independent from the state and dominant actors in national and global markets and supported by societal allies, including other working classes, political parties, churches and NGOs, can play a decisive role in the politics of agrarian reform. However, the country case studies also show that by themselves peasant movements cannot create or implement land reform. Rather, they need state actors to launch joint and/or parallel actions, either as a reaction to social pressure from below or as an autonomous initiative for reform (see, e.g. Borras, 2001; Herring, 1983). Therefore, peasant beneficiaries should lead the process of agrarian reform, but there is nonetheless a need for it to be state-supported.

State-supported

Even where strong and persistent peasant mobilisations emerge and push for agrarian reform, as in some of the country case studies, this does not guarantee automatic implementation of their demands. Rather, it is, as the case studies show, ultimately the state that has the authority and power to carry out and implement reform demands, and especially the types of reforms that require a redistribution of wealth and power in society. Therefore, as emerges from the case studies, the availability of legal frameworks, such as, for example, a land reform law, providing institutional rules to govern the contestation processes between different groups and individuals for control over property rights, is a crucial pro-reform context, although as Franco (2005; see also van Donge, 1999) explains, land reform laws, even very progressive ones, are not self-interpreting or self-implementing. And so, while it is the actual balance of forces within the state, in society and in the state–society interaction that eventually influences policy outcomes, autonomous and pro-reform judicial and adjudication bodies within the state are also important. More generally, the autonomy and capacity of the state to formulate and implement its reform policy is equally critical. For example, the state must have the autonomy to expropriate landholdings by the powerful landed elite, or the capacity to mobilise and allocate fiscal resources for the implementation of an agrarian reform. However, as reinforced by some of the country case studies, it is also necessary to recognise that the state itself is an arena of contestation that to a greater or lesser extent can seek or not seek to govern civil society and the market and is occupied by different types of actors that either support or undermine the land reform agenda.

The interaction between state and societal forces, including civil society organisations, necessarily extends beyond the national boundary, to the international level. While the international level has always been an important extension of local–national initiatives for land reform in the past, this has become even more the case during the past two decades. The phenomenal rise in number and political influence of civil society organisations, as well as the steady resurrection of land issues in the official agendas of international multilateral and bilateral development agencies has transformed the international arena of state–society interaction into a very critical one in terms of land policy making. This is partly seen in recent important initiatives such as the International Conference on Agrarian Reform and Rural Development (ICARRD) convened by the

Food and Agriculture Organisation of the United Nations in March 2006
in Brazil. Peasant movements have also increasingly extended their policy
advocacy, lobby and mobilisation initiatives at this level, as is being done
by *La Via Campesina*, today's largest and most important transnational
rural social movement (see Borras, 2004).

In this context, then, it is important to consider the role played by state
actors: the state itself, the different agencies and groups of actors within
the state, and political parties. Here, the global neoliberal framework is of
vital importance, for two reasons. The first is that the activities of transnational capital are, by definition, more difficult for the nation-state to
govern. In the global economy there has been a deepening process of
regionalism in which national differences in the balance of forces, the
forces of production, and within capitalist classes still matter in shaping
national and international processes of capital accumulation. The capacity
of the state to manage this process is difficult, but, as the case of the East
Asian economies has convincingly demonstrated, not impossible (Bello *et
al.*, 2004). However, for the state to be able to navigate this complex
global setting, civil society allies are of vital importance; without such
allies, it is more likely that the state will simply accede to the global
balance of forces.

The second aspect of the global neoliberal framework that must be
taken into account is that, increasingly, market relations have been introduced into the activities of the state and that moreover, the mechanism by
which the state regulates markets has been transformed in the wake of the
neoliberal revolution (see Gwynne and Kay, 2004). Thus, the way in which
different agencies and groups of actors within the state and political
parties interact is increasingly shaped by markets. The result has been the
gradual emergence of what Robison (2006) terms the 'market-state' in
which state autonomy has been, to a relative extent, reduced and thus
some of the characteristics of the strong states that undertook agrarian
reform half a century ago have been partly constrained. The case studies
in this volume demonstrate that, while reformists within an increasingly
marketised state are indeed crucial to the success of a land reform, they
are not on their own capable of implementing a land reform that transforms social relations. Rather, they need allies within civil society to
sustain transformational legal frameworks and carry out reforms.

In this context, the ability of pro-reform state and societal actors to
launch joint or parallel actions that complement, not undermine, each
other's initiatives to push for the implementation of reformist land policies has great influence on the nature of land reform policy outcomes
(Borras, 2001). As the country case studies consistently demonstrate,
market forces will not by themselves (re)allocate land resources in a pro-
poor manner and poor peasants themselves do not have sufficient political power to implement and carry out reforms. Moreover, the notion of a
pro-reform alliance is consistent with the literature's rich studies on class

alliances in the context of the state and the peasantry (see, e.g. Kay and Silva, 1992). However, the key analytical point, which can be inferred from some of the country case studies, is that state reformists and social movements are both crucial actors in the dynamic processes of redefining social relationships in property rights in a way that has the potential to impact upon accumulation, poverty and social exclusion. At the same time, it is also important to note that this point is most relevant, as is emphasised in the country case studies, in national settings that are characterised by relative political openness. It has relatively less relevance in national situations marked by regimes where citizens have at best highly limited participation in national governance and where the state thus has a tighter grip over the ability of people to interact in creative and reformist ways. In this latter situation, and on the role played by the rural poor in transforming national policies and politics, Kerkvliet (2005), with specific reference to Vietnam, and to O'Brien and Lianjiang (2006) on China have strong insights on the power of everyday politics.

'Productivity-enhancing'

By themselves, beneficiaries-led state-supported approaches to redistributive and transformational agrarian reform are not sufficient to ensure capital accumulation and poverty elimination. In this light, because control over land resources remains crucial to the ability of the rural poor to construct, defend and sustain their livelihoods, it is critical that land and labour productivity gains are obtained by the beneficiaries of agrarian reform, a point that is borne out in the country case studies. Previously, it was simply assumed that the redistribution of large landed estates would automatically lead to production and productivity increases. However, this did not happen. Now, current dominant thinking is that a 'free' market is the best possible way to allocate and reallocate land resources, and that there is thus a need to construct the foundations of a free market in land so as to enhance private economic efficiency. However, the country case studies show that a market-led approach does not effect efficiency improvements or a pro-poor reform of existing land-linked social relationships. There is thus ample evidence to cast doubt on the efficacy of the market-led approach to achieve productivity improvements. Rather, experiences in different countries historically demonstrate that other, complementary, policy components to land redistribution policies have to be put in place if productivity gains are to be secured (see also Kay 2002; Griffin *et al.*, 2002). These complementary policy components can include financial assistance, as well as farm input and output market access assistance, and are state-supported.

'Growth-oriented development strategy'

Finally, land reform has to be part of a more ambitious growth-oriented development strategy. In this context, economic policies have to be geared to promoting pro-poor growth. Restrictive neoliberal economic policies have been an impediment to success in land reform because of their inability to deliver the general conditions of agricultural prosperity that would sustain redistributive reform. Securing more equitable access to landed assets is not likely to be sustainable if growth of the rural economy is impeded. The economic returns to land would remain inadequate.

A scaled-up national development strategy geared to the Millennium Development Goals (MDGs) could help provide a macro-environment able to underpin and sustain the significant shift in economic and political power that a broad-based land reform programme would entail. Deprived of such a conducive environment and disconnected from a growth-oriented development strategy, land reform initiatives are likely to degenerate into slow-paced, anemic and, ultimately, ineffectual poverty alleviating – not poverty eliminating – programmes.

Emerging out of the country case studies in this book are thus a set of four interlinked themes that can assist in the construction of a transformational redistributive agrarian reform. As explained by Borras, Kay and Akram-Lodhi in the introductory chapter, these analytical themes do not romanticise the omnipotent role of peasants and land reform beneficiaries and their organisations. They also do not assign a commanding role to the central state, nor do they give sole importance to economic productivity-enhancement issues. Rather, the challenge is to analyse state, peasant movements, and the character of production not as separate groups, but as factors that are inherently linked to each other and to the global economy by their association to the politics and economics of land resources.

In closing: in this chapter the land policies examined in the ten country case studies have been analysed from a perspective that has sought to interrogate the extent to which land policy in an era of neoliberal globalisation has altered production, fostered capital accumulation, and invigorated rural politics. The country case studies demonstrate that dominant social elites still seek to alter access to land in their favour, promote transformations in rural production and foster an unleashing of rural capital accumulation. At the same time they seek to contain, where possible, through the use of the state, the potential power of rural social movements. Transnational capital does have an impact on this process. However, in the case studies the national political economy remains a significant arena of development, struggle and change, and thus the role of neoliberal globalisation is important yet highly contingent. In this light, it appears that the possibility of unleashing a pro-poor agrarian transition may depend upon the extent to which transformational reform is beneficiary-led, state-supported, productivity-enhancing, and embedded within a growth-oriented development strategy. However, it must be stressed that access to land is not a magic bullet. Rather, it is transformations in the underlying social relations of production that are contingent upon changing access to land that have, in turn, the potential to eliminate poverty and improve equality.

References

Akram-Lodhi, H. (2005). 'Vietnam's Agriculture: Processes of Rich Peasant Accumulation and Mechanisms of Social Differentiation', *Journal of Agrarian Change*, vol. 5, no. 1, pp. 73–116.

Bello, W., with H. Docena, M. de Guzman and M. Malig (2004). *The Anti-Development State: The Political Economy of Permanent Crisis in the Philippines*. Quezon City: University of the Philippines Press.

Bernstein, H. (2002). 'Land Reform: Taking a Long(er) View', *Journal of Agrarian Change*, vol. 2, no. 4, pp. 433–463.

Borras, S. Jr (forthcoming). '"Free Market", Export-Led Development Strategy and Its Impact on Rural Livelihoods, Poverty and Inequality: The Philippine Experience Seen from a Southeast Asian Perspective', *Review of International Political Economy*.

Borras, S. Jr (2004). '*La Via Campesina*: An Evolving Transnational Social Movement', *TNI Briefing Series*, no. 2004/6. Amsterdam: Transnational Institute.

Borras, S. Jr (2001) 'State–Society Relations in Land Reform Implementation in the Philippines', *Development and Change*, vol. 32, no. 3, pp. 545–575.

Franco, J. (2005). 'Making Property Rights Accessible: Movement Innovation in the Political Legal Struggle to Claim Land Rights in the Philippines', *IDS Working Paper Series*, no. 244 (June 2005) Institute of Development Studies (IDS), Brighton.

Franco, J. and S. Borras Jr (eds) (2005). On Just Grounds: Struggling for Agrarian Justice and *Citizenship Rights in the Rural Philippines*. Quezon City: Institute for Popular Democracy and Amsterdam: Transnational Institute.

Ghimire, K. (ed.) (2001). *Land Reform and Peasant Livelihoods: The Social Dynamics of Rural Poverty and Agrarian Reform in Developing Countries*. Geneva: UNRISD and London: ITDG.

Griffin, K., A. R. Khan and A. Ickowitz (2002). 'Poverty and Distribution of Land', *Journal of Agrarian Change*, vol. 2, no. 3, pp. 279–330.

Gwynne, R. and C. Kay (2004). *Latin America Transformed: Globalization and Modernity*, 2nd edn. London: Arnold.

Herring, R. (1983). *Land to the Tiller: The Political Economy of Agrarian Reform in South Asia*. New Haven, CT: Yale University Press.

Kay, C. (2002). 'Why East Asia Overtook Latin America: Agrarian Reform, Industrialization and Development', *Third World Quarterly*, vol. 23, no. 6, pp. 1073–1102.

Kay, C. and P. Silva (eds) (1992). *Development and Social Change in the Chilean Countryside: From the Pre-Land Reform Period to the Democratic Consolidation*. Amsterdam: CEDLA.

Kerkvliet, B. (2005). *The Power of Everyday Politics: How Vietnamese Peasants Transformed National Policy*. Ithaca, NY: Cornell University Press.

King, R. (1977). *Land Reform: A World Survey.* London: B. Bell and Sons Ltd.

O'Brien, K. J. and Lianjiang, Li (2006). *Rightful Resistance in Rural China.* Cambridge: Cambridge University Press.

Petras, J. (1998). 'The Political and Social Basis of Regional Variation in Land Occupations in Brazil', *Journal of Peasant Studies*, vol. 25, no. 4, pp. 124–133.

Petras, J. and H. Veltmeyer (2001). 'Are Latin American Peasant Movements Still a Force for Change?', *Journal of Peasant Studies*, vol. 28, no. 2.

Robison, R. (2006). *The Neoliberal Revolution: Forging the Market State.* London: Palgrave.

Scott, J. (1986). *Weapons of the Weak: Everyday Forms of Peasant Resistance.* New Haven, CT: Yale University Press.

Spoor, M. (ed.) (2003). *Transition, Institutions, and the Rural Sector.* New York: Lexington.

Tarrow, S. (1998). *Power in Movement: Social Movements and Contentious Politics,* 2nd edn. Cambridge: Cambridge University Press.

Tuma, E. (1965). *Twenty-Six Centuries of Agrarian Reform: A Comparative Analysis.* Berkeley: University of California Press.

van Donge, J. K. with L. Pherani (1999). 'Law and Order as a Development Issue: Land Conflicts and the Creation of Social Order in Southern Malawi', *Journal of Development Studies*, vol. 36, no. 2, pp. 48–70.

Wright, A. and W. Wolford (2003). *To Inherit the Earth: The Landless Movement and the Struggle for a New Brazil.* Oakland, CA: Food First Books.

Index